THE
GREEK HERITAGE
IN
VICTORIAN BRITAIN

THE
GREEK
HERITAGE
IN
VICTORIAN
BRITAIN

Frank M. Turner

NEW HAVEN & LONDON

YALE UNIVERSITY PRESS

Published with assistance from the foundation
established in memory of Philip Hamilton McMillan
of the Class of 1894, Yale College

Designed by Sally Harris
and set in VIP Bembo type.
Printed in the United States of America by
Halliday Lithograph Corp., West Hanover, Mass.

Library of Congress Cataloging in Publication Data

Turner, Frank Miller.
  The Greek heritage in Victorian Britain.

  Includes bibliographical references and index.
    1.   Great Britain—Civilization—Greek influences.
  2.   Great Britain—Civilization—19th century.
  I.   Title.
DA533.T87   941.08   80–24013
ISBN 0–300–02480–0
ISBN 0–300–03257–9 (pbk.)

10   9   8   7   6   5   4   3   2

For
my mother and sister
and
in memory of my father

CONTENTS

ILLUSTRATIONS

PREFACE

"Two great principles," wrote Lord Acton sometime near 1859, "divide the world and contend for the mastery, antiquity and the Middle Ages. These are the two civilizations that have preceded us, the two elements of which our's is composed. All political as well as religious questions reduce themselves practically to this. This is the great dualism that runs through our society."[1] Acton's comment delineated not only a major characteristic of the historical sensibility of the West since the Renaissance but also one of the most basic and significant presuppositions of Victorian intellectuals in Great Britain and in Europe generally. Antiquity and the Middle Ages, Hellenism and Hebraism, Jerusalem and Athens, Socrates and Christ symbolized a perceived though much oversimplified polarity in contemporary ideals and values.

The conflict was an old one, but the men and women of the nineteenth century pursued it on the terms of their day and with the concerns and purposes of that moment. Within the existing historiography only the Christian, or medieval, aspect of the dualism has received much attention. Scholarly works of distinction have appeared on the Gothic revival, the Tractarian and Cambridge movements, the Pre-Raphaelites, Newman, Pugin, Carlyle, Ruskin, and Morris. However, except for a few notable books such as Douglas Bush's *Mythology and the Romantic Tradition in English Poetry* (1937), M. L. Clarke's *Greek Studies in England, 1700–1830* (1945), Warren D. Anderson's *Matthew Arnold and the Classical Tradition* (1965), David J. DeLaura's *Hebrew and Hellene in Victorian England* (1969), and Richard Jenkyns's *The Victorians and Ancient Greece* (1980), there are almost no major studies on the Victorian treatment of the classical world; and those cited concentrate primarily on the relationship of antiquity to English literature. None of these works attempts to explore Victorian

1. Quoted in Herbert Butterfield, *Man on His Past: The Study of the History of Historical Scholarship* (Boston: Beacon Press, 1960), p. 212.

commentary on antiquity as a means of more fully understanding Victorian intellectual life itself.

The present volume is an attempt to redress that balance. The classical world stood at the heart of major areas of Victorian thought, political philosophy, theology, and formal education. Moreover, except perhaps for work in the physical sciences, no other field of Victorian intellectual endeavor was so thoroughly European. Important intellectual cross-fertilization occurred between writers on the Continent and those in Britain. Although the Victorians obviously did not discover the classics, they did make the antique past and its peoples uniquely their own. Classical literature—philosophy, mythology, and history—provided a means for achieving self-knowledge and cultural self-confidence within the emerging order of liberal democracy and secularism. For the Victorians the figures from antiquity were not the "Ancients" but distant contemporaries who had confronted and often mastered the difficulties presenting themselves anew to the nineteenth century.

Put most simply, the question I have attempted to answer is "What did the Victorians say about antiquity?" In probing what they said, I have come to frequently surprising conclusions about why they said it. Initially I had hoped the story could be told in a single book, but both the large quantity of printed material and the generally separate sets of scholars writing about Greece and about Rome have required separate considerations. This volume is devoted entirely to Greece. Further reason for this choice is that intellectuals in England had long been familiar with the classical Roman past whereas the interest in ancient Greece commenced on a significant scale only in the late eighteenth century.

Three topics that readers may expect to find covered in these pages are absent. I have not discussed the use of Greek mythology or allusions to Greek culture as displayed in Victorian poetry and literary prose. This is an immense subject in itself and not one that fitted into the patterns of thought, analysis, and scholarship that concerned me. Second, with certain exceptions I have not considered in detail the role of the classics in Victorian education. Much of the literature I examine was used in the schools and universities, but how it was used is difficult to ascertain and what students may have gleaned from it is even more obscure. Historians of education may wish to probe that subject further. Finally, this book is not a study of technical linguistic or philological scholarship. Only a classicist could carry out such an examination of Victorian editing and translations. I have attempted to understand why the classics, and more particularly the Greek classics, were perceived as useful. Having done that, I would hope that others might undertake more technical studies of the philology and translation of Greek.

I hope this book will prove interesting and informative to historians, classicists, literary critics, and the general reader. Persons from any one of these groups may feel that I have explained questions or issues that are already quite clear to them. I have done so because what the historian knows so well about Victorian politics is often quite unfamiliar to the classicist, and what the latter knows so well about Homer or Athens is normally foreign to the general scholar of Victorian Britain.

Readers will also note that from time to time I refer to classical studies of the last quarter-century to illustrate either how they have confirmed or revised nineteenth-century views or how they still reflect them. Although I admire much of this recent work and have learned much from it, I would not wish my references to be taken as evidence or suggestion that the final conclusions have been attained. The modern dialogue with Greek antiquity that commenced in the late eighteenth century will continue well past the end of the twentieth.

While writing this book I have received generous support twice from the National Endowment for the Humanities and from the Morse Fellowship Fund and the A. Whitney Griswold Fund of Yale University. Librarians of the Sterling Memorial Library, the British Library, University College London Library, the Bodleian Library, Balliol College Library, Trinity College Library, Kings College Library, Newnham College Library, the Cambridge University Library, the National Library of Scotland, and St. Andrews University Library offered friendly aid. I acknowledge the permission of the master and fellows of Balliol College to quote from the manuscripts of Benjamin Jowett.

Every author should be so fortunate as to have a publisher as encouraging as the Yale University Press. Edward Tripp both professionally and personally has supported this project from its inception. Laura Pease and Maura Tantillo have patiently overseen its final production.

Colleagues at Yale University and elsewhere have been unfailingly helpful and occasionally no doubt amused by the intellectual quandaries in which I found myself and into which I unhesitatingly drew them. Jerome Pollitt, John Herington, Hans Frei, Alvin Bernstein, Dwight Culler, Peter Gay, Joseph Hamburger, Heinrich von Staden, Ramsay MacMullen and R. K. Webb each read one or more chapters. Steven Ozment listened to and criticized my ideas throughout the writing. My particular thanks and sense of appreciation must be extended to Franklin Baumer, whose support has been constant, and to Donald Kagan, who has answered more questions about Greece than I had any right to pose to him. These friends through their kindness and generosity have allowed me to experience something of what Aristotle meant by the fellowship of the good life and the felicity thereof. For the errors from which they have saved me I am grateful, and for those that remain I am responsible.

New Haven, Connecticut
June 1980

THE
GREEK HERITAGE
IN
VICTORIAN BRITAIN

1
THE VICTORIANS AND GREEK ANTIQUITY

Throughout much of the European intellectual community of the last century there flourished an immense fascination for ancient Greece. From Goethe, Hegel, and Shelley to Kierkegaard, Arnold, Grote, and Fouillée, through Nietzsche, Fustel de Coulanges, and Frazer, the list of poets, critics, philosophers, historians, and scholars concerned at one time or another with the Greeks reads like an index of the major contributors to the intellectual life of the age. The results of their probing of the Greek experience were impressive on every score. Greek revival buildings came to dot the rural and urban landscape from Ireland to Russia. Ancient temples, theaters, marketplaces, palaces, and tombs buried for over two millennia were unearthed and their remains transported hundreds of miles to the west for display in museums designed to resemble Greek temples and dedicated to the modern muses of popular enlightenment. Whole fields of learning, scholarship, and teaching about Greek antiquity entered the life of European universities for the first time. New scholarly societies and schools for archaeology were established. In libraries and on private bookshelves there slowly accumulated a vast array of books and journals concerned with Greece. And in the learned imagination of Europe the ancient Hellenic achievement assumed a vitality and sense of relevance previously entertained in the minds of only a fewscore Renaissance humanists.

The extensive nineteenth-century concern with ancient Greece was essentially a novel factor in modern European intellectual life. Although Greek philosophy had influenced some Renaissance writers and Aristotelian categories still informed science and logic, until the late eighteenth century most educated Europeans regarded their culture as Roman and Christian in origin, with merely peripheral roots in Greece. Europe had a Roman past, and European civilization was congruent with Latin Christendom. Caesar had recorded the conquest of Gaul and the invasion of Britain, and Tacitus had described the life of the ancient Germans. Roman law and Roman literature, as well as the Latin church fathers, had dominated Europe's cultural experience. Roman walls, forts, bridges, baths, theaters, roads, and aqueducts could be found in Britain and across the Continent. In contrast to this visible, tangible, and pervasive Roman influence, the Greeks simply had not directly touched the life of Western Europe. Even the broad Enlightenment appeal to antiquity had concentrated on Rome.

Greek antiquity began to absorb the interest of Europeans in the second half of the eighteenth century when the values, ideas, and institutions inherited from the Roman and Christian past became problematical. The search for new cultural roots and alternative cultural patterns developed out of the need to understand and articulate the disruptive political, social, and intellectual experience that Europeans confronted in the wake of the Enlightenment and of revolution. In some cases the appeal to Greece served to foster further change, in others to combat the forces of disruption. In both cases the turn to Greece on the part of scholars, critics, and literary figures constituted an attempt to discern prescriptive signposts for the present age in the European past that predated Rome and Christianity. These writers were, of course, actually erecting new landmarks.

Greek antiquity first assumed major intellectual significance in Germany. There, from approximately 1750 on, poets, literary critics, and historians of art looked to ancient Greece as an imaginative landscape on which they might discover artistic patterns, ethical values, and concepts of human nature that could displace those of Christianity and ossified French classicism.[1] The discontinuity between Greece and modern Christian Europe rendered the Greek experience all the more valuable and useful. Greece could represent almost any value or out-

---

1. Henry Hatfield, *Aesthetic Paganism in German Literature from Winckelmann to the Death of Goethe* (Cambridge, Mass.: Harvard University Press, 1964); Walter Rehm, *Griechentum und Goethezeit* (Bern: Francke Verlage, 1952); Humphrey Trevelyan, *Goethe and the Greeks* (Cambridge: Cambridge University Press, 1952); Martin Vogel, *Apollinisch und Dionysisch: Geschichte eines genialen Irrtums* (Regensburg: Gustav Bosse Verlag, 1966), pp. 37–94.

look that a writer wished to ascribe to it. The moral variety in Greek culture, which was fully recognized at the time, further contributed to the breadth of its perceived relevance, as in the works of Winckelmann, Lessing, Goethe, Schiller, Hölderlin, and others. Writers used the values they discerned in the Greek experience either to throw off the asceticism of the Christian tradition and the restraints of French academic rules or to find an alternative secular confirmation for modes of taste and moral experience that were normally buttressed by Christianity or modern aesthetics. Things Greek thus contributed both to the devising of new myths and to the sustaining of old values in novel guises.

Contemporary with this well-known German literary activity there arose the less familiar but ultimately perhaps more important early historical and philological scholarship of the University of Göttingen. From it developed the major critical approaches to both pagan and Christian antiquity that characterized German theological and historical endeavors for the next century and that became models for other European and American scholars.[2] Following the lead of Christian Gottlieb Heyne, German scholars began to study ancient texts in a critical manner that took into consideration questions of linguistics, history, and textual integrity. The flowering of this *Neue Humanismus* opened fundamentally new dimensions to the understanding of the classical past and to the criticism of its literature. Those same methods held shattering implications for the study of the Bible and the historical origins of Christianity. The classical and religious studies were repeatedly to become intertwined.

A third factor independently contributing to the sense of the relevance of ancient Greece to modern Europe was the stirring of liberal democracy that began with the American Revolution. Whether the age of revolution between 1760 and 1815 was one of genuinely democratic revolution may remain a vexing question, but there can be no doubt that the revolutionary experience roused on an unprecedented scale the intensive examination of the ancient Greek democracies and

---

2. Herbert Butterfield, *Man on His Past: The Study of the History of Historical Scholarship* (Boston: Beacon Press, 1960), pp. 32–61; Christian Hartlich and Walter Sachs, *Der Ursprung des Mythgosbegriffes in der Modernen Bibelwissenschaft* (Tübingen: J. C. B. Mohr, 1952); Carl Diehl, *Americans and German Scholarship, 1770–1870* (New Haven: Yale University Press, 1978), pp. 6–48.

particularly that of Athens. The polemical writing of Greek history began in England in the 1780s, well before the expeditions of the Philhellenes in aid of the Greek revolution. The specter of a contemporary Greek democracy fascinated and inspired the romantic liberals who went to fight in its cause, but it was the possibility for conservative polemic presented by the turbulent history of the ancient Athenian democracy that occasioned the first major studies of that subject and that often determined the framework for later studies as well.

Although the focus on Greece was a change from the previous emphasis on Rome, the reorientation was a relatively simple cultural accomplishment because it occurred within literate classes already familiar with the ancient world as a source of prescriptive values and of illustrative moral and political allusions. The inheritance of the humanist education enjoyed by the educated classes in Britain since the Renaissance made the appeal to and the use of Greek antiquity both possible and effective. In 1856 John Grote, professor of moral philosophy at Cambridge and the brother of the Greek historian, observed,

> Classical study . . . is a point of intellectual sympathy among men over a considerable surface of the world, for those who have forgotten their actual Greek and Latin bear still generally with them many traces of its influence, and in fact it is this which, more than anything, makes them, in common parlance, educated men. That any one subject should be thus extensively cultivated, so as to make such sympathy possible, is a most happy circumstance, supposing it simply historical and accidental. The destruction or disuse of it will destroy one bond of intellectual communion among civilized men, and will be, in this respect, a step not of improvement. And though studies more definitely useful might succeed it, there is an utility lost, and one which will hardly be considered trifling.[3]

That now dissipated general familiarity with the classics was once one of the distinguishing and self-defining marks of the social and intellectual elite of Europe. It had originated in thoroughly aristocratic times and endured through the first century of the liberal democratic

---

3. John Grote, "Old Studies and New," in *Cambridge Essays: 1856* (London: John W. Parker and Son, 1856), p. 114.

age. To no small extent knowledge of the classical world and acquaintance with the values communicated through the vehicle of classical education informed the mind and provided much of the intellectual confidence of the ruling political classes of Europe. The great enterprises of translation undertaken during the nineteenth century in part represented attempts to preserve that frame of cultural and intellectual reference for an expanding, but not always classically trained, political elite. And the effort succeeded well until the social and political impact of the First World War thoroughly undermined the vestiges of the aristocratic life in Europe.

The structures of classical education made possible and largely sustained the study of Greek civilization and the application of that study to contemporary life. In England until after World War I a knowledge of Greek was required for admission to both Oxford and Cambridge.[4] This requirement set the major pedagogical pattern for the public schools and all other secondary institutions that hoped to send students to those universities or to provide the veneer of an elite education. The examinations for the Home Civil Service, the Indian Civil Service, and the Royal Military Academy afforded considerable advantage to students who could score well in Greek. Consequently, a knowledge of Greek (even if rarely mastery) and a familiarity with Greek culture were characteristic of a large portion of the British political elite as well as of the leaders and clergy of the Church of England. So long as this educational situation prevailed, discussions of Greek history, religion, literature, and philosophy provided ready vehicles for addressing the governing classes of the country and could be expected to find in them a potentially receptive and possibly responsive audience. Indeed, in 1865 the major commentator on Homer as well as a major translator of the poet, the chief critic and historian of Greek literature, the most significant political historians of Greece, and the authors of the then most extensive commentaries on Greek philosophy either were or had recently been members of the House of Commons or the House of Lords.

Throughout the century the profound influence on the English educated classes of the Oxford school of *Literae Humaniores* reenforced the

4. See "Memorandum of the Council of the Society for the Promotion of Hellenic Studies on the Place of Greek in Education," *Journal of Hellenic Studies* 36 (1916): lxix–lxxii.

use of both Greece and Rome as points of cultural and intellectual self-reference. This deservedly famous program of study involved then, as now, the careful, detailed translation and criticism of a set list of texts—the Greats—that changed somewhat during the course of the century. The program required two different sets of examinations. The first, known as Moderations, was taken at the end of the two years and tested primarily linguistic ability and knowledge of Greek and Latin literature. The second examination, written at the end of four years, was topically oriented and covered history, ethics, metaphysics, and political philosophy. One result of the character of the latter examination was, as R. W. Livingstone observed in 1932, a "tendency to study the classics not in and for themselves, but in relation to modern thought and modern life."[5]

During the nineteenth century the modern thought to which the classics were related at Oxford and elsewhere changed from decade to decade. As Francis Cornford of Cambridge wrote in 1903; "The ancient classics resemble the universe. They are always there, and they are very much the same as ever. But as the philosophy of every new age puts a fresh construction on the universe, so in the classics scholarship finds a perennial object for ever fresh and original interpretation."[6] Early in the century the Greeks and their philosophy were often related to the thought of Anglican theologians, such as Bishop Butler. By the thirties the patristic revival associated primarily with the Tractarian movement at Oxford stimulated interest in the relationship of Greek and Christian thought and helped to foster new approaches to the study of Plato. The same decade witnessed the major impact of German scholarship in the British universities and the publication in English in 1840 of Müller's *History of Greek Literature,* even before it was published in German. The scholarship of the Continent also led to a more critical tone in the writing of Greek history in Britain. At mid-century utilitarian and rationalist writers established a major claim to Greek studies with the publication of George Grote's *History of Greece*. The German influence reappeared in the sixties with the Aryanism of F. Max Müller's theories of myth and, more impor-

5. Richard W. Livingstone, "The Position and Function of Classical Studies in Modern English Education," *Vorträge der Bibliothek Warburg* (1930–31), p. 258.

6. Francis Macdonald Cornford, *The Cambridge Classical Course: An Essay in Anticipation of Further Reform* (Cambridge: W.H. Heffer & Sons, 1903), p. 19.

tant, in the Hegelianism of Jowett's introductions to Plato. Thereafter, archaeology and anthropology began to transform Greek studies, and by the turn of the century social psychology and French sociology had begun to make themselves felt in works on Greek religion, philosophy, and politics. Throughout the century the tradition of critical editing and commentary, inherited from Richard Porson as much as anyone, continued to be influential in the publication of Greek texts that permitted new and often revisionist commentary and emendation. In this regard one thinks of James Frazer's editing of Pausanias and the latter's attention to varieties of ritual observance that would become so important for Frazer's later work.

A final reason for the impact of contemporary concerns on the British evaluation of Greece was the largely undefined nature of classics as a discipline. Except for linguistic ability in Greek and Latin, the analytical tools and categories employed to examine a question or problem from Greek antiquity were almost invariably derived from other modern disciplines or modern religious and philosophical outlooks. Modern aesthetics guided the consideration of Greek sculpture. Modern religious sensibilities and anthropological theories determined the interpretation of Greek myths. Modern biblical scholarship influenced the reading of Homer. Modern political thought and anxieties were brought to bear on the Athenian democratic experience. Greek philosophers were judged before the bar of modern epistemology and political philosophy.

The overwhelmingly amateur character of the Victorian scholars who undertook the enterprise exacerbated this use of modern nonclassical disciplines for interpreting the Greek experience. Their work in the classics was almost always derivative of theological or ecclesiastical concerns or related directly to matters of current politics, morals, or aesthetics. A Hampshire squire, an Anglican bishop, and a City of London banker pioneered the study of Greek political history. A chancellor of the exchequer contributed the major mid-century study of Homer. A school inspector made "Hellenism" and "Hebraism" terms of common literary and cultural usage. These and others who wrote and commented on Greece approached their subjects less from an interest in the past for its own sake than from a firm conviction that what they said about Greece would have an impact on contemporary political, religious, philosophical, and moral discourse. The paradox of professional humanistic scholarship—a growing body of knowledge attained by precise methodology but tied to a shrinking sense of its perceived relevance—had happily not overtaken the Victorian study of Greece.

For all of these reasons the nineteenth-century exploration of Greek antiquity constantly manifested the wider intellectual life of the day and opens the latter for more complete consideration. Writing about Greece was in part a way for the Victorians to write about themselves. The most famous and perhaps still the most widely consulted book in English on nineteenth-century Hellenism bears the title *The Tyranny of Greece over Germany*.[7] Whatever the merits or faults of the rest of that volume, its title has fundamentally misled most subsequent consideration of the subject. What actually constituted the primary and most striking feature of Victorian Hellenism wherever it appeared was the tyranny of the nineteenth-century European experience over that of Greek antiquity. In a perceptive essay written shortly after World War II, W. H. Auden noted, "It is the unlikeness of the Greeks to ourselves, the gulf between the kind of assumptions they made, the kind of questions they asked and our own that strikes us more than anything else."[8] The reaction of nineteenth-century writers to ancient Greece had been just the opposite as again and again, in the most unexpected and sometimes perverse manner, Greek subjects were made to conform to contemporary categories of thought, culture, and morality. Across the Western world Victorian authors and readers were determined to find the Greeks as much as possible like themselves and to rationalize away fundamental differences.

Although the Hellenic revival of the nineteenth century involved an international community of scholars and writers, many of whom appealed to the wisdom of Greece in terms of a universal human experience or some concept of uniform human nature, the study and interpretation of Greek antiquity nonetheless occurred within the context of national intellectual communities whose characters bore the distinctive imprints of their respective political structures, university organization, and religious confession. In each of these intellectual

7. Eliza Marian Butler, *The Tyranny of Greece over Germany* (Boston: Beacon Press, 1958; first published, 1935).

8. W.H. Auden, "Introduction," W.H. Auden, ed., *The Portable Greek Reader* (1948; reprint ed., New York: The Viking Press, 1955), p. 16.

communities the exploration and criticism of Greek life reflected the particular political, religious, and philosophical preoccupations of the national culture. Scholars in the various European countries read each other's books and articles, but the manner in which they evaluated those ideas and incorporated them into their own work often depended on factors outside the realm of classical scholarship proper. For this reason, as well as because of the sheer mass of evidence and documentation, the present volume will be devoted exclusively to the study of Greek antiquity in nineteenth-century Britain. It may, however, also prepare the way for similar studies of other nations so that in time a comparative understanding of the role of antiquity in the intellectual life of the century may emerge.

Thus far, the words *Greeks, Greek antiquity,* and *the classics* have been used as general terms. Some important Victorian critics, such as Matthew Arnold and his disciples, did regard them in this way. Because Arnold's prose, especially portions of *Culture and Anarchy*, have entered the literary canon, there has been a tendency to equate his version of Hellenism—one often imperfectly understood—with the entire British and European consideration of Greece. This interest in Arnold has obscured broader, more important explorations of Greek civilization by other Victorian commentators. Most nineteenth-century scholars and critics of Greece, in contrast to Arnold, dealt with specific and well-defined areas of Greek life rather than with general phenomena or an extracted Hellenic essence. The self-generating engines of critical scholarship and political controversy assured a more differentiated portrayal of Greece than the one that flowed from the German literary Hellenists to whom Arnold was so much indebted.

To become more adequately acquainted with the Victorian use and abuse of Greek antiquity, one must perform an exegesis upon an exegesis. That is, one must look at the literature in which nineteenth-century critics, historians, editors, and commentators actually discussed Greek topics. This large body of materials includes histories of Greece, formal commentaries on Greek literature, authors and philosophers, the extensive introductions and footnotes to editions of the texts and translations of major Greek works, university lectures, textbooks, review essays, major encyclopedia articles, and discussions of archaeology, anthropology, and comparative religion. When these little-examined documents are studied, they reveal a world of Victorian discourse possessing considerable integrated unity and one replete with surprises and unexpected intellectual twists and turns. To read these now neglected and frequently dust-covered volumes is also to discover how correctly John Grote grasped the cultural and intellectual function of classical studies in his society. Discussions of Greek antiquity provided a forum wherein Victorian writers could and did debate all manner of contemporary questions of taste, morality, politics, religion, and philosophy.

The university-educated and other widely read classes of Great Britain often felt that a profoundly intimate relationship existed between themselves and the ancient Greeks. In a typical statement of that sentiment J. P. Mahaffy, an Anglo-Irish scholar of Trinity College, Dublin, wrote in 1874:

> Every thinking man who becomes acquainted with the masterpieces of Greek writing, must see plainly that they stand to us in a far closer relation than the other remains of antiquity. They are not mere objects of curiosity to the archaeologist, not mere treasure-houses of roots and forms to be sought out by comparative grammarians. They are the writings of men of like culture with ourselves, who argue with the same logic, who reflect with kindred feelings. They have worked out social and moral problems like ourselves, they have expressed them in such language as we should desire to use. In a word, they are thoroughly modern, more modern than the epochs quite proximate to our own.

A few paragraphs later Mahaffy continued in the same vein.

> If one of us were transported to Periclean Athens, provided he were a man of high culture, he would find life and manners strangely like our own, strangely modern, as he might term it. The thoughts and feelings of modern life would be there without the appliances, and the high standard of general culture would more than counter balance sundry wants of material comfort.... Some of the problems which are still agitating our minds were settled by the Greeks, others, if not settled, were at least discussed with a freedom and acuteness now unattainable. Others, again, were solved in strange violation of our notions of

morals and good taste; and when such a people as the Greeks stand opposed to us, even in vital principles, we cannot reject their verdict without weighing their reasons.[9]

What is of particular significance about Mahaffy's statement and what can be replicated from scores of other writers was the conviction that the Greeks had been like the Victorians and that the historical situations of the two civilizations were essentially similar. Although this attitude did not survive much beyond the first quarter of the twentieth century, it was fundamental to Victorian intellectual life and determined the outlook of much Victorian scholarship, criticism, and commentary on the Greeks.

The appeal to the affinity between the Victorian and the Greek experience was rarely made in a casual manner. There almost always existed a particular motivation for drawing the direct relationship. There was, however, no single motivating interest but rather a cluster of them, many of which were quite unrelated. Furthermore, writers convinced of one set of relationships often remained unconvinced by other approaches and uninfluenced by the authors who pursued them. For example, numerous Victorian commentators sought in one way or another to relate Greek antiquity to Christianity. They had virtually no impact on other scholars whose concerns lay with the implications of Athenian democracy for modern politics. Yet both groups were part of the larger picture of the Victorians and Greek culture. Because of the diverse approaches of the nineteenth century to the study of ancient Greece, two questions repeatedly present themselves: Why the Greeks? and Which Greeks?

The question Why the Greeks? has a fairly straightforward answer. The political parallel between ancient democracy and modern democracy established in English writing by 1790 was of major significance, as was the possibility of contrasting the ideal of Greek heroism and the Greek appreciation for beauty with bourgeois humdrum and philistinism. But authors who made these uses of Greek culture and those who appealed to Greek antiquity for other polemical purposes usually believed their analysis appropriate because of one of four general philosophical approaches to the past. These concepts of history gave

9. John Pentland Mahaffy, *Social Life in Greece from Homer to Menander* (London: Macmillan and Co., 1874), pp. 1, 2–3.

them the confidence to draw the parallels. From the viewpoint of Christian providential history, the Greeks had played an important linguistic and philosophical role in preparing the world for the Gospel. Christian writers also often regarded the Greeks as having displayed the highest moral character that human nature could assume without the light of the Gospel. The second theory, which informed several significant discussions, was a version of Viconian cycles in which certain ages of Greek history (usually the fifth century B.C.) were seen as analogous to certain periods of modern history—and thus subject to the drawing of relevant parallels. This view was particularly attractive to liberal Anglicans about the middle of the century. A third idea that defined the Victorians' approach to the Greeks was Auguste Comte's law of the three stages of intellectual development. Adherents to this theory, or to a modified version thereof, tended to conceive Greek religious and philosophical life as a microcosm of the Comtean pattern of development. These writers invariably favored positivistic epistemology and chose their intellectual heroes among the Greeks according to that standard. Finally, Hegel's concept of the historical development of Greek philosophy also suggested that Greek thought and culture held particular relevance for the Victorian experience. Nineteenth-century writers who accepted his view of the passage from *Sittlichkeit* to *Moralität* in Greek civilization discerned a similar development in their own time.

These several philosophies of history did not function in hermetically sealed compartments. For example, Benjamin Jowett seems to have found the Hegelian pattern operative because he also accepted the Viconian concept of analogous ages. Some writers adhered to the connection between Greece and Britain without a specific understanding of the theory of history from which their views derived or that informed the thought of another scholar upon whose thought they drew. Yet, however construed or misconstrued, these theories provided the major framework by means of which Victorian writers sustained their belief that the experience of Greece was directly significant for their own culture.

The answer to the question Which Greeks? is more difficult and elusive. In 1939 George Boas noted, "Every age of European culture, like every individual of the intellectual classes, has gone back to the Greeks for inspiration ever since there were any Greeks to go back to. But what Greeks they selected as '*The Greeks*,' and what ideas and manners and standards they chose as typically Hellenic have varied from age to age and from individual to individual."[10] Boas's claim to the timeless appeal of the Greeks is much exaggerated but not his assertion about the variety of human experience they have been used to illustrate. Which Greeks a Victorian writer intended to denote frequently depended on which secondary authors he had read as much as upon his familiarity with the ancient Greek literary sources. The image projected upon the Hellenes also changed with the discovery of new evidence and with the application of new conceptual frameworks. The Greeks of Matthew Arnold were simply not those of James Frazer.

Victorian and Edwardian commentators were generally aware of these changing perceptions. In 1897, looking back over the past century of British and continental Greek studies, Gilbert Murray commented:

> The "serene and classical" Greek of Winckelmann and Goethe did good service to the world in his day, though we now feel him to be mainly a phantom. He has been succeeded, especially in the works of painters and poets, by an aesthetic and fleshly Greek in fine raiment, an abstract Pagan who lives to be contrasted with an equally abstract early Christian or Puritan, and to be glorified or mishandled according to the sentiments of his critics. He is a phantom too, as unreal as those marble palaces in which he habitually takes his ease. . . . There is more flesh and blood in the Greek of the anthropologist, the foster-brother of Kaffirs and Hairy Ainos. He is at least human and simple and emotional, and free from irrelevant trappings. His fault, of course, is that he is not the man we want, but only the raw material out of which that man was formed; a Hellene without beauty, without the spiritual life, without the Hellenism. Many other abstract Greeks are about us, no one perhaps greatly better than another; yet each has served to correct and complement his predecessor; and in the long-run there can be little doubt that our conceptions have become more adequate.[11]

10. George Boas, "Preface," George Boas, ed., The Greek Tradition (Baltimore: The Johns Hopkins Press, 1939), p. v.

11. Gilbert Murray, A History of Ancient Greek Literature (London: William Heinemann, 1897), pp. xiv–xv.

There had not been and there could not have been a single Victorian image of Greece and the Greeks. Considerable variety was inherent in the Greek experience itself. The several Victorian concepts of Greek culture represented appeals to different portions of that experience and the assimilation of new evidence, but they also embodied transformations in Victorian moral and religious sensibilities that permitted a new appreciation for evidence previously available. The Victorians' conceptions of what the Greeks had been or should have been changed as their own comprehension of the physical world, of history, and of human nature changed; and as educated Victorians began to understand themselves in more complex terms, they came to ascribe a similar complexity to the Greeks.

Matthew Arnold as portrayed in a *Vanity Fair* caricature of 1871

The Elgin Marbles as displayed while still a private collection, Park Lane, 1810 (from a sketch by C. R. Cockerell) (By permission of the Trustees of the British Museum)

Richard Westmacott, Jr.
(National Portrait Gallery, London)

Percy Gardner (Elliott & Fry)

2

VARIETIES OF
VICTORIAN HUMANISTIC
HELLENISM

During much of the nineteenth and well into the twentieth century the critical and moral tradition of humanism provided the primary channel through which the civilization of ancient Greece became transformed into a useful past for a large portion of the educated British public. In Great Britain that intellectual tradition dated from the early sixteenth-century labors of Christian humanists such as John Colet and Thomas More. They and their Continental friends and counterparts, including Erasmus, had regarded the eloquence and good letters of antiquity as vehicles for reforming the literature and through that the social and moral sensibilities of the day. Later spokesmen for this tradition included Milton, Swift, Pope, Johnson, Reynolds, Burke, Coleridge, Newman, Arnold, Eliot, and Leavis. These writers have been the great generalists of English literature and criticism. With the passage of time their emphasis tended to become somewhat less distinctly Christian and more particularly humanistic, although an Anglican or Anglo-Catholic element often remained prominent in their work. For these critics, literature held significance more as an ethical than as an aesthetic enterprise, and the moral or normative use of the past as a guide to the human condition in the present predominated over other possible uses of historical experience.

Despite differences in time, personal temperament, and specific views on particular questions this humanistic coterie shared certain intellectual traits and championed a common moral stance. They usually accepted the idea of the uniformity of human nature and the belief that the experience of human beings at one time and place could provide, within limits, instruction for human beings in a later time and place. Although tending to regard human nature as corrupt, they nonetheless still considered it capable of dignity and humane behavior. They affirmed the moral responsibility of human beings for their own actions and rejected concepts of human nature that simplified its character or ignored its complexity and even mystery. These writers and critics regarded mind and imagination as the most basic of human attributes. They also stressed that first and foremost human beings are creatures of value. As Paul Fussell, one of the most perceptive commentators on this tradition, has noted, "The English humanist is . . . obsessed by ethical questions. He sees man not primarily as a maker or even as a knower, but rather as a moral actor. Prescription rather than description is the humanist's business."[1] In their prescriptive capacity the humanists often deplored the moral values or intellectual tenor of their own society without, however, in most cases, criticizing its fundamental structure. Their major polemical targets were excessive commercialism, individualism, materialism, scientific reductionism, and other patterns of thought that in one way or another subordinated social and spiritual values to selfish materialistic accomplishment. With no less fervor they also attacked what they regarded as excessive subjectivism and relativity in morality, religion, and aesthetics. They were almost always political and intellectual elitists.

During the nineteenth century this humanist tradition informed three major interpretations of Greek civilization. The first, and the most familiar, was an idealized depiction of Greek life in the fifth century B.C. that embodied many of the values perennially associated with English humanism. The most influential exponent of this interpretation of Greece was Matthew Arnold, whom at least two generations of later writers regarded as a model. Second, the aesthetic criteria according to which most Victorian critics evaluated Greek sculpture derived to a very considerable extent from the *Discourses* of Sir Joshua Reynolds, themselves one of the monuments of Augustan humanism. Both Arnold and the critics of Greek sculpture looked primarily to ancient literary sources for their knowledge of Greek life

1. Paul Fussell, *The Rhetorical World of Augustan Humanism: Ethics and Imagery from Swift to Burke* (London: Oxford University Press, 1965), p. 7. All of my remarks on the character of English humanism are deeply indebted to this work.

and culture, and they then assimilated that ancient literature and criticism into the traditional humanistic moral categories. In both cases the humanistic ideal of ancient Greek art and culture was used to combat bourgeois philistinism on the one hand and the perceived extravagances of romanticism and modernism in literature, painting, and sculpture on the other.

Victorian humanism was not, however, a static entity; and a third approach to Greece also emerged from this tradition. Many of the primary humanist assumptions encountered sharp challenges during the second half of the century when the ideas associated with historicism, the Darwinian revolution, and anthropology undermined faith in the uniformity of human nature and the image of humankind as inherently ethical beings. At the same time, the vast quantity of new information about Greece originating in professional scholarship and archaeology dissolved the possibility, always frail at best, of a unitary concept of Greek civilization. Consequently, during the last quarter of the nineteenth century and the first quarter of the twentieth there emerged what may be termed dynamic or evolutionary humanism. The values and qualities of life cherished over the centuries by the humanist critics came to be regarded as needing to be achieved anew again and again rather than as existing in some timeless manner. Writers of this new outlook tended to emphasize not only ideal values and the role of the human mind but also the interrelationship of humankind and material civilization in establishing a humane society. For these critics humane values not only existed in time but had been developed over the course of time. Through the efforts of scholars and critics such as Charles Newton, John Ruskin, Walter Pater, and Gilbert Murray, Hellenism as a source of humanistic wisdom was transformed from a static attitude toward life into a dynamic force whose values each generation must rediscover for itself and make its own. In this way humanistic Hellenism survived the evolutionary challenge and continued to provide literary and ethical ideals for the early twentieth century.

The Hellenism of Matthew Arnold

The central and most famous statement of Victorian humanistic Hellenism appeared in the fourth chapter of Matthew Arnold's *Culture and Anarchy*. First published in 1869, Arnold's exposition of the character of Hellenism in contrast to Hebraism set the tone for humanistic discussions of Greek virtues for the next fifty years. Although humanistic appreciation for Greece did not begin with Arnold's essay, many late-Victorian readers within and without the scholarly community were attracted to Greek civilization because of its alleged embodiment of the values that Arnold had championed. Later it was to Arnold's image of the Greeks that numerous intellectuals wished to return when anthropologists and archaeologists had revealed a very different version of Greek life. Selections from Arnold's discussion of Hellenism were also frequently included in anthologies of English literature and became part of the standard literary canon. To this day Arnold's remarks are what most people believe constituted the Victorian concept and understanding of Greek culture. Because his essay has overshadowed the wider, more interesting, and more complex world of the Victorian consideration of the Greek heritage, the character of Arnold's Hellenism must be considered before the larger picture can be understood on its own terms and appreciated in all its richness.

Culture and Anarchy was the climax of Arnold's crusade against the philistinism of contemporary British culture, which he had been criticizing for more than a decade. In this series of essays, written in the wake of the agitation surrounding the passage of the Second Reform Act, Arnold attacked liberal politics, Nonconformist religion, the mechanical nature of modern life, and the tumult of pluralistic society. In the spirit of Swift, Burke, and Coleridge, Arnold regarded British society as unduly concerned with means rather than ends and with commercial rather than spiritual or noble values. Reform politics, religious toleration, and commercial prosperity had become ends in themselves at the price of disregarding other, higher facets of human nature. The British citizenry was enmeshed in the narrow morality of a latter-day puritanism, and this confinement prevented them from attempting to realize their best selves and from nurturing a climate of opinion in which learning, appreciation of beauty, and a unified culture might flourish. Throughout the country people failed to understand the difference between attaining "the inward peace and satisfaction which follows the subduing of the obvious faults of our animality" and achieving "absolute inward peace and satisfaction,—

the peace and satisfaction which are reached as we draw near to complete spiritual perfection."[2] The British sought to be morally respectable and socially conventional without thinking deeply upon the character, sources, or ends of that morality.

Within the universe of mid-Victorian ethical and social tendencies Arnold denoted two under which most of the others could be subsumed. The first was "this energy driving at practice, this paramount sense of the obligation of duty, self-control, and work, this earnestness in going manfully with the best light we have." That drive he called Hebraism. Then he described "the intelligence driving at those ideas which are, after all, the basis of right practice, the ardent sense of all the new and changing combinations of them which man's development brings with it, the indomitable impulse to know and adjust them perfectly." Arnold termed that impulse Hellenism. He insisted that the final end of both Hebraism and Hellenism was "man's perfection or salvation." But in other respects the two drives were different and stood poles apart in the moral world. Hellenism embodied "spontaneity of consciousness" and the desire "to see things as they really are." Hebraism upheld "strictness of conscience" and "conduct and obedience." Both the Greeks and Hebrews had quarreled with the passions and frailties of the flesh, but the Greeks had regarded them as a hindrance to "right thinking" while the Hebrews had denounced them as obstacles to "right acting." The Hebrews had latched onto a single sure place in the universal moral order and would not be moved. In contrast, the bent of the Greeks was "to follow, with flexible activity, the whole play of the universal order, to be apprehensive of missing any part of it, of sacrificing one part to another, to slip away from resting in this or that intimation of it, however capital." Through flexibility and spontaneity Hellenism had become "invested with a kind of aërial ease, clearness, and radiancy" that manifested "sweetness and light." The difficulties involved in attaining that radiancy failed to disturb the Greek mind whereas the Hebrew confronted in the concept of sin "something which thwarts and spoils all our efforts."[3]

2. Matthew Arnold, *Culture and Anarchy,* ed. R. H. Super (Ann Arbor: University of Michigan Press, 1965), p. 100.

3. Ibid., pp. 163,164,165,167,168.

Following his memorable delineation of these two ideal types of moral outlook, Arnold suggested that Western history could be interpreted in terms of the oscillation of their influence. Although the historical record seemed to indicate that Hellenism was unsound because human beings had been unable to live according to its light and by the fourth century A.D. had opted for Hebraism and Christianity, Arnold urged that Hellenism should not on those grounds be regarded as intrinsically unsound. Rather, its initial development had been "premature." Before Hellenism could successfully flourish, a general basis for social conduct and human self-control had to be established. Hebraism had contributed mightily to the latter process after Hellenism had faded from the scene. The sixteenth century had witnessed a revival of both drives. In the secular renaissance Hellenism had again stirred the aspirations of the West. Simultaneously, the Protestant reformation had fostered a rebirth of the stern Hebraic religion, morality, and sense of sin. The moral rivalry of the fourth century A.D. had been resumed, but under quite different circumstances from the sixteenth century on. Through the rise of science and criticism, humankind had come to know itself better and to see things as they really are. Hellenism was the appropriate moral stance for this new age of intellectual daring. Yet in Great Britain, so far as the middle classes were concerned, Hebraic morality and the intellectual confinement it nurtured still prevailed. The British had failed to comprehend the forces in contemporary history that meant Hellenism should be on the ascendant and Hebraism on the decline. In their confusion the British had "made the secondary the principal at the wrong moment, and the principal they have at the wrong moment treated as secondary." The cultural, religious, and political anarchy of the day could be alleviated only "by going back upon the actual instincts and forces which rule our life, seeing them as they really are, connecting them with other instincts and forces, and enlarging our whole view and rule of life."[4] Britain required the clear Hellenic vision of things as they really are if it

4. Ibid., pp. 169, 175. It should also be noted that contemporary racial thinking played a part in Arnold's analysis. He regarded the British as part of the Indo-European racial stock and, as such, racially related to the Greeks. See Frederick E. Faverty, *Matthew Arnold the Ethnologist* (Evanston, Ill.: Northwestern University Press, 1951), pp. 162–85. In Disraeli's novel *Lothair* (1870), one of the characters articulates what amounted to Arnold's racial interpretation of Western history: " 'Aryan principles,' said Mr. Phoebus; 'not merely the study of nature, but of beauti-

was to become fully integrated into the main current of European cultural development.

Arnold's discussion of Hebraism and Hellenism was brilliantly executed and proved rhetorically convincing. As he felt at the time, it set the tone for much of the future consideration of the issues. Yet double meanings and an almost disingenuous concealment of purpose characterized the entire chapter, in which few things really were as they appeared to be. The dichotomy drawn and the historical analysis set forth were profoundly deceptive both in their content and in their apparent simplicity. Arnold's Hebrews were not Jews but rather contemporary English Protestant Nonconformists. His Greeks were not ancient Hellenes but a version of humanity largely conjured up in the late-eighteenth-century German literary and aesthetic imagination. What he meant by seeing things as they really are was not modern scientific naturalism but rather a world view that rested "on fidelity to nature,—the *best* nature—and on a delicate discrimination of what this best nature is." He sought to grasp not the laws or regularities of physical nature but rather "the intelligible law of things."[5] Hellenism for Arnold was not the experience or thought of ancient Greece but a set of more or less traditional English humanist values long employed to oppose commercialism, excessive religious zeal, dissent from Anglicanism, philosophical mechanism, political radicalism, subjective morality, and social individualism. Throughout his essay there resounded not the echoes between ancient Athens and Jerusalem but

---

ful nature; the art of design in a country inhabited by a first rate race, and where the laws, the manners, the custom, are calculated to maintain the health and beauty of a first rate race. In a greater or less degree, these conditions obtained from the age of Pericles to the age of Hadrian in pure Aryan communities, but Semitism began then to prevail and ultimately triumphed. Semitism has destroyed art; it taught man to despise his own body, and the essence of art is to honor the human frame.' 'I am afraid I ought not to talk about such things,' said Lothair, 'but if by Semitism you mean religion, surely the Italian painters inspired by Semitism did something.' 'Great things,' said Mr. Phoebus; 'some of the greatest. Semitism gave them subjects, but the Renaissance gave them Aryan art, and it gave that art to a purely Aryan Race. But Semitism rallied in the shape of the Reformation, and swept it away." *The Works of Benjamin Disraeli, Earl of Beaconsfield,* 20 vols. (London and New York: M. Walter Dunn, 1904), 17:168–69. George Hersey has suggested that racial thought was also closely related to Hellenism in Victorian painting; see George Hersey, "Aryanism in Victorian England," *Yale Review* 66 (1976): 104–13.

5. M. Arnold, *Culture and Anarchy*, pp. 178,184.

those between what Coleridge once termed the "old England, the spiritual, Platonic old England" and the new "commercial Britain."[6]

As David DeLaura has shown, the content of Arnold's Hellenism was largely uninformed by recent classical scholarship. Arnold had read widely in Greek literature, but not deeply in contemporary classical studies. From his earliest prose works through the discussion in *Culture and Anarchy* Arnold's concept of Hellenism and of what the Greeks had been like combined the intellectual elements of English humanism and German aesthetic Hellenism. In the 1853 "Preface" to his *Poems* Arnold had drawn upon Sir Joshua Reynolds's *Discourses* to emphasize the need for poetry to embody noble subjects, general truth, wholeness, and a grand style in contrast to the subjective extravagance of romantic poetry. Arnold had there claimed that in their actions and literature the Greeks had displayed those very traits. In the "Preface" of 1854 Arnold again pointed to the Greeks as a source of relief from the contemporary intellectual confusion and cultural tumult evident in much modern literature. He urged that the classical writers of antiquity and particularly those of Athens

> can help to cure us of what is, it seems to me, the great vice of our intellect, manifesting itself in our incredible vagaries in literature, in art, in religion, in morals; namely that it is *fantastic*, and wants *sanity*. Sanity,—that is the great virtue of the ancient literature; the want of that is the great defect of the modern, in spite of all its variety and power. It is impossible to read carefully the great ancients, without losing something of our caprice and eccentricity; and to emulate them we must at least read them.[7]

Already in 1854 in his sharp attack on the romantics the selective Hellenism that would emerge fully developed in *Culture and Anarchy* was well under construction. Description was becoming prescription as the values of English humanism coalesced into a vision of ancient

6. Samuel Taylor Coleridge, *Anima Poetae*, ed. E. H. Coleridge (Boston: Houghton Mifflin, 1895), p. 128.

7. David J. DeLaura, *Hebrew and Hellene in Victorian England: Newman, Arnold, and Pater* (Austin: University of Texas Press, 1969), pp. 171–91; Edward Alexander, *Matthew Arnold, John Ruskin, and the Modern Temper* (Columbus: Ohio State University Press, 1973), pp. 136–40; Matthew Arnold, *On the Classical Tradition*, ed. R. H. Super (Ann Arbor: University of Michigan Press, 1960), p. 17.

Greece and as that vision became a metaphor for those values. They would later serve as the basis for his critique of philistinism.

Like other of his educated contemporaries, Arnold was fully aware that Greek life had not been wholly sane or rational, and some of his own early poetry reflected that knowledge.[8] But the assertion of the rational, calm character of ancient Greek culture allowed Arnold to embrace a moral spirit more flexible than that of Christianity without seeming to encounter moral license. The natural Greek untouched by Christianity, though by no means uncorrupt, still possessed by virtue of his reason a guide for admirable moral conduct and for a creative culture. Arnold's confidence in the moral rationality of the Greeks derived in large measure from the image of Greece communicated by Herder, Humboldt, Goethe, and Heine. Although he knew some of the German Hellenists only at second hand, he regarded them, and particularly Goethe, as having pointed the way to a whole, healthful approach to life and to a genuinely European sense of culture. Moreover, he saw the spiritual health and sane intellectual vitality of those Germans as having originated in their intimacy with Greek culture. Needless to say, Arnold had read the Germans as selectively as he had the Greeks.

Not only was Arnold's image of Greece largely derived from the German writers, but his own specific concept of Hellenism and its function developed through his criticism of their works rather than of Greek literature. In his essay "Heinrich Heine" (1863) Arnold ascribed the spirit of what he would later call Hellenism to both Goethe and Heine. They had contributed mightily to "the awakening of the modern spirit" whereby Europeans found themselves confronted with a vast social and intellectual inheritance that "by no means corresponds exactly with the wants of their actual life." The primary

8. Warren D. Anderson, *Matthew Arnold and the Classical Tradition* (Ann Arbor: University of Michigan Press, 1965), pp. 30–49. At mid-century, in European intellectual circles, there existed a general knowledge of the nonrational character of much of Greek culture; see Max L. Baeumer, "Nietzsche and the Tradition of the Dionysian," James C. O'Flaherty, Timothy Sellner, and Robert M. Helm, eds., *Studies in Nietzsche and the Classical Tradition* (Chapel Hill: University of North Carolina Press, 1976), pp. 165–89; Walter Rehm, *Griechentum und Goethezeit* (Bern: Francke Verlage, 1952); Henry Hatfield, *Aesthetic Paganism in German Literature from Winckelmann to the Death of Goethe* (Cambridge, Mass.: Harvard University Press, 1964).

solvent to that inheritance and the chief vehicle for establishing new values was the critical attitude of mind most fully personified in the nineteenth century by Goethe. His "imperturbable naturalism" proved fatal "to all routine thinking" because he had located the standard of moral and social judgment "once for all, inside every man instead of outside him." Though initially destructive that spirit of critical naturalism would eventually lead men and women to see things as they really are, and this perspective was for Arnold a fundamental feature both of Hellenism and of a unified sense of culture. Heine had been the writer who most fully continued the tradition of Goethe. In his "life and death battle with Philistinism" Heine had defined the contemporary cultural enemy and held high the standards of beauty and reason.[9] By stripping away the sham of the present age without calling for a return to the feudal past, Heine had pointed the way to a higher mode of human excellence. Heine had furthermore discerned the perennial moral tension between Hebraism and Hellenism that Arnold would later elaborate, including the resurgence of their cultural rivalry in the Renaissance. By the close of "Heinrich Heine" Arnold had enunciated the major features of the dualism between Hellenism and Hebraism that appeared in a more elaborate form in *Culture and Anarchy*. He had done this with no extensive reference to the life, literature, or culture of ancient Greece itself. He simply assumed the German writers had assimilated the Greek spirit.

The German background establishes what Arnold understood to be the character of Hellenism, but it does not explain why he believed Greek civilization was so directly relevant to British life in his own day. Arnold was not the first British writer to contrast ancient Greece with Christian morality, romantic subjectivism, or contemporary liberalism and utilitarianism. As will be seen, critics of Greek sculpture had frequently drawn the aesthetic contrast. Romantic poets and Anglican clergymen, for different reasons and from different standpoints, had appreciated the more fleshly qualities of Greek pagan life in comparison with Judeo-Christian asceticism. Even John Stuart Mill had considered one use of ancient literature to be its presentation of values absent from modern commercial society. As he explained,

9. Matthew Arnold, *Lectures and Essays in Criticism*, ed. R. H. Super (Ann Arbor: University of Michigan Press, 1962), pp. 109,110,111.

Not only do those literatures furnish examples of high finish and perfection of workmanship, to correct the slovenly habits of modern hasty writing, but they exhibit, in the military and agricultural commonwealths of antiquity, precisely that order of virtues in which a commercial society is apt to be deficient; and they altogether show human nature on a grander scale: with less benevolence but more patriotism, less sentiment but more self-control; if a lower average of virtue, more striking examples of it; fewer small goodnesses, but more greatness and appreciation of greatness; more which tends to exalt the imagination, and inspire high conceptions of the capabilities of human nature.[10]

Yet there was a significant difference between Mill's appreciation of the contemporary function of classical literature and the view of history that informed Arnold's Hellenism. Random didactic comparisons of ancient Greece and nineteenth-century Britain, such as Mill's, or nostalgic yearnings for a vanished pagan past, such as that in Shelley's poetry or Schiller's "Götter Griechenlands," served to emphasize the differences and distance of Greece from the present day.[11] No necessary or intimate relationships were set forth to make the comparisons apt or intrinsically relevant. In contrast, after 1853 Arnold asserted a direct, intrinsic, and immediate cultural relevance of fifth-century Greece for the life of modern Britain. That relationship was by no means self-evident. What permitted Arnold to regard Greece in this light was the modified Viconian theory of history set forth by his father Thomas Arnold and other liberal Anglican historians of his father's generation.

Throughout Western Europe during the late eighteenth century a burgeoning historicism cast into doubt both the Christian and the Enlightenment assumption of the uniformity of human nature. This historicist awareness was, of course, particularly influential in Germany, but it was also present to a somewhat lesser extent among Scottish conjecturalist historians. By the 1820s a group of Anglican

10. John Stuart Mill, *Dissertations and Discussions: Political, Philosophical, and Historical*, 2 vols. (London: John W. Parker and Son, 1859), 2:69n.

11. For an important example of the comparison of modern life with the life of Greece that foreshadows Arnold and was also influenced by his German sources, see Augustus William and Julius Charles Hare, *Guesses at Truth by Two Brothers*, New Edition (London: Macmillan and Co., 1878; originally published, 1827), pp. 64–70.

historians in Britain including Thomas Arnold, Henry Hart Milman, and Connop Thirlwall began to develop a theory of history that accepted certain historicist presuppositions while at the same time allowing meaningful lessons to be drawn from the past. Deeply indebted to the thought of Vico and Barthold Niebuhr, these Anglicans suggested that all nations developed through a series of organic stages that resembled the stages of individual human growth, maturation, and decay. History was the record of the cycles of nations, which, however, did not require the same amount of time in every case. Although within each national cycle a period of intellectual and material progress occurred, there had not been within overall human history a linear course of progressive development. On the basis of this analysis these Anglican writers concluded that the spiritual salvation and moral improvement of humankind must have originated not in its own accomplishments and growth but in the providence of God imposed from without upon the cycles of merely human development.[12]

Thomas Arnold set forth his version of this Viconian theory in sermons and articles, in his *History of Rome* (1838–43), and in the notes and essays that accompanied his important Greek edition of Thucydides (1830–35). Although the elder Arnold suggested that human beings in one particular stage of growth shared few, if any, traits with those in a different stage of development, he still thought it possible to make valid comparisons and to draw significant parallels between the experiences of two separate nations if analogous periods of historical development were involved. Once the similarities between analogous periods had been discerned, the past could properly illustrate lessons for the present. As he explained, "The knowledge of these periods furnishes us with a clue to the study of history, which the continuous succession of events related in chronological order seems particularly to require."[13] Thomas Arnold went so far as to claim that

12. Duncan Forbes, *The Liberal Anglican Idea of History* (Cambridge: Cambridge University Press, 1952); Klaus Dockhorn, *Der Deutsche Historismus in England: ein Beitrag zur englishen Geistesgeschichte des 19. Jahrhunderts* (Göttingen: Vanderhoeck and Ruprecht, 1950), pp. 15–26.

13. Thomas Arnold, ed., *The History of the Peloponnesian War by Thucydides*, 3 vols., 4th ed. (Oxford: John Henry and James Parker, 1857), 1:503. See also Forbes, *Liberal Anglican Idea of History*, p. 48; Lionel Trilling, *Matthew Arnold* (New York: W. W. Norton and Co., 1939), pp. 36–76; Peter Allan Dale, *The Victorian Critic and the Idea of History* (Cambridge, Mass.: Harvard University Press, 1977), pp. 91–100; P. W. Day, *Matthew Arnold and the Philosophy of Vico* (Auckland: University of Auckland Press, 1964), Bulletin no. 70, English Series no. 12.

two civilizations standing thousands of years apart in time might have far more in common than ones separated by only a few centuries.

In drawing historical analogies between different ages, Arnold fervently contended, "The period to which the work of Thucydides refers belongs properly to modern and not to ancient history."[14] This belief as well as his father's general theory of history deeply influenced Matthew Arnold's view of the relevance of Greece for his age. As early as the "Preface" of 1853 he described late-fifth-century Greece as a time when "the dialogue of the mind with itself has commenced; modern problems have presented themselves; we hear already the doubts, we witness the discouragement, of Hamlet and of Faust."[15] A more important and direct use of the elder Arnold's theory of history occurred four years later in Matthew Arnold's inaugural lecture as professor of poetry at Oxford. In that address, published in 1869 as "The Modern Element in Literature," Arnold made an elaborate case for the common modernity of Periclean Athens and nineteenth-century Europe. Both ages were "modern" eras that could look back on earlier ancient times. The absence of war, a spirit of tolerance, an increase in the conveniences of life, and a wide opportunity for leisure in refined pursuits characterized both "modern" epochs. Most significant, as "modern" periods both ages displayed "the intellectual maturity of man himself; the tendency to observe facts with a critical spirit; to search for their law, not to wander among them at random; to judge by the rule of reason; not by the impulse of prejudice or caprice."[16] Here Matthew Arnold clearly reflected the influence of his father's contention that the transition from an ancient to a modern period of history represented "the transition from an age of feeling to one of reflection, from a period of ignorance and credulity to one of inquiry and scepticism."[17] These features of the emergence of the modern mind were identical with those that in 1863 Matthew Arnold would associate with the critical thought of Goethe and Heine. The analogy that Thomas Arnold had led his son to discern between fifth-century Athens and nineteenth-century Europe served to reenforce the latter's conviction of the intellectual affinity between the

14. T. Arnold, *History of the Peloponnesian War by Thucydides,* 3:xiv; see also 1:522.
15. M. Arnold, *On the Classical Tradition,* p. 1; see also T. Arnold, *History of the Peloponnesian War by Thucydides,* 1:519; 3:xiv.
16. M. Arnold, *On the Classical Tradition,* p. 24.
17. T. Arnold, *History of the Peloponnesian War by Thucydides,* 3:xiv.

writings of the German Hellenists and the experience and outlook of ancient, enlightened Greeks.

For Matthew Arnold, the common position within the cycle of nations of Periclean Athens and contemporary Britain meant that the Greek classics afforded an immediately relevant point of departure for comprehending Victorian intellectual and spiritual perplexities. Greek literature therefore could provide the current age with "a mighty agent of intellectual deliverance." Such deliverance was now required, Arnold explained in the inaugural lecture,

> because our present age has around it a copious and complex present, and behind it a copious and complex past; it arises, because the present age exhibits to the individual man who contemplates it the spectacle of a vast multitude of facts awaiting and inviting his comprehension. The deliverance consists in man's comprehension of this present and past. It begins when our mind begins to enter into possession of the general ideas which are the law of this vast multitude of facts. It is perfect when we have acquired that harmonious acquiescence of mind which we feel in contemplating a grand spectacle that is intelligible to us; when we have lost that impatient irritation of mind which we feel in presence of an immense, moving, confused spectacle which, while it perpetually excites our curiosity, perpetually baffles our comprehension.[18]

This much-needed comprehension was a deliverance from confusion, from incertitude, and from what Arnold would later call anarchy. Pattern and position, if not design, could be perceived in the seemingly undifferentiated manifold of modern life. To grasp the position of Periclean Athens and its culture in the cycle of the maturation of nations was to begin to set the present age into its own perspective and to hail the Greeks across the interposing centuries as spiritual and intellectual contemporaries.

In the lecture written in 1857 Arnold employed the idea of the common modernity of Periclean Athens and Victorian Britain to assert the direct relevance of the literary achievement of Greece for British literary life. Athenian literature, as exemplified by the works of

---

18. M. Arnold, *On the Classical Tradition*, p. 20.

Pindar, Aeschylus, Sophocles, and Aristophanes, had provided the kind of adequate expression of intellectual needs and difficulties that Arnold hoped contemporary British authors would seek to achieve. Surprisingly, Arnold regarded the ancient poets as more interesting and significant for the manner in which they had accommodated inherited ideas and values to modern tendencies of thought than for the actual quality of their poetry.

> Aeschylus and Sophocles represent an age as interesting as themselves; the names, indeed, in their dramas are the names of the old heroic world, from which they were far separated; but these names are taken, because the use of them permits to the poet that free and ideal treatment of his characters which the highest tragedy demands; and into these figures of the old world is poured all the fulness of life and of thought which the new world has accumulated. This new world in its maturity of reason resembles our own; and the advantages over Homer in their greater significance for *us*, which Aeschylus and Sophocles gain by belonging to this new world, more than compensates for their poetic inferiority to him.[19]

Unlike Euripides, whom Arnold conspicuously did not mention, the two earlier tragedians had, like Goethe in the nineteenth century, set forth constructive rather than destructive criticism. Even if they were lesser poets than Homer, their positive cultural function in their own modern age rendered them figures worthy of attention and emulation in the present. Perceived significance and relevance rather than any disinterested criteria of excellence constituted the touchstone of Arnold's and of the general Victorian interest in Greek antiquity.

Arnold further clarified the relevance he attached to Greece in the long closing paragraph to "Pagan and Medieval Religious Sentiment" (1864), his last major pronouncement on Hellenism before *Culture and Anarchy*. There he argued that between 530 B.C. and 430 B.C. the Greeks had experienced an epoch "of the highest possible beauty and value." And it had been the life of that century that "by itself goes far towards making Greece the Greece we mean when we speak of Greece,—a country hardly less important to mankind than Judea."

19. Ibid., p. 31.

During those decades, through the works of Simonides, Pindar, Aeschylus, and Sophocles, poetry had made "the noblest, the most successful effort she has ever made as the priestess of the imaginative reason, of the element by which the modern spirit, if it would live right, has chiefly to live."[20] Although Arnold never adequately explained, nor perhaps could he explain, exactly what he meant by the imaginative reason, it was for him the faculty or particular functioning of the mind embracing the imagination of childhood and the understanding of adulthood that produced poetry of the noblest character.[21] The imaginative reason flourished at those moments in the Arnoldian scheme of historical development when human nature displayed its most nearly self-perfected intellectual and spiritual life. During such epochs, of which Periclean Athens was a major example, the human spirit took satisfaction in itself and in the relatively full play of its own faculties. This strictly human achievement of Greece loomed large for writers, such as Arnold, who found traditional modes of Christianity untenable. If, as they suspected, human life were finite and limited to temporal existence, the Greek example might suggest the best spiritual accommodation that human beings could make to their situation. The sane, measured, but vital humanity of the Greeks provided a model for the moral and spiritual sensibilities for a new critical modern age. It was for that reason that Arnold regarded Greece as "a country hardly less important to mankind than Judea." Greece as a metaphor—"the Greece we mean when we speak of Greece"—symbolized the source of a distinctly human revelation sought after by those who could no longer look to Judea.

Read in the context of these earlier essays and of his Viconian view of history, Arnold's exploration of Hellenism in *Culture and Anarchy* must be regarded as a statement of radical Victorian humanism. In his own fashion he was continuing the Renaissance deification of humankind. Whereas Thomas Arnold had looked to some mode of divine explanation for the ultimate meaning of the cycles of historical development, Matthew Arnold looked no further than the cycles themselves and tacitly accepted the finitude of the human situation. History itself and by itself constituted the major revelation of the destiny and

20. M. Arnold, *Lectures and Essays in Criticism*, p. 230.
21. DeLaura, *Hebrew and Hellene in Victorian England*, pp. 64–65, 205–06.

character of humanity. Humankind was its own creator and mover, and a correct understanding of the cyclical historical record allowed humankind itself to stand as the best example of its own perfection. By urging the wisdom of Hellenism, Arnold implicitly directed ethical values away from divine commandments and future rewards and pointed toward values that promised fulfillment and reward in this life. Culture was to be pursued less because of its intrinsic excellence than because it was the only mode of meaningful perfection open to human beings. Moreover, because of the stage of historical development in which Europeans now lived, culture, or Hellenism, might be nurtured without fear of encountering the moral collapse many of Arnold's contemporaries expected to result from the demise of Christianity and which he associated with the excesses of romanticism. Arnold's championship of Hellenism, with its portrayal of history as a source of objective values, in effect represented nothing less than a militant call to secular living that promised little or no moral trauma as traditional religious values were abandoned.

In his inaugural lecture of 1857 Arnold had presented Greek civilization as an instrument of intellectual deliverance from the confusion of contemporary life. But in point of fact, over the years just the opposite process took place in the intellectual life of his nation. Greek life, thought, and culture acquired meaning for the Victorians as the novel political problems and moral and religious anxieties of the nineteenth century provided points of departure for examining Greece. This was as true of Arnold's Hellenism as it was of other aspects of the study of antiquity. Rhetorically and emotionally the special character and appeal of his Hellenism originated in its explicit contrast with the evangelical morality that permeated public and private life. Greece viewed for its own sake or as a prescriptive model for a complete moral life, without many of the constraints of the Hebraic heritage, made most Victorians uneasy. Arnold himself could sound so confident about the wisdom of Hellenism because he basically assumed the permanence of the Hebraic moral achievement and because the Germans whose thought he equated with the Hellenic turn of mind had themselves retained vestiges of Judeo-Christian morality. Among the reading public Hellenism within these often-unspoken limits struck a responsive chord. But as soon as a literary critic, such as John Addington Symonds in *Studies in the Greek Poets* (1873), suggested the independent moral sufficiency of the Greek experience, staid reviewers quickly retorted:

> Nothing can be more charming than Hellenism as a literary habit; but it does not fully account for Greeks and their doings as described by themselves.... You cannot go on long regarding Greeks as pure "Hellenists," or beautiful ideal children, if ever you read a book of Thucydides.[22]

Victorian Hellenism could flourish only within the limits of conventional taste and polite morality. Hellenism could break the bounds of evangelical morality but not that of Anglican gentility.

The conflict between Hebraism and Hellenism eventually came to seem less acute as British Christianity became more liberalized. The character of the dualism as it posed itself to late Victorian intellectuals was perhaps best set forth by S. H. Butcher, the editor and translator of Aristotle's *Poetics*. Writing in 1891, he observed:

> The two tendencies summed up in the world's Hebraism and Hellenism are often regarded as opposing and irreconcilable forces; and, indeed, it is only in a few rarely gifted individuals that these principles have been perfectly harmonised. Yet harmonised they can and must be. How to do so is one of the problems of modern civilization;—how we are to unite the dominant Hebrew idea of a divine law of righteousness and of a supreme spiritual faculty with the Hellenic conception of human energies, manifold and expansive, each of which claims for itself unimpeded play; how life may gain unity without incurring the reproach of onesidedness; how, in a word, Religion may be combined with Culture.[23]

In the end, transformations in religion reconciled it to culture. Among intellectual circles religion came to be regarded as a manifestation of human culture, and Hebraism became tempered. In the early nineties Richard Jebb, the Cambridge scholar who more than any other late-century professional classicist championed the Arnoldian tradition,

22. Richard St. John Tyrwhitt, "The Greek Spirit in Modern Literature," *Contemporary Review* 29 (1876–77): 554.
23. Samuel Henry Butcher, *Some Aspects of the Greek Genius* (London: Macmillan and Co., 1916; first published, 1891), pp. 45–46.

declared there existed "no necessary antagonism, between the ideal broadly described as Hebraic, and the permanent, the essential parts of Hellenism." The "essential" character of the latter was its purity and its ability to correct aberrations in modern taste. Jebb discerned "no inherent conflict between true Hellenism and spiritualized Hebraism, such as is contained in Christianity."[24] Neither a new nor a revised reading of the literature or of the experience of Greece accounted for this judgment. Rather, the liberal theological examination of the Old Testament as a document exemplifying only one of many possible modes of religiosity and morality had permitted the two elements of Arnold's dichotomy to shade off into each other. What Jebb termed "spiritualized Hebraism" was not simply Christianity, but a theologically liberalized Christianity largely shorn of bibliolatry and excessive asceticism.

If the function of Hellenism as a foil against evangelical morality declined by the turn of the century, its relevance as a conservative ideological weapon against commercialism, pluralistic, liberal politics, and subjective morality remained. Hefty prescriptions of traditional English humanist values directed against the perceived social ills of the day lay rather poorly concealed in several surveys of Greek civilization published in the decade before World War I. One of the best examples of these tracts, which were designed to preserve both genteel values and classical education, was R. W. Livingstone's *The Greek Genius and Its Meaning to Us* (1912).

Livingstone, who eventually became vice chancellor of Oxford, wrote on a wide variety of subjects. The Oxford tradition of Arnold, Jebb, and Jowett informed his thought and appreciation of Greece. Livingstone saw Greece as the prototype for a moderate conservatism that supported the concepts of a unified state and of traditional political elites against the radical liberalism of Edwardian England. In the Athens portrayed in Pericles' funeral oration was to be found a political life quite different from that of the era of Henry Asquith, David Lloyd George, and Edward Carson.

There is no talk of class jealousy and class selfishness, to be remedied by a system of checks and balances and counter-balances,

24. Richard Claverhouse Jebb, *Essays and Addresses* (Cambridge: Cambridge University Press, 1907), pp. 567, 569.

no talk of compulsory military service necessary to inculcate patriotism and to discipline and direct the irregular energies of the mob, no talk of contributory pensions desirable to breed an idea of thrift, or of a licensing bill designed to protect citizens from drunkenness, of Church schools and a religious education, without which man will relapse into the mud from which he came.[25]

In other words, Periclean Athens was a world without the disruptive pluralistic conflicts of pre-World War I Britain. Livingstone did not mention the earlier Athenian tyrants, the political rivalries of Pericles, the revolution of Corcyra, the massacre of the Melians, or the rule of the Thirty Tyrants. He knew about them, but they were not germane to his purpose nor compatible with the static, unified political ideal he wished to project and to realize.

Livingstone also suggested that Athens had had a healthier intellectual life than British society. Athenian citizens did not suffer from the influence of writers—such as William Butler Yeats, Oscar Wilde, Arnold Bennett, John Galsworthy, and the French symbolists. The Greeks had cultivated neither art for art's sake nor the intellect for the intellect's sake. What Livingstone termed "the morbid pathology and the charming affectations of modern literature" were wholly foreign to the Greek mind. The ancient Greek author brought into being a literature that provided "a representation of some event or emotion which has been felt with vivid exactness and pictured in a full clear light." Those Greeks had "looked straight at life and put down exactly what they saw, exactly as they saw it."[26] In that manner Greek literature avoided all queerness and quaintness. This image of Greek literature, of course, ignored the skepticism and passion of Euripides, the ecstatic concept of poetry in the *Phaedrus*, and the sexuality in Sappho's poetry. But Livingstone's interpretation, like Arnold's attack on romanticism, aligned the Greek literary genius with the traditional English humanist quest for the general and the ideal in literature and art, and his view allowed prescriptive patterns for a literature of moral uplift and sanity to be found in the works of Greek writers.

Near the close of his meditation on the Greek genius Livingstone

25. Richard W. Livingstone, *The Greek Genius and Its Meaning to Us* (Oxford: Clarendon Press, 1912), pp. 66–67.

26. Ibid., pp. 168,180.

probed the question of religion, which more than any other issue seemed to make the Greeks perennially relevant to humanistic intellectuals. Greece was of the highest possible significance to the present day because its people had looked only to themselves for guidance through life.

> Greece . . . stands for humanity, simple and unashamed, with all the variety of its nature free to play. The Greek set himself to answer the question how, with no revelation from God to guide him, with no overbracing necessity to cramp or intimidate him, man should live. It has been a tendency of our own age to deny that heaven has revealed to us in any way how we ought to behave, or to find such a revelation in human nature itself. In either case we are thrown back on ourselves and obliged to seek our guide there. That is why the influence of Greece has grown so much. The Greeks are the only people who have conceived the problem similarly; their answer is the only one which has yet been made.[27]

No one has better stated the particular function that Arnold had expected Hellenism to play in the emerging modern age in Britain. Intellectuals who were loath to look to science as a source of ethical wisdom and who desired to preserve a considerable portion of the values of Western literature and art in the wake of modern social, political, and religious turmoil found hope in the Greek example of human nature creating on its own a humane and orderly culture.

The selective portrayal of Greece that commenced with Arnold afforded Livingstone and others of his generation a sense of cultural and ethical confidence about the possibility of a life of dignity, decency, and restraint outside the intellectual and moral boundaries of religion. The metaphor of Greece opened a humanistic path toward the secular—a path along which most traditional religious landmarks were absent but from which other traditional values still able to address the problems of society and art could be dimly perceived. For Victorian and Edwardian intellectuals, looking to Greece as a guide to humane civilization was a way of looking to themselves for higher values and ideals. Yet just as their selectivity in describing Hellenism

27. Ibid., pp. 247–48.

did not allow them to see ancient Greece truly or to see it whole, neither did it permit them to probe the inner depths and nether side of human nature. Their Hellenism almost denied the existence of the nonrational, aggressive, and self-destructive impulses in humankind. Arnoldian Hellenism promised that an embracing of the secular and the finite would carry no significant social or psychological cost. As a consequence, while the voices of that mode of Hellenism and of humanism have been unfailingly eloquent and nobly intentioned, their thought and their prescriptions for modern culture have been rendered impotent by the larger events of this century.

Humanistic Hellenism in the Criticism of Greek Sculpture

Besides its literature, the major remains of Greek civilization were its architecture, sculpture, and decorated implements of everyday life such as vases and coins. These works of plastic art and the ancient opinions about them awakened humanistic appreciation for the Greeks as a people embodying qualities that sharply contrasted with those of the age of steam, improvement, and utility. For example, one of the characters in Thomas Love Peacock's Crotchet Castle (1831) declared:

> Sir, ancient sculpture is the true school of modesty. But where the Greeks had modesty, we have cant; where they had poetry, we have cant; where they had patriotism, we have cant; where they had anything that exalts, delights, or adorns humanity, we have nothing but cant, cant, cant. And, sir, to show my contempt for cant in all its shapes, I have adorned my house with the Greek Venus, in all her shapes, and am ready to fight her battle against all the societies that ever were instituted for the suppression of truth and beauty.[28]

This image of Greece and its sculpture as symbolizing an antagonism to the harshness, materialism, and sham of modern life would persist throughout the century. What would not persist among Victorian commentators on Greek art was the warm appreciation for statues of Venus "in all her shapes." Later writers much preferred the unseen

28. Thomas Love Peacock, Crotchet Castle (London: J. M. Dent, 1891), p. 92. I am indebted to Heinrich von Staden for drawing my attention to this passage.

beauty of the lost Phidian images of Zeus at Olympia and of Athena in the Parthenon.

Throughout the century British commentators on Greek art urged the aesthetic moral imperative of emulating the purity, the strength, and especially the reserve of Greek sculpture. Just as Arnold used Hellenism to oppose social and political pluralism, romantic literary excess, and subjective morality, the commentators on Greek art used Hellenism as a basis for attacking what they regarded as extravagance, sensuality, particularity, and individualism in contemporary art. In contrast to Arnold, though by no means in opposition to him, these critics tended to emphasize Greek restraint and to ignore Hellenic vitality. Furthermore, they did not share Arnold's historicized concept of the peculiar appropriateness of the Greeks to the present age. For the critics of art the Greeks symbolized a mode of timeless, universal beauty that was more or less foreign to Arnold's Hellenism. At its best, Greek sculpture had in their opinion embodied eternal rules of beauty and good art and had exemplified the application of rules that led the artist to produce work in accordance with both good taste and high morality.

Before the late eighteenth century no tradition for the criticism of ancient art really existed in Britain. There, as elsewhere in Europe, opinions on Greek artistry derived either from the surviving ancient descriptions and evaluations of sculpture or from examination of the very few statues then available for public scrutiny. Most of the latter, including the Laocoön, the Apollo Belvedere, the Venus de Milo, and the dying Gladiator, exemplified very late Greek work. But before a critical literature could develop, British interest in Greek sculpture had to be awakened.

Even in the late Middle Ages a few Greek marbles seem to have made their way to England.[29] In the seventeenth century Thomas Howard, Earl of Arundel, had actively collected Greek works. Only in the mid-eighteenth century, however, did the taste for Greek art grow rapidly and extensively. The prime mover in this development was the Society of Dilettanti. This group of young aristocrats who had

29. Adolf Michaelis, *Ancient Marbles in Great Britain* (Cambridge: Cambridge University Press, 1882), pp. 1–80; Stephen A. Larrabee, *English Bards and Grecian Marbles: The Relationship between Sculpture and Poetry Especially in the Romantic Period* (New York: Columbia University Press, 1943), pp. 1–65.

made the Grand Tour organized themselves during the 1730s into a society to encourage the appreciation of antiquity. Not unexpectedly, most of their early interest was concentrated on Italy. But in 1751 the Society of Dilettanti sponsored the journey of James Stuart and Nicholas Revett to Athens.[30] There the two young artists made drawings of the various artistic and architectural remains of the ancient city. Four years later they returned to Britain and prepared to publish their work. In 1762 the first volume of *The Antiquities of Athens, Measured and Delineated* was published, and three subsequent volumes appeared in 1789, 1794, and 1830. In 1769 the Society of Dilettanti patronized the publication of *Ionian Antiquities; or Ruins of Magnificent and Famous Buildings in Ionia*. Numerous travel books soon followed these widely circulated artistic and architectural studies. By the turn of the century increasing numbers of wealthy or well-patronized Englishmen hazarded the physical and political perils involved in traveling to Greece and the Turkish portions of the Ottoman Empire. Lord Byron and the other noted Philhellenes of the first quarter of the nineteenth century were a late generation of such travelers.

The visitors to Greece and Ionia published their reports and recounted their experiences. Later, geographers such as William Gell and W. M. Leake carried out elaborate studies of the topography of Greece. From these publications and reports stemmed the rise of neoclassical architecture and decoration in Great Britain. Some architects, such as C. R. Cockerell, actually went to Greece to study the ancient ruins at first hand; others simply used the published drawings, floor plans, and measurements. The buildings of classical Edinburgh, churches, museums, banks, townhouses, university structures in London, Cambridge colleges, and civic buildings and country houses throughout the provinces stand as monuments to the various stages of the neoclassical revival that extended through the 1840s. The second great treasure brought to Britain as a result of this initial wave of

30. Lionel Cust and Sidney Colvin, *History of the Society of Dilettanti* (London: Macmillan and Co., 1898), pp. 68–106; Bernard Herbert Stern, *The Rise of Romantic Hellenism in English Literature, 1732–1786* (Menasha, Wis.: George Banta Publishing Co., 1940), pp. 17–38; Larrabee, *English Bards and Grecian Marbles*, pp. 66–98; Terence Spencer, *Fair Greece, Sad Relic: Literary Philhellenism from Shakespeare to Byron* (London: Weidenfeld and Nicholson, 1954), pp. 126–70; James Osborn, "Travel Literature and the Rise of Neo-Hellenism in England," *Bulletin of the New York Public Library* 67 (1963): 279–300.

travelers to Greece was the Elgin Marbles from the Parthenon.[31] Lord Elgin had carried away that statuary shortly after the turn of the century, but only in 1816, after fierce public controversy did a Parliament agree to purchase them for a price that was about half that of Elgin's expenses.

Travelers, artists, architects, aristocrats, and, later, archaeologists brought the images of ancient Greece or the ruins themselves before the British public; but the attitudes and categories through which they were interpreted originated elsewhere. The first source for critical British appreciation of Greek sculpture was the ancient criticism of that artistry.[32] Both eighteenth-century and nineteenth-century commentators drew directly and often quite literally upon the accounts and judgments of ancient sculpture recorded in Pliny's *Natural History*, Quintilian's *Institutio Oratoria*, and Cicero's *Brutus* and *Orator*. These works were consulted directly or as presented in *The Painting of the Ancients* (1638) by Franciscus Junius. Some writers used the Latin, others the translated, version of Junius's compendium of ancient commentaries on ancient art. These sources continued to be cited by British critics of Greek art well past the middle of the nineteenth century, and most of those critics were much more familiar with these ancient literary sources of Greek art history and criticism than they were with either actual Greek statues or even later reproductions.

The second source from which the British criticism of ancient sculpture derived, and one of the lenses through which the literary evidence became read, was the work of Johann J. Winckelmann. His essays on the character of Greek art were contemporaneous with the travels of Stuart and Revett. In 1755 he published *Thoughts on the Imitation of Greek Art in Painting and Sculpture,* which was followed nine years later in 1764 by his *History of Ancient Art.* These works

31. Joseph Mordant Crooke, *The Greek Revival: Neo-classical Attitudes in British Architecture, 1760–1870* (London: John Murray, 1972); Albert Edward Richardson, *Monumental Classical Architecture in Great Britain and Ireland during the Eighteenth and Nineteenth Centuries* (London: B. T. Batsford, 1914); William Linn St. Clair, *Lord Elgin and the Marbles* (London: Oxford University Press, 1967); Theodore Vrettos, *A Shadow of Magnitude: The Acquisition of the Elgin Marbles* (New York: Putnam, 1974).

32. For an important recent discussion of the ancient criticism of art, see Jerome J. Pollitt, *The Ancient View of Greek Art: Criticism, History, and Terminology* (New Haven: Yale University Press, 1974), pp. 12–85.

constituted one of the major turning points in the history of Western taste. Almost single-handedly Winckelmann made the Greek experience alive and vitally interesting to intellectuals and creative writers throughout Germany and the rest of Europe even though he never visited Greece himself. Only the humanists of the Renaissance had previously stirred such fascination with the ancient Greek world.

Winckelmann contended that the most important feature of Greek art was "a noble simplicity and silent greatness."[33] His interpretation of the classical restraint and harmony in fifth- and fourth-century sculpture derived from his reading of the literature of that period rather than from examination of its sculpture. The statues with which he was actually acquainted were Hellenistic. This situation made his thought all the more influential since his readers were themselves normally more familiar with Greek literature than with Greek statuary. Winckelmann's essays and books, which were translated and discussed in Britain by the late 1760s, made two key contributions to the later nineteenth-century interpretation of Greek art. These were his ideas about the character and environment of the ancient Greek people and his view of the particular mode of beauty achieved by their sculptors.

Winckelmann associated the artistic achievement of the Greeks with their particular physical climate and cultural environment.[34] The warm air and plentiful sunshine allowed, and the gymnastic exercises required, them to go about nude or with little clothing on numerous occasions. As a result, their artists had frequent opportunities to observe the natural beauty of the human body. Moreover, Greek statues were closely related to the life of the community because they were erected in commemoration of athletic victories or in connection with

---

33. Elizabeth Gilmore Holt, *A Documentary History of Art*, 3 vols. (Garden City, N.Y.: Doubleday, Anchor Books, 1958), 2:349. See also Hatfield, *Aesthetic Paganism in German Literature*, pp. 1–23; Henry Hatfield, *Winckelmann and His German Critics, 1755–1781: A Prelude to the Classical Age* (New York: King's Crown Press, 1943); Rehm, *Griechentum und Goethezeit*, pp. 23–55; Eliza Marian Butler, *The Tyranny of Greece over Germany* (Boston: Beacon Press, 1958), pp. 9–48; Larrabee, *English Bards and Grecian Marbles*, pp. 90–91; Stern, *The Rise of Romantic Hellenism*, pp. 78–119; Johann J. Winckelmann, *Winckelmann: Writings on Art*, David Irwin, ed. (New York: Phaidon, 1972), pp. 3–57.

34. Johann J. Winckelmann, *The History of Ancient Art*, 2 vols., trans. G. Henry Lodge (Boston: James J. Osgood and Co., 1880), 1:286–89; 2:241.

religious rites. There thus existed both a communal exemplification and a communal appreciation of beauty. Most important for Winckelmann, the political independence of Greece had helped to nurture artistic excellence and had allowed it to flourish. And the passing of that liberty accounted for the decline of Greek art.

Winckelmann's views on the character and environment of the Greek people were transmitted to Britain partly through translations of his books and partly through the works of later German writers, including Lessing, Schiller, the Schlegel brothers, and Goethe. Although these authors may have disagreed with Winckelmann on particular points of aesthetic theory or judgment, they agreed with his essentially classical interpretation of Greek art. They also frequently portrayed the Greeks as an aesthetic people who resembled children and who were in fact the intellectual and artistic children of Western civilization. In contrast to modern culture that was informed by false social values, inhibiting aesthetic rules, and ascetic Christian morality, Greece functioned as a metaphor for a golden age inhabited, if not by prelapsarian human beings, at least by natural children who made use of their imagination to comprehend the world and their reason to restrain their passions against excess.

This idyllic view of the Greeks, originating with Winckelmann and popularized by later German Hellenists, was a fundamental influence on British thinking about Greece. Writers as varied in opinion as William Hazlitt, John Henry Newman, George Grote, John Stuart Mill, J. A. Symonds, and Walter Pater in one way or another invoked the image of the childlike character of the Greeks. The metaphor of childhood was used variously to mean that the Greeks actually thought like children, or that because of their earlier position in history their civilization was the figurative childhood of later cultures, or that as children they had not possessed a full knowledge of the passions or emotional difficulties of life. Most often when representing the Greeks as childlike, a British writer was simply regarding them as exemplifying human virtues and normal healthy impulses that were repressed in an evangelical Christian culture. For example, in *Modern Painters* Ruskin asserted:

> The Greek lived, in all things, a healthy, and, in a certain degree, a
> perfect life. He had no morbid or sickly feeling of any kind. He

was accustomed to face death without the slightest shrinking, and to undergo all kinds of bodily hardship without complaint, and to do what he supposed right and honorable, in most cases, as a matter of course.[35]

Although less well informed writers of more popular works carried the image of the Greeks as children to various levels of bathetic and sentimental insipidity, this interpretation was an exceedingly useful and influential fiction. On the one hand it served as a foil to modern moral values, and on the other it indirectly served to reenforce the Christian view that modern human beings were more decayed from sin than their progenitors.

Winckelmann's second major impact on the British appreciation and criticism of Greek sculpture was his concept that Greek art embodied ideal beauty. He argued that because of the frequent opportunities afforded Greek artists to view the nude body, the ancient sculptors had been able to copy the finest parts of various bodies as models for their statues. The resulting works of art consequently embodied not the beauty of a single individual model but rather the ideal beauty that could be created through selective observation. The collection of data from a host of models and the synthesis of those observations into a work of art that surpassed the natural object had led the Greeks "to universal beauty and its ideal images."[36] Later German Hellenists of Goethe's generation repeated Winckelmann's emphasis on the ideal and intellectual beauty in Greek art. Those judgments received further reenforcement and refinement in the more scientific and archaeologically oriented nineteenth-century criticism of K. O. Müller, Heinrich Brunn, and J. Overbeck, all of whose works were read and studied in Britain.[37]

35. John Ruskin, *The Works of John Ruskin*, 39 vols., ed. E. T. Cook and Alexander Wedderburn (London: George Allen, 1903–12), 5:230.

36. Holt, *Documentary History of Art*, 2:344. See also Winckelmann, *History of Ancient Art*, 1:308–17.

37. The idealist interpretation, with some modification, also continued to appear in the later German scholarship on Greek art that was consulted by British critics. See Karl Otfried Müller, *Ancient Art and Its Remains; or A Manual of the Archaeology of Art*, trans. John Leitch (Edinburgh, 1847; first German edition, 1835); Heinrich Brunn, *Geschichte der Griechischen Künstler* (Stuttgart; 1857); Johannes Adolf Overbeck, *Geschichte des Griechischen Plastik* (Leipzig, 1857–58). Each of these went through more than one edition and was later revised. See also Ernst Langlotz, *Über das Interpretieren Griechischen Plastik* (Bonn: H. Scheur, 1947).

Winckelmann had also contended, however, that the achievement of ideal beauty had occurred only during the highest stage of Greek art. Following in detail the scheme of art history set forth by Quintilian and Cicero, Winckelmann portrayed four periods in the development of Greek sculpture. The first had predated Phidias and was characterized by the "straight and hard." The age of Phidias had seen the "grand and square" style. That mode had been followed during the Praxitelean era by "the beautiful and flowing" style that added grace to the grand style of the previous generation. Finally, with the demise of political liberty, Winckelmann saw Greek sculpture as declining into an "imitative" period when sculptors merely copied nature or earlier statues without attempting to attain an ideal beauty.[38] British critics later repeated this same pattern in their accounts of the rise and fall of Greek art. Its origin in the ancient critics of art, and Winckelmann's repetition of the scheme, convinced them of its validity.

Winckelmann's emphasis on the ideal character of Greek sculpture allowed British commentators to graft his criticism onto the existing aesthetics of British humanism. These were embodied in the *Discourses* of Sir Joshua Reynolds, delivered to the Royal Academy of Art between 1769 and 1790. Reynolds, like Winckelmann, stood in the aesthetic tradition of the seventeenth-century critic Giovanni Pietro Bellori who had regarded the attainment of ideal beauty as the highest goal of art. Part of Bellori's work suggested that ideal beauty was achieved through the selective portrayal of actual nature while other portions suggested that ideal beauty existed only in the mind of the artist.[39] Winckelmann had drawn upon the former approach; Reynolds tended to emphasize the latter. As he declared to the Academy:

> The Art which we profess has beauty for its object; this it is our business to discover and to express; the beauty of which we are in

38. Winckelmann, *History of Ancient Art*, 2:130, 153. See Quintilian *Institutio Oratoria* XII, x, 1–10, and Cicero *Brutus* 70. For information on earlier uses of this pattern of development in ancient art by the early modern humanist Joseph Scaliger, consult Rudolf Pfeiffer, *History of Classical Scholarship from 1300 to 1850* (Oxford: Clarendon Press, 1976), pp. 113–19.

39. Holt, *Documentary History of Art*, 2:93–196; R. W. Lee, "Ut Pictura Poesis: The Humanistic Theory of Painting," *Art Bulletin* 22 (1940): 203–10, 261–63.

quest is general and intellectual; it is an idea that subsists only in the mind; the sight never beheld it, nor has the hand expressed it: it is an idea residing in the breast of the artist, which he is always laboring to impart, and which he dies at last without imparting; but which he is yet so far able to communicate, as to raise the thoughts and extend the views of the spectator; and which, by a succession of art, may be so far diffused, that its effects may extend themselves imperceptibly into public benefits, and be among the means of bestowing on whole nations refinement of taste; which, if it does not lead directly to purity of manners, obviates at least their greatest deprivation, by disentangling the mind from appetite, and conducting the thoughts through successive stages of excellence, till that contemplation of universal rectitude and harmony which began by Taste, may, as it is exalted and refined, conclude in Virtue.[40]

Reynolds commended the portrayal of the general rather than the particular and urged students to study the works of great artists of the past instead of only resorting to natural models. For Reynolds, the work of the artist must be infused with a moral intent. The gratification of the senses directly opposed the pursuit of ideal beauty, and the more art appealed to the senses the further it stood removed from this beauty and from the moral experience that such beauty could foster. Winckelmann had defined ideal beauty somewhat less metaphysically than Reynolds and had presented it as less wholly separated from the artist's observation of nature. The German critic convinced British commentators of the ideal character of Greek sculpture, but Reynolds furnished the specific meaning they attached to the concept of the ideal.

In the early nineteenth century British artists and critics who questioned the ideal nature of major Greek sculptures did so in terms of opposition to the aesthetics of Reynolds. In 1816, members of a select parliamentary committee charged with advising about the desirability of purchasing the Elgin Marbles for the nation asked witnesses drawn from the artistic community whether the statuary partook of ideal beauty. The artists and sculptors who were consulted, and who in-

40. Joshua Reynolds, *Discourses Delivered to the Students of the Royal Academy,* ed. Roger Fry (London: Seeley and Co., 1905), p. 264.

cluded Joseph Nollekins, John Flaxman, Richard Westmacott the elder, Francis Chauntry, Charles Rossi, Thomas Lawrence, and Benjamin West, admired the statues and thought they would prove beneficial to the advancement of British art. But they were divided in their opinions about the ideal beauty of the Parthenon sculptures. Several of the artists thought the Apollo Belvedere and the Belvedere torso were more nearly ideal works of art than the Elgin Marbles, even if the former were, as then believed, Roman copies. Others contended that the Elgin Marbles were of higher value than the Apollo because, in Westmacott's words, they embodied "that which approaches nearest to nature, with grand form."[41] The majority of the artists testifying, as well as Benjamin Robert Haydon, the foremost champion of the Elgin Marbles, upheld an aesthetics of actual rather than ideal nature and regarded the marbles of the Parthenon as exemplifying that truth. But which view of the sculptures a person advocated depended largely on his opinion of Reynolds's theories. As William Hazlitt bluntly declared in an article for the *Examiner* in 1816, "The Elgin Marbles are the best answer to Sir Joshua Reynolds's Discourses. . . . Art is the imitation of nature; and the Elgin Marbles are in their essence and their perfection casts from nature—from fine nature, it is true, but from real, living, moving nature."[42] Parliament the same year voted to purchase the Elgin Marbles without comment on the division of opinion among the artists. But the majority opinion in this debate and the concept that true art imitates actual nature subsided from considerations of Greek sculpture for almost half a century until revived by John Ruskin—again in opposition to Reynolds. Even then it remained a minority point of view. For most Victorian and Edwardian critics, the ideality and not the realism or naturalism of Greek art constituted its foremost excellence and virtue.

The association of naturalism with sensuality and the continuing emphasis in German commentaries on the ideal character of the Greek achievement largely accounted for the retreat from the evaluations of

41. *Report from the Select Committee of the House of Commons on the Earl of Elgin's Collection of Sculptured Marbles* (London: John Murray, 1816), pp. 83–84. See also Frederick J. Cummings, "Benjamin Robert Haydon and the Critical Reception of the Elgin Marbles" (Ph.D. diss., University of Chicago, 1967); Bernard Ashmole, *The Classical Ideal in Greek Sculpture* (Cincinnati: The University of Cincinnati, 1964), pp. 33–44.

42. Willliam Hazlitt, *The Complete Works of William Hazlitt*, 12 vols. (London: J. M. Dent and Sons, 1930), 18:100.

1816. Another reason for this was the reliance of the Victorian critics on the ancient critics whose views of the development of Greek sculpture meshed with their own moral sensibilities. For example, Philip Smith wrote the articles on sculpture for the important and widely consulted *Dictionary of Greek and Roman Biography and Mythology* (1844–49) edited by his father William Smith. The younger Smith drew extensively upon the standard ancient sources, including Quintilian and Pliny, and his comparison of Phidias and Praxiteles clearly reflected the opinions of the ancient critics.

> The contrast was marked in their subjects as well as in their style. The chryselephantine statue of Zeus at Olympia realised, as nearly as art can realise, the illusion of the actual presence of the supreme divinity; and the spectator who desired to see its prototype could find it in no human form, but only in the sublimest conception of the same divinity which the kindred art of poetry had formed; but the Cnidian Aphrodite of Praxiteles, though an ideal representation, expressed the ideal only of sensual charms and emotions connected with them, and was avowedly modelled from a courtesan. Thus also the subjects of Praxiteles in general were those divinities whose attributes were connected with sensual gratification, or whose forms were distinguished by soft and youthful beauty,—Aphrodite and Eros, Apollo and Dionysus.[43]

The ancient criticism of Phidias and Praxiteles served to confirm the modern moral aesthetics derived from Reynolds. These ancient views and descriptions allowed Smith to infuse the major qualities praised by Reynolds into the vanished statues of Phidias and to condemn the style, subject, models, and intention of the mode of sculpture that had commenced with Praxiteles—whose statues had violated Reynolds's canons by permitting the mind of the observer to revel in sensual beauty.

The most extensive mid-Victorian discussion of Greek sculpture appeared in the commentaries of Richard Westmacott the younger, who was a sculptor and professor of sculpture at the Royal Academy. His father had testified in favor of purchasing the Elgin Marbles on the

---

43. Philip Smith, "Praxiteles," William Smith, ed., *Dictionary of Greek and Roman Biography and Mythology*, 3 vols. (London: Taylor, Walton, and Maberly; and John Murray, 1849), 3:519.

grounds of their affinity with natural beauty. Between 1841 and 1860 the younger Westmacott wrote three major and quite similar articles that appeared in *The Penny Cyclopaedia, The English Cyclopaedia,* and the eighth edition of the *Encyclopaedia Britannica.*[44] He later expanded the *Britannica* essay and published it separately in 1864 as *Handbook of Sculpture.* Westmacott, like Philip Smith, merged the moral aesthetics of Reynolds with the ideal interpretation of Greek art derived from the ancient sources, from Winckelmann, and from K. O. Müller's *Ancient Art and Its Remains* (1835; translated, 1847). This combination of thought marked most discussions of Greek sculpture for the rest of the century and drew consideration of the subject directly into the English humanist tradition and into the categories of British academic art criticism. Westmacott ascribed the perfection of the Greek artistic achievement to the peculiarly Greek "sensibility to, and appreciation of the beautiful in all its various aspects." The Greeks had been the first nation to grasp that sculpture was an "imitative" rather than a "symbolical" art. That recognition meant they could copy nature and then select from nature to create "*ideal* Beauty." Because of the special sensibility of the Greeks to "beauty in all its forms," the public opinion that regulated the endeavors of the sculptor was also attuned to ideal beauty and prevented excesses of eccentric individualism on the part of the sculptor. During its best age under the collective opinion and patronage of the city-state, sculpture had been no "mere mechanical pursuit" but an art with a genuinely moral influence through which "mind was made to illumine matter."[45] In those terms the statues of the age of Phidias had epitomized the highest collective ideals of the Greek people.

Westmacott, like other British and Continental commentators, regarded Greek sculpture after the era of Phidias as infected with moral and aesthetic decay. Winckelmann had explained that decline in terms of a growing imitation that carried sculpture away from the ideal beauty and grand style of Phidias. He had also linked the loss of creativity directly to the political fortunes of the Greek cities. What

44. Consult the articles under "Sculpture" in the *Encyclopaedia Britannica,* 8th ed.; *Penny Cyclopaedia of the Society for the Diffusion of Useful Knowledge,* 27 vols. (London: 1833–43); and *The English Cyclopaedia: A New Dictionary of Universal Knowledge,* 23 vols. (London: Bradbury and Evans, 1854–62).

45. Richard Westmacott, *Handbook of Sculpture: Ancient and Modern* (Edinburgh: Adam and Charles Black, 1865), pp. 78, 79, 84, 85.

Winckelmann had described as an aesthetic and political decline, Westmacott interpreted, as did Philip Smith, in terms of moral decadence, with Praxiteles as the chief villain. Westmacott portrayed the work of that fourth-century sculptor as "soft and meretricious" and as having exemplified a movement toward sensuality and reality in artistic production. This naturalism and realistic beauty of Praxiteles' statues, in particular his Cnidian Venus, had been remarked by the ancient critics. To those opinions Westmacott added the observation that as such art emerged, "The object now was not so much to elevate and instruct as to please, by the representation of what was simply physically beautiful and seductive; and the result was, of course, to induce a lower standard of taste and fancy in the public."[46] This moral aesthetics was typically Victorian, but, more important, it derived directly from the thought of Joshua Reynolds.

Reynolds had on one occasion told the Royal Academy, "Whatever abstracts the thoughts from sensual gratifications, whatever teaches us to look for happiness within ourselves, must advance in some measure the dignity of our nature." For Westmacott, who had perhaps seen a copy of the Cnidian Venus but who had definitely read the ancient sources, such as Pliny's report of the attempted nocturnal rape of that statue, the sculpture of Praxiteles represented art executed in direct opposition to Reynolds's injunction. Praxiteles had introduced the portrayal of "voluptuous form with the most exquisite surface-executions of the marble." The charm of the polishing of the stone and the portrayal of "attractive and exciting, rather than elevating subjects" constituted the particular character of his sculpture. Westmacott concluded, "It is impossible not to feel that this was an indication that sculpture was already leaving its higher and nobler purpose." There could be "no doubt that a less pure and a less elevated feeling for art was induced by it." Beyond appealing to sensuality through his technique, Praxiteles had also conceived "the essence of sculpture" as "truth of imitation applied to the best and most perfect class of form" and had then "selected for its expression the voluptuous female and the youthful male character, in its fullest beauty, to the sacrifice of the higher aesthetic quality which was dominant in the more severe works of Phidias."[47] In other words, Praxiteles had carved statues of nude

46. Ibid., pp. 143, 176.
47. Reynolds, *Discourses*, p. 263; Pliny *Natural History* XXXVI, 21; Westmacott, *Handbook of Sculpture*, pp. 177, 178, 205.

men and women that were sensuously and sexually beautiful and that did not lead the observer to moral experience or contemplation beyond the immediate and presumably pleasurable reactions of his senses.

To no small extent Westmacott intended his criticism not only to illustrate the character of Greek art but also to prescribe rules for contemporary sculptors. He was particularly interested in driving sensuality from mid-century British sculpture. His attack on the sensuous led him into a long digression on the subject of polychromy, or the coloring of statues, a practice long known to have prevailed among the Greeks. The paint had long vanished from the Greek statues that remained to posterity and that had been held up as patterns for later sculptors. However, during the 1840s the English neoclassical sculptor John Gibson, whose studio was in Rome, had begun to carve statues to which he applied paint. One of these was a figure of Queen Victoria; another was a statue of Venus that is now in the Liverpool Museum.[48] Westmacott's father had adorned certain portions of the statuary above the entrance to the British Museum with gold paint. In his commentary on Greek sculpture the younger Westmacott criticized this modern practice with almost untamed aesthetic fury and in doing so revealed an important and typical function of the mid-Victorian discussions and explorations of Greek culture.

Westmacott could not deny that many ancient statues had been painted, but he could and did deny the wisdom of the practice. He contended that polychromy had originated not with the civilized Greeks but during an earlier, more barbarous age and that it had not been characteristic of the best period of Greek sculpture. Even if some artists had applied paint to sculpture during the fifth century, polychromy represented a vestigial remnant and constituted no part of the essential achievement of high Greek art. Westmacott thought that the Elgin Marbles and the works surviving from the Hellenistic period would not be improved nor the aesthetic experience of the observer heightened if they stood before the world as originally painted. He went on to assert, "It is obvious that if sculpture could by any possibility be subjected to the transformation that the Polychromy of the ancient kind would effect, all the known principles by which it is now

48. Gisela Richter, "Polychromy in Greek Sculpture," American Journal of Archaeology, 48 (1944): 321–33; Lady Elizabeth Eastlake, ed., The Life of John Gibson (London: Longmans, Green, and Co., 1870), pp. 123–29; 209–14.

judged, as an art of form, must undergo also a total change." These "known principles" to which Westmacott alluded had in large measure been set forth by Reynolds in his Tenth Discourse, with specific comments on the question of the coloration of statues. Reynolds had deplored the application of color to stone on the grounds of its sensual appeal and subsequent lowering of the morality of sculpture.

> If the business of sculpture were to administer pleasure to ignorance, or mere entertainment to the senses, the Venus of Medicis might certainly receive much improvement by colour; but the character of Sculpture makes it her duty to afford delight of a different, and perhaps, of a higher kind; the delight resulting from the contemplation of perfect beauty: and this, which is in truth an intellectual pleasure, is in many respects incompatible with what is merely addressed to the senses, such as that with which ignorance and levity contemplate elegance of form.[49]

By associating his criticism of Greek art with such views, Westmacott set the appreciation of Greek sculpture firmly within the bounds of academic rules and taste. The Greek achievement was not to form the basis for a challenge to the rules of conventional taste and morality in the present day. Art was to improve the mind and raise the morality of the nation, but that would not be accomplished by appeal to the senses or by use of paint on marble or by abandoning the aesthetic wisdom of Sir Joshua Reynolds.

Westmacott's rather undistinguished volume, and more particularly his remarks on sensuality and polychromy, reveal an important tension within Victorian humanistic Hellenism. The Greeks were to lead nineteenth-century men and women beyond Christian asceticism and utilitarian humdrum, but they were not to lead them beyond the limits of established good taste and reasonable morality. In the plastic arts polychromy was the equivalent of the irrational Greek impulses Matthew Arnold ignored after the period of his early poetry. It was also on a parallel with the slavery, democratic injustice, and homosexuality that were other moral blots on the Greek experience. In their prescriptive function the Greeks could be regarded as natural only so long as they did not display the entire range of natural or artistic

49. Westmacott, *Handbook of Sculpture*, p. 155. Reynolds, *Discourses*, p. 269.

impulse. Within the ethical stance of humanism Greek art and, by inference, Greek culture were intended to prescribe what F. T. Palgrave in 1870 quite simply termed "propriety"—the quality that he associated with the sculpture of the Phidian age.

Speaking of course of the two or three centuries before the "decadence," there is no straining, either after effect or novelty; no affectation; whether we look at the material side of the art, as vase-decoration, or at the choice of subject, or the management of the design, everything is found to be quietly and unostentatiously right, as if by operation of natural law. A certain high pleasure, as the end of all art, is uniformly kept in view; hence the last impression left is always beauty; never the grotesque, or the piquant, or the baldly natural, or the repulsively powerful, as in modern art. It is unfantastic; it is moderate; it is sane; it rejects what goes no further than mere suggestion; it hates the vague and the introspective;—in a word, Greek art is opposed to many popular tendencies, and proves the validity of its opposition to them by the permanent superiority of its own productions.[50]

Greek sculpture represented the beautiful and the balanced in art as opposed to an unselective realism or a naturalism that selected for representation the ugly or unseemly elements of life.

The sense of what was appropriate in art and in life generally formed the major thrust of the Victorian interpretation of Greek culture during the third quarter of the century. Writers appealed to Greece as an allegedly universal human experience, but the moral and social values of genteel upper-class English society set the parameters of that prescriptive experience. Critics transferred this moral outlook, which originated largely in the Augustan humanism of the eighteenth century, to the ancient past and then, in accordance with their humanist aims, upheld that past as a source of wisdom for current ethical and cultural conduct. Once so transferred, these traditional values assumed the guise of a higher, more ancient, and universal cultural heritage that critics of art and society could portray as the proper models for contemporary artistic endeavor.

This morally prescriptive mode of criticism continued through the

50. *The Academy* 1 (1870): 117.

last quarter of the century and into the first decades of the twentieth. The new examples of Greek sculpture unearthed by the archaeologists only marginally modified the critical approach. Commentary on Greek sculpture now became a device for combating both realism and formlessness in contemporary art and for championing collective rather than individualistic values in artistic creation. This new emphasis allowed the list of morally acceptable Greek sculptors to be extended to include Praxiteles. Walter Copeland Perry, an educator and popularizer who spent much of his life in Germany, published *Greek and Roman Sculpture: A Popular Introduction* in 1882. Perry, who made no claims for critical originality, ascribed an "ineffable nobleness, dignity, and grace" to the ancient Greek mind; and he associated those qualities with Praxiteles as well as with earlier sculptors. In contradiction to Westmacott's accusation of voluptuousness, Perry argued, probably from his examination of better Roman copies, that the Cnidian Venus stood "before the mind's eye solely as the highest representation of the loveliness of woman, without any higher attribute of mind or character, and incapable of inspiring any sublime or heroic sentiment." Such simple, unadorned female loveliness was in itself a positive good because Praxiteles had avoided the portrayal of female sensuality and had rather delineated "the beauty of tender, loving, or pathetic emotions, expressed in graceful forms and lovely features." That achievement meant he should be numbered "among ideal artists, because he did not rest in beauty as a sufficient end in itself, but employed it for the representation of thought and feeling."[51] In so defending Praxiteles, Perry was attempting to define acceptable and unacceptable modes of naturalism. There was nothing intrinsically wrong either morally or aesthetically in the portrayal of the nude female body, but the intent of the artist must be moral and the mode of portrayal must avoid, as had Praxiteles, degrading naturalism and realism. Within contemporary art Perry might well have made a similar comparison between the softly wistful female nudes in the classical Greek scenes painted by Lord Leighton and the paintings of similar subjects being produced on the Continent with emphasis on the sensuality of women portrayed in classical settings.

51. Walter Copeland Perry, *Greek and Roman Sculpture: A Popular Introduction to the History of Greek and Roman Sculpture* (London: Longmans, Green, and Co., 1882), pp. 300, 446, 461.

Perry also attempted to refute the notion that the presence of grace
and the absence of severity in fourth-century Greek sculpture were
indications of moral decay. He regarded the more nearly human
fourth-century statues of the gods as reflecting a new feeling of need
for divine companionship rather than new sensualism. As a consequence, whatever sculpture may have lost "in dignity and sanctity," it
had gained "in tenderness and grace." Furthermore, "the field of
beauty, mirth, and love" had been opened for artistic portrayal. Although "earnest and religious spirits" might regret the shift in taste,
"to the majority of mankind the vivid emotions, the tender grace, the
variety and brilliant coloring of the new school will more than com-
pensate for the calm dignity, the religious sanctity and severity, and
the divine sublimity of the old."[52] An Anglican Broad Churchman
might very well have used the same vocabulary to describe and defend
the theological transformation of the severe Christian God of the
Evangelicals into the loving, tender God of late-century religious liberals. The introduction of distinctly human and even sentimental
characteristics into either Greek sculpture or contemporary religion
did not necessarily imply a decline in morality or religious seriousness
in either age. A loving deity or a statue of graceful beauty might prove
genuinely beneficial and morally uplifting to the human spirit.

Jane Harrison in *Introductory Studies in Greek Art* of 1885 intensified
the use of Greek sculpture simultaneously to attack contemporary
realism in art and to uphold thoroughly humanistic values. Harrison
belonged to that first generation of Newnham College graduates who
made such a significant impact on British life and the intellectual
emancipation of British women. Later, as a major exponent of the
anthropological approach to the Greeks and as an advocate for the
recognition of the irrational in Greek art and religion, she would
become one of the most important and controversial classical scholars
of Edwardian Britain. But in 1885 she was still a very young scholar
who had only recently liberated herself from the evangelical training
of her Yorkshire childhood, and her aesthetic ideas were still for the
most part those of her teachers. She was just beginning the difficult
task of finding a place in a scholarly and artistic world dominated by
men and had not yet begun the study of Greek vases at the British

52. Ibid., p. 373.

Museum or the examination of Greek myths and anthropology that would carry her thoughts in directions very different from those of her first book.

In *Introductory Studies in Greek Art* Harrison advocated an extremely idealist interpretation of Greek sculpture, the purpose of which went beyond mere exposition of ancient art. She wrote that she would be satisfied, "if, by the help of the wisdom of Plato, I can show any of the citizens of our state why, eschewing the dry bones of symbolism and still more warily shunning the rank, unwholesome pastures of modern realism, they may nurture their souls on the fair sights and pure visions of Ideal art." The specter of Joshua Reynolds and the heritage of the humanist tradition were again present in a work criticizing Greek sculpture. Harrison argued that the Greek artist had not attempted to make symbols of the gods as had the Assyrians and Egyptians, nor had he merely copied nature. Rather, the artists of Greece had idealized and created images that transcended nature. Their ideal art had avoided both the harshness of realism and the dangers of extravagant individualism.

> There seems every opportunity for the development of realism, but the Greek deliberately and consciously rejects it. His democratic instinct resented the over-pre-eminence of the individual, and his religious instinct imposed strict limits of self-exaltation. What was personal in the triumph ode, in the votive statue, was always regarded with suspicion; it was not that in which the god delighted. What of beauty and strength was large, universal, human, that was the proper glory of the victor. We see here the promptings of that instinct for generalization, that rising from the particular to the universal, which for the Greek issued ultimately in the highest idealism.[53]

Like many other contemporary writers, Harrison equated Greek thought generally with that of Plato, whose desire to purify the arts of his day found a parallel among those late Victorians who eschewed the moral and aesthetic implications of more advanced contemporary artistic movements. In many cases these critics would seem to have derived their aesthetic outlook from the idealist tradition of Bellori,

53. Jane Ellen Harrison, *Introductory Studies in Greek Art* (London: T. Fisher Unwin, 1885), pp. vii, 189.

Winckelmann, and Reynolds and then found confirmation for those views in the text of Plato.

Similar critical sentiments found their way into Charles Waldstein's *Essays on the Art of Pheidias* which, like Harrison's volume, appeared in 1885. Waldstein, who changed his name to Walston during World War I, had been born in the United States and educated in Germany. He then settled in Great Britain where he was long associated with King's College and where he served at various times as Slade Professor of Art at Cambridge, Director of the Fitzwilliam Museum, and leader of archaeological expeditions for the American School in Athens.[54] Waldstein's commentary on Phidias was a direct assault on both artistic realism and art for art's sake. For Waldstein, art properly understood constituted a moral medium and an enterprise that

> does not deal with *whatever is*, it does not take all things as they happen to present themselves (as science must do); but it chooses and selects among all things in accordance with principles inherent in the human mind, and creates a state not of "what is," but of "what ought to be."

Art was not a path for advancing human knowledge or a means of opening new frontiers of human experience; it was an ethical endeavor aimed toward the ideal presentation of truth. To the Greeks, Waldstein thought, this ethical impulse had come naturally because they possessed "the childlike imagination of an essentially artistic people" that allowed them to look at objects with an inner eye. Appreciation of their artistic excellence that had portrayed an "idealised nature" and that had attained "the highest generalization of form" did not depend on a particular mood or on particular qualities of the individual modern observer. The sculptures of the Greeks were "valid for all sane men, all men of a certain physiological constitution of their senses, surrounded by man and nature relatively the same."[55] Perhaps no other critic so boldly meshed the idealism of Greek art asserted by Winckelmann with the aesthetic moral imperative set forth by Reynolds.

54. *Who Was Who, 1916–1928* (London: Adam and Charles Black, 1929), p. 1088; *King's College Annual Report,* November 19, 1927, pp. 1–2. Waldstein's papers are in the library of King's College, Cambridge.

55. Charles Waldstein, *Essays on the Art of Pheidias* (Cambridge: Cambridge University Press, 1885), pp. 43, 75, 395.

Many, though not all, of the aesthetic currents in contemporary art disturbed Waldstein. In his lectures *Greek Sculpture and Modern Art,* delivered just before World War I, he criticized contemporary artists for "their opposition to what they call beauty." He regretted that "their work becomes often a puerile—or, at all events, an exaggerated—protest against that which has hitherto been considered worthy of artistic effort." Greek artists, on the contrary, had cultivated the ideal beauty of nature "freed from individual accidence of one place or one period, of one individual or of one situation; free also from the accidence of individual perception on the part of man, and thus corresponding to the laws which govern man's perception and man's fundamental desire for harmony."[56] The humanist outlook was here fundamental. What is true for art is true for all times and all places. The Greeks had discovered a part of that truth, engrained it in marble, and left it as an aesthetic lesson for later peoples. For Waldstein and other commentators, the sculpture of the Greeks might restore health to contemporary art. As a reviewer in *The Academy* wrote in 1896, "It is on the diffusion of the spirit of Greek art . . . that the best hopes for European art in the future must rest. To an intelligent understanding of that spirit we must look for deliverance from the petty prettyness of our toys and the smart vulgarity of our galleries."[57] This was the same role that Arnold had assigned to Greece in regard to poetry in 1854.

The major Edwardian advocates of the sanity and balance of Greek art as a prescriptive contrast to the work of modern artists and the artistic pluralism and romanticism of modern culture were the Gardner brothers, Percy and Ernest. Both were distinguished professional classical scholars who wrote widely on Greek sculpture, coins, and archaeology. Unlike many previous critics of ancient sculpture, they were thoroughly familiar with several areas of Greek civilization. Nonetheless, once either of them departed from strictly technical analysis, he became a spokesman for academic art, conventional taste, and traditional humanistic values. Percy Gardner also wrote exten-

56. Charles Waldstein, *Greek Sculpture and Modern Art* (Cambridge: Cambridge University Press, 1914), pp. 34, 48. Waldstein seems not to have been opposed to all modern art but rather to what he saw as art that embodied unseemly extremes. See Charles Waldstein, *Art in the Nineteenth Century* (New York: Macmillan Company, 1903).

57. *The Academy*, 49 (1896): 369.

sively as a Christian layman on topics of liberal theology and biblical criticism. In this capacity he described himself as "a member of the school of Jowett and Arnold, of Maurice and Stanley." Percy Gardner regarded the period of the flourishing of Greek civilization as one of the eras before Christ "when a large outpouring of the divine spirit had taken place."[58] These religious considerations and the ethical outlook they embraced thoroughly permeated his normative evaluation of Greek art.

In 1905 Percy Gardner published *A Grammar of Greek Art* (later reprinted as *Principles of Greek Art*) that remained for many years a standard work on the subject. Not unexpectedly, Gardner presented a strongly idealist interpretation of the subject, but rather more fully than previous commentators he rooted the Greek artistic achievement in the collective life of the polis. He declared, "Idealism in Greece is not individual, but social; it belongs to the nation, the city, or the school, rather than to this or that artist."[59] The ethos of the ancient polis had provided the soil for the ideas and ideals that came to be embodied in the work of the artist. In a later essay Gardner's admiration for the collective genius of the polis, an attitude perhaps derived from Alfred Zimmern's *The Greek Commonwealth* (1911), led him to question the primacy even of the genius of Phidias. Gardner there observed: " . . . the Parthenon is less the work of individuals than the highest artistic bloom of a city and a period. Every worker on it seems to have partaken of a common inspiration, which worked rather in the unconscious than in the conscious strata of his mind."[60] The shared values and moral expectations of the polis provided both an ethical ideal that the artist might strive to express and a cultural restraint on the excessive individualism that might separate him and his activity from his audience.

Gardner's particular concept of the moral character of the polis owed much to Edwardian historians of Athens and commentators on Greek political thought who in turn were indebted to collectivist social

58. Percy Gardner, *The Growth of Christianity* (London: Adam and Charles Black, 1907), pp. vi, 3. See also Percy Gardner, *Autobiographica* (Oxford: Basil Blackwell, 1933), passim.

59. Percy Gardner, *A Grammar of Greek Art* (New York: Macmillan Co., 1905), p. 14.

60. Percy Gardner, *New Chapters in Greek Art* (Oxford: Oxford University Press, 1926), p. 69.

theorists. His views also stemmed from the social and political thought of the Broad Churchmen, including Arnold whom he so deeply admired. They had looked to a reformed Church of England that could embrace the entire nation and enunciate a collective social ideal to inhibit economic and political individualism. The absence of such a collective sense of identity among the citizens of Edwardian Britain accounted, Gardner thought, for the failure of modern artists to attain beauty in their enterprise.

> In our days the sculptor ordinarily works from a single model, and the works exhibited at the Royal Academy show that the models accepted by modern sculptors are often of a very poor type, ill-nourished and ill-trained. Among a people predominately urban, and living under unhealthy conditions, the admiration of robust beauty in man and woman is apt to give way to admiration of what is fashionable or smart. The danger of physical degeneracy hangs low over all the nations of Europe. Our continual competitions, our restless travellings, our reckless sacrifice of all that restrains, in our endeavours to reach certain ends, make a gospel of rhythm and moderation seem to us dull and poor. It does not spur our jaded energies, or rouse us with a stimulating appeal. And yet, as it seems to me, unless the English-speaking races return in some measure to the artistic ideals of Greece, they are in the long run doomed.[61]

Gardner's remarks incorporated the traditional humanist critique of getting and spending as well as the post–Boer War fear of physical degeneracy. His solution to those problems was a revival of Winckelmann's belief that Greek sculpture was the creation of artists who had been able to observe a beautiful, healthy people dwelling in a unified, free community. To champion the Greek ideal was, for Gardner, to call for the collective nurturing of a healthy, patriotic citizenry that would provide artists with models after whom sculpture of ideal beauty might be patterned. Better art required a better society.

61. P. Gardner, *Grammar of Greek Art*, p. 102. Several years later (1911) Gardner told the Society for the Promotion of Hellenic Studies, "The Greek feeling for corporate life, of the continuity of the race, and the Greek love of balance and moderation are even now the most potent forces to keep society from dissolution." Gardner, *New Chapters in Greek Art*, p. 355.

Humanistic writers had not only frequently criticized excessive commercialism and subjectivity; they had also questioned the primacy of empirical science as the chief mode of perceiving and interpreting the world. This attitude also informed Gardner's evaluation of the ideal character of Greek art. Like Reynolds, he urged upon his readers the possibility of an aesthetic truth transcending that available through sense knowledge alone. The Greek artists, he explained, had "aimed not at a rigid adherence to the truth, but at producing a certain effect on human beings." They had understood that the realm of nature existed for humankind only as "reflected in the human mind," and their recognition of that truth constituted "the first law of art of all practical pursuits in the world." Gardner encouraged modern artists to emulate their Greek forebears and to pursue a "higher naturalism" that would portray nature in its state nearest to perfection. That aesthetics necessarily required the artist to possess "judgment, which discriminates between good and bad, and emotion, which leaves the good and rejects the bad." Pursuit of the higher naturalism would overcome "the aesthetic nihilism" of artists who were "willing to copy whatever nature may offer." In achieving their own mode of higher naturalism, Greek sculptors had sought to perpetuate not the "spontaneous variations in the evolution of man" but rather "such variations as spoke of purpose and ideality in the forces which were moulding man." They had quite properly understood their task to be that of "adding a certain degree of moral and spiritual elevation to mere physical beauty."[62] The values to be imparted through their artistry had originated in the ethos, or collective values, of the Greek community. The truth communicated through their sculpture and awakened in the observer was the prescriptive moral truth of the polis rather than mere description of physical nature.

A similar emphasis on collective social life informed Ernest A. Gardner's criticism of Greek art. He was disturbed by the growing separation of taste between the Edwardian artist and the general public and believed that this problem originated in the refusal of the contemporary artist to pay proper respect to the function of convention in art. The flight from convention and toward extreme individualistic expression accounted for "the chaos which we see in a modern exhibi-

62. P. Gardner, *Grammar of Greek Art*, pp. 40, 100, 104.

tion of sculpture" and constituted one of the chief reasons "why the modern public is so bewildered in its study of modern sculpture." To produce works of dignity and originality, the artist could not depend on his own instincts and observations alone. To do so was to leave himself "at the mercy of fortuitous and often disadvantageous surroundings, instead of having to guide him a tradition, which, if it sometimes confines him too narrowly, saves him from losing his way altogether." The Greek sculptors had comprehended that truth and had happily succeeded in combining "tradition and observation." As Ernest Gardner argued, through the wise combination of tradition and observation Praxiteles had avoided sensuous realism in his Cnidian Venus. In that controversial statue the sculptor had expressed his individuality, but it was "the individuality of a character realised within his mind by the artist, not merely copied from the human model he set before him."[63] What had sustained such idealism in his art and prevented Praxiteles from taking satisfaction in possibly prurient thoughts was his close relationship to the community and the subordination of his own individualism to the religion of the polis and the traditional conventions of his craft.

The Gardner brothers were the major Edwardian advocates of the traditional humanist interpretation of classical Greek sculpture. They were aesthetically and morally enraptured by the rational order and beauty of those statues. They were equally convinced of the validity of the major ethical and intellectual premises that had long informed British humanism. For the Gardners, the sculpture of Greece constituted a mighty cultural weapon for the defense of art and morality against the assault of the modern, the relative, and the chaotic. The individualism, experimentation, lack of obvious form, and apparent irrationality of much contemporary artistic enterprise manifested a kind of aesthetic disorder that paralleled the social and political disorder censured by R. W. Livingstone in his book on the Greek genius. All that the early Greeks had meant to indicate by the word *chaos* seemed very real and impending to the Gardner brothers and others of their outlook. In classical Greek sculpture they perceived the achievement of order and an ideal ethical vision over an earlier and possibly

63. Ernest A. Gardner, *Six Greek Sculptors* (London: Duckworth and Co., 1910), pp. 11, 13, 16; Ernest A. Gardner, *Religion and Art in Ancient Greece* (London and New York: Harper and Brothers, 1910), p. 102.

ever-recurring disorder. Believing in a world of moral essences that seemed about to dissolve, they hoped to halt that process by infusing into the eternal marbles of Greece the values and human qualities they thought would sustain a stable, humane, and civilized society in the midst of strife. Theirs was a curiously materialistic solution to a spiritual problem.

Evolutionary Humanistic Hellenism

Both Matthew Arnold and the major critics of Greek sculpture concentrated on the culture of Greece and Athens during the fifth and fourth centuries B.C. Their treatment was highly selective. They not only ignored morally distasteful elements in Athenian life but also disregarded the history of earlier Greek civilization, except for the required reverence toward Homer. In both cases the portrait of Greece that emerged tended to be static, just as the moral values and intellectual outlooks projected onto Greek antiquity tended to support stability rather than change in art and human affairs. Nevertheless, after mid-century the discoveries of archaeologists, and later the theories of anthropologists, began to challenge a Hellenism that conceived of Greece in terms of timeless values. The excavations proved that classical Greece itself had a still more ancient past. The newly unearthed remains of Greek daily life and popular religion revealed a civilization in which Arnoldian sweetness and light were more nearly the exceptions than the rule.

Spokesmen for a humanistic Hellenism met this challenge in two ways. The first was to ignore the new information or to debate its meaning or to admit that only a selective image of Greece was being drawn. The second approach was to accept the new information and to substitute a humanism of becoming for the more traditional humanism of being. A concept of perennial human impulses and skills that displayed themselves in varying fashions at different times and places replaced the concept of the uniformity of human nature. Some of those impulses were regarded as positive and constructive, others as destructive. Humanistic values were attached to the former, and their manifestations in Greece received prescriptive commendation. This latter mode of humanistic Hellenism, developed in the second half of the century, paralleled the older humanism of essences, and continued to characterize the humanistic appreciation of Greece well into the twentieth century. It was a Hellenism of dynamic, evolutionary, civilizing human activity as contrasted with the Hellenism of simplicity and ethical severity.

As early as the 1770s the British critics of Winckelmann, such as James Barry, had questioned the special, idyllic character ascribed to the Greeks. Barry saw them as having been normal human beings and not possessed of special genius or moral qualities. If modern artists were placed in the same physical and social circumstances, they would produce works of equal merit. Almost a half-century later John Flaxman, professor of sculpture at the Royal Academy from 1810 until his death in 1826, also emphasized the normality of the Greeks. Flaxman himself held an exceedingly ideal view of art, and accepted most of Winckelmann's aesthetic opinions, but he also believed that the aesthettic achievement of the Greek sculptors rested on their mastery of technical skills. He told the students of the Royal Academy:

> ... the Greeks were enabled to represent the [human] figure with precision, boldness, and character, from their general knowledge of its internal structure and parts, the harmony of its proportions, and the laws of its mechanical motion. These principles of science they derived from the instructions of Hippocrates, and the schools of Pythagoras and Plato. This mode of proceeding was rational and true, founded on the order of nature, and accounting for effects by their causes, and showing the causes in their effects; it was consequently the most successful, and its superiority is proved by the excellence it has produced.[64]

For Flaxman the beauty of the Greek sculptors' work was ideal insofar as they had rationally understood the forms and operation of physical nature. Yet they had been very much human workmen and human beings, and their products were still statues. They had faced the same kind of technical problems that any nineteenth-century sculptor faced. They had conquered those problems through observing and understanding nature and by mastering the requisite technical knowledge

64. James Barry, *An Inquiry into the Real and Imaginary Obstructions to the Acquisition of the Arts in England* (London, 1775); John Flaxman, *Lectures on Sculpture, As Delivered before the President and Members of the Royal Academy*, 2nd ed. (London: Henry G. Bohn, 1838), pp. 108–09.

and craftsmanship. This outlook, voiced by so many of the artists in 1816 in regard to the Elgin Marbles, refused to assume that the Greeks had been larger than life or that their sculptors had possessed a special inner vision of beauty.

There were those, however, who feared that new, detailed, mundane information about Greece and Greek art might lower the Greeks in the estimation of the general public. Such was the apprehension of Charles T. Newton in the middle of the century. Newton was a pioneer in British archaeology and museum science. As a young man he had become deeply interested in archaeology as a tool for the more complete understanding of ancient civilization. He entered the foreign service and used his appointments throughout the Levant as an opportunity to gather materials for the British Museum. As a practicing archaeologist, he excavated Halicarnassus, Cnidus, and Branchidae, wrote extensively about his work, and brought many treasures back to the British Museum, where he served as the Keeper of Antiquities.[65] Newton displayed a lively and learned curiosity about the ancient past, but unlike most critics of Greek art he had little or no desire to use the classical past to combat the moral confusion or aesthethic corruption of the modern world.

Newton wanted his contemporaries to regard ancient Greece more as an example of a total civilization than as a museum of particular, select civilized masterpieces. Through examination of the full range of Greek endeavor in the plastic arts, Newton believed, the modern student might come to appreciate the *achieving* as well as the achievement of fifth-century art. In arranging the collections at the British Museum, Newton intended the development of Greek art to be readily apparent to the visitor. In 1853 he explained:

> If the sculptures of the Parthenon were presented to us completely isolated and detached from the rest of the monuments of art which remain to us from antiquity; did we not know the fact that Greek sculpture passed through a long course of transitions and preparatory stages before it attained perfection in the hands of Phidias; that he did not create art by miracle, but that he had the

65. Charles Thomas Newton, *A History of Discoveries at Halicarnassus, Cnidus, and Branchidae*, 3 vols. (London: Day and Son, 1862–63); see also *Dictionary of National Biography, Supplement,* s.v. "Newton, Charles Thomas."

genius to surpass the utmost efforts of his predecessors; if, I re-
peat, the sculptures of the Parthenon were presented to us without this preliminary knowledge, would the lesson they would
then convey be more instructive to the people generally, and
more encouraging to the young artist, than if they were exhibited
in connection with the whole development of Greek art?
Museums should not merely charm and astonish the eye by the
exhibitions of marvels of art; they should, by the method of their
arrangement, suggest to the mind the causes of such phenomena.
In our admiration of the sculpture of Phidias, or the paintings of
Raphael, we should not forget what these great masters owed to
their predecessors; we should turn from the contemplation of
their immortal works with a fresh and lively interest to the study
of the earlier schools, out of which such excellence was slowly
developed.[66]

Newton was advocating nothing less than a developmental approach
to Greek art and civilization. His outlook was analogous to the uni-
formitarianism of Charles Lyell's geology, and Newton saw nothing
less worthy in the sculpture of the fifth century B.C. for its having
roots in more primitive art than Charles Darwin would later see in the
human race for having origins in more brutish ancestors.

Newton believed that the children of Greece had grown up. And as
with any achievement of maturity, the process had been a difficult
one, deserving of both understanding and respect. He looked at the
Greek artistic experience in a manner almost the exact reverse of that
which Ernest Gardner would advocate sixty years later. Gardner admired the fifth-century sculptors for their adherence to convention
and tradition. Newton admired the earlier forging of traditions and
conventions that served later artists so well. Furthermore, he thought
that many of the skills required to formulate those traditions leading to
ideal art had been achieved in the course of meeting the practical
requirements of civilized life. The Gardner brothers, as well as Waldstein, Perry, and Westmacott, regarded Hellenism as a set of qualities to
be preserved or models to be emulated. Newton and those who advo-

66. Charles Thomas Newton, *Essays on Art and Archaeology* (London: Macmillan
and Co., 1880), pp. 69–70. See also Charles Thomas Newton, *On the Method of the
Study of Ancient Art* (Oxford: John Henry Parker, 1850).

cated an evolutionary or developmental mode of humanistic Hellenism saw Greece as exemplifying the process of civilization and the emergence of the humane from the primitive and barbaric.

Newton's views were not widespread at mid-century. He was not a man of letters, and he did not write commentaries on Greek art. Nor were his views of Greek art and life particularly derivative of the art criticism in ancient literature. He was rather one of the first British critics to form his opinions in large measure from an examination of the actual plastic remains and artifacts outside the realm of sculpture. John Ruskin also strongly advocated this approach to the Greek artistic experience. His treatment of Greece was eclectic and by no means wholly consistent. Yet throughout his various comments on the Greeks he introduced a strong infusion of the romantic intellectual and aesthetic heritage. He was interested in the particularities of Greek culture rather than generalizations from it. He admired the direct relationship of the Greeks with nature rather than their alleged achievement of ideal beauty by abstraction from nature. As demonstrated by the passage quoted earlier in this chapter, Ruskin could, and on some occasions did, view the Greeks in the idyllic fashion of the Germans. But in 1870 he delivered a set of lectures at Oxford in which he departed sharply from that tradition.

In this lecture series, entitled *Aratra Pentelici*, Ruskin condemned what he considered to be the degraded state of contemporary British sculpture and ascribed its low quality to the double idolatry of the day—of money and of a narrow interpretation of the Scriptures. To overcome these idols, so frequently condemned by Victorian humanists and moralists, Ruskin urged contemporary artists to use their imaginations and pointed to the Greeks as exemplifying the proper liberating function of the imagination. Other ancient peoples, such as the Assyrians and Egyptians, had produced works of art that merely reflected the religious idolatry of their own time and culture. In this respect the Greeks were different because they stood as "the first people that were born into complete humanity." They had fought the battle against the centaurs and had emerged as recognizable human beings. That struggle had forged the central characteristic of the Greek race—"the being born pure and human out of the brutal misery of the past, and looking abroad, for the first time, with their children's eyes, wonderingly open, on the strange and divine world." Those children of Hellas continued to mature, and they soon approached nature directly and sought to portray it as it actually presented itself to them. The qualities of "rightness and reality" guided and informed their sculpture, and their high excellence originated in this correct portrayal of nature. Ruskin flatly repudiated the idealist interpretation of Greek art, telling his audience:

> You are constantly told that Greece idealized whatever she contemplated. She did the exact contrary: she realized and verified it. You are constantly told she sought only the beautiful. She sought, indeed, with all her heart; but she found, because she never doubted that the search was to be consistent with propriety and common sense. And the first thing you will always discern in Greek work is the first which you *ought* to discern in all work; namely, that the object of it has been rational, and has been obtained by simple and unostentatious means. [67]

This passage reflected the earlier outlook of Hazlitt and Flaxman. The genius and excellence of the Greek artist lay in his capacity to present the world as it appeared to him, without mystery and without undue complication of thought.

Ruskin's attack on the idealist interpretation of Greek sculpture was a continuation of the polemic against the aesthetics of Joshua Reynolds that he had begun in the first volume of *Modern Painters* (1843). There Ruskin had argued, "Nature is so immeasurably superior to all that the human mind can conceive, that every departure from her is a fall beneath her." He denied that what was characteristic of the general could be false in regard to the specific and contended that it was "the distinctiveness, not the universality of the truth, which renders it important." He later urged that the true grand style, in contrast to that advocated by Reynolds, "is based on the *perfect* knowledge, and consists in the simple, unencumbered rendering, of the specific characters of the given object, be it man, beast, or flower." A quarter-century later in *Aratra Pentelici* Ruskin portrayed the sculptors of Greece as having achieved that true grand style. The Greek sculptor had represented the plain truth of nature and had informed it with his own emotions and feelings. But he had attempted neither to improve upon nature nor to transform it according to some general, abstract ideal.

67. Ruskin, *Works of John Ruskin*, 20:248, 302.

And as he strove only to teach what was true, so, in his sculptured symbol, he strove only to carve what was—Right. He rules over the arts to this day, and will for ever, because he sought not first for beauty, not first for passion, or for invention, but for Rightness; striving to display, neither himself nor his art, but the thing that he dealt with, in its simplicity.... The essential Hellenic stamp is veracity:—Eastern nations drew their heroes with eight legs, but the Greeks drew them with two;—Egyptians drew their deities with cats' heads, but the Greeks drew them with men's; and out of all fallacy, disproportion, and indefiniteness, they were, day by day, resolvedly withdrawing and exalting themselves into restricted and demonstrable truth.

Through such a truthful approach to nature the Greek had begun to comprehend the world and to discover his own humanity therein. Wherever truthfulness to nature appeared in the plastic arts, as in a delicate Japanese carving of a fish that he examined, Ruskin saw the embodiment and realization of the Greek artistic ideal.[68]

For Ruskin the realm of Greek art included a vast array of complex and delicate craftsmanship that displayed artistic capacities and moral sensibilities far more extensive than those associated with the much-lauded simplicity and calm of high Greek sculpture. He projected onto the coins, temple ornamentation, and decoration of metallic objects that had adorned ancient Greek stone statues the same romantic love for the particularities of nature and the same respect for quality in craftsmanship that he championed in his own day. Through their decoration of such relatively small objects the Greeks had mastered not only "all broad, mighty, and calm conception, but... all that is divided, delicate, and tremulous." In the detailed, complex artistry that appeared on the reins of horses, on gold molding, in the carving of ivory, and in the use of colors, the Greeks stood forth "as masters of human order and justice, subduing the animal nature, guided by the spiritual one." The Greek was a genuine workman as well as an artist, and "as a workman, he verily did, or first suggested the doing of, everything possible to man."[69] The Greek world had been beautiful not because those ancient people had probed some underlying Platonic reality but because they had been alive to the immediate beauty and

68. Ibid., 3:137, 152, 25; 20:347, 288–89.
69. Ibid., 20:350, 351.

spiritual qualities of nature and had copied them directly in their art. If modern British art, and particularly sculpture, were again to create that which was beautiful, it must also thrust off contemporary material and religious idolatry and approach nature directly in the spirit of that ancient craftsmanship.

Whereas Arnold and most of the other critics of Greek sculpture viewed Hellenism as an island of calm in a multitudinous society, Ruskin believed the Greeks could teach his troubled countrymen how to transform that society, how to turn the drudgery of work into the beauty of craftsmanship, and how to forge a more beautiful world and a better quality of life. The Greek experience and achievement were both relevant and potentially normative because the natural beauty the Greeks had perceived and replicated in their art could still be seen and copied by modern artists and craftsmen. That approach to Greek art had led Ruskin to examine the subject more deeply in a developmental perspective and more broadly in cultural context than had most of his contemporaries. But while Ruskin discerned and delineated new dimensions and complexities in Greek culture, he did not embrace or seek out the whole of Greek life. Nor did he attempt to integrate conceptually or technically the world of Greek craftsmanship with that of fifth- or fourth-century sculpture.

Of late Victorian commentators on Greek culture as an artistic and moral entity, only Walter Pater attempted to provide an integrated interpretation of the Greek experience. Over the course of his career Pater wrote substantial essays on Greek sculpture, religion, and philosophy. His opinions and conclusions about these topics modified as his personal intellectual viewpoint passed from an intense skepticism and relativism based on Hegelian thought and British empiricism to a religious humanism founded on Plato and late-century high Anglican theology. This personal evolution rendered his concept of Hellenism both complicated and protean, yet certain generalizations are possible. Pater held an agonistic concept of Greek culture that resembled Jacob Burckhardt's.[70] Both writers thought Greek civilization had been characterized by substantial internal tension and struggle. David De-

70. Henry Hatfield, *Clashing Myths in German Literature from Heine to Rilke* (Cambridge, Mass.: Harvard University Press, 1974), pp. 43–61; Arnaldo Momigliano, *Essays in Ancient and Modern Historiography* (Middletown, Conn.: Wesleyan University Press, 1977), pp. 295–306.

Laura has correctly argued that Pater's Hellenism was in large measure "a deliberate response to, and modification of, Arnold's view of the Greeks."[71] Pater was not caught up in Arnold's concept of analogous stages of historical development. His view of history, so far as he had one, derived from Hegel and from contemporary anthropologists. For him the human spirit manifested itself throughout the entire past, and all facets of civilization seemed vital and potentially interesting. Pater's entire consideration of Greek civilization also had a more secure foundation in recent scholarship and archaeology than Arnold's. Archaic as well as Periclean Greece fascinated Pater, who perceived and accepted the presence of those irrationalities in Greek life and art that Arnold chose to ignore. Pater brought more imagination, empathy, and perhaps even more sweetness and light to the subject. As demonstrated by the "Conclusion" to *Studies in the Renaissance*, he dared to experience the intellectual and ethical flux that Arnold and others like him dreaded and feared. Consequently, when Pater did eventually champion the spirit of order, his appreciation for it was more hard won than Arnold's, and his praise and enthusiasm for it partook of the conviction of experience rather than the aloofness of chiseled classicism.

Although Pater discussed Greek art in largely Hegelian terms in "Winckelmann" (1867), he made his most complete and systematic commentary in three essays that although published in 1880 had possibly been written as lectures delivered at Oxford about 1879.[72] The title of the first two—"The Beginnings of Greek Sculpture"—was significant. It was an acknowledgment that the art of the Greeks had a past as well as a present. This emphasis on origins permeated classical studies after 1870 and fundamentally challenged the older prescriptive mode of Hellenism. As Percy Gardner, who regretted the develop-

71. DeLaura, *Hebrew and Hellene in Victorian England*, p. 177.

72. Walter Pater, "The Beginnings of Greek Sculpture," *Fortnightly Review* 33 (1880): 190–207; 422–34; "The Marbles of Aegina," *Fortnightly Review* 33 (1880): 540–48. These were reprinted in a somewhat revised form in Walter Pater, *Greek Studies* (London: Macmillan and Co., 1901; first published, 1895), pp. 187–268. On Pater's Oxford lectures, see Lewis R. Farnell, *An Oxonian Looks Back* (London: Martin Hopkinson, 1934), pp. 76–77. For discussions of the Hegelian elements in Pater's early Hellenism, consult Peter Allan Dale, *The Victorian Critic and the Idea of History*, pp. 217–45, and Bernard Fehr, "Walter Pater und Hegel," *Englische Studien* 50 (1916–17): 300–08.

ment, wrote in 1908, "It is a Darwinian age, when the search for origins seems to fascinate men more than the search for what is good in itself."[73] The interest in origins and the emphasis on development embraced the spirit of ethical and cultural relativism that Gardner and others of his persuasion sought to combat through the appeal to Hellenism. Pater, in contrast, believed that it was possible to regard Greece from a developmental standpoint and still discern in Greek art and experience something that would prove lasting and of contemporary relevance and worth. To the extent that he succeeded, Pater provided an alternative pattern for the humanistic appreciation of Greece during the next fifty years.

Throughout his essays on Greece, Pater stressed the variety that had been present in Greek life. The Greeks during their entire history had confronted as much multitudinousness and potential for disorder as people in the nineteenth century did. What Pater termed "the romantic spirit" had informed Greek culture, brought complexity into its life, and been manifest in superstition, unsavory rituals, idol worship, and other irrational behavior in Greek religion. Directly countering Matthew Arnold's contention that Greek religion, in contrast to medieval, had lacked a sense of sorrow, Pater argued about 1878 in a revision of an earlier essay:

> . . . this familiar view of the Greek religion is based on a consideration of a part only of what is known concerning it, and really involves a misconception, akin to that which underestimates the influence of the romantic spirit generally, in Greek poetry and art; as if Greek art had dealt exclusively with human nature in its sanity, suppressing all motives of strangeness, all the beauty which is born of difficulty, permitting nothing but an Olympian, though perhaps somewhat wearisome calm. In effect, such a conception of Greek art and poetry leaves in the central expression of Greek culture none but negative qualities; and the legend of Demeter and Persephone, perhaps the most popular of all Greek legends, is sufficient to show that the "worship of sorrow" was not without its function in Greek religion; their legend is a legend made by and for sorrowful, wistful, anxious people; while the

---

73. Percy Gardner, "Preface" to Adolf Michaelis, *A Century of Archaeological Discoveries*, trans. Bettina Kahnweiler (London: John Murray, 1908), pp. viii–ix.

most important artistic monuments of that legend sufficiently prove that the Romantic spirit was really at work in the minds of Greek artists, extracting by a kind of subtle alchemy, a beauty, not without the elements of tranquillity, of dignity and order, out of a matter, at first sight painful and strange.[74]

In this manner Pater was urging the commensurability of Greek religion and culture to the present age and to the full range of human emotions. Not only had he discerned the romantic, sorrowful, irrational elements in Greek poetry and legends, but, more important, he had found them physically present in the remains unearthed by archaeologists. He pointed out that the sanctuary of Demeter at Cnidus, excavated by Charles Newton, provided evidence of both the intellectualized side of the legend and of the popular Greek religious practices involving fetishes and superstitious idolatry.[75] In the face of such concrete evidence it was difficult, if not impossible, to sustain a unified, ideal, rational image of Greece.

In the essays "The Beginnings of Greek Sculpture" and "The Marbles of Aegina" Pater, like Ruskin before him, emphasized the sensuous qualities and workmanship of Greek statues. Although readily admitting that a strong intellectualized element was present in major Greek sculpture, he understood the origins of that sculptured beauty to lie outside the reflective faculties. Of the masterpieces of Greek statuary, Pater observed

> ... in them, that profoundly reasonable spirit of design which is traceable in Greek art, continuously and increasingly, upwards from its simplest products, the oil-vessel or the urn, reaches its perfection. Yet though the most abstract and intellectualized of sensuous objects, they are still sensuous and material, addressing themselves, in the first instance, not to the purely reflective faculty, but to the eye; and a complete criticism must have approached them from both sides—...

To be properly and thoroughly appreciated, Greek sculpture had to be viewed against the background of the lovely and intricate utensils of

---

74. Pater, Greek Studies, pp. 110–11; see also Walter Pater, The Renaissance: Studies in Art and Poetry (New York: The Macmillan Co., 1905), pp. 214–15.
75. Pater, Greek Studies, pp. 140–44.

everyday life. The exquisite urns, vases, boxes, cups, and chests had been the vehicles through whose manufacture the skills requisite for and aesthetic taste embodied in later sculpture had been achieved. Within those small, practical objects there lay "as *designed* work, that spirit of reasonable order, that expressive congruity with the adaption of means to ends, of which the fully developed admirableness of human form is but the consummation." To grasp fully the genius and accomplishment of Greek art it was necessary to cultivate a "constant appreciation of intelligent *workmanship* in work, and of *design* in things designed, of the rational control of matter everywhere."[76]

Pater's evaluation of Greek art amounted to little less than a paean to material civilization and to reason as applied to practical needs. The intellectual and spiritual achievement of Greek sculpture rested on a foundation of lesser practical skills and of the sensuous accomplishments of Greek craftsmen. For Pater, it was not the civility of Greece but the civilizing of its culture that merited the respect and wonder of later generations. The forging of design and material order where they had not previously existed was the momentous achievement of Greece and the feature of its civilization that deserved emulation. Greeks of the sixth and fifth centuries had held that perspective on their own civilization, and Pater helped to reinvest British classical studies with an appreciation for a similar evaluation of the Greek genius.

Yet, as Pater argued, the early world of archaic ornamentation and rational design was not wholly satisfactory or complete. Nowhere amidst the "exquisite craftsmanship, touching the minutest details of daily life with splendour and skill" did there exist any genuine sense of humankind itself or of the possibility of expressing such a form and through it the human soul. The supreme accomplishment of later Greek sculpture had been the development of the ability to perceive and to render that expression. This moral insight and this ability originated in the influence of the Dorian, or European, impulse in Greek life. This was the cultural tendency "which finding human mind the most absolutely real and precious thing in the world, enforces everywhere the impress of its sanity, its profound reflexions upon things as they really are, its sense of proportion." Apollo was the

76. Ibid., pp. 190, 220–21.

patron god of the Dorian impulse. In combination with the Ionian or Asian influence that was patronized by Hephaestus and that had accounted for the emergence of design, the Dorian impulse fostered the final insights required for high Greek sculpture. Into the realm of early handicraft developed in Ionia, the "Dorian, European, Apolline influence introduced the intelligent and spiritual human presence, and gave it its true value, a value consistently maintained to the end of Greek art, by a steady hold upon and preoccupation with the inward harmony and system of human personality."[77] The first statues to exhibit this combination of Ionian skill and Dorian proportion were the Aegina marbles then, as now, exhibited in Munich.

Pater on more than one occasion interpreted higher Greek culture as a product of the creative, almost dialectical, relationship between the Ionian and Dorian impulses. The Ionian influence, which Pater considered "centrifugal" in character, accounted for the mechanical skills and the tendency toward particularism in life, politics, and philosophy. The Dorian influence, which Pater termed "centripetal," was a force for order and for solidarity. By their combination they had nurtured not merely civilization in Greece but a particular quality of life. Without the positive, necessary contributions of both impulses, Greek culture would have possessed a very different character. Nevertheless, in spite of his high praise and appreciation for Ionian craftsmanship, Pater still discerned "the true Hellenic influence" as residing in the religion of Apollo and the sense of Dorian order.[78] The latter impulses had allowed humankind to become an object to itself and to portray itself in its various manifestations through the material and artistic skills nurtured by the Ionian experience.

Although Pater clearly favored the benefits of the Dorian impulse, his concept of their range was much wider than that suggested by other contemporary critics of Greek sculpture. Pater explained that through the influence of Apollo Greek art had "attained, in its reproductions of human form, not merely to the profound expression of the highest indwelling spirit of human intelligence, but to the expression also of the great human passions, of the powerful movements as well as of the calm and peaceful order of the soul." This was a Hellenism far

77. Ibid., pp. 224, 253, 256.
78. Ibid., pp. 252, 256.

more complex, rich, and dynamic than that of Winckelmann, Arnold, or the Victorian critics of Greek art. Pater's humanism and Hellenism were not a set of essential values or attitudes to be preserved in good society; they consisted, rather, of an appreciation for the role of material civilization in providing a necessary foundation for the life of reason. Pater understood Hellenism to be just that dialectical combination of material and spiritual forces making for reason and human adaptation and growth. As he had written in "Winckelmann," the higher modes of Hellenic culture were "a sharp edge of light" that cut through the gloom of chthonian religion and that amidst the surrounding darkness defined the possibility of a self-determined aspiration and moral direction in human nature. For that reason Pater could urge, "Hellenism is not merely an absorbed element in our intellectual life; it is a conscious tradition in it."[79] Hellenism was the perceived human capacity to forge and order the world and to determine the character of the cultural and ethical environment. It was the basis for creating a civilization in which the human spirit could make itself at home in the world.

Whereas the Hellenism of Arnold with its recapturing of the Greek experience, and that of the art critics with its preservation of good taste, had been conservative in their bias, Pater's was generally progressive. The latter outlook began to characterize numerous general studies of Greek culture from the 1890s through the mid-twenties of this century. This point of view reflected a determination to associate Greece with positive forces for change and human improvement as well as with the preservation of the enduring moral and social values. It also was a strategy whereby classical scholars who were confronted with information about Greece presented by anthropology could continue to maintain that Greece held valuable lessons for modern life. For example, in 1891, S. H. Butcher observed:

> From Greece came that first mighty impulse whose far-off workings are felt by us to-day, and which has brought it about that progress has been accepted as the law and goal of human endeavour. Greece first took up the task of equipping man with all that fits him for civil life and promotes his secular wellbeing; of unfolding and expanding every inborn faculty and energy, bodily

79. Ibid., p. 255; Pater, *The Renaissance*, pp. 215, 209.

and mental; of striving restlessly after the perfection of the whole, and finding in this effort after an unattainable ideal that by which man becomes like to the gods.

Shortly before the turn of the century, in his often reprinted *The Greek View of Life*, G. Lowes Dickinson declared that the "specific achievement of the Greek spirit" had been "to humanize barbarism and enlighten superstition."[80] Butcher and Dickinson, and others of similar outlook, wanted to see Greece as standing on the side of the future rather than as a rear-guard outpost of the past. Such had also been the view of Walter Pater.

The interpretation of Greece from a progressive standpoint became attractive not only as archaeology and anthropology divested Greek civilization of much of its sane, rational, classical outlines but also as the upheaval of World War I made the spirit of classicism seem too aloof and passive a perspective to be immediately relevant. The onset of war and the political and social conditions accompanying it brought the progressive image to the forefront. For example, in 1921 Gilbert Murray attempted to associate Greece with the hopes of European liberals by praising its progressive character.

> We must listen with due attention to the critics who have pointed out all the remnants of savagery and superstition that they find in Greece: the slave-driver, the fetish-worshiper and the medicine-man, the trampler on women, the bloodthirsty hater of all outside his own town and party. But it is not those people that constitute Greece; those people can be found all over the historical world, commoner than blackberries. It is not anything fixed and stationary that constitutes Greece: what constitutes Greece is the movement which leads from all these to the Stoic or fifth-century "sophist" who condemns and denies slavery, who has abolished all cruel superstitions and preaches some religion based on philosophy and humanity, who claims for women the same spiritual rights as for man, who looks on all human creatures as his brethren and the world as "one great City of gods and men." It is that movement which you will not find elsewhere, any more than the

80. Butcher, *Some Aspects of the Greek Genius*, pp. 41–42; G. Lowes Dickinson, *The Greek View of Life* (New York: Doubleday, Page, and Co., 1913; originally published, 1896), p. vi.

statues of Phidias or the dialogues of Plato or the poems of Aeschylus and Euripides.[81]

This was the spirit of Greece that had created an image of humankind
and human society that reasonable and humane men and women must
seek to realize once again in a world newly threatened with barbarism.
It should also be noted that those values of civility that Murray ascribed to Greece were those that could be associated with the liberal
political and intellectual tradition of nineteenth-century Britain. Both
Greece and Victorian England were tarnished ideals in 1921, and
Murray was in effect suggesting that the genius of each had been the
capacity for self-criticism and reform.

It is at once ironic and significant that Gilbert Murray, the foremost
British champion of Hellenism in this century, should also have been
deeply attached to the modernist spirit in literature and art. During the
1890s he had read Ibsen to his classes in Glasgow, and after the turn of
the century he had fought against the censorship of the London stage.
He was also deeply involved with the application of anthropology to
Greek art and literature. All of those activities and the ideas associated
with them challenged the varieties of humanistic Hellenism championed by Arnold, Westmacott, Waldstein, and the Gardner brothers.
Because of his modernist stance, Murray, like Walter Pater before
him, was profoundly aware of the darker side of human nature and the
social and psychological tensions of civilized life. For Murray, the
glory of Greece lay not in its provision of a sense of artistic and moral
propriety that would stand against bad taste and philistinism but in its
example, however frail and imperfect, of human reason taming in
some measure human bestiality. Just as he wrote that Greece was not a
fixed entity, Murray also understood that civilization itself was not
something fixed or certain. It had to be forged again and again so that
reason might be allowed to continue its struggle against superstition,
chauvinism, anti-intellectualism, bigotry, and hatred. It was this
struggle rather than the preservation of propriety that would become
most pressing for Europeans of the twentieth century.

81. Gilbert Murray, "The Value of Greece to the Future of the World," Richard
W. Livingstone, ed., *The Legacy of Greece* (Oxford: Clarendon Press, 1928; first
published, 1921), p. 15.

George Grote
(John Murray Collection)

F. Max Müller

John Addington Symonds
(National Portrait Gallery, London)

Jane Ellen Harrison as portrayed by Augustus John
(By permission of the Principal and Fellows of Newnham College)

James George Frazer
(T. and R. Annan and Sons, Glasgow)

Lewis Farnell

3
GREEK MYTHOLOGY AND RELIGION

An Inheritance Spurned

Early Victorian classicists, commentators, and historians, as well as the reading public at large, were more familiar with the Greek myths than with any other single aspect of Hellenic culture. Numerous versions of the myths and channels of information about them already existed. Throughout the eighteenth century the Homeric epics had enjoyed a wide readership in the original and in translation. A considerable number of handbooks and dictionaries of classical myths were readily available. Mythological scenes were commonplace in painting and sculpture, and from Renaissance, neoclassical, and romantic poets the early Victorians had inherited a literature rich in allusions to the Greek myths.[1]

The romantic poets in particular had turned to the myths as a means of interpreting the spiritual problems and aspirations of modern life and thought.[2] Wordsworth, Coleridge, Keats, and Shelley, as well as many lesser figures, had regarded the Greek myths and mythical thought in general as constituting not mere conventional window

1. Richard Chase, *The Quest for Myth* (Baton Rouge: Louisiana State University Press, 1949), pp. 7–21; Burton Feldman and Robert D. Richardson, *The Rise of Modern Mythology 1680–1860* (Bloomington: Indiana University Press, 1972); Albert C. Yoder, *Concepts of Mythology in Victorian England* (Ann Arbor, Mich.: University Microfilms, 1971); James Kissane, "Victorian Mythology," *Victorian Studies* 6 (1962): 5–28; Janet Burstein, "Victorian Mythography," *Victorian Studies* 18 (1975): 309–24.

2. Douglas Bush, *Mythology and the Renaissance Tradition in English Poetry,* rev. ed. (New York: W. W. Norton and Co., 1963); Douglas Bush, *Mythology and the Romantic Tradition in English Poetry* (New York: W. W. Norton and Co., 1969).

dressing for literature but rather forms and symbols once alive in the human mind and spirit and still capable of new life. For the romantics, mythical thinking was an alternative to an overly rationalized Christianity and the thoroughly mechanized world view of Newtonian physics. Victorian poets of all literary statures continued to employ the myths and to incorporate classical themes in their writing. However, the vital link between myth and the autonomous poetic imagination languished in the climate of scientific rationalism and empirical inquiry, and the myths again became primarily conventions or allegories. In 1822 Hartley Coleridge described myths as pertaining to the childhood of the race and reluctantly concluded: "That youth is flown for ever. We are grown up to serious manhood, and are wedded to reality."[3] Not until the emergence of Yeats at the close of the century would the mythologizing function of the poet again assert itself, and then it did it so through the Celtic rather than the classical myths. Between the flowering of romantic poetry and the Celtic revival, myths, and especially Greek myths, passed from being a matter of inspired imagination to being one of mere fancy.

Closely related to this demise was the rejection of a body of syncretic studies of myth that had flourished in the late eighteenth century and that had provided source materials for several romantic poets. Among the more important of these was Jacob Bryant's *A New System, or an Analysis of Ancient Mythology* (3 vols., 1774), which derived all ancient myths, including those of Greece, from the traditions of the Amonian family, the descendants of Ham. William Blake had frequently consulted this work.[4] After the turn of the century several books in the same tradition by George S. Faber were published: *Horae Mosaicae* (1801), *A Dissertation on the Mysteries of the Cabiri* (1803), and *The Origin of Pagan Idolatry* (3 vols., 1816).[5] These volumes traced the

3. Hartley Coleridge, "On the Poetical Use of the Heathen Mythology," *London Magazine* 5 (1822): 119.

4. Jacob Bryant, *A New System, or an Analysis of Ancient Mythology* (London, 1774); Edward B. Hungerford, *Shores of Darkness* (New York: Columbia University Press, 1941), pp. 3–34; Albert J. Kuhn, "English Deism and the Development of Romantic Mythological Syncretism," *PMLA* 71 (1956): 1094–116; Northrop Frye, *Fearful Symmetry* (Boston: Beacon Press, 1962), pp. 173–75; Feldman and Richardson, *Rise of Modern Mythology*, pp. 241–43.

5. George S. Faber, *Horae Mosaicae, or a View of the Mosaical Records with Respect to Their Coincidence with Profane Antiquity...and Their Connection with Christianity* (Oxford, 1801); *A Dissertation on the Mysteries of the Cabiri* (Oxford, 1803); *The*

archetype of all myths to Noah and the ark. Such studies, along with others of a similar character dealing with Celtic myths, constituted the British parallel to the mystical, allegorical, or symbolic interpretations of myth that on the Continent were associated with Friederich Creuzer's *Symbolik und Mythologie der alten Völker* (1810). Although until the 1860s reviewers complained about the continuing use of Bryant, there is little evidence that his ideas or Faber's exercised any appreciable influence.[6] The same climate of opinion that brought low the poetic imagination also smothered the symbolic and mystical concepts of the myths. Studies such as K. O. Müller's *Introduction to a Scientific Study of Mythology* (1825; translated, 1844) carried the day. Serious British commentators on classical myths, including Thomas Keightley, the Irish writer of textbooks and author of *The Mythology of Ancient Greece and Italy* (1831), and William Smith, editor of the *Dictionary of Greek and Roman Biography and Mythology* (1844–49), specifically repudiated the syncretic approach in favor of the newer empirical, historical method.[7]

The Victorian mythographers also abandoned two other eighteenth-century attitudes toward the Greek myths. Unlike some earlier writers they saw no reason to fear that any substantial consider-

---

Origin of Pagan Idolatry (London, 1816); Hungerford, *Shores of Darkness,* pp. 3–34; William D. Paden, *Tennyson in Egypt,* University of Kansas Publications in Humanistic Studies, no. 27 (Lawrence, Kan., 1942), pp. 75–88, 154–59; Feldman and Richardson, *Rise of Modern Mythology,* pp. 397–99.

6. George Eliot, "Mackay's *Progress of the Intellect,"* *Westminster Reivew* 54 (1851): 181; Benjamin Edward Pote, "Ancient Figurative Language," *Foreign Quarterly Review* (American edition) 23 (1839): 34–46; T. S. Baynes, "Cox's Aryan Mythology," *Edinburgh Review* 132 (1870): 331; John Stuart Blackie, *Horae Hellenicae: Essays and Discussions on Some Important Points of Greek Philology and Antiquity* (London: Macmillan and Co., 1874), pp. 167–69; Henry Gay Hewlett, "The Rationale of Mythology," *Cornhill Magazine* 35 (1877): 407–23.

7. Karl Otfried Müller, *Introduction to a Scientific Study of Mythology,* trans. John Leitch (London: Longman, Brown, Green, and Longmans, 1844). This work also provides a valuable commentary on other contemporary German theories of myth. See also G. C. Lewis, "Mythology and Ancient Religion of Greece," *Foreign Quarterly Review* 7 (1831): 33–52; review of Müller's *Introduction to a Scientific Study of Mythology,* *Fraser's Magazine* 35 (1847): 301–07; Thomas Keightley, *The Mythology of Ancient Greece and Italy,* Second Edition, Considerably Enlarged and Improved (London: Whittaker and Co., 1838), pp. 1–14; William Smith, ed., *Dictionary of Greek and Roman Biography and Mythology,* 3 vols. (Boston: Charles C. Little and James Brown, 1849), 1:ix.

ation of paganism as an alternative to Christianity would follow from an interest in the myths. Books such as William Godwin's *Pantheon* (1806), published under the pseudonym of Edward Baldwin, John Bell's *New Pantheon* (1790), and Lampriere's *Dictionary* tended to remove serious religious dimensions from the myths by relating the stories in a mundane fashion and by rendering their content a matter for reference books. During most of the nineteenth century whatever serious religious consideration the myths received originated with writers, such as Elizabeth Barrett Browning, who regretted the Greek lack of Christian faith, or F. D. Maurice, who looked for evidence of knowledge of the true God among the gentile nations.[8] Otherwise, not until anthropologists began to study primitive myths late in the century did Victorian commentators consider the genuinely religious character of the Greek mythical narratives.

But the enlightenment rationalism of the philosophes was an even more important eighteenth-century attitude toward myth rejected or at least much modified by the Victorians. From Bayle to Hume, the philosophes had used the stories from Greek and other non-Christian myths to attack contemporary Christianity. Parallels between Christian and pagan myths allowed them to suggest that Christianity was neither historically unique nor morally pure. Like the writers of the Enlightenment, the Victorian commentators regarded myths as phenomena arising naturally from human experience, but they differed from the philosophes' analyses. For example, Hume had argued that myths and religion arose "from a concern with regard to the events of life, and from incessant hopes and fears, which actuate the human mind."[9] In his view, religious myths, whether ancient or modern, manifested the dominance of the passions over reason. Consequently, the roots of religion, with all its undesirable results, origi-

8. Alex Zwerdling, "The Mythographers and the Romantic Revival of Greek Myth," *Publications of the Modern Language Association* 79 (1964): 448–56; Bush, *Mythology and the Romantic Tradition in English Poetry*, pp. 266–72; Frederick Denison Maurice, *The Religions of the World and Their Relations to Christianity* (London: John W. Parker, 1847), pp. 113–18.

9. David Hume, *The Natural History of Religion*, ed. H. E. Root (Stanford: Stanford University Press, 1967), p. 27; Frank E. Manuel, *The Eighteenth Century Confronts the Gods* (New York: Atheneum, 1967), pp. 3–12, 168–83; James Collins, *The Emergence of Philosophy of Religion* (New Haven: Yale University Press, 1967), pp. 29–48; Chase, *The Quest for Myth*, pp. 7–21.

nated not in an isolated past or in a mistaken interpretation of physical nature but rather within human nature itself and in the human situation. Nineteenth-century rationalists would not accept this analysis because it undercut their expectation of human progress through the accumulation of scientific knowledge. For their part they historicized myth and the myth-making mentality to an earlier epoch of human development. In this manner they sought to explain the presence of myths in the human past while banishing them from the present except as vestigial cultural artifacts.

Finally, Victorian writers spurned the view of myths proffered by R. Payne Knight. In *A Discourse on the Worship of Priapus* (1786) and in *An Inquiry into the Symbolical Language of Ancient Art and Mythology* (1818) Knight traced the origin of myth and religion to various modes of phallic worship.[10] Victorian classicists wanted little or nothing to do with this theory. Even James G. Frazer's late-century remarks on the sexual character of myths lay veiled in polysyllabic descriptions. Before Frazer's work, most commentators either rationalized or excised the sexuality of the myths. Indeed Connop Thirlwall, a not illiberal scholar, trained at Cambridge, praised Thomas Keightley's rendition of the Greek myths for having made the subject fit for ladies. Among other examples, Keightley simply recorded that Cronos had "mutilated" his father and so ignored the fact of the castration of Uranos. He softened the impact of incest among the gods by a reminder that incest was not uncommon among certain Asiatic peoples. Charles Kingsley in *The Heroes* (1856), a book written for children, simply told his youthful readers that some parts of the stories were "too terrible to speak of here," but that they might learn of them when they grew up.[11]

Victorian scholars, historians, philologists, and compilers of handbooks on the classics knew about either all or most of these earlier

10. Richard Payne Knight, *A Discourse on the Worship of Priapus* (London, 1786); *An Inquiry into the Symbolical Language of Ancient Art and Mythology* (London, 1818); Feldman and Richardson, *Rise of Modern Mythology*, pp. 249–51.

11. Connop Thirlwall, *A History of Greece*, 8 vols. (London: Longman, Rees, Orme, Brown, Green, and Longman and John Taylor, 1835), 1:192n; see also Thomas Keightley, *The Mythology of Ancient Greece and Italy for the Use of Schools*, 11th American Edition, Enlarged and Improved (New York: D. Appleton and Co., 1845), pp. viii–ix, 22–23; Charles Kingsley, *The Heroes; or, Greek Fairy Tales* (Cambridge: Macmillan and Co., 1856), p. 151.

approaches to the Greek myths. They were not ignorant of the sexual and gloomy side of ancient religion. They còuld read Homer, Hesiod, Pausanias, Ovid, and the other ancient sources of the myths. Most of them were also reasonably well informed about German research. Yet on the whole, Victorian commentators who took up the subject of Greek myths repudiated their inheritance from the eighteenth and early nineteenth centuries. That choice has often been criticized. For example, two recent historians of modern mythography have observed:

> If the romantic reappraisal of myth included an affirmation of the Dionysian, the violent, the sexual, and the darkly fatalistic elements of myth, it therefore included within its approval the whole irrational side of myth. . . . But the Victorian revaluation of myth largely ignored or rejected this entire side of myth, and in filtering myth through a mesh of decorous and sunny gentility, robbed the subject of much of its seriousness, much of its dignity, much of its capacity to nourish tragedy, and many of its deep connections with what Melville called the "underformings of the mind."[12]

As a description, this statement is correct; but its implicit negative judgment on the Victorian treatment of myth is markedly ahistorical. It condemns the repudiation of previous modes of interpretation without asking why such a change in perception, analysis, and sensibility took place.

That transformation occurred not because Victorian commentators sought to rob myths of their seriousness but because they saw a new kind of seriousness attaching to them. A remark made by A. C. Bradley in 1881 about the function of myths in poetry is applicable to the more general Victorian consideration of the subject. "The problem," Bradley explained, "is so to reshape the material they give us, that it may express ideas, feelings, experiences interesting to *us,* in a form natural and poetically attractive to *us.*"[13] Contemporary concerns were always the major touchstone for the Victorians. The major link between their treatment of the Greek myths and their culture was

---

12. Feldman and Richardson, *Rise of Modern Mythology,* p. 301.
13. Andrew Cecil Bradley, "Old Mythology in Modern Poetry," *Macmillan's Magazine* 44 (1881): 30.

the matter of religion itself. Whether as orthodox believers, unorthodox liberals, or agnostics, most Victorian mythographers took contemporary religion seriously. They approached Greek religion with no less seriousness of purpose. They recognized that what they said about the Greek myths and religious experience might bear directly on Christianity and the moral and intellectual life derived from it. Consequently, to the extent that they wished to debunk Christian myths and Christian beliefs or to liberalize their interpretation or character or to relieve their oppressive hold on contemporary intellectual life, the Victorian commentators tended to do the same with the myths of Greece. In that respect the ancient myths had perhaps rarely been treated with more seriousness.

George Grote and the Past Which Never Was Present

Beginning in the late seventeenth century, European intellectuals began to employ the tools of critical reason and positivistic history to analyze the myths, fables, and legends of Israel, Greece, Rome, and the Christian church. This generally skeptical movement of thought involved new ways of reading, questioning, and evaluating existing literary evidence and often led to frequent interplay between works dealing with secular history and those dealing with sacred history. Scottish writers, including Adam Smith, Adam Ferguson, and John Millar, had contributed thoroughly naturalistic analyses of the development of human society, but by the end of the eighteenth century the German universities had become the center for historical and theological studies in the critical mode. Christian Gottlieb Heyne at the University of Göttingen had initiated an interpretation of classical myths that eventually culminated in David Friedrich Strauss's application of mythic analysis to the life of Jesus.[14] The publication of F. A. Wolf's *Prolegomena ad Homerum* in 1795 spawned a century of controversy over the *Iliad*. During 1811 and 1812 B. G. Niebuhr published his multivolume *History of Rome* in which he rejected the historical validity of the early Roman legends related by Livy. By the mid-twenties K. O. Müller presented an empirical theory of myth in the *Introduction to a Scientific Study of Mythology*. In addition to these

14. Christian Hartlich and Walter Sachs, *Der Ursprung des Mythosbegriffes in der Modernen Bibelwissenschaft* (Tübingen: J. C. B. Mohr, 1952).

major works, there were a large number of other books and articles by figures such as C. A. Lobeck, the main thrust of which was rationalistic, historicist analysis. An examination of this literature reveals two more or less distinct stages in the treatment of Christian and classical myths. During the first, writers tended to rationalize or eradicate the irrational elements in the stories in hope of discerning some remaining kernel of historical fact. In the second stage, the critics rejected the myths and legends themselves as possessing no basis in factual historical events.

The German influence began to be felt in Great Britain when Julius Hare and Connop Thirlwall translated Niebuhr's history into English between 1828 and 1832. Thomas Arnold incorporated Niebuhr's skeptical views of early Roman legends into his own *History of Rome,* which began to appear in 1838. Henry Hart Milman's *History of the Jews* (1829) and *The History of Christianity from the Birth of Christ to the Abolition of Paganism in the Roman Empire* (1840) approached the Old Testament and early Christian narratives in a similarly critical and naturalistic fashion. Samuel Taylor Coleridge and a few other writers whom he influenced had begun to read the Bible in a critical manner by the late twenties. Similar treatment of the Greek myths and legends developed much more slowly. During the 1780s John Gillies and William Mitford wrote histories of Greece in which they used the mythical narratives as historical background to the later Greek ages. Although Wolf's *Prolegomena* roused controversy, the first round of the debate in England saw the champions of a unitary, historical Homer carry the day. In 1824 Fynes Clinton in his much-respected chronology of ancient history *Fasti Hellenicae* provided dates not only for the Trojan War but also for the expedition of the Argonauts. Thirlwall, who was deeply read in German scholarship, voiced guarded skepticism about the myths and legends in his *History of Greece* (1835). He urged that care be exercised in sifting through them for true events, but he finally concluded that some residue of genuine historical fact might be gleaned from them. For example, the Argonaut narrative seemed "to exhibit an opening intercourse between the opposite shores of the Aegean." Still other writers during the twenties and thirties suggested that the myths represented allegories formulated by various orders of ancient pagan priests. Only Thomas Keightley broached the possibility that "the heroes, like the gods, of

Greece were the pure creation of imagination."[15] He argued that case in 1831 without attracting followers.

Such was the situation in British scholarly circles when Victoria ascended the throne in 1837, but it did not prevail much longer. Among the members of her first Parliament sat the person who would not only transform British thinking about Greek myths but also redirect the course of the fledgling British study of Greek religion, history, and philosophy for over fifty years. George Grote, later known as "the historian of Greece," was in 1837 the intellectual and tactical leader of the philosophic radicals in the House of Commons.[16] Originally he had been a successful banker in the City of London, but during the twenties he became deeply involved with radical political and intellectual circles and became a close associate of both James and John Stuart Mill. After intense activity in support of the First Reform Act, Grote entered the reformed House of Commons where he achieved the most renown for his long, unsuccessful effort to secure the use of the ballot in parliamentary elections. His home and his brilliant wife Harriet were the nucleus for strategy sessions among the radical party. Of that group, within and without Parliament, only John Stuart Mill rivaled Grote for breadth of reading, penetration of insight, and sheer intellectual power.

Following the triumph of Peel in the election of 1841, Grote withdrew from politics in the belief that the reorientation of political life he

15. Barthold Georg Niebuhr, *The History of Rome,* trans. Connop Thirlwall and Julius Hare (Cambridge: J. Taylor, 1828–32); Thomas Arnold, *History of Rome,* 3 vols. (London: B. Fellowes; J. G. and F. Rivington, 1838–43); Henry Hart Milman, *The History of the Jews,* 3 vols. (London, 1829); *The History of Christianity from the Birth of Christ to the Abolition of Paganism in the Roman Empire,* 3 vols. (London, 1840); Henry Fynes Clinton, *Fasti Hellenicae: The Civil and Literary Chronology of Greece from the LVth to the CXXIVth Olympiad,* 2nd ed. with additions (Oxford: Clarendon Press, 1827; first edition, 1824); Thirlwall, *History of Greece,* 1:149; Keightley, *Mythology of Ancient Greece and Italy* (1838 ed.), p. 498. See also Samuel Taylor Coleridge, *Miscellanies, Aesthetic and Literary to Which Is Added the Theory of Life,* ed. T. Ashe (London: George Bell, 1885), p. 150; M. H. Abrams, *The Mirror and the Lamp: Romantic Theory and the Critical Tradition* (W. W. Norton and Co., 1958), pp. 290–97; John W. Burrow, *Evolution and Society: A Study in Victorian Social Theory* (Cambridge: Cambridge University Press, 1968), pp. 77–78.

16. Harriet Grote, *The Personal Life of George Grote,* 2nd ed. (London: John Murray, 1873); Martin Lowther Clarke, *George Grote, a Biography* (London: University of London, Athlone Press, 1962); Joseph Hamburger, *Intellectuals in Politics: John Stuart Mill and the Philosophic Radicals* (New Haven: Yale University Press, 1965), passim.

had expected from the Reform Act had failed to develop. He continued to be active in public life and served as an energetic trustee for both the British Museum and University College London. But after his retirement from politics Grote devoted most of his attention to the writing of *A History of Greece,* a project he had initially contemplated and begun in the early 1820s. The first two volumes of that work appeared in 1846 and the eleventh and twelfth in 1856. Thereafter he published a three-volume study, *Plato, and the Other Companions of Socrates.* A posthumous two-volume work on Aristotle appeared in 1872. With the exception of aesthetics and art there was almost no area of the study of ancient Greek civilization upon which Grote failed to leave a distinctive mark. For that reason his name and achievement figure more prominently in the Victorian history of Greek studies in Britain than those of any other single author. From the forties on Grote was the one scholar with whom any aspiring British classicist had to contend, either directly or indirectly. Later students of Greece continued to react to the people who had reacted to Grote. It is difficult to think of another Victorian scholar or man of letters who made such extensive contributions to any other field of learning outside the physical sciences.

Although Grote lacked the elegant style of Macaulay and the gift for passionate invective of Carlyle, he possessed a commanding power for reasoned argument and lucid explication. Grote was as much an ideological historian as he had been an ideological politician. He regarded the writing of history as didactic in purpose and critical in method, an intellectual outlook that owed much to his Benthamite associations and to his broad familiarity with the literature of the Enlightenment. He was an enemy of sinister interests in politics, an empiricist in psychology, and a rationalist in religion.[17] To the end of his life in 1871 contemporary critics and reviewers persisted in regarding Grote primarily as a brilliant political radical who had ventured into the writing of history and in analyzing his work in terms of his political career and his early political associations. That viewpoint obscured the expansive purview of Grote's intellect. He was a thoroughly European scholar and cosmopolitan thinker whose mind

17. Philip Beauchamp, *Analysis of the Influence of Natural Religion on the Temporal Happiness of Mankind* (London, 1822). Jeremy Bentham wrote this work, and George Grote edited it.

was open to ideas and information culled from a wide variety of intellectual traditions, as his copious footnotes in Greek, Latin, Italian, French, and German bear witness. Although his native predilection lay with the Enlightenment, he was also familiar with the German idealists and romantics whose thought in no small measure shaped his own.

Grote's intellectual eclecticism brilliantly manifested itself in the analysis of Greek myths and legends that appeared in the two opening volumes of *A History of Greece* published in 1846. As the title of the most important chapter indicated, he sought to present the "Grecian Mythes, as Understood, Felt, and Interpreted by the Greeks Themselves." His discussion stood directly in the mainstream of the historicist tradition of nineteenth-century scholarship.[18] He drew upon the rationalist bias of the philosophes, the critical mythography of Müller, Lobeck, and other Germans, the developmental theories of Vico, the Scottish conjecturalist historians, and Comte, and the comparative mythography of writers such as the Grimm brothers. The result of this wide reading was a new departure for the British study of Greek myths and history—a historicist analysis of the function of myth in ancient societies and a learned polemic against the derivation of alleged historical fact from the evidence provided by the Greek myths. His eclecticism meant that no single historical theory dominated his work and also allowed later writers of diverse intellectual outlooks to find significant parts of his analysis compatible with their own purposes.

Grote performed for Greek history the task that Niebuhr had performed for Roman history. Drawing upon Müller's *Introduction to a Scientific Study of Mythology,* Grote broke the link between Greek myths and Greek history that his most learned British and European predecessors had been unwilling to sever.[19] He contended that no

18. Klaus Dockhorn, *Der deutsche Historismus in England: ein Beitrag zur englishen Geistesgeschichte des 19. Jahrhunderts* (Göttigen: Vanderhoeck and Ruprecht, 1950), pp. 48–57; Duncan Forbes, "*Historismus* in England," *Cambridge Review* 4 (1950–51): 387–400.

19. John Stuart Mill, "Grote's History of Greece," *Edinburgh Review* 84 (1846): 347–48. Prior to Grote, Thomas Keightley had used Müller's view of myth to say that the Greek myths were the product of the Greek imagination. However, Keightley had not drawn any substantial conclusions about the relationship of the myths to the writing of Greek history. See Keightley, *Mythology of Ancient Greece and Italy* (1838 ed.), pp. 1–14.

satisfactory empirical evidence existed in the mythical narratives to say anything about the history of Greece before 776 B.C., the year of the first Olympiad. The events narrated in the myths of creation up through those told about the Trojan War and its aftermath he characterized as taking place in "a past which never was present,—a region essentially mythical, neither approachable by the critic nor measurable by the chronologer." It was impossible to discern true from false information in these stories because the authors of the myths had themselves made no such discernment. Sorting through the myths for some kernel of plausible truth simply obscured the fundamental fact that myth constituted the total mode of thought and consciousness for people living in an era and state of society where there existed "no records, no philosophy, no criticism, no canon of belief, and scarcely any tincture either of astronomy or geography." The myths were not history or allegory or symbols. They were the facts of everyday belief and consciousness for the minds of Greeks living during the most ancient epoch of that civilization. The only way in which those myths could be properly understood was through the difficult process of identifying "ourselves with the state of mind of the original mythopoeic age." That effort would require the adoption of "a string of poetical fancies not simply as realities, but as the governing realities of the mental system" and would "only reproduce something analogous to our own childhood."[20]

For Grote, the Greek myths were the intellectual product of an "age of historical faith, as distinguished from the later age of historical reason." Strangers to positive philosophy and science, the originators of the myths had been guided "by vivacity of imagination and by personifying sympathy" in providing themselves with interpretations of natural phenomena, ethical precepts, and a plausible account of the

20. George Grote, *A History of Greece,* A New Edition (London: John Murray, 1869) (unless otherwise noted, all references are to this edition), 1:43, 434, 341–42. Grote also drew upon Vico's *Scienza Nuova* for the idea of myth as representative of a mentality analogous to childhood and included in the first edition of *A History of Greece* (London: John Murray, 1846) a four-page quotation from Vico in a footnote (1:473–76). By the 1869 edition Grote had condensed the quotation (1:341–43). He seems to have paid little or no attention to the essential features of Vico's historical theory other than the analogy with childhood. See *The Autobiography of Giambattista Vico,* trans. Max Harold Fisch and Thomas Goddard Bergin (Ithaca: Great Seal Books, 1962), pp. 91–93.

past. Myth might resemble history in being narrative and philosophy in being illustrative, but "in its essence and substance, in the mental tendencies by which it is created as well as in those by which it is judged and upheld, it is a popularised expression of the divine and heroic faith of the people." Grote argued that for modern historians the empirical fact was not the detail of the myth but the existence of faith in it. No doubt the Eleusinians had unquestionably believed the myth of Demeter and Persephone. Yet the undisputed fact of their honestly held faith in those figures did not make

> the less certain that they were simply mythes or legends, and not to be treated as history either actual or exaggerated. They do not take their start from realities of the past, but from realities of the present, combined with restrospective feeling and fancy, which fills up the blank of the aforetime in a manner at once plausible and impressive. What proportion of fact there may be in the legend, or whether there be any at all, it is impossible to ascertain and useless to inquire; for the story did not acquire belief from its approximation to real fact, but from its perfect harmony with Eleusinian faith and feeling, and from the absence of any standard of historical credibility.[21]

Later observers have noted the parallel between Grote's rejection of the historical validity of myth and that of David Friedrich Strauss in *Leben Jesu* (1835).[22] Both scholars emphasized the role of community feeling in validating the original mythical narratives. Both also regarded myths as evidence only of the state of mind that gave rise to them. Consequently, modern writers could not properly employ either Greek or New Testament myths as critical historical sources for events that by their very nature myths could not explain or give account of. Grote may have read Strauss and would certainly have appreciated his analysis, but the more probable reason for their agreement was their common reading in the advanced German mythography that stemmed from the work of Heyne and his later disciples.

21. Grote, *History of Greece*, 1:viii, 332, 428, 42.
22. Hewlett, "Rationale of Mythology," p. 409; John M'Clintock, ed., *Cyclopaedia of Biblical, Theological and Ecclesiastical Literature* (New York: Harper and Brothers, 1894), 3:806. I am indebted to Yoder, *Concepts of Mythology in Victorian England*, p. 92, for these references.

To provide a further buttress to his rejection of the historical character of the Greek myths, Grote drew upon contemporary comparative
mythology. In a chapter entitled "The Grecian Mythical Vein Compared to that of Modern Europe" he pointed out the similar men-
talities displayed in the Greek myths and in the myths of medieval
Europe. In this effort Grote was highly dependent on the Grimm
brothers and other writers who had examined the German sagas.[23]
Both the medieval lives of the saints and the stories of chivalrous
heroes corresponded in character and purpose to the Greek myths as
"stories accepted as realities, from their full conformity with the
predispositions and deep-seated faith of an uncritical audience, and
prepared beforehand by their authors, not with any reference to the
conditions of historical proof, but for the purpose of calling forth
sympathy, emotion, or reverence." The vividly present hand of God in
those narratives "brings us even back to the simple and ever-operative
theology of the Homeric age." The medieval mythopoeic age had
originated in the turmoil of the fifth and sixth centuries of the Christian era when the dissolution of the Greek and Roman critical mentality had left "the mind free to a religious interpretation of nature not
less simple and *naïf* than that which had prevailed under Homeric
paganism."[24] Modern historians recognized the mythic character of
these stories and did not look to them for historical information. They
should come to treat the myths of Greece in the same manner.

Grote's analysis of the mythopoeic age had genuinely partaken of
the spirit of German historicism. No less than the German Hellenists
did he believe that the inhabitants of ancient Greece had truly felt the
presence of the gods and had perceived the world in a fashion wholly
unlike that of modern men and women. But unlike most of the German Hellenists and English romantics, Grote was anything but re-
gretful about the demise of the mythopoeic mentality, which had
occurred sometime after the completion of the Homeric epics through
"a silent alteration in the mental state of the society." In 1843, while
directly criticizing the nostalgia of Schiller's "Götter Griechenlands,"

23. Grote's major sources for his discussion of the Middle Ages included Jacob
Grimm's *Deutsche Mythologie*, François Guizot's *Cours d'Histoire Moderne* (1839), L.
F. Alfred Maury's *Essai sur les Légendes Pieuses du Moyen Age* (1843), and J. J. A.
Ampère's *Histoire Littéraire de la France* (1839–40).
24. Grote, *History of Greece*, 1:453, 455, 456.

Grote observed, "Estimated by a poetical standard, the loss has been serious indeed; but it has been far more than compensated by the acquisition of lasting and substantial benefits."[25] Understanding and appreciation of the mythic frame of mind did not require its commendation.

Grote portrayed the progressive modification in Greek thinking that resulted in rationalism and material improvement as having originated in "the expansive force of Grecian intellect itself." Contact with physical nature such as described in Hesiod's *Works and Days* meant the Greeks of that era became "more deeply enlisted in the world before them, and disposed to fasten on incidents of their actual experience" than had been those of Homer's day. Some of them must have begun to observe the regularity of natural phenomena. Expansion of trade began to nurture "an historical sense" as the Greeks discovered whole civilizations unaccounted for by their myths. The growth of cities demonstrated the inadequacy of the social relations and ethics grounded in the Olympian myths. These changing facts and experiences of everyday life required a new mode of thought because they could not be readily accommodated into the fabric of the myths. The physical philosophies of Thales, Xenophanes, and Pythagoras marked the first attempt in Greece "to disenthral the philosophic intellect from all-personifying religious faith, and to constitute a method of interpreting nature distinct from the spontaneous inspirations of untaught minds." By setting aside the personal view of nature and regarding it as an object, these philosophers had initiated the metaphysical stage of Greek thought; but they still had not achieved empirical categories of analysis. In the fifth century, however, with the appearance of Anaxagoras, Hippocrates, and Socrates, something resembling a scientific outlook had emerged; and with it "that radical discord between the mental impulses of science and religion" had become manifest.[26]

25. Ibid., p. 346; George Grote, "Grecian Legends and Early History," *Westminster Review* 39 (1843): 328. This is a very important article in which Grote outlined the ideas he explored more fully in *A History of Greece*.

26. Grote, *History of Greece*, 1:350, 353, 354, 356, 362. See Georg Wilhelm Friedrich Hegel, *Lectures on the History of Philosophy*, 3 vols., trans. E. S. Haldane and Frances H. Simson (New York: The Humanities Press, 1968), 1:149–350, for a very different account of Greek intellectual development. This comparison makes particularly clear Grote's dependence on Comte and the Scottish historians.

In accounting for this "native growth of the Hellenic youth into an Hellenic man," Grote had abandoned his use of the German writers and had turned to Comte and the Scottish school of conjecturalist history represented by Adam Smith, Adam Ferguson, and John Millar.[27] Grote described the results of the intellectual transformation of Greece in largely Comtean terms and accounted for its occurrence through the conjecturalist categories of unconsciously directed economic and material advance. These developmental frameworks, unlike those of Germany, allowed Grote, in a manner later more fully undertaken by anthropologists such as Edward Tylor, to abandon a concept of uniform human nature without also abandoning rationality as the proper end of eventual human advance.[28] As J. W. Burrow has maintained, for such writers "mankind was one not because it was everywhere the same, but because the differences represented different stages in the same process."[29] By associating myth with specific material conditions of social life that were subject to change and improvement, Grote was in effect arguing that mythical thinking did not necessarily constitute a permanent feature of the human situation. Social and economic progress could eradicate the situation that allowed myths to flourish. Even so, this measured optimism—or mitigated pessimism—appeared fragile in light of Grote's portrayal of the renewed mythic outlook of the Middle Ages and his later portrayal of the impact of religious thought on Greek politics.

Although mythic thinking had largely disappeared among certain superior minds of the fifth and fourth centuries, Grote argued that the myths themselves had remained very much facts of culture and general consciousness. Even the more advanced thinkers could not completely erase from their minds myths they "had imbibed in their childhood from the poets, and by which they were to a certain degree unconsciously enslaved." Moreover, those enlightened writers still had to function in a larger society where many and perhaps most people still deeply believed the myths. Consequently, figures such as Pindar, Herodotus, Thucydides, Anaxagoras, Socrates, Plato, Aeschylus, Sophocles, and Euripides had sought not to destroy the myths

27. Grote, History of Greece, 1:446.
28. Duncan Forbes, " 'Scientific' Whiggism: Adam Smith and John Millar," Cambridge Review 7 (1953–54): 643–70; Burrow, Evolution and Society, pp. 10–23, 42–64.
29. Burrow, Evolution and Society, p. 98.

but rather to remove them as obstacles to further progressive thought by accommodating the stories "to an improved tone of sentiment and a newly created canon of credibility."[30] For example, Herodotus had rejected current supernatural explanations while preserving reports of them in the past, and the dramatists had attempted to raise the ethical and moral relationship between the gods and humankind presented by the myths.

These various reforms constituted a recasting of the myths that forced "them into new moulds such as their authors had never conceived." The reform, purification, and explanation of the inherited stock of myths that had continued through the later Hellenistic age meant that from the fifth century onward a novel character and new functions came to be ascribed to the ancient myths by the Greeks themselves. As Grote explained:

> It was from the... strong necessity, of accommodating the old mythes to a new standard both of belief and of appreciation, that both the historical and the allegorical schemes of transforming them arose; the literal narrative being decomposed for the purpose of arriving at a base either of particular matter of fact, or of general physical or moral truth.

From the assumption by enlightened Greeks, such as Euhemerus, that the ancient myths must have had some original meaning long obscured by the passage of time there had emerged "a string of allegorised phenomenal truths" and "a long series of seeming historical events and chronological persons." Yet both the allegories and purported histories had been "elicited from the transformed mythes and from nothing else."[31] Previous modern scholars had failed to grasp this ancient transformation of the mythic inheritance and had thus misconstrued the actual character of the myths and of the mythopoeic age. They had also failed to comprehend the tendencies of intellectual activity in Greece after the fifth century.

The confusion about the allegedly historical content of the myths had fostered further errors in the writing of Greek history. The outlook of enlightened Greeks toward their myths had not been shared by the general population. Beginning in the fifth century, a cultural

30. Grote, *History of Greece*, 1:364.
31. Ibid., pp. 364, 407–08, 412.

schism had divided Greece and especially Athens. Advanced thinkers might have looked for history in the myths, but for a much larger portion of the population the myths and religious ceremonies continued to provide a primary mode of thought and imagination. This point was very important for Grote's later analysis of Greek politics and had been fundamental to his desire to repudiate the historical validity of the myths. So long as the myths continued to be regarded as sources of factual information about the legendary age, there was little possibility for modern scholars to examine them as modes of thought that could have detrimentally affected the functioning of democratic political structures during the classical period of Greek history. In his preface of 1846 Grote told his readers:

> ... it must be confessed that the sentimental attributes of the Greek mind—its religious and poetical vein—here appear in disproportionate relief, as compared with its more vigorous and masculine capacities—with those powers of acting, organising, judging, and speculating, which will be revealed in the forthcoming volumes. I venture however to forewarn the reader that there will occur numerous circumstances in the after political life of the Greeks which he will not comprehend unless he be initiated into the course of their legendary associations. . . . The occasion will indeed often occur for remarking how these legends illustrate and vivify the political phenomena of the succeeding times.[32]

Until the true character of myths and mythical thinking had been discerned, the later pernicious impact of such thought and feelings on the political life of Greece could not be perceived. As Grote related the political history of Greece, he would defend Greek democratic structures from their alleged frailties by blaming instead the survival of a religious frame of mind in the citizens of the democracy. Those issues will be more fully explored in chapter five.

The Assimilation of Grote's Theory of Greek Myth

For almost a quarter-century the two opening volumes of Grote's *History of Greece* constituted the most extensive and learned discussion

32. Ibid., pp. xi–xii.

of Greek myth and of mythic thought generally to appear in English. As such, the work enjoyed a broad though often unrecognized influence both within and without the realm of classical studies. Students in other fields of learning could apply his analysis to non-Hellenic primitive societies. This appears to have been the case with certain anthropologists during the third quarter of the century.[33] It was also possible for writers on Greek antiquity to accept Grote's views of the character of myth without accepting his theory of human intellectual development. For example, his concept of myth as the product of the imagination became a major factor in the aesthetic criticism of Greek myths by John Ruskin, Walter Pater, and J. A. Symonds. His discussion of the confrontation by fifth-century Athenian intellectuals with their mythic inheritance led to a novel appreciation of those ancient figures as religious reformers whose cultural situation paralleled that of liberal Victorian Christians.

Two features of Grote's work allowed this radical, utilitarian, positivist author to exercise such a paradoxical influence over essayists such as Ruskin and Pater who were so deeply moved by the sheer beauty of Greek literature and art. The first was Grote's contention that myth pertained to the childhood of the race. Although he usually equated that childhood with Comte's theological stage of intellectual development, he had also frequently enough described the mythopoeic age in the language of the German Hellenists to permit other writers to associate the mythopoeic mentality with the carefree, innocent Greeks imagined by many of the Germans. The connection received further encouragement from passages in which Grote had used the metaphor of growth from childhood to adulthood to portray Greek intellectual progress.

The second connecting link was Grote's location of the origin of myth in the functioning of the imagination. Although the creative imagination as a concept is usually associated with romanticism and belief in transcendental knowledge, rationalist and associationist psy-

33. "Myth is not to be looked on as mere error and folly, but as an interesting product of the human mind. It is sham history, the fictitious narrative of events that never happened." Edward Burnett Tylor, *Anthropology: An Introduction to the Study of Man and Civilization* (London: Macmillan and Co., 1881), pp. 387, 379. See also Alexander Bain, "The Intellectual Character and Writings of George Grote," in George Grote, *The Minor Works of George Grote,* ed. Alexander Bain (London: John Murray, 1873), pp. 74–75.

chology also entertained a theory of the imagination that recognized a
significant role for the feelings and for sympathy. John Stuart Mill
once explained this associationist mode of imagination as it related to
poetry.

> At the center of each group of thoughts or images will be found a
> feeling; and the thoughts or images are only there because the
> feeling was there. All the combinations which the mind puts
> together, all the pictures which it paints, the wholes which Imag-
> ination constructs out of the materials supplied by Fancy, will
> be indebted to some dominant *feeling,* not as in other natures to a
> dominant *thought,* for their unity and consistency of character—
> for what distinguishes them from incoherencies.[34]

Mill's statement succinctly captures the mode of imagination that
Grote attributed to the mythopoeic age. Rather than thought or empirical experience, feelings that implied nothing transcendental provided the grounds for accepting the imagination as the interpreter of
nature, morals, and history. Almost in spite of himself, Grote had
provided a useful finite concept of myth and imagination for writers
who were profoundly troubled by the difficulty for creative imagination in human experience limited strictly to the realm of sensations.
Grote had demonstrated that human beings so circumscribed could
create, and in the legendary age of Greece had created, a mental realm
of beauty and fanciful animation that answered to the deeper needs of
the human situation. During the second half of the century, under the
impact of Darwinian thought and naturalistic psychology, aesthetically minded writers embraced this finite concept of the imagination
rather than a romantic or Coleridgean one.

John Ruskin's views of myth went through several stages of development. In Volume III of *Modern Painters* (1856) he drew upon
Grote's exposition for his own chapter "Of Classical Landscape." To
present a salutary contrast to the pathetic fallacy that ascribed human
attributes and emotions to physical nature, Ruskin looked to the
Greeks who, he contended, had personified nature in a true rather than
in a false spirit. Their myths had not been flowery or fanciful allegories

---

34. Quoted in Abrams, *Mirror and the Lamp,* p. 178.

but sincere projections onto nature of personalities such as their own. As Ruskin asserted in *Modern Painters:*

> ... when Diana is said to hunt with her nymphs in the woods, it does not mean merely, as Wordsworth put it, that the poet or shepherd saw the moon and stars glancing between the branches of the trees, and wished to say so figuratively. It means that there is a living spirit, to which the light of the moon is a body; which takes delight in glancing between the clouds and following the wild beasts as they wander through the night; and that this spirit sometimes assumes a perfect human form, and in this form, with real arrows, pursues and slays the wild beasts, which with its mere arrows of moonlight it could not slay; retaining, nevertheless, all the while, its power and being in the moonlight, and in all else that it rules.[35]

The Greek could perceive nature in no other fashion than to find divine personality immanent throughout, and that personality always resembled his own. This projection of self into nature, with its creation of humanlike deities, meant that the Greeks had been able to live comfortably in their natural environment, in their physical bodies, and with their gods who were never absolutely different in kind from themselves. The Greeks had consequently experienced few of the emotional restraints, inward forebodings, and outward asceticism of modern men and women, who, like Ruskin himself, had been reared in narrow versions of Christianity. Although Grote had thoroughly rejected such nostalgia for the mythopoeic age, his analysis of the myths and particularly his rejection of their allegorical or historical character served to provide a new dimension of historical reality for an age in which the human imagination had freely, creatively, and healthfully functioned. This outlook validated Ruskin's contrast of the mentality of the Greeks with the false values and perceptions of moderns. The world and the human experience could be and once had been approached differently.

John Addington Symonds and Walter Pater carried the implications

---

35. John Ruskin, *The Works of John Ruskin,* 39 vols., ed. E. T. Cook and Alexander Wedderburn (London: George Allen, 1903–12), 5:226–27. See also Raymond Edward Fitch, *The Golden Furrow: John Ruskin and the Greek Religion* (Ann Arbor, Mich.: University Microfilms, 1965), pp. 39–42, 66–72.

of Grote's mythography further than Ruskin had. In *Studies of the Greek Poets* (1873) Symonds urged that "the truth to be looked for in myths is psychological, not historical, aesthetic rather than positive." This statement represented Grote's position precisely, and, as James Kissane has urged, it probably epitomized the mid-Victorian concept of Greek myth.[36] For writers such as Symonds and Pater, who had surrendered their Christian faith and who were convinced of the finitude of human experience and its imprisonment in the world of the senses, Grote's concept of myth could and did suggest that even a world composed solely of matter and energy need not be a realm without loveliness.

Pater's major comments on myth occurred between 1867 and 1876. In his essay "Winckelmann" (1867), which was included in *Studies on the Renaissance* and which was deeply informed by both Hegel's aesthetics and modern anthropology as well as by Grote's work, Pater discerned "a universal pagan sentiment" from which all religion had arisen. That sentiment indicated humankind's acute awareness of its vulnerability in the natural world.

> This pagan sentiment measures the sadness with which the human mind is filled, whenever its thoughts wander far from what is here, and now. It is beset by notions of irresistible natural powers for the most part ranged against man, but the secret also of his fortune, making the earth golden and the grape fiery for him. He makes his gods in his own image, gods smiling and flower-crowned, or bleeding by some sad fatality, to console him by their wounds, never closed from generation to generation.

Through the myths, human beings sought to make themselves less estranged from nature and by religious ritual to exercise some vague control over it. In Greece as elsewhere those rituals had been frequently cruel, bloody, and repulsively superstitious. Then, perhaps echoing Grote's comparison of the ancient mythopoeic epoch and the Christian Middle Ages, Pater declared, "Scarcely a wild or melancholy note of the medieval church but was anticipated by Greek poly-

36. John Addington Symonds, *Studies of the Greek Poets,* 3rd ed. (London: Adam and Charles Black, 1893), 1:51; James Kissane, "Victorian Mythology," *Victorian Studies* 6 (1962): 14–15.

theism." However, Greek religion, in contrast to Christianity, had been privileged "to be able to transform itself into an artistic ideal." Greek religion and myth in conjuction with "the perfect animal nature of the Greeks" had fostered an ideal art that was appropriate to the finitude of the human situation.[37]

In 1876 Pater published an essay on Demeter and Persephone and another on Dionysus, both of which more directly reflect the influence of Grote. There Pater described the myths as rising in a "world of vision unchecked by positive knowledge." In the cases of Demeter and Dionysus that vision incorporated "the whole productive power of the earth ... and the explanation of its annual change" in terms of corn on the one hand and the vine on the other. Again following Grote quite closely, Pater termed Demeter the "Mater Dolorosa" of the Greeks and suggested that in some cases ritual observances may have preceded the myths that explained them. However, Pater embraced much of Grote's theory in order to transform it, turn it on its head, and urge a role for new mythic thought in the contemporary age of positivistic science. Drawing upon Heine and upon commentaries on the poet, Pater suggested that the modern world might become re-populated with deities of the Greek variety. The ancient myths rooted in the human imagination illustrated the kind of religion possible within the confines of positivist epistemology.

The myth of Demeter and Persephone ... illustrates the power of the Greek religion as a religion of pure ideas—of conceptions, which having no link on historical fact, yet, because they arose naturally out of the spirit of man, and embodied, in adequate symbols, his deepest thoughts concerning the conditions of his physical and spiritual life, maintained their hold through many changes, and are still not without a solemnising power even for the modern mind, which has once admitted them as recognized and habitual inhabitants; and, abiding thus for the elevation and purifying of our sentiments, long after the earlier and simpler races of their worshippers have passed away, they may be a pledge to us of the place in our culture, at once legitimate and

37. Walter Pater, *The Renaissance: Studies in Art and Poetry* (New York: The Macmillan Co., 1905), pp. 211, 212, 214, 215, 218.

possible, of the associations, the conceptions, the imagery, of Greek religious poetry in general, of the poetry of all religion.[38]

For Grote the myths illustrated a state of psychological consciousness in humankind at a particular stage or moment in its intellectual development. For Pater the myths expressed something more akin to existential images of perennial needs and aspirations of human beings. Their lack of historical basis made them all the more directly relevant. Although the gods of Greece may have vanished, the human imagination that had given them birth and sustained their life remained. Furthermore, the myths themselves remained as witnesses of the capacity of the imagination to address the spiritual needs of finite human beings and to foster the conditions for an ideal art appropriate to such beings. Pater thus adopted much of Grote's analysis of myth while rejecting most of its implicit plea for rational intellectual progress.

Pater's essays of 1876, like so much of his other writing, were more suggestive than satisfying. He set forth his themes with subtle touches rather than with bold strokes. One senses that he felt and knew things about both Greek and contemporary religion that he dared not say. It sufficed to alert his age that the Greek myths embodied human feelings, emotions, and inner powers that still dwelled in the world. Three years earlier in *Studies of the Greek Poets* John Addington Symonds had been more forthright. Although Symonds is now best known as a historian of the Renaissance, his two volumes on the Greek poets were for many years the standard work on the subject. Symonds's description of the mythopoeic age, his portrayal of the Greeks as children, his comparison of the legendary age of Greece with the Christian Middle Ages, and his contention that the Greek myths were "the parents of philosophies, religions, politics" lead one to suspect that he wrote his lectures with Grote's first volume open before him on his desk. Yet Symonds did not merely parrot Grote but used the latter's approach to myth to comment on the problems of the faltering of religious faith in the third quarter of the nineteenth century. He drew specific parallels between the qualities of Greek myths and the stories in the Judeo-Christian tradition. He described Empedocles as a person who resem-

---

38. Walter Pater, *Greek Studies,* ed. Charles L. Shadwell (New York: The Macmillan Co., 1903), pp. 22, 6, 116, 155–56. See also Grote, *History of Greece,* 1:40, and John S. Harrison, "Pater, Heine, and the Old Gods of Greece," *Publications of the Modern Language Association* 39 (1924): 655–86.

bled a modern agnostic. And in words that might have been applied to contemporary liberal Christians he praised Pindar as "the fine flower of Hellenic religion, free from slavish subservience to creeds and ceremonies, capable of extracting sublime morality from mythical legends, and adding to the old glad joyousness of the Homeric faith a deeper and more awful perception of superhuman mysteries." The age of Pindar had witnessed the emergence of both a destructive skepticism and a constructive purified theism that existed side by side. The former deteriorated into mere skepticism and the latter into mystical metaphysical speculation. But between the hopeful commencement and dreary close of this critical movement, the Greek tragedians had attempted to set forth a reformed religious synthesis. Disturbed by the immorality and unpredictability of the gods, Aeschylus and Sophocles had attempted to purify the myths and to present images of the gods worthy of the power they possessed. Symonds regarded Aeschylus's conviction "that what a man sows he will reap, and that the world is not ruled by blind chance" to be "in one sense or another, the most solid ethical acquisition of humanity." Sophocles had carried the reformist impulse a step further by spiritualizing religion and making it "more indefinite." In so doing, he had hoped to render religion "more impregnable within its stronghold of the human heart and reason, less exposed to the attacks of logic or the changes of opinion."[39]

Symonds's interpretation of the dramatists today seems rather dated, quaint, and exceedingly Victorian. It was in fact very much Victorian, because only after the publication of the first volume of Grote's *History of Greece* were liberalizing religious functions and goals ascribed to Aeschylus and Sophocles. Grote's analysis of the ancient modes of interpreting and reforming the mythic inheritance permitted liberal Victorian religious writers such as James Anthony Froude, John Stuart Blackie, Richard Jebb, Evelyn Abbott, and E. H. Plumptre, as well as Symonds and others to see their own contemporary role as religious reformers prefigured in the enlightened writers and philosophers of fifth-century Athens. Like their ancient predecessors, they were forcing their inherited religious myths "into new moulds such as their authors had never conceived."[40]

39. Symonds, *Studies of the Greek Poets*, 1:2, 327, 414, 427.
40. Grote, *History of Greece*, 1:364.

For all practical purposes early Victorian commentaries on Greek literature and drama had ignored the religious character of those works and their intent to reform the myths. The redirection of criticism came about only after the publication of Grote's work. In 1850 R. W. Mackay, in *The Progress of the Intellect as Exemplified in the Religious Development of the Greeks and Hebrews,* employed a concept of myth largely based on Grote's and noted the attempts of both Pindar and Aeschylus to purify the mythic narratives. The same year John Stuart Blackie, a prolific classicist and professor of Greek at Edinburgh, set forth a similar theme in the introduction to his translation of Aeschylus, as did F. A. Paley of Oxford in his commentary on his Greek edition of the dramatist in 1855. Matthew Arnold voiced the same outlook in his lecture "The Modern Element in Literature" (1857). Sophocles attracted increasing attention as Christian writers looked for evidence of true faith and morals in the Greek dramatists. This viewpoint achieved its most fulsome expression in Dean E. H. Plumptre's evaluation of Sophocles.

> Nowhere, even in the ethics of Christian writers, are there nobler assertions of a morality divine, universal, unchangeable, of laws whose dwelling is on high . . . [which] written on the hearts of all men, are of prior obligation to all conventional arrangements of society, or the maxims of political expediency.

According to Plumptre, Sophocles had taken the inadequate mythology of Homer and, so far as possible, had transformed it into "an instrument of moral education" to "lead men upwards to the eternal laws of God, and the thought of His righteous order." With somewhat less enthusiasm but still within the same vein Evelyn Abbott, a late-century Oxford Greek historian, explained that the tragedians had aided the development of the Greek intellect by refusing to allow "the mythology which stood to them in the place of doctrine to restrain them from the endeavour to bring their conception of the Supreme Being into harmony with their conceptions of justice and law."[41] It would be difficult to discover a more succinct statement of the intention of liberal Victorian Christians in regard to their own mythic inheritance.

41. Robert William Mackay, *The Progress of the Intellect, As Exemplified in the Religious Development of the Greeks and Hebrews* (London: John Chapman, 1850),

Such interpretations of the major literary figures of Greece and Athens allowed many Victorians to feel a particular kinship with their experience. Young James Anthony Froude in 1849 defended his skeptical novel *The Nemesis of Faith* by an appeal to the Greek experience.

What Plato says of the mythology of the Greeks, I say of that of the Hebrews. I do not mean that Hebrew mythology is *as* insulting to the pure majesty of God, or *as* injurious in its direct effects to those who are brought to believe it. But I am sure that it contains things which *are* both insulting and injurious—and because, to all thinking persons who consciously use the faculties which God has given them, large portions of it have become equally incredible with the Greek, it may, therefore, indirectly be even more injurious, as permitting the mind to cling to it with an attachment which will render the struggle at parting more violent and more convulsive.[42]

The problems of the enlightened Greeks were the problems of enlightened Victorians. The stance of the ancient Greeks in regard to their myths, as interpreted by Grote and further confirmed later by Matthew Arnold's concept of an analogous stage of cultural development in Athens and Britain, gave Victorians the intellectual confidence to take a similar stance. Those liberal Christians failed to see,

---

1:215, 452–53; John Stuart Blackie, trans., *The Lyrical Dramas of Aeschylus,* 2 vols. (London: J. W. Parker, 1850), 1:xxxvii–lviii; Frederick Apthorp Paley, *The Tragedy of Aeschylus re-edited with an English Commentary* (London: Whittaker and Co., 1855), pp. xvi–xxx; Matthew Arnold, *On the Classical Tradition,* ed. R. H. Super (Ann Arbor: University of Michigan Press, 1960), p. 31; Edward Hayes Plumptre, trans., *The Tragedies of Sophocles* (New York: George Routledge and Sons, 1881; first edition, 1865), pp. lxxvi, xciv; Evelyn Abbott, "The Theology and Ethics of Sophocles," Evelyn Abbott, ed., *Hellenica: A Collection of Essays on Greek Poetry, Philosophy, History, and Religion* (London: Rivingtons, 1880), p. 38. See also Brooke Foss Westcott, *Essays in the History of Religious Thought in the West* (London: Macmillan and Co., 1891), pp. v–vi, 51–141, for discussions of the religious dimensions of Aeschylus and Euripedes, and Richard Claverhouse Jebb, *Sophocles: The Plays and Fragments with Critical Notes, Commentary, and Translation in English Prose* (Amsterdam: A. M. Hakkert, 1962–67; originally published, 1894) for further consideration of Sophocles. An examination of previous commentaries on the Greek dramatists and of the standard encyclopedia and reference book articles revealed no treatment of these writers as religious reformers prior to the appearance of Grote's *History of Greece.*

42. James Anthony Froude, *The Nemesis of Faith,* 2nd ed. (London: John Chapman, 1849), p. v.

however, that such was possible because they themselves had largely created the cultural parallel that sustained their courage.

F. Max Müller—Myth as the Disease of Language

No doubt the most famous Victorian student of myth was Mr. Casaubon in George Eliot's *Middlemarch,* who devoted his life to the discovery of a key to all mythologies. Much ink has been spilled and many academic dinner parties enlivened in learned attempts to ascertain who among George Eliot's numerous acquaintances was the pattern for this character. Happily it is unnecessary to continue those speculations here. There was, however, one scholar in Britain whose professional endeavor did very much resemble Mr. Casaubon's amateur efforts. This was Friedrich Max Müller, professor of Sanskrit at Oxford. Unlike old Casaubon who was married to the young, idealistic Dorothea, this German transplanted into Oxford enjoyed a very happy marriage to a woman nearly his own age. But like the fictitious scholar, Müller believed that in philology he had discovered the key, if not to all, then to nearly all myths. During the second half of the century his theory was the major rival to Grote's and probably the most influential academic view of myth to appear before the turn to anthropological theory.

Müller was one of those figures who have given nineteenth-century scholarship its reputation for heroic enterprise.[43] He combined his native German erudition and industry with a clear English style and an insatiable capacity for writing books and articles. That much of his work was repetitive seems almost beside the point in light of his translations of the *Rig-Veda,* his numerous volumes on mythology and philology, and his four sets of Gifford Lectures. His reputation was so high that when it appeared he might leave Oxford, he was relieved of all teaching duties. George Grote once refused Gladstone's offer of a peerage because acceptance seemed incompatible with his

---

43. *The Life and Letters of the Right Honourable Friedrich Max Müller,* edited by his wife (London: Longmans, Green, and Co., 1902); Chase, *Quest for Myth,* pp. 44–48; Jan de Vries, *The Study of Religion: An Historical Approach* (New York: Harcourt, Brace and World, 1967), pp. 86–90; Richard Dorson, "The Eclipse of Solar Mythology," in Thomas A. Sebeok, ed., *Myth: A Symposium* (Bloomington: Indiana University Press, 1974), pp. 25–63.

political principles. Müller refused the offer of a knighthood from the Crown because it was a minor British honor and he had already received higher awards from other European nations. In 1899, just two years before his death, he did, however, agree to be made a Privy Councillor. It is necessary to provide these indications of contemporary assessments of Müller's achievement because today he and his theory are largely forgotten or disregarded. Mr. Casaubon is now more famous than Max Müller.

Müller's personal and intellectual reputation also illustrates the important and little explored relationship between the British and German intellectual communities. From the twenties on, British students, scholars, and clergymen visited Germany and studied German philosophy, theology, science, philology, and classical scholarship. Numerous important German works in these fields were translated into English. A key figure in this interchange was Baron Bunsen, the Prussian ambassador to Britain.[44] A scholar himself, Bunsen cultivated friendships and contacts within the British intellectual and university communities. It was Bunsen who brought Müller to Britain at the age of twenty-five to complete the translation of the *Veda* under the financial patronage of the British East India Company. It was Müller's expertise in Sanskrit and philology that eventually led him to the study of the Greek myths.

During the late eighteenth and early nineteenth centuries much speculation had arisen in both Britain and Germany about the possible oriental influence on Greek culture. Heyne had suggested that a possible common geographical center from which later nations had become dispersed might account for the similarities among the myths of different cultures. Creuzer had contended that the Greek myths were stories brought to the eastern Mediterranean by a group of Indian priests. The great orientalist Sir William Jones of Great Britain had made similar suggestions, but except for Edward Pococke's eccentric and little noticed *India in Greece: or, Truth in Mythology* (1852) there had been almost no discussion in Britain about the possibility of an oriental origin of the Greek myths.[45] Müller changed that situation,

44. Dockhorn, *Der deutsche Historismus in England,* passim.
45. William Jones, *Asiatic Researches* (London, 1799); Manuel, *The Eighteenth Century Confronts the Gods,* pp. 272–80; Edward Pococke, *India in Greece: or, Truth in Mythology* (London: J. J. Griffin and Co., 1852).

and he did so in a fashion that seemed to provide a scientific basis for what had previously been religious or romantic speculation.

In 1856 in the paper "Comparative Mythology" published in *Oxford Essays* Müller outlined the theory of myth that he repeated and expanded for the remainder of the century. Using etymological tables, he derived the names of several Greek mythical characters from Sanskrit roots. To these etymological derivations he attached an elaborate theory of linguistic and anthropological development linking India and Greece. Like Heyne, Müller postulated a mythopoeic age during which the race from whom all later Aryan peoples sprang had occupied a single geographical area and had spoken a single, now-unknown, language. During this period the ancestors of the Aryans had described the various phenomena of nature with different words.

> These words were all originally appellative; they expressed one out of many attributes, which seemed characteristic of a certain object, and the selection of these attributes and their expression in language, represents a kind of unconscious poetry, which modern languages have lost altogether.[46]

In this primordial naming of natural objects by an unknown people using a lost language lay the origin of later myths.

The ancestors of the Aryans had dispersed across Asia and into Europe. As they migrated, their language changed. The original meanings of the words describing nature were forgotten and new meanings attached to them. As the carriers of language forgot or changed the original meanings of the words, myths resulted. As Müller explained in 1856, "In order to become mythological, it was neces-

---

46. Friedrich Max Müller, *Chips from a German Workshop*, 4 vols. (New York: Charles Scribner and Co., 1869), 2:52. "In the sense in which I use *mythological*, it is applicable to every sphere of thought and every class of words, though, from reasons to be explained hereafter, religious ideas are most liable to mythological expression. Whenever any word, that was at first used metaphorically, is used without a clear conception of the steps that led from its original to its metaphorical meaning, there is danger of mythology; whenever those steps are forgotten and artificial steps put in their places, we have mythology, or if I may say so, we have diseased language, whether that language refers to religious or secular interests." Friedrich Max Müller, *Lectures on the Science of Language, Second Series* (New York: Scribner, Armstrong, and Co., 1874), pp. 375–76.

sary that the radical meaning of certain names should have been obscured and forgotten in the language to which they belong." Whereas for Grote the interpretations of the myths by later Greeks constituted deviations from the original mythopoeic mentality, for Müller the myths themselves were the deviation. In 1861 Müller told an audience of the Royal Institution:

> Mythology, which was the bane of the ancient world, is in truth a disease of language. A myth means a word, but a word which, from being a name or an attribute, has been allowed to assume a more substantial existence. Most of the Greek, the Roman, the Indian, and other heathen gods are nothing but poetical names, which were gradually allowed to assume a divine personality never contemplated by their original inventors.[47]

Language that had expressed the early thoughts of humankind had taken on a life and existence of its own that had little or no relationship to the thoughts originally enunciated through it.

Of all the objects that had been named in primeval times none had attracted more attention or received a larger number of poetic appellatives than the sun in its various relationships to other natural phenomena. The sun had been the central object of interest to the ancestors of the Aryans, and Müller concentrated his own speculations on it. According to his theory, the words originally simply descriptive of the sun eventually came to have narrative stories associated with them. For example, he traced the names Apollo and Daphne to Sanskrit words for the dawn and argued that the later myth of Apollo and Daphne had originated in observations of the sun overcoming the dawn. Although Müller considered his theory applicable to all Aryan myths, he drew most, though not all, of his examples from the Greek myths. He led readers and lecture audiences through one myth after another, relating the stories to every conceivable appearance or function of the sun. Coming to the close of Heracles' labors, he announced, "Another magnificent sunset looms in the myth of the death of Heracles."[48] He then explained how the tales of the hero's labors had

47. Müller, *Chips from a German Workshop*, 2:74; Friedrich Max Müller, *Lectures on the Science of Language, First Series,* from the Second London Edition, Revised (New York: Scribner, Armstrong and Co., 1875), p. 21.
48. Müller, *Chips from a German Workshop,* 2:88.

undoubtedly derived from a primeval description of the tireless sun in its daily journey across the heavens.

The solar theory invited all manner of parody and criticism. One especially ungenerous detractor composed an essay proving Max Müller himself to have been merely a solar myth.[49] Others faulted the theory from an anthropological point of view, and more recent critics have continued to demonstrate and to delight in its inadequacies. However well merited in some respects, this criticism of Müller has ignored the role of the solar theory in the broader context of his thought. Müller conceived of religion as the product of "a faculty of faith" that, functioning "independent of, nay in spite of sense and reason, enables man to apprehend the Infinite under different names, and under varying disguises."[50] The early names given to natural objects had arisen out of that innate religious faculty; the later myths represented the decay of that early and presumably pure religious intuition of humankind. Both Grote and Müller deplored mythic thought. Grote regarded it as bad science, hindering the progressive development of the human intellect; Müller saw it as obscuring a correct understanding of true religion and human nature.

Müller hoped to establish the foundation of religion in the fundamental character of humankind. His theory of an innate "faculty of faith" stood in opposition both to theories that derived religion from special revelation and to others, like Grote's, that regarded it as an early, mistaken mode of thought. Müller believed that separating religion from myth and grasping the essentially decayed nature of myths would reveal the brilliance of the initial religious thoughts of humankind.

> Like an old precious medal, the ancient religion, after the rust of ages has been removed, will come out in all its purity and brightness: and the image which it discloses will be the image of the Father, the Father of all the nations upon earth; and the superscription, when we can read it again, will be, not in Judea only, but in the languages of all the races of the world, the Word of God, revealed, where alone it can be revealed,—revealed in the heart of man.

49. Dorson, "Eclipse of Solar Mythology," p. 55, n. 22.
50. Friedrich Max Müller, *Introduction to the Science of Religion* (London: Longmans, Green, and Co., 1873), p. 17.

Religion was innate to humankind, and the philological analysis and study of ancient religions would reveal "more clearly than anywhere else, the *Divine education of the human race.*"[51] Thus comprehended, pure religion would remain safe from the attack of zealous orthodox Christians and scientific critics.

Müller in effect challenged the progressionist interpretation of intellectual development. He had combined Lessing's concept of the education of humankind with a watered-down version of a romantic theology of feeling. He hoped thereby not only to save religion from its contemporary enemies but also to prove that human beings had not descended, in a progressive evolution, from savages. Müller maintained that his philological interpretation of myth assured that "the idea of a humanity emerging slowly from the depths of an animal brutality can never be maintained again." Near the end of his life he wrote:

> What . . . I consider as the most important outcome of Comparative Mythology is the conviction which it leaves in our minds that the ancestors of the Aryan races were not mere drivelling idiots, but that there was a continuous development in the growth of the Aryan mind as in the growth of the surface of the earth. . . . It is to me the same relief to know that the gods of Greece and India were not mere devils or the work of devils or fools, but that they also, even in their greatest degradation, had a rational meaning and a noble purpose.[52]

Despite the crudity, indecency, irrationality, and immorality in the myths of their descendants, the original, primitive Aryan peoples had not been anything other than a noble, civilized race. That conviction, sustained by philology and the solar theory of myth, was intended to hold off the onslaught of Darwinism.

Despite criticism Müller made few revisions in his theory and pressed the solar concept with all the zeal, tediousness, and humorlessness of a mind seemingly possessed by a single idea. Yet he was a moderate in the cause of the solar theory when compared to George

---

51. Ibid., pp. 67, 226.
52. Müller, *Chips from a German Workshop,* 2:7; Friedrich Max Müller, *Contributions to the Science of Mythology* (London: Longmans, Green, and Co., 1897), pp. 21–22.

Cox, his major British disciple. Throughout a long series of books and manuals for children and adults, Cox carried Müller's interpretation of the Greek myths to extremes that even its originator criticized.[53] In *The Mythology of the Aryan Nations* (1870), translated into French by Mallarmé,[54] Cox reduced all the myths of local and national heroes such as Perseus, Jason, and Theseus to varieties of an original myth in the Vedic hymns

> which tells us of the Sungod robbed of his cows in the west, of the mission of Saramâ to discover the fastnesses where the thieves have hidden them, of their resistance until Indra draws nigh with his irresistible spear, of his great vengeance and his beneficent victory. Carrying us back yet one step further, these legends . . . resolve themselves into phrases which once described with a force and vividness never surpassed, the several phenomena of the earth and the heavens.[55]

Whereas Müller tended to refer to Indian and Greek myths only when he could find what he considered genuine etymological derivations, Cox simply collected myths that were similar and assumed that there existed an etymological connection that could be worked out. Cox far more than Müller was responsible for an almost totally solar interpretation of the Greek myths. Many a young reader who would never have ventured near any of Müller's heavy tomes easily read Cox's manuals without realizing they constituted an unmitigated apology for the solar theory.

Müller's ideas and Cox's extensive popularizations provided a major channel whereby a very unsavory side of Greek civilization was domesticated for educated Victorians. One myth after another related incidents of theft, murder, lying, incest, adultery, homosexuality, promiscuity, sodomy, and castration among the gods and heroes. These features of the stories deeply troubled many Victorians. On an

53. Müller, *Chips from a German Workshop*, 2:168–69.

54. Stéphane Mallarmé, *Les Dieux Antiques: Nouvelle Mythologie d'après George W. Cox* (Paris: Librairie Gallimard, 1925; 1st ed., 1880).

55. George W. Cox, *The Mythology of the Aryan Nations* (London: Longmans, Green, and Co., 1870), 1:207. See also Müller, *Chips from a German Workshop*, 2:76, Dorson, "Eclipse of Solar Mythology," pp. 39–47, and (for the most extensive discussion of Müller's British disciples) Richard Dorson, *The British Folklorists* (London: Routledge and Kegan Paul, 1968), pp. 160–201.

unconscious level Victorian readers may have experienced anxiety over the affinity of their own thoughts with the immoralities in the myths. The linguistic and solar theory relieved the otherwise largely admirable Greeks of the burden of having followed an irrational and immoral religion. The myths had not commenced as immoral stories told by a highly sensual people but were the result of an inevitable decay of language. Cox explained to young readers and their parents in his *Manual of Mythology:*

> You may be sure that in all these tales there is nothing of which, in its old shape, we ought to be ashamed, and that, when you have lifted the veil which conceals them, you will find only true and beautiful thoughts which are as much ours as ever they were the thoughts of men who lived in that very early time.

The "disagreeable features" were merely distortions arising from the decay of words.[56] Although such assurances failed to explain why the Greeks had persisted in recounting those indecent tales, the explanation did permit the Victorians who were so inclined to regard the myths as harmless solar stories, whether the ancient Greeks had viewed them so innocently or not.

Müller's considerable academic reputation and the mid-century interest in the Aryan culture allowed the influence of the solar theory to become quite widespread and enduring. Paintings of mythical themes, such as those by G. F. Watts and Lord Leighton, portrayed childlike, often passionless, innocent deities who were close to the natural order and inordinately fascinated by the sun. The theory also quickly penetrated the literary world. It was reasonably compatible with Grote's denial of the historical content of the myths, which Müller also denied, but at the same time it allowed writers to ascribe a moral meaning to the stories. For example, in "Pagan and Medieval Religious Sentiment" (1864) Matthew Arnold related the story of Adonis told in the fifteenth idyll of Theocritus. Arnold explained there

56. George W. Cox, *A Manual of Mythology in the Form of Question and Answer,* First American from the Second London Edition (New York: Leypoldt and Holt, 1868), pp. 17, 18. Cox wrote a large number of other popular works, two of which—*Tales from Greek Mythology* (1861) and *Tales of the Gods and Heroes,* (1862)—were combined by the Everyman's Library into *Tales of Ancient Greece* (London and New York, 1915) and frequently reprinted. I owe this reference to Dorson, "Eclipse of Solar Mythology," p. 59, n. 66.

was "not a particle" of religious sentiment in the story as there given, but he further observed:

> And yet many elements of religious emotion are contained in the beautiful story of Adonis. Symbolically treated, as the thoughtful man might treat it, as the Greek mysteries undoubtedly treated it, this story was *capable of a noble and touching application, and could lead the soul to elevating and consoling thoughts.*

Arnold went on to say that Adonis was the sun in both its winter and summer course, that during the passage the sun experienced both a time of triumph and a period of defeat, but the defeat was not final. So interpreted, Adonis became "an emblem of the power of life and the power of beauty, the power of human life and the bloom of human beauty" heading toward decay but not without hope of renewal. Arnold left unstated whether any Greek had interpreted the myth in this fashion or whether his explanation was a modern view imposed on the old story. In *The Queen of the Air* (1869) John Ruskin somewhat modified his previous Grotean interpretation of myth and acknowledged the new influence of the philologists. He suggested that the solar theory indicated that a spiritual, moral approach to nature was still possible even in an age of materialistic science and economics. If modern men and women could conceive of the power and beauty of the sun as had the Greeks, then they might "soon over-pass the narrow limit of conception which kept that power impersonal, and rise with the Greek to the thought of an angel [i.e., Apollo] who rejoiced as a strong man to run his course, whose voice, calling to life and to labour, rang round the earth, and whose going forth was to the ends of heaven."[57] Nature could again exist for the moral sustenance of humankind and not merely as a theater of economic exploitation.

Although the solar theory helped Arnold and Ruskin to avoid the moral problems of the myths and to draw religious and spiritual lessons from the stories, John Addington Symonds regarded the theory as a device that squeezed the essential vitality from ancient Greek life. An unswerving Grotean, Symonds argued in 1873 that to interpret the myths as a disease of language inhibited or foreclosed exploration

57. Matthew Arnold, *Lectures and Essays in Criticism*, ed. R. H. Super (Ann Arbor: University of Michigan Press, 1962), p. 222 (my italics); Ruskin, *Works of John Ruskin*, 19:302–03. See also Fitch, *The Golden Furrow*, pp. 218–352.

of the psychological facts of human existence to which the myths bore
witness.

> . . . it is surely a poor way of whitewashing the imagination of the
> ancients to have recourse to a theory which sees in myths nothing
> better than a mange or distemper breaking out in language and
> tormenting the human mind for a season. Nor can the theory be
> stretched so far as to exonerate the nation from its share of interest
> in these stories. The people who made the supposed linguistic
> mistakes, delighted in the grotesque and fantastic legends which
> were produced. . . . The real way of exculpating the conscience of
> the Greeks, indicated both by philosophy and common sense, is
> to point out that, in the age of reflection, the tragic poets
> moralised these very myths, and made them the subject-matter of
> the gravest art, while the sages instituted a polemic against the
> confusion of fabulous mythology with a pure notion of Godhead
> obtained by reflection. . . .

The myths of Greece *did* reflect the content as well as the power of the
human imagination. The character of that content might be regretted
or criticized, but it could not truthfully be denied or removed. Heap-
ing contempt on Müller's implicit emasculation and desexualization of
the gods of Greece, Symonds declared, "The deities are male and
female, not because their names have genders, but because the thinking being, for whom sex is all-important, thinks its own conditions
into the world outside it."[58] Throughout their myths the vibrant,
healthy, and natural Greeks had given vent to the fundamental fact of
human sexuality that Müller and many other educated Victorians
wished to repress or at the very least not to mention.

Symonds's critique of Müller's theory illustrates two important
limitations to the mid-Victorian domestication of the Greeks. The
first was that the classical documents and artifacts themselves sometimes proved intractable. Texts could be stretched or read selectively
to fit a particular purpose only so far as the integrity of the scholarly
community permitted. There were nearly always a few gadflies who
criticized a heavy-handed use of the Greek past. There was also considerable general agreement about the empirical facts of Greek life,

58. Symonds, *Studies of the Greek Poets*, 1:56–57, 59.

politics, literature, and philosophy. At issue was the matter of interpretation. Müller and Cox might rationalize certain obscenities, but
the obscenities remained. Few people went so far as to deny their
presence. The naturalism and sensuality of Greek life still lay behind
the veil, and the veil could always be lifted. The ever-growing body of
archaeological evidence also provided further information that made
difficult a reading of the past that ignored the empirical facts too
facilely.

The second limitation was that the process of domestication and the
reading of contemporary moral propriety into the Greek experience in
and of themselves led to a reaction. As the values of a peace-loving,
respectable, bourgeois society and liberal state were projected onto the
ancient Greek world, people who wished to protest or escape those
values could do so by revising or rejecting that image of Greece.
Symonds's volumes on the Greek poets provide a striking example of
Hellenism breaking beyond the bounds of respectable domestication.
Symonds had, like other writers, explored the spirituality of the Greek
tragedies, but he also pointed to the "Phallic ecstasy" of the comedies.
The latter implied the presence in Greek culture of "a profound
sympathy with nature in her large and perpetual reproductiveness, a
mysterious sense of the sexuality which pulses in all members of the
universe and reaches consciousness in man."[59] The Greeks had understood that neither the physical nor the spiritual side of humanity could
be considered in isolation.

Through their acceptance of the totality of human nature, the
Greeks, Symonds believed, had produced "a well-balanced and complete humanity, the bloom of health upon a conscious being, satisfied,
as flowers and beasts and stars are satisfied, with the conditions of
temporal existence." They had proved by their example that human
beings aware of the finite character of their lives could be joyous,
creative, and capable of noble feats. Modern human beings could also
achieve that healthy Hellenic harmony but not from mock contemplation of nature or an attempted recreation of the Greek mentality.

We must imitate the Greeks, not by trying to reproduce their
bygone modes of life and feeling, but by approximating to their
free and fearless attitude of mind. While frankly recognizing that

59. Ibid., 2:159; 1:59

much of their liberty would for us be license, and that the moral progress of the race depends on holding with a firm grasp what the Greek had hardly apprehended, we ought still to emulate their spirit by cheerfully accepting the world as we find it, acknowledging the value of each human impulse and aiming after virtues that depend on self-regulation rather than on total abstinence and mortification.

In this and similar passages Symonds sought to defend his own homosexual orientation, which put him at odds with contemporary culture. But his championing of the free Greek spirit went beyond that personal goal.[60] By pointing to the sensuality in Greek culture and its compatibility with spirituality, in writers such as Aeschylus, Sophocles, and Plato, Symonds hoped to demonstrate that a similar moral synthesis was possible for the nineteenth century. What had been true for the Greeks in regard to sex, love, and spirituality could also be true for contemporary British society. However, in the third quarter of the century Symonds's opinions about sex and the Greeks represented a distinctly minority viewpoint and were largely lost in the polite brilliance of Müller's solar theory.

The Turn to Anthropology

During the first three quarters of the nineteenth century classical scholars, historians, and commentators had discussed Greek myths, religion, history, and culture primarily on the basis of evidence from literary sources, ancient sculpture, and surviving coins. This situation changed markedly and rapidly during the last three decades of the century as fresh archaeological evidence and new theoretical frameworks became available. Jane Ellen Harrison captured the atmosphere of this turn of events in one passage of her autobiography.

Looking back over my own life, I see with what halting and stumbling steps I made my way to my own special subject. Greek literature as a specialism I early felt was barred to me. The only field of research that the Cambridge of my day [the seventies] knew was textual criticism, and for fruitful work in that my

60. Ibid., 2:377, 385; Phyllis Grosskurth, *John Addington Symonds: A Biography* (London: Longmans, 1964), pp. 163–64.

scholarship was never adequate. We Hellenists were, in truth, at that time a "people who sat in darkness", but we were soon to see a great light, two great lights—archaeology, anthropology. Classics were turning in their long sleep. Old men began to see visions, young men to dream dreams. I had just left Cambridge when Schliemann began to dig at Troy. Among my own contemporaries was J. G. Frazer, who was soon to light the dark wood of savage superstition with a gleam from *The Golden Bough.* . . . [Edward] Tylor had written and spoken; Robertson Smith, exiled for heresy, had seen the Star of the East; in vain, we classical deaf-adders stopped our ears and closed our eyes; but at the mere sound of the magical words "Golden Bough" the scales fell—we heard and understood. Then Arthur Evans set sail for his new Atlantis and telegraphed news of the Minotaur from his own labyrinth; perforce we saw this was a serious matter, it affected the "Homeric question".[61]

These developments were neither so smooth nor so systematic in their coming as Harrison suggested, but her irony does convey the mixed emotions of many British classicists. The results of the archaeological discoveries, which Hugh Kenner has termed "Renaissance II," in conjunction with the theories of anthropology, required that classical studies be extensively revised. As Sheldon Rothblatt has observed, that revision allowed the study of the classics to assume a more nearly scientific character just at the time that literary studies in the universities came under attack.[62] The new sciences also considerably modified the Victorian image of Greek religion. The veil that Grote had so tightly drawn across the prehistoric age of Greece was rent asunder, and the cloak that the solar theorists had so carefully laid across the nakedness of Greek sexuality and irrationality was thrust aside.

Despite these changes in method and outlook major continuities remained between the mid-century and late-century considerations of Greek religion and mythology. These elements of continuity should be emphasized because most studies of Victorian mythography usually

61. Jane Ellen Harrison, *Reminiscences of a Student's Life,* 2nd ed. (London: The Hogarth Press, 1925), pp. 82–83.

62. Hugh Kenner, *The Pound Era* (Berkeley: University of California Press, 1971), pp. 41–53; Sheldon Rothblatt, *Tradition and Change in English Liberal Education: An Essay in History and Culture* (London: Faber and Faber, 1976), pp. 168–170.

halt before the turn to anthropology or regard it as uncharacteristic of the Victorian approach to myth. This separation is simply incorrect. In the first place most of the anthropological theory that redirected Greek studies well into the twentieth century originated in the seventies and eighties. Second, most of the major British advocates of the anthropological study of Greek culture—Andrew Lang, J. G. Frazer, Jane Harrison, Gilbert Murray, A. B. Cook, and Lewis Farnell—were educated and had reached intellectual maturity well before the turn of the century. There was also a continuity of thought from Grote to these later writers in their common naturalistic approach to the phenomena of myth and in their common rejection of myth as a source of narrative history. Several of the later scholars also shared with Grote a subordination of their analysis to French sociological theory, and where they differed from Grote was often where later French sociologists, such as Émile Durkheim, differed from Comte. Finally, much of the new outlook on myths stemmed from the examination of vases and other pottery that Charles T. Newton had gathered into the British Museum about mid-century and which he taught younger students, including Jane Harrison, to use as sources for investigating Greek religion. As early as 1850 Newton had predicted that a very different portrait of Greek life would emerge once those remains had been carefully and systematically examined.[63]

Although Pater's essays reflected a knowledge of anthropology, Andrew Lang was the first British writer to apply the science to Greek myth and religion in an extensive manner. Like so many other people who wrote on the classics during the nineteenth century, Lang was a multitalented figure who in addition to commenting on the myths also translated Homer, wrote three books on the poet, published numerous works on primitive religion, and wrote about Shakespeare, sports, and psychical research. As a student at Oxford he had imbibed Müller's solar theory, but he rejected that approach in the early seventies when he read deeply in the anthropology of Tylor, Spencer, and M'Lennan. Soon he published a number of journal articles attacking Müller. These culminated in his essay "Mythology" prepared for the ninth edition of the *Encyclopaedia Britannica*. His volumes *Custom and*

63. Charles Thomas Newton, *Essays on Art and Archaeology* (London: Macmillan and Co., 1880), pp. 20–23, 53–56.

Myth (1885) and *Myth, Ritual, and Religion* (1887) largely repeated his earlier arguments.[64]

Lang applied the comparative method of folklore to the explication of the Greek myths. He attempted to compare "the seemingly meaningless customs or manners of civilized races with the similar customs and manners which exist among the uncivilized and still retain their meaning," and he assumed that "similar conditions of mind produce similar practices, apart from identity of race or borrowing of ideas and manners." Lang looked to the American Indians, the Australian aborigines, the African Bushmen, and the Eskimos for a key to the mind of the early Greeks. For example, he suggested that the myth of Cronos represented a variation of a myth describing the severance of the earth and sky that could be found in other forms from China to South America. Moreover, for Lang there was no escape from the unsavory content of the myths. No matter where one traced the origins of the Greek stories, what would ultimately be discovered were "myths cruel, puerile, obscene, like the fancies of the savage mythmakers from which they sprang."[65] The tales reflected the minds of their originators and not the decay of their language.

For all the bravado and cheerful embracing of savagery, Lang's approach to the myths was hardly less an example of intellectual prudery than Müller's. Lang's analysis also displayed clear analogies with Grote's earlier explication of the myths. Like the anthropologists upon whose theories he so heavily depended and who in their turn seem to have drawn on Grote, Lang recognized the savage intellect in order to banish its influence from civilized life. For the anthropologists, religious or irrational social practices existing in the midst of generally rational societies represented dysfunctional survivals from a previous stage of social evolution.[66] Lang simply applied this analysis to the Greeks. During the savage stage of their intellectual and social development the myths had originated. Through the conservative character of religious instincts and practices, those myths survived

64. Roger Lancelyn Green, *Andrew Lang, A Critical Biography* (Leicester: E. Ward, 1946); Andrew Lang, "Mythology," *Encyclopaedia Britannica*, 9th ed.; *Custom and Myth* (New York: Harper and Brothers, 1885); *Myth, Ritual, and Religion*, 2 vols. (London: Longmans, Green, and Co., 1887); Richard Dorson, "Eclipse of Solar Mythology," pp. 25–63.

65. Lang, *Custom and Myth*, pp. 21, 28.

66. Burrow, *Evolution and Society*, pp. 101–36.

into the civilized age. Consequently Lang could claim that "the whole of Greek life yields relics of savagery when the surface is excavated ever so slightly" and that Greek myths "bear the indelible stain of the savage fancy" without also arguing that fifth-century Athenians were uncivilized.[67] The irrational and savage pertained to the past stages of Greek culture, and the myths were simply survivals of that age. The admirable achievements of Greece arose from its rationality and its escape from mythic thought.

Lang has been properly credited with achieving the overthrow of the solar theory, but at his best he was only a gifted amateur and at his worst a polemical bore. He was not the person to establish a permanent connection between anthropology and the classics. The scholar who welded that link and redirected thought about the Greek myths for over a generation was, of course, James G. Frazer, author of the twelve volumes of *The Golden Bough* which began to appear in 1890.[68] That seminal work commenced as a study of a particular Roman cult and expanded into an extensive survey of various manifestations of primitive religion. So far as Greek religious practices were concerned, Frazer's commentary was rooted in an intimate knowledge of Pausanias, whose work he had edited and whose text is filled with descriptions of rites and abandoned temples and sanctuaries that had received little attention from earlier Victorian students of the myths. In Frazer's volumes what Walter Pater had termed the "gloomy side" of Dionysian worship stood revealed in all its splendid terror.[69] Mid-century commentators had domesticated Dionysus into the happy god of the vine whose worshipers resembled the pastel bucolic Bacchae of Lord Leighton's painting, but Frazer told his readers that in the worship of Dionysus the animal symbolizing the god was consumed as ecstatic votaries tore apart and ate the uncooked flesh of the creature. Frazer concluded that although some elements of Dionysian worship had been rendered less harmful as the god was assimilated into Greece, "neither the polished manners of a later age, nor the glamour which Greek poetry and art threw over the figure of

67. Lang, *Myth, Ritual, and Religion*, 1:258 and *The Academy* 25 (1884): 134.
68. Robert Angus Downie, *Frazer and the Golden Bough* (London: Victor Gollancy, 1970); John Vickery, *The Literary Impact of "The Golden Bough"* (Princeton: Princeton University Press, 1973), pp. 3–106.
69. Pater, *Greek Studies*, p. 44.

Dionysus, sufficed to conceal or erase the deep lines of savagery and cruelty imprinted on the features of this barbarous deity."[70] For Frazer savagery, cruelty, and irrationality had survived well into the classical age of Greece not only in the stories of the myths but in the rituals of the religious life of the people.

Although previous Victorian scholars had been less than comfortable with Dionysus, they had with rare unanimity approved of Demeter. Grote, Pater, and Lang had regarded her as the Mater Dolorosa of Greek mythology, and Tennyson had portrayed her as the epitome of motherhood. Frazer, in contrast, described both Demeter and Dionysus as mere "personifications of cultivated plants." The touching story of Demeter's search for Persephone told of nothing more than "the decay and revival of vegetation." The mother represented the corn of last year, the daughter the seed sown in the spring. In their origins Frazer considered it probable that

> Demeter and Persephone, those stately and beautiful figures of Greek mythology, grew out of the same simple beliefs and practices which still prevail among our modern peasantry, and that they were represented by rude dolls made out of the yellow sheaves on many a harvest-field long before their breathing images were wrought in the bronze and marble by the master hands of Phidias and Praxiteles.[71]

The reductionism that characterized so much late-Victorian rationalism thus worked its will on the gods of Greece as Frazer transformed Demeter and Persephone into wheat-sheaf dolls.

Frazer's analysis of Greek religion was highly revisionist, but his direct comments on the subject were relatively few. So far as the future consideration of Greek myth and religion was concerned, he exercised two important influences. First, by relating primitive religion to anxiety over securing an adequate food supply, he tended to focus on the social rather than the intellectual origins of myth. Second, his archetypal system in which the concept of the dying and reborn deity figured so prominently provided a frame of reference for further new interpretations of Greek myth and ritual. The major impact of his

70. James G. Frazer, *Spirits of the Corn and of the Wild,* 2 vols. (London: Macmillan and Co., 1912), 1:34.
71. Ibid., 1:v, 35, 208.

concepts on Greek studies came through the development of his ideas in the works of the so-called Cambridge school of ritualistic interpretation.[72] The major figures in this group were Jane Ellen Harrison, Francis Cornford, A. B. Cook, and the Oxonian Gilbert Murray. They urged that myths were the product of ritual practices that predated the formulation of the myths. Both the rituals and the later myths arose from and were largely determined by the collective thought of the particular social group under investigation. Under the influence of these writers the image of the ancient gods became as transformed intellectually as it was artistically about the same time in the sculpture of Jacob Epstein. Their work, controversial then and later, represented a major drive toward modernism in classical study.

The intellectual lineage of the Cambridge group is difficult, if not impossible, to trace. All of them generally regarded Frazer as a major forebear, but he was less than approving of their theories. He was a rationalist who investigated irrational behavior; some of the ritualists, particularly Harrison and Cornford, attempted to set the irrational at the heart of human nature and of authentic human experience. The Cambridge ritualists drew heavily upon the work of the biblical critic William Robertson Smith and upon the writings of Émile Durkheim. They were also aware of Continental scholars such as Fustel de Coulanges, who as early as 1860 in *The Ancient City* had emphasized the religious basis of Greek society, and Wilhelm Mannhardt, who had written extensively about ritual, cults, and myths prior to Frazer.[73] Perhaps as important as any particular set of books read by the ritualist interpreters was their determination to explore corridors of the human experience and of Greek culture that the rationalism and sense of propriety of their forebears had closed to serious examination.

72. Robert Allen Ackerman, *The Cambridge Group and the Origins of Myth Criticism* (Ann Arbor, Mich.: University Microfilms, 1969) is the most extensive study of these writers. See also Harry C. Payne, "Modernizing the Ancients: The Reconstruction of Ritual Drama, 1870–1920," *Proceedings of the American Philosophical Society* 122 (1978): 182–192; Robert Allen Ackerman, "Jane Ellen Harrison: The Early Work," *Greek, Roman, and Byzantine Studies* 13 (1972): 209–30; Robert Allen Ackerman, "Frazer on Myth and Ritual," *Journal of the History of Ideas* 36 (1975): 115–34.

73. Numa Denis Fustel de Coulanges, *The Ancient City: A Study of the Religion, Laws, and Institutions of Greece and Rome,* trans. Willard Small (Garden City, N.Y.: Doubleday, Anchor Books, n.d.; originally published, 1864; 1st English trans., 1873); Wilhelm Mannhardt, *Wald- und Feldkulte* (Berlin, 1875–77).

In 1889 William Robertson Smith, who had come to Cambridge from Aberdeen after a long public controversy over his views on the higher criticism of the Bible, published his immensely influential *Lectures on the Religion of the Semites*. The central argument of this exploration of the religious practices of the Old Testament was that ancient religions had possessed nothing resembling theology and had instead consisted of ritual observance.

> Belief in a certain series of myths was neither obligatory as part of true religion, nor was it supposed that, by believing, a man acquired religious merit or conciliated the favor of the gods. What was obligatory or meritorious was the exact performance of certain sacred acts prescribed by religious tradition.[74]

Religion had been neither a private, individual matter nor an intellectual, cognitive activity. Traditional ritual practices had little or nothing to do with the saving of souls but were directed toward preserving the well-being of the society. Religion and social life were intimately intertwined and could not be separated. Frazer warmly acknowledged his indebtedness to Smith and incorporated many of Smith's ideas into *The Golden Bough,* but he later dissociated himself from the ritualist school.[75] It was Jane Ellen Harrison who more than any other late-century classical scholar adapted Smith's philosophy of religion to the study of Greek myth and ritual. What had been true of ancient Hebraism became true for ancient Hellenism.

As noted in the previous chapter, Harrison, who was born in 1850, had been educated at Cambridge and then worked for a number of years at the British Museum.[76] Her *Introductory Studies in Greek Art* (1885) presented a traditional idealist interpretation of the subject, but her ideas began to change as the result of her study of the collection of Greek vases at the British Museum. The portrayal of myths and other religious images on the ancient pottery differed markedly from the character of the gods portrayed in the sculpture. She discovered, as her mentor Charles Newton had predicted at mid-century, that the vases

74. William Robertson Smith, *Lectures on the Religion of the Semites* (Edinburgh: Adam and Charles Black, 1889), p. 19.
75. Ackerman, "Frazer on Myth and Ritual," pp. 115–34.
76. Francis MacDonald Cornford, *The Dictionary of National Biography, 1922–1930,* s.v. "Harrison, Jane Ellen."

displayed the penetration of Greek religion into all details of daily life and revealed religious practices and stories not included in the traditional myths. To this new mode of documentation from ancient artifacts Harrison added ideas that she drew, often uncritically, from Nietzsche, Durkheim, Bergson, and others associated with the turn-of-the-century revolt against positivism.

Harrison published *Mythology and Monuments of Ancient Athens* in 1890. It was a hastily written volume in which she set forth two themes that marked all of her later work. First, she urged that there had been "no more fertile source of absurd mythology than *ritual misunderstood.*" The myths of Greece had arisen out of the rites of the primitive religious cults, and once those ritual origins had been investigated, it would become evident that the primary function of Greek religion had been the fending off or appeasing of a class of spirits alien to the traditional myths. The vast role of such spirits in Greek religion was her second theme. She contended that close examination of the cult worship of Greece would reveal "a classical world peopled, not by the stately and plastic forms of Zeus, Hera, Artemis, Apollo, Athene, and Hephaistos, but by a motley gathering of demi-gods and deified saints, household gods, tribal gods, local gods,..." evidence for which was to be found on the vases, temple remains, and other inscriptions discovered at the sites of cult worship.[77] The glory and serenity of the Olympians had been a late development in Greek religious life and one that rested on the foundation of rather ugly daemons, ghosts, and spirits. Harrison's exploration of this region of Pre-Homeric and Pre-Olympian religion was analogous to the archaeological penetration of Mycenaean and Minoan culture. Each of these endeavors delved into the substructures of the more familiar Homeric and classical Greek civilizations.

Harrison developed these initial ideas more fully and tied them more directly to Smith's concept of the social function of ancient religion in her two later books *Prolegomena to the Study of Greek Religion* (1903) and *Themis* (1912). Like so many other scholars of her generation, Harrison thought the standard literary sources could no longer provide a satisfactory account of either Greek mythology or

77. Margaret de G. Verrall and Jane Ellen Harrison, *Mythology and Monuments of Ancient Athens* (London: Macmillan and Co., 1890), pp. xxxiii, iv. See also *Classical Review* 4 (1890): 376; Grote, *History of Greece,* 1:61; Pater, *Greek Studies,* p. 122.

Greek religious practices. In the *Prolegomena,* however, she went even further and condemned not only dependence on literature, but also and more important "our modern habit of clear analytic thought" as a major stumbling block to an understanding of ancient myth. In order to comprehend the undifferentiated world of primitive apprehension and fear over the requirements of physical survival, that rational habit of thought must be abandoned. Pre-Homeric Greek religion had not been a matter of Olympian cheerfulness but rather was permeated by an atmosphere of "fear and deprecation" wherein the objects of worship "were not rational, human law-abiding *gods,* but vague, irrational, mainly malevolent, *daimones,* spirit-things, ghosts and bogeys and the like, not yet formulated and enclosed into god-head." The ancient religious rites had been desperate attempts to control such spirits and to appease the forces that seemed to threaten the survival and continuation of the community. Furthermore, the iconography of Greek sculpture, vases, and tomb decoration provided evidence that even fifth-century religious life had more to do with chthonic worship than Olympian serenity. Every major Olympian festival of the classical age, such as the Diasia of Zeus, the Thargelia of Apollo and Artemis, and the Anthesteria of Dionysus, had incorporated rituals that had no obvious connection with the Olympian gods. Inscriptions and artwork clearly linked the Olympians with animals and plants that pertained to chthonic worship. The Olympians were merely a civilized veneer over the still present and, as presented in Harrison's prose, almost pulsating chthonic practices.[78]

Previous scholars had recognized the chthonic elements in Greek religion, but Harrison portrayed them more extensively and set them directly into the life of the classical age. Even more important, she questioned whether the movement toward the anthropomorphizing of the Olympians had been desirable or even genuinely religious in character. With unconcealed contempt she remarked, "Anthropomorphism provides a store of lovely motives for art, but that spirit is scarcely religious which makes of Eros a boy trundling a hoop, of Apollo a youth aiming a stone at a lizard, of Nike a woman who stoops to tie her sandal."[79] In a manner reminiscent of Nietzsche, with

78. Jane Ellen Harrison, *Prolegomena to the Study of Greek Religion* (Cambridge: Cambridge University Press, 1903), pp. 162, 7, 10–11.
    79. Ibid., p. 258.

whose work she was familiar, Harrison regarded the gods of Olympus as decadent and as severed from the genuine source of religion and life. By implication she was also directly attacking contemporary humanistic criticism of Greek sculpture, such as her own early work, that looked to the statues of anthropomorphic gods as prescriptive embodiments of the kind of rationalism, naturalism, and propriety that should inform modern art and society. For Harrison, rationalism and propriety were incommensurable with the full expression and realization of the human spirit.

Harrison believed that the Greeks themselves had sensed the inadequacy of their anthropomorphic gods when they turned first to the worship of Dionysus and then to Orphic rites, the spirit of which represented "an impulse really religious." Whereas James Frazer had found Dionysus offensive to his sense of decorum, gentility, and rationality, Harrison regarded the deity as symbolic of a return to nature and of the constant interplay between the physical and the spiritual. The drunkenness and ecstasy of Dionysian worship should not interfere with the modern understanding of the attraction and perennial significance of such ritual. Moreover, even in ancient times most of those moral difficulties had been addressed through the Orphic reformation. The Orphic cults had advanced beyond chthonic worship and embraced the basic impulses of Dionysian religion without incorporating the latter's more reprehensible features. Harrison contended, "The religion of Orpheus *is* religious in the sense that it is the worship of the real mysteries of life, of potencies (. . .) rather than personal gods (. . .); it is the worship of life itself in its supreme mysteries of ecstasy and love."[80] Orpheus had espoused the Dionysian hope that human beings might become like the gods and had spiritualized it by rejecting drunkenness in favor of abstinence and purification as the path to divine life and unity with the vitality of nature. Olympian religion had signified the impossibility of that attainment, and the art embodying Olympian religion similarly stressed the limitations on the human spirit.

Almost a decade later, in *Themis: A Study of the Social Origins of Greek Religion,* Harrison resumed her diatribe against the Olympians. The book was an extended analysis of the Hymn of the Kouretes,

80. Ibid., pp. 365, 658.

discovered on Crete after the turn of the century. Harrison interpreted the hymn as a portrayal of the annual life-and-death cycle of the Eniauto-Daimon or year-spirit. Her discussion drew heavily on the sociology of Durkheim and the philosophy of Bergson. She understood religion as a social phenomenon that involved the projection of group emotion and the social structure of the group in question. The myths were dependent upon rituals, and the rituals in turn were derived from the structure of the society. In a modification of her earlier views, she urged that the real significance of the worship of Dionysus was less the sense of total identification with the deity than the sense of total identification with and submergence into the social group that was achieved through his worship. That sense of identity had allowed ancient worshipers to experience what Bergson called *durée,* unity with the vital forces of nature and life. This mode of worship arose in a matrilinear society which, by its structure, constituted a collective group in which social relationships were grounded in real life and where thinking itself was collective.[81]

According to Harrison's interpretation, the later triumph of the Olympians reflected the dissolution of that vital group identity and constituted the collective projection of a patrilinear society. The social bonds of the latter were inherently weak because the structure itself fostered the dissolution of the bonds between parents and those between parents and children. The Olympians had been fashioned "on the highly personalized, individualized self, and the essence of the sense of self is separateness, or consciousness of the severance of one self from other selves, and of that self as subject and distinct from objects." For that reason the gods of Olympus always seemed surrounded by a "chill remoteness." Harrison regarded the ascendancy of the Olympians as symbolizing the demise of the intimate relationships

---

81. Jane Ellen Harrison, *Epilegomena to the Study of Greek Religion and Themis: A Study of the Social Origins of Greek Religion* (New York: University Books, 1962), pp. 490–505 (hereafter cited as *Themis*). (This edition was a reprint of the second edition, revised, of *Themis,* published in 1927.) For the most extensive contemporary review of the work, see *Revue de L'Histoire des Religions* 69 (1914): 323–71. Harrison did not originate the matrilinear theory, which in England had first been set forth by John Ferguson M'Lennan in *Primitive Marriage* (1865) and *Studies in Ancient History* (1876). By the turn of the century, this view of early Greek society had been widely criticized. See Lewis R. Farnell, *The Higher Aspects of Greek Religion* (New York: Charles Scribner's Sons, 1912), pp. 25–26.

between human beings and of human beings with nature that was fostered by chthonian worship and the religions of Dionysus and Orpheus. Of the Olympic deities she wrote:

> The Greek Gods, in their triumphant humanity, kicked down that ladder from earth to heaven by which they rose. They reflected, they represented the mood of their worshippers, which tended always to focus itself rather on what was proper to humanity than on what was common to man and the rest of the universe.[82]

The Olympians reflected the triumph of humankind over the dangers of the environment, achieved at the cost of repressing humankind's full emotional nature. The gods and those who worshiped them had become as spiritually cold as the winds of Olympus itself. By clear implication Harrison was condemning the mode of humanistic Hellenism that sought to create an ideal image of rational humanity living without the disturbing influences of emotion, passion, and ecstasy.

There was exceedingly little evidence for the alleged transformation of Greek society from a matrilinear to a patrilinear structure, and Harrison's theory was widely criticized. But by this stage in her career she admitted to having become more interested in religion than in classical studies proper. She was simply employing her very imaginative and often uncritical analysis of Greek religion as an apology for the mysterious, the mystical, and the untamed impulses of the human soul. In her admiration for the ecstatic this gifted woman, who was over sixty years old when *Themis* appeared, was at one with the much younger Edwardian poets and novelists such as Yeats and Lawrence, the latter of whom read her works with much interest.[83] Indeed, her major influence was on creative writers and literary critics rather than on classicists, who frequently faulted her scholarship. Yet in her emphasis on the idea that religion stemmed from ritual and art, which were in turn largely determined by the structure of primitive society, she came to be numbered among the first of those whom Geoffrey Hartman has described as the "modern and inspired structuralists."[84]

82. Harrison, *Themis*, pp. 473, 476.

83. Vickery, *Literary Impact of "The Golden Bough,"* pp. 280–302.

84. Geoffrey Hartman, *Beyond Formalism: Literary Essays 1958–1970* (New Haven: Yale University Press, 1970), p. 7. See especially Harrison, *Themis*, pp. 480–92.

She yearned for a fuller appreciation of the unity of life and of the connectedness of things than either traditional rationalism or traditional Hellenistic humanism could afford. In that respect she struck a responsive chord with one of the major impulses of early twentieth-century intellectual life.

Harrison's close friends Gilbert Murray and Francis Cornford also trod the path of early structuralism. Murray contributed a chapter to *Themis* that traced the ritual origins of tragedy. Cornford in 1914 made similar claims for comedy in *The Origins of Attic Comedy*.[85] Cornford had also followed Harrison's lead by examining the nonrational as well as the structural sources of enlightened Greek thought. In *Thucydides Mythistoricus* (1907) Cornford sharply criticized the general nineteenth-century interpretation of the historian as a rational, scientific thinker. He argued that in fact Thucydides had moved within an intellectual climate "which we should recognize to be poetical and mythical."[86] Thucydides' thought was nearer to that of the tragedians than to that of rational thinkers, and behind his analysis of events lay the mythic concepts of Fortune, Eros, Elpis, and Nemesis. Although he had recognized the importance of empirical fact, he lacked a fully rational framework by which he might interpret those facts. In effect Cornford challenged the rather facile Victorian equation of the elite intellectual life of fifth-century Athens with that of modern Britain. In *From Religion to Philosophy* (1912) he carried his argument even further. There, drawing extensively upon Durkheim and acknowledging Nietzsche, he contended that the modes of thought that were clearly articulated in Greek philosophy had been "already implicit in the unreasoned intuitions of mythology"[87] which had originated in the collective projections of the social structure. Though adopting much of Harrison's framework, Cornford differed from her in that he displayed little regret over the emergence of rational thought in Greece.

85. Gilbert Murray, "Excursus on the Ritual Forms Preserved in Greek Tragedy," in Harrison, *Themis,* pp. 341–63; Francis MacDonald Cornford, *The Origins of Attic Comedy* (London: E. Arnold, 1914).

86. Francis MacDonald Cornford, *Thucydides Mythistoricus* (Philadelphia: University of Pennsylvania Press, 1971; 1st ed., 1907), p. xi.

87. Francis MacDonald Cornford, *From Religion to Philosophy: A Study in the Origins of Western Speculation* (New York: Harper, Torchbook, 1957; first published, 1912), p. v. See British Library Add. Mss. 58427 for the Cornford-Murray correspondence.

Although the fascination with the irrational and its portrayal as a positive force in human life and society were the most striking changes between Edwardian and mid-Victorian mythography, the Olympians and rationality were not without their defenders among late-century commentators on the myths. In 1894 Edward Caird, in the context of a Neohegelian analysis of religious development saw the Olympian mythology as representative of humankind overcoming nature through use of its intelligence, and he argued:

The gods of Greece are powers that make, perhaps we may not say strictly, "for righteousness," but certainly for civilization. They are man's forerunners in the work of taming and subduing nature into his servant; and it is his glory that he can follow them in their labors.

In his popular and often reprinted *Greek View of Life* (1896) G. Lowes Dickinson regarded the Olympians as allowing the Greeks of the classical age to feel "at home in the world." Those deities had transformed the foreboding natural forces surrounding the Greek into creatures that resembled himself. Interestingly enough, however, the foremost defenders of Olympian mythology and the religion it fostered were two scholars whose work embraced anthropology and whose portraits of Greek religion were quite as much cluttered with local cults and daemons as Jane Harrison's. The first was Lewis Farnell,' an Oxford don and later vice-chancellor of the university; the other was Gilbert Murray, Regius Professor of Greek at Oxford. Both, in the words of Murray, felt that "the besetting error of the anthropologists has been a tendency to confuse Greek religion proper with the swamp of barbarism from which it arose."[88] Both writers attempted to draw the anthropological analysis of Greek religion into the current of late Victorian and Edwardian humanistic Hellenism discussed in the previous chapter.

Differences in scholarly rigor, imagination, and temperament separated Farnell from Harrison. He disliked female scholars and in 1896 had opposed the admission of women to Oxford. That attitude was typical of a conservatism bordering on priggishness that carried over

---

88. Edward Caird, *The Evolution of Religion,* 2nd ed., 2 vols. (New York: Macmillan and Co., 1894), 1:266; G. Lowes Dickinson, *The Greek View of Life* (New York: McClure, Phillips, and Co., 1906; 1st ed., 1896), p. 9; Gilbert Murray, "Olympian Houses," *Albany Review* 2 (1907–08): 205.

into his evaluation of Greek religion. Farnell had initially encountered Greek mythology through Müller's solar theory. Lang's work introduced him to anthropology, but he never abandoned the search for genteel values in Greek culture that had marked the writings of the solar theorists. Throughout the five volumes of *The Cults of the Greek States* (1896–1909) and his numerous other books Farnell argued that "while Greek mythology was passionate and picturesque, Greek religion was, on the whole, sober and sane."[89] Like Müller, he was embarrassed by the moral character of the myths, but he looked to their later ethical interpretation rather than to their allegedly pure origins to excuse their immortality. Farnell felt, as did Percy Gardner, that recognition of the dark and superstitious roots of Greek religion should not lead to the neglect of "the flowers and the fruit which derive their nutriment from those roots."[90]

Farnell admired practically all of those aspects of Olympian religion that Harrison deplored. The Olympians had nurtured reason, civilization, and propriety in Greek life. They embodied new, higher ethical ideals that had contributed to genuine social progress. Following the earlier lead of Richard Claverhouse Jebb, Farnell especially emphasized the service of the cult of Apollo. The rites of that god had provided ritual purification for homocide, which led to the demise of the code of revenge, and the same cult had developed "the sense of religious purity" that aided the emergence of a concept of individual conscience.[91] Moreover, as the various Olympian cults penetrated the different Greek states, those religions tended to dissolve local tribal loyalties and made possible a more nearly Panhellenic life. Whereas Harrison had stressed the chthonic survivals of the Olympian festivals, Farnell urged recognition of the civic functions of those annual observances. Worship of the Olympians sanctified marriage and fam-

89. Lewis R. Farnell, *The Cults of the Greek States,* 5 vols. (Oxford: Clarendon Press, 1896–1909), 1:ix. See also Lewis R. Farnell, *An Oxonian Looks Back* (London: Martin Hopkinson, 1934), and Farnell's review of *Themis* in the *Hibbert Journal* 11 (1912–13): 453–58. The letters of Jane Harrison to Gilbert Murray that are preserved in the Newnham College Library, Cambridge, contain numerous critical comments on Farnell and his work.

90. Percy Gardner, "A New Pandora Vase," *Journal of Hellenic Studies* 21 (1901): 9. See also Ernest A. Gardner, *Religion and Art in Ancient Greece* (New York: Harper and Brothers, 1910).

91. Farnell, *Cults of the Greek States,* 4:252. See also Jebb *Sophocles,* 6:xii–xiii, and Farnell, *Higher Aspects of Greek Religion,* passim.

ily life and thus forged strong links among the citizens of the states. The shared religious experience and participation also helped to curb the excessive individualism that for Farnell was incompatible with civilized life. This civic religion and its ethical ideals provided the Greek artists with materials worthy of their talents and allowed them to dedicate their works to the gods. In turn the statues of the classical age with their remarkable ideal beauty had refined more primitive religious ideas and made the higher Olympian religion attractive to larger numbers of citizens. Harrison, by contrast, regarded the art of the classical age as symbolizing the end of vital religion in Greece, but Farnell portrayed it as permitting civic freedom to flourish in the absence of fanaticism. In that manner the Olympians had made possible both the art and the civic life from which the propriety of Greek culture sprang.

Gilbert Murray's was a more problematical defense of the Olympians. In his *Four Stages of Greek Religion* (1912), later extended to five stages, he drew extensively from Harrison's work and fully portrayed "the half-lit regions . . . the dark primeval tangle of desires and fears and dreams from which [the Olympians] drew their vitality." However, Murray found little to admire in chthonic religion and its later remains, and he championed the very functions of the Olympians that Harrison faulted. For Murray the coming of the Olympians had effected "a religious reformation" that eradicated much, if not all, superstition and that furthered the development of the polis and of Panhellenism. Furthermore, he thought the patrilinear Olympian deities were on the whole preferable to their matrilinear predecessors with "their polygamy and polyandry, their agricultural rites, their sex-emblems and fertility goddesses."[92] That the Olympian reformation was incomplete Murray did not deny. Each separate locality worshiped its own particular Zeus, as became clear in excruciating detail in A. B. Cook's multivolume study *Zeus*.[93] Although the Olympian world was less chaotic than that of the chthonic spirits, it had not constituted monotheism. But for all the Olympian failure to create a perfect religion or to alleviate the political isolation of the polis, the

92. Gilbert Murray, *Four Stages of Greek Religion* (New York: Columbia University Press, 1912), pp. 27, 78.

93. Arthur Bernard Cook, *Zeus: A Study in Ancient Religion*, 2 vols. (Cambridge: Cambridge University Press, 1914–25).

Olympians had possessed the supreme religious virtue of having "issued no creeds that contradicted knowledge, no commands that made man sin against his own inner light."[94] The gods of Greece had not been fully rational creatures, but they had not stood as barriers against the achievement of rationality.

Although in many respects Murray was in agreement with Farnell, different spirits lay behind their work. Farnell understood Olympian art and civic religion as a kind of goal toward which Greek culture had long been moving. His analysis was analogous to that of the art critics who prescriptively traced the rise of naturalism in Greek sculpture and its attainment of ideal forms. Murray regarded the Olympian reformation as an example of the striving of the human spirit toward a more nearly perfect fulfillment—a striving that had to be repeated again and again in human history.

> The Olympian gods as we see them in art appear so calm, so perfect, so far removed from the atmosphere of acknowledged imperfection and spiritual striving, that what I am now about to say may ... seem a deliberate paradox. It is nevertheless true that the Olympian Religion is only to the full intelligible and admirable if we realize it as a superb and baffled endeavour, not a *telos* or completion but a movement and effort of life.[95]

For Murray, unlike Farnell and those who wrote in his tradition, the human experience was open-ended and by its very nature contingent and indeterminate.

That fragile contingency had strikingly manifested itself in the history of Greece. Reversing Farnell's interpretation, Murray argued that the life of the polis itself had made possible the beneficial qualities of Olympian religion. He went so far as to claim that "the real religion of the fifth century was ... a devotion to the City itself." The polis itself had provided the security that its citizens believed they attained through the worship of their beautiful gods. When the polis was crushed under the Macedonian invasion, the reasonably sane civic life and the worship of the Olympians collapsed. Thereupon ensued the rise of new religions founded on mysteries, mysticism, and a rejection of the notion of humankind as the forger of its own world.

94. Murray, *Four Stages of Greek Religion*, p. 99.
95. Ibid., p. 81.

It is a rise of asceticism, of mysticism, in a sense, of pessimism; a loss of self-confidence, of hope in this life and of faith in normal human effort; a despair of patient inquiry, a cry for infallible revelation; an indifference to the welfare of the state, a conversion of the soul to God. It is an atmosphere in which the aim of the good man is not so much to live justly, to help the society to which he belongs and enjoy the esteem of his fellow creatures; but rather, by means of a burning faith, by contempt for the world and its standards, by ecstasy, suffering and martyrdom, to be granted pardon for his unspeakable unworthiness, his immeasurable sins. There is an intensifying of certain spiritual emotions; an increase of sensitiveness, a failure of nerve.[96]

This failure of nerve could be avoided not by the preservation of the sense of propriety alone but, more important, by the preservation of those political and social structures that made humane social life and humane values themselves possible. Murray understood that every generation must fight the battle of the Olympians against the chthonic spirits, who might be defeated but never permanently vanquished. Like Grote, Murray feared intellectual and social regression; and like Pater, but without his intent, Murray thought the ancient gods and spirits could exercise a perennial, beneficent influence over human life. What must be nurtured and sustained was a human society in which nerve would be unlikely to fail and in which men and women would be more likely to follow their rational than their irrational impulses. It was the fragility of such a society that Murray recognized and that the vagaries of European politics would soon shatter.

The careers of Harrison, Farnell, and Murray following World War I were not unrelated to their writings on Greek myth. Harrison despaired of the future of civilization. She left England for many years, seems not to have opened a classical text for a decade, and became wholly enamored with the thought of Russian mystics. Farnell assumed for a time the duties of vice chancellor of Oxford and devoted much of his effort to combating what he regarded as the Communist menace confronting the university and Western civilization as a whole. Murray, who had supported the conflict against Germany after earlier deploring the Boer War, threw much of his energy into an

96. Ibid., pp. 96, 103. See also *Revue de L'Histoire des Religions* 69 (1914): 259–62.

attempt to make the League of Nations a viable institution for keeping the peace. To no small extent the actions of each scholar might have been predicted from their attitudes toward Greek religion, the function of the Olympians in Greek life, and the role of human reason implied in their commentaries on those subjects.

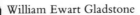
William Ewart Gladstone

John Stuart Blackie
(National Portrait Gallery, London)

Richard Claverhouse Jebb

Gilbert Murray
(National Portrait Gallery, London)

4

THE READING
OF HOMER

The Victorian reading and criticism of the Homeric epics furnish the best example of the appropriation of a well-known, previously translated, and widely read ancient Greek author to specifically nineteenth-century preoccupations. Since the Renaissance, the *Iliad* and the *Odyssey* had provided a challenge to British translators and an inspiration to British poets and artists. The English renderings of Homeric verse by Chapman and Pope stood as minor monuments of English literature. Long before the young John Keats, hundreds of Englishmen had heard Chapman "speak out loud and bold." Gauged in terms of circulation, Pope had spoken out even more boldly. The criticism occasioned by Pope's translation, as well as the quarrel between the ancients and moderns, had brought various problems of Homeric poetry before the eighteenth-century reading public. Homer had also conveyed much of the information about Greek myth and religion. Neoclassical artists such as John Flaxman had created memorable illustrations of the events surrounding the lives of the Homeric heroes.[1]

Through the influence of Thomas Blackwell's *Enquiry into the Life and Writings of Homer* (1735) and Robert Wood's *Essay upon the Original Genius and Writings of Homer* (1775), eighteenth-century British Homeric criticism became markedly historical in character.[2] As the neoclassical concern over the value and character of Homer as a poet diminished, new controversies arose over the historical conditions

1. Maynard Mack et al., "Introduction," Alexander Pope, *The "Iliad" of Homer I–IX*, ed. Maynard Mack (New Haven: Yale University Press, 1967), pp. xxxv–ccil.
2. Donald M. Foerster, *Homer in English Criticism: The Historical Approach in the Eighteenth Century* (New Haven: Yale University Press, 1947), pp. 26–40, 63–113.

that had permitted his genius to flourish, the similarity of his verse to that of Ossian, features of Homeric geography, and the nature of Homeric society. As a result of these controversies, a sense of concrete particularity came to characterize British discussions of Homer. Furthermore, the reports of travelers, such as Lady Mary Wortley Montagu and Wood, confirmed the faithfulness of Homer to the details of the actual landscape. His world was real. The winds he had described still blew over the Troad where the Scamander flowed.

Later British criticism of the epics continued to be deeply rooted in the eighteenth-century conviction of the realism of Homer's poetry. Except for adherents to the solar theory of myth, every significant Victorian commentator believed that in describing and criticizing Homeric characters, religion, or society, he was dealing either with events that had actually occurred or with a society that had actually existed. Even George Grote, who understood "the real Trojan war" to have been only a legendary tale that provided later generations of Greeks with "a grand and inexhaustible object of common sympathy, common faith, and common admiration," nonetheless defended the accuracy of the details of political and social customs described in the *Iliad* and *Odyssey* as truthful records of the poet's own age.[3] For, as he explained in regard to the mythical narratives:

> ... the very same circumstances which divest their composers of all credibility as historians, render them so much the more valuable as unconscious expositors of their own contemporary society. While professedly describing an uncertified past, their combinations are involuntarily borrowed from the surrounding present. For among communities, such as those of the primitive Greeks, without books, without means of extended travel, without acquaintance with foreign languages and habits, the imagination even of highly gifted men was naturally enslaved by the circumstances around them to a far greater degree than in the later days of Solon or Herodotus; insomuch that the characters which they conceived and the scenes which they described would for

3. George Grote, *A History of Greece,* New Edition, 12 vols. (London: John Murray, 1869), 1:311.

that reason bear a stronger generic resemblance to the realities of their own time and locality.[4]

Since by its very nature the poetic imagination was descriptive, or passive, rather than creative, Homeric verse had portrayed its society in terms of existing forms and categories.

This realistic and historical appreciation of the Homeric epics was the first and most important eighteenth-century legacy to Victorian commentators on Homer. Unlike most of the eighteenth-century approaches to myth, it was not repudiated. In fact, for many nineteenth-century writers Homer was to be read and valued more nearly for his worth as a truthful historical narrator or recorder than as a poet. For example, in 1850 Colonel William Mure observed in his widely read and frequently cited *Critical History of the Language and Literature of Antient Greece:*

> Could it ... be established that the events which Homer exhibits as great national enterprises, or the heroes by whom they were conducted, were but the dreams of his own imagination or of that of his ancestors, the result would be, or ought to be, a proportional diminution of our interest in the character and fate of those heroes.

Mure was, of course, replying to Grote's reduction of the incidents and personalities of the Trojan war to "essentially a legend and nothing more."[5] In his diluted, Gradgrind fashion Mure thought the epics more worthy and valuable as historical accounts than as products of a creative poetic imagination, and he was by no means alone in that opinion. It colored practically all Victorian considerations of the poems.

4. Ibid., 2:58. This passage should be compared with Adam Ferguson, *An Essay on the History of Civil Society,* ed. Duncan Forbes (Edinburgh: Edinburgh University Press, 1966; originally published, 1767), p. 77. Grote cites Ferguson in *History of Greece,* 1:436.

5. William Mure, *A Critical History of the Language and Literature of Antient Greece* (London: Longman, Brown, Green, and Longmans, 1850), 1:33. (This attitude is by no means a thing of the past. See Denys Page, *History and the Homeric Iliad* (Berkeley: University of California Press, 1959), p. 258.); Grote, *History of Greece,* 1:312.

The second eighteenth-century legacy to Victorian commentary on Homer and one intimately related to the historical approach was the Homeric question. In 1795, F. A. Wolf, a student of Heyne, published his *Prolegomena ad Homerum*.[6] This epochmaking work of classical scholarship was an introduction to the Greek text of the *Iliad*. It addressed the question of how the text itself had come into being. Wolf was among the first scholars to appreciate the philological implications of the Venetian Scholia published in 1788 by Villoison. After studying this text of Homer, the product of the best mediaeval Byzantine scholars, Wolf understood that it was impossible ever to recover the original text of the Homeric epics. In the course of explaining the difficulties of textual transmission, he followed the lead of Robert Wood's *Essay upon the Original Genius and Writings of Homer* and argued that the art of writing had not existed during the period when Homer had allegedly written the *Iliad*. Wolf thought it unlikely, if not impossible, for a single person to have composed so long a poem from memory. Nor did it seem that a rude society could have provided sufficient opportunities for recitation of so extensive an epic. Instead of having been composed by a single poet, the *Iliad,* according to Wolf, had originated in a number of shorter lays sung by a group of wandering poets called rhapsodists. The rhapsodic lays had been collected and collated into one long epic poem during the regime of the Athenian tyrant Pisistratus. Wolf's essay, originally published in Latin and later translated into German but not into English, provoked within German scholarly circles a controversy of heroic proportions that persisted throughout the next century. In the course of the dispute "Wolfian" was a term that came to be applied to almost anyone who questioned the unity of Homeric authorship whether on Wolf's original grounds or on some other basis.

In Great Britain skeptical theories about Homeric authorship made little headway, despite the acknowledged English influence on Wolf.

6. Friedrich August Wolf, *Prolegomena ad Homerum* (Halle, Saxony, 1795); Georg Finsler, *Homer in der Neuzeit von Dante bis Goethe* (Leipzig and Berlin: B. G. Teubner, 1912), pp. 458–72; Marshall Montgomery, *Friedrich Hölderlin and the German Neo-Hellenic Movement* (London: Oxford University Press, 1923), pp. 107–99; Mark Pattison, *Essays,* 2 vols. ed. Henry Nettleship (Oxford: Clarendon Press, 1889), 1:337–414.

About the turn of the century, Jacob Bryant had started a brief pamphlet war by suggesting on geographical premises that the *Iliad* was historical fantasy. This idea had no appreciable impact, however, and the whole matter was soon forgotten. Later, Coleridge privately and Carlyle publicly accepted the multiple authorship of the *Iliad*. Examinations given at Cambridge during the late twenties suggest that Wolf's theory had been expounded in order to be promptly refuted. In 1831 the liberal Anglican historian Henry Hart Milman observed that German theories had hardly begun to stir the thought of British writers. During the forties the *Encyclopaedia Britannica*, the *Encyclopaedia Metropolitana*, and William Smith's *Dictionary of Greek and Roman Biography and Mythology* explained the theories of Wolf and his followers in a generally evenhanded fashion.[7] No broad British dispute over the matter had arisen.

Yet by the middle decade of the century a lively controversy—though not of the porportions of the one in Germany—had developed. But it occurred for reasons that had little to do with Wolf, or for that matter with Homer. As John Stuart Blackie noted in 1866:

> If the Wolfian theory with regard to the origin and composition of the Homeric poems be looked at beyond the surface, it will be

7. Jacob Bryant, *A Dissertation concerning the War of Troy, and the Expedition of the Grecians, as described by Homer: Showing that No Such Expedition Was Ever Undertaken, and That No Such City of Phrygia Existed* (London, 1796); John Bacon Sawrey Morritt, *A Vindication of Homer, and of the Ancient Poets and Historians Who Have Recorded the Siege and Fall of Troy* (Eton, 1799); Thomas Falconer, *Remarks on Some Passages in Mr. Bryant's Publications, Respecting the War of Troy* (London, 1799); (see also Grote, *History of Greece*, 1:320n); Samuel Taylor Coleridge, *The "Table Talk" and "Omniana" of Samuel Taylor Coleridge*, ed. T. Ashe (London: George Bell and Sons, 1909), pp. 74–75. On Carlyle and other Victorian literary critics, see Donald M. Foerster, *The Fortunes of Epic Poetry: A Study in English and American Criticism, 1750–1950* (Washington, D.C.: The Catholic University of America Press, 1962), pp. 56–76, 116–32; *Classical Examinations; or, A Selection of University Scholarships and Other Public Examination Papers, and of the Questions on the Lecture Subjects of the Different Colleges in the University of Cambridge* (Cambridge: W. P. Grant, 1830), pp. 390, 404, 407–10, 423; Henry Hart Milman, "Origins of the Homeric Poems," *Quarterly Review* 44 (1831): 126; *Encyclopaedia Britannica*, 7th ed., (1842), s.v. "Homer"; *Encyclopaedia Metropolitana* (London, 1845), s.v. "Homer and Hesiod," and "Homerus," William Smith, ed., *Dictionary of Greek and Roman Biography and Mythology* (London: Taylor, Walton, and Maberly and John Murray, 1844–49), 2:500–12.

found to underlie a great number of the most important literary, historical, and theological questions that stir the mind of England at the present hour.[8]

The matters to which Blackie alluded included the problems of taste and translation disputed by Matthew Arnold and Francis Newman in 1861 and the question of how to evaluate the validity and content of ancient historical documents that had divided historians since Niebuhr's day. But the most significant contemporary issue upon which Homeric scholarship touched was the implication of Wolfian or skeptical approaches to Homer for the reading, study, and appreciation of the Bible.

Homer and the Bible

That the Homeric epics constituted the Bible of the Greeks was a truism for nineteenth-century commentators. The *Iliad* and the *Odyssey* had furnished the Greeks of the classical age, as the Old Testament had similarly provided later generations of Hebrews, with myths, heroes, and historical narratives wherein lay both a store of moral precepts and the foundation of a sense of cultural unity. Eighteenth-century critics had transformed the Homeric poems into ancient historical accounts of real wars and real heroes that were more or less contemporary with those of the Old Testament. They had also made casual comparisons between the epics and the Old Testament in matters of language, social customs and religious observances. In his *Lectures on the Sacred Poetry of the Hebrews* (1753) Bishop Robert Lowth had encouraged further literary comparison by treating major portions of the Old Testament as poetry. In Germany Herder and Heyne had contributed to a similar mode of thought. Consequently, for British readers and critics Homer and the Bible had already become somewhat intertwined.

Matthew Arnold, in the third quarter of the nineteenth century, regarded the role that the Homeric epics had played among the Greeks of the classical age as a model for the use of the Bible in modern British society. He defended his own frequent use of biblical quotations and

8. John Stuart Blackie, *Homer and the "Iliad,"* 4 vols. (Edinburgh: Edmonston and Douglas, 1866), 1:184.

allusions on the ground that the Bible was "the only book well enough known to quote as the Greeks quoted Homer." He compared the reading of the Bible in British schools with the reading of Homer in ancient Greek schools. This perception of the cultural function of Homer among the Greeks also entered into Arnold's famous exchange with Francis Newman over the proper translation of the epics. Newman thought archaic Greek words in the English translations of the epics should be rendered so as to sound as unfamiliar to a modern English audience as the original verse had sounded to Greek listeners centuries after Homer. To that end he included Anglo-Saxon and archaic English words in his translation of the *Iliad*. Arnold contended that the archaic Greek of Homer must have sounded no more unfamiliar to the citizens of Periclean Athens than the words of the King James version of the Bible sounded to nineteenth-century Englishmen. Thus, the language of the Authorized Version was the most appropriate rhetoric for Homeric translation. Still later in the century, S. H. Butcher and Andrew Lang defended the English archaism of their translation of the *Odyssey* by arguing that "the Biblical English seems as nearly analogous to the Epic Greek, as anything our tongue has to offer."9

Had the parallel between the two ancient books functioned in so simple a literary fashion, the story would have been neither significant nor particularly interesting. What was novel in the British treatment of Homer and the Bible during the nineteenth century was the problematical situation into which German historical and philological criticism had thrust both ancient texts. The Homeric question came alive to British writers once they saw its relationship to the fate of the Bible. It was concern over the latter that sparked critical interest in the former. The character of this relationship is illustrated in a statement from George Rawlinson's preface to the Bampton Lectures of 1859, which were entitled *The Historical Evidences of the Scripture Records*.

9. Matthew Arnold, *Democratic Education,* ed. R. H. Super (Ann Arbor: University of Michigan Press, 1962), p. 359n; Francis W. Newman, *The "Iliad" of Homer Faithfully Translated into Unrhymed English Metre,* 2nd edition revised (London: Trübner and Co., 1871; 1st ed., 1856), p. viii; Matthew Arnold, *On the Classical Tradition,* ed. R. H. Super (Ann Arbor: University of Michigan Press, 1960), pp. 155–56; Samuel Henry Butcher and Andrew Lang, trans., *The "Odyssey" of Homer Done into English Prose* (London: Macmillan and Co., 1929; 1st ed., 1879), p. ix.

Rawlinson, who was also a scholar of Herodotus, regarded his task as
that of meeting and defeating examples of

> that latest phase of modern unbelief, which, professing a rev-
> erence for the name of the person of Christ, and a real regard for
> the Scriptures as embodiments of what is purest and holiest in
> religious feeling, lower Christ into a mere name, and empty the
> Scriptures of all their force and practical efficacy, by denying all
> historical character of the Biblical narrative.[10]

Rawlinson's statement would have been equally valid and timely for
much contemporary Homeric criticism if the name of Homer had
been substituted for Christ, the Homeric epics for the Scriptures, and
literary excellence for religious feelings. Although there is little evidence that in writing the *Prolegomena ad Homerum* Wolf had intended
to imply questions about the historical credentials of the Bible, his
methods and the kinds of questions he posed were cut from the same
cloth as contemporary German criticism of the Scriptures and the
critical discussions of biblical mythology that had originated with
Heyne.[11] Because of this common national and methodological origin, the criticism of Homer and the criticism of the Bible became
intermeshed. The enemies of the Bible were the skeptics of Homer,
and the doubters of Homeric unity were the enemies of the Bible.
Initially the British defense of Homer against skeptical analysis tended
to imply a similar defense for the Bible. By the close of the century,
however, the critical reading of the Scriptures had come to be employed in support of the relevance and humanity of the *Iliad* and
Odyssey.

   The opening volumes of George Grote's *History of Greece* (1846) set
the Homeric question and its implicit relationship to the Bible before
the British reading public and permanently associated the issues with
rationalist, radical, and utilitarian thought. In his first volume Grote
assigned the narrative content of the Homeric epics to that mythical
"past which never was present" and thus drew his analysis of the

---

10. George Rawlinson, *The Historical Evidences of the Truth of the Scripture Records,
Stated Anew, with Special Reference to the Doubts and Discoveries of Modern Times* (London: John Murray, 1859), p. v.

11. Hans Frei, *The Eclipse of Biblical Narrative* (New Haven: Yale University Press,
1974); Christian Hartlich and Walter Sachs, *Der Ursprung des Mythosbegriffes in der
Modernen Bibelwissenschaft* (Tübingen: J. C. B. Mohr, 1952).

poems into the ambience of a theory of myth that held skeptical implications for Christian history as well as for the Greek legendary age. In
the second volume Grote denied the unity of Homeric authorship but
not on strictly Wolfian premises. With Wolf he agreed that the art of
writing probably had not existed during the period of Homeric composition and that the poems had been transmitted orally until committed to writing about the middle of the seventh century B.C., when a
literate class appeared in Greece. However, Grote made certain significant departures from Wolf. Grote regarded as "nowise admissable"
the Wolfian view of a recension of the *Iliad* from previously disconnected lays at the time of Pisistratus. There were simply too few
elements from that late period in the existing poem. Furthermore, in
contrast to Wolf who had concentrated on the *Iliad,* Grote devoted
considerable attention to the *Odyssey* as well. The character of the
Odyssey seemed to prove that a long, unified, premeditated epic could
arise in a rude, primitive age and be transmitted successfully to a later
literate period. Grote even suggested, "If it had happened that the
Odyssey had been preserved to us alone, without the Iliad, I think the
dispute respecting Homeric unity would never have been raised."[12]

Grote thought the strict Wolfians had boxed themselves into an
untenable position. There was an obvious, if clearly imperfect, unity,
or at least organization, to the *Iliad.* The problem was to account for
both the observable unity and the departures from it. The Wolfian
solution presented what Grote regarded as an inelegant historical explanation. As he commented, "The idea that the poem as we read it
grew out of atoms not originally designed for the places which they
now occupy, involves us in new and inextricable difficulties when we
seek to elucidate either the mode of coalescence or the degree of existing unity." Grote's approach was to look at the obvious coherence in
the epic and to consider the work, as much as was possible, as a unity.
He contended that the *Iliad* was a poem that had outgrown its original
purpose and organization. According to his analysis, Books 1, 8, and
11 through 22 inclusive constituted "the primary organization of the
poem, then properly an Achilleis."[13] These books concentrated on the
exploits and wrath of Achilles. Books 2 through 7 inclusive and 10,
23, and 24 had been added later to transform the Achilleis into a poem

12. Grote, *History of Greece,* 1:43; 2:143, 165.
13. Ibid., 2:174, 176.

encompassing a larger scope—an *Iliad*. Book 9, which relates the embassy from Agamemnon to Achilles, Grote considered to be spurious. Had that generous offer of reconciliation been proffered, Achilles would no longer have had a just cause of offended honor to support his continued absence from the Greek camp. Moreover, the fact of the embassy would also have rendered several later speeches of Achilles wholly inappropriate or out of character. In this manner, Grote did see more than one hand as having constructed the text of the *Iliad*. However, except for Book 9 and a few other lesser interpolations, he thought it perfectly possible that the original author of the Achilleis might himself have composed most or all of the later, expanded *Iliad*.

As was true of so much of his monumental history, Grote's analysis of the Homeric question was a masterpiece of shrewd criticism and common sense. His theory received support and considerable acceptance in Germany soon after it was published in 1846. Within British scholarly circles, however, his theory and textual analysis were largely ignored for over thirty years. William Mure, William Ewart Gladstone, Matthew Arnold, Francis Newman, and John Stuart Blackie either disregarded or attacked them. Not until the publication in 1878 of William Geddes's *The Problem of the Homeric Poems* did a British scholar of stature strongly urge acceptance of the Grotean approach to the Homeric question. By the close of the century Grote's concept of an original core to the *Iliad*—the actual elements of which remained in dispute—that was later expanded upon and interpolated into had become orthodox opinion in the widely influential works of Richard Claverhouse Jebb and Walter Leaf.[14]

The major sources of mid-century resistance to Grote's Homeric criticism would seem to have been the low level of British scholarship and political and religious prejudice. The Homeric question had re-

---

14. Ludwig Friedländer, *Die Homerische Kritik von Wolf bis Grote* (Berlin: Georg Reimer, 1853); William D. Geddes, *The Problem of the Homeric Poems* (London: Macmillan and Co., 1878); John Pentland Mahaffy, "Recent Homeric Studies," *Macmillan's Magazine* 38 (1878): 405–16; Richard Claverhouse Jebb, *Homer: An Introduction to the "Iliad" and the "Odyssey,"* 6th ed. (Boston: Ginn and Co., 1904; 1st ed., 1887), p. 164; Walter Leaf, *The "Iliad," Edited with Apparatus Criticus, Prolegomena, Notes, and Appendices,* 2nd ed., 2 vols. (Amsterdam: A. M. Hakkert, 1971; 1st ed., 1901–02), 1:xxi, 370, 423, 526; Henry Browne, *Handbook of Homeric Study* (London: Longmans, Green, and Co., 1908), p. 151; Alan John Bayard Wace, "The Higher Criticism of Homer," *Edinburgh Review* 230 (1919): 161–71; John A. Scott, *The Unity of Homer* (Berkeley: University of California Press, 1921), pp. 39–72.

ceived so little previous scholarly examination in Britain that the philological grounds of Grote's discussion were rarely fully appreciated. John Stuart Mill made some brief criticisms in his review of the second volume of *History of Greece* and noted the considerable distance that separated Grote from Wolf.[15] Other writers were much less perceptive. They confused the issue of the unity of Homeric authorship with that of the historical reality of the epic narrative. William Mure's *Critical History of the Language and Literature of Antient Greece* (1850), the first major British work in the field to appear after Grote, largely ignored Grote's textual analysis and attacked his assignment of the Trojan War to an origin in the primitive mythopoeic mentality. Gladstone in *Studies on Homer and the Homeric Age* (1858) similarly pressed the argument for the realism of the epics. Both of these critics felt confident of the unity of authorship. Even writers, such as John Stuart Blackie, who took note of Grote's Achilleis theory, generally associated it with Wolf whose theory was then often equated with political radicalism either directly or by innuendo. For example, Mure placed Wolf's essay in the revolutionary climate of the 1790s and suggested that within Homeric studies the appearance of the *Prolegomena ad Homerum* might be compared to the publication of "a pamphlet, containing spurious revolutionary doctrines, in a hitherto tranquil state, at the moment when the minds of men were ripe for political change."[16] It was a simple matter for readers to pass from Wolf's implied political radicalism to the well-known and acknowledged radicalism of Grote.

Grote's reputation for religious rationalism did nothing to assuage existing fears that legitimization of a critical approach to Homer would encourage a similar approach to the Bible. As early as 1841 Thomas De Quincey, defending the unity of Homer, noted that Wolfian techniques were also being applied to the Bible. Gladstone, re-

15. John Stuart Mill, "Grote's *History of Greece*," *Edinburgh Review* 84 (1846): 362–68. Other major reviews fell into rather predictable opinions. *The Westminster Review*, 46 (1846): 393–415, generally supported Grote's analysis and the Wolfian approach. Such would be expected from this radical journal. A more conservative and critical discussion was published in *The Quarterly Review* 78 (1846): 113–44 by Henry Hart Milman.

16. Mure, *A Critical History of the Language and Literature of Antient Greece*, 1:197. See also William Mure to John Stuart Blackie, 26 July 1854, J. S. Blackie Papers, 2624, p. 42, National Library of Scotland.

viewing the work of Wolf's disciple Lachmann for the *Quarterly Review* in 1847, voiced warnings about German skepticism. Three years later another writer for the *Quarterly Review* went even further and declared that

> ... the doctrine revived and developed by Wolf as to Homer, was an offset from the determined warfare against the Bible which throughout the last century occupied so many of the liveliest intellects in Europe. Homer has been not unjustly called, by Wolf himself, the Bible of the Greeks; and it would be easy to show in how many ways the Antichristian conspiracy might have hoped to see its proper object forwarded by the collateral—however in many cases undesigned—co-operation of those who essayed to shake everything that had been for thousands of years accepted as to the origin, construction, and authority of the literary monument which approached nearest in claims of antiquity to the Hebrew Scriptures, and had exerted an influence only inferior to theirs on the religious belief of nations, besides directing and governing, far more than any other writings whatever, the general sentiment and taste of the cultivated world.

In 1854 E. B. Pusey, the great Tractarian leader and Oxford professor of Hebrew, bluntly asserted, "The scepticism as to Homer ushered in the scepticism on the Old Testament." For Pusey, an archconservative churchman who had studied briefly with Heyne in the 1820s, the critical approach to Homer epitomized the more general frame of mind that called into question all traditional belief and authority. He was largely correct. For as T. H. Huxley later observed, criticism of Homer was a manifestation of the scientific spirit that examined the previously unexamined idols of the day.[17]

17. Thomas DeQuincy, "Homer and the Homeridae," *Blackwood's* 50 (1841): 414; William Ewart Gladstone, "Lachmann's *Essays on Homer*," *Quarterly Review* 81 (1847): 381–82; John Gibson Lockhardt, "Homeric Controversy," *Quarterly Review* (American ed.), 87 (1850): 236–37; Edward Bouverie Pusey, *Collegiate and Professorial Teaching and Discipline in Answer to Professor Vaughn's Strictures* (Oxford and London: John Henry Parker, 1854), p. 62; (Another Tractarian leader, John Keble, had vigorously defended the unity of Homeric authorship in *Lectures on Poetry, 1832–1841*, 2 vols., trans. E. K. Francis, (Oxford: Clarendon Press, 1912), 1:97–99); Thomas Henry Huxley, *Collected Essays*, 9 vols. (New York: D. Appleton and Co., 1895), 5:32–33.

Some commentators raised the skepticism supposedly nurtured by the Homeric question to an even higher level. They suggested that doubt about the unity of Homeric authorship might also imply doubt about the existence of God. Supposedly at issue was the theistic argument from design. Just as an orderly universe required the presence of a creator, so also a long, designed poem demanded the existence of an author. One of the characters in Mrs. Browning's *Aurora Leigh* (1857) quipped:

> Wolf's an atheist
> And if the Iliad fell out, as he says,
> By mere fortuitous concourse of the old songs,
> We'd guess as much, too, for the universe.

Poetic license might justify this caricature of Wolf's views, but such was not the case with John Stuart Blackie, who blatantly used religious apprehensions to forestall serious consideration of Grote's theory of Homer. In 1866 Blackie incorrectly and unjustly argued that if Grote's views were correct, "the Wolfian theory is triumphant." He had previously stated, "Those who believe in a great poem cannot avoid thinking that the Wolfians are engaged in a perverse attempt, closely analogous to the meagre method of explaining the world without a God, in which certain incomplete intellects have in all ages found an unnatural delight."[18] By portraying both Wolf and Grote as much more radical than either had actually been and then refuting their falsely construed arguments, Blackie made an indirect case for the Bible and theism through the criticism of Homer and simultaneously hindered a critical approach to the poet by appeal to religious anxiety.

Blackie's remarks on Wolf and Grote are somewhat curious when compared with his own views of the *Iliad*. His interpretation of the epic was restrained and not nearly so far removed from Wolf as his rhetoric might have led readers to suppose. He accepted the absence of writing during the period of epic composition. Blackie's Homer, like Blackie himself, was a folklorist whose great poem was a compilation of earlier ballads, and Blackie translated the poem in ballad verse. He admitted that the personalities and incidents of the *Iliad* were based upon legends and had only the most fragile basis in actual historical

18. Elizabeth Barrett Browning, bk. 5; Blackie, *Homer and the "Iliad,"* 1:247, 245n.

events. Blackie's position in classical studies and religious thought was not unlike that of Anglican Broad Churchmen. He could not acquiesce in Grote's analysis because he still wanted some kind of Homer and some kind of genuine historical foundation for the epic, no matter how weak, just as he and others wanted to believe in some kind of God and in biblical truth, no matter how diffuse. Blackie, like the liberal Anglicans, pursued a moderate rationalism. That course meant they must strongly object to more extreme rationalistic writers as a way of denying that their own moderate goals might lead to conclusions they could not accept. In that regard Blackie's reading of Homer was not unlike Matthew Arnold's reading of the Bible in *Literature and Dogma*.

Picking up the stick from the other end, Victorian commentators sometimes employed the reading of the Bible as a guide to the appreciation of Homer. Blackie, for example, suggested the vast influence of the English Bible proved that a book originally written in an ancient language could become a living reality to a modern nation. Other writers observed that the multiple authorship of the Bible and of the Book of Common Prayer meant that committee or multiple authorship could produce works of elevated spiritual and ethical meaning not lacking art or beauty. In *Social Life in Greece* (1874), a book that went through numerous printings during the last quarter of the century, the Anglo-Irish scholar J. P. Mahaffy of Trinity College, Dublin, contended that a comparison of the modern reading of the Bible and the ancient reading of Homer would explain why the inconsistencies in the epics that had plagued modern readers since Wolf had not bothered Greek readers. In reading Homer, the ancient Greeks had assumed the poems to have been composed with a moral intention. Modern men and women read the Bible with a similar assumption. Consequently, "... the [biblical] incidents which are in accordance with our moral sense are utilised and insisted upon, the other matters are forgotten, and so the whole annals of a race in some respects unfit for our instruction are taught as the inspired word of God written for our Learning." The ancients had perused Homer with a similar selectivity that had been determined by their own sense of the morality of their gods.[19]

19. Ibid., 1:vii; Browne, *Handbook of Homeric Study*, p. 86; Walter Leaf, *A Companion to the "Iliad" for English Readers* (London: Macmillan and Co., 1892), p. 18; John Pentland Mahaffy, "Recent Homeric Studies," p. 412. John Pentland Mahaffy, *Social Life in Greece from Homer to Menander* (London: Macmillan and Co., 1874), p.

It is possible to make too much of these mid-century comparisons between problems of biblical and Homeric criticism. Hermeneutical methods were not applied to Homer. Comparisons between the two bodies of ancient literature were unsystematic, fairly rude, and often polemically opportunistic. Nevertheless, the perceived relevance of the Homeric question for biblical studies does seem to have limited the extent of candid acceptance and exercise of rational analysis of the Homeric poetry. There also exists a clear chronological parallel between the appearance and assimilation of the higher criticism of Homer and the Bible in Britain. Certain Anglicans had been familiar with both modes of analysis in the 1820s and 1830s, but their impact was smothered by the Tractarian movement. Major skeptical works touching both documents then appeared during the 1840s in radical political and intellectual circles. Grote discussed Homer. George Eliot and Unitarian writers translated and introduced the German criticism of the Bible. There followed about a quarter of a century of controversy, conservative attack, and gradual assimilation of the skeptical analyses of both texts in the universities and among liberal Anglican and Scottish Presbyterian scholars. By the final quarter of the century the critical reading of Homer and the Bible had been incorporated into the thought and publications of the major intellectual and scholarly circles of the nation. But Homer's epics became subject to the critical analysis of Geddes, Jebb, and Leaf only after more or less free discussion of the Bible had become a fact of British intellectual life. In that regard, the career of Homer and the Bible was quite similar to the discussions of Hebraism and Hellenism during the same period. In both cases Christian concerns tended to determine the consideration of the Greek subjects.

The intimate connection of biblical and Homeric criticism still continued to flourish when the inhibiting effect of concern for the Bible on British Homeric scholarship had ceased. This development was not

---

328. Victorian critics did not argue that the Bible had been the Homer of the Hebrews. The closest that any writer came to urging that position was Edwin Hatch when he explained that Jews who became familiar with Greek philosophy found themselves compelled to reinterpret the Pentateuch much as later Greek philosophers had undertaken a new interpretation of Homer. See Edwin Hatch, *The Influence of Greek Ideas on Christianity* (New York: Harper and Brothers, 1957; originally published, 1890), pp. 65–66. Hatch delivered his lectures on this subject in 1888.

limited to Britain. As Ulrich von Wilamowitz-Moellendorff declared in his dedication of *Homerische Untersuchungen* (1884), "Moreover, the Bible and Homer must be understood and analyzed first of all in terms of themselves, and even the nature of their transmission, the history of the texts, demands the use of parallel analysis."[20] The impact of other explanatory factors on textual analysis contributed further to the already existing linkage between Homer and the Bible. Archaeology throughout the eastern Mediterranean revealed both Homeric and biblical culture to have been more complex than had once been thought. Each ancient society had itself developed from a still more ancient past. The eager acceptance of the concept of evolution that characterized so much late nineteenth-century thought favored a developmental approach to the composition of both the Bible and the Homeric epics. Finally, if the epics were not the work of a single poetic genius and the Bible were not the inspired word of God, scholars dealing with them needed to suggest other reasons for the continued appreciation and intellectual utility of both works.

All of these threads of influence were woven into the fabric of Gilbert Murray's *The Rise of the Greek Epic* (1907), written initially as a set of lectures delivered at Harvard University in 1906. Drawing upon contemporary literary criticism, Murray contended that the *Iliad* and the *Odyssey*, like the Bible, the *Song of Roland*, the Arthurian legends, and the *Niebelungenlied*, were traditional books that embodied "not the independent invention of one man, but the ever-moving tradition of many generations of men."[21] Over the course of several centuries different writers took a received narrative, expanded and reworked it, reformed its contents to conform to current moral and aesthetic sensibilities, and thus renewed the life and usefulness of the story. Of these various traditional books Murray regarded the Bible as the one best suited for comparison with the Homeric epics.

Murray's selection of the Bible was not a random one. The recent work of Robertson Smith and S. R. Driver on the Pentateuch provided his acknowledged model for examining the emergence of a traditional book and for presenting that development as one of pro-

20. Ulrich von Wilamowitz-Moellendorff, *Homerische Untersuchungen* (Berlin, Weidmannsche Buchhandlung, 1884), p. iii (my translation). The dedication was to the biblical scholar Julius Wellhausen.

21. Gilbert Murray, *The Rise of the Greek Epic* (Oxford: Clarendon Press, 1907), p. 154.

gressive moral achievement. According to Smith and Driver in their several studies of Old Testament literature, the Pentateuch was the product of a composite effort of numerous writers who during different periods of Hebrew history had responded to the immediate political, religious, and moral developments of the nation.[22] As a result of their effort to impose an increasingly monotheistic theology on works that had originally contained much polytheistic material, each major book of the Pentateuch had gone through numerous editions, reformations, and expurgations. The presence of incomplete expurgations, such as the retention of the story of Cain's rejected sacrifice, and of poorly executed ones, such as the two creation narratives, bore witness to the occurrence of the expurgatory process. The story of the discovery of the book of Deuteronomy during the reign of King Josiah (II Kings 22:8) suggested the way in which one imposition of a new edition of a traditional book on the Hebrew nation had taken place.[23]

Murray contended that the text of the Homeric poems reflected an expurgatory development similar to that of the Old Testament. The very kind of moral and religious reform of those poems that Plato urged in his dialogues had actually been performed on earlier editions of the *Iliad* and the *Odyssey*. To sustain this argument, Murray posited the existence of a large body of ancient verse, now lost, but originally containing much morally repugnant material that over the course of time and through a series of editings and reworkings had come to constitute the present Homeric epics. The unknown editors who had carried out this process embodied what Murray termed the "Homeric spirit." Through their collective work the Greek epics had become "a force and the embodiment of a force making for the progress of the human race" because over the course of centuries the Homeric spirit had raised the concept of humanity held by the Greeks.[24] In effect, Murray was reversing the analysis of the solar theorists, such as Max Müller, who had posited an ancient noble people whose moral life had undergone a process of decay.

It was Murray's contention that the various expurgations and inter-

22. William Robertson Smith, *The Old Testament in the Jewish Church* (New York: D. Appleton and Co., 1881); Samuel Rolles Driver, *The Book of Genesis with Introduction and Notes,* 11th ed. (London: Methuen and Co., 1920; 1st ed., 1904).

23. Murray, *The Rise of the Greek Epic,* pp. 101–15.

24. Ibid., pp. 116, 1.

polations displayed both what the ancient editors had rejected from traditional knowledge and what they had put in its place. From extrapolating the character of those expurgations, Murray set forth the main features of the Homeric spirit, which, when all was said and done, rather resembled the spirit of the Victorian Mrs. Grundy. For example, there was considerable evidence that "certain forms of sexual irregularity" had existed during the age of the original composition of the Homeric poems. Murray could not bring himself to use any more explicit term to refer to homosexuality, but he argued:

> Early Greek traditions testify both to the existence and the toleration of these practices. Now Homer has swept this whole business, root and branch, out of his conception of life. Exactly the same spirit is seen at work when we compare the rude ithyphallic Hermae of ancient Greek cults with the idealized messenger of the Gods in the Odyssey.[25]

The Homeric spirit was happily heterosexual and tolerated only the ideals of chivalrous friendship and loyalty in combat between males. The same progressively civilizing spirit had also removed from the original traditional stories barbarous military practices and had replaced them with a code of limited chivalry. For example, the bodies of fallen warriors in Homer's narrative were generally stripped of armor, but not of their tunics. There were no poisoned arrows in Homeric battles, although Murray thought certain lines in the poems suggested that such arrows had been included in the original story.

Limits did exist to the expurgations of the Homeric spirit. The desecration of Hector's body could not be removed since that incident was an indelible part of the traditional story. Such incomplete expurgation arose inevitably from "various disturbing influences" indigenous to the character and situation of traditional literature.[26] These included the storyteller's instinct, tribal feeling, attachment to or identification with a particular character or event, and incidents in the traditional narrative that were so much a part of common knowledge that their removal would destroy the story. These limitations in themselves illustrated both the tension and the cooperation between the poets and their audience because the audience had to approve of the

25. Ibid., pp. 118, 116–17.
26. Ibid., p. 109.

changes that were being made. Whereas George Grote had regarded the audience as a check on the accuracy of the poet's political and social details, Murray saw it as confirming the poet's moral revision.

The most significant expurgation illustrating the bond between the reforming poet and the approving audience had related to Greek religion. In *The Rise of the Greek Epic* the Homeric spirit was presented as the vehicle that had carried out much of the Olympian reformation Murray would later discuss in the *Four Stages of Greek Religion* (1912). Over the course of time the Homeric spirit no longer tolerated the worship of chthonic deities or the practice of human sacrifice, practices that James Frazer and Jane Harrison had outlined in their works. In suppressing those ancient rites, the Homeric spirit not only had halted repugnant ritual but also had implicitly recognized that men and women are human beings and not gods. That recognition—the "clear realization that man was not a god, and that it was no use calling him so"—constituted "a remarkable achievement of the Hellenic intellect" and laid the foundation for the humanism that emerged in Greek culture. For Murray that achievement, which had required "such clearness of sight, such daring, such humanity," represented the acceptance of human finitude and the beginning of the possibility of articulating distinctly human and humane values.[27] In this analysis, as elsewhere, Murray directly opposed the opinions of his friend Jane Harrison, whose admiration for chthonic worship stemmed from the ancient mythical vision of human beings becoming divine.

The moral achievements of the Homeric spirit, as reflected in the final text of the epics, provided Murray with his major defense for the lasting value of the poems. Just as Driver in his commentary on Genesis urged that the ancient Hebrew document retained religious and spiritual value and worth despite its collective composition, problematical historical accuracy, and mistaken cosmology, so Murray, having surrendered the idea of a unitary Homer and the historical reality of the Trojan War and its heroes, could still appeal to the *Iliad* and the *Odyssey* as monuments to the achievement of civilized humanity in the West.[28] The impact of the biblical analysis was even more intimate. With the demise of faith in the Bible as a source of revealed

27. Ibid., p. 129.
28. Driver, *Book of Genesis,* pp. lvii–lxxiv.

truth and knowledge, the moral lessons of the *Iliad* and the *Odyssey* could and did assume all the more importance and significance for a scholar such as Murray. In effect, his progressionist interpretation of the Homeric epics substituted those poems for the Hebrew Bible as the source of major ethical values for modern European culture. In his view the epics of the Greeks recorded the emergence and construction of a distinctly human culture from an earlier human barbarism. Throughout Murray's several books that achievement was hailed as the lasting lesson of Hellenism and the perennial moral challenge presented by the Greeks to each new generation of Europeans.

Murray's analysis of the *Iliad* and the *Odyssey* as providing evidence of the emergence of civilization and the human spirit in the West also represented (probably unwittingly) the last significant statement of another connection between Homer and the Bible previously forged by certain Victorian commentators. For those writers the Homeric epics were to the record of profane history what the Old Testament was to the record of sacred history. They looked to the poems for knowledge of humankind's secular development that could supplement the story of religious development narrated in the Old Testament.

The Homeric Epics as a Secular Bible

In 1830 Henry Nelson Coleridge, the nephew and son-in-law of the poet, published an *Introduction to the Study of the Greek Classic Poets.* This small volume was the first post-romantic period study of the subject and may properly be regarded as the earliest Victorian commentary on Homer. Written primarily for students, it set forth a number of theses that would reverberate through later Victorian studies of the Homeric epics. While firmly encouraging the mastery of Greek, Coleridge thought it better that Homer and other classics be read in translation than remain unread. Textual commentary should elucidate issues and problems beyond those of vocabulary and syntax. The historical context should always be taken into account, and the historical information in Homer should be appreciated. Throughout his own discussion Coleridge incorporated the historical considerations of Homeric poetry explored by Continental writers and especially by Vico. These general ideas and practices characterized most nineteenth-century British classical commentaries and allowed them to introduce readers and students not only to the culture of the Greeks but also to much contemporary Continental thought and to the commentators' own views of the relevance of the classical world.

Coleridge also developed another idea that became one of the persistent themes in the mid-Victorian appreciation of Homer. Echoing eighteenth-century critics, he suggested the presence of a peculiar historical and cultural relationship between the Homeric poems and the Bible. While examining the *Iliad,* Coleridge observed:

> Being then so ancient a book, it should be read with patience and a simple mind. Nay, more—we should approach it with something of the kind of reverence which we yield to the Hebrew Genesis, and be perpetually familiar with its contents, as with the secular Bible of mankind. So vivid are the rays which flow from this globe of light, and so strong its power of attraction, that we neither see nor measure the thousands of years which have rolled away since its creation and to-day—we forget the extreme antiquity in the uncommon luminousness of Homer, and almost believe that the Iliad, like the Bible, is collateral with all time, is for now and for ever.

Extrapolating from Vico, Coleridge regarded both Homeric and Old Testament society as standing apart both from the initial savage state of humankind and from its later artificial condition of commerce and manufacture. In the patriarchal social structures, in the mutual hospitality to strangers, and in the similar modes of agriculture and religious sacrifice there existed a very real "correspondence of spirit and manners." Although the moral qualities of Homer's heroes were below those of biblical characters, Coleridge nevertheless contended, "He who has the longest studied, and the most deeply imbibed, the spirit of the Hebrew Scriptures, will the best understand, and the most lastingly appreciate, the tale of Troy Divine."[29]

The reading of the Homeric epics as "a secular Bible of mankind" was in part an emulation of the patristic embracing of pagan civiliza-

29. Henry Nelson Coleridge, *Introduction to the Study of the Greek Classic Poets Designed Principally for the Use of Young Persons at School and College,* 2nd ed. (London: John Murray, 1834), pp. 176–77, 179, 180. See also Henry Alford, *Chapters on the Poets of Ancient Greece* (London: Whittaker and Co., 1841), pp. 17–18.

tion for Christian purposes. However, this mode of interpretation also
reflected the anxiety of Victorian Christians over the secularization of
history by non-Christian writers. If portions of Homeric and Greek
culture could be drawn into providential history or could be understood as illustrating Christian truth, then all history and not just that
recorded in the Bible could be regarded as prescriptively sacred. This
effort might well be considered the historical equivalent of Carlyle's
metaphysical natural supernaturalism. Just as Carlyle had discerned
the wonder and splendor of the supernatural within finite physical
nature, so the writers who linked the Greeks and the Hebrews found
evidence of divine dispensation and perhaps even of revelation in secular history.

The modes of linkage ranged from silly, artificial juxtapositions to
more nearly serious scholarly endeavor. On the most simpleminded
level the author of a fictitious biography of Herodotus published in
1855 included an imaginary meeting in Jerusalem between the Greek
historian and the Hebrew prophet Nehemiah in order to dramatize the
connections between the sacred and secular development of the
West.[30] On a more sophisticated plane of thought liberal Anglicans
uncomfortable with the morality of the Bible and skeptical about its
historical accuracy pointed to the elevated ethical tone of Greeks, such
as Socrates and Plato, and suggested, in the spirit of certain patristic
writers, that some Greeks may have shared in the wisdom of God that
was finally revealed through Christianity. F. D. Maurice, Charles
Kingsley, and other Broad Churchmen were willing and eager to find
such divine truth imparted outside the traditional limits of the Hebrew
and Christian dispensations.

Several commentators on Homer believed the poems taught moral
lessons very similar to those of Christianity. In 1851 James Anthony
Froude, having separated himself from Anglican orthodoxy but, like
many unbelievers, remaining apprehensive about new foundations for
morality, declared:

> ... when the occasions of life stir the feelings in us on which
> religion itself reposes, if we were as familiar with the Iliad as with

---

30. James Talboys Wheeler, *The Life and Travels of Herodotus*, 2 vols. (London:
Longman, Brown, Green, and Longmans, 1855), 1:v. In 1823 another author, writing for the Royal Society of Literature, had suggested, with possible dependence on

the Psalms, the words of the old Ionian singer would leap as naturally to our lips as those of the Israelite king.

He went on to urge that in Homer the supreme divine power was "the same immortal lover of justice and the same hater of iniquity" as that conceived by Christians in the nineteenth century. Moreover, in the Homeric epics, he thought, "Justice means what we mean by justice, and iniquity what we mean by iniquity." The epics might thus provide an acceptable, if not perfect, source for wise moral precepts. A few years later in 1865 George Musgrave, a translator of the *Odyssey*, maintained that the poem encouraged an "entire submission to and humble reliance upon a Divine and merciful and overruling Providence" and exemplified "the defeat of wickedness and vice, and the condign destruction of evil doers" that must be viewed only with astonishment emanating as it did "from the head and heart of a Heathen." As late as 1908 the classical scholar James Adam would urge that "the entire *Odyssey* may be regarded as one great drama by the first of tragic poets intended 'to justify the ways of God to man' by showing how Justice is in the end triumphant over Sin."[31]

Other writers claimed to have discovered evidences of distinctly Christian truth in Greek literature and particularly in Homer. The *Iliad* and the *Odyssey* as secular documents contained or bore witness to the doctrines or providential historical vision present in the Bible. The early church fathers, including Justin Martyr and Eusebius of Caesarea, had frequently constructed elaborate theories about the preparation for the Gospel within pagan times or about the elaboration of the Gospel truth before the coming of Christ.[32] Several Victorian commentators on Homer undertook a similar venture. It was proba-

---

patristic sources, that Homer and Moses were one and the same person and that the incidents in Homer were disguised versions of Old Testament stories. See *Blackwood's* 14 (1823): 343–46.

31. James Anthony Froude, *Short Studies of Great Subjects*, 2 vols. (London: Longmans, Green, and Co., 1867), 2:170, 171; George Musgrave, *The "Odyssey" of Homer Rendered into English Verse*, 2 vols. (London: Bell and Daldy, 1865), 1:xxvi; James Adam, *The Religious Teachers of Greece*, ed. Adela Marion Adam (Edinburgh: T. & T. Clark, 1908), p. 41.

32. Henry Chadwick, *Early Christian Thought and the Classical Tradition: Studies in Justin, Clement, and Origen* (New York: Oxford University Press, 1966), pp. 10–22; Jaroslav Pelikan, *The Emergence of the Catholic Tradition* (Chicago: University of Chicago Press, 1971, pp. 27–41.

bly not happenstance that such authors were frequently Tractarian in sympathy and thus often quite familiar with patristic literature. In *The Christian Scholar* (1849) Isaac Williams, an Oxford movement poet, translated passages from pagan philosophers and poets that might illustrate Christian truths. He then explicated those passages through additional poetic commentaries. For example, after describing the vengeance of Odysseus on Penelope's suitors, Williams explained,

> There falls a light on this illumin'd page,
> And as I ponder with delightèd eyes
> Upon the holier lore of earlier age,
> Something I read of higher mysteries,
> Of One who hath descended from the skies,
> And wanders here in His own kingly hall,
> A *stranger*,—and in *prison* often lies,
> And on His brethren's charities doth call,
> Yet weighs and watches each, the God and Judge of all.[33]

Another religious commentator saw in the Homeric narrative the typology for Jewish history. In 1843 Archdeacon John Williams, rector of the Edinburgh Academy, published *Homerus,* a four-hundred page volume in which he explicated the *Iliad* "as an exoteric Poem, exemplifying the mode in which a great nation is signally punished for national sins." Troy was the evil nation. The sinful leaders were Priam and his sons who sacrificed the prosperity and happiness of their city to defend the sensuality of Paris. According to Williams, the fate of Troy was a model of the fate of all nations who disobeyed God and in particular a model of the fall of Jewish Jerusalem to Rome in 70 A.D.[34]

The moral and Christian allegorical interpretations of the *Iliad* and the *Odyssey* had little or nothing to do with either the Homeric question or the historical reality of the events in the narrative. Rather, to use Heinrich Heine's terms, these approaches represented the imposition of a "romantic" reading on a "classical" text. In *Die Romantische*

---

33. Isaac Williams, *Poetical Works,* 6 vols. (Oxford: J. Parker and Co., 1874), 4:148.

34. John Williams, *Homerus* (London: John Murray, 1842), pp. 118, 132, 427. For a hostile review of this work, see William Mure, "Archdeacon Williams's *Homerus,*" *Edinburgh Review* 77 (1843): 44–71. See also John Williams, *Essays on Various Subjects* (London: John Russell Smith, 1858), pp. 282–83.

Schule (1835) Heine had explained, "Classical art only had the finite to represent, and its images could be identical with the idea of the artist. Romantic art had infinite or purely spiritual relations to represent or rather to imply."[35] Given the finite character of classical literary vision, Heine suggested no one could read the *Odyssey* and think the hero was anything but the son of Laertes and the spouse of Penelope. But Heine's concept of a romantic projection of numerous levels of meaning onto a text had long been practiced with the allegorical and symbolic reading of the Bible, and in both Hellenic and Hellenistic Greece interpreters had attached mystical and allegorical meanings to Homer's poetry. Seventeenth-century British commentators had combined the two traditions, as had certain of the church fathers, and had looked for esoteric symbols, allegories, or interpretations of the Bible in the Homeric epics. John Williams and Isaac Williams simply revived that earlier tradition of Homeric interpretation.[36] The revival of such a reading of Homer in the early nineteenth century would seem to reflect the impact of romanticism on religious life, new familiarity with medieval and patristic literature, and a predisposition in many Christian circles toward dispensationalist theology.

In *Literature and Dogma* (1873) Matthew Arnold contended that the finding of a "secret sense in Homer proves to be a mere dream" as he also thought to be true of "the noting of a secret sense in the Bible."[37] The seeking of reserved meanings from both ancient documents declined simultaneously among the higher intellectual circles in Britain. However, that demise did not reach a conclusion before William Ewart Gladstone combined an historical reading of Homer with a dispensationalist reading of the Bible to produce the most curious of all serious Victorian interpretations of Homeric poetry.

Gladstone's interest in Homer was peripheral neither to Victorian Homeric criticism nor to his own intellectual life. Between 1847 and his death in 1898 he produced seven volumes on Homer and a very

35. Heinrich Heine, *Die Romantische Schule* (Munich: Wilhelm Goldmann, 1964), p. 17 (my translation). Homer is the subject of this passage.

36. I. Williams, *Poetical Works*, 4:xiii–xix; Félix Buffière, *Les Mythes d'Homère et la Pensée Grecque* (Paris: Société d'Edition "Les Belles Lettres," 1956), pp. 7–13, 251–57, 410–18, 583–90; Noémi Hepp, *Homére en France au XVIIe Siècle* (Paris: Librairie C. Kincksieck, 1968), pp. 319–34.

37. Matthew Arnold, *Dissent and Dogma*, ed. R. H. Super (Ann Arbor: University of Michigan Press, 1968), p. 378.

large number of articles. The books included *Studies on Homer and the Homeric Age* (3 vols., 1858), *Juventus Mundi* (1869), *Homeric Synchronism* (1876), *Homer* (1878), and *Landmarks of Homeric Study* (1890). For better or for worse, his works on Homer constituted the single most extensive body of Victorian Homeric commentary.[38] The main concerns of his writings stemmed from his anxiety over the fate of Christianity as a revealed religion in an increasingly secular and skeptical age. His study of the Homeric texts gave him the confidence in later life to undertake the defense of the Bible against T. H. Huxley.[39] However, his initial major foray into Homeric scholarship grew out of his activity in the reform of Oxford University. He hoped to prove that a curriculum in which classical studies, and the study of Homer in particular, played a major role would not necessarily mean the abandonment of distinctly Christian education and that such train-

38. William Ewart Gladstone, *Studies on Homer and the Homeric Age,* 3 vols. (Oxford: Oxford University Press, 1858); *Juventus Mundi: The Gods and Men of the Heroic Age* (London: Macmillan and Co., 1869); *Homeric Synchronism: An Enquiry into the Time and Place of Homer* (London: Macmillan and Co., 1876); *Homer* (New York: D. Appleton and Co., 1879); *Landmarks of Homeric Study* (London: Macmillan and Co., 1890); "Lachmann's *Essays on Homer,*" *Quarterly Review* 81 (1847): 381–417; "On the Place of Homer in Classical Education and in Historical Inquiry," *Oxford Essays* (1857), pp. 1–56; "Homer and His Successors in Epic Poetry," *Quarterly Review* 101 (1857): 80–122; "Homeric Characters in and out of Homer," *Quarterly Review* 102 (1857): 204–51; "Shield of Achilles," *Contemporary Review* 23 (1874): 329–36; "Homer's Place in History," *Contemporary Review* 24 (1874): 1–22, 175–200; "Reply of Achilles to the Envoys of Agamemnon," *Contemporary Review* 23 (1874): 841–48; "Homerology," *Contemporary Review* 27 (1876): 632–49, 803–20; 28 (1876): 282–309; "The Isis of Homer, and Her Relation to Genesis IX:11–17," *Contemporary Review* 32 (1878): 140–52; "The Slicing of Hector," *Nineteenth Century* 4 (1878): 752–64; "On Epithets of Movement in Homer," *Nineteenth Century* 5 (1879): 463–87; "The Olympian System versus the Solar Theory," *Nineteenth Century* 6 (1879): 746–68; "The Great Olympian Sedition," *Contemporary Review* 51 (1887): 757–72; "The Greater Gods of Olympus," *Nineteenth Century* 21 (1887): 460–80, 748–70 and 22 (1887): 79–102; "Universitas Hominum; or the Unity of History," *North American Review* 145 (1887): 589–602; "The Homeric Herê," *Contemporary Review* 53 (1888): 181–97; "Olympian Religion," *North American Review* 154 (1892): 231–41, 365–76, 489–502, 613–25. This list of articles may be incomplete. See also John L. Hammond, "Gladstone and the League of Nations Mind," *Essays in Honour of Gilbert Murray* (London: George Allen and Unwin, 1936), pp. 95–118; John L. Myres, *Homer and His Critics,* ed. Dorothea Gray (London: Routledge and Kegan Paul, 1958), pp. 94–122; Hugh Lloyd-Jones, "Gladstone on Homer," *Times Literary Supplement,* 3 January 1975, pp. 15–17.

39. William Ewart Gladstone, *The Impregnable Rock of Holy Scripture* (London: William Isbister, 1890), pp. 3–4.

ing was even required for a correct understanding of the Bible and of human nature and society.

As member of Parliament for Oxford and chancellor of the exchequer Gladstone had been deeply involved during the 1850s in all stages of the debate over the reform of the University. Although the reform measures imposed on Oxford by the parliamentary act of 1854 had related primarily to internal structure and organization, Gladstone knew that the questions of lay versus clerical control and religious versus secular education had been fundamental to the entire consideration of the future of the university. Opponents of reform such as E. B. Pusey had contended that any departure from the religious character of Oxford education would lead to the kind of scholarship that in Germany had fostered a critical reading of Homer and the Bible and skepticism in the minds of students.[40] Gladstone had pursued a policy of moderate reform that would allow the university to accommodate itself to new social and political realities without surrendering its own distinctive character. In 1857 he began publishing essays and books on Homer, in part to reassure his Christian friends that secular studies were a necessary complement to religious education and if properly pursued could provide a new bulwark for the faith.

Gladstone belonged to the unitarian and realist schools of Homeric scholarship. With the exception of a review article published in 1847, he discussed the Homeric question itself only in a marginal fashion.[41] He was familiar with Wolfian studies but thought they had been thoroughly refuted by later scholars. He felt the unity of plot and character in the *Iliad* strongly suggested authorship by a single poet. Gladstone's conviction of the historical realism of Homer arose from prejudice, faith in the text, and intuitive judgment, based on his own public experience, that the speeches and orations in the epics rang true to life. Those convictions led him to reject Grote's mythical view of Troy and allowed him long before Schliemann's discoveries to write about the Homeric age with a familiarity and particularity that foreshadowed the writing of archaeologists and anthropologists. Gladstone regarded the *Iliad* and *Odyssey* as still-life portraits of a dynamic

40. *Report and Evidence upon the Recommendations of Her Majesty's Commissioners for Inquiry into the State of the University of Oxford* (Oxford: Oxford University Press, 1853), Evidence, pp. 4–24.

41. Gladstone, "Lachmann's *Essays on Homer*," pp. 381–417.

and developing society. The idea that Homeric society had a past—a concept that came to predominate only late in the century through the discoveries of archaeology—was already present in Gladstone's work largely because of his Burkean sense of organic historical development.

This estimate of Homer's historical realism was fundamental to the use that Gladstone envisioned for the poet in university education. The Oxford Examination Statute of 1850 had made Homer one of the authors required for the moderations examination normally written by students after two years of study at the university.[42] In an article entitled "On the Place of Homer in Classical Education and in Historical Inquiry" published in the Oxford Essays of 1857 Gladstone urged that the study of Homer not only examine the literary excellence of the work but also consider in a comprehensive fashion the social, political, and religious life portrayed by the poet. The historical details of the epics that presented early humankind "in the free unsuspecting play of his actual nature" would permit students to observe natural human beings dwelling and growing outside the perimeters of the special dispensation of divine revelation and mission entrusted to the Hebrew nation and recorded in the Old Testament. The information in Homer provided additional knowledge about humankind and about the broader purposes of God for the human race. Gladstone asked his readers, "How is it possible to over-value this representation of the human race in a complete, distinct, and separate form with its own religion, ethics, polity, history, arts, manners, fresh and true to the standard of its nature . . . ?"[43]

Gladstone's approach to Homeric society reflected a more general attitude of Victorian Christians and one epitomized by novelist Charlotte Yonge's remark, "The history of the Jews shows what God does for men; the history of Greece shows what man does left to himself."[44] Gladstone thought that nowhere was this constrasting information more important than in regard to religion. Some British critics, such as John Stuart Blackie, had attempted to reduce the myths and religious practices recorded in the Homeric poems to a static theology.[45]

42. George Robert Michael Ward and James Heywood, trans., Oxford University Statutes, 2 vols. (London: William Pickering, 1851), 2:294.
43. Gladstone, "On the Place of Homer in Classical Education," pp. 5, 4.
44. Charlotte Yonge, Young Folks's History of Greece (Boston: D. Lothorp and Co., 1879), p. 133.
45. John Stuart Blackie, "On the Theology of Homer," Classical Review 7 (1850): 414–58.

Gladstone, on the contrary, regarded the religious materials in the epics as an eclectic collection of disparate beliefs and rituals that reflected the mixture of peoples involved in the expedition against Troy. A profusion of cults existed in the various armed camps. The several gods in Homer's narrative had been originally the particular gods of different peoples living throughout the eastern Mediterranean.

For Gladstone, religious life in the time of the Homeric epic was a transitional moment in the larger span of Greek religious development. There was evidence, on the one hand, that the religious practices of the various peoples on the Troad differed from an earlier, primitive nature worship. In that respect, what Gladstone termed the Olympian system of anthropomorphic gods had been a humanization of those earlier beliefs and practices. On the other hand, the Homeric deities, in contrast to the later portrait of the same gods in Hesiod, were highly, if imperfectly moral. Consequently, at the outset of their career among the Greeks the Olympians had acted as a force for humanity and probably for civilization even if they did later become morally degraded. In this analysis Gladstone somewhat prefigured the views of scholars, such as Jane Harrison and Gilbert Murray, who also saw the Olympians as a late religious development that displaced much of the chthonic worship.[46] It is necessary to point out these sensible elements of Gladstone's discussion of Homeric religion so that the judicious side of his thought does not become wholly obscured by his further interpretation of the Olympian system.

Gladstone combined this concrete historical approach to Homeric society with a dispensational reading of the Old Testament. He believed, in accordance with ancient Christian writers, that God had revealed his plan for redemption and salvation to humankind before the covenant with Abraham.[47] The basis for belief in this primitive

46. Gladstone's most succinct presentation of his views appears in an important letter to F. Max Müller (28 September 1864) that was published in Friedrich Max Müller, *Lectures on the Science of Language,* 6th ed. (London: Longmans, Green, and Co., 1871), 2:440–44. The original letter is in the Bodleian Library, Max Müller papers, Dep. d. 170. See also Jessie Stuart, *Jane Ellen Harrison: Portrait from Letters* (London: The Merlin Press, 1959), p. 66.

47. This interpretation of Genesis was very ancient. Modern writers upon whom Gladstone may have drawn for his particular ideas were John Leland, *The Advantage and Necessity of the Christian Revelation Shewn from the State of Religion in the Ancient Heathen World* (London, 1768); Bishop Samuel Horsley, "Dissertation on the Prophecies of the Messiah Dispersed among the Heathen," in Samuel Horsley, *Nine Sermons* (London, 1815), pp. 3–117; William Peach, *The Probable Influence of Revela-*

revelation was the promise recorded in the third chapter of Genesis that the child of the woman would bruise the head of the serpent. This promise was interpreted as prefiguring the coming of Christ through human birth to destroy the power of Satan. Gladstone, who assumed as historical events both this promise and the communion of God with various peoples before the covenant with Abraham, concluded that knowledge of the messianic promise had not been limited to the Hebrews, whom God had later chosen as the particular vessel for the fulfillment of the promise. From 1858 on Gladstone contended that a careful examination of the Homeric epics and their myths provided

> a very strong presumption, that the Hellenic portion of the Aryan family had for a time preserved to itself, in broad outline, no small share of those treasures, of which the Semitic family of Abraham were to be the appointed guardians, on behalf of mankind, until the fulness of time should come.[48]

Gladstone first enunciated this thesis in the second volume of *Studies on Homer and the Homeric Age* and never wholly abandoned the idea.[49] Though never able to satisfy himself as to how the most ancient people of the Greek race had initially received knowledge of the promise, he still held fast to his conviction that they had known of it.

Within the Homeric portrait of religious practices and beliefs Gladstone discerned three major residual elements of the primitive promise of a redeemer. These were the existence in Homer of a godhead, of the presence of an Evil One, and of the concept of a deliverer born of woman. Jupiter (Gladstone insisted on the Roman names) was "the administrator of sovereign power" and represented the "unity and supremacy of the Godhead." The common parentage but separately governed realms of Jupiter, Neptune, and Pluto suggested the idea of a Trinity. There was much less evidence for a

---

tion on the Writings of Heathen Philosophers and on the Morals of the Heathen World (Cambridge, 1819); George Chandler, *The Scheme of Divine Revelation Considered Principally in Its Connection with the Progress and Improvement of Human Society* (Oxford, 1825). See also *The New Catholic Encyclopaedia*, 1st ed., s.v. "Revelation, Primitive."

48. Gladstone, *Juventus Mundi*, p. 288.

49. Near the close of his life, Gladstone was working on a long study that would discuss the Olympian system. Notes for that work suggest he had not abandoned his hope of linking Homer and the primitive revelation. British Library Add. Mss., 44711, 44712, 44713.

concept of an Evil One, but Gladstone undauntedly pointed to the Titans. He also thought that Homer's portrayal of evil through deceit, or *Até,* might represent a very disintegrated form of a principle of evil.[50]

The figure of the Redeemer or Deliverer in Homeric religion presented a much more complicated issue. In Jewish tradition the Redeemer was to be born of the seed of woman but was also to be a spiritual Logos. In the epics Gladstone believed Apollo and Athena embodied this concept. Both stood apart from the other Olympians as the only children of Jupiter possessing extraordinarily great power. Generally their wills were in agreement with that of Jupiter. Their moral characters were of a higher quality than their fellow Olympians. Most important, their respective births conformed to the necessities of the primitive revelation. Apollo was the son of Leto, whom Gladstone identified as the woman of the promise. Athena sprang from Jupiter's head. She had no mother and was therefore equivalent to the principle of the Logos. Gladstone concluded, " . . . the differences between the birth of Athené and that of Apollo, according to Homer, correspond with the differences between the two forms of the Messianic tradition represented respectively in the Logos, and the Son of the Woman."[51] These elements of primitive tradition had been present in the religious beliefs from which Homer had constructed the anthropomorphic Olympian mythology that Gladstone felt had contributed to the overcoming of the earlier Greek worship of nature.

Needless to say, reviewers and critics universally condemned these speculations that were termed by a later biographer of Gladstone "the most fantastic in which a student could indulge."[52] Yet despite the criticism and ridicule Gladstone persisted in his views. Near the end of his life he was heard to say that proving the connection between the Olympian religion and the Hebrew revelation vied for importance only with solving the Irish question. The problem for the historian is

50. Gladstone, *Studies on Homer,* 2:42, 43, 45.

51. Gladstone, *Juventus Mundi,* p. 270. See also, Gladstone, "The Isis of Homer," pp. 141–49; Gladstone, *Studies on Homer,* 2:43–49, 130–31 and Müller, *Lectures on the Science of Language* (1871), 2:440–44.

52. *Dictionary of National Biography, Supplement,* s.v. "Gladstone, William Ewart." See also Alexander Bain, "The Intellectual Character and Writings of George Grote," in George Grote, *The Minor Works of George Grote* ed. Alexander Bain (London: John Murray, 1873), pp. 76–79.

to understand why Gladstone, in the face of evidence and learned opposition, continued to press for a connection between the Olympian mythology and an interpretation of Genesis that, as E. A. Freeman observed, had come into Jewish tradition only well after the age of Homer.[53] The issue might be dismissed as an example of Gladstone's well-known proclivity to eccentricity and stubbornness, but there is another more interesting, if nonetheless perplexing, solution.

Gladstone's reading of Homer differed from that of other commentators who from at least the seventeenth century on had attempted to link the Bible and Homer. Gladstone did not think the characters in Homer were disguised biblical personalities nor that the events in the epics derived from those in the Bible or presented a biblical typology. Rather, within the text of his own commentary, Gladstone stressed that the alleged elements of the primitive messianic tradition in Homer constituted *"a true theology falsified."*[54] Paradoxically, such a falsified or decayed system of true theology was exactly what Gladstone wanted to find.

Like Christian writers from the earliest days of the Church, Gladstone thought the history of Greek religion "demonstrated our inability to tread the way of righteousness and pardon without the Redeemer." But he also wanted to assert something more subtle than the traditional Christian attitude toward other faiths. He intended his remarks on Homer to confirm the argument from his work *The Church in Its Relations with the State* (1838) that pagan history demonstrated "how inadequate is the simple power of truth to produce permanently beneficial results on our corrupted nature, without the covenanted influences of divine grace."[55] The vessels of that grace had been the patriarchs, the Jews, and finally the Christian church with its scriptures, creeds, and, rites. The demise of true, revealed religious knowledge among the most ancient ancestors of the Greeks, as shown

53. Mrs. Humphrey Ward, *A Writer's Recollections* (London: L. W. Collins Sons and Co., 1918), p. 238; Edward A. Freeman, *Historical Essays, Second Series,* 2nd ed. (London: Macmillan and Co., 1880), pp. 71–72.

54. Gladstone, *Studies on Homer,* 2:9 (italics mine); see also Finsler, *Homer in der Neuzeit,* pp. 141–47.

55. Gladstone, *Studies on Homer,* 2:528; William Ewart Gladstone, *The State in Its Relations with the Church,* Fourth Edition, Revised and Enlarged, 2 vols. (London: John Murray, 1841), 2:369. See also *Studies on Homer,* 2:43.

by the decayed elements of genuine religious truth in the Homeric epics, demonstrated the inability of even the most gifted of human peoples to care for or to achieve through their own efforts the most significant of all knowledge without divine aid and divinely ordained institutions.

Gladstone's highly unusual and obscure apologetic was a direct reply to other alternative theories of religion. True religion could not arise from the natural exercise of human imagination or from the reasoned contemplation of nature. Religious truth must originate outside human nature and human experience and must be protected by some special vessel or institutional tradition. The vestigial elements of the primitive messianic tradition in Homer suggested that, contrary to Grote, myth was a matter not of imagination but rather of historical revelation and historical development. Imagination alone had not constructed the theological mixture present in the Homeric epics.

However, Gladstone was less concerned by outright rationalist attacks on religion, such as Grote's, than by liberal religious theorists who believed that human beings were naturally religious creatures but who had no inclination to defend Christian orthodoxy. Here the philological and solar approaches to myth and religion were Gladstone's chief targets. As early as his study of 1858 he voiced skepticism about the philological analysis of myth. He took a much stronger stand on the subject after George Cox criticized his views in a series of articles and in the *Mythology of the Aryan Nations* (1870). In 1879 Gladstone characterized the solar theory of myth as representative of the "anti-traditional" movement in contemporary thought that undermined religious authority by looking for the origins of religion in the reactions of human beings to nature or in other aspects of human psychology. Müller's "faculty of faith" was one such attempt to explain religion in terms of subjective human psychology. These approaches to myth and religion ignored the documents of revelation, provided no center for monotheism, ascribed power to physical rather than to moral entities, and allowed no place for sin in human nature.[56] Moreover, Gladstone argued that if the analysis of Müller

56. Gladstone, *Studies on Homer*, 2:30–32; George W. Cox, *The Mythology of the Aryan Nations* (London: Longmans, Green, and Co., 1870), 1:10–25; "The Historical Credibility of the Homeric Poems," *Fortnightly Review* 7 (1867): 567–80; "The Origin and Character of the Homeric Poems," *Fortnightly Review* 9 (1868): 419–36;

and Cox were correct, Greek religion should have become morally better rather than worse over the course of the centuries. The post-Homeric degradation of popular Greek religion and mythology, as well as the failure of the best minds of Greece to acquire full religious truth through the functioning of their natural mental and moral faculties, bore witness to the necessity of revealed religion and of an institution to protect that revelation. These were the reasons that Gladstone attached such importance to establishing a link between the Olympian system of Homer and the messianic promises of Genesis.

Although in Gladstone's mind the link between Homer and the book of Genesis vindicated the necessity of revealed religion, he thought that other implications of that connection demonstrated the inadequacy of the Old Testament as a guide to humankind's political, intellectual, and aesthetic character. Gladstone contended that by choosing the Hebrew nation as the instrument for the appearance of the promised messiah, God had effectively "removed it, for the time of its career, out of the family of nations." Israel's messianic mission had qualitatively separated that chosen people from the purposes for which God had originally created the human race. The task of the Hebrews had not been that of supplying "the Christian ages with laws and institutions, arts and sciences, with the chief models of greatness in genius or in character." It was, in fact, essential to their covenanted role that the ancient Hebrew nation *not* contribute to the achievement of intellectual, artistic, or material progress. As Gladstone explained his view:

> An unhonoured undistinguished race, simply elected to be the receiver of the Divine Word, and having remained its always stiffnecked and almost reluctant guardians, may best have suited the aim of Almighty Wisdom; because the medium, through which the most precious gifts were conveyed, was pale and colourless, instead of being one flushed with the splendours of Empire, Intellect, and Fame.[57]

Gladstone, "The Olympian System versus the Solar Theory," pp. 747, 749; See also George W. Cox, "Homeric Mythology and Religion," *Fraser's Magazine* 20 (1879): 798–807, and Albert Reville, *Prolegomena to the History of Religion*, trans. A. S. Squire (London: Williams and Norgate, 1884), pp. 40–48.

57. Gladstone, *Studies on Homer*, 2:525, 530, 533.

Had the Redeemer arisen in a nation skilled in the arts of civilization, then, Gladstone argued, Christianity might have come to be regarded merely as a product of a natural state of human development.

Gladstone's interpretation of the Jewish messianic mission thoroughly denigrated the possible contributions of Hebraism to the more general secular development of human culture. In particular, the special function of the Jewish nation in history rendered Old Testament society and politics inappropriate models for emulation by other nations and peoples. In his rector's address of 1865 at Edinburgh, Gladstone explained that while the Jews had been fulfilling their particular God-ordained mission, "there was other work to do, and it was done elsewhere." Much of that work had been accomplished by the Greeks. The development of their language and philosophy—"the secular counterpart of the Gospel"—later permitted the diffusion of Christianity throughout the Mediterranean world.[58] The Greeks had also nurtured certain fundamental potentialities in human nature that the messianic mission of the Hebrews prevented the chosen people from realizing. These included the capacity for art, science, philosophy, commerce, government, and all those other human activities that provided for the quality of life on earth. Those secular activities were natural to humankind as creatures of God and were as important to the fulfillment of its created nature as the plan of redemption described in the Old Testament. It was toward an understanding of humankind's first endeavors in those secular but still God-ordained labors that the Homeric epics could provide information necessarily excluded from the Old Testament record.

Through these speulations and long discussions of Homeric society and government Gladstone employed the *Iliad* and the *Odyssey* not only to champion the necessity of revealed religion but also to defend the Christian propriety of secular callings, knowledge, and progress. Gladstone sought to counter those Christians, found in both the evangelical and high-church wings of the Anglican church, who wished to confine all areas of human endeavor within the limits of biblical models and precepts. His much-belabored analysis of the epics allowed Gladstone to reconcile his own personal commitment to the Christian faith with his dedication to a political career and policies of

58. William Ewart Gladstone, *Gleanings of Past Years* (New York: Charles Scribner's Sons, n.d.), 7:81, 77.

moderate progress. Both were part of the larger plan of God for humankind. Faith in Christ and in a plan of providential redemption did not foreclose a belief in the temporal amelioration of the human condition, the moderate extension of liberty within human society, and the pursuit of beauty and knowledge in this life. Furthermore, this outlook meant that the teaching of the classics in the universities and the lessening of traditional religious instruction and influence need not indicate that those reformed institutions were any the less committed to a calling approved by God.

Gladstone's arguments produced ironic results. Just as his liberal political policies diminished the role in British life of his beloved Anglican church, his Homeric criticism made clear—as did that of no other writer of the age—the practical futility of attempting to maintain the division of history into sacred and profane orders. Gladstone had unwittingly prepared the way for a wholly humanistic appreciation of the Homeric record on the part of later commentators, such as Gilbert Murray, who no longer gave any serious consideration to providential or redemptive purposes in human history. By allowing the history of the Old Testament record to pertain so exclusively to human salvation, Gladstone made the natural achievements of the Greeks appear prescriptively adequate for temporal life. Gladstone had portrayed the Greeks of Homer's age as representative of humanity emerging toward civilization under its own direction, and by the turn of the century that was the only way British intellectuals thought civilization could emerge.

Realism, Homer, and Victorian Society

The realism that so thoroughly permeated Victorian Homeric criticism invited frequent contrasts between the society of Homer's day and that of the nineteenth century. For many readers one of the strongest attractions of the epics was the contrast their narratives provided with the quieter life of the emerging bourgeois, liberal state. The primitive, even savage, life portrayed in the poems possessed a vitality and sense of human strength not present in the midst of Reform Bill debates, mechanics institutes, and evangelical reform societies. In 1831 Professor James Wilson, writing under the pseudonym of Christopher North, waxed eloquent over the hearty days of old.

Reader, beautiful or brave! lend us your ears, while again we seek
to hold with you converse high about old Homer and the Heroic
Age. These are mechanical times in which we live; those knew of
no machinery but of the gods. Now, Science, the son of Intellect,
is sole sovereign; then, the Muses, daughters of Memory, queen-
like reigned on earth. Three thousand years ago, Rhapsodists
roamed o'er continent and isle—all last summer we saw not so
much as a poetical peddler. Reason is our idol now—we bow
down to it, and worship it; and Imagination, though she still have
a dwelling-place in the world of Poetry, has been banished from
life.[59]

Such anti-intellectual interpretations of Homer and a search for prescriptive heroic or noble values appropriate for nineteenth-century life
were a major strain in Victorian Homeric commentary. Thanks to
Grote's strong defense of the accuracy of the social and political details
in the poems, even the consideration of the Homeric question did not
intrude upon the prescriptive reading of the epics. Homer furnished
James Anthony Froude, John Stuart Blackie, John Addington
Symonds, and Matthew Arnold with copious materials to uphold the
values and social vitality they felt were missing or endangered in
contemporary liberal society.

This particular line of criticism, with its emphasis on action, nobility, and moral and physical strength, owed much to the thought of
Thomas Carlyle and his praise for the heroic life. For example, in
1851, urging along Grotean lines that "the poet is the truest historian"
and that "whatever is properly valuable in history the poet gives
us—not events and names, but emotion, but action, but life," Froude
suggested that Carlyle might well have looked to the Homeric age
rather than the Christian Middle Ages for solutions to the social problems delineated in *Past and Present*. In Homer's time human beings
were still intimately associated with their daily work, and even nobles
understood the sacramental character of labor.

The wise Ulysses built his own house, and carved his own bed.
Princes killed and cooked their own food. It was a holy work with
them—the way of saying grace for it; for they offered the animal

59. James Wilson, "Sotheby's *Homer*," *Blackwood's* 29 (1831): 829.

in his death to the gods, and they were not butchers, but sacrificing priests.

Setting aside the facets of life improved by Christianity, Froude contended it would be "difficult to point to a time when life in general was happier, and the character of man set in a more noble form."[60] In this manner Froude read into the Homeric age the qualities that Carlyle had associated with the Middle Ages. The younger writer found this transposition necessary because his own experience with the catholicizing tendencies of the Tractarian movement had made the Catholic Middle Ages anathema to him. Homeric society provided an alternative historical model upon which he could project the virtues of an organic social order.

John Stuart Blackie's comments on Homeric life similarly reflected Carlylean imperatives. Like his more famous fellow Scot, Blackie had revolted against the secular, commercial ethic of the Scotland of his youth and against the skepticism that had arisen out of the Scottish enlightenment. They also shared an admiration for Germany and a thorough distaste for the character of human life created by liberal political and economic values. Blackie's ballad-collecting Homer, while sympathetic to the poor and the humble, nonetheless maintained "a loyal admiration for kings and a just horror of democracy." More important, Homer had recognized that war could be a most effective school for national virtue. That lesson was of intense importance for the present age "when a belief in the sacredness of human life is in such favour as to have assumed the character of a beautiful disease rather than a healthy instinct." The combats and the physical prowess of the Homeric heroes displayed the importance and nobility of physical strength, which had come to be too little appreciated in the third quarter of the nineteenth century. Blackie declared:

> We are too bookish in our notions, and apt to think that by arming the brain with certain retail formulas of learning and science, and giving an examiner's certificate accordingly, we send out a proper man to the world, fit for any encounter. . . . I feel always, when I read Homer, that one of my chief pleasures consists in having to do with such lusty-bodied men, who, though

60. Froude, *Short Studies,* 2:164, 179–80, 190.

they sometimes fight to excess, are never feeble; who nowhere tell of their stomachs and their nerves, and never torture their brains with incalculable theories and unfathomable speculations.[61]

Blackie's comments on Homer as a counterweight to liberal values were published in 1865 and partook of the contemporary militant spirit displayed in *Tom Brown's School Days,* muscular Christianity, the volunteer movement, and the defense of Governor Eyre.

Within classical studies, nothing so clearly epitomized the drive toward bourgeois respectability that Blackie destested as the solar theory of myth. The philological theorists had not hesitated to apply their formula to the Homeric tales and to scorch Homer's heroic vitality in the burning rays of the sun. In 1864 Max Müller had explained, "The siege of Troy is but a repetition of the daily siege of the East by the solar powers that every evening are robbed of their brightest treasures in the West." As usual, George Cox carried the solar interpretation to a further degree of insipid gentility. In his *Manual of Mythology* he interpreted the vengeance of Achilles as "the victory of the sun, when, at the end of a stormy day, he comes forth from the mists and tramples on the clouds which have veiled his splendours." The savage duel between Achilles and Hector that had stirred the emotions and imaginations of readers for centuries represented

the mighty battle of the vapors and the sun, which seems to trample on the darkness, just as Achilles tramples on the body of Hector: and as this victory of the sun is gained just as he is sinking into the sea, so the death of Achilles is said to follow very soon after that of Hector.[62]

---

61. Blackie, *Homer and the "Iliad,"* 1:148, 156, 157–58. The last passage may well owe something to John Ruskin's chapter "Of Classical Landscape," *Modern Painters,* vol. 3. See John Ruskin, *The Works of John Ruskin,* 39 vols., ed. E. T. Cook and Alexander Wedderburn (London: George Allen, 1904), 5:221–47.

62. Friedrich Max Müller, *Studies on the Science of Language,* New Edition (London: Longmans, Green, and Co., 1885), 2:515; George Cox, *A Manual of Mythology in the Form of Questions and Answers,* First American from the Second London Edition (New York: Leypoldt and Holt, 1868), pp. 212–13. For a major critique of Müller and Cox from a historical standpoint, see John P. Mahaffy, *Prolegomena to Ancient History* (London: Longmans, Green, and Co., 1871), pp. 43–95.

The flight from vigor, health, and heroism could not go much further. Achilles' character clearly so repulsed Cox's sensibility and was so repugnant to the values he approved that the heroic personality had to be denied reality. Cox and Müller were led to these explications by the logic of the solar theory, but their adherence to that theory, as well as the substance of its application, reflect the attempt to flee the darker, passionate depths of human nature.

The most vehement opponent of this solar interpretation of Greek life was John Addington Symonds. In *Studies of the Greek Poets* (1873) Symonds forcefully denied that Achilles was a setting sun. The subject of the *Iliad* was not clouds or vapor but "the Passion of Achilles"—his passionate anger against Agamemnon and his passionate love for Patroclus. Those superhuman passions could no more be reduced to solar myths than could the sexual energies present in other mythic narratives.

> The Mythus of Achilles may possibly in very distant ages have expressed some simple astronomical idea. But for a man to think of this with the actual *Iliad* before his eyes would be about as bad as botanising on his mother's grave. Homer was not thinking of the sun when he composed the *Iliad*. He wove, as in a web, all elements of tragic pity and fear, pathos and passion and fateful energy, which constitute the dramas of nations and of men.

The qualities of Achilles pertained to the epoch when the human race was emerging from barbarism toward civilization. There was nothing small, mean, petty, or soft about that hero who became the ideal of a race that, despite all Victorian attempts at domestication, had "subordinated morals to art, and politics to personality."[63]

Symonds attributed to Achilles the mode of heroism that Carlyle had made familiar to mid-Victorian readers. Achilles stood larger than life and by his very nature had to dwell beyond the morality that applied to ordinary people.

> To Achilles, to Alexander, to Napoleon, we cannot apply the rules of our morality. It is, therefore, impossible for us, who must aim first at being good citizens, careful in our generation, and

63. John Addington Symonds, *Studies of the Greek Poets,* 3rd ed. (London: Adam and Charles Black, 1893), 1:80, 82, 96.

subordinate to the laws of society around us, to admire them
without a reservation. Yet, after all is said, a great and terrible
glory does rest upon their heads; and though our sentiments
of propriety may be offended by some of their actions, our
sense of what is awful and sublime is satisfied by the contemplation of them. No one should delude us into thinking that true
culture does not come from the impassioned study of everything,
however eccentric and at variance with our mode of life, that is
truly great. Greatness, of whatever species it may be, is
always elevating and spirit-stirring.[64]

Symonds was here replying not only to the solar theorists, but also to
the purveyors of domesticated Hellenism, such as Gladstone and Arnold, who were unwilling to confront the full moral implications of
Homer's epics. Gladstone had once described the Homeric kings as
being similar to Christian gentlemen.[65] Arnold had sought to impose
the values of traditional neoclassical humanism on the poems. Both
writers wanted to partake of the idealism of the Homeric age without
embracing its heroism and savagery. Symonds recognized, like
Nietzsche, that the Homeric Greeks had dwelled beyond the moral
boundaries of modern life and presented an image of humanity altogether different from the nineteenth-century bourgeois vision.

The contrast between Gladstone's and Symonds's prescriptive discussions of Homeric society emerged very clearly in regard to the
women in the poems. According to Gladstone, Homeric Greek society tolerated neither prostitution nor homosexuality. Its manners
were equally restrained, and its laws of marriage recognized
monogamy, prohibited degrees, and "the natural perpetuity of the
marriage contract." There were no examples of divorced couples.
Paris was never described by the Greeks as the husband of Helen, and
Menelaus received her back. Penelope through all the long years remained faithful to Ulysses.

The Heroic age has left no more comely monument, than its
informal, but instinctive, and most emphatic sense, thus recorded
for our benefit, of the sanctity of marriage, of the closeness of the
union it creates, and of the necessity of perpetuity as an element of

64. Ibid., p. 107.
65. Gladstone, *Studies on Homer,* 2:467.

its capacity to attain its chief ends, and to administer a real discipline to the human character.

It was no wonder that Gladstone was accused of carrying his crusade
against the Divorce Act of 1857 into his commentary on the epics. He
even contended that the concubinage of the chiefs besieging Troy
constituted, "especially if the connections were single, the mildest and
least licentious of all the forms in which the obligations of the marriage
tie could be relaxed."[66] Although this double standard was not extended to women, Gladstone thought it significant that widows had
remained free to marry.

A direct line of descent would seem to extend from Gladstone's
portrait of domestic morality in the Homeric epics to Gilbert Murray's
concept of a priggish "Homeric spirit" expurgating immorality from
earlier versions of the poems.[67] Both Gladstone and Murray sought to
discover in Homeric society a tendency toward natural moral progress,
and both found that tendency confirmed in the sexual conduct of the
Homeric heroes. Gladstone had hoped to demonstrate that natural
reason and revelation need not differ on moral issues. He also had to
prove that the substance of natural Homeric morality did not differ too
extensively from the moral code of the Old Testament if he were to
convince clerical Oxford of the utility of Homer. Gladstone's influence lingered over the study and teaching of Homer. His books would
naturally have been consulted by teachers at Oxford when Murray
studied there, and even by the turn of the century his work remained
the most extensive English commentary on Homeric society and politics. His theology aside, Gladstone's commentaries also appealed to
late nineteenth-century and early twentieth-century liberals who believed in progress and cosmopolitan attitudes in international relations. Finally, Gladstone unlike Arnold and his followers, had portrayed the Greeks of Homer's day as achieving civilization rather than
epitomizing timeless noble values.

Gladstone was able to provide or invent mitigating interpretations
of questionable social customs in Homer, but the moral qualities of the
heroes and heroines in the epics were less easy to gloss over. The major

66. Ibid., pp. 487, 489, 497, See also Herman Merivale, "Mr. Gladstone's
Homeric Studies," *Edinburgh Review* 108 (1858): 531.
67. Gladstone, *Studies on Homer*, 2:467.

difficulty was the character and conduct of Helen of Troy. Her situation and motivations were highly problematical. Had Paris forced her to leave the court and bed of Menelaus or had she forwarded the action and been a willing victim? William Mure called her "the fair adulteress" and declared that she and Paris stood as "unprincipled votaries of sensual enjoyment; both self-willed and petulant, but not devoid of amiable and generous feeling." Gladstone, who walked the streets of London to rescue prostitutes, dissented from Mure's judgment and pointed to the "vast space between a faultless and a worthless woman." For him it was simply inconceivable that Homer would have portrayed a multitude of Greek heroes embarked on a long, drawn-out war to avenge a worthless woman. In the epics themselves everyone regarded Helen as essentially blameless. Moreover, Gladstone felt she compared quite favorably to the biblical Bathsheba who was not recorded as grieving over the death of Uriah as Helen was over the fallen Greek warriors. Although Helen was not made of the stuff of martyrs nor possessed of the highest moral sense, she still remained "endowed with much tenderness of feeling, with the highest grace and refinement, and with a deep and peculiar sense of shame for having done wrong." In all classical literature nothing approached "so nearly to what Christian theology would term a sense of sin, as the humble demeanor, and the self-denouncing, self-stabbing language of the Argeian Helen."[68] In effect Gladstone transformed Helen into the repentant fallen woman of the Victorian domestic novel. She was a morally acceptable character only to the degree that she resembled not a Greek woman but rather a Hebrew maiden of a properly ascetic disposition.

Symonds's commentary on Homer's women was not lacking in certain strains of conventionality, but on the whole he still recognized and admired the genuinely pagan elements in Helen's character. For Symonds, Helen did possess a conscience and could recognize the nobility of Hector and the ignobility of Paris. Yet Helen was not to be regarded as a model for other women. Symonds felt, ". . . there is no woman who, reading the *Iliad,* would not choose to weep with Andromache in Hector's arms, rather than to smile like Helen in the laps of lovers for whom she little cared." Helen was bound as if by chains

68. Mure, *A Critical History of the Language and Literature of Antient Greece,* 1:344, 358; Gladstone, *Studies on Homer,* 3:572, 576–77, 584–85.

to the service of Aphrodite, and the lack of steadfast love in her life was one cost of that service. Over the centuries Helen had remained symbolic of "the indestructible Hellenic spirit" that had never learned the lesson of the fall of man in the garden of Eden. The continuing attraction of Helen for later ages was just the very freshness of this paganism. The other women of Homer displayed a similar freedom of spirit that even in its chasteness was perennially attractive. Penelope, whom Symonds compared to a Hebrew heroine, in her guile, prudence, and tenacity represented nothing less than humanity itself. In Nausicaä he saw "the most perfect maiden, the purest, freshest, lightest-hearted girl of Greek romance." In her encounter with Ulysses she proved herself to be "as free from coquetry as she is from prudishness."[69] For Symonds, all of these women dwelled in that golden childhood of the race described by the German Hellenists. They flourished in such remarkable beauty because social convention and spiritual asceticism had not constrained their inner humanity.

Matthew Arnold had, of course, drunk at the same springs of German Hellenism, but he had become less heady than Symonds. Arnold also had looked to Homeric poetry as a corrective to the humdrum mediocrity of bourgeois life. But in contrast to Symonds or Blackie, Arnold had thought Homer's poetry could fulfill that mission only if it were drawn into the cultural and literary tradition of classical Greece. In light of Arnold's Viconian concept of history and analogous ages, such a reading was necessary if Homer were to be relevant to the nineteenth century. Arnold had outlined his views on the character of Homeric poetry and its proper style of English translation in his *Lectures on the Translation of Homer* (1861). The target of those lectures was the translation of the *Iliad* by Francis Newman, the brother of John Henry Newman and a teacher at University College London. Francis Newman was one of the great Victorian eccentrics, and his translation of the *Iliad* is today remembered primarily for its having used the meter of "Yankee Doodle" and for having been attacked by Arnold. However, it was more than a disagreement over taste that elicited Arnold's criticism. Newman, explaining in 1856 the ideas behind his translation, described Homeric culture as being in a "half-developed condition" and Homeric verse as "direct, popular, forcible,

69. Symonds, *Studies of the Greek Poets*, 1:115, 125, 134, 136.

quaint, flowing, garrulous," and "similar to the old English ballad."[70] He also argued that the language of Homer, like the society it portrayed, had been very different from that of Periclean Greece. In his translation Newman had attempted in his own curious manner to convey the spirit and to suggest the rhetoric of that archaic age.

Arnold countered Newman on almost every point. He pursued a moderately unitary approach to Homeric authorship and rejected the ballad or rhapsodist origins of the epics and consequently Newman's style of translation based on that theory. He denied that the Homeric epics were popular poetry and argued that Homer had written to please an aristocratic or noble audience. The distinctive qualities Arnold discerned in the author of the poems were

> that he is eminently rapid; that he is eminently plain and direct, both in the evolution of his thought and in the expression of it, that is both in his syntax and in his words; that he is eminently plain and direct in the substance of his thought, that is, in the matter and ideas; and finally, that he is eminently noble.

The *Iliad* and the *Odyssey* throughout bore the stamp of the grand style that arose in poetry "when a noble nature, poetically gifted, treats with simplicity or with severity a serious subject."[71] Newman's translation obscured all these qualities as well as the moral impact they might have on the reader. His theories and translations also improperly separated Homeric poetry from its clear connection with the classical age. There were archaisms in Homer, but they had not been more unfamiliar to the reader of fifth-century Athens than was the language of Elizabethan England to the English reader of the mid-nineteenth century.

Arnold was determined to rescue Homer from eccentric translators and from a mode of historicized reading that would remove the epics from the realm of Hellenic culture. His particular defense of the Hellenic and classical character of Homer was reminiscent of those critics

---

70. Francis W. Newman, "Preface," Francis W. Newman, *The "Iliad" of Homer Faithfully Translated into Unrhymed English Metre* (London: Walton and Maberly, 1856), p. iv. See also Francis W. Newman, *Homeric Translation in Theory and Practice: A Reply to Matthew Arnold, Esq.* (London: Williams and Norgate, 1861). Newman's preface to the second edition of his translation of the *Iliad* (1867) is the most concise statement of his views on Homeric poetry.

71. Arnold, *On the Classical Tradition*, pp. 102, 188.

who a century earlier had championed Pope's translations against detractors and historical critics. For Arnold, Homer as a living poet must represent nobility and good taste. In the major critical circles it was primarily Arnold's views that triumphed. Homer came to be seen as a source of those restrained Hellenic values that Arnold and his followers hoped might flourish in British culture and society. In *Homer* (1887), probably the most widely read late-century guide to the poet, Richard Claverhouse Jebb maintained that "the Homeric poems are the oldest documents of Hellenic life" and that "the Homeric Greek exhibits all the essential characteristics and aptitudes which distinguish his descendant in the historical age."[72] Homer and humanistic Hellenism seemed firmly linked. Homer had become a purveyor of sweetness and light to the middle classes.

This interpretation of Homer and the social elitism attached to it led to a surprisingly paradoxical situation among British Homeric scholars during the last two decades of the century. For most readers and students of Homer, the unearthing of Troy, Mycenae, and Tiryns provided a happy confirmation to one degree or another of the historical reality of Homeric times. However, for others like Jebb, who along with Arnold regarded the Homeric epics as the fountainhead of Hellenic culture, confrontation with the ruins of Homeric civilization was not necessarily a happy experience. It was unclear that the cities discovered by Schliemann and others could have fostered a culture with the values the English humanistic critics wished to make prescriptive. More important, the civilization of Mycenae seemed distinctively different from that of the classical age. The discoveries of the archaeologists in effect separated Homer, his verse, and his society from later Hellenic civilization.

Jebb was the British literary scholar most disturbed by the implications of archaeology. The predominant realism of British Homeric criticism meant he could not easily defend a Hellenic Homer on poetic or imaginative grounds. He and Arnold had argued that real historical links existed between the Homeric and classical ages. Nor could he join Max Müller in denying any historical basis for Homer's narrative. Rather, to preserve the Hellenism of Homer, Jebb had to question the integrity of the interpretation of the archaeological discoveries. Suffi-

72. Jebb, *Homer: An Introduction to the "Iliad" and "Odyssey,"* p. 38.

cient disagreement existed among all concerned for a lively debate to ensue. The major question was not whether the cities unearthed were exactly those described by Homer but rather whether they were of the same civilization. The conflict eventually settled on the unlikely issue of the architecture of the Homeric house.[73] Several writers evaluating the evidence believed the buildings unearthed at Tiryns were similar to those described in the poems. If true, this discovery meant that Homeric culture was quite different from Hellenic culture. Jebb argued that the houses were not the same, and for a time, until proved wrong, he suggested that much of the Tirynsian ruins were actually Byzantine. The debate over the Homeric house continues and has taken on a scholarly life of its own. However, no small part of its instigation was the desire on the part of Jebb to preserve Homer as part of the literary armory of Arnoldian Hellenism.

By the nineties scholars had taken another approach to defending the nobility of the Homeric poems. At this time Walter Leaf, who had been educated at Cambridge but spent most of his life in banking, was probably the most ditinguished Homeric scholar in Great Britain. His edition of the *Iliad* and his earlier commentary on the epic summarized the textual and historical scholarship of the century. In *A Companion to the "Iliad" for English Readers* (1892) Leaf contended that the epic was not Hellenic but Mycenaean. But the change in the cultural origin of the poem did not detract from its essential nobility nor did it mean that the work had in any sense been popular. Leaf explained:

> The Iliad and Odyssey are essentially and above all court poems. They were composed to be sung in the splendid palaces of a ruling aristocracy, and the commonality have no part or lot as actors in them. . . . [T]he poems are aristocratic and courtly, not popular.

Furthermore, Leaf argued, the poems should not be associated with "a young and primitive people." They were rather "the offspring of an

73. Friedrich Max Müller, "Dr. Schliemann's Book on Troy," *The Academy* 5 (1874): 39–41; John Linton Myres, *Homer and His Critics*, pp. 154–56, 165–72. See also Charles Thomas Newton, "Dr. Schliemann's Discoveries at Ilium Novum," *The Academy* 5 (1874): 173; Philip Smith, "Discoveries at Troy," *Quarterly Review* 136 (1874): 526–66; Richard Claverhouse Jebb, "Schliemann's *Ilios*," *Edinburgh Review* 15 (1881): 514–47; Richard Claverhouse Jebb, "The Ruins at Hissarlik, and Their Relation to the *Iliad*," *Journal of Hellenic Studies* 3 (1882): 202.

advanced civilization, the growth of centuries."[74] In this manner the *Iliad* and *Odyssey* retained the aristocratic excellence required of them for prescriptive use in the schools and also represented the product of a high civilization that could be relevant to readers living in a later high civilization. Leaf thus linked nobility to archaeological realism.

Nonetheless, the new disciplines of archaeology and, to a lesser extent, anthropology spelled the end of the noble vision of Homeric society and poetry that had been shared by most late-century commentators. For writers influenced by anthropology, the epics became examples of the folktales or *Märchen* that were told in many primitive societies.[75] The continuing impact of archaeology upon the existing realistic tradition of British criticism led to a triviality of discourse of which the debate over the Homeric house was an example, to commentary on the poems through pictures or drawings of the archaeological remains, and finally to the transformation of Homeric characters into bourgeois British subjects. As Geoffrey Hartman has observed in another context, "When empathy becomes conventional, and the new or alien loses its aureole of sacred danger, it is increasingly difficult to admit transcendent personality or real difference."[76] The choice that seemed to confront late-century critics and commentators was to conceive Homer and his society as totally different from the present day and in effect to deny any direct cultural relevance or to transform Homeric society into a mirror image of the contemporary world. In both cases there occurred a flight from the text and from the imagination of Homer himself.

In several books on Homer published between 1893 and 1910 Andrew Lang followed the first course. Representing what might be termed Homeric fundamentalism, Lang argued that the epics had been composed during a single period by no more than two authors. Lang's

---

74. Leaf, *A Companion to the "Iliad" for English Readers,* pp. 2, 3; See also Walter Leaf and M. A. Bayfield, *The "Iliad" of Homer Edited with General and Grammatical Introductions, Notes and Appendices,* 2 vols. (London: Macmillan and Co., 1898), 1:ix–xv and Leaf, *The "Iliad," Edited,* 1:xv–xix.

75. Frank Byron Jevons, *A History of Greek Literature from the Earliest Period to the Death of Demosthenes* (London: Charles Griffin and Company, 1886), p. 19; David Binning Monro, ed., *Homer's "Odyssey," Books XII–XXIV, with English Notes and Appendices* (Oxford: Clarendon Press, 1901), pp. 289–92.

76. Geoffrey Hartman, *Beyond Formalism: Literary Essays 1958–1970* (New Haven: Yale University Press, 1970), p. 70.

return to a modified unitarian position foreshadowed the general course of twentieth-century Homeric criticism, though not its basis, which was developed later by Milman Parry. Lang's volumes were full of pictures of archaeological remains, shields, weapons, and clothing that to a large extent constituted his proof for the integrity of the poems. No matter how much he protested his admiration for the glory of the verse, the grounds for his exaltation were exceedingly mundane. This evidence may well have suggested, in line with Grote's view, a poet who could correctly report what he had seen but certainly not one who could have produced a monument of the literary imagination. This emphasis on the everyday realism of the epics rendered Lang's Homer little more than a quaint curiosity and a good reporter of ancient times. His society, his clothes, his religion were simply too different and too far removed from the late nineteenth century to suggest much contemporary value for English readers. The same judgment would also be true of the effect of more scholarly works such as *The Early Age of Greece* (1901) by William Ridgeway of Cambridge and *Homer and History* (1915) by Walter Leaf.[77] Homer, his imagination, his heroes, and his poetry were lost under a welter of archaeological evidence and theories.

The second course was to interpret Homer through the categories of contemporary British literary realism. Samuel Butler, the author of *Erewhon* and *The Way of All Flesh* and the critic of Charles Darwin's intellectual integrity, exemplified this approach. In *The Authoress of the "Odyssey"* (1897) Butler pursued Homeric realism with a vengeance. He argued that the epic had been written by a young, unmarried woman who had lived near Trapani in Sicily. His young authoress had composed her poem with the same attention to the intimate detail of real life and social setting that generally characterized Butler's own novels. The theory of the female authorship of the *Odyssey* has evoked

---

77. Andrew Lang, *Homer and the Epic* (New York: AMS Press, 1971; 1st ed., 1893); *Homer and His Age* (London: Longmans, Green, and Co., 1906); *The World of Homer* (London: Longmans, Green, and Co., 1910); Adam Parry, "Introduction," Milman Parry, *The Making of Homeric Verse: The Collected Papers of Milman Parry*, ed. Adam Parry (Oxford: Clarendon Press, 1971), pp. ix–lxii; William Ridgeway, *The Early Age of Greece* (Cambridge: Cambridge University Press, 1901), pp. 336, 683–84; Walter Leaf, *Homer and History* (London: Macmillan and Co., 1915). See also Walter Leaf, *Troy: A Study in Homeric Geography* (London: Macmillan and Co., 1912).

much humor ever since Butler proposed it; however, there can be no question as to Butler's sincerity. The quest for the authoress became nothing less than an obsession with him during the latter part of his life. With admiralty charts, maps, and his camera Butler spent several years tracing what he thought to be the route of Odysseus in the vicinity of Sicily. Jane Harrison in her autobiography recalled Butler's having badgered her with his views in the restaurant of an Athenian hotel.[78]

Although *The Authoress of the "Odyssey"* may seem an odd book, it nonetheless fits directly into the context of Victorian Homeric commentary and criticism. Butler combined Gladstone's intense domestication of Homeric society with Symonds's rejection of bourgeois values. He based his theory of female authorship directly on his own expectations of normal male and female behavior. The "whitewashed" character of Penelope provided the key evidence for the female authorship of the epic. For Butler, only a woman could portray another woman surrounded by more than a hundred suitors pestering her for years and refraining from seeking other wives until she had made her decision. Such vanity flowed naturally from the feminine character. The fear that scandal might touch Penelope and the absence of driving passion on her part and on the part of the suitors suggested that the writer of the *Odyssey* could not possibly "have even the faintest conception of the way in which a man feels towards a woman he is in love with, nor yet much (so far as I may venture to form an opinion) of what women commonly feel towards the man of their choice." Such naive ignorance suggested the writer of the epic was a relatively young, unmarried woman. Butler's long list of reasons for believing in female authorship concluded with the observation, "When Ulysses and Penelope are in bed and are telling their stories to one another, Penelope tells hers first. I believe a male writer would have made Ulysses' story come first and Penelope's second."[79] All the domestic relations that Gladstone had suggested were present in Butler's portrait, but the privacy and sense of decorum were mis-

78. Henry Festing Jones, *Samuel Butler, Author of Erewhon (1835–1902): A Memoir* (London: Macmillan and Co., 1919), 2:264–81; Jane Ellen Harrison, *Reminiscences of a Student's Life,* 2nd ed. (London: The Hogarth Press, 1925), p. 70.

79. Samuel Butler, *The Authoress of the "Odyssey," Where and When She Wrote, Who She Was, the Use She Made of the "Iliad," and How the Poem Grew Under Her Hands* (London: J. Cape, 1922; 1st ed., 1897), pp. 127–28, 157.

sing. Penelope and Ulysses were all too real and all too much like the local tradesman and his spouse—neither better nor worse nor more nor less admirable.

Butler's ironic bourgeois reduction of the characters in the *Odyssey* made a significant contribution to the future appreciation of Homer. Butler had simultaneously vanquished both the Hebraic and the Hellenic reading of the poem. He had also denied the presence of the heroic. In Butler's analysis the central fact of the *Odyssey* was that of "a bald elderly gentleman, whose little remaining hair is red, being eaten out of house and home during his absence by a number of young men who are courting the supposed widow—a widow who, if she be fair and fat, can hardly also be less than forty."[80] Butler in his rather offhanded fashion transformed the *Odyssey* into a story whose hero was in fact an antihero and into a work the realism of which was confirmed by its attention to the trivialities and dullness of everyday life.

Unlikely though it may seem, it was Butler's mode of realism that helped to carry the Homeric epics into the mainstream of twentieth-century literature. Late nineteenth-century novelists and their successors had difficulty in dealing with the heroic upheld by Blackie and Symonds, with the virtuous so admired by Gladstone, and with the noble as advocated by Arnold. The new novelists looked to realism and championed the antihero. Butler was one of the persons who transmitted the Homeric heritage to that new generation. James Joyce read *The Authoress of the "Odyssey"* and may also have used Butler's translation of the epic. There is also reason to believe that Joyce's confidence in his ability to recreate the Dublin of his youth literary brick by literary brick stemmed in part from his reading of Butler's volume.[81] It would be wrong and perhaps even silly to claim any

80. Samuel Butler, *Collected Essays,* 20 vols. (London: Jonathan Cape, 1925), 2:270. For another writer who also treated Homer's women without romance, see F. Melian Stawell, *Homer and the "Iliad": An Essay to Determine the Scope and Character of the Original Poem* (London: J. M. Dent and Co., 1909), pp. 109–29.

81. Hugh Kenner, "Homer's Sticks and Stones," *James Joyce Quarterly* 6 (1969): 292–97; Hugh Kenner, *The Pound Era* (Berkeley: University of California Press, 1971), pp. 46–51; William Bedell Stanford, *The Ulysses Theme,* 2nd ed. (New York: Barnes and Noble, 1964) p. 276n; Michael Seidel, *Epic Geography: James Joyce's Ulysses* (Princeton: Princeton University Press, 1976), pp. x, 47, 84–86. Robert Graves adopted Butler's theory of a female author of the *Odyssey* for his novel *Homer's Daughter* (New York: Doubleday and Co., 1955), pp. 7–9.

major influence for *The Authoress of the "Odyssey"* on Joyce's *Ulysses*.
Yet without attempting to press a point further than is warranted, it is
worth noting that Butler's book was the only commentary in English
that discussed the *Odyssey* without either Hebraicizing or Hellenizing
it. Moreover, though lacking both Joyce's genius and industry, Butler
had transformed the story of the epic into the tale of an antihero and
into categories of late nineteenth-century domestic life. In other
words, Butler, as the eccentric heir to Victorian Homeric commentary
and as a great despiser of respectable social and intellectual conventions, so disposed of the materials of the epic as to leave them ready for
a new modern literary genius to retell.

George Grote with a folio volume containing his note slips for *A History of Greece*
(National Portrait Gallery, London)

William Mitford

G. B. Grundy

5
THE DEBATE OVER
THE ATHENIAN
CONSTITUTION

In 1915 when it became apparent that the war with Germany would involve a prolonged conflict, new posters appeared in the advertising slots on London buses. ·The placards displayed excerpts from the funeral oration Pericles had delivered in 431 B.C. over the bodies of Athenian soldiers who had fallen during the first year of the Peloponnesian War.[1] To the university-trained civil servants charged with the propaganda effort, the call of Pericles for steadfastness against Sparta seemed to provide appropriate inspiration for modern citizens of a liberal, commercial nation engaged in a struggle with a largely absolutist, militaristic state. The spirit and values of the ancient Athenian polis so memorably set forth by Pericles symbolized in the minds of many educated people the social and political solidarity to which the modern British democracy should aspire. The Athenian ideals of equality before and obedience to the law, of the participation of the citizenry in public life, of government by open discussion, and of appreciation for the good and the beautiful as well as for the strong and the useful epitomized the civic experience and achievement for which a generation of Britons would perish in the Flanders mud. No doubt many of the young officers in the trenches understood and admired the literature of classical Athens more than that of England. They also may very well have identified more intimately with the victors at Marathon and Salamis, and later perhaps with the victims of the Syracusan folly, than they did with the knights of Agincourt, the

1. Graham Wallas, *Our Social Heritage* (New Haven: Yale University Press, 1921), p. 166.

187

victors against the Armada, the sailors at Trafalgar, the troops at Waterloo, or the soldiers at Sevastopol.

During the nineteenth century the perception of a close relationship between the political history of ancient Athens and Great Britain had emerged as an almost unquestioned assumption for numerous British intellectuals. John Stuart Mill had once declared, "The battle of Marathon, even as an event in English history, is more important than the battle of Hastings." Lord Acton, a more conservative Victorian liberal, had suggested that modern Britain shared with Periclean Athens "the idea that the object of constitutions is not to confirm the predominance of any interest, but to prevent it; to preserve with equal care the independence of labour and the security of property; to make the rich safe against envy, and the poor against oppression." Matthew Arnold's essays had presented Periclean Athens as an example of what a modern state should seek to achieve in the cultural and political life of its people. Near the close of the century Gilbert Murray claimed that "the reasoned daring" of Athenian "social and political ideals" appealed to late Victorians more strongly than those of eighteenth-century Britain. During the turbulence of the Edwardian years Richard Livingstone could point to the stability of Athens and the absence of party strife as an ideal toward which modern political life should strive. By 1915, Alfred Zimmern, a university classicist recruited to the civil service for the war effort, wrote in all seriousness:

> Greek ideas and Greek inspiration can help us to-day, not only in facing the duties of the moment, but in the work of deepening and extending the range and the meaning of Democracy and Citizenship, Liberty and Law, which would seem to be the chief political task before mankind in the new epoch of history on which we have suddenly entered.[2]

Various books that appeared shortly after the war echoed similar sentiments.

2. John Stuart Mill, "Grote's *History of Greece*," *Edinburgh Review* 84 (1846): 343; Lord Acton, *Essays on Freedom and Power*, ed. Gertrude Himmelfarb (Boston: Beacon Press, 1948), p. 39; Gilbert Murray, *A History of Ancient Greek Literature* (New York: D. Appleton and Co., 1897), p. 1; Alfred E. Zimmern, *The Greek Commonwealth: Politics and Economics in Fifth Century Athens*, 2nd ed. (Oxford: Clarendon Press, 1915), p. 5.

Such favorable commentary on the Athenian political experience and its prescriptive linkage to British political life would have seemed nothing less than impossible a century earlier. Eighteenth-century and early nineteenth-century political commentators had consistently pointed to Athens as a key example of civic lawlessness, political disorder, and the absence of personal security. The authors of the first substantial English narrative histories of ancient Greece intended their books to serve as unabashedly antidemocratic polemics. In 1786 John Gillies, the historiographer-royal of Scotland and a prolific author of classical studies directed toward contemporary political issues, expressed the hope that his description of the Athenian democracy might demonstrate "the incurable evils inherent in every form of Republican polity" and "the inestimable benefits" of "hereditary Kings, and the steady operations of well-regulated Monarchy."[3] The movement of thought from the strictures of Gillies to the effusion of Zimmern is in part the story of the transformation of commentary on Athenian politics from a stronghold of conservative polemic into a model of liberal political development and behavior. But it is also the story of the transformation of British political thought itself.

The Image of Athens in the Eighteenth Century

During the first three quarters of the eighteenth century Athens captured neither the political nor the historical imagination of British intellectuals. The experience of Rome loomed much more prominently in their thought and writing. A few histories of Greece with extensive treatments of Athens did appear, including Temple Stanyan's *The Grecian History* (1739), the volumes of *An Universal History* (1744), and Oliver Goldsmith's *The Grecian History* (1774). The message of these books was more or less uniformly one of praise for Sparta and condemnation of Athens. In the view of these writers, as in that of more important Continental authors, among them Montesquieu and Rousseau, Sparta appeared as a strong, stable polity immune from the political unrest, party factions, and turbulent leader-

3. John Gillies, *The History of Ancient Greece, Its Colonies, and Conquests from the Earliest Accounts till the Division of the Macedonian Empire in the East Including the History of Literature, Philosophy, and the Fine Arts*, 3rd ed., 2 vols. (London: A. Strahan and T. Cadell, 1792), 1:iii.

ship that had marked Athenian political life. For example, Stanyan attacked the constitution that Solon had constructed for the citizens of Athens.

> Since therefore they would admit of no Government, but a *Democracy*, he [Solon] form'd his Laws according to that Model. It did not indeed come up to that of *Sparta* laid down by Lycurgus; and the Difference is easily accounted for, from the Temper of the *Athenians*, which was too delicate, and capricious, to be brought to those grave and regular Austerities; and without considering the great Sway the People bore in the Execution of the Laws, the Laws themselves were more numerous and confus'd, and could not therefore be so religiously observ'd as they were at *Sparta*.

The same writer also condemned the institution of ostracism, the failure of the Athenians to appreciate gifted leaders, and their vulnerability to demagogues such as Cleon. By such arguments Stanyan hoped to convince his English readers that "our Liberty is better secured to us, than it could be in any of the Republics of Greece."[4]   The favoring of Sparta over Athens was a long-standing tradition in European thought. In eighteenth-century Britain it had derived further support from the political ideology of the Country party. Numerous recent studies have made clear the significance of this mode of thought in eighteenth-century politics. Spokesmen for these ideas drew upon concepts from Polybius, Machiavelli, and James Harrington to urge the necessity of a balanced constitution for the preservation of liberty.[5] In their view, each component of the constitution had to maintain its

4. Temple Stanyan, *The Grecian History from the Original of Greece to the End of the Peloponnesian War,* 2 vols. (London: J. & R. Tonson, 1739), 1:180–81; 2: Preface, n.p.

5. Elizabeth Rawson, *The Spartan Tradition in European Thought* (Oxford: Clarendon Press, 1969); Zera Silver Fink, *The Classical Republicans: An Essay in the Recovery of a Pattern of Thought in Seventeenth Century England* (Evanston, Ill.: Northwestern University Press, 1945); Caroline A. Robbins, *The Eighteenth-century Commonwealthman: Studies in the Transmission, Development and Circumstances of English Liberal Thought from the Restoration of Charles II until the War with the Thirteen Colonies* (Cambridge, Mass.: Harvard University Press, 1959); Bernard Bailyn, *The Ideological Origins of the American Revolution* (Cambridge, Mass.: Harvard University Press, Belknap Press, 1965); Isaac F. Kramnick, *Bolingbroke and His Circle: The Politics of Nostalgia in the Age of Walpole* (Cambridge, Mass.: Harvard University Press, 1963); John G. A. Pocock, *Politics, Language and Time: Essays in Political Thought and History* (New York: Atheneum, 1971), pp. 104–47; John G. A. Pocock, *The Machiavellian Moment: Florentine Political Thought and the Atlantic Republican Tradition* (Princeton: Princeton University Press, 1975), pp. 333–461.

independence of the others. It was particularly important that men of property in the Commons remain independent of the influence of the monarchy. The specter of corruption of the constitutional balance haunted these thinkers. They believed that such corruption had been occurring in England since 1688, especially since Walpole's ascendancy. Its instruments were government-sponsored placemen in Parliament, standing armies, excessive taxes that put vast sums of money at the disposal of the monarchy, and excessive commercial prosperity that led to factional politics and political influence independent of real property. In the eyes of some writers who promoted this ideology, Athens provided an example of such a thoroughly corrupted, unbalanced political regime. Edward Wortley Montagu, Jr. (or possibly his tutor, who may have written parts of the book) in *Reflections on the Rise and Fall of Antient Republics Adopted to the Present State of Great Britain* (1759) portrayed the "truly democratic" government of Athens with its "giddy and fluctuating populace" as illustrative of the danger of government by faction.[6] Montagu feared that mid-century politicians would sell away British liberty through political jobbery as Pericles had sold Athenian liberty through the payment of juries, which amounted to bribing the people.

Even advanced eighteenth-century reformers who sought a more representative parliamentary system and who thus might have seemed predisposed to defend Athens did so only in the most backhanded manner. Joseph Priestley, the politically radical scientist and Unitarian minister, would only claim that "the convulsion of Athens, where life was in some measure enjoyed, and the faculties of body and mind had their proper exercise and gratification, were, in my opinion, far preferable to the savage uniformity of Sparta."[7] The crimes of the democracy in Athens still far outweighed its virtues even in the eyes of reformers. The infrequent mention of Athens by radicals suggests they knew that the history of the city provided no strong defense for their position and that it had not actually exemplified the mode of government they sought to achieve in Britain.

All of these remarks and opinions were stated fleetingly in undistin-

6. Edward Wortley Montagu, Junior, *Reflections on the Rise and Fall of Antient Republics Adopted to the Present State of Great Britain* (London: A. Miller, 1759), pp. 74, 85.

7. Joseph Priestley, *An Essay on the First Principles of Government; and on the Nature of Political, Civil, and Religious Liberty* (London, 1768), p. 132.

guished histories or political pamphlets. Athens was not a fundamental concern for any of these writers. But during the last quarter of the century the American Revolution, the radical movement for reform in Parliament, and later the French Revolution awakened a new interest in the Athenian experience on the part of defenders of the political status quo. During those years *democracy* or genuine *republicanism* could denote no existing European polity.[8] Consequently, when the American colonies began to form a government without a monarch, it was not unnatural for some writers to look to the classical Greek republics for indications of what the future might hold for the Americans. In 1778 John Gillies warned that if any people should ignore the unhappy history of Greece and, "disdaining to continue happy subjects of the country under whose protection they have so long flourished, would set on foot a republican confederacy, let them tremble at the prospect of those calamities, which, should their designs be carried into execution, they must both inflict and suffer." Three years later Josiah Tucker, the irascible dean of Bristol, with both the Americans and their British supporters in mind, attacked the Lockean concept of government by compact and consent in hope of rousing in "every true Friend to Liberty an Abhorrence of the Idea of an Athenian Common-Wealth." In 1797 Gillies voiced a similar warning against government based on consent in his introduction to Aristotle's *Politics.*[9] In this manner there emerged a conservative polemical strategy of portraying the ends of the American revolt and of the Yorkshire Association reform movement as democratic in character and then decrying democracy through enumeration of the disasters and crimes of Athens. This conservative response to the revolutions of the late eighteenth century provided the occasion for the first major English narrative history of Greece.

William Mitford and the Indictment of Athenian Democracy

The most influential of the antidemocratic commentators on Athens was William Mitford, a Hampshire country gentleman who had at-

8. Robert Roswell Palmer, *The Age of Democratic Revolution,* 2 vols. (Princeton: Princeton University Press, 1959–64), 1:13–20.

9. John Gillies, "Introduction," John Gillies, trans., *The "Orations" of Lysias and Isocrates,* 2 vols. (London: J. Murray, 1778), pp. lxii–lxiii; Josiah Tucker, *A Treatise*

tended Oxford, where he was a member of an undergraduate break-
fast club whose number also included Jeremy Bentham.[10] Although
Mitford left the university without taking a degree, he remained long
enough to hear William Blackstone's lectures on the British law and
constitution. These lectures and his own later experiences as a county
magistrate and member of Parliament convinced him of the wisdom
and near-perfection of the British polity. After leaving Oxford he
traveled for some time in France where he became acquainted with the
political ideas of the French philosophes who admired the much-
discussed balance of the English constitution and to some extent the
republics of antiquity. Mitford was more than casually familiar with
these writers, among whom, it must be recalled, supporters of
monarchy or aristocracy rather than of democracy predominated. On
returning to England, he settled on his family's estate at Exbury in
Hampshire and attached himself to the South Hampshire militia in
which he became a colonel. The association was fortuitous because
Edward Gibbon served in the same company. On one occasion Gibbon, perhaps impressed by Mitford's knowledge of Greek at a time
when that language enjoyed little of its later vogue, suggested that he
write a history of Greece. Mitford did just that. The first volume
appeared in 1784 and the tenth in 1810.

Since the mid-nineteenth century, neither Mitford nor his work
have received much attention. J. P. Mahaffy of Trinity College, Dublin thought the volumes important primarily for having stimulated in
Grote "a great successor to write his famous antidote." More recently,
Mitford's *History of Greece* has been considered significant primarily
for having provided occasion for the sharpening of the young
Macaulay's historical criticism. However, despite later deprecations
and corrections, Mitford's history constituted a turning point of no
small consequence in British intellectual history. His was the first

Concerning Civil Government (New York: Augustus M. Kelley, 1967; originally published, 1781), p. 226; John Gillies, trans., *Aristotle's "Ethics" and "Politics," Compris-
ing His Practical Philosophy*, 2 vols. (London, 1797), 2:3–6.

10. *Dictionary of National Biography*, s.v. "Mitford, William"; Lord Redesdale,
"Memoir of the Author," in William Mitford, *The History of Greece*, A New Edition
with Numerous Additions and Corrections, 10 vols. (London: T. Cadell, 1835),
1:ix–lii; Arnaldo Momigliano, *George Grote and the Study of Greek History* (London: H.
K. Lewis & Co., 1952), pp. 4–10.

major narrative history of Greece to appear in English, and his volumes withstood the potential rivalry of Gillies's history which appeared in 1786. They remained the standard work on Greek history until the publication of Connop Thirlwall's *History of Greece* in 1835. In Mitford's pages Lord Byron, Thomas Arnold, John Stuart Mill, and William Ewart Gladstone first encountered the political experience of the Greek commonwealths. Arnold later paired Mitford with Niebuhr as one of "the giants who first cut through the rocks and penetrated the tangled thickets of the forest" of ancient history. Writing much later in the century, Edward A. Freeman came closer to the mark when he condemned Mitford as "a bad scholar, a bad historian, a bad writer of English," but he nonetheless also recognized him as "the first writer of any note who found out that Grecian history was a living thing with a practical bearing."[11]

The latter part of Freeman's comment is highly significant. It was Mitford who more than anyone else legitimized the use of Athenian history as a vehicle for debating in detail the wisdom and viability of modern democratic government. Because his work held the field essentially unchallenged for almost half a century, Mitford's concept of the Greek political experience directly or indirectly influenced every history of Greece written in English for over one hundred years. Even historians and political writers who completely rejected Mitford's ideology and interpretations still in one degree or another accepted his contention that the political experience of Athens possessed some relevance for the modern British situation. Just as concerns with the Bible determined the nineteenth-century criticism of Homer, the problems of contemporary political debate shaped the writing of Greek history. In nineteenth-century England Greek history would always mean political history that was as profoundly involved with the present as with the past.

Like most eighteenth-century historians, Mitford conceived his work didactically. His volumes on Greece were a panegyric, largely derived from Country party ideology, on the virtues of the balanced

---

11. John Pentland Mahaffy, "A Critical Introduction," in Victor Duruy, *History of Greece and of the Greek People from the Earliest Times to the Roman Conquest,* 8 vols. (Boston: Ester and Laurial, 1890), 1:4–5; John Clive, *Macaulay: The Shaping of the Historian* (New York: Knopf, 1973), p. 137; Thomas Arnold, "Early Roman History," *Quarterly Review* 32 (1825): 72; Edward A. Freeman, *Historical Essays: Second Series,* 2nd ed. (London: Macmillan and Co., 1880), p. 127n.

English constitution and a polemic against those who would undermine that balance in the name of democracy, the people, or antique
precedents. The people who wanted to reform governments either at
home or abroad through emulation of the ancient Greek republican
political institutions were simply wrongheaded. Those commonwealths, unlike polities with balanced constitutions, had failed to establish practices that nurtured security of persons and property or a
general long-range stability. In a departure from most previous
analyses of ancient politics, Mitford contended that all the Greeks,
including the usually praised Spartans, had lacked any real capacity for
successful government.

> Able in war, skilfull, perhaps to the utmost of human ability, in
> political intrigue and political negotiation, in leading fellow-
> citizens, in bargaining with strangers, the Greeks were unfortu-
> nately deficient in the more important science of framing that
> great machine which we call a Government; harmonizing the
> various ranks of men of which a nation must consist; providing,
> at the same time, security for property, and equal justice for those
> who have no property; establishing, for the well-disposed of
> every rank, an interest in the preservation of the constitution,
> and, for the unprincipled and turbulent, strong coercion to secure
> it against disturbance; reconciling the protection of private rights
> with the maintenance of public force, and making a general pri-
> vate interest in the support of the existing order of things the basis
> of patriotism, and the source of general concord and public
> spirit.[12]

In other words, freedom, as an eighteenth-century English country
gentleman understood the word, had been nonexistent in the cities of
Greece.

According to Mitford, the history of Greece was the story of balanced Homeric monarchies declining into various modes of unhappy
republican life whose well-being was eventually sustained only
through the fortunate conquest by Macedonia with its own mixed or
balanced constitution. Later critics would scorn Mitford for the praise
he heaped on the Homeric and Macedonian monarchies and would

12. Mitford, *History of Greece,* 5:6.

portray him as the champion of every form of political oppression. Yet in his own mind Mitford thought the presence of primitive councils of nobles and chieftains suggested the elements of a genuinely balanced polity such as adherents to Country party ideology prized. The uncertainty surrounding Telemachus's succession to his father's throne not only presupposed political turmoil but also, and more important, seemed "plainly to admit a right of the people to interfere, and direct the succession."[13] By *people* Mitford would seem to indicate persons of some property and substance.

During the dark ages after the Homeric record ceased, the "vigorous principles of democracy, which had always existed in the Grecian governments, began to ferment," and they eventually triumphed everywhere except in Sparta, which retained its two kings. But the small size and, more important, the slavery of those republican or democratic polities prevented them from serving as models for modern political structures. As Mitford described the situation, the frequent, direct participation of Greek citizens in political life made slavery "absolutely necessary." Only with slaves performing the greater part of the productive labor could the whole free citizenry attend to the affairs of government. Yet this slavery by its very nature meant that a considerable segment of the population was wholly "excluded from any interest in the country."[14] Persons so excluded from the public realm could have no concern for the public good or the defense of the commonwealth. The availability of slaves also meant that rich free citizens did not require the labor of poor free citizens, so the latter could rarely benefit from the prosperity of the rich. The mutual interdependence and social reciprocity that at least in theory characterized economic interests in eighteenth-century Britain were absent from Greece and, by implication, from any democracy. Mitford's sensitivity to the evil of ancient slavery set him far ahead of the nineteenth-century liberal historians of Greece who turned their eyes from slavery in Greece, as they did from the plight of the contemporary poor.

Mitford's objection to slavery was primarily political, and for that reason he reserved his harshest criticism for Sparta. Slavery was an institution without which the Lycurgan constitution could not have

13. Ibid., 1:105.
14. Ibid., pp. 225, 339, 226.

functioned, as it in effect "required that every Lacedaemon should be, in the strictest sense of the modern term, a gentleman, without business." Equality in Sparta meant that the slaves were the collective property of all free citizens and that no compromise could relax the rigor of their repression. Consequently, "never was human nature degraded by system to such a degree as in the miserable Helots." Furthermore, the threat of a slave revolt required a standing military force in Sparta, which fostered a lust for conquest and command that was "a disease inherent in the vitals" of the Lycurgan system. Later critics of Mitford tended to ignore these strictures of Spartan society They regarded Mitford as simply a reactionary opponent of emerging political liberalism. They were mistaken. Mitford was a late voice of the Country party ideology whose spokesman had consistently opposed standing armies, such as Mitford discerned was required by Spartan slavery, on the grounds that they always posed a danger to liberty and that armed conquest could corrupt free republics into militaristic empires. Moreover, a historian of this outlook could hardly countenance other of the institutions founded by Lycurgus whose "fundamental principle was that the commonwealth was all in all; that individuals were comparatively nothing; that they had no right of property, nor even of life, but in subordination to the wants of the common parent."[15] The whole intent of the eighteenth-century Country party had been the preservation of liberty and the rights of independent persons and property against the tyranny of an all-powerful central government, whether the latter be an unlimited monarchy or a democracy.

Whatever the faults of Sparta, and they were many, Mitford considered those of Athens worse and of more immediate danger to the British polity. The history of Athens exemplified all the follies of the democratic government that he saw being urged on Britain through calls for parliamentary reform by the Yorkshire Association and being undertaken by the former colonies in America. Democracy, not Spartan uniformity, was the pressing threat to the mixed constitution of Britain, and it was the pitfalls of democracy as manifested in the Athenian experience that had to be exposed.

15. Ibid., pp. 254, 265, 271, 258–59. See also Adam Ferguson, *An Essay on the History of Civil Society,* ed. Duncan Forbes (Edinburgh: Edinburgh University Press, 1966; originally published, 1767), p. 56.

For Mitford democracy in Athens began with the reforms of Solon in the early sixth century B.C. Explained most simply, Solon created four orders of citizens ranked according to wealth from among whom only members of the three upper orders could hold major offices. He vested primary powers of government in the Assembly consisting of all citizens, in a Council of Four Hundred of whom each tribe elected a hundred, and in the ancient Areopagus, a court whose membership consisted of former archons.[16] Mitford thought that the Council and the Areopagus had been intended to balance the Assembly. However, Solon had nullified the potential balance of his constitutional structure by the egregious error of committing "to the whole free population in assembly, where every free Athenian had his equal right to vote and speak" the supreme authority of the commonwealth. He had thereby put "unlimited power into the hands of those least capable of properly exercising any power." In the absence of the representative principle, the members of the Assembly were responsible to no one. Hence, for all his attempts at balanced government, Solon had in reality erected nothing less than "A TYRANNY IN THE HANDS OF THE PEOPLE."[17]

The activity of political factions in Athens insured that the potential fallacies in Solon's constitution would emerge as realities. The factional conflict existed because the Athenians and the Greeks in general failed to acknowledge the sound English principle that "the aggregate of private good constitutes public good, and its corollary, that the rights of individuals, once established by law, should be ever held sacred."[18] In place of that salutary principle the Greeks had fallen victim to the Lycurgean idea that the public good and the private good are at least antagonistic, if not necessarily opposed to each other. Consequently, no Athenian faction felt it could trust the government to recognize its needs unless it controlled the machinery of government. A faction would attempt to capture control of the government under the guise of carrying out the public good when in fact it was seeking realization of its own selfish ends. The existing regime was thus always considered a threat to those out of power, and they to it.

16. For a recent survey of Greek consitutional and political development, see Raphael Sealey, *A History of the Greek City States, 700–338 B.C.* (Berkeley: University of California Press, 1976).

17. Mitford, *History of Greece,* 1:335, 343, 5:9 (Mitford's emphasis).

18. Ibid., 5:34.

These factional machinations eventually gave rise to and justified the appearance of the Greek tyrants, whom Mitford admired almost without reservation and whom he portrayed as an acceptable alternative to the imbalance resulting from democratic politics. He regarded them as figures perhaps resembling Bolingbroke's Patriot King though he did not use the term, and as a means for overcoming the hopeless corruption stemming from factional interests.

> The import of the term Tyrant, among the Greeks, differed greatly from what it bears in modern languages. Not limited, as in these, to express an atrocious character, it meant generally a citizen of a republic who by any means, whether legal or generally allowed, or otherwise, acquired sovereignty over his fellow citizens, or the sole direction of the executive government. History has recorded Grecian Tyrants as men of extraordinary virtue, who used their power in strict conformity to established law, and ever advantageously for the people they governed.... Ursurper, therefore, is not a convertible term: though in general the Grecian tyrants were usurpers. Without a favouring among the people, no man could rise to the tyranny: therefore, a man of universal bad character could not become a tyrant.

Although initially the head of a faction, a tyrant might, through personal influence and the need for broader political support, eventually rise above his own factional base and rule for the benefit of all. According to Mitford, the Athenian tyrant Pisistratus had epitomized the wise monarch who observed the law, cared for the poor, encouraged industry, and patronized the arts. His political excesses, including imprisonment of the children of opponents, had not been wholly evil and might even be considered "singularly mild" if "compared with what we hereafter shall find usual in revolutions in Grecian cities."[19] Whatever the errors of Pisistratus, political and private life for most Athenian citizens had been more secure under his rule than under the fleeting despotism of later democratic factions or oligarchical cliques, such as the Thirty Tyrants.

No single topic treated by Mitford so roused the ire of his nineteenth-century critics as the discussion of the tyrants. But his remarks must, in part, be understood once again in the context of the

19. Ibid., 1:360–61, 368.

Country party ideology. After the middle of the eighteenth-century, and influenced by Bolingbroke's later writing, there were many people who felt that the corruption of a previously balanced constitution could be overcome only through the leadership of some extraordinary person who would restore constitutional balance and civic virtue in place of factional strife and selfishness.[20] Mitford's rehabilitation of the much-abused tyrants was closely analogous to the later attempt by George Grote to present a favorable portrait of the demagogues. In both cases, the historians sought to turn a potential embarrassment into a polemical advantage. In the long run neither proved particularly successful.

For Mitford, the wisdom of tyranny was confirmed by the history of Athens after Pisistratus. Following the expulsion of Hippias, the last of the Pisistratid tyrants, various quarreling factions again governed Athens. Mitford relegated Cleisthenes, whom Grote and other later historians considered the founder of Athenian democracy, to the status of an inept, would-be tyrant who achieved power only by appealing to the lower orders in the Assembly to change the consitution. His reforms amounted merely to establishing the selfish hegemony of his own faction.

The single most insidious instrument of post-Cleisthenean government was ostracism. No other feature of Athenian politics roused more criticism during the eighteenth century and later. Dean Tucker had declared, "Nothing could have been better calculated for gratifying the Caprice and Licentiousness of a Mob, or for indulging the Spleen and Jealousy of a Rival, or for concealing the Wiles and Intrigues of a pretended Patriot, than this very Project." Mitford regarded ostracism primarily as an instrument of "democratical jealousy" by which ambitious men might "make popular passion serve their private purposes" and repress the superiority that ability and high character might acquire in the republic. Ostracism was indicative of the corruption that the institutions of democracy imposed on even virtuous leaders. For example, to avoid potential ostracism, Cimon had not only to win battles but also to maintain his own faction in the Assembly through favors to the lower orders. His political conduct necessarily involved "a continual preparation for an election;

20. Pocock, *Machiavellian Moment,* pp. 483–86.

not as in England, to decide whether the candidate should or should not be a member of the legislature; but whether he should be head of the commonwealth or an exile." Similar democratic pressures relating to the threat of ostracism led Ephialtes and Pericles to adopt a new policy that permanently undermined the political life of the city. To broaden their popular support, they bribed the people by using public funds to pay juries and to construct great public buildings. The power of the Areopagus, which was composed of conservative former archons, blocked this appropriation of public monies. Consequently, to maintain their dominance, Ephialtes and Pericles successfully persuaded the Assembly to degrade the power of the ancient court.

> This was the finishing stroke to form at Athens that union of all the powers of government, legislative, executive, financial, and judicial, in the same hands, which, according to the sage Montesquieu, constitutes the essence of despotism; and hence the term tyrant was, even in that age, applied to the assembled Athenian people.[21]

Through this final corruption of political balance there emerged a democratic tyranny that lacked the wisdom, moderation, and respect for existing political institutions and laws that Mitford associated with the Pisistratid tyrants. The full-fledged democracy sought neither the public good nor the sum of individual private goods as henceforth ever-changing factional alignments ruled.

So long as a person of Pericles' ability remained the "prince of Athens," the worst excesses of that "community of lordly beggers" could be staved off. Yet even Pericles encountered grave difficulties when the Peloponnesian War commenced, and with his passing a new breed of far more undesirable political figures emerged. These were the demagogues of whom Cleon—"as remarkably born for the depression of Athens as Miltiades, Themistocles, Aristides, Cimon, and Pericles for its exaltation"—was the most infamous. The very nature of the radical democracy allowed the demagogues to play on public passions and to lead the people into villainies such as the afterward-repealed condemnation of the Mytilenians. For, as Mitford explained, " . . . where neither one person nor a select body was responsible, but

21. Tucker, *Treatise Concerning Civil Government*, p. 220; Mitford, *History of Greece*, 2:145, 303, 318.

the whole people, truly despotic, were the common authors of every public act, the shame of flagitious measures was so divided that it was disregarded."[22] The demagogues could not advise prudence for fear of losing their support in the Assembly; the Assembly would not turn toward more responsible leadership for fear of losing its own predominance.

The corruption of the Athenian polity was complete. Although the city may have possessed the forms of political liberty, the reality did not exist. Amidst the factional strife, the social bonds and sense of common civic interest disintegrated so that "for maintaining civil order and holding the state together, flattery and bribes alone could persuade the multitude, and the only alternative was violence." The poor who envied the rich sought to bring the latter to trial in order to receive bribes, confiscated property, or at least jury fees. The social compact no longer consisted "in the security of every one against injury from others, but in the power of every one to injure others." Property and persons enjoyed neither security nor protection, and "the satisfaction . . . of an Englishman in considering his house and his field more securely his own, under the protection of the law, than a castle defended by its garrison, or a kingdom by its armies, was unknown in Attica."[23] The Athenian democracy possessed no means of reforming itself, restraining its ambitions, or protecting the class of society from which wise, judicious leaders might emerge.

Because of this characterization of the Athenian democracy, Mitford, to the astonishment of most of his contemporaries, heaped lavish praise on the Macedonian conquest. In part he was writing out of the tradition of the cult of Philip of Macedonia that flourished briefly in the late eighteenth century, but more directly his favorable treatment of Philip's conquest of the corrupt Greek democracies reflected the belief that in a thoroughly corrupt polity reform and reconstruction could only come from the outside.[24] Mitford regarded Macedonia as a reasonably pure descendant of the more ancient balanced monarchies. In that northern realm the monarch was "supreme, but not despotic."

The chief object of his office, as in the English constitution, was to be conservator of the peace of his kingdom: for which great

22. Mitford, *History of Greece*, 2:253; 3:25, 152; 4:131.
23. Ibid., 5:29, 11, 25.
24. Momigliano, *George Grote and the Study of Greek History*, p. 5.

purpose he was vested with the first military and the first judicial authority; as in the governments described by Homer, he commanded the army, and presided over the administration of justtice. But he was to command and to judge according to established laws. He had no legislative authority but in concurrence with the assembled people; and condemnation, and the decision of all more important causes, rested with popular tribunals; in which, as among our forefathers, in what thence bears yet the title of King's Bench, the king presided in person, but the court gave judgment.

Although Macedonia was plagued by problems of the succession similar to those of England before the Tudors, the Macedonian civil wars had not taken so many lives proportionally as the civil strife in the Greek democracies. Mitford, therefore, regarded the invasion by Philip—"the popular king of a free people"—as having afforded the best opportunity for Greek unification against Persia and as having brought to a close the desultory activities of the southern democratic states.[25] It is quite possible that in the Macedonian imposition of a balanced monarchical polity on lawless democracies Mitford also saw the prototype of the British campaign against the forces of the French Revolution and Napoleon.

In 1819 *Blackwood's Magazine* congratulated Mitford for having produced "a history of Greece in the true English spirit" and for having surveyed "everything in the bright PAST of antiquity with an eye cooled and calmed by the reflection and experience of the troubled PRESENT in which himself [*sic*] has lived."[26] The journal may have confessed more than it intended. Although Mitford's *History of Greece* was a strong and not unpersuasive antidemocratic polemic, the work was not, as nineteenth-century critics would assert, informed by a reactionary sentiment. Mitford did not appeal to Burkean traditionalism or to religious bias. Politics was for him a thoroughly human activity, and its goal was the maintenance of what he and many others of his generation in England understood by the free polity of a balanced constitution. He condemned Athens and the other Greek states for not having preserved such a government and presented them

25. Mitford, *History of Greece,* 7:232, 231; 8:388.
26. *Blackwood's* 5 (1819): 443.

as warnings to his fellow countrymen of the dangers of abandoning the existing framework of government. Nor did Mitford appeal to some mode of authoritarian government as the alternative to democracy. Unlike John Gillies, his Scottish counterpart in the writing of Greek history, Mitford did not look to the enlightened absolutist rulers on the Continent with their standing armies and strict bureaucracies as the model for effective government and healthy civic life. His ideal was nothing more and nothing less than the existing, theoretically balanced constitution of England. Even in his curious admiration for the Greek tyrants and for Philip of Macedonia, Mitford had seen a mixed polity as the structure to be restored by those improbable figures.

Mitford's influence lasted long into the nineteenth century. His work was immediately incorporated into tracts against the French Revolution, such as Robert Bisset's *Sketch of Democracy* (1796). These associations did much to give Mitford's *History of Greece* its reactionary reputation. The volumes commanded the attention and readership of all sections of the reading public. Liberal critics, such as Lord Brougham and others, might criticize the treatment of the Greek tyrants and Macedonia; but in the absence of alternatives even the political radical James Mill gave Mitford's history to his son John Stuart along with strict instructions to ignore its conservative bias.[27] However, Mitford's most significant impact was more subtle. So complete had been his condemnation of the character of the Athenian state and so widespread was the acceptance of his views that he had in effect also established the grounds on which the reputation of Athens would have to be restored. The civic virtues that Mitford denied Athens had possessed and, by implication, that a democratic polity could possess were features of government prized by Englishmen of various political persuasions. Later liberal historians consequently had to prove that Athens and, by implication, democracy had actually achieved those virtues. Only with difficulty would the debate over the Athenian constitution escape the parameters that Mitford had set.

Commentary on Athens during the Years of Reform

The ascendancy of Mitford's *History of Greece* continued without serious check until 1824 when the young Thomas Babington Macaulay,

27. *Edinburgh Review* 12 (1808): 478–517; *Quarterly Review* 5 (1811): 33 and 25

in *Knight's Quarterly,* addressed himself to it as "a book which enjoys a great and increasing popularity" for want of serious examination and criticism.[28] Two years later there appeared in the radical *Westminster Review* an equally critical essay on Mitford's *History* by a young City banker named George Grote. In these youthful essays the great liberal and radical historians set forth the political principles and concepts of historical criticism that about twenty years later would become more fully manifest in their respective histories of England and Greece. These essays also display the liberal and radical minds contemplating the same object with equally critical acumen but with differing ideological solutions for the problems they perceived.

In phrases of characteristic vituperative sarcasm Macaulay attacked Mitford's scholarship as imprecise, his prose as awkward, his spelling as curious, and his politics as unacceptable. He accused Mitford of approaching ancient Greek politics, as he would later accuse James Mill of approaching contemporary English political life, in an a priori manner that failed to recognize "that a good government, like a good coat, is that which fits the body for which it is designed." Of the Exbury squire Macaulay complained:

> He is a vehement admirer of tyranny and oligarchy, and considers no evidence as feeble which can be brought forward in favour of those forms of government. Democracy he hates with a perfect hatred, a hatred which, in the first volume of his history, appears only in his episodes and reflections, but which, in those parts which he has less reverence for his guides, and can venture to take his own way, completely distorts even his narration.[29]

Either Macaulay had not read Mitford's volumes with care, or he purposefully distorted their contents. He portrayed Mitford as an unmitigated champion of Sparta and failed to mention the historian's strictures on that state which Grote in his later review both noticed and approved. Macaulay also contended that Mitford had been a consistent champion of oligarchy when in fact he had favored a mixed constitution.

(1821): 154–74; John Stuart Mill, *Autobiography* (New York: New American Library, Signet, 1964), p. 32.

28. *The Works of Lord Macaulay Edited by His Sister, Lady Trevelyan* (London: Longmans, Green, and Co., 1871), 7:683.

29. Ibid., p. 687.

Macaulay's hostile misreading of Mitford's volumes, as well as the appearance of other reviews of the work during the twenties, suggests that the Greek history completed in 1810 had assumed a somewhat new ideological identity and usage. During the period of the French wars Mitford's championship of a balanced polity had constituted a generally mainline, patriotic defense of the political status quo in Britain. However, by the third decade of the nineteenth century when the lines for and against domestic political reform were more sharply drawn, Mitford's position stood at the distinctly reactionary end of the contemporary political spectrum. Those who upheld it generally opposed any significant political change, and they had become more extreme in their views since 1815. Macaulay's review was an attempt by a moderate reformer associated with the Whigs to undermine and to shake the credibility of a work that helped to sustain the inflexible conservative polemic against accommodation with the new political realities of the age.

Macaulay intended his essay to redirect consideration of Athenian history so as to remove the subject from current political discourse, to which it contributed only confusion. Ancient democracy was not a positive political model for persons of Macaulay's persuasion. During the later Commons debate over the Reform Bill he urged members to understand that the measure would not establish an Athenian-style democracy.[30] Continuation of the Mitfordian analysis of ancient politics simply distorted perceptions of contemporary political options. Macaulay saw the choice in his own day as lying not between a balanced constitution and lawless democracy but rather between timely, moderate reform and revolution. Athenian history, as interpreted by Mitford and lesser followers, simply sustained the misperception of the contemporary political scene. Consequently, in 1824 Macaulay called for a new history of Greece that would be free from adherence to abstract political principles and that would include "a complete record of the rise and progress of poetry, philosophy, and the arts." For the latter endeavors had exhibited "in its noblest form, the immortal influence of Athens."[31] This demand for a cultural history of Greece has been correctly regarded as an important attempt to redirect the writing of history in Great Britain away from a narrow political base and toward exploration of other facets of the human experience. How-

30. Hansard's *Parliamentary Debates, 1830–1831,* 2:1201.
31. *Works of Lord Macaulay,* 7:699, 703.

ever, that call was also no less an effort to remove Athens as a subject of political debate that by its frame of reference almost inevitably distorted the goals of moderate political reformers.

George Grote's discussion of Mitford in 1826, like his Benthamite politics, led to conclusions quite different from Macaulay's. Grote could not dismiss Athens from political discourse because he and his Benthamite friends were essentially seeking to democratize British politics, and the Athenian example was of considerable significance to their political goals. Grote thought Mitford's history required major corrections of both fact and interpretation. Mitford had failed to explain that the poor citizens of Athens were simply those less wealthy than the very rich. He had also refused to acknowledge the oligarchical machinations within the Athenian democracy. However, more important than these and other simple faults of scholarship, Mitford's *History of Greece* was fundamentally distorted by the author's uncritical admiration of English political institutions. Because Mitford possessed a mind "priding itself on adherence to everything English," he had been unable to judge the Athenian democracy on the philosophical grounds of what might constitute the best regime. His standard of the allegedly mixed contemporary constitution of Britain was philosophically and practically inadequate. The powers, personalities, and institutions that Mitford believed constrained the monarch actually constituted

> a set of adjuncts interested in bad government just as much as himself; who prevent him, not from misgovernment, but from appropriating to himself all the fruits of misgovernment; and who, in reality, limit very considerably his power of doing well, and without at all limiting his power of doing ill.

History written from such a mistaken standpoint and taught in the universities by men who were themselves beneficiaries of corruption and sinister interests prevented the story of Greek democracy from being "employed to unfold the mechanism of society, and to bring to view the various illustrations which Greek phenomena afford of the principles of human nature."[32]

Grote called for the writing of a new history of Greece, but unlike

32. George Grote, "Mitford's *History of Greece*," *Westminster Review* 5 (1826): 282, 331.

Macaulay he wanted a continuation of polemical history with only the perspective of the polemic changed. A future history of Greece should be based on "both philosophy and research" which would liberate it from the unphilosophical British bias of Mitford. So written, such a history would, in Grote's view, demonstrate that "it is to democracy alone (and to that sort of open aristocracy which is, practically, very similar to it), that we owe that unparalleled brilliance and diversity of individual talent which constitutes the charm and glory of Grecian history." Rather than a work issuing from Whiggish commonsense and compromise, Grote looked toward a history of Greece informed by democratic ideology and naturalistic philosophy. He readily understood that "the extraordinary interest which the classical turn of English education bestows upon all Grecian transactions, and the certainty that a Grecian history will be more universally read than almost any other history" would allow such a new scholarly work to propagate radical political ideas.[33]

A few years after these two reviews appeared, Macaulay would defend the Reform Bill as preventing revolution and protecting existing institutions. Grote would consider the measure as providing the occasion for an ideological reorientation of British political life. Their differing stances at that time had been implicit in their discussions of Mitford.

Despite the criticisms of Macaulay and Grote, it was Mitford's history that still continued to carry the day. His ideas found their way into textbooks such as Arthur Thomas Malin's *History of Greece* published in 1829 by the Society for the Diffusion of Useful Knowledge and Thomas Keightley's *History of Greece* of 1839. Mitford's interpretation of Athens also permeated articles in the *Encyclopaedia Metropolitana,* whose authors regarded Athenian citizens as "open to the grossest flattery" and possessed of "vanity and self-conceit . . . only to be paralleled by their levity and cruelty." While behaving as tyrants toward their most gifted citizens, the Athenians had permitted the republic under Pericles to be "rendered completely a dictatorship."[34]

33. Ibid., p. 280.

34. *Encyclopaedia Metropolitana* (London, 1845), s.v. "History of Greece," "Pericles." The latter statement echoed a previous charge made by an eighteenth-century writer. See John Trenchard, *Cato's Letters: or Essays on Liberty, Civil and Religious, and Other Important Subjects,* 3rd ed. (London, 1723), 2:73–74.

Similar derogatory comments occasionally crept into Smith's *Dictionary of Greek and Roman Biography and Mythology* (1844–49) and the seventh and eighth editions of the *Encyclopaedia Britannica*.

The critical editions of the comedies of Aristophanes published by Thomas Mitchell during the second quarter of the century also strongly perpetuated Mitford's image of Athens. Mitchell's introductions and notes restated Aristophanes' criticisms of Athenian political and intellectual life and went on to interpret them in largely Mitfordian terms. For example, he characterized Periclean Athens as a city beleaguered by

> that fatal compact, silent but not the less effectually made between Pericles and the Athenian people—the one bargaining for amusement, pay, outward splendour, and nominal sovereignty, the other contenting himself with the possession of unostentatious but real power, and secretly no doubt reserving to himself the right of transmitting that power under a more substantial title to his children—the extrinsic decoration was gradually wearing off, and the real deformity daily developing itself.[35]

Mitchell not only presented Mitford's analysis in a somewhat exaggerated form but also contributed to the continued uncritical acceptance of Aristophanes as a primary source of information on political activity in fifth-century Athens.

Other works of the 1830s also continued to suggest an intimate link between Athenian and British politics. Philosophically, the most important of these was the three-volume critical edition of Thucydides that Thomas Arnold published between 1830 and 1835. In addition to drawing numerous contemporary parallels, such as his comparison of the speeches of Cleon with the agitating journalism of William Cobbett, Arnold set forth the Viconian analysis of Greek political and intellectual development that would so profoundly influence his son's concept of Hellenism. Thomas Arnold believed that contemporary Europe and fifth-century Greece stood in the same phase of cyclical development, as each had emerged from an aristocratic age to confront strife over politics based on property or numbers. But the elder

35. Thomas Mitchell, ed., *"The Frogs" of Aristophanes, with Notes Critical and Explanatory, Adapted to the Use of Schools and Universities* (London: John Murray, 1839), p. iii.

Arnold was not wholly satisfied with some of the parallels that could be drawn from that argument. For example, certain important differences had to be noted between ancient and modern aristocrats.

> We must not transfer to the higher orders of the cities of Greece, notions derived from our experience of the nobility and gentry of England in our own days....In order to get a right notion of the aristocracies of Greece, we must take what are in our own mere monstrosities and exceptions; the excesses of individual folly, or some lingering remains of a past state of oppression and iniquity, which the full tide of improvement has not yet washed away.[36]

Arnold might also have argued by implication, though he did not, that a similar differentiation should be made between the *people* in the ancient Greek democracies, with their passionate excesses, and the people in the emerging liberal democratic states.

Two years after the last of Arnold's volumes of Thucydides had appeared, Edward Bulwer-Lytton in *Athens: Its Rise and Fall* (1837) attempted, like Macaulay, to remove the Athenian democracy from contemporary political debate. Perhaps following Mackintosh who in *Vindiciae Gallicae* (1791) had denied any analogy between Athens and revolutionary France,[37] Bulwer-Lytton regarded the small size, the slavery, and the absence of the concept of representation in ancient Athens as precluding any meaningful parallel between its political experience and that of modern states. Yet Bulwer-Lytton, who was also a novelist, a social critic, and a Whig, could not deny all relevance of Athens for the present age. The city had possessed wise nobles who made timely concessions to popular opinion and thus retained their position of leadership.

> Athens in this respect . . . resembled England, and as now in the later state, so then in Athens, it was often the proudest, the wealthiest, the most high-born of the aristocrats that gave dignity and success to the progress of democratic opinion.[38]

36. Thomas Arnold, ed., *The History of the Peloponnesian War by Thucydides*, 4 vols. (Oxford: J. Parker, 1830), 1:471, 669–70.

37. James Mackintosh, *The Miscellaneous Works of the Right Honourable Sir James Mackintosh* (London: Longman, Brown, Green, and Longmans, 1846), 2:103–04.

38. Edward Bulwer-Lytton, *Athens: Its Rise and Fall; with Views of the Literature, Philosophy, and Social Life of the Athenian People*, 2 vols. (New York: Harper & Brothers, 1837), 2:179; 1:152–53.

Perhaps in answer to an unflattering implicit parallel drawn between Pericles and Lord Grey at the time of the Reform Bill,[39] Bulwer-Lytton portrayed those ancient Whigs, including Cimon, Aristides, and Pericles, as temperate leaders who had maintained the position of their order by wisely responding to change.

Bulwer-Lytton's two volumes might have constituted the opening of a new history of Greece somewhat resembling that for which Macaulay had called in 1824. Bulwer-Lytton did devote considerable attention to cultural matters, and he certainly was not directed by rigid political doctrines. However, he abandoned his study after the appearance of the first two of four projected volumes because he realized that Connop Thirlwall's *History of Greece* (8 vols., 1835–45) would quickly supplant anything he might yet publish. Thirlwall was the first British historian to bring the vast accomplishments of German classical scholarship into the service of Greek history.[40] His extensive reading in primary and secondary sources and his high critical standards made Mitford's volumes obsolete, and after 1838 the latter were not reprinted.

Although Thirlwall avoided overt political polemics, he implicitly neutralized Athens as a stock weapon in the conservative armory. If not an enthusiastic supporter of Athenian democracy, he was clearly sympathetic. He believed that ostracism had been a useful and not necessarily a pernicious institution. Cleon was a person whose blunt language and resolute counsels allowed him to gain "credit for plain good sense and honest patriotism, while he watched for every turn of the popular inclination, that he might not anticipate or go beyond it." Although he was not to be really admired, neither was he to be wholly condemned. Thirlwall on occasion chastised the actions or policies of the Athenians, but he did not blame their political institutions. For example, of the condemnation of Melos he observed:

> The conduct of the Athenians in the conquest of Melos is far less extraordinary than the openness with which they avow their principles. But, unjust as it was, it will not to a discerning eye appear the more revolting, because it wanted the varnish of sanc-

39. John Williams, "Subversion of Ancient Governments," *Quarterly Review* 45 (1831): 453.

40. John Connop Thirlwall, *Connop Thirlwall, Historian and Theologian* (New York: The Macmillan Co., 1936).

tity, by which acts of much fouler iniquity have been covered in ages which have professed to revere a higher moral law.[41]

Thirlwall simply would not ascribe moral failure in human behavior to the democratic polity or suggest that some other constitutional arrangement would have avoided the failure. Nor by the same token would he ascribe the achievement of human virtue to a democratic constitution.

In the preface to *A History of Greece* George Grote said that had he not been already so deeply involved in his own research, the publication of Thirlwall's volumes would have halted his own work. That generous remark by one former schoolmate to another has obscured the very serious differences that separated Grote's history from Thirlwall's. Thirlwall had liberated himself from Mitford's anglophilia and displayed in the words of the *Eclectic Review,* "no disposition to try the politicians of Greece by maxims drawn from Magna Charta." Yet, as John Stuart Mill remarked, Thirlwall had not produced "a Philosophical history" in the positivist or politically radical sense. Thirlwall had used evidence from myths to portray the early history of Greece. He not only had failed, or refused, to vindicate democracy but also had reserved the warmest remarks of his eight volumes for Alexander the Great whom he characterized as one of the earth's greatest sons and "one of the benefactors of his kind."[42] But most important, Thirlwall wrote from the liberal Anglican view of history. For him, nations experienced natural and necessary cycles of growth and decay. Their salvation and the source of human moral redemption lay outside of time. His providential view of history meant that for him politics could achieve only a relative mode of human virtue. Consequently, he necessarily rejected the primacy of politics in human affairs and the view that the political community was the arena for the achievement and exercise of virtue. George Grote accepted both of these latter beliefs, which stemmed from the civic humanism of the Renaissance. Excellent as Thirlwall's *History of*

41. Connop Thirlwall, *A History of Greece,* 8 vols. (London: Longman, Rees, Orme, Brown, Green, & Longman and John Taylor, 1835–45), 3:186–87, 361–62.
42. George Grote, *A History of Greece,* A New Edition (London: John Murray, 1869), 1:iii–iv; *Eclectic Review* 69 (1839): 104; John Stuart Mill, "Grote's *History of Greece,*" p. 346; Thirlwall, *History of Greece,* 7:110.

Greece was, a Greek history written in accordance with radical ideology, such as Grote had demanded in 1826, was still to appear.

George Grote: The Apotheosis of the Athenian Democracy

George Grote's *History of Greece* (12 vols., 1846–56) was the single most enduring contribution to the debate over the Athenian constitution. Through Grote's description, analysis, and argument the Athenians became transformed into the ancient equivalent of modern Englishmen who had mastered the art of self-government and who had achieved a civilization wherein artistic excellence, positivistic thought, and individual liberty had largely, if not always perfectly, flourished. E. A. Freeman described Grote's work as "one of the glories of our age and country" and declared that "to read the political part of Mr. Grote's history . . . is an epoch in a man's life." For after the appearance of Grote's *History of Greece* Englishmen looked at the Athenians and saw in large measure the reflection of their own best selves. Moreover, Grote rapidly attained a European reputation. As one twentieth-century classicist has commented, "All the German studies on Greek History of the last fifty years of the nineteenth century are either for or against Grote."[43] As a work of scholarship and of political education Grote's volumes must stand as one of the chief monuments of mid-Victorian intellectual life.

Grote's concern with the political history of Greece had grown directly out of his activity in radical politics during the 1820s. In 1826 when he had called for a new history of Greece that would demon-

---

43. Edward A. Freeman, "Grote's *History of Greece*," *North British Review* 25 (1856): 172; *Historical Essays: Second Series*, p. 169; Momigliano, *George Grote and the Study of Greek History*, p. 13. See also Karl Christ, *Von Gibbon zu Rostovtzeff* (Darmstadt: Wissenhaftlische Buchgesellschaft, 1972), pp. 79, 226–27; N. Loraux and P. Vidal-Naquet, "La formation de l'Athènes bourgeoisie: essai d'historiographic, 1750–1870," and H. O. Pappé, "The English Utilitarians and Athenian Democracy," in *Classical Influences on Western Thought, A.D. 1650–1870*, ed. R. R. Bolgar (Cambridge: Cambridge University Press, 1979), pp. 169–222, 295–308; *Revue des Deux Mondes* 69 (1848): 428–40; 72 (1849): 846–56; 76 (1850): 699–705; *Heidelberger Jahrbücher der Literatur* 39 (1846): 641–52; 41 (1846): 816–29; Eduard Meyer, *Geschichte des Alterthums* (Stuttgart: J. G. Cotta'sche Buchhandlung Nachfolger, 1901), 3: 292–94; Robert Pöhlman, *Aus Altertum und Gegenwart: Gesammelte Abhandlungen* (Munich: C. H. Beck'sche Verlagsbuchhandlung, 1895), pp. 315–43. I am indebted to Ms. Rosario Perez for the last two references.

strate the positive benefits of democracy, he had already begun extensive reading for such a project, but set the work aside as he became deeply involved in agitation for the Reform Bill. In 1833 he had entered the reformed House of Commons where he became a leader of the philosophic radicals. This coterie, whose political philosophy derived primarily from Bentham, James Mill, and the classical political economists, was the only ideologically oriented group in the reformed Parliament.[44] They consciously sought to effect a realignment of existing political alliances into parties that would represent what they conceived to be the real political divisions of the nation—a selfish aristocracy versus the people or the general community interest. After the election of 1840, Grote and his circle, by then much reduced through a series of electoral losses, recognized their failure to reconstruct English politics. Their ideological vision and the concrete reality of the political situation simply would not mesh. The Whigs had not become more radical. Various radical middle-class and working-class pressure groups pursued their own selfish ends rather than the general interest. Discouraged by these developments and seeing little hope for immediate improvement, Grote retired from political life and resumed work on the Greek history that he had commenced writing about eighteen years earlier.

Grote's *History of Greece* began to appear in 1846, and, as he had demanded twenty years earlier of a work on this subject, it assumed an ideological and political orientation very different from Mitford's. But despite obvious differences, Grote's history was nevertheless conceptually a direct descendent of the earlier study. Both writers conceived their histories as vehicles for contemporary political polemics, and both distorted their evidence and arguments to that end. Both believed that some kind of direct analogy could be drawn between the government of ancient Athens and the liberal state emerging in Great Britain. Grote's use of such analogies was actually much more extreme than Mitford's. Ironically, nothing so clearly testified to the impact of Mitford's view of Athens and the benefit Grote indirectly

44. Harriet Grote, *The Personal Life of George Grote,* 2nd ed. (London: John Murray, 1873), pp. 82–142; Martin Lowther Clarke, *George Grote: A Biography* (London: University of London, The Athlone Press, 1962); Joseph Hamburger, *Intellectuals in Politics: John Stuart Mill and the Philosophic Radicals* (New Haven: Yale University Press, 1965).

derived from it than the critical reception of Grote's history. Over the years one reviewer after another characterized Grote as a writer uniquely qualified by virtue of his service in the reformed Parliament to provide modern readers with special insight into the politics of the ancient Greek democracies. It had been Mitford more than any other single person who had convinced his fellow countrymen that a liberally reformed House of Commons would resemble the Athenian Assembly.

Paradoxically, while refuting Mitford's indictment of Athens, Grote embraced as his own many, though by no means all, of the political virtues that Mitford had espoused. Whereas Mitford had seen democracy as endangering those values, Grote presented democracy as fostering them. Grote, like his predecessor, sought to explain how a republic could sustain itself against internal turmoil, moral corruption, and civic decay. Mitford had looked to a mixed constitution to achieve those ends. Grote, however, vigorously argued that only democratic structures could foster the achievement of a "constitutional morality" that sustained

> a paramount reverence for the forms of the constitution, enforcing obedience to the authorities acting under and within those forms, yet combined with the habit of open speech, of action subject only to definite legal control, and unrestrained censure of those very authorities as to all their public acts.[45]

Public life as sanctioned by constitutional morality incorporated government by consent, discussion and due process that guaranteed the liberty of the individual, freedom of thought, fair administration of justice, public responsibility of officials, and security of property. Grote believed the constitutional morality of a democratic state would prevent the abuse of power that the balance of the parts was purported to achieve, but did not, in a mixed polity. All citizens of a democracy would presumably support its basic institutions even while contesting for political power among themselves because they understood that those structures afforded them more protection and more rights than other possible alternatives. For Grote, democratic freedom was the best guarantor of both stability and civic virtue.

45. Grote, *History of Greece*, 4:81.

Mitford had condemned modern liberal democratic politics by equating it with the lawlessness of ancient Athens. A half-century later Grote reversed the analysis. He vindicated democratic Athens by arguing that it had achieved the kind of stability and constitutional morality that the British liberal state enjoyed in the mid-Victorian age. To make his case, Grote frequently applied to Athenian politics terminology associated with British political development from the Stuarts to his own day and in effect portrayed Athenian political history as an evolution from an absolutist state to parliamentary democracy. In a parenthetical phrase he would usually acknowledge the tentative validity of such terminology, but would then ignore the problems it presented as he developed his case. For example, according to Grote the Homeric kingdoms had not been mixed monarchies as Mitford had contended. Rather, they were governments "founded (*if we may employ modern phraseology*) upon divine right as opposed to the sovereignty of the people, but requiring, as an essential condition, that the king shall possess force, both of body and mind, not unworthy of the exalted breed to which he belongs." Those kingdoms should not be associated with modern monarchies in which power for mischief was circumscribed by means of "representative constitutions acting under a certain force of manners, customs, and historical recollection." Consequently, the hatred of kings so often manifest in early Greek history constituted at that time a laudable virtue that flowed from the "deep conviction of the necessity of universal legal restraint."[46] That worthy conviction in conjunction with the excessive claims of royal authority inevitably led to political instability and the absence of constitutional morality.

Having asserted the divine-right character of the early monarchies, Grote proceeded to tell the story of the rise of Greek liberty. The ancient oligarchs eventually tamed the power of the kings. Yet, having protected their rights from the potentially unchecked power of monarchy, the oligarchs failed to provide similar security to lesser persons in the society. The resentment aroused by the oligarchs among the lower orders had in turn called forth the "despot," Grote's translation of the word *tyrannos*. The rule of the despots also failed to establish long-range stability and social peace. Resistance to the gov-

46. Ibid., 3:5 (italics mine), 12.

ernment, followed by political chaos and personal insecurity, were the eventual outcomes of despotism. Consequently, before the fifth century there was little or nothing commendable or stable about Greek political life. Monarchy, oligarchy, and despotism each had proved itself incapable of fostering constitutional morality.

Grote's solution to this political dilemma was, of course, democracy; but here he had to be very careful. The Solonian reforms wherein both Mitford and Thirlwall had seen the beginning of Greek democracy had proved only marginally successful. They had also involved the redistribution of property and had been followed by a period of despotism under the Pisistratids. This scenario too closely resembled the confiscation of property during the French Revolution and Napoleon's later tyranny to suit Grote's polemical purposes. Consequently, he denied Solon the honor of having founded the democracy. Instead Grote portrayed Solon's major achievement as the structuring of a new system of credit in Athens. By his *Seisachtheia* Solon had abrogated existing debts and made it henceforth illegal for a debtor to become the property of a creditor because of failure to meet financial obligations. Thereafter, banking, coinage, and contracts became more secure in Athens, even during its later democratic age, than anywhere else in the ancient world and more so than in most European kingdoms until very recent times. Despite these economic reforms, however, Solon's overall political policy was fundamentally undemocratic since it "left the essential powers of the state still in the hands of the oligarchy."[47] Through this interpretation of Solon's rule, Grote implicitly argued first that Greek democracy had not commenced with changes in property arrangement and second that property and contracts established under a nondemocratic regime would not necessarily be endangered by the emergence of democratic government. Property and democracy were, in his opinion, absolutely compatible. Property might be even more secure under democracy than under alternative modes of government because democracy encouraged stability through constitutional morality.

Grote acknowledged that Solon had planted the seeds of democratic government and had allowed censure of officials by the Assembly and Council. Yet under the Solonian constitution Athenian political life

47. Ibid., p. 128.

amounted to little more than a series of oligarchical rivalries. There was little or no citizen loyalty to the political structure.

> In the age of Solon there was no political idea or system yet current which could be assumed as an unquestionable datum—no conspicuous standard to which the citizens could be pledged under all circumstances to attach themselves. The option lay only, between a mitigated oligarchy in possession, and a despot in possibility; a contest wherein the affections of the people could rarely be counted upon in favour of the established government.

The almost inevitable result of this situation was the Pisistratid despotism which represented the victory of one oligarchical party over all others. Again it was crucial that Grote construe Solon's constitution as essentially undemocratic in order to suggest that oligarchy rather than democracy had fostered the Pisistratid despotism under which Athenian political structures became "a mere empty formality, working only in subservience to the reigning dynasty, and stripped of all real controlling power."[48] Under the coercive leveling power of the despot the distinction between citizen and noncitizen became obscured, and neither personal nor moral sentiments attached the people to the institutions of government.

However, during the turmoil following the expulsion of Hippias in 510 B.C. Cleisthenes transformed this situation and injected a new and unprecedented vitality into political life. Aligning himself with the more popular elements in the Assembly, Cleisthenes abolished one mode of political association—the four Ionic tribes based on family, religion, and geography—and constructed another—the ten Athenian tribes whose existence was based on their position in Athens' new civic life. Each new tribe was composed of *demes* forced into *trittyes,* units of local government that were not usually geographically contiguous with others from the same tribe. Cleisthenes also admitted numerous metics and superior slaves into citizenship.

According to Grote, through these reforms "the Athenian people, politically considered, thus became one homogeneous whole." When the members of a *deme* (he almost wholly ignored the *trittyes*) functioned politically as part of a tribe composed of other *demes* from

48. Ibid., 3:146; 4:57.

all over Attica, they could have no "separate hope or fears apart from the whole state." Cleisthenes had thus devised structures whereby the political life of Athens could function free of the sinister or particular interests that originated in local oligarchy, family prejudice, or "factions arising out of neighborhood." Grote regarded these reforms as the "real and important revolution" that had created the Athenian democracy and the atmosphere of constitutional morality it nurtured. Through the functioning of the reformed Assembly

> men were . . . trained to the duty both of speakers and hearers, and each man, while he felt that he exercised his share of influence on the decision, identified his own safety and happiness with the vote of the majority, and became familiarised with the notion of a sovereign authority which he neither could nor ought to resist. This was an idea new to the Athenian bosom. With it came the feelings sanctifying free speech and equal law . . . together with that sentiment of the entire commonwealth as one indivisible, which always overruled, though it did not supplant, the local and cantonical specialities.

The ideas of liberty and equality and "the grand and new idea of the sovereign People, composed of free and equal citizens" produced an "electric effect" on the Athenians, as in modern times it had on the French, and fostered "a host of sentiments, motives, sympathies, and capacities, to which they had before been strangers." There arose within the citizens of the democracy qualities of loyalty and sentiments of patriotism "disposing them to the voluntary action and suffering on its behalf, such as no coercion on the part of other governments could extort."[49]

In tracing the beginning of genuine Athenian democracy and civic virtue to the reforms of Cleisthenes, Grote's analysis delineated in the Greek experience the successful application of political ideals that he had previously urged upon his own nation. The critical point of juncture between British and Athenian politics was the issue of community versus particular, or sinister, interests. In 1831 Grote published the pamphlet "Essentials of Parliamentary Reform" in which he argued that the existing British constitution had "lost its hold on our

49. Ibid., 4:59, 61, 60, 55, 67, 104, 105.

moral feelings." It no longer served the general interest of the nation but rather a variety of corrupt particular interests. As Grote explained:

> Now the general interest, far from being composed of various local and professional interests, is not only distinct from, but exclusive of, every one of them. The interest of an individual by himself apart—the interest of the same man jointly with any given fraction of his fellow-citizens—all these are distinct objects, abhorrent and irreconcilable in general, coinciding occasionally by mere accident.... And a governing body which would promote the universal interest, must discard all inclination to the separate interest of any class whatever.

The general interest could predominate only "when it stands forth prominently and conspicuously as the single purpose of delegation—when it enters into every man's feelings of duty—and when it is least traversed and overlaid by other objects of pursuit." Toward achieving that goal, Grote suggested that in addition to reform of Parliament and introduction of the secret ballot, there should also be devised "a proper distribution of electoral bodies and places of voting" that would help to dissolve local geographical and corporate ties.[50] By these devices the critical reason of each individual voter could be brought to bear with genuine independence on the issues being decided by an election. With such care for restoring the general interest, the reformed constitution would presumably again command the moral feelings of the nation. In the fourth volume of *A History of Greece,* published in 1847, Grote portrayed the reforms of Cleisthenes as having in effect vindicated the wisdom of the kind of radical reform program that he had proposed in 1831. Moreover, whereas the moderate Reform Act of 1832, which Grote regarded as incomplete, had been followed by the particularistic politics of the Anti-Poor Law Movement, Chartism, and the Anti-Corn Law League, the revolution of Cleisthenes had fostered new unity and patriotism in Athens.

The political arrangements that Grote advocated in 1831, and major portions of *A History of Greece,* displayed certain affinities with the politics of Rousseau as well as of Bentham and the philosophic radi-

50. George Grote, *The Minor Works of George Grote* ed. Alexander Bain (London: John Murray, 1873), pp. 3, 30, 31–32, 34.

cals.[51] Like Grote, Rousseau had been exceedingly sensitive to the danger that private interests posed to a healthy civic life. In the *Social Contract* and other works Rousseau had consistently argued that a person's "particular interest may speak to him quite differently from the common interest." The major achievement of wise social and constitutional arrangements was the transformation of self-love into community loyalty, and actual participation in civic life constituted for Rousseau a major means of education for common citizenship. Furthermore, he had also advocated some kind of electoral machinery whereby citizens might vote in complete civic independence rather than as members of particular associations because he held that it was "essential, if the general will is to be able to express itself, that there should be no partial society within the State, and that each citizen should think only his own thoughts."[52] Grote's pamphlet of 1831 and his great House of Commons speech on the ballot in 1833 echoed similar political sentiments, which he expressed in more extreme rhetoric than had Rousseau. In a private letter of 1837 to Lord Brougham Grote also wrote of the need to multiply "independent wills" and to exclude "the influence of those private hopes and fears which deprive a man of his free agency at the moment of polling."[53]

Grote employed Rousseau's thought eclectically and unsystematically, as he did that of so many other Continental writers. Grote hoped

51. It is difficult to ascertain Grote's exact familiarity with Rousseau, but certain links can be established. It is certain that he had studied *Lettres écrites de la montagne* (which included a summary of the *Social Contract*) because his notebooks contain a long passage from this work dealing with particular and general political interests. *George Grote Papers,* British Library, Add. Mss. 29529, pp. 31–32.

52. Jean-Jacques Rousseau, *The Social Contract and Discourses,* trans. George Douglas Howard Cole (New York: E. P. Dutton and Co., 1950), pp. 17, 27. It is probable that Grote's translation of *tyrannos* as *despot* throughout *A History of Greece* also derives from the *Social Contract* in which Rousseau stated, "In order that I may give different things different names, I call him who usurps the royal authority a *tyrant,* and him who usurps the sovereign power a *despot.* The tyrant is he who thrusts himself in contrary to the laws to govern in accordance with the laws; the despot is he who sets himself above the laws themselves. Thus the tyrant cannot be a despot, but the despot is always a tyrant" (p. 87; French text also consulted). Mitford had presented the *tyrannos* as a tyrant in the Rousseauean sense. Grote portrayed the *tyrannos* as a Rousseauean despot because laws required the assent of individual moral feeling and the *tyrannos* always smothered that feeling and was content with mere formal observance of law.

53. George Grote to Lord Brougham, 31 July 1837, Brougham Papers, 10623, University College London.

for the realization of the general interest without suppressing the private self of citizens. For that reason, in sharp contrast to Rousseau, he praised Athens and condemned Sparta. Grote portrayed Cleisthenes as an almost Rousseauistic legislator who had nurtured the triumph of the general interest in Athens without fostering the Spartan frame of mind that had been so "deeply possessed with the feelings of command and obedience" and "comparatively insensible to the ideas of control and responsibility." In Grote's view, Cleisthenes' reforms had permitted the functioning of "the sentiment of the entire commonwealth as one indivisible"—something resembling the general will— liberated from pernicious particularistic interests but within a climate of open discussion, civic equality, enlightened thought, individual initiative, and secure property.[54] In other words, Grote believed that a democratic moral commonwealth could be established and had been established in Athens without requiring the extensive personal sacrifices that Rousseau had demanded. This outlook would eventually lead Grote into considerable difficulty in accounting for the absence of fervent patriotism at the time of the Macedonian onslaught. But initially he accounted for the failure of Athenians to pursue the general interest by appealing in Comtean fashion to intellectual backwardness rather than personal selfishness on their part.

Detractors of Athenian democracy never wearied of reciting examples of irrational, immoral, and vicious political behavior and misjudgment that filled the annals of the city. These always included the confusion surrounding the launching of the Syracusan invasion, the persecution of the victorious generals after the battle of Arginusae, the condemnation of Socrates, and the failure to stave off the Macedonian conquest. Grote acknowledged all of these errors, but he denied that any of them originated in the democratic character of the constitution. Rather, he drew upon his analysis of the survival of mythic thought into the fifth century to defend the democracy against its critics. He portrayed the Athenians as committing most of their political blunders when they behaved in accordance with surviving mental habits, moral sentiments, or political deference whose origins predated the establishment of the democracy and that suggested that the process of democratization had been somewhat incomplete. The crimes of the

54. Grote, *History of Greece*, 3:7; 4:67.

city occurred when the Athenians acted as men rather than as genuinely democratic citizens. Like Rousseau, Grote did not equate every majority decision with an expression of the general will or general interest. The general interest of the democratic community could express itself only when citizens were properly informed and could act according to reason. Those conditions had not prevailed each time the Athenian Assembly gathered, especially if the vestiges of the mythic frame of mind were operative. The latter situation prevailed during the recall of Alcibiades from the expedition against Syracuse.

In 415 B.C., shortly after the Athenian Assembly had approved the invasion of Sicily, the Hermae, images of household gods, that stood outside homes were mutilated during the night. Alcibiades, among others, was linked to the crime and charged with profaning the Eleusynian mysteries. He denied the charges, and the expedition set sail. But soon the Assembly recalled Alcibiades to stand trial. On the return voyage he defected to Sparta. In Athens itself other citizens were imprisoned, tried, and executed. The dreary affair had traditionally provided conservatives with a major example of the fickleness of the Athenian democracy and its capacity for mob action.

Not unexpectedly, Grote looked at the matter differently.[55] There was no reason to think the Spartans or citizens of another oligarchical polity would have behaved differently from the Athenians. In the climate of religious terror, it had seemed absolutely necessary that the culprits be apprehended to secure the city from the wrath of the gods. Those driving religious fears were the product of predemocratic Greek culture rather than of the democratic polity of Athens. Furthermore, Alcibiades' detractors were members of the oligarchical party who, having failed to destroy him before launching the invasion, consciously exploited the religious unrest for their own particular ends. Grote also observed in a footnote that the ancient Athenians were actually less culpable morally and politically than the seventeenth-century Englishmen who had prosecuted the Popish Plot. In Athens a real conspiracy had defaced the Hermae, whereas in Stuart England, except in the mind of Titus Oates, there had been no plot.

The second moral enormity often cited to exemplify the mob action

55. Ibid., 7:52–54.

and ingratitude of the Athenian democracy was the illegal condemnation of the eight generals who, after winning the naval battle of Arginusae in 406 B.C., had allowed several hundred Athenian sailors to
drown. Casting aside proper legal procedures, the Athenian Assembly
sentenced the generals to death. Grote regarded this incident as the
darkest of all events in the record of the Athenian democracy. The
explanation of its occurrence provided the occasion for his most significant exploration of the kinds of sacrifice that democratic citizenship
might entail.

The charges against the generals had initially been raised before a
meeting of the Athenian Assembly. Some days later a meeting of the
Council of Five Hundred was held, at which it ruled illegally that the
final judgment should be imposed collectively on the eight men and
only with regard to the evidence presented in the previous Assembly
meeting. Between the gathering of the Assembly and the Council
meeting, the festival of Apaturia had taken place, during which were
observed major rites of family life, including marriage and commemoration of the dead. Grote regarded the festival as nothing less than an
atavism on the democratic landscape.

> This was the characteristic festival of the Ionic race; handed down
> from a period anterior to the constitution of Cleisthenes, and to
> the ten new tribes each containing so many demes—and bringing
> together the citizens in their primitive unions of family, gens,
> phratry, etc., the aggregate of which had originally constituted
> the four Ionic tribes, now superannuated.[56]

Apaturia celebrated the very modes of familial, religious, and local
association that Cleisthenes had attempted to exorcise from politics
through the new, moral association of citizenship.

During this ancient festival in 406 B.C., a large number of men
(possibly with plan but Grote thought more probably spontaneously)
had appeared in mourning clothes and with shaven heads as a sign of
outrage against the deaths of the sailors who were now absent from the
family circle. It had been after this incident that the eight generals were
condemned. Clearly, Grote argued, that heinous action had not originated in the democratic polity.

56. Ibid., p. 433.

The true explanation is different, and of serious moment to state. Political hatred, intense as it might be, was never dissociated, in the mind of a citizen of Athens, from the democratical forms of procedure: but the men, who stood out here as actors, had broken loose from the obligations of citizenship and commonwealth, and surrendered themselves, heart and soul, to the family sympathies and antipathies; feelings, first kindled, and justly kindled, by the thought that their friends and relatives had been left to perish unheeded on the wrecks—next, inflamed into preternatural and overwhelming violence by the festival of Apaturia, where all the religious traditions connected with the ancient family tie, all those associations which imposed upon the relatives of a murdered man the duty of pursuing the murderer, were expanded into detail and worked up by their appropriate renovating solemnity.

In that state of mind—both prerational and predemocratic—the Athenians had thrust off constitutional morality and condemned the generals. "Such," Grote acidly commented, "is the natural behavior of those who, having for the moment forgotten their sense of political commonwealth, become degraded into exclusive family-men."[57] The predemocratic bonds of religion and family sympathy had roused a primitive fanaticism that temporarily dissolved the bonds of citizenship and the civic morality of a democratic commonwealth.

The analysis of this incident revealed the genuinely radical nature of Grote's vendetta against modes of human association other than the ties of citizenship. His ideal citizens were essentially atomistic individuals who enjoyed few substantial social relationships other than mutual membership in the commonwealth. Only in *A History of Greece* did Grote fully explain how literally he had meant in 1831 that the general interest was "not only distinct from, but exclusive of, every" particular interest in the society. His remarks on the pernicious quality of family relationships in the body politic also prove how far from the mark were those later British writers and foreign socialist critics who regarded Grote as a mere spokesman for middle-class politics and morality. On the contrary, George Grote, in the words he once used to describe Plato, looked "to nothing short of a new genesis of the man and the citizen, with institutions calculated from the begin-

57. Ibid., 448, 449.

ning to work out the full measure of perfectibility."[58] Democracy for him had not been merely a matter of electoral devices but rather a vehicle for moral transformation.

The character of genuine democratic life that Grote delineated in regard to Athens explains his failure to take any particular pleasure in the adoption of the ballot in 1870. He told Mrs. Grote that even with the ballot British politics would never operate "upon a clear or enlightened perception of *general interests.*"[59] Nothing more than a struggle for party supremacy would ensue because of the partisan organization of the electorate. Forty years earlier he had hoped the ballot would reorient and revive British public life as Cleisthenes' reforms had stirred Athens. By 1870 he had decided that the modes of particularistic association that from time to time led Athens into crimes and errors would also continue to infect British politics. Grote retreated from the ballot not because he had become more conservative but because he had come to understand more clearly the social and intellectual changes required for the proper functioning of a radical democracy.

In the early forties Grote and other philosophic radicals ascribed the failure of their political program largely to the continuing impact of religion, the aristocracy, and particular class interests on British political life after the passage of the Reform Act. By appealing in the main to those same pernicious influences to explain the major errors of the Athenian democracy, Grote redirected the debate over the Athenian constitution. Previously, Athens had stood as an example of the danger of democracy to stable political activity. Grote reversed the analysis and portrayed the post-Cleisthenian experience of Athens as an object lesson in the threat that religion, aristocracy, and particularism posed to a democratic state. Democracy had accounted for the constitutional morality and patriotism of Athens. And when other evil influences had undermined that morality or sapped that patriotism, it was those institutions of the democracy most often condemned by the conservatives—popular juries, ostracism, and the demagogues—that had provided for its internal stabilization.

For Grote, as for earlier historians, Pericles' degradation of the

58. Ibid., 8:198.
59. H. Grote, *Personal Life of George Grote,* p. 313.

Areopagus and his institution of the payment of juries constituted "the consummation of the Athenian democracy." The new juries brought the wealthy under the rule of law by making bribery difficult. The system nurtured constitutional morality by imparting "a sentiment of dignity to small and poor men, through the discharge of a function exalted as well as useful—in calling forth the patriotic sympathies, and exercising the mental capacities of every individual."[60] The popular juries thus helped to produce real equality among citizens and respect for the general interest, and they served as institutions of civic education. Although the Athenian dikasteries might, in Grote's opinion, have been improved by certain guidance from judges so as to avoid popular prejudice, they still had provided the best opportunity for a fair trial that had existed in the West prior to the experience of British and American citizens during the past century.

The most significant danger to the stability of Athens originated not in the alleged corruption of juries but in the pride and ambition of overpowerful citizens who might seek to undermine the constitution for selfish ends. Despotisms or oligarchies could use their armies to protect themselves against such overmighty subjects, but that alternative was not open to democracies, whose magistrates might use an army for their own selfish purposes. The Athenian institution that protected the emerging democratic constitution from internal disruption by private citizens was the much maligned practice of ostracism—"the safety-gun of the republic." Because it banished a dangerous or allegedly dangerous person by peaceful, constitutional means, ostracism brought tranquility to public debate in Athens. In casting a vote of ostracism, no citizen had to "depart from the constitution or lose his reverence for it." Rather than a manifestation of party politics, ostracism was "an expression of deliberate public feeling." The domestic tranquility achieved through this wise institution meant that eventually the Athenians were able "to dispense with that exceptional security which ostracism offered." The folly of exiling Damon and Hyperbolus, who were in no sense enemies of the constitution, had led the Athenians to recognize that ostracism was no longer necessary. They then abandoned it. Meanwhile, it had served an "inestimable tutelary purpose."[61]

60. Grote, *History of Greece*, 5:236, 245.
61. Ibid., 4:78, 86, 85, 86, 89.

Grote's case for the benefits of ostracism—one of the most carefully argued sections in the history—was a rationally convincing brief such as a lawyer might submit to a court or, perhaps more appropriately, such as a banker might expect to receive from a person requesting a loan for a dubious undertaking. His argument amounted to a *post hoc ergo propter hoc* proposition that ostracism had permitted the democracy to grow "from infancy to manhood without a single attempt to overthrow it by force."[62] But, as Evelyn Abbott pointed out later in the century, Grote failed to present a single example to support his contention.[63] Nor did Grote admit that ostracism provided no security against attempts by followers of an exiled leader to disrupt constitutional procedures in order to return their chief. Grote himself seems to have recognized that for all his rationalization ostracism remained an affair of factions that might have operated as unjustly as conservative critics charged. His answer to such underlying doubts was merely an *ad hominem* argument. Conservative governments had themselves excluded pretenders to thrones, such as the current Duke of Bordeaux or Napoleon, or a century earlier Charles Edward Stuart. But, Grote declared, "No man treats this as any extravagant injustice, yet it is the parallel of the ostracism."[64] In this fashion Grote may have exposed the double political standard of the conservatives, but he did not prove that ostracism had been either just or pragmatically useful.

To contemporary readers the most astonishing feature of Grote's rehabilitation of the Athenian democracy was his vigorous defense of the demagogue Cleon. That portion of *A History of Greece* also most clearly displayed Grote's stategy of making Athens an object lesson in the dangers posed by conservative forces in a democracy. Previous antidemocratic writers, such as Mitford, had argued that a modern liberal democratic state would resemble lawless Athens. Reversing the analogy, Grote presented ancient, democratic Athens as almost a mirror image of the stable, liberal mid-Victorian polity. By imposing the

---

62. Ibid., p. 86.

63. Evelyn Abbott, *A History of Greece*, 2nd ed., 1893 (London: Longmans, Green, and Co.; reprinted., 1911), 1:483n. The possible utility of ostracism in the liberal state did impress some later readers. H. G. Wells reported that Gilbert Murray once suggested to him that ostracism might have averted the Ulster crisis of 1914 by ridding the political arena of Edward Carson. H. G. Wells, *The Outline of History* (Garden City, N.Y.: Garden City Publishing Co., 1925), p. 262.

64. Grote, *History of Greece*, 4:88.

nineteenth-century parliamentary context on the ancient Athenian institutions, Grote allowed and practically compelled his readers to associate the Athenian Assembly with structures, procedures, and a
sense of decorum that had never existed there. More important, he
could portray the same types of political influences he saw interfering
with the contemporary parliamentary system as those that had undermined Athens.

Grote's transformation of the character of the Athenian Assembly
was the single most stunning example of Victorian domestication of
Greek life and in large measure accounted for the profound sense of
intimacy that later writers perceived between Athens and Britain. A
few years later Mommsen would similarly modernize late Republican
Rome. Grote described Pericles as the "prime minister," and he
portrayed the Assembly as divided between "the party of movement
against that of resistance, or of reformers against conservatives."
Within that parliamentary framework, which Grote confessed was
not wholly applicable, the demagogue Cleon stood as "a man of the
opposition, whose province it was to supervise and censure official
men for their public conduct." Cleon's methods were those required
of one whose social position could not automatically command the
attention of the Assembly as could that of wealthy speakers or those
from established families. Cleon, a leather seller, had to work harder,
attend meetings more assiduously, and display more audacity than
members of the well-organized political clubs. Although his tone may
have been bitter and his invective extreme, he rigidly adhered to the
forms of the constitution. Previous historians had generally viewed
Cleon through the eyes of Thucydides and Aristophanes, his ancient
enemies. However, continuing the analogy with the modern scene,
Grote argued that such a practice made no more sense than "judging
Sir Robert Walpole, or Mr. Fox, or Mirabeau, from the numerous
lampoons put in circulation against them."[65]

The more just and proper way to evaluate Cleon was to compare
him with a contemporary noble or oligarchical Athenian leader. For
that foil, Grote chose Nicias, who had long enjoyed an unblemished
reputation for piety, honesty, patriotism, and bravery. But as Grote
dissected the record of Nicias with the keenest of polemical blades,

65. Ibid., 5:225, 218; 6:69, 260.

little of his former reputation survived. Grote went so far as to declare, "Never did any man at Athens, by mere force of demagogic qualities, acquire a measure of esteem so exaggerated and so durable, combined with so much power of injuring his fellow-citizens as the anti-demagogic Nicias." In his superstitious piety the oligarchical general eschewed the philosophers of the day and surrounded himself with prophets who guided his decisions "just as the government of Louis XIV and other Catholic princes has been modified by the change of confessors."[66] Nicias used his personal fortune to purchase the popular esteem of the citizenry. He had been party to allowing Cleon to rush the Assembly into a war policy in the pernicious hope that an ensuing military defeat would discredit the demagogue. On military campaigns Nicias displayed carelessness and bad judgment. Yet the allegedly fickle Athenian people never swerved in their devotion to him even after the dreary performance in Sicily.

The blind democratic deference to oligarchical leaders in Athens provided the best defense for the activities of the demagogues. Such deference represented still another instance of the predemocratic mode of association and of political thought interfering with the successful functioning of the democracy. Only a demagogue, such as Cleon, only a spokesman for a constitutional opposition, might have been able to expose the folly of the decision to invade Sicily as urged by Alcibiades or to point out the incompetence of Nicias's military leadership.

> Happy would it have been for Athens had she now had Cleon present, or any other demagogue of equal power, at that public assembly which took the melancholy resolution of sending fresh forces to Sicily and continuing Nicias in the command! The case was one in which the accusatory eloquence of the demagogue was especially called for, to expose the real past mismanagement of Nicias—to break down the undeserved confidence in his ability and caution which had grown into a sentiment or routine—to prove how much mischief he had already done, and how much more he would do if continued.[67]

66. Ibid., 7:191; 6:67.
67. Ibid., 7:123.

Of course the absence of a genuine opposition speaker in the debates on the Sicilian invasion (Nicias's role being ambiguous at the initial discussion) undermined Grote's previous contention that there existed an actively recognized opposition in the Assembly. However, the presence or absence of an opposition in Athens had not really been his point. His fundamental argument was that democratic governments could not reach correct decisions unless the bonds of deference were broken. Deference to the nobility and the monetary corruption practiced by the nobility had interfered with the exercise of citizens' independent judgment and had undermined the Athenian democracy just as, in Grote's opinion, they were corrupting the modern British liberal state.

In the closing volumes of *A History of Greece* Grote continued to portray the pernicious influence of allowing particular interests to triumph over the general interest in a democracy. The decline of the Athenian democracy from the momentary enthusiasm and patriotism following the reforms of Cleisthenes became most fully manifest in the failure to meet the challenge of the Macedonian threat.

> All depended upon her will: upon the question, whether her citizens were prepared in their own minds to incur the expense and fatigue of a vigorous foreign policy—whether they would handle their pikes, open their purses, and forego the comforts of home, for the maintenance of Grecian and Athenian liberty against a growing, but not as yet irresistible, destroyer. To such a sacrifice the Athenians could not bring themselves to submit; and in consequence of that reluctance, they were driven in the end to a much graver and more irreparable sacrifice—the loss of liberty, dignity, and security.[68]

In a sense this comment suggested that in Athens democracy and citizenship had not, except perhaps at the time of the Persian invasion, been the dominant mode of association or of personal self-definition. Democracy had not failed as a form of government in Athens, but it had not succeeded fully in transforming the men of Athens into citizens. Whereas earlier commentators had blamed the democratic in-

68. Ibid., 11:82.

stitutions of Athens for its defeat at the hands of Macedonia, Grote blamed the men of Athens.

Grote had been able and more than eager to defend Athenian democracy against its conservative and aristocratic enemies, but he could not defend the Athenians against themselves. The institutions of democracy in and of themselves had been incommensurable with human nature. In the Assembly of Demosthenic Athens Grote could only perceive private interests in conflict with each other. As might be expected, he championed Demosthenes but with less vigor and enthusiasm than he had defended Cleon. By the age of Demosthenes it was almost impossible to identify the forces actually supporting civic virtue. To describe that situation, Grote reverted to an extended organic metaphor that would have been more nearly appropriate to Thirlwall's history than to his own.

> The Demosthenic Athenian of 360 B.C. had as it were grown old. Pugnacity, Panhellenic championship, and the love of enterprise, had died within him. He was a quiet, home-keeping, refined citizen, attached to the democratic constitution, and executing with cheerful pride his ordinary city-duties under it; but immersed in industrial or professional pursuits, in domestic comforts, in the impressive manifestations of the public religion, in the atmosphere of discussion and thought, intellectual as well as political. To renounce all this for foreign and continued military service, he considered as a hardship not to be endured, except under the pressure of danger near and immediate. Precautionary exigencies against distant perils, however real, could not be brought home to his feelings; even to pay others for serving in his place, was a duty he could scarcely be induced to perform.[69]

Ultimately the Athenian democracy had not produced citizens who would save themselves. Private interests at last presided over the demise of the general interest and the liberty of the city. The late, uncertain response to Macedonia and the final conquest of Athens stood as a warning of the fate of a liberal state in which religion, deference, and particularism hindered the formation of a genuinely democratic frame of mind.

69. Ibid., p. 83–84.

Although Grote has traditionally and correctly been numbered among the major nineteenth-century defenders of democratic government, the character of his democratic vision has rarely received much attention. Initially he believed that electoral reform would redirect political life for the good and foster the general interest. His own political experience then led him to believe that an intellectual transformation of residual social and religious attitudes was required. This faith in institutional and intellectual reform led him, like so many other nineteenth-century liberals and radicals, to avoid the question of fundamental social change in establishing the moral bonds of democracy. Furthermore, so eager was he to prove that democracy was less coercive than alternative governments and less tyrannical than its opponents charged that he ignored those elements of actual or potential coercion that pertain to governments simply by virtue of their being governments. He tended to portray democracy as providing benefits that would naturally stimulate patriotism rather than as either requiring or demanding sacrifice that might not always flow forth automatically. His early Benthamite belief in the more or less automatic identity of interests if unhindered by sinister interests left him ill-equipped to deal with the selfish particularism of both the mid-Victorian liberal state and the fourth-century Athenian democracy.[70]

Grote has also been unquestioningly regarded as the foremost champion of Athens. He did defend Athens from unjust and misconceived conservative attacks, but he did not in fact champion Athenian democracy. The democracy that he championed had no precedent, past or present. His model was the community that under better cricumstances Athens might have become after the reforms of Cleisthenes and that Britain might still achieve. Grote's democratic community in which the general interest would predominate over religion, deference, and particularism lay in the future. It belonged to the tradition of radical rationalist utopias, though it remained outside the social utopian vision. However, Victorian readers missed the radical

70. The question of whether Benthamism urged the automatic or artificial identity of social or political interests remains a vexing one. Both elements are present in the thinking of the members of the Benthamite coterie and sometimes in the same person. For this reason, the utilitarian circle was the source for the idea of a centralized state and for a libertarian vision. Grote's thought on the whole pertains to the latter point of view although he frequently demonstrates frustration with the impact of selfish interests on public life.

thrust of *A History of Greece* just as Victorian voters had earlier spurned Grote's radical political program. They remained content with the moderate liberalism of the First Reform Act, and for many years they admired Athens for the resemblance Grote had convinced them the ancient city bore to their own national polity. The great history that Grote had hoped might stir his countrymen to self-criticism and reform instead provided frequent occasion for political narcissism.

Gladstone versus Grote: The Homeric Polity and Victorian Politics

Grote's *History of Greece* achieved immediate and long-standing acclaim. Distinguished reviewers of the various volumes, including John Stuart Mill, A. P. Stanley, and George Cornewall Lewis, praised the power of argument, the prodigious scholarship, and the familiarity with Continental sources. For at least a half a century the work remained the standard study in English on Greek history and profoundly influenced other scholarly histories and popular textbooks at home and abroad. Near the close of the century Richard Claverhouse Jebb told an audience that Grote's *History of Greece* had done more than any other single book "to invest his subject with a vivid, an almost modern interest for a world wider than the academic."[71] Despite its reservations about the late Athenian democracy, which contemporaries either ignored or failed to understand, the basic impact of Grote's study was to persuade large segments of the articulate Victorian reading public that Athenian history was the story " . . . of a richly endowed people, learning the arts of self-government and free inquiry with the rapidity of an infant prodigy, and springing in a little more than a century from the depths of ignorance and political degra-

71. Richard Claverhouse Jebb, *Essays and Addresses* (Cambridge: Cambridge University Press, 1907), p. 534. The examples of four rather different works suggest the manner in which Grote's views became diffused: see *History of Ancient Greece,* in Chambers Educational Courses (London: W. and R. Chambers, 1855); Rev. James White, *Landmarks of the History of Greece* (London: G. Routledge & Co., 1857), dedicated to the Ventnor and Bonchurch Mechanics Institute; William Smith, *A History of Greece from the Earliest Times to the Roman Conquest* (London: John Murray, 1854), the key one-volume textbook of the second half of the century; and William Watkins Lloyd, *The Age of Pericles: A History of the Politics and Arts of Greece from the Persian to the Peloponnesian War* (London: Macmillan and Co., 1875), a sophisticated popular history for middle- and upper-middle-class audiences.

dation to the loftiest heights of intellectual greatness and constitutional freedom."[72] In other words, they saw in Athens the British achievement.

Although some contemporaries dissented from one or more of the particulars of Grote's defense of Athens and radical democracy, only one English writer attempted to criticize the fundamental basis of Grote's argument and political philosophy. That person was Gladstone, whose discussion of politics in *Studies on Homer and the Homeric Age* (1858) was a direct reply to Grote. Gladstone's consideration of Homeric politics was a Peelite critique of the presuppositions of radical Victorian political thought. Without returning to Mitford's concept of a mixed constitution, Gladstone offered a conservative interpretation of Homeric political life that cast doubt on Grote's view of the Athenian democracy and on the virtues of democracy in general. Mid-Victorian readers seem to have failed to perceive the relationship between Gladstone's Homeric studies and Grote's history because Gladstone's arguments were typically convoluted and because his treatment of Homeric mythology and religion so thoroughly detracted from the seriousness with which his work was received.

Although Grote had denied the historical validity of the events of the Homeric narrative, he had defended the accuracy of the descriptions of political and social life recorded in the epics. Using the Homeric kings as one point of contrast with the later Greek democracies, he had portrayed Homeric political life as lacking all those virtues that he associated with healthy politics. Those monarchs were absolute rulers in a society where the sinister interests of the few stood out in stark contrast to the good of the many. The most striking feature of Homeric politics was the "omnipotence of private force tempered and guided by family sympathies, and the practical nullity of that collective sovereign afterwards called *The City*." Debate and discussion were conspicuous by their absence, and the Homeric Council and Agora displayed a "nullity of positive function." There was clearly little role for opposition or criticism.

The fate which awaits a presumptuous critic, even where his virulent reproaches are substantially well-founded, is plainly set

72. James Talboys Wheeler, *The Life and Travels of Herodotus in the Fifth Century before Christ: An Imaginary Biography Founded on Fact,* 2 vols. (London: Longman, Brown, Green, and Longmans, 1855), 1:247–248.

forth in the treatment of Thersites; while the unpopularity of such a character is attested even more by the excessive pains which Homer takes to heap upon him repulsive personal deformities, than by the chastisement of Odysseus—he is lame, bald, crook-backed, of misshapen head and squinting vision.

Information flowed only from the monarch to the people. Most important, within Homeric government there existed no "idea of responsibility to the governed," but rather "the main-spring of obedience on the part of the people" consisted "in their personal feeling and reverence towards the chief."[73] There also appeared to be little evidence of rational consent to political decision or rational bases of legitimacy for the political processes and institutions.

Gladstone approached the Homeric age from a very different perspective than did Grote. He intended his consideration of Homeric politics to contribute to the more extensive historical and civic study of the classics in the reformed universities. One source of resistance to such study was the widespread feeling that the ancients had not provided political models proper for English life. The ancient states of Greece had seemed to swerve between repressive personal rule and democratic tyranny. Moreover, by mid-century Mitford's concept of mixed Homeric monarchies was no longer relevant to British politics or to conservative thought. Gladstone's analysis of Homeric politics paralleled the conservative accommodation to reform era politics that Robert Peel had accomplished as the conservative leader in the House of Commons. That policy, which Gladstone supported in the forties and continued to pursue in the fifties after Peel's death and the split in Conservative party ranks, consisted of the preservation of traditional political and religious institutions through moderate administrative reforms that removed egregious abuses and renewed public loyalty. In a sense it had been the success of Peel's strategy, as attested by the conservative victory in 1840, that had convinced George Grote to abandon political life. Gladstone's discussion of Homer once again posed a confrontation between a Peelite and a radical vision of politics.

In still another example of the Victorian domestication of the Greek experience, one no less striking than Grote's imposition of par-

73. Grote, *History of Greece,* 2:93, 67, 72, 61.

liamentary life on Periclean Athens, Gladstone contended that Homeric political structures were the institutions of ancient politics most "in harmony with the fundamental conceptions and even institutions, of the English-speaking races of the world." The Homeric heroes had themselves dwelled in an age of transition quite analogous to that of Victorian England. The patriarchal Homeric monarchies had to accommodate themselves to new realities of expanding commerce and economic competition. Those features of Homeric life meant that

> it should be easier for the English, than for the nations of most other countries, to make this picture real to their own minds; for it is the very picture before our own eyes in our own times and country, where visible traces of the patriarchal mould still coexist in the national institutions with political liberties of more recent fashion, because they retain their hold upon the general affections.[74]

Gladstone then proceeded to discern in the politics of the Homeric age of transition the wisdom of the Peelite policy of avoiding both unthinking reaction and heady liberalism or radicalism.

Gladstone's analysis of the Homeric polity essentially refuted Grote's interpretation point by point. If Grote could be shown to be wrong about the Homeric kingdoms, then the later development of radical Athenian democracy might be regarded as unwise or unnecessary. By analogy, if the Peelites were correct about policy for Britain, then solutions of political radicals, such as Grote, would also appear mistaken. Whereas Grote had regarded the Homeric monarchs as absolute rulers, Gladstone portrayed them as multitalented officials governing by implicit consent, careful attention to public opinion, and proper fulfillment of the moral expectations of the society. Their government had been tempered by "publicity and persuasion." Although usually portrayed as heroic fighters, every Homeric king had also been "emphatically a gentleman, and that in a sense not far from the one familiar to the Christian civilization of Europe." These Christian gentlemen had not imposed thier wills on repressed subjects, but had

---

74. William Ewart Gladstone, "Universitas Hominum; or the Unity of History," *North American Review* 145 (1887): 599; William Ewart Gladstone, *Studies on Homer and the Homeric Age,* 3 vols. (Oxford: Oxford University Press, 1858), 3:31.

ruled through genuine assent that flowed from the perennial laws of politics.

> The Homeric king reigns with the free assent of his subjects—an assent indeterminate, but real, and in both points alike resembling his kingly power. The relation between ruler and ruled is founded in the laws and conditions of our nature. Born in a state of dependence, man, when he attains to freedom and capacity for actions, finds himself the debtor both of his parents and of society at large; and is justly liable to discharge his debt by rendering service in return.[75]

This social reciprocity from which assent arose stemmed not from utility or rational calculation but from a natural and presumably innate sense of gratitude for previous service and a recognition of continuing dependence. Such assent was not a product of reflection but rather the result of natural sociability and a sense of the organic nature of human relationships.

The concept of sinister interests controlling political institutions for selfish ends—the problem that so haunted Grote and other philosophic radicals—was simply absent from Gladstone's purview. The Homeric king embodied the public perception of public problems and issues. He was "uplifted to set a high example, to lead the common counsels to common ends, to conduct the public and common intercourse with heaven, to decide the strifes of individuals, to defend the borders of the territory from invasion." Homer had believed that wise kings in partnership with wise councillors could and should decide what constituted the common good. On the other side of the coin, Homer possessed no concept of any domestic group that might "require repression or restraint from the government."[76] There were no natural domestic enemies of the monarchy or of the polity in general.

A major reason for the absence of domestic threats to the Homeric monarchies, in Gladstone's view, was the wise process of legislative discussion and collective decision-making achieved in the Council and the Agora, or Assembly. Although Homer portrayed the Council only as a military body, Gladstone thought there was evidence that it also functioned during peacetime. The Council was composed of

75. Gladstone, *Studies on Homer*, 3:7, 47, 67–68.
76. Ibid., p. 69.

those persons who, if not consulted, possessed sufficient private power to be able to cause the monarch difficulty. In that sense, the Homeric Council operated very much like the British cabinet and

> seems to have been a most important auxiliary instrument of government; sometimes as preparing materials for the more public deliberations of the Assembly, sometimes intrusted, as a kind of executive committee, with its confidence; always as supplying the Assemblies with an intellectual and authoritative element, in a concentrated form which might give steadiness to its tone, and advise its course with a weight adequate to so important a function.[77]

Gladstone believed Homer's descriptions of the debates of the chieftains proved that the Council had thoroughly debated issues before taking them to the Assembly. This process of Council debate rang true to public life as he had experienced it himself, and this particular congruity between Homer's description and his own day-to-day political activity was a major influence in convincing him of the historical accuracy of the Homeric epics.

Gladstone similarly believed that the Assembly had also been a genuinely deliberative body. The incidents of Book 2 of the *Iliad,* in which Agamemnon set before the troops the question of returning home, suggested to Gladstone that the soldiers were accustomed to hearing policy debated and then reaching some collective decision. The Assembly,

> instead of being the simple medium through which the king acted, was the arena on which either the will of the people might find a rude and tumultary vent, or, on the other hand, his royal companions in arms could say, as Diomed says, "I will use my right and resist your foolish project in debate; which you ought not to resent."

Such debate in the Assembly proved there had existed a large measure of free speech and persuasion in the Homeric polity. Nor should the harsh rebuking of Thersites be regarded as the usual treatment of opposition spokesmen because his example represented "railing" rather than "reasoning."[78]

77. Ibid., p. 98.
78. Ibid., pp. 100, 124.

Furthermore, that only a very few people in the Assembly actually participated in debates did not indicate that the remaining members were necessarily subject to misgovernment. In an exceedingly revealing comment Gladstone reminded his readers:

> Even in the nineteenth century, it very rarely happens that a working man takes part in the proceedings of a county meeting: but no one would on that account suppose that such an assembly can be used as the mere tool of the class who conduct the debate, far less of any individual prominent in that class.[79]

This was clearly the sentiment of a person who had rarely if ever felt constrained to remain silent during a county meeting. Furthermore, that remark displayed the incapacity of an honest conservative leader to understand that a political structure that favored the life of his own class might not also benefit the lower orders. Gladstone, like so many Peelite conservatives and liberals who rejected political radicalism, could not grasp that a social or political interest group could be sinister without being deliberately sinister.

Other serious problems also existed for Gladstone's extrapolation of a responsive political structure from Homer's descriptions of the conduct of ancient chieftains. Gladstone recognized in particular that there were no examples of actual voting or divisions in the councils and assemblies of the *Iliad* and *Odyssey*. Not unnaturally, Grote had supposed the absence of voting indicated that those institutions possessed no substantial power. Gladstone dissented from that opinion, and in a passage that must have gladdened the hearts of his conservative Oxford University electors he vigorously denounced decision-making by majorities.

> Decision by majorities is as much an expedient, as lighting by gas. In adopting it as a rule, we are not realizing perfection, but bowing to imperfection. We follow it as best for us, not as best in itself. . . . Decision by majorities has the great merit of avoiding, and that by a test perfectly definite, the last resort to violence; and of making force itself the servant instead of the master of authority. But our country still rejoices in the belief, that she does not decide all things by majorities. The first Greeks neither knew the

79. Ibid., p. 129.

use of this numerical dogma, nor the abuse of it. They did not employ it as an instrument, and in that they lost; but they did not worship it as an idol, and in that they greatly gained. . . . There could not be a grosser error than to deny every power to be a real one, unless we are able to measure its results in a table of statistics, and to trace at every step, with our weak and partial vision, the precise mode by which it works towards its end.[80]

This statement was a direct attack on the radical concept of democracy. Majority decisions might avoid conflict (achieve "constitutional morality" in Grote's analysis), but they were no guarantee of correct or just decisions, as Gladstone might well have argued, but did not, from the text of Grote's history. Gladstone's critique of decisions by majorities echoes Burke in its rejection of the rationalizing, calculating spirit in politics and looks forward to Arnold's denunciation of politics concerned with machinery rather than with the nurturing of cultured citizens. Gladstone in the 1850s understood intuitively what most political theorists did not recognize until the turn of the century—that politics must deal with the intangible and the nonrational as well as with the rational and predictable. He also understood, perhaps with an eye to the plebiscites of Napoleon and Louis Napoleon, that voting majorities do not necessarily ensure freedom for the voters.

Gladstone's remarks on majorities and popular participation in government were part of the broader debate on democracy that took place in Britain during the fifties and sixties. They were also significant documents in accounting for his personal intellectual and political transformation from the conservative member for Oxford into the "People's William." That important story belongs more properly in a biography of Gladstone, and it has been told many times. However, the volumes on Homer present evidence that has not been previously considered. Although in the study of Gladstone's home at Hawarden there were separate desks for political writing and for literary and theological essays, the same person worked at each. The views of political behavior presented in Gladstone's Homeric studies illustrate how he could pass from conservatism to the advocacy of greater democracy, just as Grote's *History of Greece* explains in large measure

80. Ibid., pp. 116–17.

how the political radical who supported the ballot in the thirties regretted its enactment by the Gladstone ministry in the seventies.

In *Studies on Homer and the Homeric Age* Gladstone emphasized the necessity for political leaders to respond to public opinion. Responsiveness to the public had been a hallmark of Homeric rulers. "In heroic Greece," Gladstone contended, "the King, venerable as was his title, was not the fountainhead of the common life, but only its exponent. The source lay in the community, and the community met in the Agora." When Homer wished to denote a spokesman from the Agora, he used the word *Tis,* meaning in this instance "someone" or "somebody." Gladstone urged, "The *Tis* of Homer is, I apprehend, what in England we now call public opinion."[81] Moreover, throughout his discussion of Homeric and modern oratory Gladstone portrayed the political leader as responding to a particular audience and formulating his opinions from it as well as for it. These views from his volumes of 1858 suggest that he thought popular opinion and popular expectations could and should modify political decisions and the stands of political leaders. As public opinion about further electoral reform changed in the early sixties, and as his constituency changed from Oxford to Lancashire, Gladstone modified his political opinions, as his study of Homer had suggested a wise leader should do.

In *Juventus Mundi,* published in 1869 as a condensation and revision of his earlier Homeric volumes, Gladstone made significant changes in the previously quoted attack on majorities. He reduced the long discussion to a single sentence: "There is no decision by numbers [in Homer]; the doctrine of majorities is an invention, an expedient, of a more advanced social development." The ridicule of majorities has disappeared and decision by majorities is even made to sound progressive. However, his apprehension over atomistic political majorities remained. In the new book on Homer Gladstone introduced the concept of "reverence"—which constituted "that powerful principle, the counter-agent to all meanness and selfishness, which obliges a man to have regard to some law or standard above that of force, and extrinsic to his own will, his own passions, or his own propensities." Gladstone portrayed this principle as having provided the moral glue for Homeric society. Reverence assured respect for the deity, recogni-

81. Ibid., p. 141.

tion of reciprocal rights among neighbors and fellow citizens, good faith, friendly relations beyond the limits of one's own class, and the integrity of the institution of marriage. Reverence was channeled toward parents, kings, the old, the beautiful, the opinions of other persons, the weak, the poor, and the dead. Gladstone declared that the emotion and habit of reverence represented to "the Greek mind and life what the dykes in Holland are to the surface of the country; shutting off passions as the angry sea, and securing a broad open surface for the growth of every tender and genial product of the soil."[82] Reverence in effect inhibited excessive selfishness and antisocial individualism.

Gladstone wrote those words on reverence a few months before he entered upon his first and greatest ministry. They were the last sentence in a chapter that had begun with a declaration of the similarity between the best ideas of Homeric and British government.

> Among the soundest of them we reckon the power of opinion and persuasion as opposed to force; the sense of responsibility in governing men; the hatred, not only of tyranny, but of all unlimited power; the love and the habit of public in preference to secret action; the reconciliation and harmony between the spirit of freedom on the one hand, the spirit of order and reverence on the other; and a practical belief in right as relative, and in duty as reciprocal. Of these elements, whether in ancient or in modern times, great governments have been made.[83]

By stressing reverence and qualities of political restraint, Gladstone was pleading for civility among citizens of the recently extended democracy and for patient questioning of existing practices and institutions. He was hoping to elicit those qualities that years before Grote had associated with the phrase "constitutional morality." However, Gladstone's path to such morality differed from Grote's.

Both men admired order and civility in public life, but Grote, haunted by the images of the sinister, selfish, antisocial drives in human nature, had by the end of his life come to despair over the possibility of suppressing those drives through political institutions.

82. William Ewart Gladstone, *Juventus Mundi: The Gods and Men of the Heroic Age* (London: Macmillan and Co., 1869), pp. 434, 449, 449–50.

83. Ibid., p. 413.

He had advocated the suppression of human selfishness through the swath of the majoritarian general interest cutting across all other personal and family loyalties for the sake of the good of the commonwealth. Grote had looked for something very nearly resembling the redemption of human nature through politics and had discovered it in neither London nor Athens. Gladstone, under no delusions about the potential goodness of temporal human nature, sought to alleviate political conflict and the possible tyranny of the majority through healthy traditional secondary associations to which citizens might devote as much or more loyalty as they did to the state. He upheld reverence for all those personal, family, religious, and local social ties that Grote abhorred and regarded as inhibitions to the proper functioning of democracy. For Gladstone those associations not only prevented the perversion of democracy and the atomization of its citizens but also allowed human nature properly to fulfill itself. The political testimony of Homer, which Gladstone read as a prescriptive narrative of early humankind flourishing in the freshness of its own humanity, taught the fundamental importance and wisdom of such human institutions, just as the residual elements of the primitive messianic tradition that Gladstone discerned in the epics taught him to look outside the political arena for the redemption of humankind. Thus armed with his faith in the Homeric record, Gladstone did not flinch from the face of the emerging democratic age. Its possible imperfections did not discourage him because unlike Grote he had never looked for the perfection or substantial moral improvement of human nature on earth.

Late-Victorian and Edwardian Reflections on Athens

Gladstone had been the only major mid-century British writer to question the fundamental political presuppositions of Grote's history, but his attack was so circuitous and so deeply embedded among other quite eccentric views of Homeric life that it exerted no perceptible influence on the consideration of Athenian and English politics. Most of Grote's reviewers, critics, and immediate imitators were exceedingly generous to the historian, and their exuberance for the Athenian constitution often far outstripped Grote's most favorable remarks and generally ignored his implicit radical critique of the city. For example,

E. A. Freeman, later professor of history at Oxford, declared that a fair examination of Athenian political institutions would lead to nothing less than the conclusion that "this mob clothed with executive functions made one of the best governments which the world ever saw." Participation in the Athenian Assembly assured the presence of a larger number of citizens fit to exercise power than had any other political system. Moreover, according to Freeman, "The average Athenian citizen was, in political intelligence, above the average English member of Parliament."[84]

Freeman's comments reflected both the persuasiveness of Grote's rehabilitation of the Athenian polity and the early signs of intellectual discontent with the mid-century liberal state. As this discontent grew, the evaluation of Grote's portrait of Athens became somewhat more critical. British politics became more complicated and more confused during the latter part of the century, and the treatment of Athenian politics often reflected that new complexity. Furthermore, as late-century political scientists and sociologists probed more deeply into the social and psychological foundations of democratic life, many of the attitudes, values, and institutions that Grote had most detested in ancient life came to be those most highly regarded by Edwardian scholars. Although by the First World War many commentators had come to believe that Athens and Britain had little in common, most would still have agreed with the historian who in 1927 argued that, despite the differences, Athenian political experience had nonetheless provided "a good rallying point round which we may sort out our political ideas."[85]

Although Grote's *History of Greece* had answered many of the earlier criticisms of Athens, it had left one issue largely unprobed. That was the question of slavery. As early as Jeremy Bentham English reformers had questioned whether any state with so extensive a slave population should be regarded as a democracy. Grote had tended to ignore Athenian slavery and had concentrated his major criticism on the helot system in Sparta. His reviewers quickly spotted the lacuna in his history and addressed themselves to the slavery issue. Generally speaking, their remarks revealed the willingness of mid-century liberals to exclude large portions of a population from political participation, their incapacity to confront the contemporary social question, and their reluctance to admit the close relationship between political and social structures in either the past or the present.

In 1850 George Cornewall Lewis, a liberal Whig cabinet minister and a distinguished classical scholar, suggested, no doubt with the Second French Republic in mind, that slavery had allowed Athens to escape two dangers that plagued modern, fully democratic states. Because the Athenian population included a large number of slaves who carried out much ordinary labor, Lewis explained, the term "poor citizen" appearing in ancient histories denoted a group of people "altogether unlike the populace of our large cities, or even the operatives of our manufacturing towns." In other words, slavery meant that the Athenian democracy even with its "poor citizens" had functioned without the direct political influence of the social residuum that mid-century Victorian liberals feared would tyrannize the state if the franchise were too broadly extended. Also, according to Lewis, the institution of slavery insured that a large segment of the Athenian population received their sustenance through private households and thereby the city was relieved from having to confront those "important questions, which are now comprehended under the name of *socialism*."[86] Lewis, who had earlier written an important book entitled *Remarks on the Use and Abuse of Political Terms* (1832), clearly understood that the evil indicated by the word *slavery* would be far outweighed in the minds of his middle-class readers by the intense anxiety and the specter of disorder roused by the term *socialism*.

John Stuart Mill was less complacent about Athenian slavery three years later in his review of Grote's *History of Greece,* but he still attempted to rationalize the institution and even suggested that some benefits may have acrued from it. Mill hesitantly agreed to regard Athens as a democracy because despite the presence of slaves the city had had a government directed "by a multitude, composed in majority of poor persons" and one also characterized by "boundless publicity and freedom of speech." Slavery undoubtedly represented "the greatest blot" on the record of the city, but in Mill's view Athenian slavery had been less evil than the slavery in modern America or the West Indies. In Athens the slaves had not been a separate race. They

86. George Cornewall Lewis, "Grote's *History of Greece,*" *Edinburgh Review* 91 (1850): 142.

could be freed and absorbed into the citizenry or made citizens in new colonies. The Greeks had also believed their slaves were possessed of moral personalities. Most important, the institution of slavery had not rendered manual labor dishonorable to the free classes of the Athenian population. Mill also suggested that slavery in ancient times should not receive a blanket condemnation because "as a temporary fact, in an early and rude state of the arts of life" the insitution may have been "a great accelerator of progress." The real evil of slavery was less the iniquity "of first introducing it, as of continuing it too long."[87] In this manner, Mill rooted Athenian slavery in the economic and social conditions of the time and separated it from the democratic political structure. He used a progressionist historicism to remove the moral obloquy of slavery from the ancient democracy just as Grote had appealed to a progressionist epistemological historicism to present religious mentality rather than political structures as the cause of harmful decisions by the democracy.

With the passage of the Second Reform Act in 1867 and the growing participation of the working class in political life, it became difficult, if not impossible, for scholars to suggest, as Lewis had, that there had been political benefits from slavery or to rationalize it as had Mill. Moreover, the awakening of genuine social concern and a sense of social guilt among university students and intellectuals led to a more forthright condemnation of the slavery in Athens. In 1880 A.C. Bradley of Oxford, who later became an influential Shakespearean critic, bluntly attacked Athenian slavery and those earlier commentators who had attempted to excuse it.

> This institution and the contempt even for free labour are the most striking proofs that the Hellenic solution of social problems was inadequate; modern writers find in them the "dark side" of Greek life, or even the "blot upon their civilization." But the latter expression at least is misleading, since it implies that such defects had no organic connection with the strength and beauty of this civilization; whereas, in fact, the life of "leisure," devoted to politics and culture or to war would have been impossible without them, and general conclusions drawn from Greek history which do not take them into account are inevitably vitiated.

87. John Stuart Mill, "Grote's *History of Greece,* IX, X, XI," *Edinburgh Review* 98 (1853): 439, 429, 430.

A few years later in a very thoughtful textbook on Greek history, which repeatedly betrayed contemporary political and social concerns, Arthur Grant argued that slavery in ancient cities, such as Athens, meant that "the democracies of the ancient world do not deserve the name according to our modern ideas." In contrast to its ancient counterpart, modern democracy, Grant observed, clearly implied "the dignifying of labour by the entry of labourers into the circle of citizenship."[88] Such sympathy and concern with social democracy meant that the Athenian political experience and, more especially, Grote's interpretation of it, seemed on the whole neither useful nor commendable to socialists and to many of the new liberals of the late century. The primacy that Grote and others of his generation had attached to politics as a vehicle of moral transformation simply could not be accepted by later writers concerned with more immediate social reform.

However, the eagerness with which these writers condemned Athenian slavery and with it Athenian democracy played directly into the hands of late-century conservative writers. The most important of these was G. B. Grundy of Oxford. Before assuming his teaching duties at Oxford in 1893, he had for a time served as an army tutor, and he remained a strong supporter of the military establishment and its values. Grundy was no less devoted to the Conservative party. In 1925 he successfully mobilized conservative political sentiment at Oxford to prevent the election of Herbert Asquith as chancellor of the university because he would not forgive the former prime minister for having carried the House of Lords Act in 1911.[89] Full of contempt for democracy, hatred of socialism, and admiration for aristocratic, military values, Grundy's major books, *The Great Persian War and Its Preliminaries* (1901) and *Thucydides and the History of His Age* (1911), attempted a fundamental revision of the nineteenth-century humanistic and radical interpretations of Athenian democracy. Against the Arnoldians Grundy argued that Greek politics had been a highly parti-

88. Andrew Cecil Bradley, "Aristotle's Conception of the State," Evelyn Abbott, ed., *Hellenica: A Collection of Essays on Greek Poetry, Philosophy, History, and Religion* (London: Rivingtons, 1880), pp. 185–86; Arthur J. Grant, *Greece in the Age of Pericles* (New York: Charles Scribner's Sons, 1893), pp. 8–9.

89. George Beardoe Grundy, *Fifty-Five Years at Oxford: An Unconventional Autobiography* (London: Methuen & Co., 1945), pp. 63, 142–45.

san affair involving much social conflict. Against Grote and his followers Grundy urged that Athenian democracy had not protected Greece from the Persians, that it had not achieved constitutional morality, and that it had directly contributed to the defeat of the city by Macedonia. Grundy contended that such a revisionist approach was necessary to prevent modern political leaders from drawing inherently mistaken conclusions from the Athenian experience.

For Grundy, the major democratization of Athens had occurred not with the Cleisthenian reforms but after the battle of Marathon. Grundy, in fact, denied that Marathon had been "a crowning victory for the new democracy," and bluntly declared, "The opposite was rather the case."[90] At the time of the Persian invasion, he explained, the democratic party in Athens actually hoped for the restoration of Hippias, the deposed Pisistratid tyrant. Miltiades, the victor of Marathon, was not a democrat but the leader of aristocratic forces who had taken control of the Cleisthenian political structures. The Athenian democrats had been preparing for a coup d'état when Miltiades left the city to meet the Persians. However, the early appearance of Spartan reenforcements for Miltiades compelled the Persians to fight before their Athenian sympathizers could execute the coup. Consequently, the battle of Marathon was a victory for the aristocracy of Athens and their nondemocratic Spartan allies. The folly of the English nation depending on nonaristocratic leadership to preserve English liberty and security, and the implication of probable lack of patriotism on the part of modern liberals, could hardly have been made plainer.

As a direct result of the post-Persian War prosperity, according to Grundy, rich Athenian citizens began to invest their new capital in large numbers of slaves. This marked expansion of the slave population caused intense competition between slaves and free laborers. The hard-pressed and increasingly unemployed groups of free ablebodied workmen, whom Grundy always called the proletariat (the term by which he also translated *demos*), became the major domestic political

90. George Beardoe Grundy, *The Great Persian War and Its Preliminaries: A Study of the Evidence, Literary and Topographical* (London: John Murray, 1901), p. 170. With acknowledgment, Grundy took his account of the events surrounding Marathon from J. Arthur R. Munro, "Some Observations on the Persian Wars: I—The Campaign of Marathon," *Journal of Hellenic Studies* 19 (1899): 185–97.

problem for fifth-century Athenian statesmen. Their solution to this difficulty was payment of citizens for participation in various democratic political activities, such as jury duty, and for service in the navy. Possession of citizenship guaranteed receiving this aid, which was financed by taxes levied against the wealthy citizens, who presumably owned numerous slaves and profited from their labor. During the regime of Pericles the ranks of the citizenry were repeatedly expanded in order to make more and more unemployed persons content with their lot by opening to them the financial benefits of citizenship. Grundy contended that because of this policy "Greek democracy was intensely communistic... because the problem of Greek life could only be solved by such means."[91] Poor citizens always attempted to use their political power to tap further the wealth of rich citizens and easily found leaders ready to help them in that effort. Consequently there had always been conflict between the rich and the poor in Athens.

Grundy saw this class conflict as vitiating the picture of the polis as an ideally unified social entity. Party loyalty almost always took precedence over loyalty to the polis as each individual and class pursued its own economic interest. This situation meant that by the fourth century neither the wealthy nor the poor citizens were actively loyal to the city. The quest for social and political equality also prevented the Athenians from acknowledging effective leaders. In Grundy's opinion,

> The Greek was a political monomaniac. His political ideal would only have been realized permanently in a world where all were of equal ability and equal honesty. It was an ideal which in practical life tended to bring the second-rate man to the control of the affairs of the state.

The folly of democratic politics most fully manifested itself in the fourth century when through the Macedonian conquest "the superior race which had intrusted its fortunes to politicians succumbed utterly to a race which, though inferior to it in nearly every department of life,

91. George Beardoe Grundy, *Thucydides and the History of His Age* (London: John Murray, 1911), p. 106; see p. 147 for the translation of *demos* as "proletariat."

was directed by the master-minds of statesmen."[92] This last contention embodied the elitist and authoritarian political thought characteristic of so much conservative and social imperialistic literature in
Edwardian England. Implicit in it was the much-discussed anxiety
about whether a liberal state, such as Britain, could successfully confront Germany. Grundy and many others of his generation believed
that the divisive politics of the opening decade of the century had
sapped the unity of the British state and the moral and military strength
of the nation.

The slavery question did much to prevent the emergence of new
defenders of Athenian democracy and opened the way for Grundy's
fierce condemnation of Athens. However, no less important for the
debate over the Athenian constitution was the political science of the
late century that also reoriented the evaluation of Athenian democracy. Although books on political life in Greece still frequently used
modern terms, such as *prime minister,* to describe ancient officials, the
fundamental grounds of Grote's analogy between ancient and modern
democratic states were, at least in theory, repudiated. Students of and
participants in the democratic politics of England in the last third of the
century repeatedly denied that modern democracy resembled the democracy in Athens.

In *Essays on Reform,* published in 1867, James Bryce contended that
so many differences existed between England and the ancient democracies "that no arguments drawn from their experience are of any
value as enabling us to predict its possible results here." Ten years later
Thomas Erskine May, a Whig historian, political commentator, and
clerk of the House of Commons, suggested that very few relevant
political lessons might properly be drawn from the history of the
Greek republics because their political and social structures were so
different from those of modern times.

> Their society consisted . . . of privileged citizens, foreigners, and
> slaves. It was without the multiplied grades of modern society, its

92. Ibid., p. 5. On Edwardian social imperialism and authoritarian thought, see
Bernard Semmel, *Imperialism and Social Reform* (Garden City, N.Y.: Doubleday and
Co., 1968); Robert J. Scally, *The Making of the Lloyd George Coalition* (Princeton:
Princeton University Press, 1975); and Frank M. Turner, "Public Science in Britain,
1880–1919," *Isis* 71 (1980):589–608.

territorial nobles and country gentlemen, its learned professions, its independent gentry, its church establishments and universities, its standing armies, its merchants and manufacturers, its traders, artificers, and free labourers. . . . Representation was unknown: there was no separation of legislative, executive, and judicial functions: there were no effective checks upon the sovereign power: there was no body of trained judges, magistrates, and public officers: there was no sense of political or moral responsibility: there was no religious creed to teach the generous and forbearing spirit of charity.

John Robert Seeley, Henry Sidgwick, Benjamin Jowett, Frank B. Jevons, and W. L. Newman drove home similar points in numerous articles, books, and commentaries on modern political science and ancient political theory.[93] For those writers, Grote to the contrary, Athens had not been like England and England should not model itself on Athens. In particular, the representative system in modern democracy separated it, and wisely so, from its ancient counterpart.

Despite the best efforts of these authors, the Athenian constitution continued to provide a useful tool for the polemics of political commentators. Paradoxically, in the closing years of the century it was the work of a conservative historian that derived the most benefit from the close analogy, established by Grote, between the Athenian and British democracies. Evelyn Abbott was an Oxford scholar who achieved a very productive career in spite of a lifetime of paralysis incurred in a riding accident. He published a three-volume history of Greece (1888–1900) and a major biography of Pericles (1891), as well as more specialized classical studies. His outlook was typical of the grow-

---

93. James Bryce, "The Historical Aspect of Democracy," in *Essays on Reform* (London: Macmillan and Co., 1867), p. 263; Thomas Erskine May, *Democracy in Europe: A History* (London: Longmans, Green, and Co., 1877), 1:127–28; John Robert Seeley, *Introduction to Political Science: Two Series of Lectures* (London: Macmillan and Co., 1908), pp. 79–82, 313–14; Henry Sidgwick, *The Development of European Polity* (London: Macmillan and Co., 1903), pp. 100–19, and *Elements of Politics,* Second Edition, Revised Throughout (London: Macmillan and Co., 1897), pp. 604–22; Benjamin Jowett, trans. and ed., *The "Politics" of Aristotle* (Oxford: Clarendon Press, 1885), pp. ix–cxlv; Frank B. Jevons, *The Development of the Athenian Democracy* (London: C. Griffin & Co., 1886); William Lambert Newman, *The "Politics" of Aristotle,* 4 vols. (Oxford: Clarendon Press, 1902), l:xl–lviii.

ing conservatism of late-century university intellectuals.[94] Many of them had been relatively liberal during the 1860s and had supported the Second Reform Act and a freer religious and intellectual life in the universities. But by the 1880s they had become disenchanted with the Liberal Party and with the new and more radical course charted by Gladstone. They thoroughly distrusted the prospect of any further democracy, and after the Home Rule debate of 1886 they often drifted into Liberal Unionist and sometimes into Conservative party politics.

Abbott seems to have admired the British constitution as it stood about 1870 when political corruption had been attacked and a moderately democratic franchise established. The traditional institutions of the nation remained intact as order and progress seemed to have been reconciled through typical English political genius. In *A History of Greece* and *Pericles and the Golden Age of Athens* Abbott transferred his admiration for that achievement to the constitutions of Solon and Cleisthenes. Both ancient reformers had retained the ancient Areopagus and had thereby preserved "the best practical wisdom, and the most tried moral and political worth in the city." Even under the advanced Cleisthenian constitution with its pernicious institution of ostracism, the Athenians had still remained "a people, not a rabble, a state, not a city; they were animated by a noble public spirit, not by a selfish greed; they desired liberty, not aggrandisement."[95] That civic spirit, fostered by wise political structures, had been what allowed Athens to achieve its victory over Persia and to maintain the liberty of its citizens.

Those structures had remained essentially sound, if not without defect, until they were undermined by the machinations of Pericles, of whom Abbott declared it was "impossible to deny that he destroyed a form of government under which his city attained to the height of her prosperity and that he plunged her into a hopeless and demoralizing war." It seems quite certain that Abbott saw Pericles as the ancient prototype of Gladstone. After 1886 Gladstone moved increasingly in a radical direction and was associated with political figures who were demanding the reform of the House of Lords and its reconstruction on a more democratic basis. Abbott portrayed Pericles' attack on the

94. J. Roach, "Liberalism and the Victorian Intelligentsia," *Cambridge Historical Journal* 13 (1957): 58–81; Christopher Harvie, *The Lights of Liberalism: University Liberals and the Challenge of Democracy, 1860–1886* (London: Allen Lane, 1976).

95. Abbott, *History of Greece*, 1:415, 485.

ancient Areopagus in terms that suggested a clear parallel to contemporary criticism of the Lords. Abbott argued:

> The Areopagus was worth attacking by a democratical reformer, because the existence of it involved two principles which democracy could not tolerate. The members held office for life; and they were not responsible to any higher authority for the proper discharge of their duties.

The popular juries that Pericles also had instituted would not tolerate a searching review of their decisions such as the Areopagus would undertake. The Periclean radicalization of Athenian politics consequently demanded the abolition of the ancient court so that there would exist "no serious check on the administrative action of the assembly."[96]

In the absence of that check on the Assembly, the wisdom of Athenian government depended solely on the quality of the leaders the citizenry were willing to acknowledge. However, when political power came to depend for its authority on the constant approval of the people, a leader could not be expected to function wisely. Abbott warned, "A democracy ruled by a great man is an admirable form of government; but a democracy with rulers absorbed in maintaining their own position is incapable of governing itself or others: at home it is distracted by parties; abroad it is inconsistent or tyrannical." Both flaws manifested themselves in Athens during Pericles' own lifetime. Although Pericles attempted to meet the material demands of the people through the payment of juries and a program of public works, the unending demands of the citizenry led eventually to war. Whereas most earlier historians who wished to illustrate the tenor of Athenian democracy had quoted from Pericles' funeral oration, Abbott concentrated on his final speech to the city, recorded in Book II of Thucydides. In that oration Pericles had justified the maintenance of the Athenian empire even while admitting that it may not have been justly gained or administered. This policy, in Abbott's opinion, exhibited "a love of domination which was most dangerous to the freedom of Greece" and which "nourished the most selfish passions of the

---

96. Evelyn Abbott, *Pericles and the Golden Age of Athens* (London: G. P. Putnam's Sons, 1891), pp. v, 80; Abbott, *History of Greece*, 2:397.

Athenian people."[97] The war into which those passions led the city had ended in its defeat. For Abbott, an unchecked radical democracy could not sustain its own freedom or independence. The lessons for the contemporary late-Victorian political scene were relatively clear.

The emphasis that Abbott, and Grundy after him, placed on foreign policy indicated that still another shift in the conservative criticism of modern democracy through the Athenian example had taken place. Just as Gladstone's Homeric studies had revealed a transition from the Mitfordian conservatism of the balanced polity to the Peelite position, the work of Abbott and Grundy reflected the movement from Peel to the new conservatism of Salisbury, Balfour, and Chamberlain, with their emphasis on strong military defense, maintenance of effective empire and Irish union, and protection of the various economic, social, and intellectual elites that were threatened by the forces of radical and social democracy. Foreign and military policy at the close of the century remained one of the last political strongholds of the traditional and liberal British elites. Abbott and Grundy employed their histories to maintain that situation. In this regard, the conservatism of their classical studies resembled that of Eduard Meyer, the contemporary German historian of ancient Greece, whose books urgently questioned the possibility of an effective nationalist foreign policy in a radically democratic state.[98]

While Abbott and Grundy continued the longstanding conservative critique of Athens, certain British classicists for the first time began to set forth the character of Athenian politics and society in a genuinely prescriptive manner. Radical political reformers, discontent with the limited liberal state and the individualism of British society, found in Athenian democracy and the social community of the polis a model against which the British democratic experience could to some extent be measured and found wanting. Grote had defended Athens by making it resemble England. These later writers thought that English politics might be improved through the emulation of Athens.

As early as 1863 E. A. Freeman had suggested that the citizen in the Athenian Assembly could function more wisely than the English member of Parliament because the former "could not shelter himself

97. Abbott, *History of Greece*, 3:152, 131.
98. Christ, *Von Gibbon zu Rostovtzeff*, pp. 286–333.

under those constitutional theories by which, in the case of the average English member, blind party voting is looked upon as a piece of political duty, and an independent judgment is almost considered a crime."[99] His comment reflected the liberal university intellectual's distaste for the increasingly partisan character of Victorian politics. As that tendency grew in political life, radical as well as conservative discontent with the institutions of the late-century democracy also arose.

The classical study that most directly criticized Victorian politics by an appeal to the Athenian experience was *Election by Lot in Athens* (1891). Its author, J. W. Headlam, thought that Grote's analogy between Athenian and British institutions had contributed to a significant misunderstanding of both and that it had particularly obscured the nature of Athenian politics. In terms of citizenship, Headlam explained, Athens had been thoroughly aristocratic but in terms of actual government and administration perfectly democratic. The *demos,* composed of citizens, had in fact actually governed itself, administered its laws, and conducted its foreign policy without devolving significant power and authority on any other secondary political body.

According to Headlam's analysis, the keystone of Athenian democratic government was the curious institution of election by lot, which secured the supremacy of the Assembly and prevented the predominance of any single citizen. Headlam claimed, "Mediocrity in office was its object, because this was the only means of ensuring that not only the name but also the reality of power should be with the Assembly." Election by lot assumed that each citizen had the duty to hold office and to answer to the Assembly for his official conduct. The questioning and criticism of officials that in modern states occurred at elections took place in Athens through the courts, where "political trials were really an opportunity for the expression of popular favor or distrust." The verdict on a person rendered by the courts was "a vote of confidence or non-confidence given by the people as a result of their observation of his political career, a vote of the same kind as that which

---

99. Edward A. Freeman, *History of Federal Government from the Foundation of the Achaian League to the Disruption of the United States* (London and Cambridge: Macmillan and Co., 1863), 1:47.

in England is given at a general election."[100] In contrast to Grote, Headlam regarded the institutions of Athens as structurally different from but functionally similar to those of England. Yet he believed the contrasts in structure were more significant than the similarities in function.

Headlam felt that the more perfectly contemporary readers understood the real character of the Athenian government, the more fully they would comprehend "how far any modern country is from being a true democracy." Sixty years earlier, it will be recalled, Macaulay had declared that the First Reform Bill would not create an Athenian-style democracy. Had he known of the remark, Headlam would have fully concurred and would have said the same about the Second and Third Reform Acts. The Athenian state as a genuinely self-governing democracy possessed certain virtues that Headlam found necessarily absent from modern liberal political structures.

> The Greek had no doubt what he meant by a Democracy; it was a city in which the people gathered together at a definite place in one large visible assembly governed the whole state. When we speak of popular government we mean by "people" a great mass of men living long distances apart from one another who have never seen one another and who never will. The Greeks meant a very limited number of men who were accustomed to come together in a definite place. People with us is a vague idea; the demos to an Athenian was a concrete thing which he had often seen and heard. . . . [B]y "government" we mean a vague ill-defined control of the government. In no modern country does the people govern; it is incapable of doing so, it is not sufficiently organised; the work of government is too complicated. Parliament, or Ministers, or the President, govern; the people appoint them and more or less control them. But at Athens the demos did govern.[101]

Headlam's analysis directly implied that the dangers to liberty and security in the modern state with its potentially unresponsive representative institutions dominated by lawyers, bureaucracies, armies,

100. James Wycliffe Headlam, *Election by Lot at Athens* (Cambridge: Cambridge University Press, 1891), pp. 32, 36, 37.
101. Ibid., pp. 179, 29.

and political parties, were very different from those portrayed by the earlier nineteenth-century critics who had regarded radical Athens as the frightening prototype of the emerging liberal governments. Headlam perceived too little rather than too much democratic control and direction might be one of the chief problems for the citizenry of the late-century liberal state.

Headlam's monograph was contemporaneous with works by American, British, and Continental political scientists and sociologists who were attempting to understand why the liberal state did not function in the rational manner that its earlier nineteenth-century theorists had projected. They began to examine the role of parties, bureaucracies, and the nonrational social and psychological elements operative in political life; they also took much more interest in collective social and political activity than in the individual citizen. The social tensions in their societies made them more concerned with what held people together than with what permitted individualistic activity. Although their studies were empirical and their analysis rational, these social scientists regarded human reason as only one among many factors in social and political activity. The book that first brought this point of view to bear on ancient history was *La Cité Antique* by Fustel de Coulanges. Published in 1864 and translated into English in 1873, this volume analyzed both Greek and Roman cities as having been organized around the family and religion and as having sustained their strength and nurtured patriotism through those institutions. Explicit in this analysis was a rejection of the rationalism and positivism that had characterized French and English social thought during the first half of the century. It exercised considerable influence over the late-century French social theorists who carried Fustel de Coulanges's revolt against positivism even further. [102]

Fustel de Coulanges believed his interpretation of ancient civic institutions would establish the inappropriateness of drawing comparisons between them and those of modern times. He had not, however, counted on the ingenuity of English writers. Although apparently

102. Numa Denis Fustel de Coulanges, *The Ancient City: A Study of the Religion, Laws, and Institutions of Greece and Rome,* trans. Willard Small (Garden City, N.Y.: Doubleday, Anchor Books, n.d.), pp. 11–14. For an important discussion of this work see Arnaldo Momigliano, *Essays in Ancient and Modern Historiography* (Middletown, Conn.: Wesleyan University Press, 1977), pp. 325–44.

unfamiliar with *La Cité Antique,* Matthew Arnold, five years after its appearance, appealed to the ideal unity of the Greek polis as the means of overcoming modern democratic pluralism. That attitude dominated many literary and humanistic studies of Greece for the rest of the century, but its advocates provided little or no substantive analysis of the sources of the unity of the polis. The first British writers to examine that issue were the various scholars of Greek myth and religion. They owed much to French anthropologists who had themselves studied the work of Fustel de Coulanges. Harrison, Farnell, Murray and others for all their disagreements still portrayed religion, ritual, and family life as having directly contributed to the character of Greece in the classical age and as probably having led to the demise of civil strife and the emergence of a law-abiding society. All of this, of course, directly contrasted with Grote's concept of constitutional morality achieved through radical political reform.

Nonetheless, late-Victorian political historians, with the exception of George Cox, tended to ignore the social life of Greece and the nonrational bonds of that society.[103] Not until 1911 did a major study appear in Great Britain that attempted to synthesize the religion, economics, politics, and social structures of the Athenian experience. The book was *The Greek Commonwealth* by Alfred Zimmern of Oxford. The title of the volume in itself suggested the new tone and emphasis that his analysis brought to the study of Greek life. Previous historians and critics had admired Athenian art and detested its politics, or defended its politics by decrying its slavery. Zimmern attempted quite heroically and with considerable success to conceive Athenian society as a unit. In a sense he sought to create a portrait of "what fifth-century Athens was really like" in the same fashion that his contemporary James Joyce attempted to create a portrait of early-twentieth-century Dublin.[104] It is no accident that both writers admired Samuel Butler's work on Homer and the *Odyssey* because for all three of them the particularity of everyday life was paramount.

Zimmern achieved his synthesis by combining classical studies with

103. George W. Cox, *A History of Greece,* 2 vols. (London: Longmans, Green, and Co., 1874), 1:18, 184–85; see also Richard Claverhouse Jebb in *The Academy* 5 (1874): 600–01.

104. Zimmern, *Greek Commonwealth,* pp. 6, 90. See also William Warde Fowler, *The City-State of the Greeks and Romans* (London: Macmillan and Co., 1893).

the pioneering social psychology of Graham Wallas. Wallas, in contrast to earlier radical, utilitarian thinkers, believed the experiences of modern democracies and the implications of Darwinian thought indicated that citizens should not be thought of as persons whose natural rationality was inhibited by sinister interests and ignorance but rather as creatures governed by reason, habit, and numerous other ineradicable psychological factors acquired through inheritance and the social environment. If a good or as he termed it a "great society" were to be attained, reformers must take into account all of these psychic elements.[105] Wallas also believed that the great society, if realized, would resemble the ancient polis described by Aristotle and praised by Pericles. That was the mode of social unity and citizen integration Wallas hoped might be achieved in the twentieth century.

Alfred Zimmern had studied Greek with Wallas and later remained a close friend. He drew upon Wallas's thought as he attempted "to analyse the different strands of feeling which attached the Greek citizen to his state." In exploring those feelings, Zimmern also curiously echoed the opinions of Gladstone. At one point, Zimmern explained, "Greek patriotism had fused the emotions of school and family, of inheritance and early training, of religion and politics—all the best of boyhood with all the best of manhood—into one passionate whole." That patriotism resulted from the mingling of people in the marketplace, but it grew even more from the Greek awareness that human life was both richer and more secure when lived collectively in a city. In the city a Greek could benefit from what Zimmern, using a favorite Edwardian political term, called "efficiency." Greek collective life had also not required its citizens to surrender other substantial social associations. In particular, the family and religion remained the core of their existence. Secure in their family circles and religious institutions, the citizens of Athens had been able to enjoy both the innovations achieved through critical reason and the wisdom of the past sustained by "reverence." Those latter inherited moral codes and expectations had nurtured the fundamental unity of the Greek commonwealth.

> For they went down to levels which reason had not yet plumbed
> and embodied the elemental unselfishness—the sense of one

105. Martin J. Wiener, *Between Two Worlds: The Political Thought of Graham Wallas* (Oxford: Clarendon Press, 1971), pp. 61–127; Wallas, *Our Social Heritage,* p. 168.

human being's natural relation to another—which was the germ of Greek citizenship as of all good citizenship since. Fraternity sits ill on the banner of the anarchist; there is no true fraternity which does not grow, as it grew in Greece, out of the plain primaeval emotions of friendship or family.[106]

In effect, for Zimmern the secret of the Greek social genius and the patriotism of the polis had been the very absence of the primacy of politics that Grote and others had tried to find there.

Zimmern's analysis was suggestive of Burke's criticism of early political liberalism, but it was more basically rooted in Edwardian social psychology and political theory. Zimmern contended that the Athenians had loved and defended their city not because its democratic structures guaranteed a set of rights but because the democracy succeeded in meeting its citizens' perceived material needs. He insisted that the Athenians had known "that government does not consist of rights, irrespective of their exercise, but of something a great deal more practical."[107] Athenians had been loyal to their commonwealth because it allowed them to live well, to pursue their interests, to mix freely with one another, and to improve their lot in life. The polis had allowed them to become more completely human, and this realization of the Aristotelian concept of the fellowship of the good life and the felicity thereof was what had sustained Athenian patriotism. This was also the lesson that the Greek commonwealth had bequeathed to modern democracies.

Zimmern attempted to direct the debate over the Athenian constitution beyond the parameters of the nineteenth-century discussion. He had discovered in the Athenian commonwealth a sense of the good civic life that modern democratic states might wisely seek to emulate. He vigorously denied conservative arguments that the Athenian government had been irrational and necessarily founded on slavery.[108] He

106. Zimmern quoted in Wiener, *Between Two Worlds,* p. 176; Zimmern, *Greek Commonwealth,* pp. 65, 82, 84, 70.

107. Ibid., pp. 157–58. See also Alfred Zimmern, "Political Thought," Richard W. Livingstone, ed. *The Legacy of Greece* (Oxford: Clarendon Press, 1957; first published 1921), pp. 321–52.

108. Zimmern, *Greek Commonwealth,* pp. 154–177; Alfred Zimmern, *Solon and Croesus and Other Greek Essays* (London: Humphrey Milford, 1928), p. 119; see also pp. 105–64 and *Greek Commonwealth,* pp. 378–94.

also strongly refuted Grote's view that Athens had achieved wise government only insofar as it had repudiated its social and religious heritage. Zimmern, like others of the Edwardian generation, preferred to measure the wisdom and effectiveness of government by the services rendered to its citizens and by the human qualities and talents that political structures elicited from the governed. In a moment of unguarded enthusiasm he declared:

> The Athenian community during the Periclean time must be regarded as the most successful example of social organization known to history. Its society, that is, was so arranged ("organized" is too deliberate a word) as to make the most and the best of the human material at its disposal. Without any system of national education, in our sense of the word, it "drew out" of its members all the power and goodness that was in them. . . . We are apt to forget that we owe the Parthenon sculptures not merely to the genius of Phidias but also to the genius of the social system which knew how to make use of him.[109]

Here was the voice of Edwardian collectivism and efficiency. It was clearly the statement of a writer who, like his mentor Graham Wallas, sought to foster a great and good society rather than independent, self-directing individuals.

Zimmern's *The Greek Commonwealth* was, and in its later revisions remains, one of the most sensitive, eloquent, evocative, and humane works ever written about Athens in this language. At the same time the volume marked in a real sense the close, or more properly the transcendence, of the debate over the Athenian constitution. Zimmern upheld politics as a matter primarily of administration and the meeting of practical material needs to insure a life of quality rather than as a continuing dialogue over rights, limitations on political power, and the question of who should govern. In that respect his thought may lie near to Aristotle's but it stands far from the world of Victorian political discourse, just as British political life itself by 1911 had largely passed away from those nineteenth-century problems. Democracy had become a fact, and the issues of the new century seemed

109. Zimmern, *Greek Commonwealth*, pp. 365n–66n.

to revolve primarily around the quality of life and the character of the social community that democracy might foster.

Throughout the nineteenth century *democracy* had been one of those "masked words" that Ruskin once portrayed as capturing consciences and evoking a host of expectations, apprehensions, and terrors. The examination of the political life of Athens had been one of the ways whereby some of the masks had been set in place and others removed. The early conservative historians of Athens had determined the manner in which its democracy would be considered and examined, and in doing so, they largely established which problems of democratic government would be considered though discussions of Athens. This situation meant that the debate over the Athenian constitution was primarily a debate over the conservative image of democracy and not over democracy itself. The association of the conservative interpretation of Athenian politics with modern democracy persistently distorted the understanding and analysis of both. From the work of William Mitford through that of Alfred Zimmern the vices perceived in Athens and the virtues eventually discerned therein were those that British scholars, historians, politicians, and political scientists either feared or hoped might become manifest in the political structures of their own day. During World War I Ernest Barker observed, "The problems of Greek citizenship touch us to-day because they are ours; and they are ours because the experience of the Greeks has passed into our substance and merged into our being."[110] He would have been nearer the mark had he written that the problems and anxieties of British citizenship had passed and merged into the being of the Greeks.

110. Ernest Barker, *Greek Political Theory: Plato and His Predecessors* (London: Methuen, 1951; first published, 1918), p. 16.

6

SOCRATES AND
THE SOPHISTS

For the Victorian age the most famous citizen of Athens was Socrates, the philosopher-teacher who had urged his contemporaries to reexamine the quality and presuppositions of their lives and whose career as the self-proclaimed gadfly of the city ended with judicial condemnation and execution. Socrates' rise to prominence as a problematical figure in nineteenth-century scholarship and commentary came about for three reasons. First, the ancient sources displayed substantial disagreement about him. Second, his life and message and his fate at the hands of his fellow citizens were considered relevant for the modern age. Finally, controversy swirled about Socrates because of the stature and reputation of the philosophers and historians who discussed and evaluated his story.

Four major ancient documentary sources and a host of lesser ones of varying quality recorded the life and work of Socrates. The basic texts were those of Xenophon, Plato, Aristophanes, and Aristotle. In these as well as in the lesser documents there was sufficient information to elicit interest and numerous questions—too little to assure certainty of conclusion but more than enough to arouse confusion and controversy because there were discrepancies in both fact and emphasis. The Socrates of Xenophon displayed tendencies toward commonsense morality and reformist religion but possessed a somewhat dull personality. Plato's Socrates ranged over the entire field of sophisticated philosophical discourse. In Aristophanes's *Clouds* Socrates was a figure portrayed as interested in physical science and, like the Sophists, as posing a threat to traditional Athenian morality. The Socrates discussed by Aristotle had originated induction and definition but had contributed nothing else original to philosophy. The other more

fragmentary Socratic sources made clear that in addition to the followers of Plato and Aristotle numerous other diverse schools of later
Greek philosophy had traced their origins to the conversations of
Socrates. Consequently, depending on which of the ancient texts informed a modern writer's point of view, very different portraits and
evaluations of Socrates could and did emerge.

The question of sources would probably have remained little more
than the subject of learned, but limited, debate had it not appeared as
the classical and secular equivalent to the problems surrounding the
historical Jesus. In 1873 Benjamin Jowett of Balliol College, Oxford
told a class, "The two biographies about which we are most deeply
interested (though not in the same degree) are those of Christ and
Socrates."[1] He went on to explain that neither teacher had left his own
writings and that in both cases modern knowledge depended on
widely divergent sources that portrayed rather different personalities.
It would seem that Jowett and others hoped that since the textual
discrepancies cast little doubt on the historical Socrates, a similar sympathy might be extended to the texts recording the life of Jesus.[2] It is
difficult, if not impossible, to know how substantial a role the parallel
with the historical Jesus played in the Victorian concern with Socrates,
but it is certain that the matter was present in the minds of not a few
liberal Christians. Too many other parallels were established between
Socrates and Christ for the issue of disputed sources not to have been
considered.

As a potential ally in numerous other nineteenth-century disputes,
Socrates was the most protean of all Greek figures. He received favorable attention from spokesmen for naturalism, rationalism, liberal
religion, and idealism. Usually such writers portrayed the conflicts
between Socrates and the Sophists or between Socrates and the Athenians as the ancient counterpart of a particular modern intellectual
debate. In this regard, the character of the Sophists became as problematical as that of Socrates. The Victorian debate over democracy
also involved appeals to the fate of Socrates. If the circumstances
surrounding his trial and death could be demonstrated to stem directly

1. Notebook on Pre-Socratics—Lent Term, 1873, p. 39, Benjamin Jowett Papers, Balliol College Library, Oxford, Box B.
2. Arthur Penrhyn Stanley, *Lectures on the History of the Jewish Church: Third Series*
(London: John Murray, 1876), p. 222.

from the nature of democratic society, his case could furnish a prime example of democratic injustice and suppression of the pursuit of truth and individual expression. Later, other writers who prized the supremacy of the state and traditional morality used Socrates to demonstrate the potential political and moral danger of any citizen seeking to set himself above the law and customs of the community.

The appropriation of an ancient intellectual figure to support or clarify some modern cause was not new. However, during the nineteenth century more important European philosophers, historians, and essayists concerned themselves with Socrates than at any time since he had drained the cup of hemlock and become the subject of intense philosophical speculation in the fourth century B.C.[3] Although some of this interest flowed from the high eighteenth-century estimate of Socrates, the fountainhead of nineteenth-century investigation was Friedrich Schleiermacher's definition of the problem of the ancient historical sources and Hegel's interpretation of the historical and philosophical significance of Socrates' career. Later critics, such as Eduard Zeller, Friedrich Nietzsche, and Sören Kierkegaard, in one manner or another responded to the Hegelian analysis. The French philosophers, Victor Cousin, Emile Boutroux, and Alfred Fouillée among others, addressed themselves to the subject of Socrates, and in Great Britain, R. D. Hampden, G. H. Lewes, Connop Thirlwall, Alexander Grant, George Grote, Benjamin Jowett, John Stuart Mill, Walter Pater, J. B. Bury, John Burnet, and A. E. Taylor found reason to comment, often extensively, on his life and character. The stature of these writers and their involvement in diverse areas of thought meant

3. V. de Magalhaes-Vilhena, *Le Probleme de Socrate: Le Socrate Historique et Le Socrate de Platon* (Paris: Presses Universitaires de France, 1952) is a wide ranging discussion of the literature on Socrates. Some of the major non-British works of the nineteenth century include Sören Kierkegaard, *The Concept of Irony with Constant Reference to Socrates,* trans. Lee M. Capel (Bloomington: Indiana University Press, 1968; original edition, 1841); Victor Cousin, *Histoire générale de la philosophie depuis les temps les plus ancient jusqu'au XIXe siècle* (Paris: Dider et cie, 1861); Cousin also edited a major French edition of Plato that included extensive commentary on Socrates; Charles Renouvier, *Manuel de la Philosophie Ancienne,* 2 vols. (Paris: Paulin, Libraire, Editeur, 1844); Alfred Fouillée, *La Philosophie de Socrate,* 2 vols. (Paris: Librairie Philosophique de Ladrange, 1874); Emile Boutroux, *Études d'histoire de la philosophie* (Paris, 1897) pp. 11–94; Eduard Zeller, *Die Philosophie der Griechen: Eine Untersuchung Über Charakter, Gang und Hauptmomente Iher Entwicklung,* (Tübingen: Ludwig Friedrich Fues, 1842), vol. 2. There were also numerous lesser accounts, as well as the work of Hegel and Nietzsche discussed in this chapter.

that their discussions of Socrates commanded attention and elicited replies from other Victorian intellectuals.

In certain respects the Victorian examination and criticism of Socrates resembled the consideration of Homer. In both cases British writers entered into genuine discussion with Continental scholars and philosophers, but the end result in both instances proved to be a rather parochial resistance to the implications of Continental analysis. For example, one of the first significant British essays on Hegel's thought dealt with his concept of Socrates and the Sophists. However, the purpose of the discussion was to refute Hegel's analysis in order to retain Socrates as a voice in support of moderate liberal Anglicanism. Even when scholars, such as Alexander Grant and Benjamin Jowett, incorporated Hegel's historical framework into their presentations of Greek philosophy, they did so selectively and modified it to make Socrates more acceptable to their own moral position. George Grote's discussion of Athenian intellectual life led to a seminal analysis of both the Sophists and Socrates, but for all its brilliance the rationalist earnestness of his discussion now makes it seem somewhat dated. The Edwardian critics Burnet and Taylor saw in Socrates a fervent religiosity of character and thought that might better have suited an early nineteenth-century Methodist or one of Matthew Arnold's righteousness-seeking Hebrews.

In short, throughout the nineteenth century the British treated the most ironic of all the Greeks without a trace of irony. Generally lacking such a sense of irony themselves, Victorian commentators on Socrates seem to have been unable to discern it in antiquity. Their Socratic studies, which in scholarly terms were often superior to those of now more frequently read Continental philosophers, revealed the essential comfortableness of British intellectual life and the relative ease with which even radical critics were assimilated into the prevailing culture. Both the critics and champions of that culture believed that answers to social, political, and intellectual problems existed. Consequently, the ironic stance was absent from the British evaluation of Socrates. Either he or his opponents had a legitimate cause. There was little sense of a clash between two utterly irreconcilable positions nor a recognition that the Socratic critique might have called into doubt an entire social or intellectual reality. The empirical bias of these British writers led them to see Socrates and his relationship to

Athens in the same particularistic terms by which they viewed their relationship to their own society rather than with the universalistic wholeness of writers whose thought derived from Hegel. All of which is to say that British culture produced Hampden, Thirlwall, Grote, and Mill rather than Kierkegaard or Nietzsche. It is, however, important to remember that the two latter philosophers and their ironic concept of Socrates received widespread acceptance and accommodation only in the twentieth century when irony became hardly less than a way of life for many Western intellectuals. To come to grips with the mainstream of nineteenth-century British thought, irony and the ironic Socrates must for a time be set aside and the earnestness of religious conviction and rationalist optimism taken up.

The Liberal Anglican Socrates

Early Victorian commentary on Socrates was limited to a few pamphlets, encyclopedia articles, and occasional lectures or books on the history of philosophy or of Greece. Liberal Anglican clergymen-scholars authored the largest number of these, with the most complete treatment being R. D. Hampden's essay for the seventh edition of the *Encyclopaedia Britannica* published in 1842. In addition to Hampden, who had taught at Oxford and later became bishop of Hereford, the more important of these writers were Charles James Blomfield, an editor of Thucydides and later an eminent bishop of London, W. A. Butler of Dublin University, F. D. Maurice of Kings College, London, and Connop Thirlwall. All of these clergymen were sound scholars and representatives of the latitudinarian tradition of Anglicanism that since the seventeenth century had opposed materialism and excessive rationalism on the one hand and religious enthusiasm and irrational fanaticism on the other. As might be expected, these clerical scholars assimilated Socrates into their own camp.

The liberal Anglicans predicated their image of Socrates on the received opinion that the ancient Sophists who had appeared in a number of fifth-century Greek cities had exercised a decidedly bad and probably immoral influence. Aristophanes and Plato had voiced this opinion, which had received further ancient confirmation in the works of the church fathers. Such a negative connotation for the words *sophist* and *sophistry* remained commonplace and informed all early nineteenth-century British comments on the subject. In 1818 Samuel Taylor Coleridge spoke of the sophist as "a wholesale and retail *dealer* in wisdom—a *wisdom-monger,* in the same sense as we say, an iron-monger." This creature had introduced a pernicious mode of corruption into the moral being of his students.

> The understanding was to be corrupted by the perversion of the reason, and the feelings through the medium of the understanding. For this purpose all fixed principles, whether grounded on reason, religion, law, or antiquity, were to be undermined, and then, as now, chiefly by the sophistry of submitting all positions alike, however heterogeneous, to the criterion of the mere understanding, disguising or concealing the fact, that the rules which alone they applied, were abstracted from the objects of the senses, and applicable exclusively to things of quantity and relation.

Sophistry had led to a morality based on sense knowledge alone. A few years later Thomas Morrell explained that through the influence of the Sophists "the faculty of reason was perverted from its important and legitimate object—the discovery of truth—to technical forms and modes of discussion favourable to the propagation of error and falsehood." Similar opinions appeared in Thomas Mitchell's introduction of 1820 to the comedies of Aristophanes.[4]

The liberal Anglicans perpetuated this viewpoint, which they and others derived from Tennemann's *Manual of the History of Philosophy* as well as from the ancient sources. Blomfield portrayed the Sophists as "pernicious teachers" who taught "there was no inherent nor essential difference between right and wrong." Thomas Arnold declared

---

4. Samuel Taylor Coleridge, *The Friend,* ed. Barbara E. Rooke (Princeton: Princeton University Press, 1969), 1:436, 439; Thomas Morell, *Elements of the History of Philosophy and Science from the Earliest Authentic Records to the Commencement of the Eighteenth Century* (London: B. J. Holdsworth, 1827), pp. 147–48; Thomas Mitchell, trans., *The Comedies of Aristophanes* (London: John Murray, 1820), 1:xlvi–lxxxi. See also Joseph Priestley, *Socrates and Christ Compared* (London: J. Johnson, 1803), pp. 14–17; *Encyclopaedia Britannica,* 6th and 7th eds., s.v. "Sophists"; J. Forster, "The First Philosophers of Greece" and "Socrates and the Sophists of Athens," *Foreign Quarterly Review* 30 (1842–43): 61–92 and 331–368; Karl Otfried Müller and John William Donaldson, *A History of the Literature of Ancient Greece* (London: John W. Parker and Son, 1855), 2:93–102, 161–72.

that "not the wildest extravagance of atheistic wickedness in modern times can go further than the sophists of Greece went before them." The loss of moral direction in Greece, which Blomfield and Arnold saw naturally leading to the deterioration of Athenian democracy at the close of the Peloponnesian War, was the dark result of a society riddled by sophistic thought. Hampden, whom the Oxford movement leaders considered a rank liberal but who adopted a purely Mitfordian view of Athens, argued that the Sophists and their immoral philosophy were the outcome rather than the cause of Athenian misgovernment. In his Dublin lectures, Butler termed the Sophists "philosophic hirelings" whose teaching served only political ambition. F. D. Maurice basically agreed with this analysis in his mid-century history of philosophy.[5]

To these writers the Sophists represented an affront to the conviction that reason could perceive the existence and comprehend the nature of the unchanging moral truth that was the law of God. The vitriolic rhetoric applied to those ancient teachers stemmed from their resemblance to the skeptics of the Enlightenment and of later times who, in the opinion of even liberal clergy, had employed reason to undermine belief in humankind's innate moral and spiritual nature. When these Anglicans came to portray Socrates and his relationship to the Sophists and to Athenian society, not surprisingly the image they drew very much resembled themselves. Socrates was a philosopher mediating between the extreme rationalism and egoism of the Sophists and the ignorant superstitition and enthusiasm of traditional religionists. In this difficult middle position Socrates stood forth as a rational liberal deist, the founder of natural religion, the upholder of a universal moral law, and the advocate of a moderate inductive view of philosophy and morality resembling Francis Bacon's.

Although liberal Anglicans thought Socrates had attempted to

---

5. *Encyclopaedia Metropolitana* (London, 1845), s.v. "Socrates"; Thomas Arnold, ed., *The History of the Peloponnesian War by Thucydides*, 4th ed., 3 vols. (Oxford: John Henry and James Parker, 1857), 3:xv; R. D. Hampden, *The Fathers of Greek Philosophy* (Edinburgh: Adam and Charles Black, 1862), pp. 297–305 (This volume comprised his articles "Socrates," "Plato," and "Aristotle" that had appeared in the seventh and eighth editions of the *Encyclopaedia Britannica*. His revisions were negligible.); William Archer Butler, *Lectures on the History of Ancient Philosophy*, 2 vols., ed. William Hepworth Thompson (Cambridge: Macmillan and Co., 1856), 1:367; Frederick Denison Maurice, *Moral and Metaphysical Philosophy*, New Edition with Preface (London: Macmillan and Co., 1872; first published, 1850), 1:121–30.

undermine ancient sophistry by leading his fellow citizens to recognize their own ignorance, they did not think that Socratic doubt was the path to skepticism. As Hampden explained, "He threw doubts on what was doubtful, that there might be the less doubt and uncertainty about what remained when the doubtful was removed from a subject." In this fashion Socrates led some of his contemporaries to reasoned morality and to the understanding that genuine knowledge and lasting moral achievement originated not in the cultivation of the intellect for mental exercise but with the "*education* of the mind and character." He had himself blocked the potentially skeptical conclusion to his own philosophy by regarding natural religion and independently existing moral laws as pillars of truth, knowledge, and wisdom. According to Hampden:

> He felt that there was a reality in the principles of piety, justice, benevolence, and other moral sentiments, which no sophistry could impugn. He not only felt their reality within himself, but he had observed, that however invisible to the outward eye, they produced real effects in the world; that they were not only evidenced in the constitution of Nature, but also recognized in those unwritten laws which were found everywhere the same, independently of positive institution, as well as in the enactments of particular states. He looked for the original of these sentiments to the perfect nature of the Divinity; and he held them to be invariable and true. Hence he would allow no proper and adequate power of causation but moral design. Material or mechanical causes were in his view but of instrumental efficacy. It was moral sentiment only, the love and pursuit of good, that possessed real power.

As "a genuine philosopher" in contrast to the false Sophists, Socrates could understand and see that a moral agency permeated the physical universe. That perception set limits on his skeptical use of reason, prevented subjective sentiment from informing all of his religious experience, and provided a sound foundation for his concept of the virtuous life. Although Hampden regarded the moral instruction of Socrates as imperfect, particularly the extreme emphasis on knowledge as virtue, he nevertheless thought that Socratic morality bore "strongly the marks of the law written by the finger of God."[6]

6. Hampden, *Fathers of Greek Philosophy*, pp. 423, 315, 423–24, 373, 408.

What Hampden termed Socrates' "good sense" had led the philosopher to oppose not only the skepticism and moral expediency of the Sophists but also the religious superstition that pervaded Athenian life. For Hampden the Athenian festivals, oracles, and temple priests constituted the ancient equivalent of modern sacerdotal religion based on tradition, priestcraft, and an authoritarian church. The superstition pervasive in Athens was the ancient counterpart of the Roman Catholic Church and of Oxford Tractarian theology whose latter advocates would relentlessly persecute Hampden.

> Resting their belief of a Divine agency in the world on Tradition and Authority, men omitted to explore the witness of God in their own nature, and in the world around them. . . . As infidelity in these days finds its refuge in the belief of infallibility in the Church, and is itself in its turn the miserable refuge from the despotism of the very infallibility before which it crouches in silence; so among the votaries of heathen superstition, the doubts and misgivings of the thoughtful intellect and the troubled heart, were left to prey on themselves, shut up in abject submission to an external authority, and unprepared for their own defence and support.

Socrates' call for self-examination, his dependence on his own internal feelings for guidance—Hampden's interpretation of the Socratic daimon—, and his urging the Greeks to look to the operation of nature for knowledge of the rationality and benevolence of God had directly challenged their superstition. But ultimately the "spirit of the Heathen Religion" and "the genius of Intolerance" had prevailed in Athens and brought about the death of Socrates.[7] Hampden and others of his opinion hoped for a better outcome in their own battle against religious superstition.

For liberal churchmen, several other happy conclusions followed from their interpretation of Socrates in addition to the belief that tempered reason was compatible with the Christian faith. The life of Socrates and his noble, if still imperfect, moral theory suggested that God had not totally abandoned the pagan world. As God had given prophets to Israel, so among the heathen, argued Hampden,

7. Ibid., pp. 385, 430, 340, 370.

He appears to have raised up, from time to time, individuals, from among themselves, heathen still, yet gifted with a purity of moral vision beyond their contemporaries, to retrace the Divine outline of their original nature, amidst the ruins and crumbling monuments of its former greatness; and to declare almost authoritatively, the indelible but forgotten law of Truth and Righteousness.[8]

This belief that God had from time to time spoken through certain heathen personalities was an alternative to the concept of a decayed primitive revelation later supported by Gladstone. Like the revelation postulated by Gladstone, it dated from the patristic age and had no historical evidence to support it by the critical standards of the nineteenth century. However, Hampden's position held some attraction during the thirties and forties for Christians troubled by the moral character traditionally ascribed to their God. It suggested to them that God had not callously or arbitrarily excluded the pagan world from his love and concern by restricting his revelation to the Jews and the Christian church.[9] By the fifties a few liberal churchmen, in particular F. D. Maurice, would carry the argument to the logical conclusion that God had in some manner revealed his truth in all religions.

Most Anglicans, including the liberals, would not have agreed with Maurice. While voicing warm admiration for Socrates and claiming that God may have used him to speak to the heathen, these clergymen-scholars usually left no doubt about the superiority of the Christian revelation. Socrates' failure to encourage sexual purity, his approval of sensual indulgence, and his countenancing retaliation against enemies, as reported by Xenophon, led Charles Blomfield to contend that

... it is a strong argument of the necessity which existed, before the time of our Saviour, of a divine revelation, that a philosophy so pure and rational as that of Socrates, enforced as it was by the ablest and most eloquent writers of antiquity, had but little effect

8. Ibid., p. 434.
9. Adolf Harnack, "Sokrates und die alte Kirche," in Adolf Harnack, *Reden und Aufsätze* (Gieszen: J. Ricker'she Verlangsbuchhandlung, 1904), 1:27–48; Howard R. Murphy, "The Ethical Revolt against Christian Orthodoxy in Early Victorian England," *American Historical Review* 60 (1955); 800–17.

in improving the religious or moral character of the most acute and ingenious people of the heathen world.[10]

The other Anglican commentators agreed with Blomfield. The wisdom of Socrates and its possible relationship to the divine had not diminished his need or that of Greek culture generally for the higher truth of God revealed in Christ.

The liberal Anglican portrait of Socrates as an ancient moralist who had embraced reason without spurning all vestiges of religion and intuition remained alive well past the middle of the century. Hampden's original article reappeared in the eighth edition of the *Encyclopaedia Britannica* (1853-63) and was published separately as part of *The Fathers of Greek Philosophy* in 1862. The image of a moderately rational Socrates served as a model for those clergy who wished to move toward progressive thought without burning all the moral and intellectual bridges to the Christian past. The clergymen who established this view of Socrates were very much European intellectuals. They were particularly drawn to Germany. Many of them read German well and were aware of the important developments in German philology, theology, and philosophy. By the late thirties some of them had begun to study Hegel. By the middle of the next decade they perceived that Hegel's interpretation of Socrates clashed with their own and required refutation on both philosophical and historical grounds.

Hegel had explicated his concept of Socrates in his *Lectures on the History of Philosophy* published posthumously in 1832 and with a more definitive text in 1840. He had also discussed Socrates' career in *The Philosophy of History,* which a few English scholars seem to have read in the forties. Hegel's consideration of Socrates was probably the most significant of the century and aroused criticism, commentary, and reaction throughout Europe. Today the most famous of these responses is Kierkegaard's *Concept of Irony,* which remained practically unknown until the present century. During the nineteenth century Eduard Zeller's *History of Greek Philosophy* was the most widely consulted reply to Hegel's analysis of ancient thought. In Great Britain the *Lectures on the History of Philosophy* stirred the first major criticism of Hegel's work, in the form of an incisive appendix to the fourth volume

10. *Encyclopaedia Metropolitana* (London, 1845), s.v. "Socrates."

of the second edition of Thirlwall's *History of Greece* published in 1847.

Unlike so much of his philosophy, Hegel's discussion of Socrates and the Sophists is reasonably clear and for the most part unambiguous. For Hegel, both Socrates and the Sophists marked a fundamental turning point in the development of the Greek mind. The Sophists were "the teachers of Greece through whom culture first came into existence in Greece, and thus they took the place of poets and of rhapsodists, who before this were the ordinary instructors." By *culture* Hegel meant the organization of the empirically experienced world into categories determined by subjective, reflective reason as opposed to collective, prereflective religious categories. *Culture* implied that ideas and beliefs were to be investigated rather than simply believed. It was the equivalent of "the so-called enlightenment of modern times."[11]

According to Hegel, the Sophists' reward for having taught people to exercise critical judgment was a not wholly deserved reputation for moral evil. Their actual practice of training young men "for common Greek life, for citizenship and for statesmen" had been neither immoral nor pernicious. The alleged immorality of instructing persons to deduce various and varied conclusions from a single body of evidence should not have been imputed "to any special quality in the Sophists, but to reflective reasoning." A reflective, critical culture, such as the Sophists nurtured in Greece, must "necessarily lead beyond implicit trust and unrestricted faith in the current morality and religion." That such reflective criticism led to skepticism was not a moral fault of the Sophists themselves but pertained to the stage of the world's historical development during which they lived. Their use of reflective reason was as yet unrestrained or undetermined by the limitations that Socratic and, more particularly, Platonic philosophy would establish in the ancient world and that Christianity furnished in the nineteenth century. The work of the Sophists, however, had been a necessary step toward those later developments. Hegel still believed, nonetheless, that sophistry could and did exist in the modern world whenever thinkers allowed their reason to be directed merely by

11. Georg Wilhelm Friedrich Hegel, *Lectures on the History of Philosophy*, 3 vols., trans. E. B. Haldane and Francis H. Simson (London: Kegan Paul, Trench, Trubner and Co., 1892), 1:355, 356.

self-will without regard for the determined truths of religion and philosophy. [12] In that regard he agreed with those writers who equated the critical qualities of the philosophes and their followers with the spirit of sophistry. Through this analysis Hegel both defended the reputation of the ancient Sophists and criticized modern intellectuals whose thought did not extend beyond the achievement of the Sophists.

Hegel argued that Socrates, through his appeal to reflection and his reference of personal judgment to conscious reasoning, represented a further and more profound development of the sophistic movement. Socrates had separated natural and reflective morality and thus precipitated the evolution of moral sensibility from *Sittlichkeit* to *Moralität*. According to this famous Hegelian distinction, *Sittlichkeit* constituted the morality residing in the unreflective custom and religion of the ancient community. *Moralität* was the reflective morality that developed as the individual subjective consciousness looked within itself to discover what objective truth would have moral authority over it. Socratic philosophy gave birth to the latter.

> We now see Socrates bringing forward the opinion, that in these times every one has to look after his own morality, and thus he looked after his through consciousness and reflection regarding himself; for he sought the universal spirit which had disappeared from reality, in his own consciousness. He also helped others to care for their morality, for he awakened in them this consciousness of having in their thoughts the good and true, *i.e.,* having the potentiality of action and of knowledge. [13]

By this process the Greeks had abandoned the religion of the poets and the moral customs of the polis and had turned to their own subjective reason to find direction for life. The Sophists, whose reliance on subjective judgment Socrates had imitated and furthered, had not gone beyond the diversity of individual self-interest attained through subjectivity. Socrates, and Plato after him, were not content to rest in mere subjectivity but believed that through subjective reason there might be attained an objective authoritative knowledge that could prove as binding on action as had been natural morality.

12. Ibid., pp. 358, 369, 365, 367–68.
13. Ibid., p. 409.

Nevertheless, in this dialectical development from *Sittlichkeit* to *Moralität* to a new objective morality, Socrates remained for Hegel a transitional figure. The Socratic principle was "that man has to find from himself both the end of his actions and the end of the world, and must attain to truth through himself." Yet Socrates could not simply say and did not even fully realize that he was now making his own individually reasoned moral decisions. His own perception of his reflective subjectivity manifested itself to him as an unconscious impulse that assumed the form of his daimon, which Hegel termed the Socratic "Genius" and which he interpreted as an appeal to a personal religious oracle. Hegel contended,

> The Genius of Socrates stands midway between the externality of the oracle and the pure inwardness of the mind; it is inward, but it is also presented as a personal genius, separate from human will, and not yet as the wisdom and free will of Socrates himself.[14]

Appeal to this private religious experience was bound to lead Socrates into conflict with his fellow Athenians because it epitomized the individual consciousness in conflict with the collective consciousness.

Hegel contended that the Socratic "Genius" did represent a new god and that Socrates was genuinely guilty of introducing new deities. Moreover, by questioning existing social and intellectual authority, he had also interfered with the morality of family life in Athens. Hegel went so far as to assert that the Socratic principle had been the fundamental cause of the decay of the Greek state in the fourth century because the flourishing of the principle of subjectivity had undermined the spirit and bonds of the polis community which eventually was replaced by the authority of monarchy after the Macedonian conquest.[15] Consequently, for Hegel Socrates was in fact guilty of the charges brought against him at his trial, and the Athenians had been correct in perceiving him as a threat to their mode of morality and social life.

However, Hegel did not regard Socrates' guilt as the reason for his death. A very small majority of the Athenian jury had convicted him, and the conviction did not necessarily entail execution. The capital

14. Ibid., pp. 386, 425.
15. Ibid., pp. 407–35; see also Georg Wilhelm Friedrich Hegel, *The Philosophy of History*, trans. J. Sibree, (New York: Dover Publications, 1956), pp. 269–72.

sentence had been imposed only after Socrates refused to compromise by suggesting a reasonable alternative. By that steadfast refusal he had in effect set his own conscience above and in direct opposition to the collective conscience of the Athenian community. His defiance was the logical outcome of his advocacy of subjective reflection and the discovery of morality from subjective sources. The Athenians had correctly understood that moral subjectivity was a clear and present danger to the values and mores of the state. Socrates' death, therefore, was not unjust but rather essentially tragic because "in what is truly tragic there must be valid moral powers on both the sides which come into collision; this was so with Socrates."[16] This aesthetic judgment of Socrates' fate and the role of the Athenian people therein was highly reminiscent of Hegel's analysis of *Antigone,* according to which the heroine's tragedy originated in conflicting loyalties to the equally valid laws of state and of religion.

On the Continent the Hegelian approach to Socrates, either through acceptance or rejection, was fundamental to the work of Kierkegaard, Nietzsche, and Eduard Zeller, the great historian of Greek philosophy. In Britain the Hegelian interpretation ran headlong into the empirical historical analysis and moral outrage of Connop Thirlwall who denounced Hegel's portrait of the philosopher as "a sad tissue of miserable sophistry, a series of outrages against historical truth, right feeling, and the first principles of justice and common sense."[17] Thirlwall's important critical essay of 1847 on the Hegelian Socrates seems to have escaped most later notice because it was hidden in an appendix to his history of Greece, a work soon eclipsed by Grote's. However, Grote referred to Thirlwall's critique and the tenor of the commentary on Socrates and Sophists by Alexander Grant and Benjamin Jowett also suggests familiarity with it.

For Thirlwall, Hegel had been historically and morally mistaken about Socrates. The historical misinterpretation tended to reenforce the moral errors. For persons of Thirlwall's turn of mind, there were right and wrong uses of reason. Socrates epitomized the former, the Sophists the latter. Except for their appeal to the faculties of critical reason, the Sophists and Socrates had little in common. Socrates had

16. Hegel, *Lectures on the History of Philosophy,* 1:446.
17. Connop Thirlwall, *A History of Greece,* New Edition, 8 vols. (London: Longman, Brown, Green, and Longmans, 1847), 4:547.

used his reason "to establish certain principles of moral conduct by which men might be surely guided to what was right and good." The Sophists on the other hand had "only endeavoured to furnish every man with grounds or pretext for following his own inclination, and sacrificing all law and right to selfish instincts." Whereas these teachers had undermined morality and existing institutions by pointing to their conventional nature, Socrates had obeyed the law, observed existing religious rites, and told other people to do the same. He had been a firm ally of those "institutions which tended to put a wholesome restraint on the selfish appetites and passions of the citizens, and to regulate their conduct with a view to the public good."[18] In other words, Socrates had stood as a pillar of traditional religion and morality tempered by a moderate use of rationality. He was neither antisocial nor antireligious so far as the life and customs of Athens were concerned.

Thirlwall questioned the rigid scheme of moral development that Hegel had imposed on the ethical thought and experience of Greece and particularly the distinct turning point in Greek morality that he ascribed to the influence of Socrates. In Thirlwall's judgment:

> Hegel's notion of the principle of simple faith, and unreflecting obedience, with which he supposes the philosophy of Socrates to have come into collision, appears to me, if not wholly false, at least so vague and exaggerated, as to be quite inapplicable to this or any other question; and if Hegel could have been induced to qualify it so as to make it more consistent with the truth, he would probably have found it useless for his argument.

There was no question that the bulk of the Athenians in Socrates' day, as well as most people at any time, guided their moral lives according to instinct, prejudice, reverence, and religion rather than strict rational principles. But Thirlwall thought such nonrational practices were "not of so delicate a texture" that the assaults of either Socrates or the Sophists could quickly or decisively rend them asunder. Furthermore, the public life and debates of Athens rather than the teachings of the philosophers had been the major vehicles whereby the laws and customs of the city came into question. The laws of Athens had never

18. Ibid., pp. 549, 529.

been simply "the objects of passive, unreflecting obedience," but had always been subject to criticism, question, and revision. Solon himself had been permitted to recast the laws of the city according to no other light than that of his own reason.[19]

The alleged Hegelian dualism between the individualistic, subjectively reflective Socrates who established a law unto himself and a public opinion that was rigidly devoted to scrupulous observance of existing legal and customary procedures also disintegrated under close scrutiny. The trial of the generals after the battle of Arginusae provided Thirlwall with the case in point. On the first day of the trial, when the opponents of the generals first attempted to convict them as a group, Socrates was president of the Prytany, one of the few times he took an active part in civic life. At great personal risk he stood firm against the popular will and refused to allow the Assembly to decide the illegal question. Yet, observed Thirlwall, with all-too-obvious sarcasm,

> Hegel wishes us to believe that the same people who on this occasion threatened him with death for his resistance to their arbitrary will, afterwards actually condemned him, on the ground that the majesty of the law was in their eyes a thing too sacred to be touched by philosophical argument, even for the purpose of supporting it when it seemed to totter.[20]

This memorable incident clearly cast doubt on Socrates' alleged threat to Athenian law and upon the monolithic unity of law, custom, and religion that Hegel had seen existing in the polis. The incident also cast doubt on the moral legitimacy of the Athenians' later condemnation of Socrates for what Hegel saw as their perception that he was endangering their existing customs and institutions.

Thirlwall also took Hegel to task for his interpretation of the Socra-

19. Ibid., p. 530.
20. Ibid., p. 531. See pp. 223–25 for Grote's interpretation of this incident. He dissented from Thirlwall's position in part because he believed the Athenians voted against the generals out of religious fanaticism. In that sense Grote saw Socrates as opposing religion and custom as well as upholding the law. Grote also, however, differed from Hegel's view that law and political institutions were the concrete embodiments of will or a religious mentality. For Grote the genius of the Athenian democratic political structures was the manner in which they overcame religious and family ties.

tic *daimon*. Hegel had improperly referred to it as Socrates' "Genius"—a term indicating a personal guardian spirit or formal deity that was not really denoted by the word *daimon* or by the other terms Plato and Xenophon used to describe it. Those two ancient writers had not suggested the presence of a guardian spirit, nor had they presented the psychological phenomenon as an oracle. Thirlwall also denied that the Socratic *daimon* could validly be interpreted as symbolizing the substitution of personal moral judgment for that of the oracles. Oracles and other modes of divination had never been the sole factor but only one of many guiding intelligent Greeks in making any particular decision. There was no formal antithesis between an appeal to an oracle and the use of private judgment. Furthermore,

> the occasions, either public or private, on which the aid of divination was called in at all, were infinitely rare, in comparison with those on which men followed the suggestions of their own judgment. We do not find for instance that in the debate on the massacre of the Mitylenaeans, or the Melians, it was proposed to suspend the execution until the pleasure of the gods had been ascertained.

Hegel had incorrectly made "the exception the rule" and built "his theory on its supposed universality."[21] In spite of certain discrepancies in their accounts, both Xenophon and Plato portrayed the *daimon* as only occasionally influencing Socrates' action. Yet even then the *daimon* did not replace oracles; the situations in which Socrates reportedly followed the guidance of the *daimon* were not those in which a Greek would ordinarily have consulted an oracle or any other mode of divination.

From these criticisms Thirlwall moved to Hegel's analysis of the trial of Socrates. He flatly declared that Hegel had been "so possessed with his own view of the case, that he is constantly confounding the charge which he himself brings against Socrates, and could have suggested to his accusers, with that which Anytus and Melitus, in their ignorance of this History of philosophy, actually brought." The accusers had not presented the *daimon* as a principle superceding all existing religious observances. Nor had Socrates presented it as a god.

21. Thirlwall, *History of Greece,* New Edition, 4:539.

Considered in terms of ordinary Greek modes of divination it was not particularly unorthodox nor suggestive of atheism. Moreover, although the accusers of Socrates had said that he corrupted the youth, the alleged corruption had related to particular advice to the son of Anytus and not to a more general habit of teaching young men to think for themselves and to rely on their own private judgment. For Thirlwall, Hegel's interpretation of Socrates' trial as a tragedy with moral right on both sides simply could not be made congruent with the facts. Thirlwall regarded the moral truth of the situation as quite plain and uncomplicated. As he argued in another context, " . . . there never was a case in which murder was more clearly committed under the forms of legal procedure than in the trial of Socrates." Hegel's contrary analysis represented nothing less than "an unjustifiable sacrifice of historical truth to a philosophical speculation."[22]

Thirlwall himself might well stand accused of having sacrificed much of the subtlety and insight of Hegel's interpretation of Socrates to his own religious and philosophic scruples. In particular, he too closely equated the moral and religious ethos of Athens, which was fundamental to Hegel's discussion, with the civic institutions and law of the city. Behind Thirlwall's polemic lay the liberal Anglican conviction of the essential unity of truth. That concept was incompatible with Hegel's idea that equally valid modes of conceiving the moral world could clash as the mind of God and the human spirit developed. For Thirlwall, true religion, properly understood, and right reason could not stand in necessary or tragic conflict either in Athens or in nineteenth-century Britain. The moral relativism implicit in Hegel's analysis had to be resisted. Socrates, for all his affinity with the Sophists, nonetheless differed from them in his belief in "man as a rational being—capable of distinguishing truth from error, and of giving an intelligent preference to that good which most properly belongs to his nature, over every other end."[23] This was the position liberal Anglicans embraced in regard to modern thought, and it was the outlook they believed would vindicate Christianity to their age and perpetuate it into the next. For that reason Thirlwall had brought the most histor-

22. Ibid., pp. 541, 556, 542.
23. Ibid., pp. 533–34. For Thirlwall's original discussion of Socrates, see his *History of Greece,* 8 vols. (London: Longman, Rees, Orme, Brown, Green, & Longman and John Taylor, 1835–45), 4:257–80.

ically minded of all philosophers to the bar of empirical historical judgment to prove him wanting and to preserve Socrates as an example of the possible synthesis of rationality, reverence, and moderation in religion and social life.

When Thirlwall published his essay in 1847, it was German philosophy that seemed to pose the major challenge to the liberal Anglican idea of Socrates. But in 1850 the eighth volume of Grote's *History of Greece* appeared. There in the midst of his narrative of Greek political history lay two chapters on the Sophists and Socrates that soon redirected both British and Continental scholarship on the subject. The image of Socrates as a moderate, Broad Church Anglican rapidly gave way to the image of Socrates as a radically critical rationalist.

The Victorian Rationalist Socrates

Since antiquity, rationalist and scientifically minded writers had regarded Socrates as an ambiguous figure. That ambiguity had become even more pronounced during the Enlightenment. At issue was the character and extent of Socrates' rationalism. During the eighteenth century and later, strongly skeptical rationalists had respected and praised Socrates as a questioner of things established, as an enemy of prejudice, and as the highest example of philosophic courage in the face of death. However, his separation of physical science and morality disturbed those rationalists because they often hoped to mesh science and morality, with the latter frequently subordinate to the former.[24] More moderate religious rational thinkers, particularly in Britain, often compared Socrates' search for rational moral truth with Bacon's demand that an inductive examination of nature replace sterile scholastic reasoning. During most of the nineteenth century, moderate rationalists, like the liberal Anglicans, and the more extreme rationalists, like the utilitarians and the positivists, often disagreed with each other in numerous fields of thought. Although early in the century Socrates had remained largely in the preserve of the Anglican moderates, by 1850 after a hesitant start, secular rationalists attempted

24. Peter Gay, *The Enlightenment: An Interpretation* 2 vols. (New York: Alfred A. Knopf, 1966, 1969), 1:81–82, 2:85–88; Benno Böhm, *Sokrates im achtzehnten Jahrhundert: Studien zum Werdegange des moderner Persönlichkeitsbewusstseins* (Neumünster: Wachholtz, 1966).

to draw Socrates directly into the traditions of analytic science and modern critical rationalism.

The tension in the minds of the secular rationalists displayed itself in the portrait of Socrates presented in G. H. Lewes's *Biographical History of Philosophy,* first published in 1845. This work, which went through several editions and revisions, was a rather sophisticated history of philosophy written from a Comtean standpoint and the first study of any kind in English to review the philosophy of Hegel and to take some account of Hegel's analysis of ancient Greek intellectual life. Lewes's point of departure was Comte's law of the three stages of intellectual development—religious, metaphysical, and positivist. Philosophers were considered good or bad, advanced or retrograde in the degree to which they either represented or contributed toward the realization of positivist, scientific philosophy.

Lewes repudiated previous British treaments of Greek philosophy by discussing the Sophists in a favorable light. According to Lewes, "The Sophists were hated by some because powerful, by others because shallow. They were misrepresented by all." Plato's image of the Sophists was a "caricature," and his discussion provided only "the *reductio ad absurdum* of what they had thought." Nothing less than "a thorough revision" of the opinion of their firmest ancient opponent was required.[25] The Sophists, like other skeptics of the age, had abandoned the speculations of the Ionic natural philosophers. The Sophists had not, however, simply reveled in skepticism, but rather they had turned from nature to a consideration of politics and rhetoric, where they believed some possibility of more nearly certain truth existed.

Although Lewes thought the social philosophy of the Sophists important and much less pernicious than had previous commentators, he was more interested in their renunciation of the Ionic physical philosophy, which he regarded as one of the major sources of all the later metaphysical systems that had for so long interfered with the attainment of genuine science. The Sophists had realized that the Ionian approach to physical nature failed to answer fundamental philosophical questions. However, even though the Sophists had attained the ability and insight to spot a really bad idea, they had still lacked the

25. George Henry Lewes, *A Biographical History of Philosophy,* 2 vols. (London: Charles Knight and Co., 1845), 1:158, 171, 173.

capacity to correct the idea or to eliminate it altogether. They had not achieved the insight of a Bacon.

> In them we see the first energetic protest against the possibility of metaphysical science. This protest, however, must not be confounded with the protest of Bacon—must not be mistaken for the germ of positive philosophy. It was the protest of baffled minds. The science of the day led to scepticism; but with scepticism no energetic man could remain contented. Philosophy was therefore denounced, not because a surer, safer path of inquiry had been discovered, but because Philosophy was found to lead nowhither. The scepticism of the Sophists was a shallow scepticism in which no great speculative intellect could be drowned.

Whatever faults or shortcomings the Sophists displayed were intellectual rather than moral. For all of their courage they had failed to smother metaphysical philosophy. That failure soon permitted Socrates to saunter forth as "a knight-errant of philosophy" who attacked numerous religious and intellectual prejudices but who in the end advocated a new and mistakenly subjective view of nature and morality.[26]

Socrates repudiated the Sophists' wise denial of moral truth and embarked on a search for "moral certitude" which was "the rock upon which his shipwrecked soul was cast." Although guided by the highest of intentions and posing the important question of "the nature and condition of Science," Socrates had nonetheless led his disciples and many later philosophers in the wrong direction and one counter to that later set forth by Bacon. As Lewes explained:

> The aim and purpose of Socrates was confessedly to withdraw the mind from its contemplations of the phenomena of nature, and to fix it on its own phenomena: truth was to be sought by looking inwards, not by looking outwards. The aim and purpose of Bacon's philosophy was the reverse of this.

Lewes thus agreed with Hegel's interpretation of the direction of Socrates' thought, but, as would be expected from a positivist author, he

26. Ibid., pp. 179–80, 200. By "philosophy" Lewes always meant metaphysical or nonempirical thought and speculation.

vigorously dissented from the philosophic idealism implicit in Socrates' method. Moreover, Lewes argued that Socratic induction com-
pounded the initial error by reasoning from analogy and by confusing
words with things in the search for precise definitions. Socrates had
propounded the egregiously mistaken idea of considering a correct
definition as "a true description of the Thing *per se,* and the *explanation
of terms* as equivalent to the *explanation of things,* and *the exhibition of the
nature of any thing in a definition* as equivalent to the *actual analysis of it in
a laboratory.*" That fundamental misconception had carried over into
the philosophies of Plato and Aristotle and still flourished "in all the
metaphysical systems of the present day."[27] The career of Socrates had
not been the fountainhead of true science, and, by implication, those
who associated Socrates with science remained confused about the
character of science in both ancient and modern times.

George Grote favored a modern rational, scientific world view no
less than Lewes, but he regarded Socrates as one of the founders of that
mode of thought. Two factors led Grote's analysis and his own largely
Comtean interpretation of Socrates to differ from that of Lewes. First,
for Grote Western history had displayed the achievement of positive
knowledge more than once, whereas Lewes had tended to posit a
single line of progressive development that culminated in Comte.
Grote saw intellectual evolution in Greece as a distinct compartment
of history. The ancients had experienced all three of Comte's stages
and had then regressed under the impact of superstition and Christianity. Second, as stressed previously, Grote subordinated his analysis of
Greek life and thought to politics. And it was primarily in connection
with the Greek political experience that he appropriated the Sophists
and Socrates to the rationalist tradition.

Grote commented extensively about Socrates and the Sophists on
three separate occasions. He first discussed them in volume eight of *A
History of Greece,* published in 1850. He further clarified his position in
several new footnotes to the third edition of the history that appeared
in 1855. He continued and in many ways added to his analysis in *Plato,
and the Other Companions of Socrates* (1865). These later discussions
sharpened and somewhat extended his original argument but did not
significantly change its main thrust.

27. Ibid., pp. 200, 221, 215, 218.

Chapter sixty-seven of Grote's *History of Greece* may well have been the single most influential section in all twelve volumes and to this day remains one of the major points of scholarly departure for interpreting the Greek Sophists. There he set out to exorcise from studies of ancient philosophy the concept of *"Die Sophistik,"* by which he meant the negative image of the Sophists and their activity then predominant among Anglican commentators and especially among Continental historians of philosophy such as Ritter, Brandis, and Zeller. Grote objected to this traditional, unfavorable portrayal of the Sophists because it was predicated on an antidemocratic interpretation of Athenian history. According to this interpretation, the Sophists were either the cause or the manifestation of the decay of late fifth-century Athenian democracy. Grote contended, first, that such decay had not appeared at that time and that constitutional morality had never functioned more usefully than in the aftermath of the collapse of the Thirty Tyrants. Second, and more important, he urged that the thought and work of the Sophists had helped to foster the climate of constitutional morality.

Grote argued that the chief cause for the immoral reputation and misunderstanding of the Sophists lay in the backward projection of the modern derogatory meaning of the words *sophist* and *sophistry* into the climate of fifth-century Athens. This anachronism received an erroneous justification by the uncritical acceptance of Plato's works as the primary source of information about the Sophists' activity. In an argument quite similar to one previously set forth without perceptible impact by John Gillies in 1778, Grote explained that *Sophist* had originally denoted "a wise man—a clever man—one who stood prominently before the public as distinguished for intellect or talent of some kind."[28] Quite soon the envy and anti-intellectualism rooted in the apprehension of superior minds by persons with inferior ones associated "a certain invidious feeling" with the term. After 450 B.C. the various teachers of music and rhetoric who had achieved importance and stature in the democracy came to be designated by the old established word *Sophist*. According to Grote, there was little that was new about these later teachers except that they taught better than their

28. George Grote, *A History of Greece,* New Edition, 12 vols. (London: John Murray, 1869), 8:151. See also John Gillies, trans., *The "Orations" of Lysias and Isocrates* (London: J. Murray and J. Bell, 1778), pp. cxxix, 14n–17n.

predecessors, attained greater prestige, and, most important, received pay for their efforts. The profession of public instruction rather than any particular set of ideas united these figures and meant that they could be perceived as a distinct group. In his dialogues, however, Plato took the word *Sophist* out of current circulation, dwelled on its unpleasant connotations, and to these added all the features of philosophy that he disliked. Neither the Sophists nor their function was novel; "What was new was the peculiar use of an old word; which Plato took out of its usual meaning, and fastened upon the eminent paid teachers of the Socratic age."[29] By the nineteenth century the word had accumulated further unpalatable connotations that in turn were read back into the Greek experience.

Yet, Grote contended, even if one granted the Platonic meaning of the term, Plato's dialogues failed to support the usual unfavorable portrait of the Sophists. In Plato's presentation of the Sophists' teachings nothing intrinsically immoral appeared. On the contrary, Prodicus, a Sophist, was the author of the unquestionably moral tale of the Choice of Hercules. Protagoras appeared as a moral and not unworthy teacher. Except for the alleged fallacies intrinsic to rhetoric itself, Plato brought no charges of moral turpitude against Gorgias. And Callicles, whose harsh view on power in the *Gorgias* was frequently taken to exemplify the political danger of sophistry, was not regarded as a Sophist by Plato. Nor did the accusations of the Sophists' flattering of the people stand up to scrutiny, for surely the profoundly antidemocratic ideas of Callicles and Thrasymachus hardly played to the democratic crowd.

So far as Athenian civic life was concerned, the Sophists, by Grote's account, were neither indications nor causes of political decay. Rather they were "Professors or Public Teachers" who immeasurably helped to create a viable democratic culture in the city. They were highly useful citizens who actively promoted constitutional morality by inculcating in citizens the skills of persuasion and discussion without which some political groups in the city might have resorted to armed force. In their educative capacity the Sophists were the advocates and perpetuators of the political status quo in Athens. In a description of their activity that closely paralleled Hegel's but that appears to have

29. Grote, *History of Greece*, 8:153, 156.

been developed independently Grote portrayed the Sophists as relatively conservative democratic educators.

> They professed to qualify young Athenians for an active and honourable life, private as well as public, *in Athens* (or in any other given city): they taught them "to think, speak, and act," *in Athens;* they, of course, accepted, as the basis of their teaching, the type of character which estimable men exhibited and which the public approved, *in Athens*—not undertaking to recast the type, but to arm it with new capacities and adorn it with fresh accomplishments. Their direct business was with ethical precept, not with ethical theory: all that was required of them as to the latter, was, that their theory should be sufficiently sound to lead to such practical precepts as were accounted virtuous by the most estimable society *in Athens*. It ought never to be forgotten, that those who taught for active life were bound by the very conditions of their profession to adapt themselves to the place and the society as it stood.

Grote firmly adhered to this concept of the conservative function of the Sophists, and in a footnote of 1855 he implicitly endorsed A. P. Stanley's conclusion that the Sophists had been the "established clergy" of the Athenian democracy. Furthermore, by arguing that it was as unfair to judge the Sophists from the point of view of Plato as to judge "the present teachers and politicians of England or France from that of Mr. Owen or Fourir," Grote rather subtly reminded his readers that it had been Plato rather than the Sophists who had advocated a radical restructuring of property holding, marriage, and child rearing.[30]

Grote's analysis of the Sophists bore some resemblance to Hegel's. Both saw the Sophists as educating the Greeks in the skills of enlightened thought and in the capacities of civic life and statesmanship. Both regarded that intellectual and civic culture as in one way or another displacing more traditional religious beliefs and social mores. And both believed the Sophists had been unjustly misrepresented by contemporary observers and by later historians. There is, however, no evidence that at the time Grote wrote the eighth volume of the

30. Ibid., pp. 164, 159, 204n, 200.

History of Greece he knew more about Hegel's view of the Sophists than the information available in Thirlwall's critique of 1847 and in German histories of philosophy.[31] It seems unlikely that Grote drew upon Hegel without acknowledgment since he did fully acknowledge other German sources. Nor did he make any further references to Hegel in the footnotes of 1855. By the time he wrote *Plato, and the Other Companions of Socrates,* however, Grote had read Hegel's *History of Philosophy,* which he cited and praised.

Moreover, there were certain significant differences of emphasis between Grote's view of the Sophists and Hegel's. In annotations to Albert Schwegler's *Handbook of the History of Philosophy* (1867) James Hutchinson Sterling, an early British advocate of Hegelian thought, noted Grote's divergence from Hegel's analysis. He criticized Grote's rather rigid application of Comte's three stages to Greek intellectual development and regretted Grote's use of only those German sources inspired by the Enlightenment: "Mr. Grote's philosophy extended only to what of *Aufklärung* the Germans contained, and not to—the last lesson—their correction of it."[32] In other words, Grote had embraced the destructive use of reason, which Hegel had equated with modern sophistry, and had not qualified that application of reason by any appeal to German idealist philosophy or, in particular, to Hegel. The latter omission was, from Sterling's standpoint, fatal to Grote's position.

Sterling argued that Grote had vindicated the activity of the Sophists for the same reasons that Hegel himself had advocated.

> Mr. Grote, then, is evidently right so far. But this *so far* is only one half. Defence of the rights of the subject, this is one half of the action of the Sophists, and in this they are defensible, justifiable, laudable. Denial of the rights of the object, again, this is the other half of the action of the Sophists, and in that they are indefensible, unjustifiable, and positively censurable. Now Hegel and the rest [of the historians of Greek philosophy] see this latter half quite as prominent as the other one. . . . Mr. Grote alone accentuates the rights of the subject and a warranted relativity; Mr. Grote alone

31. Ibid., pp. 298n–299n.
32. Albert Schwegler, *Handbook of the History of Philosophy,* 3rd ed., ed. and trans. James Hutchison Sterling (Edinburgh: Edmonston and Douglas, 1871), p. 346.

forgets, knows not, or names not, the rights of the object, and a warranted irrelativity.[33]

The very relativity implicit in the Sophists' critique of traditional Greek life, which Hegel regarded as the major fault of their activity and as the flaw that Socrates and Plato had begun to correct, was for Grote the major contribution of the Sophists and a mode of thought that deserved emulation in modern politics and philosophy. The critical, rationalist skills imparted by the Sophists to the Athenians and by the Enlightenment to modern times dissolved those religious and moral prejudices that Grote saw undermining and interfering with democratic institutions. Furthermore, the subjective, intuitive approach to knowledge advocated by Hegel and foreshadowed for him in the Socratic and Platonic corrections to the Sophists was the kind of thinking that Grote considered most antithetical to freedom and democracy.

Finally, Sterling quite correctly perceived that Grote's analysis of the Sophists and his commendation of critical skepticism led directly to civic individualism rather than to the construction or development of a state that, in Hegelian terms, would provide a new universal morality.[34] Hegel believed the spirit of sophistry had eventually resulted in the demise of the polis. Grote believed on the contrary that the Sophists had contributed in the most fundamental manner to the strength of the democracy. However much Hegel and Grote's thought may have converged in regard to the function of the Sophists, their analyses radically diverged in their evaluations of the contribution of the ancient teachers to Greek life and in their understanding of what constituted wise political structures. There was no bridge between idealism and critical empiricism.

Grote made no reply to Sterling and may not have been aware of his comments. He did, however, answer a criticism from F. D. Maurice, the most distinguished liberal Anglican theologian of the mid-century, who in a manner similar to Sterling's accused the Sophists of encouraging selfishness, unlimited personal ambition, and extreme individualism. Maurice had set forth his views in his *History of Moral*

33. Ibid., pp. 381–82.
34. Ibid., p. 394. See also Alfred William Benn, *The Greek Philosophers,* 2 vols. (London: Kegan Paul, Trench, & Co., 1882), 1:104–07.

and Metaphysical Philosophy published in 1850. In a long footnote of 1855 Grote observed that selfishness and political ambition in Greece certainly predated the Sophists. Political ambition in Athens was not qualitatively different from that in the British Houses of Parliament. The skills taught by the Sophists both allowed ambitious leaders to pursue their ends peacefully and ensured that a variety of ambitious politicians would be present to counteract each other. What the Sophists represented was "intellectual and persuasive force, reflecting and methodized so as to operate upon the minds of free hearers, yet under perfect liberty of opposition: persuasion against the ambitious man, as well as by him or for him." The political choice lying before any society was between politics based on persuasion or politics based on coercion. When the instruments of persuasion were discredited, there remained "open no other ascendency over men's minds, except the crushing engine of extraneous coercion with assumed infallibility."[35] The Sophists and the competitive political individualism they fostered, and that by implication rationalists nurtured in modern liberal states, prepared the way for a free society and one in which the state could not dominate the lives of its citizens.

If despite certain affinities Grote's interpretation of the Sophists differed from Hegel's, this was even more the case with Grote's treatment of Socrates. Grote's most surprising strategy in defense of the Sophists was his inclusion of Socrates himself within their number as he observed:

> . . . it is certain, that if, in the middle of the Peloponnesian war, any Athenian had been asked,—"Who are the principal Sophists in your city?"—he would have named Socrates among the first; for Socrates was at once eminent as an intellectual teacher, and personally unpopular—not because he received pay, but on other grounds . . . : and this was the precise combination of qualities which the general public naturally expressed by a Sophist.[36]

Except for the rehabilitation of Cleon, no passage in Grote's history more astonished nineteenth-century British readers. Furthermore, the connection that Grote perceived between Socrates and the Sophists

35. Grote, *History of Greece,* 8:162n.
36. Ibid., p. 155.

was not casual but fundamental and intimate. The Sophists had taught the rhetorical and persuasive skills necessary for democratic institutions. Socrates had laid the moral foundations necessary for citizens to develop a mode of thinking that would permit them to function as democratic citizens rather than as men dwelling in traditional modes of intellectual outlook and social association.

Socrates had distinguished "between that which was, and was not, scientifically discoverable: an attempt, remarkable, inasmuch as it shows his conviction that the scientific and the religious point of view mutually excluded one another, so that where the latter began the former ended." Through that distinction—his "capital innovation"—and through his example of the questioning, critical intellect, Socrates had imparted to his fellow citizens the method whereby customary and religious habits of mind that had led the democracy to commit its greatest crimes and blunders might be eradicated and supplanted by more nearly scientific analysis. He had denounced "the semblance and conceit of knowledge without real knowledge" that supported prejudice, prescription, and deference in matters of morality and politics. In this respect, Grote thought Socrates' role in Greek intellectual development was reminiscent of the role Bentham had played in English legal philosophy. Socrates had awakened the "analytical consciousness" of his fellow citizens to encourage effective social and political action, and he had carried that skill into the study of ethics in the manner again normally associated with Bentham.

> To study Ethics, or human dispositions and ends, apart from the physical world, and according to a theory of their own, referring to human good and happiness as the sovereign and comprehensive end; to treat each of the great and familiar words designating moral attributes, as logical aggregates comprehending many judgements in particular cases, and connoting a certain harmony or consistency of purpose among the separate judgements; to bring many of these latter into comparison, by a scrutinising dialectical process, so as to test the consistency and completeness of the logical aggregate or general notion, as it stood in every man's mind:—all these were parts of the same forward movement which Socrates originated.

Grote's language echoes John Stuart Mill's essay "Bentham," and the analysis of Socrates as leading philosophy from undifferentiated inquiry to the differentiation of questions into species, general and individual, paralleled the accomplishment Mill ascribed to Bentham's genius. According to Grote, Socrates' break with the logical analysis of earlier Greek philosophy marked the beginning of the development of logic that was expanded by Plato, systematized by Aristotle, and, with considerable modification in light of later scientific knowledge, recast in modern times by Mill.[37]

Grote went further than any other British author of the century in setting Socrates into the scientific and Baconian tradition of inductive thought. In his preface of 1850 he described Socrates as the "originator of the most powerful scientific impulse which the Greek mind ever underwent." He portrayed Socrates as clearing away the same kind of intellectual idols that had plagued Bacon.

> It is a process of eternal value and of universal application. That purification of the intellect which Bacon signalized as indispensable for rational or scientific progress, the Socratic Elenchus affords the only known instrument for at least partially accomplishing. However little that instrument may have been applied since the death of its inventor, the necessity and use of it neither have disappeared, nor ever can disappear.

By his logical examination of commonplace opinions Socrates had provided an intellectual solvent to custom, sham knowledge, and unexamined opinions. He had in this manner attempted "to create earnest seekers, analytical intellects, foreknowing and consistent agents, capable of forming conclusions for themselves and of teaching others."[38] As a moral reformer, who spurned the transcendentalism of his pupil Plato, Socrates had based his intellectual and moral reformation on the empirical facts and realities of social life and human nature. Socrates was one of that line of thinkers who had led others to see the world as it really is and to do so without illusion and without fear.

In *Plato, and the Other Companions of Socrates* Grote intensified the critical stance attributed to Socrates and further suggested that the

37. Ibid., p. 227, 242, 230, 232–33, 233–34.
38. George Grote, *History of Greece* (London: John Murray, 1850), 8:iv; 8:298, 257 (1869 ed.).

negative criticism and skepticism traditionally associated with the Sophists had actually been the primary feature of Socrates' own mission. What most Continental writers termed *Die Sophistik* should, Grote argued, be more properly termed *Die Sokratik*.[39] As Eduard Zeller commented, "If Hegel . . . attacked the common notion of the disagreement of Socrates and the Sophists, because Socrates, in one respect, agreed with the Sophists, Grote attacks it for the very opposite reason, because the most distinguished of the so-called Sophists are at one with Socrates." In this later study Grote presented Socrates as a radical, self-conscious opponent of "King Nomos," or the rule of custom, religion, emotion, and prescription, which Hegel had associated with *Sittlichkeit*. For Grote, Socrates' goal had been nothing less than an attempt "to eliminate affirmative, authoritative exposition, which proceeds upon the assumption that truth is already known—and to consider philosophy as a search for unknown truth, carried on by several interlocutors all of them ignorant."[40] Socrates' agnosticism, like that later to be popularized by Huxley, appeared as a fundamental challenge to a culture dominated by religion. Throughout the relevant passages of his work on Plato, Grote was far more pessimistic about the intellectually oppressive character of public opinion than he had been in the *History of Greece*. The reasons for this new turn of mind would seem to have been the acknowledged influence of Mill's *On Liberty*, Grote's own growing disillusionment with the continuing role of religion and deference in English politics, and perhaps the difficulties with religious authorities encountered by British liberal theologians and scientific writers during the sixties.

Despite his condemnation of King Nomos Grote did not portray the trial and death of Socrates as either a tragedy, as had Hegel, or a

39. George Grote, *Plato, and the Other Companions of Socrates*, 3rd ed., 3 vols. (London: John Murray, 1875), 1:260n. This analysis of the relation of sophistic thought to Socratic teaching was carried further by Henry Sidgwick of Cambridge University in two important essays originally published in the *Journal of Philology* (vols. 4 and 5) in 1872 and 1873 and reprinted in Henry Sidgwick, *The Philosophy of Kant and Other Essays*, ed. James Ward (London: Macmillan and Co., 1905), pp. 323–71. Sidgwick contended that many of the doctrines and philosophical methods most closely associated with Sophistry appeared in Athens only after Socrates had taught and were direct offshoots of his philosophic method.

40. Eduard Zeller, *Socrates and the Socratic Schools*, Newly translated from the 3rd German ed. by O. J. Reichel ed. (London: Longmans, Green and Co., 1885), p. 189; Grote, *Plato*, 1:257, 296, 238.

clash between the individual and his society, as had Mill. Grote's conviction of the progressive nature of knowledge prevented his seeing the situation as having been one in which two equally valid moral positions associated with different intellectual stages came into tragic conflict. His commitment to democracy made him chary of a simple individual-against-his-society analysis. Rather, Grote blamed the final condemnation of Socrates on the philosopher's eccentric personality and his religious zeal. Grote would have agreed with Macaulay's private assessment:

> I do not much wonder at the violence of the hatred which Socrates had provoked. He had, evidently, a thorough love for making men look small. There was a meek maliciousness about him which gave wounds such as must have smarted long, and his command of temper was more provoking than noisy triumph would have been.

The ancient sources convinced Grote that only the sincere belief, derived from the Delphic oracle, that the gods had sent him on his mission of intellectual reformation had given Socrates the courage to question his fellow citizens about their beliefs and values. Socrates "was not simply a philosopher, but a religious missionary doing the work of philosophy."[41] For Grote, Socrates' conviction of a rational mission had not required a rational psychological source, and it had been the personal religious fervor informing Socrates' life and activity that had ultimately made him anathema to many Athenians.

Blaming Socrates' death on a religious factor permitted Grote to exonerate the Athenian democracy from any particular guilt in the case. So far as the democracy was concerned, the astonishing fact was the period of almost fifty years during which the Athenians had tolerated the man, his methods, and his never ending impertinent questions. The record of those years proved that Athens had been truly a place of free thought and open discussion. More important, such a long period of toleration suggested that only very special circumstances could have occasioned Socrates' condemnation. Anytus had a personal grudge against the philosopher, and Socrates' association with Alcibiades and Critias also must have told against him. But

41. George Otto Trevelyan, *The Life and Letters of Lord Macaulay* (1908; reprint ed. London: Longman's, 1959), p. 603; Grote, *History of Greece*, 8:220; see also 8:268.

Socrates himself had provided the crucial factor leading to his own death. Any fair-minded reader of the sources must conclude, Grote argued, that "no such verdict would have been given unless by what we must call the consent and concurrence of Socrates himself." He had claimed a divine mission and had displayed the kind of intellectual insolence that had its political counterpart in Alcibiades. Furthermore, Socrates had treated his trial as "the fittest of all opportunities for manifesting, in an impressive manner, both his personal ascendency over human fears and weakness, and the dignity of what he believed to be his divine mission."[42] His own personal, religiously rooted fanaticism had caused his death. Indeed, one might say that Grote sought to make the gods themselves responsible for the condemnation and execution of Socrates. In any case, neither the Athenian people nor their polity were responsible for the end of Socrates' mission.

As already observed in regard to Grote's previously discussed defenses of Athens, a case for the innocence of the democracy had been made but not necessarily proved. Grote did not ask if a judicial system that allowed such a willing miscarriage of justice was free from blame. He did not ask whether every insolent defendant had been or should have been found guilty. Moreover, as his critics at the time pointed out, Grote had ignored cases of other philosophers, such as Anaxagoras, who had been driven from Athens for their opinions.[43] Alexander Grant, the major Victorian editor of Aristotle's *Ethics,* suggested that a reading of the ancient sources in Grote's manner led to the conclusion that the death of Socrates "must be regarded as little else than a judicial suicide."[44] Though convincing and seminal in its parts, Grote's portrait of Socrates was less than satisfying as a whole.

No major commentators or historians in Britain or on the Continent accepted the validity of Grote's entire discussion of Socrates and the Sophists. Rather, they developed or emphasized particular aspects of it and incorporated those with other approaches to the subject. Aside from criticism, such as E. M. Cope's, that simply rejected Grote's analysis, two separate interpretations of the rationalist Soc-

---

42. Grote, *History of Greece,* 8:280, 291.
43. William Mure, *A Critical History of the Language and Literature of Antient Greece,* 4 vols. (London: Longman, Brown, Green, and Longmans, 1853), 4:519–22.
44. Alexander Grant, *The "Ethics" of Aristotle Illustrated with Essays and Notes,* 2 vols. (London: John W. Parker and Son, 1857), 1:118.

rates and his relationship to the Sophists and Athens emerged in the wake of Grote's *History of Greece*.[45] The first, closely associated with Oxford scholars, assimilated Grote's views into a modified version of the liberal Anglican Socrates. The second approach fully embraced the view of a radically skeptical Socrates and associated him with modern rationalism and naturalism.

In 1850 Arthur Penrhyn Stanley, a Rugby and Oxford graduate, the biographer of Thomas Arnold, and later the liberal dean of Westminster Abbey, reviewed volume eight of Grote's *History of Greece* for the *Quarterly Review*. He republished the essay in a somewhat revised form in 1876. Stanley regarded Socrates as a "Prophet of the Gentile world" and a major figure in "the religious history of all mankind." In contemplating Socrates, he found himself transported "from the glories of Hellenic heathenism into the sanctities of Biblical religion." Although Stanley fairly and clearly explicated Grote's analysis, he made certain extrapolations from it that confirmed much of the liberal Anglican portrait. He accepted Grote's view of the Sophists as a conservative force in Athenian life and of Socrates' affinity with them, but he used that interpretation to suggest a Christian parallel. Socrates might properly be regarded as a Sophist, just as St. Paul had been a rabbi. Yet neither teacher was a typical example of their respective orders, and both had gone beyond the intellectual and religious standpoint of their contemporaries. Although a Sophist, Socrates had become "the champion of all that was most true and most holy." Stanley eagerly embraced Grote's portrait of Socrates as both a deeply religious person and a philosopher of critical rationalism and presented him as "the first great example of the union between vigorous inquiry and profound religious belief." In that respect the career of Socrates provided Stanley with "the rare satisfaction" of knowing

45. For critical assessments of Grote's interpretation of the Sophists, see Edward Meredith Cope, "The Sophists," *Journal of Classical and Sacred Philology* 1 (1854): 145–88, and "The Rhetoric of the Sophists," *Journal of Classical and Sacred Philology* 2 (1855): 129–69; 3 (1857): 34–80, 253–88; John Stuart Blackie, *Horae Hellenicae: Essays and Discussions on Some Important Points of Greek Philology and Antiquity* (London: Macmillan & Co., 1874), pp. 197–216; Robert William Mackay, "Introduction," R. W. Mackay, *The "Sophistes" of Plato: A Dialogue on True and False Teaching, Translated, with an Introduction on Ancient and Modern Sophistry* (London: Williams and Norgate, 1868), pp. 1–64. Henry Sidgwick strongly supported Grote's position; see Sidgwick, *Philosophy of Kant*, pp. 323–71, as did Henry Jackson in "Sophists," *Encyclopaedia Britannica* (9th ed.) and Alfred Fouillée in *La Philosophie de Socrate*, 2:319–51.

"that the boldest philosophical enterprise ever undertaken was conceived, executed, and completed, in and through a spirit of intense and sincere devotion."[46] Broad Churchmen believed a similar spirit could inform modern critical speculation.

Although Stanley's essay was not the last extended comparison of Socrates and Christians nor the last analysis of Socrates as a religious philosopher, it was the final portrait drawn more or less according to the traditional liberal Anglican pattern. Thereafter, commentators of that outlook tended to employ a modified Hegelian analysis and related Socrates less closely to Christianity. The person most responsible for this development was Benjamin Jowett, professor of Greek at Oxford, the major Victorian translator of Plato, and after 1870 the influential master of Balliol College. Deeply attracted to German thought and biblical criticsm, he had introduced Hegel's philosophy to Oxford by the late forties. During the next decade he achieved a personal reputation for religious liberalism and unorthodoxy. The Hegelian pattern for the emergence of Greek philosophy allowed Jowett to outline a general evolution of the human mind and of religion without specifically discussing revelation or having to look for supposedly Christian truth in non-Christian religion. The historical approach to philosophy and theology not only helped to elucidate ideas but also emancipated "the human mind from the past by explaining the past."[47] To grasp that philosophy and theology possessed histories was to understand that they must be ever changing and that new concepts could and should be set forth.

Although Jowett accepted and taught Hegel's broad scheme of Greek intellectual development, he dissented from the German philosopher's evaluation of the Sophists and Socrates. Although Jowett disputed Grote's claim of absence of uniformity in the use of the

46. Stanley, *Lectures on the History of the Jewish Church: Third Series,* pp. xvii, 195, 196, 224, 228. For the original essay see *Quarterly Review* 88 (1850–51): 41–68. Stanley delivered part of the revised essay as a lecture in the early seventies and evoked a critical reply in *Dean Stanley and Saint Socrates: The Ethics of the Philosopher and the Philosophy of the Divine* by H. Highton (London: Elliot Stock, 1873). For an essay that seems to have drawn upon both Grote and Stanley by a former headmaster of Rugby, see Edward Meyrick Goulburn, "Socrates: a Lecture," in *Lectures Delivered before the Young Men's Christian Association* (London: James Nisbet and Co., 1859), pp. 364–420.

47. Notebook on Pre-Socratics–Lent Term, 1873, p. 17, Benjamin Jowett Papers, Balliol College Library, Oxford, Box B.

word *Sophist* in Greece and Grote's insistence that Plato misrepresented his enemies, he fully agreed with Grote's contention that the Sophists had upheld the moral and intellectual status quo. But Jowett suggested that this very activity had been pernicious to morality. In lecture notes of the 1850s he wrote, "No other class of teachers ever took in their naked way the actual maxims and practices of life as the basis of philosophy."[48] The Sophists had simply confirmed the morality of the society in which they dwelled and had not sought to improve it. They had in effect advocated the lowest common denominator of morality in daily and public life. Jowett criticized the Sophists not for having upheld evil, immoral, skeptical, or radical ideas, but rather for having by the very conservative character of their teaching inhibited and consciously obstructed the pursuit of higher or improved moral truth. The life and mission of Socrates stood as a stirring protest against the sophistic dedication to moral complacency and mediocrity. The "whole idea of Socrates' teaching," Jowett noted in 1873, had been "the evolution of a man out of himself." That process meant "a moral change from the love of opinion to the love of knowledge."[49] Whereas the Judeo-Christian tradition had portrayed that transformation as one from darkness to light, Socrates had described it as the passage from ignorance to knowledge. In this fashion Jowett used Grote's analysis of the Sophists to reassert a rather Platonic view of Socrates and the necessity of the radical moral reformation that Plato had demanded in his dialogues.

Jowett's published essays on the Sophists and Socrates appeared only in the seventies, as part of his extensive commentary on Plato. The impact of his teaching, however, first displayed itself in Alexander Grant's introduction to the *Ethics* of Aristotle, the first edition of which appeared in 1857. Grant was a more thoroughgoing Hegelian than his teacher Jowett and a worthy opponent of George Grote. In good Hegelian fashion Grant posited three stages of Greek morality—unconscious, transitional, and conscious. The Sophists had initiated the transitional era, and Socrates the conscious period. Grant

48. Notebook on Pre-Socratic Philosophy, 1850s, p. 3, Benjamin Jowett Papers, Balliol College Library, Oxford, Box B. See also Benjamin Jowett, trans. and ed., *The Dialogues of Plato Translated into English with Analysis and Introductions,* Third Edition Revised and Corrected Throughout, 5 vols. (New York: Macmillan and Co., 1892), 4:283–90.

agreed with Grote that the Sophists had been a set of teachers rather than a school of thinkers and that their contemporaries had badly misrepresented them. However, he differed from Grote on two key points reflecting the influence of both Hegel and Jowett. First, Grant had no doubt that the ancient Sophists had been guilty of sophistry in the modern sense of the term. With something of the charlatan about them, the Sophists had tampered and trifled with moral convictions and had represented "the pretence of philosophy" rather than a genuine search for truth. If such advocates of the absence of fixed opinion had not dwelled and taught in Athens, the whole thrust of Plato's philosophy would lose its meaning and the relevance that contemporaries had discovered therein would be inexplicable. Second, Grant questioned whether Grote was correct in his assessment of the contribution of sophistical rhetoric to civic life. With the Sophists rhetoric had amounted to stressing form over content and to being able to make "a harangue upon any given subject."[50] More important, the rhetoric of the Sophists had often involved various modes of fallacious reasoning. This criticism cast into doubt Grote's claim that the rhetoric of the Sophists had constructively aided the democratic life of Athens.

Grant regarded the era of the Sophists "as a necessary, though in itself, unhappy step in the progress of the human mind." The subjective side of knowledge had come into necessary conflict with popular morality. But the challenge to such morality eventually "merged into the deeper philosophy and constructive method of Socrates" whose thought had been "necessitated by that of the Sophists." Here Grant also decisively differed from Grote. Socrates had perhaps externally appeared similar to the Sophists, but

> looking at the internal character and motives of the man, his purity, and nobility of mind, his love of truth, his enthusiasm(...), his obedience to some mysterious and irresistible impulse, and his

49. Notebook on Pre-Socratics—Lent Term, 1873, pp. 79–81, Benjamin Jowett Papers, Balliol College Library, Oxford, Box B.

50. Grant, *The "Ethics" of Aristotle*, 1:82, 97 (see note 24 in chapter 7 for the variations in the several editions of this work); Alexander Grant, *The "Ethics" of Aristotle Illustrated with Essays and Notes*, Third Edition, Revised and Partly Rewritten (London: Longmans, Green, and Co., 1874), 1:128. In this edition Grant's criticism of Grote was more systematic and less uncompromising than in the first edition.

genius akin to madness,—we must call him the born antagonist and utter antipodes to all Sophistry.

The Socratic dialectic, like that of the Sophists, frequently disturbed popular morality. However, it differed fundamentally from that of the Sophists. Socrates' questioning normally implied that some new mode of higher and truer moral knowledge might be attained. He always sought to find permanent and secure ideas in the fluctuating thought and perceptions of the moment. And finally, a conversation with Socrates always "left the impression that the most really moral view must after all be the true one." The distinctions that Grant drew between Socrates and the Sophists were not those Hegel had drawn, though the analysis was based on a Hegelian view of intellectual development. There was little of the Hegelian subjective search for moral truth in Grant's Socrates. More nearly like the earlier Anglican Socrates, Grant's philosopher was convinced "that the broad distinctions of right and wrong are more objective and permanent than anything else, more absolutely to be believed in than even the logic of the intellect."[51]

Jowett and Grant, despite their protests to the contrary, had assimilated much of Grote's analysis of the Sophists, but on the whole they rejected the idea that Socrates had been a Sophist and a philosopher of scientific morality. Their view became widespread in the latter part of the century, since Jowett was the authority on Plato and Grant on Aristotle for many editors of school editions of the two ancient philosophers. In those text books of the late century the Sophists were generally treated gently; one commentator compared them to university extension lecturers.[52] Those same works tended to present Socrates as an example of a heroic individual daring to be a nonconformist in a democratic society that would not tolerate him. Adherents to this approach tended to accept Grote's view of Socrates as a strong rationalist but rejected his opinion that Socrates had come to his death because of obedience to the gods.

51. Grant, The "Ethics" of Aristotle (1857 ed.), 1:110, 100, 121, 127, 109.
52. C. S. Fearenside and R. C. B. Kerin, eds., Plato: The "Phaedo" (London: W. B. Clive & Co., 1891), p. 165. The concept that the Sophists had been a group of teachers rather than a philosophical sect had become almost universally accepted by late in the century.

The treatment of Socrates as a rationalist martyr was a revival of the Enlightenment view of him and a secularization of the Liberal Anglican portrait. Secular public opinion replaced heathen religion as the culprit, and scientific thought replaced divine wisdom as the intellectual principle personified by Socrates. This image of Socrates appeared in *On Liberty* as Mill paired him with Christ as an example of a martyr for wisdom and righteousness dying because of the demands of conformist public opinion.[53] Mill's view received approval in Grote's study of Plato and appeared in several later short introductions to schoolbook editions of the *Apology*. For example, George Stock, the editor of numerous school editions of classical texts, portrayed Socrates as a martyr for philosophy whose *Apology* from the pen of Plato "shows us philosophy tried before the bar of passing public opinion, condemned to drink the bitter juice of the hemlock, and justified before the ages."[54] This line of interpretation, which was never particularly subtle, may be said to have culminated in *The Greek Philosophers* by A. W. Benn, published in 1882. For Benn, Socrates was the symbol of freedom of thought in all its forms. Of Socrates' trial he declared:

> Here, in this one cause, the great central issue between two abstract principles, the principle of authority and the principle of reason, was cleared from all adventitious circumstances, and disputed on its own intrinsic merits with the usual weapons of argument on the one side and brute force on the other. On that issue Socrates was finally condemned, and on it his judges must be condemned by us.[55]

Benn thus pressed on his readers the very conclusion of the injustice of the Athenians that Grote had purposely avoided. No manner of rationalization could vindicate the Athenians. They had destroyed the

53. John Stuart Mill, *On Liberty* (Indianapolis: Bobbs-Merrill Co. 1956), pp. 29–30.

54. St. George Stock, ed., *The "Apology" of Plato with Introduction and Notes* (Oxford: The Clarendon Press, 1887), p. 5. See also Henry Cary, ed. and trans., *Dialogues of Plato containing the "Apology of Socrates," "Crito," "Phaedo," "Protagoras"* (London: George Bell & Sons, 1888), p. v; Frederick John Church, *The Trial and Death of Socrates being the "Euthyphron," "Apology," "Crito," and "Phaedo" of Plato* (London: Macmillan and Co., 1880), p. xxvi.

55. Benn, *The Greek Philosophers*, 1:167.

wisest person ever to stand in their midst, and they had done so on the
grounds of prejudice and unreasoning intellectual authority.

A variation of this theme, also departing from Grote, regarded
Socrates as a fierce critic and enemy of Athenian democracy. G. H.
Lewes had suggested as much in 1845 and described Socrates' condemnation as the result of "a political trial." The most influential
spokesman for this position was Rev. James Riddell who composed an
extensive and thoughtful introduction to the complete Greek text of
Plato's *Apology* that appeared in 1867. He fully embraced Grote's
view of Socrates as a serious analytical philosopher. However, the
very nature of that rationalist approach to the world turned Socrates
into an enemy of the democracy itself and not merely of the prescriptive moral ideas held by Athenian citizens. Throughout his life Socrates had been critical of the fact and presuppositions of democracy,
the flaws of which were intrinsically connected in his mind with the
profound intellectual faults he saw in Athenian life.

> To him the alarming symptoms were such as these,—that this
> [democratic political] system extolled as so perfect could exist
> with an utter abeyance of principles; could be carried on by men,
> who, in knowledge of it, were mere empirical adventurers; that it
> neither undertook nor directed education; that much might be
> going wrong with it, without its giving any check or warning;
> that morality might share the general wreck and not be
> missed;—and that, all this while, the Athenian mind should
> throw itself without misgiving into such a system, and find all its
> wants satisfied, and its self-complacency encouraged; that while
> intolerance was stimulated, the belief in any unwritten law of
> right beyond and above the positive enactments of the state had
> all but died out, and a belief in divine sanctions was scarcely felt.[56]

Although there are expected echoes of the liberal Anglican Socrates in
this passage, particularly in the suggested compatibility of rationality
with divine sanctions, Riddell's Socrates was far more a critic of the
intellectual presuppositions of democratic citizens than of the Sophists. When Socrates did not temper that criticism in the wake of reac-

56. Lewes, *Biographical History of Philosophy,* 1:205; James Riddell, ed., *The
"Apology" of Plato with a Revised Text and English Notes, and a Digest of Platonic Idioms*
(Oxford: The Clarendon Press, 1867), p. xxx.

tion following the fall of the Thirty Tyrants, he was condemned as an enemy of the democracy. Riddell's interpretation, often in some form of combination with Mill's, also frequently appeared in the introductions to school editions of the *Apology,* whose editors had used his version of the Greek text as the source for their own selections. Riddell's approach was on the whole more convincing than the account provided by Grote largely because it directly confronted the very unpleasant likelihood that figures such as Socrates would always encounter a less than friendly reception in democratic states. Those late-century university intellectuals who increasingly felt incapable of influencing the British democracy also often identified with the role into which Riddell cast Socrates.

For most of the last third of the century Socrates' mission was championed over that of the Athenians who had condemned him. However, by the close of the century, as political individualism began to give way to the collectivism of the new liberalism and as the communal life of the ancient polis received new recognition and commendation, writers began to vindicate the Athenians against the rational, individualistic mission of Socrates. In 1898 in a history of Greek literature Gilbert Murray reasserted the Hegelian contention that "the death of Socrates is a true tragedy."[57] Murray felt one could quite easily sympathize with the hatred Anytus held for Socrates. His son had deeply disappointed his expectations, and Socrates had seemed to be the cause of that filial dissipation. During the rule of the Thirty Tyrants Anytus had been forced to flee the city and had suffered a loss of property that he never tried to reclaim. He had then become one of the leaders who overthrew the tyranny. Socrates, on the other hand, had believed truth to be more important than politics. Although he had refused to obey certain orders from the tyrants, he had nonetheless remained in the city and had continued to carry on his conversations. The tragedy of these two people, both of whom deserved admiration, was that one had been willing to die for democracy by resisting the tyrants while the other had been willing to die for the truth. Murray thus in effect vindicated Anytus by implying that any Athenian citizen loyal to the democracy might have honestly and sincerely opposed Socrates.

57. Gilbert Murray, *A History of Ancient Greek Literature* (London: William Heinemann, 1897), p. 177.

This viewpoint received valuable independent support from J. B. Bury, a leading liberal classicist and historian from Cambridge, who in 1900 published the first edition of his still widely used textbook on Greek history. In his exceedingly ambiguous pages on Socrates there appeared considerable tension between the Socratic rationalism that Bury unquestionably valued and its possibly deleterious effect on the Athenian democracy that Bury also admired. Such intellectual tension was quite common among Edwardian liberals, and in an effort to relieve those difficulties social scientists, such as Graham Wallas, had attempted to reorient social and political thought. For Bury, as for Grote, Socrates had been the originator of the logical method that sought truth through formulating precise critical definitions. Although regarding this process as an immense accomplishment, Bury warned that its practice had of late become so commonplace that "we have rather to guard against its dangers." That qualification would not have occurred to Lewes, Grote, or Mill. Furthermore, according to Bury, Socrates had been the founder of utilitarian ethics, an unsparing critic of popular religion, and a prober of the philosophic foundations of democracy. Socrates was "the first champion of the supremacy of the intellect as a court from which there is no appeal" and was "a rebel against authority as such." Through Socratic modes of individualism the Greeks had achieved a more cosmopolitan outlook on the world and had learned to use reason as an instrument for questioning the social, political, and religious status quo. Socrates had believed the state existed for the individual rather than the individual for the state. All of these aspects of Socrates' thought had raised doubts in the minds of honest Athenians about his loyalty and patriotism.

> And from their point of view, they were perfectly right. His spirit, and the ideas that he made current, were an insidious menace to the cohesion of the social fabric, in which there was not a stone or a joint that he did not question. In other words, he was the active apostle of individualism, which led in its further development to the subversion of that local patriotism which had inspired the cities of Greece in her days of greatness.

Socrates really was guilty of the charges brought against him, and his defense answered them in an essentially unsatisfactory manner. Bury, therefore, regretfully concluded, "There have been no better men than Socrates; and yet his accusers were perfectly right."[58]

A few years later similar criticism appeared in Ernest Barker's *Political Thought of Plato and Aristotle* (1906), which portrayed Socrates as an "intellectualist" whose utilitarianism based on individualism proved a source of instability in Athens. By the middle of World War I, when the British government had turned to conscription and censorship, T. R. Glover of Cambridge University carried this line of thought to its logical conclusion. He declared that the Socratic injunction against the unexamined life constituted "the very charter of the individualist and the anarchist" and contended, "There never was any Athenian who had exercised an influence so subtly destructive of Democracy as Socrates."[59] Such remarks obviously reflected the climate of the war, but they were also indicative of the more general reaction against rationalism and political individualism that characterized many European intellectual circles after the turn of the century. As noted in the previous chapter, the Edwardian generation, including Murray, Bury, Barker, Graham Wallas, and Alfred Zimmern, were more sympathetic to forces making for social cohesion rather than for criticism and disruption. This new direction of thought inevitably led to a reappraisal of the rational, individualistic Socrates described by George Grote just as it also led to a revaluation of the Benthamite, utilitarian politics with which Grote and Mill had been associated. But significantly the Edwardian critics repudiated Grote's admiration for the rational, analytic Socrates while retaining his concept of the Socratic mission. What was at issue was less Socrates and his character than the political and intellectual worth that Grote and other mid-Victorians had ascribed to him.

The influence of Grote's analysis of Socrates on another European

58. John Bragnell Bury, *A History of Greece to the Death of Alexander the Great* (London: Macmillan and Co., 1900), pp. 578, 576, 577, 579, 581. Bury was much more sympathetic in his portrayal of Socrates in *The Cambridge Ancient History* (Cambridge: Cambridge University Press, 1958; originally published in 1927), 5:395–97 and *A History of Freedom of Thought* (New York: Henry Holt and Co., 1913, pp. 30–35.

59. Ernest Barker, *The Political Thought of Plato and Aristotle* (New York: Russell and Russell, 1959; originally published, 1906), pp. 48–53; Terrot Reaveley Glover, *From Pericles to Philip* (London: Methuen & Co., 1917), p. 278.

writer also deserves mention. Friedrich Nietzsche, from his early university lectures and *The Birth of Tragedy* (1872) through *The Twilight of the Idols* (1888), devoted considerable attention to the figure of Socrates.[60] Whether Nietzsche admired or hated Socrates is and will remain a vexing question for Nietzsche scholars. What remains certain is that Nietzsche believed Socrates marked a turning point in the history of philosophy and of the polis. It is also clear that he regarded Socrates as a rational, analytical thinker whose thought and questioning had, along with Euripidean drama, dissolved the intellectual foundations of the polis. Scholars have generally supposed that Nietzsche's ideas about Socrates derived from his reading of the ancient sources and from Hegel, Zeller, Albert Lange, and other German historians of philosophy. Although all of those influences are obviously present, the evidence for Grote's impact is also quite strong. Nietzsche began his university career in the 1860s when Grote's reputation was at its height, and he was familiar with both the *History of Greece* and *Plato, and the Other Companions of Socrates*. In lectures delivered in the early seventies on the Greek philosophers before Plato, Nietzsche cited Grote's works and generally adopted Grote's view of the character and death of Socrates.

Despite its variations over the years, Nietzsche's Socrates bore several features that were distinctly associated with Grote's interpretation. From *The Birth of Tragedy* onward the Nietzschean Socrates symbolized the logical, scientific questioning of instinct, prejudice, and received opinion. He stood forth as the prototype of the "theoretical man" whose un–Dionysian culture "believes that it can correct the world by knowledge, guide life by science, and actually confine the individual within a limited sphere of solvable problems."[61] Socrates was the master dialectician for whom virtue was easily equated with reason. Like the English utilitarians, whom Nietzsche detested and after whom Grote's Socrates was largely modeled, Nietzsche's Socrates believed that morality as such and its value were not problematical

60. Walter Kaufman, *Nietzsche: Philosopher, Psychologist, Antichrist,* 3rd ed., rev. and enl. (New York: Vintage Books, 1968), pp. 391–411; Hermann Josef Schmidt, *Nietzsche und Sokrates: Philosophische Untersuchungen zu Nietzsches Sokratesbild* (Meisenheim am Glan: Verlan Anto Hain, 1969). See also the bibliographies in these volumes.

61. Friedrich Nietzsche, *The Birth of Tragedy* in *Basic Writings of Nietzsche* trans. and ed. Walter Kaufman (New York: Modern Library, 1968), p. 109.

issues. Furthermore, in lectures composed about the same time as *The Birth of Tragedy*, Nietzsche argued that Socrates had felt a sense of divine mission and declared, with specific mention of Grote, that Socrates had welcomed his own death and cooperated in bringing it about.[62] In *The Wanderer and His Shadow* (1880) Nietzsche described Socrates as a missionary who had achieved a delicate compromise between piety and freedom of the spirit.[63] This image of the philosopher as one possessed by a sincere, even fervent religiosity as well as by a dedication to scientific truth and reasoned morality had been the keynote of Grote's analysis.

It would be tendentious in the extreme to claim that Nietzsche's Socrates was the same as Grote's or to suggest that the former could be reduced to the latter. The Socrates of Nietzsche was much more complex, interesting, and ambiguous. Nietzsche's personal philosophical relationship to the figure of Socrates was also much more intense and intimate than was Grote's. Nonetheless, today when Grote is little read and Nietzsche commands the attention of scores of scholars and thousands of students, it is not without interest and historical import that Nietzsche's understanding of Socrates in no small way depended on the work of an English utilitarian, bourgeois banker, many of whose moral and philosophical values the German writer scorned to the depths of his being. Nietzsche in part found Socrates so problematical in character and so nearly contemporary in philosophy because of the very values and modes of thought that Grote had so indelibly associated with the Athenian.

Socrates as Mystic

Grote's interpretation of Greek intellectual life and of a rationalist Socrates had been part of the more general movement toward scientific and naturalistic thought that characterized British intellectual life in the third quarter of the century. At the time and then later in the

---

62. Friederich Nietzsche, *Gesammelte Werke*, 23 vols. (Munich: Musarion Verlage, 1921), 4:363–64. See also Friedrich Nietzsche, *Twilight of the Idols* in *The Portable Nietzsche*, trans. and ed. Walter Kaufman (New York: Viking Press, 1967), pp. 473–79.

63. Nietzsche, *Gesammelte Werke*, 9:229. See also Schmidt, *Nietzsche und Sokrates*, pp. 204–07.

century much of the debate spurred by Grote's analysis reflected the opposition of idealist and religious writers to the universe of human experience as circumscribed by positivist science.

A number of classical commentators, especially those in the Scottish universities, attempted to maintain the traditional dichotomy between Socrates and the Sophists by associating the former with idealism, or intuitive thinking, and the latter with materialism and sensationalism. Philosophical prejudice displaced historical analysis. These writers seized upon Socrates' rejection of early Greek natural philosophy to draw him into the antipositivist current of European thought of which they were themselves a part. John Stuart Blackie, an outspoken opponent of scientific naturalism, told a London audience in 1869 that rather than urging the scientific study of morals, Socrates "had preached virtue as a mission, and the exercise of right reason as the only means of obtaining virtue." So characterized, the Athenian provided a figure of immense intellectual respectability whose thought and career could serve as a model for those opposed to the arrogance of modern scientific writers. Blackie declared:

> Socrates . . . was right, not only for Greece in the fifth century before Christ, but for England at the present moment, and for all times and places, when he proclaimed on the house-tops that the first and most necessary wisdom for all men is not to measure the stars, or to weigh the dust, or to analyze the air, but, according to the old Delphic sentence, to know themselves, and to realize in the breadth and depth of its significance what it is to be a man, and not a pig or a god.[64]

Cardinal Manning once similarly employed the example of Socrates to suggest that cultivation of the moral character was a more important task for education than preparation for making money or for expanding technology.[65] For such persons Socrates symbolized the predominance of the eternal moral verities over getting and spending and over matter and motion, both of which they associated with ancient and modern sophists.

64. John Stuart Blackie, *Four Phases of Morals: Socrates, Aristotle, Christianity, Utilitarianism* (New York: Scribner, Armstrong, and Co., 1872), pp. 7, 21.

65. Henry Edward Manning, *The Daemon of Socrates: A Paper Read before the Royal Institution* (London: Longmans, Green and Co., 1872), pp. 41–42.

A similar determination to retain Socrates in the antipositivist camp led other writers to compare him with Thomas Carlyle. Both Socrates and Carlyle had been unorthodox opponents of sham who called for an active life lived in accord with a true intuitive perception of spiritual realities. Both were idealists and transcendentalists who combined a certain degree of rationality with a mode of quasi-religious fanaticism. Lewes first suggested this comparison in a reply to Grote that reaffirmed Lewes's contention that Socrates had been an intuitive and subjective rather than a scientific thinker. John Stuart Mill dropped a similar hint. John Start Blackie accepted this position with much enthusiasm.[66] The Socrates-Carlyle interpretation reached its zenith in 1914 when Nichol Cross published a full-length biography of Socrates in which it was often difficult to discern whether the Athenian or the Scot was the subject. Cross paraphrased the message of Socrates in words that echoed *Sartor Resartus*.

> Get to know thyself, what thou really are, what thou really hast. Strip off all the clothing of the mind which thou hast borrowed, all these categories and formulae and ready made judgments which thou has adopted; these only prevent thee from getting into touch with the reality of thy self and of the universe.[67]

Thus to relate Socrates to Carlyle was to preserve his image as a zealous and essentially religiously minded reformer without picturing him as a precursor or symbolic supporter of positivism or scientific naturalism.

Although some religious liberals, such as J. R. Seeley, decried the traditional comparison of Socrates and Christ on the grounds that religion and philosophy and a church and a philosophic sect were very different, the parallel continued to be drawn during the latter part of the nineteenth century and the opening of the twentieth. R. M. Wen-

66. George Henry Lewes, *The Biographical History of Philosophy from Its Origin in Greece to the Present Day*, Library Edition, Much Enlarged and Thoroughly Revised (London: John Parker and Son, 1857), p. 141. This suggestion was added to Lewes's revised edition in part to refute Grote by explaining that a thinker could be critical of the morality of his society without being a rationalist. John Stuart Mill, *Dissertations and Discussions: Political, Philosophical, and Historical*, 4 vols. (London: Longmans, Green, Reader, and Dyer, 1867), 3:366; Blackie, *Four Phases of Morals*, pp. 39–41.

67. Robert Nichol Cross, *Socrates: The Man and His Mission* (London: Methuen and Co., 1914), p. 113.

ley in *Christ and Socrates* (1889) and J. T. Forbes in *Socrates* (1905) pointed to the spiritual qualities of the Athenian philosopher.[68] For such writers there was no question about the moral and religious superiority of Christ, but the spiritual life that could be ascribed to the pagan philosopher allowed a defense for the universal validity of religious matters without reference to the Christian or biblical tradition.

These efforts to assert a religious interpretation of Socrates were unsystematic and unscholarly, and they had no perceptible impact on more serious treatments of the philosopher. The important challenge to the nineteenth-century rationalist Socrates arose as a direct result of the so-called Socratic problem, that is, the question as to which major ancient source—Xenophon, Plato, Aristophanes, or Aristotle—presented the truest portrait of Socrates.[69] The problem existed because Socrates had enjoyed a reputation among both ancients and moderns for having marked a distinct turning point in Western philosophy. But the account of Xenophon, regarded since the eighteenth century as the most reliable, provided little indication why he should deserve that reputation. Scholars generally believed the much richer portrait by Plato to be historically unreliable because Plato had mixed his own thought with that of Socrates. In a seminal essay of 1818, "On the Worth of Socrates as a Philosopher," Friedrich Schleiermacher defined the problem as it confronted all writers thereafter. He asked, "What *can* Socrates have been, in spite of what Xenophon tells us of him without contradicting those traits of character which Xenophon definitely exhibits as Socratic, and what *must* he have been to have given Plato cause and justification for introducing him in the way he does in his dialogues?"[70] As the vast scholarly literature on the subject indicated in the years that followed, this proved to be anything but a simple question.

68. Robert Mark Wenley, *Socrates and Christ: A Study in the Philosophy of Religion* (Edinburgh and London: William Blackwood and Sons, 1889); J. T. Forbes, *Socrates* (Edinburgh: T. & T. Clark, 1905). See also Lewis Campbell, *Religion in Greek Literature: A Sketch in Outline* (London: Longmans, Green, and Co., 1898), pp. 315–38 and James Adam, *The Religious Teachers of Greece,* ed. Adela Marian Adam (Edinburgh: T. & T. Clark, 1908), pp. 321–29.

69. V. De Magelhaes-Vilhena, *Le Probleme de Socrate,* passim; Jean Humbert, *Socrate et les Petits Socratiques* (Paris: Presses Universitaires de France, 1967); A. R. Lacey, "Our Knowledge of Socrates," in Gregory Vlastos, ed., *The Philosophy of Socrates: A Collection of Critical Essays* (Garden City, N. Y.: Doubleday, Anchor Books, 1971), pp. 23–49.

70. Quoted in Lacey, "Our Knowledge of Socrates," p. 32.

Connop Thirlwall translated Schleiermacher's essay in 1833, but British classical historians and commentators usually acknowledged the question only to ignore it and its implications. One suspects religious discomfort caused by the textual difficulties of the Homeric question was no less present when scholars considered the Socratic problem. The differences among the several portraits of Socrates resembled the differences among the portrayals of Jesus in the Gospels, which in each case maintained itself to be a true account. The most notorious example of flight from the sources was James Frederick Ferrier, a respected Scottish philosopher, who told his students in the late fifties:

> In attempting to give a consistent and intelligible account of the Socratic system, both as it is in itself and as it stands opposed to the doctrines of the Sophists, I shall be obliged to attribute to him opinions which even Plato does not articulately vouch for as belonging to Socrates.... [A]lthough all that I shall attribute to Socrates has, I conceive, a sufficient warrant in the general scope and spirit of his philosophy, there will be something in my exposition for which no exact historical authority can be adduced. This course will, at any rate, conduce to intelligibility.... It is bad to violate the truth of history, but the truth of history is not violated, it is rather cleared up, when we evolve out of the opinions of an ancient philosopher more than the philosopher himself was conscious of these opinions containing.[71]

Then without a single reference to or quotation from any ancient source Ferrier assured his class that Socrates had been opposed to all forms of sensationalism in philosophy and had been a precursor to Scottish Common Sense Philosophy.

Other writers were more cautious, but few directly confronted the problem of the sources. William Fitzgerald made a serious examination of the Aristotelian materials and set forth a system whereby he believed it possible to distinguish references to the historical Socrates from those to the Platonic Socrates. George Grote outlined the problem, supported the primacy of Xenophon, but then proceeded to use Plato's *Apology*, as the single most important Socratic document. In *A*

71. James Frederick Ferrier, *Lectures on Greek Philosophy and Other Philosophical Remains,* ed. Alexander Grant and E. S. Lushington, 2 vols. (Edinburgh and London: William Blackwood and Sons, 1866), 1:212–213.

History of Greece his intentions and references were reasonably clear, but they became quite ambiguous in *Plato, and the Other Companions of Socrates*. A. P. Stanley noted the similarity between the Socratic problem and the problem of the historical Jesus, but drew no significant conclusions about the Socratic sources. Nevertheless, except for Fitzgerald and Jowett, the latter of whom completely rejected the historical validity of the Platonic Socrates, British writers gave the problem little hard or systematic thought.[72]

That situation prevailed until well after the turn of the century. Then in 1911 two scholars from St. Andrews issued a major challenge to the predominance of Xenophon. John Burnet in a long introduction to a Greek edition of the *Phaedo* (1911) and Alfred Edward Taylor in *Varia Socratica* (1911) contended that "the portrait drawn in the Platonic dialogues of the personal and philosophical individuality of Socrates is in all its main points strictly historical, and capable of being shown to be so." What Plato had done for his master was "not, as is too often thought, to transfigure him, but to understand him."[73] The mystical, transcendental, or Pythagorean doctrines of reminiscence, migration of the soul, and priority of form over material substance had not originated with Plato but had been taught by Socrates himself. Although the Burnet-Taylor thesis is now defunct among classical and philosophical scholars and kept alive only through warnings issued to young readers against its seductive attraction, it was revolutionary when first enunciated; and it provoked over thirty years of learned controversy.

With both Burnet and Taylor the thesis of a mystical or at least nonrationalist Socrates grew out of earlier scholarly interests. Burnet approached the subject from a background in the history of Greek philosophy, Taylor from idealist philosophy. In 1892 Burnet had published *Early Greek Philosophy* in which he attributed the origin of the Platonic theory of ideas or forms to Pythagoras and his followers. In particular, the Pythagoreans had set forth the concept of the priority of form over material substance. This view allowed him later to por-

---

72. William Fitzgerald, *Selections from the "Nichomachean Ethics" of Aristotle* (Dublin: Hodges and Smith, 1850), p. 163; Grote, *History of Greece* (1869), 8:206–10; *Plato, and the Other Companions of Socrates*, 1:281–82; Stanley, *Lectures on the History of the Jewish Church; Third Series*, p. 222; Jowett, *Dialogues of Plato*, 2:97–99.

73. Alfred Edward Taylor, *Varia Socratica: First Series* (Oxford: James Parker and Co., 1911), pp. ix, ix–x

tray Socrates as the philosophical conduit through which the theory in a more fully developed form reached Plato. As Burnet explained in *Greek Philosophy: Thales to Plato* (1914), Socrates took the concept of mathematical form from the Pythagoreans and expanded it to include metaphysical and ethical forms as well.[74] This interpretation cleared away the major obstacle to regarding the Platonic Socrates as a historical figure because previously it had been assumed on Aristotle's authority that Socrates had no connection to the theory of forms.

Like certain Continental scholars, such as Karl Joel, Burnet believed the practice of separating the Platonic Socrates from the "historical" Socrates required critical re-examination.[75] In point of fact, Xenophon had known Socrates in only the most casual way and had not been present at the trial or execution or even during many of the conversations related in the *Memorabilia*. Xenophon, unlike Plato, did not make clear his absence from reported discussions. Moreover, there was some evidence that Plato's works may have provided Xenophon with one of the sources for his own account. The usual practice of using Aristotle as a check on the information in Plato and Xenophon was unsound because there was little or no reason to believe that Aristotle possessed any significant firsthand knowledge. On the other hand, there were strong grounds for accepting the veracity of Plato. Almost all of the doctrines traditionally regarded as specifically Platonic appeared in the Socratic discourses of the *Phaedo*. Burnet thought it inconceivable, given Plato's reverence for Socrates, that he would have "falsified the story of his master's last hours on earth by using him as a mere mouthpiece for noble doctrines of his own."[76] That Aristotle, who freely criticized his teacher on other matters, did not accuse Plato of falsifying the portrait of Socrates was further evidence of a negative sort. Moreover, Plato had known Socrates well both personally and through family connections, and he had been present in Athens at crucial moments in the life of Socrates when

74. John Burnet, *Greek Philosophy: Thales to Plato* (London: Macmillan, 1968; originally published, 1914), pp. 154–79.

75. Karl Joel, *Die echte und der Xenophontishe Sokrates,* 2 vols. (Berlin: R. Gaertners, 1893–1901); L. Robin, "Les Memorables de Xenophon et notre connaissance de la philosophie de Socrate," *Année philosophique* 21 (1910): 1–47; Auguste Dies, *Autour de Platon: Essai de Critique et d'histoire,* 2nd ed., rev. and corr. (Paris: Socièté d' Edition "Les Belles Lettres," 1972; originally published 1921), pp. 127–48.

76. John Burnet, ed., *Plato's "Phaedo"* (Oxford: Clarendon Press, 1911) pp. xi–xii.

Xenophon was away. Finally, the character of the Platonic dialogues suggested that they were reports of speeches and conversations of real people. The general absence of anachronisms supported this contention. When Plato discussed his own ideas or topics of current controversy, Socrates either faded into the background or completely disappeared from the conversations.

Burnet's idea that the Platonic Socrates was the actual historical figure fundamentally challenged the nineteenth-century portrait of Socrates as a rationalist thinker who had originated induction and abandoned metaphysical and theological patterns of thought. "The truth is," Burnet commented, "that, apart from the prejudice which insists on seeing Socrates as a 'rationalist,' there is nothing to cause surprise in the fact that he was influenced by mystic doctrines." Those commentators who regarded Socrates as a rationalist or "intellectualist" failed to understand that Greek philosophy had arisen from "an effort to satisfy what we call the religious instinct" and from the belief that the individual soul must enter into communion with the divine reality of nature. The intense religiosity that Grote had discerned in Socrates' character but had separated from his philosophy had actually been intrinsic to his entire career and message. Moving well beyond the Pythagoreans, Socrates had developed his own peculiarly religious concept of the soul. In Ionia the soul had been regarded as the seat of consciousness and of moral qualities, but not as something individual. The Pythagoreans treated it as a divine entity or a fallen god that lay encased in a physical human body as a punishment. They regarded the soul as remaining unconscious during life but capable of receiving purification through the care of the person in whose body it slumbered. According to Burnet, however, Socrates had departed from the Pythagoreans and had taught that the soul was the *conscious* self within, determining good and evil, and that the most important duty of life was to look after one's soul and to maintain its purity. Through this novel doctrine Socrates had "healed the rift between science and religion which had proved so fatal to the Pythagorean Society, and it may be suggested that the significance of his teaching is not yet exhausted."[77] Socrates had drawn the care of the

77. Ibid., p. liv; Burnet, *Greek Philosophy,* p. 10; John Burnet, "Philosophy," R. W. Livingstone, ed., *The Legacy of Greece* (Oxford: Clarendon Press, 1957; originally published 1921), p. 78. See also John Burnet, "The Socratic Doctrine of the Soul,"

soul and concern for knowledge and action into a single moral and intellectual activity.

For Burnet, this doctrine of Socrates, and the teachings of the Sophists, represented reaction against an intellectualist or abstract scientific speculation in Greece that had failed to provide a place in the larger order of things for humankind and its internal spiritual impulses. In that regard, he agreed with G. H. Lewes's contention that Socrates had been an enemy of the early science in Greece and not a precursor of modern positivist science. Burnet declared, "The death of Socrates was that of a martyr, and 'intellectualism', if there is such a thing, can have no martyrs."[78] Burnet's analysis was part and parcel of the more general late-Victorian and Edwardian effort to examine sympathetically those features of Greek religion, philosophy, and society that earlier rationalist authors had largely discounted in order to discover an ancient positivist age. His repudiation of the rationalist Socrates paralleled Jane Harrison's critique of Olympian religion, Francis Cornford's denial of the scientific character of Thucydides, and Alfred Zimmern's portrayal of the religious and familial bonds of the polis.

Burnet had approached Socrates from the standpoint of a historian of Greek philosophy and as a scholar of Plato. By regarding Socrates as his own spokesman rather than as a mask for his student, Burnet believed he could establish a more consistent version of what must have been Plato's own thought. If the Platonic Socrates were also the historical Socrates, then Plato's own personally achieved philosophy was to be found primarily in dialogues such as the *Theaetetus,* the *Sophist,* the *Parmenides,* the *Timaeus,* and the *Laws.* By contrast, A. E. Taylor came to the problem of Socrates from the standpoint of a practicing philosopher who had previously written *The Problem of Conduct* (1901) and *Elements of Metaphysics* (1903), as well as briefer studies of Epicurus and Hobbes. He was also a devout Christian imbued with the idealist theology of the Lux Mundi group of high church Anglicans. Taylor, like Burnet, had studied at Oxford where

---

John Burnet, *Essays and Addresses* (London: Chatto and Windus, 1929), pp. 126–62; and John Burnet, "Socrates," James Hastings, ed., *Encyclopaedia of Religion and Ethics,* 13 vols. (Edinburgh: T. & T. Clark, 1929), 11:665–72.

78. Burnet, *Greek Philosophy,* p. 10. Ernest Barker extensively revised his earlier estimate of Socrates to accord with Burnet's views in *Greek Political Theory: Plato and His Predecessors* (London: Methuen and Co., 1918).

he had become a close friend of F. H. Bradley. He later taught for a time with Samuel Alexander at Owens College, Manchester. Both of these philosophers championed philosophical idealism and vigorously rejected positivism and scientific reductionism. Taylor joined Burnet at St. Andrews in 1908, and in a series of books and articles commencing in 1911 with *Varia Socratica* Taylor attempted to draw Socrates into the idealist and Christian camps.

Through a close analysis of the words εἶδος and ·ιδέα in pre-Platonic literature Taylor reaffirmed to his own satisfaction the argument previously set forth by Burnet that the Platonic concept of ideas had originated with the Pythagoreans. He then portrayed Socrates as a "continuator" of both the religious and the speculative features of Pythagorean philosophy. An analysis of Aristophanes' *Clouds* provided further evidence for the Socratic association with the Pythagoreans. However, Taylor based his case in larger measure on the trial of Socrates as recorded in the *Apology*. That document actually suggested that Socrates had in fact been guilty of one of the religious charges against him and that this guilt proved him to have been anything but the rationalist philosopher of nineteenth-century commentators.

Taylor contended that Socrates had successfully vindicated himself against the charges of atheism and corruption of the youth, but had not even attempted to refute the accusation of importing new gods. The latter charge had nothing to do with his *daimon*, but rather with his participation in religious cults disapproved by his fellow citizens. Socrates was guilty not of believing less than other Athenians but rather of believing more. According to Taylor:

> What he is accused of is neither atheism nor moral delinquency, in any sense we should attach to the words, but devotion to a religious cultus which has not the stamp of the State's approval, and is, in fact an unlicensed importation from abroad. As our ancestors of the seventeenth century would have put it, he frequents a foreign conventicle.[79]

79. Taylor, *Varia Socratica*, pp. 7–8. See also Alfred Edward Taylor, "Plato's Biography of Socrates," *Proceedings of the British Academy* 8 (1917–18): 93–132, for Taylor's defense of the historical credibility of Plato as a source for Socrates' life. It should also be noted that James Adam in *The Religious Teachers of Greece*, p. 94, and Jane Harrison in *Prolegomena to the Study of Greek Religion* (Cambridge: Cambridge Uni-

The last sentence is significant because throughout his analysis Taylor, whose father had been a Methodist minister, presented Socrates as the ancient equivalent of a modern British Nonconformist. Evidence in other dialogues indicated that Socrates had taught Pythagorean doctrines and that members of the cult had visited him in prison. His emphasis on the Pythagorean doctrines of the future life and the necessity of caring for one's soul challenged the Athenian and general Hellenic concept of the all-sufficient character of the polis. Other Athenians had consequently perceived Socrates as antidemocratic, and their hostility to his Pythagorean heresy was similar to the political hostility that later raged between church and state in Christian Europe.

This Pythagorean interpretation allowed Taylor to establish a line of descent from the earliest Greek philosophers through Socrates to Plato and later schools of Greek and Western philosophy and theology. Consequently, according to Taylor, Socrates did not mark a major turning point, and Plato's philosophy did not result from wholly independent speculation. For Taylor this fundamental continuity meant that the scientific and idealist traditions of European thought were compatible, since both could be traced to the Pythagoreans, who cared for their souls while seeking a more precise knowledge of nature. In opposition to Grote, Taylor contended that the religious and dialectical sides of Socrates' mission were not separate but necessarily complimentary, as they must always be for a true philosopher.

> Behind Socrates, if the main ideas of these studies contain substantial truth, we dimly discern the half-obliterated features of Pythagoras of Samos, and behind Pythagoras we can only just descry the mists which enclose whatever may be hidden under the name of Orpheus. And behind Orpheus, for us at least, there is only the impenetrable night. But it is a night in which, as we can hardly fail to recognize, the Church, the University, the organisation of science, all have their remote and unknown beginnings. They are all "houses" of the soul that, by what devious route soever, has come by the faith that she is a pilgrim to a country that

---

versity Press, 1903), pp. 512–17, compared the Orphic cults to English Dissenting sects.

does not appear, a creature made to seek not the things which are seen but the things which are eternal. . . . Philosophy . . . began as the quest for the road that leads to the city of God, and she has never numbered many true lovers among those who "forget the way."[80]

Standing at the point of the historically discernable emergence of philosophy, Socrates represented the essential unity of the scientific and religious modes of apprehending the world. Those two modes of thought were quite divided in 1911, but Taylor seemed to feel that what had been one in the beginning should not remain permanently sundered.

As Taylor more fully developed his concept of Socrates, it became increasingly Christian. He accepted Burnet's view of the distinctive character of the Socratic doctrine of the soul and stressed the Socratic injunction toward "tendance of the soul." He also argued that the Idea of the Good in Plato's dialogues was a Socratic rather than a Platonic teaching and that the Idea of the Good was the metaphysical equivalent of the Christian God. Finally, he drew Socrates closer to Christianity than had any writer of the past century. In both the mission of Socrates and the faith of the Church Taylor saw the conviction that something divine resided in human nature and that human nature "cannot but aspire to a good which is above time and mutability, and thus the right life is, from first to last, a process by which the merely secular and temporal self is re-made in the likeness of the eternal."[81] That faith, in conjunction with the conviction that the revival of Platonic thought in the Renaissance had fostered the scientific revolution, allowed Taylor to believe that in spite of all the debate that was occurring in the intellectual world around him science and faith were one.

Burnet's treatment of Socrates was part of the secular revolt against positivism. Taylor's works more properly belonged to the liberal Christian and idealist revival that occurred in British intellectual circles during the first quarter of this century. Most, if perhaps not all,

80. Taylor, *Varia Socratica*, pp. 268–69. Francis MacDonald Cornford's *From Religion to Philosophy: A Study of the Origins of Western Speculation* (New York: Harper and Row, 1957; originally published 1912) should also be consulted for a similar approach to the development of Greek thought.

81. Alfred Edward Taylor, *Plato: The Man and His Works* (London: Methuen and Co., 1926), p. 192.

present-day commentators on Plato and Socrates consider the Burnet-Taylor thesis incorrect and now refuted. The testimony of Aristotle that Socrates was responsible for the philosophic doctrines of induction and definition—and for those alone—could not ultimately be overcome. Such is the conclusion of classical scholarship. Yet the thesis itself was only partly a matter of scholarship, especially in Taylor's hands. As set forth by him, it constituted a resurrection in idealist garb of the old liberal Anglican portrait of Socrates as a link between faith and reason and between revelation and natural knowledge. It also was another example of the use of ancient philosophy to block the inroads of empirical and scientific thought. For if Burnet and Taylor saw in Socrates a continuation of the speculations of Pythagoras and Orpheus, one must see in those two modern scholars the gleam of intellectual fire and spiritual enthusiasm that had informed the thought of Shaftesbury, of Cudworth and the other Cambridge Platonists, and of the early Renaissance humanists, such as John Colet, who brought the Platonic light to Britain to illumine the inner resources of the human soul.

7

THE *ETHICS* OF ARISTOTLE

In the history of Greek philosophy Aristotle followed Plato, but in nineteenth-century Britain familiarity with Aristotle's work preceded any extensive consideration of Plato and in part determined the character of Platonic studies. Consequently, the Victorian treatment of Aristotle will be taken up before examination of the Platonic revival.

Throughout the century British study of Aristotle addressed only parts of his philosophy, and most of those received little more than minimal attention. In the *History of the Inductive Sciences* (1837), William Whewell of Trinity College, Cambridge offered an extensive discussion of Aristotle's scientific thought, and G. H. Lewes later completed a book-length study of the same subject. Lewes criticized Aristotle for scientific errors but at the same time praised him for his attempt to pose meaningful questions to the natural order. Although there was general agreement among commentators that Aristotle had not himself been an Aristotelian, it was also agreed that his science could not guide the modern study of physical nature. In regard to logic, many contemporary philosophers regarded Richard Whately, Sir William Hamilton, and John Stuart Mill as the major successors of Aristotle. Hamilton in particular drew heavily upon Aristotelian analysis for his lectures on logic and metaphysics, and in turn critics of Hamilton often used Aristotelian categories. Yet no British philosopher, logician, or classicist wrote a significant commentary on Aristotelian logic. The *Poetics* fared little better. John Henry Newman wrote an essay on that treatise when he was a very young scholar, but no further significant commentary appeared until S. H. Butcher published Aristotle's *Theory of Poetry and Fine Art* in 1894. The *Politics* had been frequently translated since the eighteenth century; major critical discussions of it, however, were lacking until Jowett's introduction to his translations of 1885 and W. L. Newman's important

four-volume edition of the Greek text with extensive notes and introductory essays that appeared in 1887.[1]

The reasons for the paucity of Aristotelian studies are not difficult to
delineate. The textual problems were less interesting than those related to Homer and Socrates, and the perceived relevance of his philosophy was less certain. Furthermore, few British scholars were actually prepared either academically or intellectually to range over as
broad an expanse of human knowledge as had Aristotle. Only Grote
dared to assume the challenge, and he died before completing the
task.[2] Many writers and classicists found Aristotle's thought both
difficult and obscure. The works themselves presented considerable
problems, and even in translations, which were not always available,
they were neither easy nor eloquent. Much of Aristotelian philosophy
was not readily teachable to students poorly grounded in Greek or in
philosophy or in both. Moreover, Bacon's condemnation of Aris-
totelianism had carried over to Aristotle as well and provided some
scholars with an easy excuse to avoid exceedingly difficult labor. Later
in the century the revival of Thomism within the Roman Catholic
Church may also have hindered the cause of Aristotelian study in
progressive, protestant Britain.[3] Finally, Aristotle's style and philosophy did not readily accomodate themselves to the goals of the university reformers who at mid-century warmly embraced Plato.

The exception to the widespread disregard of Aristotle's work was
the *Ethics,* which became the single most translated Greek philosophi-

1. William Whewell, *History of the Inductive Sciences from the Earliest to the Present
Times,* 2 vols. (London: John W. Parker, 1837), 1:41–54, 67–88; George Henry
Lewes, *Aristotle: A Chapter from the History of Science, Including Analyses of Aristotle's
Scientific Writings* (London: Smith, Elder and Co., 1864), pp. 19, 41, 108–09, 120,
381–82; Edward Poste, *The Logic of Science: A Translation of the "Posterior Analytics,"
with Notes and Introduction* (Oxford: F. Macpherson, 1850); John Henry Newman,
Essays and Sketches, new ed., 2 vols., ed. Charles Frederick Harrold (New York:
Longmans, Green, and Co., 1948), 1:55–82; Samuel Henry Butcher, *Aristotle's
Theory of Poetry and Fine Art* (New York: Dover Publications, 1951; originally pub-
lished, 1894); Marvin Theodore Herrick, *The "Poetics" of Aristotle in England* (New
Haven: Yale University Press, 1930), pp. 141–80; Benjamin Jowett, trans. and ed.,
The "Politics" of Aristotle (Oxford: Clarendon Press, 1885); William Lambert New-
man, ed., *The "Politics" of Aristotle,* 4 vols. (Oxford: Clarendon Press, 1887–1902).

2. George Grote, *Aristotle,* 2 vols., ed. Alexander Bain and G. Croom Robertson
(London: John Murray, 1872).

3. Alfred William Benn, *The Greek Philosophers,* 2 vols. (London: Kegan Paul,
Trench, and Co., 1882), 1:275–85.

cal text of the entire century. The reasons for the vitality of the *Ethics*
were in part related to the book itself but in even larger measure to the
curriculum at Oxford. After the adoption of the Examination Statute
of 1800, which established a more formal and rigorous program of
study and evaluation, the *Ethics* rapidly assumed a central place in the
Literae Humaniores program and maintained that position for the rest
of the century.[4] More Oxford students read the *Ethics,* or at least its
first four books, than any other single ancient treatise, and more tutors
had to teach it. The large number of translations was a direct result of
this curricular situation, and to no small extent commentary on the
Ethics reflected and embodied the shifting intellectual patterns at Oxford and the changes in the Greats reading list. For example, the
comparison of the *Ethics* with Bishop Joseph Butler's thought that was
common in the early nineteenth century stemmed from the presence
of works by Butler on the Greats reading list and generally ceased after
they were removed in the sixties.

The *Ethics* particularly suited the education in character rather than
scholarly accomplishment emphasized at nineteenth-century Oxford.
As a vehicle for training young men for careers in the church, politics,
and the civil service, the *Ethics* possessed both charm and evident good
sense and upheld the social elitism so much a part of Oxford life. The
book was eminently practical in content, and its constant references to
the experiences of everyday life appealed to Baconian prejudices. In
contrast to certain Platonic dialogues, the *Ethics* was a "safe" book.
Aristotle did not stir the mystical imagination of the young, and, more
important, he left men secure in their property and undisturbed in
their family circles. His praise for collective social life did not crush the
individual for the sake of the collectivity, and he encouraged citizens to
improve the quality of their society without overturning its structures
or sacrificing its existing amenities. Aristotle's emphasis on the pre-

4. Finley Melville Kendall Foster, *A Bibliographical Survey of English Translations
from the Greek* (New York: Columbia University Press, 1918), pp. 26–34; Mark
Pattison, *Essays,* 2 vols., ed. Henry Nettleship (Oxford: Clarendon Press, 1889),
1:462, 474–75; Herbert Arthur Evans, "Literae Humaniores," *Oxford Magazine* 27
(1908–09): 55–56, 90–91, 119–20, 152–53, 188–89, 220–21, 247–48; Martin
Lowther Clarke, *Classical Education in Britain 1500–1900* (Cambridge: Cambridge
University Press, 1959), pp. 98–127; W. R. Ward, *Victorian Oxford* (London: Frank
Cass and Co., 1965), pp. 13–20; David Newsome, *Two Classes of Men: Platonism and
English Romantic Thought* (London: John Murray, 1974), pp. 73–78.

scriptive role of current social opinion as the best mold for conduct served to uphold the status quo of the age. His requirement for the conditioning of the will and the formation of good habits provided significant supplements to the Socratic equation of knowledge with virtue and made Aristotle's ethical thought appear more complete and acceptable to Christians and aristocrats. The former believed ethics must involve more than intellect, and the latter felt that proper social conduct was inculcated by a particular ethos and by nurture over a long period of time rather than by intellectual endeavor. Finally, the *Ethics,* unlike most other of Aristotle's works, could be read satisfactorily as a book; and as Mark Pattison, rector of Lincoln College, once pointed out, it was a work from which examination questions could be easily culled.[5]

The long dominance of the *Ethics* at Oxford did not, however, mean it was always taught in the same fashion or that it was used always to impart the same lessons. In 1855 Mark Pattison had already discerned four stages of Aristotelian study at the university during the first half of the century. He looked back upon an initial "scholar's" period when the various works of Aristotle had been studied primarily as texts of the Greek language. Thereafter followed a time of "common sense," when teachers and students regarded the *Ethics* as "an eminently practical treatise" that "came home to our business and bosoms, and told us of the commonest things we were doing every day of our lives." That stage was succeeded by a "critical" period during which the various treatises of Aristotle were read and compared with each other in an attempt to discover a general system of thought. Finally, by mid-century a "scientific" age had dawned as the light of history, philology, and criticism was cast on Aristotle's works.[6] Pattison's remarks are important for indicating contemporary recogition of shifts in the teaching of Aristotle and for providing a modicum of information about instruction that was primarily oral and that predated most of the published commentaries on the *Ethics.*

For present purposes Pattison's scheme of four stages requires modification. The first three of his eras of Aristotelian study are better merged into a single period when a Christian or, more correctly,

5. Mark Pattison, "Philosophy at Oxford," *Mind* 1 (1876):90.
6. Pattison, *Essays,* 1:463–65.

Anglican reading of the *Ethics* predominated. The third quarter of the century, as Pattison quite correctly perceived, saw a generally critical and historicist approach to the treatise as it came to be regarded primarily as an ancient philosophical text that should be interpreted in terms of the historical epoch during which it had been written. This interpretation, as well as a contemporary utilitarian critique, raised the question of the current relevance of the *Ethics* as a moral guide. Finally, from the last quarter of the century through World War I the *Ethics* was read from the standpoint of philosophical idealism and as a text for good citizenship. During this last period, for the first time in Britain the *Ethics* and the *Politics* were read in light of each other. These three modes of interpretation in turn mirrored the intellectual and institutional life of Victorian Oxford as it made the transition from an exclusively Anglican institution where theological concerns dominated to a university where German scholarly methods had made inroads and ultimately to a place where leaders and civil servants of a modern secular democracy received their training.

The "Ethics" and Christianity

In 1857 the first volume of Sir Alexander Grant's edition of *The "Ethics" of Aristotle* was published. The appearance of this important work based on critical scholarship and numerous German sources led more than one reviewer to reflect on the manner in which the *Ethics* had previously been taught at Oxford. The critic for the *Saturday Review* bitterly denounced traditional Oxford instruction. Uncritical textual analysis had ignored the question of which books properly belonged to the *Nichomachean Ethics* and which to the *Eudemian*. Of still more serious concern, students read the *Ethics* "unhistorically," as if it were "the treatise of a modern author, written in the same philosophical language, and from the same point of view, as the treatises of other modern authors." Oxford tutors also too readily exhibited "the desire to find Christian doctrines, such as the doctrine of human corruption, in the great heathen philosopher" and to that end had twisted "Aristotle's theory of moral states into accordance with the ecclesiastical doctrine of regeneration." Each of these charges was true. Throughout the first half of the century and even into the second, the *Ethics* was read and taught with little regard for either the time or the place of its composition and as a work that had some kind of direct or indirect relationship to Christianity. The latter point of view emerged because the *Ethics* was almost invariably compared and contrasted with the works of Bishop Butler, whose *Analogy of Religion* was the only modern text on the *Literae Humaniores* reading list. Aristotle stood as the example of the highest heathen moralist and Butler as the most accomplished Christian moralist. Each in his own sphere appeared beyond significant correction or improvement. As Matthew Arnold recalled, ". . . we at Oxford used to read our Aristotle or our Butler with the same absolute faith in the classicality of their matter as in the classicality of Homer's forms."[7]

Although more than one critic of clerical Oxford repeated the accusations of Arnold and the *Saturday Review*, it is difficult to ascertain exactly what was being taught in regard to the *Ethics* during the first half of the century. There were almost no English commentaries on the treatise, and those that did find their way into print often amounted to little more than paraphrases. Nonetheless, there are a few documents that suggest the uses to which Oxford teachers and scholars put the *Ethics* prior to the impact of German scholarship.

In 1810 Edward Copleston, provost of Oriel College and later bishop of Llandaff, defended the place of Aristotle in the university by pointing to "the precision of the language, the close connection of the reasoning, the enlarged philosophical views, and the immense store of principles and maxims" contained in the *Ethics* and the *Rhetoric*. He praised those writings as "the best calculated of any single work for bringing into play all the energies of the intellect, and for trying, not merely the diligence of the scholar, but the habit of discrimination which he has formed, the general accuracy of his thoughts, and the force and vigor of his mind." Copleston felt little or no apprehension over devoting so much attention to the moral thought of a heathen philosopher because, as he explained:

> In a Christian community, Ethics is much more included within the province of Religion than that of Philosophy. Without the function of Religion, the purest system of Ethics would be com-

---

7. *Saturday Review* 4 (1857): 469; Matthew Arnold, "Bishop Butler and the Zeit-Geist," (1876) in Matthew Arnold, *Essays Religious and Mixed,* ed. R. H. Super (Ann Arbor: University of Michigan Press, 1972), p. 12.

paratively lifeless and unfruitful; and without ethical instruction, Religion itself is vapid, and even dangerous.

Copleston further argued that the Christian Gospel had been intended to correct but not "to supercede moral reasoning" and that Christianity possessed "no entire and systematic code, which renders the employment of our natural faculties in such an enquiry less needful." Finally, for Copleston the *Ethics* of Aristotle was preferable as a text to William Paley's utilitarian system because the apparent completeness of the latter might lead students to believe "that it contains *all* we think well established in Christian Ethics: whereas the Greek philosopher is always studied with a reserve in favour of Christianity, and an habitual reference is made to a more unerring standard, by which its soundness is to be tried."[8] Copleston had outlined the character of the Oxford approach to Aristotle that would last for a century. More often than not what modified that reading was the particular understanding of Christianity against which the *Ethics* was measured and compared.

Copleston's implied criticism of Paley, whose moral philosophy dominated Oxford and Cambridge in 1800, was indicative of the beginning of a shift away from Paley and toward Bishop Butler, whose thought had largely captured Oxford in 1830. Butler's emphasis on conscience and his particular defense of natural theology seemed more adequate to the growing skepticism of the age. In the early thirties R. D. Hampden successfully urged the inclusion of Butler's *Analogy of Religion* on the *Literae Humaniores* reading list.[9] Thereafter, comparisons between Butler and Aristotle became the order of the day. These appeared in a rather sophisticated form in Hampden's analysis of the ancient philosopher prepared, like his article on Socrates, for the *Encyclopaedia Britannica*.

Hampden was by all accounts the most accomplished Aristotelian scholar in the university and one also deeply versed in scholastic philosophy. He presented Aristotle as a progressive thinker who had been no less of "a reformer of the Ancient Philosophy, than Bacon was of the Scholasticism of his day." Like Bacon, he had urged an inductive

---

8. Edward Copleston, *A Reply to the Calumnies of the Edinburgh Review against Oxford,* 2nd ed. (Oxford: J. Cooke and J. Parker, 1810), pp. 141, 178, 179, 180.

9. Hamish F. G. Swanston, *Ideas of Order: Anglicans and the Renewal of Theological Method in the Middle Years of the Nineteenth Century* (Assen: Van Gorcum and Comp. B.V., 1974), pp. 1–13.

philosophy, had criticized the philosophical idols raised by Plato's system of ideal forms, and had attempted to set his age on the path to meaningful scientific analysis and discovery. As an ethical philosopher, Aristotle in a rather Baconian fashion had employed his reason to ponder human experience and to formulate a theory of conduct in light of that experience. The result was a moral philosophy that could commend itself to Christians.

> The ethical writings of Aristotle, composed amidst the darkness of heathen superstition, abound with pure and just sentiments. Instead of depressing man to the standard of the existing depraved opinions and manners, they tend to elevate him to the perfection of his nature. They may indeed be studied, not only as an exercise of the intellect, but as a discipline of improvement of the heart; so much is there in them of sound practical observation on human nature. . . . They are directed, it must be allowed, solely to the improvement of man in this present life. But so just are the principles on which he builds that improvement, that we may readily extend them to those higher views of our nature and condition to which our eyes, by the light of Divine Revelation, have been opened. And no greater praise can be given to a work of heathen morality than to say, . . . that they contain nothing with which a Christian may dispense with, no precept of life which is not an element of the Christian character; and that they only fail in elevating the heart and mind to objects which it needed Divine Wisdom to reveal, and a Divine Example to realize to the life.[10]

Just as Bacon had regarded nature as a second book of divine revelation, Hampden thought the empirical examination of the human situation could and must supplement revelation as a source of moral truth and ethical precept. As an example of such a rational supplement, Aristotle's *Ethics* possessed high value even if it did not address the question of human salvation. It was in large measure just that positive, constructive function assigned by Hampden and and other liberal Oxford Anglicans to human reason that loosed on them the tumult of the Tractarian reaction.

10. Renn Dickson Hampden, *The Fathers of Greek Philosophy* (Edinburgh: Adam and Charles Black, 1862), pp. 23, 122–23.

Hampden's analysis of the *Ethics* went beyond simple observation of Aristotle's frequent agreement with Christianity morality. Rather, he approached the *Ethics* as a manifestation of the natural reason in the same spirit that Butler in the *Analogy of Religion* had examined the order of physical nature. Butler had proposed to demonstrate "that the system of Religion, both natural and revealed, considered only as a system, and prior to the proof of it, is not a subject of ridicule, unless that of Nature be so too."[11] He had then attempted to prove that Christians believed according to revealed religion nothing about physical nature that they did not also already believe according to reason and that the modes of reasoning used in regard to nature were the same as those used in regard to the doctrines of revealed religion. To the extent that Hampden could demonstrate Christian morality or moral presuppositions to be present in the ethical philosophy that Aristotle had set forth by natural reason, those same opinions could not be cast into doubt by attacks on Christian revelation. In other words, Aristotle's *Ethics* allowed Hampden to defend Christian ethics by separating the validity of the latter from dependence on biblical authority. If Aristotle held certain moral doctrines on the grounds of natural reason, Christians could not be faulted for holding the same precepts on the grounds of revelation.

For example, Hampden suggested that Aristotle's emphasis on public opinion for ascertaining the propriety of an action in effect constituted

> a standard of right and wrong inherent in human nature, or what is equivalent to a Conscience. If all agree in praising a certain modification of the Affections, and in blaming another, it is clear that there must be some common principles in all to serve as the bases of these unanimous judgments.

Hampden also contended that Aristotle's idea that prudence was necessary for achieving the ethical mean provided grounds for a concept of duty. He pointed to the absence of calculation or utilitarian

11. Joseph Butler, *The Analogy of Religion* (New York: Frederick Ungar, 1961), p. 7.

motive in that ideal and associated it with an intuitive approach to moral action and ethical decision. According to Hampden:

> The Prudence which he teaches is no calculation of consequences. It is a practical philosophy of the heart; inseparably connected with the love of that conduct which it suggests. Whereas, when we are taught to act on the ground of interest, the prudence then inculcated is a mere intellectual foresight of consequences, independent of any exercise of the heart. . . . The heart of man leaves far behind this morality of consequences, and decides, even before the action itself has its birth, whether it is morally right or wrong.[12]

The very existence of Aristotle's theory of the mean and of prudence as the vehicle for determining it meant that a nonutilitarian morality was attainable through the use of human reason and was not dependent on revelation. The existence of this nonutilitarian ethics, rationally achieved by a heathen, served to protect the wisdom and relevance of a similar ethics based on intuition and conscience taught in the context of the revealed Christian faith. Although such arguments may seem contorted, they were familiar to all Anglicans who had studied Butler and were attractive to those who hoped to see Butler's ethics supplant Paley's and thus repulse the utilitarian morality of secular philosophers.

Hampden wrote his essay on Aristotle in 1831, and it appeared in both the seventh and eighth editions of the *Encyclopaedia Britannica* as well as in his *Fathers of Greek Philosophy* (1862). Shortly after it was written, the Tractarian movement and the sharp controversies it spawned stirred Oxford for almost twenty years. Hampden became one of the most prominent targets of the Tractarians until he left Oxford in 1847 to assume the diocese of Hereford.[13] The theological issues that divided Hampden and his detractors were also reflected to some extent in the treatment of the *Ethics*. Both Hampden and the High Church party shared the assumptions that the ancient treatise

---

12. Hampden, *Fathers of Greek Philosophy*, pp. 138, 139.
13. Owen Chadwick, *The Victorian Church*, 2 vols. (Oxford: Oxford University Press, 1966–70), 1:237–50.

bore some relationship to Christianity and to Bishop Butler's philosophy. They differed, however, over the character of that relationship and the reasons for it. The Tractarians, whose opinions on the subject must be gleaned from several short discussions rather than any major work, tended to find specific Christian doctrines in Aristotle rather than philosophical evidence that the natural reason of humankind could come to broad conclusions about human morality analogous to those delivered by revelation. Furthermore, they assumed that Aristotle's agreement with Christianity stemmed from his knowledge in a diluted form of primitive revelation.

Some sense of the tenor of this Tractarian interpretation can be obtained from a pamphlet written in 1837 by Frederick Oakeley, a fellow of Balliol, a strong Tractarian, and later a convert to Roman Catholicism. Almost twenty years later Mark Pattison cited this pamphlet as not untypical of the reading of the *Ethics* in some circles at Oxford during the thirties and early forties.[14] Oakeley's *Remarks upon Aristotelian and Platonic Ethics as a Branch of the Studies Pursued in the University of Oxford* displayed the intensely parochial intellectual atmosphere of the university during the Tractarian period. Oakeley's mental horizons stretched no further than the university examinations, the controversies over the character of the Anglican Church, and theological reasoning that attempted to make Aristotelian virtues conform to those associated with Christianity. Like Hampden, whose *Britannica* article he cited, Oakeley portrayed the *Ethics* as an alternative to a liberal, utilitarian morality based on the spirit of calculation. He saw the treatise as "exhibiting the rough draught, and faint outline, which the Gospel has filled up," and he argued that the Gospel and the *Ethics* stood in agreement in their mutual view of "man's Moral nature as capable of advancing indefinitely towards its perfection." Oakeley also urged the existence of close parallels between the *Ethics* and the moral philosophy of Bishop Butler on the issues of habit, temptation, and fatalism. Butler's writings constituted "a Christian Commentary" on the *Ethics* and demonstrated how the latter might be "vindicated from profane uses."[15] Oakeley seems to have had little or

14. Pattison, *Essays*, 1:464.
15. Frederick Oakeley, *Remarks upon Aristotelian and Platonic Ethics as a Branch of the Studies Pursued in the University of Oxford* (Oxford: J. H. Parker, 1837), pp. 48, 49, 29.

no understanding of why Aristotle and Butler might have shared elements of a common outlook. He did not, for example, suggest that Butler's possible familiarity with Aristotle was a significant factor or that categories of Greek philosophy might well be expected to inform later Christian thought. Nor did he explain, or perhaps even grasp, that just as Butler had fought modern materialism in the guise of Hobbes so Aristotle had rejected ancient materialism. Neither the history of thought nor the inner logic of either philsophy provided a context for Oakeley's comments. The only significant context was the program of reading for the *Literae Humaniores* examination.

All of these initial observations were more or less standard, but Oakeley went well beyond those facile comparisons of heathen and Christian ethics. He attempted to illustrate Aristotle's philosophy through Christian examples and in doing so attempted to assimilate Aristotle's thought into contemporary Anglican concerns. He argued that by the mean as a standard for conduct Aristotle had not intended to imply moderation in conduct. Rather, Aristotle had regarded the mean as a mode of participation in the extremes. Oakeley then presented the labors of the sixteenth-century reformers of the Catholic Church in England as illustrating what Aristotle had meant by the mean.

> The object of our Reformers, as a body, was not so much to steer clear of extremes, as to pursue Truth. They did not set to work with a salutary fear of opposite errors, but pursued their object boldly; veering round (if they saw need) from one (so called) extreme to the other; sedulous of Truth, but reckless of Opinion; to men, seeming alternately, or relatively to their own standard, Papists, or Ultra Protestants; and yet, the while, instruments, in God's hands, for the production of the Reformed Catholic System; the precise exemplification of Aristotle's "Mean Excellence." For, of course, when the Church is called a "Via Media," reference is made not to her *doctrines* only, but to her *spirit,* and practical system. The Church *temper* . . . is (in the language of Aristotle) a Mean between servile Submission, and proud Independence; or between unreasoning Belief, and unbelieving Reason; or, lastly, between Apathy and Excitement. And yet it is much liker to an Extreme, than any of the so-called extreme

systems; i.e. it much better *represents the principle,* and *realizes the professed object,* of each.[16]

Just as the *Literae Humaniores* examination determined Oakeley's comparison of Aristotle with Butler, the contemporary quarrels at Oxford over the character of the Anglican Church determined his interpretation of the concept of the Aristotelian mean. He used Aristotle's concept to uphold the Tractarian ideal of the church against that of the Oriel Noetics and the Evangelical party. In that manner, he hoped to suggest that the "Via Media" was congruent with both the injunctions of God and the wisdom of humankind.

Finally, Oakeley contended that the major Aristotelian virtues were identical or at least compatible with Christianity. For example, he saw little difference between Aristotle's concept of courage, which derived almost entirely from military experience, and the ideals of Christian courage, patience, and fortitude. He explained that Aristotelian courage

is a perfectly Christian quality. It is nothing else than the habit of mind which leads us, on proper occasions, to "quit ourselves like men." It is the frame of mind, of which Warlike Courage is only a single form, an accidental result. It is a fearlessness (not an apathy) about our duty, *whatever it may be.* About the precise nature of that duty, Christians and Heathens would, of course, disagree; but there is not need, therefore, that they should disagree about the habit of mind, which leads to such a result.

Even more surprising, Oakeley attempted to find common characteristics in the great-souled or high-minded man of Book IV of the *Ethics* and some version of Christian high-mindedness. Few elements in the *Ethics* seemed to commentators before or since more distinctly Greek and less Christian than that nobly arrogant figure. Oakeley admitted that Aristotelian magnanimity seemed quite unchristian, but he believed that Aristotle must have seen that humility was necessarily involved with true magnanimity. Oakeley also contended that there was a Chrstian version of high-mindedness analogous to Aristotle's.

Under the Christian system, a certain grateful consciousness of Moral superiority, is perfectly compatible both with Humility

16. Ibid., pp. 53–54.

and with Charity. It becomes wrong only when (as in the case of the Pharisee in the parable) it involves a *contemptuous* estimate of others. . . . One who knows himself to be in the right, will (as Aristotle says) unite manly straightforwardness with prudent reserve. He has no self-distrust; wherefore he does not hang upon the opinion of the multitude, but on all needful occasions will speak openly and without fear. And yet, distrustful of the sympathy of inferior minds, he is not prodigal of words, and ostentatious of feelings; ever dreading to profane what he cannot hope to make generally intelligible.

Although Aristotle's high-mindedness was by no means identical with the Christian quality, his discussion of the virtue nonetheless contained "a striking intermixture of most unusual truth."[17] Perhaps only Gladstone's discovery of Christian gentlemen in the Homeric kingdoms presented a more unexpected piece of domestication of Greek values. The parochialism of Oakeley's purview was as striking as the confusion of his thinking, and the latter was in no small measure the result of the former.

Perhaps the most outspoken early Victorian writer to insist upon the useful relationship between the morals of the Christian faith and those of Aristotle's *Ethics* was William Sewell, a tutor at Exeter College, Oxford, for a time professor of moral philosophy, a moderate Tractarian, and a highly orthodox churchman.[18] The most famous incident in his life was his public burning of a copy of James Anthony Froude's *Nemesis of Faith* before a class at Exeter College. In less impassioned moments Sewell introduced the study of Plato to modern Oxford and apparently attracted goodly numbers of students to his lectures on the subject. He enunciated his view of the relationship of ancient ethics to Christianity in *Christian Morals,* a work that first appeared in 1841 and afterward went through several printings in both England and the United States.

Sewell commended both Plato and Aristotle to his students and readers, but he argued that the genuine truth present in their

17. Ibid., pp. 57–58, 61, 62. John Henry Newman rejected any attempt to make Aristotle's great-souled man compatible with Christianity. See A. Dwight Culler, *The Imperial Intellect: A Study of Newman's Educational Ideal* (New Haven: Yale University Press, 1958), pp. 75–79, 201–04.

18. Lionel James, *A Forgotten Genius, Sewell of St. Columba's and Radley* (London: Faber and Faber, 1945).

philosophies had not originated with them. Generally speaking, Greek ethical thought displayed

> the human mind struggling by itself to attain its perfection—
> uttering faint cries like an infant, to signify wants which it cannot
> express—yearning for some light to fall on it, some hand to guide
> it—wandering now into the wildest errors, now reaching grand
> truths, and now arriving, by the use of reason, at paradoxes and
> mysteries.

In the good time of Providence the Christian Gospel had provided answers to those cries and solutions to those paradoxes. Sewell believed, however, that the Greeks had not lived entirely without knowledge of genuinely divine truth. He traced the more sublime and true elements of Greek moral philosophy, as exhibited in Plato and Aristotle, to unspecified Eastern sources that had been privy to the wisdom of a primitive revelation. Truth derived from those sources accounted for the agreement of Plato and Aristotle with certain elements of later Christian teaching. On these grounds Sewell concluded, "Both Christian . . . and heathen Ethics are based on a revelation from God."[19] By this argument, which originated in the patristic age, Sewell avoided the question of an independent Greek influence on Christianity and the possibility that divine wisdom might have arisen outside traditional channels of revelation or through the natural reason.

Although he admired Aristotle somewhat less than Plato, Sewell urged Christians who believed the Church adequately provided for common moral practice to resort to Aristotle to understand that morality in a more nearly scientific or carefully reasoned manner. He advised his readers to

> be prepared to correct and enlarge Aristotle by Plato; and to Plato
> you may add all the other Greek sects and modern moralists, only
> referring whatever you find in them to the doctrines of Aristotle.
> They will serve to enlarge, to balance, to qualify, to contradict, to
> illustrate, to support him. Range all the moral information which
> they offer under heads supplied by Aristotle. In this manner you
> will attain variety without confusion; you will be continually
> building upon a regular fixed foundation.

19. William Sewell, *Christian Morals* (London: James Burns, 1841), pp. 59, 45.

A person consulting Aristotle for a framework of morality would be less likely to consider the scientific claims of the modern rationalists and utilitarians whom Sewell abhorred. In contrast to the latter philosophers, Aristotle, along with Christian thinkers, had wisely refused to confound pleasure and happiness. In opposition to utilitarianism, Christian and Aristotelian ethics, according to Sewell, shared the common view that human happiness consists of "the exercise of the noblest faculties of man on the noblest of subjects." Both regarded the noblest faculty as reason and the noblest subject as "eternal, immutable truth."[20] Sewell simply confused the Christian and Aristotelian concepts of eternal truth and largely overlooked the clearly non-Christian features of the *Ethics*.

A final indication of the mode of Christian interpretation of the *Ethics* at Oxford is provided by Montagu Burrows in *Pass and Class,* an often reprinted guide to Oxford and its studies first published in 1860. In that book Burrows included an essay on the *Ethics* that is of particular interest because he based it on the notes he had made while a student during the fifties. He explained that one purpose of Oxford education was to convey a "sense of the futility of any mere intellectual education, of the inseparable connection between faith and reason, of the certain ruin of both by the neglect of the cultivation of either." The careful study of Aristotle's treatise in conjuction with Bishop Butler contributed directly to that end. Although the *Ethics* led the student to many acceptable and wise conclusions, it also presented other moral difficulties insolvable to the natural reason of even a "supremely gifted heathen." To the latter quandaries, Burrows contended, the Christian faith provided solutions.

> Thus the doctrine of the Fall of Man, the perversion of the noble nature, the overclouding of his godlike intellect, clears up the Socratic paradox which Aristotle condemns, but scarcely attempts to meet. The union of the religious inner life with outward moral activity, in whatever sphere of life a man is thrown, which is the basis of Christian teaching, removes the awkward inconsistency traceable throughout the *Ethics* between its author's notions of contemplative happiness and that of practical life. . . . The cogency of the motives to virtue laid down by Aristotle is incalculably magnified in the scheme of those to whom a

20. Ibid., pp. 116, 409.

future state has been Revealed; to say nothing of the fresh motives which have been superadded, and the Divine aid which they are taught the way to obtain. . . . The anomalies which we cannot but perceive in the application of his views on the relations of morals to politics, are removed at once when, as the common bond and means of training, we read the Church for the State.[21]

There was not a hint of criticism, historical sense, or modern theology in Burrows's comments. A parochial version of Christianity had simply been added to a parochial reading of Aristotle. But such had been the usual approach to the *Ethics* at early Victorian Oxford.

During the same years, teachers at Oxford and elsewhere also urged that Christianity provided a necessary impetus for moral conduct that was lacking in Aristotle and, by implication, in the natural reason for humankind. Edward Copleston had pointed to this happy complementary relationship between Aristotle and Christianity as early as 1810, and John S. Brewer had repeated the point in his notes to a Greek edition of the *Ethics* in 1836.[22] The person who most enthusiastically proclaimed this relationship was John Stuart Blackie. In lectures delivered at the Royal Institution in 1869, the Edinburgh professor praised "the thoroughly masculine, thoroughly manly, and thoroughly healthy" character of the *Ethics*. He also noted certain parallels between Aristotelian and Christian moral concepts. Aristotle's inclusion of passionate as well as rational tendencies in human nature suggested an understanding of original sin and recalled St. Paul's remarks about the conflict of the spirit and the flesh. But the most important feature of the *Ethics* was the doctrine of the mean, which provided a splendid supplement to the teachings of the Christian Gospel.

> The importance of Aristotle's rule arises from the fact that it is a regulative principle of universal application; and in this way it

21. Montagu Burrows, *Pass and Class: An Oxford Guide-Book Through the Courses of Literae Humaniores, Mathematics, Natural Science, and Law and Modern History* (Oxford: John Henry and James Parker, 1860), pp. 247–49. See also *Autobiography of Montagu Burrows*, ed. Stephen Montagu Burrows (London: Macmillan, 1908), pp. 200–01.

22. Copleston, *A Reply to the Calumnies of the Edinburgh Review against Oxford*, pp. 179–80; John S. Brewer, ed., *The "Nichomachean Ethics" of Aristotle with English Notes* (Oxford: Henry Slater, 1836), pp. 438n–439n.

may well be taken in the left hand, along with the golden rule in the right hand.... These two famous maxims indeed may, for practical purposes, be regarded as complementary to each other. For persons in whom the sympathetic emotions predominate are often deficient in the regulative faculty; while those whose power of regulation is great have sometimes little to regulate, and, like a great commander with few soldiers, makes a poor appearance in the battlefield. In the struggle of life, the man whose sympathetic unselfish impulses are strong will perhaps find more benefit from the constant reference to Aristotle's mean than even to the Scriptural golden rule, while the well-tempered Aristotelian will, on the other hand, find it for his advantage to inquire whether the even pace at which he goes is not as much owing to the dullness of the charger's blood as to the skill with which the rider wields the rein.[23]

Taken alone the *Ethics* lacked the spur or inducement to moral conduct that Christianity provided, but in conjunction with the Gospel the *Ethics* could genuinely improve moral behavior and lead to a fuller realization of human nature.

Burrows's essay of 1860 and Blackie's lecture of 1869 were little more than echoes of the interpretations of the *Ethics* propounded in the earlier part of the century. They and the Anglicans whose views they restated had read and taught the *Ethics* from the standpoint of personal action and personal ethical values. Because they thought human nature had not changed since the age of Aristotle, the *Ethics* remained for them current and relevant to present-day conduct. Since the *Ethics* manifested the natural reason functioning prior to the advent of Christ, whatever faults or deficiencies it might have could be remedied by the truth of the Gospel. Moreover, since these writers assumed that students would read the *Ethics* in a Christian community, Aristotle's injunction to conform to current modes of social conduct was regarded as acceptable. Most important, the *Ethics* stood as a great defense for a nonutilitarian approach to morality. All of these assumptions and the interpretations of the *Ethics* they supported received a

23. John Stuart Blackie, *Four Phases of Morals: Socrates, Aristotle, Christianity, Utilitarianism* (New York: Scribners, Armstrong, and Co., 1872), pp. 157, 161–63, 168–69.

fundamental challenge in 1857 when Alexander Grant published his edition of The *"Ethics" of Aristotle.* Suddenly, criticism, historicism, and Hegel appeared on the British Aristotelian landscape. No other single work of classical scholarship, except perhaps Grote's analysis of Greek myths, so rapidly transformed earlier opinions held in Britain on a major subject from Greek antiquity or so thoroughly exposed them as palpable nonsense.

The *"Ethics"* Historicized

Sir Alexander Grant, as noted in the previous chapter, was the major mid-Victorian commentator on Aristotle's *Ethics.* Heir to an impecunious baronetcy, Grant was educated at Oxford, where he studied with Benjamin Jowett and where for a time he was a fellow of Oriel College. In 1857 he published the first volume of his Greek edition of the *Ethics.* Two years later he left England for India, where from 1863 to 1868 he served as vice-chancellor of the University of Bombay. While living in India, Grant completed his annotations to the *Ethics;* a second edition of the work was published in 1866. He returned to Britain in 1868 to assume the duties of principal and vice-chancellor of the University of Edinburgh and remained in that post until his death in 1884. In 1874 he published an extensive revision of the *Ethics* in which he made considerable accommodation to Grote's views on the Sophists and in 1885 a fourth edition of the *Ethics* with still further revisions. Grant also wrote a small volume on Aristotle and one on Xenophon, as well as the article on Aristotle for the ninth edition of the *Encyclopaedia Britannica.*[24]

Grant's edition of the *Ethics* consisted of a series of extensive introductory essays and the Greek text supplemented with critical, expository footnotes. Grant did not translate the *Ethics.* His influence was consequently considerably more limited than that of Jowett,

24. On Grant's life, see W. Y. Sellar, "Sir Alexander Grant," *Blackwood's* 137 (1885): 133–43, and *The Academy* 24 (1884): 375. The publication of Grant's initial edition of the *Ethics* was disrupted apparently because of his departure for India. The first edition, The *"Ethics" of Aristotle Illustrated with Essays and Notes* (London: John W. Parker and Son, 1857, 1858) consisted of two volumes and an incomplete text of the *Ethics.* The first volume included his essays and the second of Books I–VI of the *Ethics,* with a very important preface that discussed influences on nineteenth-century classical studies. A third promised volume containing Books VII–X did not appear. Before the appearance of these volumes Grant had privately published two of his introductory

whose translations almost turned Plato into a contemporary writer. Moreover, again unlike his good friend Jowett, Grant approached the exposition of the *Ethics* as a scholarly and academic task rather than as an opportunity to mold the mind of the British political elite. Nevertheless, his commentary was the most complete to appear in English before the publication of J. A. Stewart's two-volume *Notes on the "Nichomachean Ethics" of Aristotle* (1892). For thirty-five years Oxford tutors, who often criticized particular features of Grant's work, continued to use it and regarded it as the major source of instruction on the subject.

Grant's edition of the *Ethics* was highly significant in British intellectual history for another reason. It was the first attempt by a British classical scholar to set a major Greek philosopher into the pattern of historical development outlined by Hegel in his *Lectures on the History of Philosophy*. The combination of historicism, rational criticism, and German philosophy set Grant's writing apart from previous British scholarship on Greek antiquity. Indeed, his model had not been a classical study but Jowett's commentary on St. Paul's Epistles published in 1855.[25] Jowett had taught him to use the tools of

---

essays in Alexander Grant, *Two Essays on the "Ethics" of Aristotle* (privately printed, 1856). The second edition, *The "Ethics" of Aristotle Illustrated with Essays and Notes, Second Edition, Revised and Completed* (London: Longmans, Green, and Co., 1866) consisted of two volumes. The first contained the essays somewhat revised, an essay on Stoicism that had first appeared in *Oxford Essays* for 1858, and Books I–II of the *Ethics*. The important preface of 1858 was omitted from this edition and from subsequent ones. For the second edition, John Purves of Balliol College revised some of the notes, but it is unclear whether Grant had passed judgment on those revisions. The third edition, *The "Ethics" of Aristotle Illustrated with Notes and Essays*, Third Edition, Revised and Partly Rewritten (London: Longmans, Green, and Co., 1874) also consisted of two volumes arranged as in the second edition. However, Grant made extensive and substantial revisions in the notes and essays. This edition contained his most thorough discussion of the Sophists. The fourth edition, *The "Ethics" of Aristotle Illustrated with Essays and Notes*, Fourth Edition, Revised (London: Longmans, Green, and Co., 1885) appeared in two volumes with a new preface that discussed primarily textual criticism and incorporated some revisions in the essays and footnotes. Unless otherwise noted, all citations are taken from the first edition.

25. Grant, *"Ethics" of Aristotle*, 1:v–vii. To see how vastly Grant's work differed from previous commentators, see William Edward Jelf, *Notes to Aristotle's "Ethics"* (Oxford: John Henry and James Parker, 1856), in which the author promised to interpret the work with as little reference as possible to earlier or later philosophers (p. 5). For a devastating critique of Jelf's commentary, consult Henry W. Chandler, *An Examination of Mr. Jelf's Edition of Aristotle's "Ethics"* (Oxford: William Graham, 1856).

critical thought and research developed in Germany, and the enthusiasm and excitement that such research elicited were evident in
Grant's preface to the second volume of his first edition of the *Ethics*,
published in 1858.

> With the present century fresh lights have gradually dawned
> upon the world, and we now look with different eyes upon an-
> tiquity. We bring to the remains of the ancient philosophers new
> ideas to guide us in our study. First among these is the historical
> spirit, the axiom that human thought can only be known by
> knowing its antecedents; second, is the critical spirit, which is
> neither hasty to accept nor to reject, but which weighs and dis-
> criminates; third, is the philosophical spirit, which has a certain
> sympathy and affinity for the speculation of the Greeks. It re-
> quires some philosophy to interpret a philosopher. Modern
> German thought, whatever may have been its extravagances,
> has, to say the least, this advantage, that it puts those who have to
> the slightest degree caught its influence on a better level for
> understanding Parmenides and Heraclitus, Plato and Aristotle.
> And thus it is only in the present century that the history of
> Grecian philosophy has been adequately written.

Previously, British historians of Greece and its intellectual life had
adopted some concept of providential development, the modified
Viconian approach of the liberal Anglicans, the Comtean model employed by Grote and Lewes, or no explicit historical framework at all.
Those earlier commentators had attempted to explain the meaning or
significance of a philosopher within a larger scheme of historical development primarily in order to give him some immediate modern
applicability or relevance. Grant, reacting against the traditional teaching of the *Ethics* at Oxford, employed his version of Hegel's historicism for just the opposite reason. He hoped to set Aristotle's work
directly into the intellectual climate of the ancient world and "to ascertain as far as possible, and to make clear, the meaning of these *Ethics*
from the point of view of their writers."[26] And for Grant the end result
of such an analysis was to understand the more or less complete in-
applicability of the *Ethics* to the modern world.

26. Grant, *"Ethics" of Aristotle*, 2:xi–xii, xiv.

Through this historicist analysis, Grant's commentary and notes single-handedly transformed the *Ethics* from a source of current moral wisdom into an object of academic study. Comprehension of the treatise through ascertaining its text, its historical milieu, and its exact ancient philosophical concepts replaced consideration of its relationship to Anglican theology and Christian revelation. Reviewers immediately saw the significance of this change, with one observing in 1857, "The interest of Aristotle's *Ethics* being mainly historical, must be mainly academic."[27] This development in classical studies paralleled the development in theology. Although Grant did not attempt to establish the exact Greek text of the *Ethics* and accepted that edited by Bekker, he did regard the treatise as a document that must be criticized first as a document rather than as a system of morality. This was the critical approach to a text that British scholars had resisted in regard to Homer from fear of its implications for the Bible. Paradoxically, the liberalization of British theology made possible the critical examination of Aristotle's *Ethics* and other ancient texts at Oxford. Once scholars, such as Jowett, applied the methods of critical philology and history to the Bible, no substantial religious obstacles remained to prevent application of similar methods to classical documents. Resistance to the latter had rarely been more than a tactic to prevent or to delay the emergence of the former. Ironically, in England many classicists learned the tools of German critical scholarship from the theologians, as Grant had from Jowett. Furthermore, the early Victorian interpretations of the *Ethics* ceased to be germane when the Christian theology with which they had been associated received new interpretation and when other theologians replaced Bishop Butler on the shelves of Anglican rectories. The removal of Butler from the *Literae Humaniores* reading list in 1864 was as important for the reading of the *Ethics* as for the future of Anglican theology.

In his textual criticism Grant decried the earlier unquestioning ac-

27. *Saturday Review* 4 (1857): 470. The promise of professional classical scholarship at Oxford heralded by Grant's edition of the *Ethics* was not fulfilled until almost the turn of the century because the research-oriented party in the university lost out to the party that emphasized teaching. See Arthur Engel, *From Clergyman to Don: The Rise of the Academic Profession in Nineteenth-Century Oxford* (Ph.D. diss., Princeton University, 1975), passim, and Sheldon Rothblatt, *Tradition and Change in English Liberal Education: An Essay in History and Culture* (London: Faber and Faber, 1976), p. 169.

ceptance by British scholars of the entire body of the *Nichomachean Ethics* as essentially uncorrupt text. He argued that the treatise was an unfinished work, the present text of which had been set by Aristotle's followers after his death. Drawing upon the textual criticism of the German scholar Ludwig Spengel and the English classicist Hugh Munro, Grant urged that Books V, VI and VII properly belonged to the *Eudemian Ethics* and had been added to the *Nichomachean*.[28] He based this contention on a comparison of both the style and the content of the two works. The three disputed books interfered with the continuity of the *Nichomachean Ethics* but not with that of the *Eudemian Ethics*. In the former work the presence of the three questionable chapters meant there were two separate considerations of pleasure, with very little relationship between them. Moreover, the contents of the last three books of the *Nichomachean Ethics* (VIII–X) contained references to the first four books but not to the three central books. For these and other more technical reasons Grant concluded that in Books I–IV and VIII–X readers possessed "an unfinished, or multilated, treatise, which so far as we possess it came straight from the hand of Aristotle."[29] The significance of Grant's analysis, which would ultimately be displaced in Aristotelian scholarship, was that for the first time a British classicist looked at the *Ethics* as a test that required textual criticism before a substantive interpretation could be set forth.

Grant argued in another of his introductory essays that not only the text of the *Ethics* but also its morality reflected a history. As explained in the previous chapter, Grant followed Hegel's *History of Philosophy* and postulated three periods of Greek morality. From an age of unconscious moral thought the Greeks had passed through a period of skepticism and then had entered an era of conscious morality inaugurated by Socrates. To understand Aristotle, Grant contended, it was necessary to be familiar with those earlier philosophies "since a system of any kind can only be properly understood by knowing its antecedents."[30] Aristotle had not, as suggested by Hampden, achieved his moral philosophy through a Baconian-like observation of human nature. The manner in which Aristotle reasoned, the questions he posed, the solutions he approved and those he rejected displayed an intimate

28. Grant, *"Ethics" of Aristotle*, 1:1–43.
29. Grant, *"Ethics" of Aristotle*, 3rd ed., 1:69.
30. Grant, *"Ethics" of Aristotle*, 1:45.

relationship to earlier Greek thought and morality. Aristotle's moral philosophy was the product of a particular time, place, and intellectual heritage. Such an analysis now seems commonplace, but in the 1850s it was quite novel and even daring.

Grant portrayed Aristotle as owing a vast intellectual debt to Plato as well as having disagreed with his mentor's philosophy. Aristotle had derived from Plato his views on the nature of politics, the concepts of the chief good and the proper function of humankind, the divisions of the human mind, the value of friendship, the relation of ignorance to vice, the mean as the standard of conduct, and the belief in the high excellence of philosophy.[31] Grant's discussion of the relationship of Aristotle to Plato was the most learned consideration of the latter to be published in Great Britain before the appearance in 1865 of Grote's *Plato, and the Other Companions of Socrates*. The clear implication of Grant's discussion was that Aristotle, whom Oxford so valued, could not be genuinely comprehended or appreciated without the intense study of Plato, whom the university still generally ignored. For Grant, again under the shadow of Jowett, it was impossible to portray Plato as a hazy idealist or mystic, as was the common early Victorian practice, and then to praise Aristotle as a practical philosopher of scientific understanding. In effect, Grant's application of the historical method to Aristotle was a spur to new historical and philosophical research on Plato.

Despite the close links between teacher and pupil, Grant acknowledged that Aristotle differed substantially from Plato. Aristotle had abandoned Plato's idea of the good as a moral ideal. For Aristotle, ethics remained first and foremost a practical matter, the guiding principle of which "must not be this absolute transcendental good, but a practical good, which he envisioned as happiness, or the end for man." This practicality indicated that Aristotle had been "more human than Plato" and that he had approached morality with more eagerness and sheer enthusiasm than had his mentor. Aristotle had also been much less hostile to the moral wisdom that might reside in the popular Greek morality which had originated in the unconscious era. Along with this appreciation for practical popular morality, Aristotle had refrained from insisting that ethical decisions stem from reasoned philosophy.

31. Ibid., pp. 139–49.

Aristotle's considerable intellectual achievement had been to understand that human beings could become moral creatures by practicing
moral habits. Through this emphasis on the inherent moral capacity of
humankind Aristotle had tended to expound "the strength [rather]
than the weakness of human nature."[32] If anything, the *Ethics,* in
contrast to Plato's dialogues, displayed perhaps "over much elation"
with the possibility of human virtue.

Grant wanted not only to trace the connection between Aristotle's
thought and earlier Greek philosophies but also to differentiate his
thought from that of later times. He was particularly determined to
end the facile equation of Aristotelian and Christian ethics. He denied
that any evidence for the Christian doctrine of human corruption was
present in the *Ethics* or that the philosopher had looked to human
existence or morality beyond earthly experience. He declared quite
bluntly: "Aristotle's theory rather comes to this, that the chief good
for man is to be found in life itself. Life, according to his philosophy, is
no means to anything ulterior." Furthermore, Aristotle's universe
was an orderly one, but unlike Paley's it required no watchmaker
deity. The order of the Aristotelian universe originated immanently,
and for that reason Aristotle could regard the world with "a kind of
natural optimism." But, as Grant explained in another passage, such
optimism should not be mistaken for a belief in a moral government of
nature such as Bishop Butler might have urged. Aristotle's concept of
nature differed markedly from that of either Butler or Paley.

> His point of view rather is that as physical things strive all, though
> unconsciously, after the good attainable by them under their sev-
> eral limitations, so man may consciously strive after the good
> attainable in life. . . . It is best, therefore, to exclude religious as-
> sociations (as being un-Aristotelian) from our conceptions of the
> ethical *telos,* and then we may be free to acknowledge that it is
> evidently meant to have a definite relation to the nature and con-
> stitution of man.[33]

Aristotle's concepts, virtues, and metaphysical presuppositions simply were not Christian nor were they Christian minus the final truth

32. Ibid., pp. 154, 164–65.
33. Ibid., pp. 194, 224, 173.

imparted through revelation. To impose Christian meanings on the *Ethics* was to forget that it was a Greek treatise of the fourth century B.C.[34]

With no less historicizing zeal Grant declared that "to try to read Aristotle's book merely as if it were a modern treatise" meant the student must ignore all the facts of the growth of the human mind since Aristotle's day. It was simply wrongheaded to ask how or if Aristotle agreed or disagreed with modern philosophers, such as Bishop Butler or Auguste Comte. To attempt to discern the approval of conscience in the pleasure that Aristotle attached to the moral *telos* was "to mix up things modern and ancient." He also explained, "Happiness with Aristotle is something different from what we mean by it. . . ." Nor could a theory of duty or the modern concept of the moral sense be said to exist in Aristotle's philosophy. Modern systems of ethics had gone beyond Aristotle and had become much more "self-conscious" than his. The questions of duty, moral obligation, and right predominated in modern ethical thought. According to Grant:

> Individual will, and therefore individual responsibility, are now the first thoughts of Ethics. It is no more a question of happiness, or, as with Aristotle, what is the chief good? but, rather, what constitutes duty? Why is anything right, and why are we obliged to do the right?

Aristotle had neither raised nor addressed these kinds of problems; they had not even occurred to him. He had written and taught during the childhood of the world when the question of obligation did not yet burden humankind and when the Comtean ideal of "the brotherhood of man had not dawned." So far as any constructive or useful relationship to current ethical inquiry was concerned, Grant drew an absolute veil across the *Ethics*. Although he admitted that certain Aristotelian terms might appear in modern ethical discourses, Grant nonetheless firmly declared, ". . . in the *matter* of morals the world has clearly outgrown the *Ethics* of Aristotle."[35] This was historicism with a ven-

---

34. Alexander Grant, *Aristotle* (Edinburgh and London: William Blackwood and Sons, 1877), p. 108.

35. Grant, *"Ethics" of Aristotle*, 1:245, 176, 175, 212; 2:96; 1:248, 249; Grant, *"Ethics" of Aristotle*, 3rd ed., 1:385, 388.

geance and historicism that embraced a wholly irreversible and non-repetitive mode of historical and intellectual development.

Grant pursued this same theme throughout his extensive notes to the Greek text and rarely hesitated to point out how far Aristotle's ethical ideals stood from modern views of right conduct. Grant particularly considered the great-souled man of the fourth book of the *Ethics,* whom Christian commentators had usually carefully ignored, as a generally reprehensible creature. The virtues Aristotle so admired in that figure bore no relationship to law or duty; and the vices the great-souled man eschewed were those that would have brought him little or no gratification in any case. Grant contended this ancient character could be neither a good man nor a good citizen in a modern society.

> Here then there is no self-subjection to a law. The great-souled man does not avoid vice because it is "wrong" (in the modern sense), but simply because it is unworthy of him. Thus he is most essentially a law to himself and above all other law....
>
> [Aristotle's] system is based on the idea of self-respect. (...) This principle goes a long way in elevating the character and purifying the conduct, but its natural development is also a dislike of all limitations of the individuality; in short, its natural development is a sort of noble pride.

Those qualities were "essentially not a human attitude," and for Grant this Aristotelian ideal offended both Christian humility and secular self-restraint.[36] In sharp contrast to so many other contemporary commentators on Greek culture, Grant made no attempt to assimilate Aristotle's *Ethics* or values into some kind of agreement with Victorian morality.

Although Grant strongly criticized the Sophists' lack of a steady moral position, a spirit of ethical and historical relativism informed his own Hegelian consideration of Aristotle in two ways. First, the historicist analysis of the *Ethics* implied that the morality of the treatise

---

36. Grant, *"Ethics" of Aristotle,* 3rd ed., 2:72. In the first and second editions, Grant's remarks were similar, but he used the term "high minded" rather than "great-souled." See ibid., 1st ed., 2:166–67. One commentator did attempt to domesticate the great-souled man by suggesting that he resembled the strong individualist of John Stuart Mill's *On Liberty;* see Edward Moore, *An Introduction to Aristotle's "Ethics,"* Second Edition, Revised and Enlarged (London: Rivingtons, 1878), p. 238.

had been commensurate with the ethical requirements of fourth-century Athens, and Grant gave no indication that Christian morality or another later ethics would have improved Greek life. Grant's framework of Greek intellectual development derived from Hegel's analysis, but Grant's interpretation of Greek thought involved a much less overt sense of teleological evolution toward an eventually secure ethical position in the form of either Christianity or idealist philosophy. His understanding of development was more open-ended and indeterminate than Hegel's. It seems likely that Grant had not fully thought through the implications of the Hegelian scheme, and most certainly he did not grasp the close relationship that Hegel understood to exist between Greek morality and the character of the polis. Second, although denying that Aristotle's moral outlook was relativistic, Grant's own language and rhetoric nonetheless implied the presence of a moral relativism that his denials failed to overcome.[37] This situation arose because he interpreted the philosophical concepts of the *Ethics* through the Hegelian terms of *in* itself and *for* itself. That approach injected into Aristotle's thought a strong element of subjectivism from which flowed relativistic implications for his morality.

Grant explained that for Aristotle human nature could fulfill itself only by realizing its *telos.* But human beings unlike other parts of physical nature achieved their ends subjectively as well as objectively.

> The ends of physical things are for other minds to contemplate, they are ends objectively. But ends of moral beings are ends subjectively, realized by and contemplated by those moral beings themselves. The final cause, then, in *Ethics,* is viewed so to speak, from the inside.

The end of human life for Aristotle was a particular satisfaction involving moral worth and goodness that the mind subjectively

37. Grant recognized that Aristotle's injunction to emulate the conduct of the best people in society might be taken to suggest the absence of any real standards. Countering that possible interpretation of the *Ethics,* Grant argued, "Aristotle usually escapes from pure indefiniteness and relativity by asserting that the standard in each case is to be found in the good, the wise, the refined man. This standard is evidently the expression of the universal reason of man. It is not to be supposed that wit, beauty, or goodness are merely matters of taste, as Aristotle would seem for a moment to imply.... When he adds afterwards that the educated man must be the standard of appeal, he means that the laws of reason must decide." Grant, *"Ethics" of Aristotle,* 3rd ed., 2:91.

experienced—"the deep moral pleasure which attaches to noble acts."
In this respect, "the end and the consciousness of the end are not
separated." The highest such satisfaction stemmed from philosophic
contemplation. However, Grant also had to note

> how in the separate parts of life, in the development of each of the
> various faculties, Aristotle considers an end to be attainable; how
> he attached a supreme value to particular acts, and idealizes the
> importance of the passing moment; how he attributes to each
> moment a capablility of being converted out of a mere means, and
> mere link in the chain of life, to be an End-in-itself, something in
> which life is, as it were, summed up.

Aristotle had attempted to work his way between presenting the good
life as found in the satisfaction of the moment, which was the doctrine
of the Cyrenaics, and the good life as found in the satisfaction of a
contemplative ideal that had little or no relationship to life as lived each
day. His solution to this dilemma, according to Grant, was to find the
chief good not as "*a* perfect life, but *in* a perfect life." Although the
good, "as it exists in and for the consciousness," was independent of
time, it still had to be experienced "in an adequate complete sphere of
external circumstances." The internal experience must in some fashion overcome the external situation. Grant contended that this theory
of happiness "requires permanence of duration, but it looks for this in
the stability of the formed mental state, which is always tending to
reproduce moments of absolute worth."[38] Both the internal and external realization of the human end-in-itself occurred strictly within a
finite world and in no manner looked beyond this life.

The subjectivism and emphasis on the experience of the moment
that despite qualifications so profoundly permeated Grant's discussion
of the Aristotelian end-in-itself came even more to the fore in his
examination of the function of *energeia* in the *Ethics*. In both the essays
and the commentary Grant translated this term as "consciousness"
although it had usually been rendered as "activity" or "energy."
Grant's novel usage led him to translate Aristotle's definition of virtue
as, "The good for man is conscious life according to the law of excellence." He defended this controversial translation, which was roundly

38. Grant, *"Ethics" of Aristotle*, 1:174, 176, 177, 179, 180.

criticized by his contemporaries, on the grounds that if viewed objectively ("for the mind") *energeia* meant "an activity desirable for its own sake." But if *energeia* were regarded subjectively ("in the mind"), the term acquired a different meaning.

> Henceforth, it is not only the rounded whole, the self-ending activity, the blooming of something perfect, in the contemplation of which the mind could repose; but it is the mind itself called out into actuality. It springs out of the mind and ends in the mind. It is not only life, but the sense of life; not only waking, but the feeling of the powers; not only preception or thought, but a consciousness of one's own faculties as well as of the external object.

Such a "conscious vitality of the life and the mind" could not be a permanent state. Rather it was "like a thrill of joy, a momentary intuition" that provided briefly "a glimpse of the divine, and of the life of God."[39]

In his discussion of *energeia* Grant further suggested that Aristotle had regarded virtue "as a regulative, rather than a primary idea" and "as subordinate, though essential, to happiness." To reduce Aristotle's ethical thought to the maxim that good acts produce good habits might suffice for everyday prescriptive injunctions but it stripped the philosopher "of all his philosophy." Aristotle had implied that *energeia* "was no mere process or transition to something else, but contained its end in itself, and was desirable for its own sake." According to Grant's analysis, that meant consciousness was desirable for its own sake. Grant explained that for Aristotle, "It is the deepest and most vivid consciousness in us that constitutes our happiness." Grant also contended that Aristotelian pleasure "proceeds rather from within than from without; it is the sense of existence; and it is so inseparably connected with the idea of life, that we cannot tell whether life is desired for the sake of pleasure, or pleasure for the sake of life." So far as the relationship between pleasure and happiness was concerned, Grant thought Aristotle made no significant distinction except to portray happiness as "something ideal and essentially moral" and as extending over a lifetime and implying the use of humankind's highest faculties.

39. Ibid., pp. 181–201; 2:34; 1:193, 193–94.

> Happiness then, as a permanent condition, is something ideal;
> Aristotle figures it as the whole of life summed up into a vivid
> moment of consciousness; or again, as the aggregate of such
> moments with the intervals omitted; or again, that these mo-
> ments are its essential part (. . .), constituting the most blessed
> state of the internal life (. . .), while the framework for these
> will be the . . . most favourable external career.[40]

Those moments of intense consciousness were coupled with the sense
of having accomplished good deeds, with the sense of awakened
friendship, or with the highest exercise of reason. For Grant, attainment of such heightened subjective consciousness rather than the formation of good habits lay at the core of Aristotle's moral philosophy.

In translating *energeia* as consciousness, Grant acknowledged that
he had used "a distinct modern term, whereas the ancient one was
indistinct." In defense of that procedure he claimed to have clarified
the conceptual difficulties that arose from Aristotle's "tendency to
confuse the subjective and the objective together" and to have made
explicit what Aristotle had left implicit. He did not say that the basis of
his explication of the term was Hegelian philosophy. Contemporaries
generally found Grant's approach to *energeia* and the implications that
followed from it neither convincing nor satisfactory. In the midst of a
generally favorable assessment of his work, the *Saturday Review* curtly
inquired, "Is it possible to depart more widely from the canons of the
historical method than by saying for a philosopher what he never says
for himself, on the ground that we see he meant it?"[41] Later interpreters of the *Ethics* did not follow Grant's lead on the explication of
energeia, but echoes of his remarks curiously appeared in Walter Pater's
notorious "Conclusion" to *Studies in the Renaissance*. This volume was
published in 1873, but the "Conclusion" had originally appeared as
part of an essay printed in 1868.[42] Pater latched onto the subjectivism

40. Ibid., 1:192, 194, 199, 200, 200–01.

41. Ibid., p. 194; *Saturday Review* 6 (1858): 619. In the third edition of his work
Grant changed the translation of *energeia* in several key footnotes (but not in the
introductory essay) from "consciousness" to "vitality." In the fourth edition he rendered Aristotle's definition of the good for humankind as "vital action according to
the law of excellence." Grant, *"Ethics" of Aristotle,* 4th ed. 1:451.

42. The "Conclusion" originally appeared at the end of Pater's review of William
Morris's poetry in *The Westminister Review* 90 (1868): 309–12.

and relativism implicit in Grant's analysis and rendered a much more extreme version of both.

Pater entered Oxford as a student in 1858 and read for the *Literae Humaniores* examination.[43] He attended lectures by Jowett and also read very deeply in Hegel's philosophy. In 1862 he was elected a fellow of Brasenose College where he trained students for the Greats examination. All of these circumstances seem to assure that he was familiar with Grant's edition of the *Ethics,* which Oxford study guidebooks encouraged students to consult. Pater was also familiar with scientific literature and positivist epistemology. The latter, in conjunction with Hegel, produced in him an almost morbid sensibility to the flux of human experience and nature. In his "Conclusion" Pater meditated on the flux that was flowing throughout physical nature and within subjective psychological experience as well. Internally the human mind encountered "the movement, the passage and dissolution of impressions, images, sensations, . . . that continual vanishing away, that strange perpetual weaving and unweaving of ourselves."[44] The chief service of philosophy, religion, and culture was to sharpen the observation of that fluctuating manifold of psychological experience.

It was in his remarks on this internal flux in the fourth paragraph of the "Conclusion" that the echoes from Grant's Aristotle commenced. Pater urged, "Not the fruit of experience, but experience itself is the end." One could receive only a limited number of sensations in life, but one should "pass most swiftly from point to point, and be present always at the focus where the greatest number of vital forces unite in their purest energy." Then followed the most famous passage of the essay.

> To burn always with this hard gem-like flame, to maintain this ecstasy, is success in life. Failure is to form habits; for habit is relative to a stereotyped world; meantime it is only the roughness of the eye that makes any two persons, things, situations, seem alike. While all melts under our feet, we may well catch at any

43. Anthony Ward, *Walter Pater: The Idea in Nature* (London: Macgibbon and Kee, 1966), pp. 25–54.

44. Walter Pater, *Essays on Literature and Art,* ed. Jennifer Uglow, (London: Dent, 1973), p. 40.

exquisite passion, or any contribution to knowledge that seems, by a lifted horizon, to set the spirit free for a moment, or any stirring of the senses, strange dyes, strange flowers, and curious odors, or work of the artist's hands, or the face of one's friend. . . . The theory, or idea, or system, which requires of us the sacrifice of any part of this experience, in consideration of some interest into which we cannot enter, or some abstract morality we have not identified with ourselves, or what is only conventional, has no real claim upon us.

Pater's emphasis on the pursuit of moments of pleasurable experience and contemplation of them from an aesthetic rather than a moral point of view were congruent with Grant's analysis of Aristotle's use of *energeia*. More important, the condemnation of habit as failure recalled Grant's contention that to equate Aristotle's theory of conduct with forming good habits was to miss the point of his philosophy. Pater's injunction to seek a variety of experiences evoked Grant's paraphrase of the meaning of Aristotelian pleasure as "the sense of life itself; the sense of the vividness of the vital powers; the sense that any faculty whatsoever has met its proper object."[45] Both Grant and Pater believed such pleasure was applicable to the mind and the physical senses. Finally, the versions of morality that Pater repudiated were just those that Grant associated with Plato and that he portrayed Aristotle as having abandoned. Throughout the "Conclusion" Pater set the same high value on the heightened state of consciousness as the source of both pleasure and happiness that Grant had argued was conveyed by a proper understanding of *energeia* in Aristotle's philosophy.

Both Pater's aestheticism and Grant's historicism shared the spirit of relativism that burst the bounds of the Victorian propriety, Christian theology, and humanistic Hellenism by which so many of their contemporaries approached both Greek culture and their own lives. Pater had interpreted art and personal psychological experience aesthetically rather than morally, and he had appropriated the parts of Grant's analysis and rhetoric that challenged contemporary morality rather than those that confirmed it. Grant's historicism strongly resembled

45. Ibid., pp. 40–41; Grant, *"Ethics" of Aristotle*, 1:198–99. See also Peter Allan Dale, *The Victorian Critic and the Idea of History* (Cambridge: Harvard University Press, 1977) pp. 173–85.

Pater's aestheticism in its refusal to reduce the *Ethics* to nineteenth-century moral categories. He set the *Ethics* apart from Victorian moral experience and concerns by observing in 1857 at the close of his essays, "... when we consider this noble treatise in relation to modern thought, we feel there is something about it that stands apart from ourselves; that its main interest is historical; that we look back on it as an ancient building shining in the fresh light of an Athenian morning."[46] No other classical scholar of the day was willing to view Greek antiquity with such detachment.

Grant's edition of the *Ethics* eventually brought an end to the Christian interpretation of the treatise, but it failed to convince later commentators that the work had little bearing on nineteenth-century morality.[47] Nor did the criticisms of the *Ethics* by utilitarian authors have any greater effect in this respect. In an undated posthumous essay George Grote praised Aristotle for having, in Grote's view, rejected "the notion of a moral sense or instinct, or an intuitive knowledge of what is right and wrong." But Grote considered the *Ethics* insufficiently consistent in its definition of happiness. That the most virtuous nature is essentially the most happy also appeared to be a "highly questionable" proposition to Grote. Aristotle had failed to establish what, in the absence of general agreement in a society, would constitute the good or the just for humankind. He should have explained how "the rule of propriety" that aided the determination of the mean came to be established in the first place. Since Aristotle had not done so, "the capital problem of moral philosophy still remains unsolved" in the *Ethics*.[48]

Henry Sidgwick of Cambridge University, who was the most distinguished moral philosopher of late-Victorian England, independently suggested a critique similar to Grote's. In *The Methods of Ethics* (1874) Sidgwick criticized the imprecision of the ethical thought of

46. Grant, *"Ethics" of Aristotle,* 1:258.

47. Edward Meredith Cope, *A Review of Aristotle's System of Ethics* (Cambridge: Deighton, Bell, and Co., 1867), pp. 50–56; Frederick Denison Maurice, *Moral and Metaphysical Philosophy,* New Edition with Preface, 2 vols. (London: Macmillan and Co., 1872), 1:219.

48. George Grote, *Fragments on Ethical Subjects,* ed. Alexander Bain (London: John Murray, 1876), pp. 134, 158, 164. The manuscript of this essay is in the Bodleian Library. Oxford, Add. D 85. It would appear to have been written during the early 1840s.

both Plato and Aristotle. Plato had not really explained how the Good was to be ascertained. And Sidgwick continued, "Nor, again, does Aristotle bring us much nearer such knowledge by telling us that the Good in conduct is to be found somewhere between different kinds of Bad. That at best only indicates the *whereabouts* of Virtue: it does not give us a method for finding it." In a later essay Sidgwick admitted that the *Ethics* provided a good portrait of the ideals of the Greek upper classes, but Aristotle had not addressed the fundamental question of ethical inquiry—What ought I to do? Useful general conclusions about making ethical decisions could not be gleaned from the treatise, and Aristotle's mode of determining the mean was often misleading and sometimes inappropriate. On occasion that imprecision had led the ancient philosopher "to such eccentricities as that of making simple veracity a mean between boastfulness and mock-modesty."[49] Such fundamental imprecision meant that although Aristotle's philosophy might have some historical value, it could not guide present-day life.

At the turn of the century, in the *Encyclopaedia of Religion and Ethics,* Henry Jackson, another Cambridge scholar who devoted most of his work to Plato, followed Grote and Sidgwick in their criticism of Aristotle. Jackson argued:

> In these two treatises, the *Nichomachean Ethics* and the *Politics,* Aristotle is an acute, and judicious student of human nature. They have a Shakespearean quality which makes them perennially interesting. But it must be clearly understood that they do not pretend to offer a theory of morality. Aristotle says nothing about the Good, about Duty, about the distinction between Right and Wrong; and very little about the faculty which discriminates them.[50]

Grote, Sidgwick, and Jackson were criticizing Aristotle for not having provided the very kind of ethics that he had clearly said he could not provide. Aristotle had enunciated the impossibility of scientific ethics

---

49. Henry Sidgwick, *The Methods of Ethics,* 7th ed., reissued (Chicago: University of Chicago Press, 1962; 1st ed., 1874), p. 376; Henry Sidgwick, *Outlines of the History of Ethics for English Readers,* with an additional chapter by Alban G. Widgery (London: Macmillan and Co., 1931; originally published, 1886), p. 64.

50. Henry Jackson, "Aristotle," *Encyclopaedia of Religion and Ethics,* 13 vols., ed. James Hastings (New York: Charles Scribner's Sons, 1908), 1:790.

and had then attempted to ascertain the next most satisfactory view of moral conduct. In explaining why Aristotle's ethical philosophy was inadequate from a nineteenth-century critical point of view, Jackson also inadvertently explained just why the *Ethics* nonetheless still continued to be useful to many modern readers. Just as a person could experience moral enlightment from Shakespeare's plays, so also could he receive a similar heightening of moral consciousness from the *Ethics*. Aristotle had understood that most people require good models rather than sound explanations of morality. So long as a broad consensus existed in Victorian society as to who were the morally best people, whether in a Christian or a secular sense, Aristotle's treatise could be deemed useful. As traditional religious defenses of morality encountered difficulty, it is possible that ethics conceived as a mode of socialization loomed more important.

For all its lack of scientific precision and its alleged historical irrelevance, the *Ethics* remained a meaningful treatise for many nineteenth-century readers. In 1867 a writer for the *Westminister Review* observed, "Let a man once read through the *Ethics* with ordinary intelligence, and he can never afterwards countenance the stupid belief in the necessary dependence of morality on revelation."[51] The young Jane Harrison, coming down to Cambridge from a strict Evangelical home in Yorkshire, found the reading of the *Ethics* just such an experience of intellectual liberation.[52] The treatise opened a realm of moral possibilities previously unknown to her. The doctrine of the mean might not be the most precise of ethical concepts and it might embody ancient and no longer germane Greek metaphysics, but for a person who had previously been familiar only with the precise injunctions of the Decalogue the Aristotelian mean provided a new beginning. People who felt this way were not uncommon in the late-Victorian universities. Nor were collegiate instructors who had abandoned Christian orthodoxy but who would not embrance the utilitarian alternative. For all of them moral conduct was more important than scientific moral philosophy, and the *Ethics* could speak to their situation. Of little less importance, acquaintance with the *Ethics* was one of

51. *Westminster Review* 87 (1867): 44.
52. Jane Ellen Harrison, *Reminiscences of a Student's Life* (London: Hogarth Press, 1925), pp. 80–81.

the cultural experiences whereby the university-trained elite defined
itself and distinguished itself from the rest of the nation.

The "Ethics" and Citizenship

During the last quarter of the century and the years before World War
I, consideration of the *Ethics* as a treatise on citizenship and politics
supplanted the previous emphasis on its relationship to Christianity.
Idealist philosophers at Oxford used the *Ethics* to renew the long-
standing university opposition to political individualism and utilitarianism. Like Hegel, whom they admired and upon whose thought they
were highly dependent, the idealists looked to the ancient polis as a
possible conceptual model for a political and social life in which the
individual citizen was thoroughly integrated with his society. This
shift of emphasis coincided with the transformation of Oxford from
a stronghold of the Church into a school for statesmen and civil servants who would serve the liberal democratic state.

The most important Oxford idealists were T. H. Green, F. H.
Bradley, John Caird, Edward Caird, and Bernard Bosanquet. These
philosophers, having left the Church of England or remaining merely
nominal members, were the nonclerical successors of the mid-century
Broad Churchmen. That earlier group of scholars had been more
responsible than any other body of intellectuals for importing modern
German philosophy and historical studies into Britain. They had attempted to make the Church of England a genuinely national institution that encompassed the widest possible spectrum of theological
opinions. Their religious liberalism had also led them to see the human
spirit as discovering moral and religious truth through a variety of
cultural channels, including Greece, rather than only through the dispensations to Israel and the Christian church. The Broad Churchmen
had been generally conservative in their social views but favored a
political elite recruited more nearly by merit than by birth. The later
idealists would also look to German philosophy, reject utilitarianism
and mechanistic views of society, nurture a concept of secular citizenship that encompassed the entire nation, emphasize morally responsible leadership on the part of the social and political elite, and view
antiquity as but one stage in the larger moral and intellectual evolution
of humankind.

The most charismatic of the Oxford idealists was Thomas Hill Green of Balliol College.[53] A young, eloquent, dynamic teacher, Green communicated to his students his personal yearning for righteousness and social reform. He spoke to those whose Christian faith was fragile or had, like his own, dissolved, and he provided them with a sense of purpose and direction toward the higher life of creating a good society for their fellow citizens. He was active in the temperance movement and, with other moral reformers of the day, believed the state should act to improve the life of its citizens. Society for Green was not a contract, but a moral community for the development and nurture of its members. Although Green died as a relatively young man in 1882 and his books appeared posthumously, his thought and his students continued to influence British intellectual and political life well past the turn of the century.

As a philosopher of ethics, Green presents the interesting case of an Oxford student who had been educated in Aristotle's *Ethics* and who then developed his own philosophy from his study of Kant and Hegel. Consequently there were distinct traces of Aristotle's moral thought in Green's work even where he was not commenting on the ancient philosopher. For example, in the *Prolegomena to Ethics* Green set forth a definition of virtue not unlike Aristotle's, although the influence of Kant's emphasis on the will and Hegel's on the community were also clearly present.

> The conception of virtue is the conception of social merit as founded on a certain sort of character or habit of will. Every form of virtue arises from the effort of the individual to satisfy himself with some good conceived as true or permanent, and it is only as common to himself with a society that the individual can so conceive of a good.[54]

Green, like Aristotle, and probably because of Aristotle, could comprehend human beings only as social creatures. Virtue and character

---

53. Melvin Richter, *The Politics of Conscience: T. H. Green and His Age* (London: Weidenfeld and Nicholson, 1964); Craig Jenks, "T. H. Green, the Oxford Philosophy of Duty and the English Middle Class," *British Journal of Sociology* 28 (1977): 481–97.

54. Thomas Hill Green, *Prolegomena to Ethics,* 4th ed., ed. A. C. Bradley, (Oxford: Clarendon Press, 1899), p. 298.

formation were possible only within society. The great moral issue of the day was the quality of life fostered by a society and the means whereby that quality of life came to be extended to ever larger numbers of people that they might more fully realize their humanity. Green was more concerned with moral character than with the making of rational moral decisions. He seems to have felt that sound moral decisions would flow almost naturally from a good moral character, and he had few doubts as to what constituted the latter. Needless to say, Green and Henry Sidgwick never really understood each other, and they quarreled politely for years at cross purposes. It is perhaps indicative of the self-perceived moral needs of late-Victorian university students that Green attracted large numbers to his classes while Sidgwick's classes were almost invariably small.

Green's remarks on Aristotle's *Ethics,* made in the course of undergraduate lectures published in 1883 as the *Prolegomena to Ethics,* displayed several strands of notable continuity with earlier Oxford commentators. Along with William Sewell and R. D. Hampden, Green related the *Ethics* to the moral teachings of Christianity and employed it to oppose utilitarianism and a Hobbesian concept of society. Following Alexander Grant, Green presented the *Ethics* as the product of the particular intellectual development and social context of Greece. However, Green implicitly dissented from Grant's view of the irrelevance of the *Ethics* for modern times. In effect, Green attempted to mesh the ethical concerns of the Christian commentators with the historical outlook of Grant and with the social concerns of idealist philosophy.

Like so many other late-Victorian intellectuals who had abandoned the Christian faith, Green hoped to provide alternative intellectual support for those Christian values that he still admired and that stood in opposition to utilitarian and commercial social values. Green's tactic was to locate the origins of those humane Christian values in the moral speculations of the Greek philosophers. He contended that from the time of Socrates onward there had emerged from Greek philosophy

> the connected scheme of virtues and duties within which the educated conscience of Christendom still moves, when it is impartially reflecting on what ought to be done. Religious teachers

have no doubt affected the hopes and fears which actuate us in the pursuit of virtues or rouse us from its neglect. Religious societies have both strengthened men in the performance of recognized duties, and taught them to recognize relations of duty towards those whom they might otherwise have been content to treat as beyond the pale of such duties; but the articulated scheme of what the virtues and duties are, in their difference and in their unity, remains for us now in its main outlines what the Greek philosophers left it.[55]

In this fashion Green separated the substance of Christian values from the historical manifestations of the faith upon which the higher criticism had cast doubt. Christianity had provided the zeal and a more nearly universal application for the values that Greek thinkers had initially set forth. Although Green had clearly abandoned the concept of a primitive revelation to account for similarities between Christian and Greek thought, behind his concept of the role of Greece in the moral evolution of humanity there still lay a sense of the providential preparation of the world by Greece and its philosophers for the more complete truth of the Gospel. For even if the natural reason could conceive virtues of the highest order, only faith could carry them into action. Here Green agreed with John Stuart Blackie.

In explaining the rise of Greek moral philosophy, Green closely trod the path prepared by Hegel and first pursued in England by Grant. However, in contrast to Grant's analysis, the specter of divine providence pervaded the background of Green's remarks. The Greek philosophers had, according to Green, articulated rather than invented morality. In that capacity they had been "really organs through which reason, as operative in men, became more clearly aware of the work it had been doing in the creation and maintenance of free social life, and in the activities of which that life is at once the source and the result." Concerned with the "citizen-life" in the polis, the philosophers brought into consciousness the morality that reason had already imparted through the formation of the family and the state.[56] Existing spiritual demands and requirements among humankind had given rise to those social institutions and to the values according to which they

55. Ibid., p. 304.
56. Ibid.

functioned. Through the vehicle of the Greek philosophers reason had yielded the new virtue of being dissatisfied with moral law that failed to articulate what actually constituted goodness, justice, and the like. In his account of the philosophers Green omitted any discussion of the Sophists, and he did not explain whether he believed their challenge to the traditional beliefs of the polis was part of the cunning of reason.

In Green's view the Greek philosophers had fostered the conviction "that every form of real goodness must rest on a will to be good, which has no object but its own fulfillment." Green contended that this same conviction informed the Christian belief that "blessed are the pure in heart, for they shall see God." This Christian belief could appeal to a larger audience than the one formulated by the Greeks, "but if those affected by it came to ask themselves what it meant for them . . . , it was mainly in forms derived, knowingly or unknowingly, from the Greek philosophers that the answer had to be given." Green believed that both Plato and Aristotle had taught the basis for purity of heart with all the clarity that Christians could desire. Moreover:

> Once for all they conceived and expressed the conception of a free or pure morality, as resting on what we may venture to call a disinterested interest in the good; of the several virtues as so many applications of that interest to the main relations of social life; of the good itself not as anything external to the capacities virtuously exercised in its pursuit, but as their full realisation.

That concept of pure disinterested moral conduct had informed "all the true and vital moral conviction" that had descended into the nineteenth century.[57] To be moral in a conscious and articulated manner was for Green to participate in the mind of Plato and Aristotle. Through this analysis Green in a very real sense demeaned the Christian faith. He sought to rescue what he understood to be the moral substance of Christianity by severing it from historical Christianity. Whereas previous Oxford commentators had attempted to make the Greeks look like Christians or like proto-Christians, Green attempted to portray the later Christians as children of Greece.

Within Green's framework major portions of the tradtional Chris-

57. Ibid., pp. 305, 305–06, 306, 308–09, 309.

tian ethical message retained their validity because the morality in question had been initially Greek and was therefore not dependent upon the validity of the Christian revelation. The major impetus for ethical reform on the principle of human brotherhood resided in the development of the human spirit rather than in Christianity. Green explained to his students:

> The idea of a society of free and law-abiding persons, each his own master yet each his brother's keeper, was first definitely formed among the Greeks, and its formation was the condition of all subsequent progress in the direction described; but with them, . . . it was limited in its application to select groups of men surrounded by populations of aliens and slaves. In its universality, as capable of application to the whole human race, an attempt has first been made to act upon it in modern Christendom. With every advance towards its universal application comes a complication of the necessity, under which the conscientious man feels himself placed, of sacrificing personal pleasure in satisfaction of the claims of human brotherhood. . . . The will to be good is not purer or stronger in him than it must have been in any Greek who came near to the philosopher's ideal, but the recognition of new social claims compels its exercise in a new and larger self-denial.

The capacity of the human soul itself had evolved since Greece to higher levels of actual and potential spiritual perfection, and that evolution meant that the definition of social good had become very different than it had been for Aristotle. Yet such beneficial ethical development "would itself have been impossible but for the action of that idea of the good and of goodness which first found formal expression in the Greek philosophers."[58] The Greeks had taught what it meant to be good in the first place, and they had taught that the theater for ethical action was the realm of citizenship.

Although Green as much as Grant accepted a historicized interpretation of Greek philosphy and Aristotle's *Ethics,* he dissented from Grant's conclusion that the substance of ethics had changed. Green admitted that "reflection on what is implied in the pursuit [of virtue]

58. Ibid., pp. 330, 341.

yields standards of virtue which, though identical in principle with those recognised by Aristotle, are far more comprehensive and wide-reaching in their demands." The expansion of the realm of moral activity, however, had not in fact changed the character of Aristotelian virtues. Green contended that many apparently Christian activities actually fulfilled Aristotelian virtues. The Christian social worker who at the risk of his own life sacrificed personal pleasure to serve the sick or ignorant exemplified the brave man of Aristotle.

> The principle of self-devotion for a worthy end in resistance to pain and fear is the same in both cases. But Aristotle could only conceive the self-devotion in some form in which it had actually appeared. He knew it in no higher form than as it appeared in the citizen-soldier, who faced death calmly in battle for his State. In that further realisation of the soul's capacities which has taken place in the history of Christendom, it has appeared in a far greater wealth of forms.

The primary difference between the modern age and Aristotle's time was the new conviction that far more people in many different social groups were capable of ethical behavior. Furthermore, economic and political changes had created more potential objects of loyalty and devotion for modern men and women than the Greek, familiar only with his own polis, could possibly have known. As Green explained, "In modern Christendom it is not merely our theories of life but the facts of life that have changed."[59] Those new facts meant the application of the ancient virtues must assume new guises.

Green had played quite fast and loose with Aristotlë's *Ethics*. He had tranformed Christian virtues into allegedly Aristotelian ones and had then associated those reshaped ancient noble values into instruments of modern social reform. Green saw the state through its enlightened administrators and active self-sacrificing citizens as combating the spirit of commerce and selfishness in the manner that conservative Broad Church reformers in the tradition of Coleridge had advocated a generation earlier. Green lodged those reform values in the thought of Greece and looked to the institution of the state as the vehicle for their realization. For all his discussion of Christianity, Green had

59. Ibid., pp. 313, 314.

thoroughly secularized the Broad Church program of conservative social reform and simultaneously secularized the Christian values that informed that program. It was the Aristotelian vision of the good life realized on earth through the political community that permitted Green to effect the transformation.

Green's philosophy cast a long shadow across late Victorian and Edwardian politial thought as philosophical idealism flourished at Oxford and elsewhere in Britain. The ideals of personal self-sacrifice and of collective social responsibility for the welfare and moral improvement of citizens appealed to many intellectuals who sought social reform without socialism. Other late-century interpretations of the *Ethics* and a renewed interest in Aristotle's *Politics* reflected this growing climate of civic morality. During the same years that historians and political scientists were emphasizing the vast differences between ancient and modern democracy, commentators on Greek political philosophy were pointing to the contemporary relevance of the ideals rather than the institutions of Athens. In an essay on the *Politics* published in 1880, A. C. Bradley wrote, "With every step in the moralising of politics and the socialising of morals, something of Greek excellence is won back." He also argued that even within the context of the British attachment to limited government, the state, through its enforcement of education, its provision of aid for the helpless, its regulation of working conditions, and its laws for the enforcement of decency, was "not only the guardian of the peace and a security for the free pursuit of private ends, but the armed conscience of the community."[60] And it was clear from his essay that he believed such activity should be continued and expanded. Jowett's long introduction to his translation of the *Politics* and W. L. Newman's commentary to his Greek edition of that work further served to emphasize the civic nature of the polis as the background for Aristotle's ethical thought. The social solidarity of the polis, which so starkly contrasted with the social tensions of the late-Victorian and Edwardian period, deeply impressed university commentators on the *Ethics*. Green's philosophy helped to convince them that such social bonds were still possible in the modern world.

60. Andrew Cecil Bradley, "Aristotle's Conception of the State," in Evelyn Abbott, ed., *Hellenica: A Collection of Essays on Greek Poetry, Philosophy, History, and Religion* (London: Rivingtons, 1880), pp. 241, 243.

The civic background of the *Ethics* also received attention in commentaries that were not overtly political in nature. In 1892 J. A. Stewart of Christ Church, Oxford published his *Notes on the "Nichomachean Ethics,"* which was and still is the most extensive treatment of the work in English. The two volumes, which did not include the text, contained over one thousand pages of footnotes accompanied neither by essays nor by any other apparatus for general commentary. Despite the inevitably disconnected character of the notes, consideration of the civic life of Greece received emphasis throughout as essential for an understanding of the *Ethics*. For example, Stewart explained:

> The maintenance... of a beautiful everyday life, according to Hellenic traditions—a life in whose varied activities one takes a personal, but not a self-aggrandising part—is Aristotle's standard of Virtue. It has the advantage of being a standard which it is not very difficult to keep in view. It is easier to see whether a particular action is in harmony with the tone of the society in which one has been brought up than to see whether it promotes the "greatest good for the greatest number."

No other commentator so bluntly set forth Aristotle's conservative attitude towards the standards of Hellenic society. Stewart, for example, contended that Aristotle had dwelled "in a glorious present which has no need of a future" and that "any radical improvement of the existing system was inconceivable to Aristotle."[61] In Aristotle's opinion the major function of a philosopher of ethics was to make clear those common opinions and traditions and to remove obscurity and confusion.

Stewart may have intended to blunt the reformist interpretation of the *Ethics* propagated by Green, but Green's work had á charm and

61. John Alexander Stewart, *Notes on the "Nicomachean Ethics" of Aristotle,* 2 vols. (Oxford: Clarendon Press, 1892), 1:204–05, 338, 352. For other examples of the civic interpretation of Aristotle's intent in the *Ethics,* see John Burnet, ed., *The "Ethics" of Aristotle* (London: Methuen and Co., 1900), pp. xxviii–xxix; W. Gough, *Notes Introductory to the Study of Aristotle's "Ethics"* (Oxford: Joseph Thornton and Son, 1915), pp. 9–14; and Harold Henry Joachim, *Aristotle: The "Nicomachian Ethics": A Commentary,* ed. D. A. Rees (Oxford: Clarendon Press, 1951), p. 17. The last volume was based on lectures delivered at Merton College, Oxford University, between 1902 and 1917.

persuasiveness that could not be denied. It was simply too useful to reformers who wanted change without radical rhetoric or radical political devices. It was also helpful to teachers such as J. H. Muirhead, author of *Chapters from Aristotle's Ethics* (1900), who wanted to give the ancient treatise immediate relevance. As an instructor at Birmingham University, located in a city renowned for its political radicalism, Muirhead not unnaturally hoped to impart a sense of contemporary utility to the *Ethics* and to associate the work with the collectivist reform philosophy current at the turn of the century. He urged that the major benefit derived from studying the *Ethics* was the concept of human nature set forth therein.

> We are here placed from the outset at the right point of view with regard to the nature of man whose ends we are investigating. It is the good of man as a citizen, or member of a community, not of man as individual, which is the subject-matter of ethics. The good of the individual ought never to be separated from the good of the whole of which he is a part—ethics from politics.

Aristotle here appeared as an advocate of the collectivism of the new liberalism, and his thought provided a weapon against the heritage of mid-Victorian individualism and social atomism. Muirhead understood as well as Green, whose influence he acknowledged, that modern society differed markedly from the ancient polis. Modern social and economic life did not, however, justify the substitution of individualism for a sense of community; rather it demanded that modern men and women enlarge their "conception of the range of man's organic connections."[62] The social union of the ancient polis should be replicated by establishing new dimensions to modern social relationships and citizenship.

Aristotle's concept of philosophy as a means of clarifying existing ethical opinions similarly provided support for intellectuals who sought to persuade the nation that all citizens deserved to share those elements of life that widely accepted social ideals designated as good, just, and beneficial. In *The Political Thought of Plato and Aristotle* (1906), Ernest Barker set Aristotle into such a tradition of reform.

---

62. John Henry Muirhead, *Chapters from Aristotle's "Ethics"* (London: John Murray, 1900), pp. 23–24, 24.

Aristotle stood with Burke in the ranks of "conservative reformers." Through his respect for popular opinions and even popular prejudices, Aristotle had assumed the stance of the defender of "the 'divine right of things as they are.' "[63] In that regard Barker agreed with J. A. Stewart. However, Barker understood Aristotle's conservatism to imply a defense of existing social and political institutions only insofar as they fulfilled social ideals and their intended moral purpose. If those institutions failed to fulfill those ends, they must be reformed. This attitude encouraged repair of the accidental flaws of a society without questioning its essential values, ideology, and structures. It was an outlook espoused by many liberal Edwardian reformers who wanted more citizens to enjoy the good life but who also had no intention of overturning the foundations of the social order.

The civic interpretation of the *Ethics* indicated a fundamental shift in British intellectual life and culture. The treatise came to be read as a civic document because the culture in which it was studied had itself become more distinctly civic in character. Democracy, empire, military preparedness, international economic rivalry, an expanding bureaucracy, national insurance, school lunches, and national education, to mention only a few political developments, had made citizenship a category of thought and association to which an increasingly large number of values and experiences adhered. The state, and citizenship therein, had largely supplemented and in many cases supplanted the early Victorian social categories of religion, estate, county, city, and class. By the reign of Edward VII the reading of the *Ethics* at Oxford had become a means of articulating and legitimizing those new civic associations, just as three quarters of a century earlier it had been an instrument for confirming Anglican theology and a paternalistic society. Yet the extent of the change of interpretation should not be overemphasized, because both the Anglican and the idealist reading of the *Ethics* served to inhibit more radical, rationalist criticism of British society.

63. Ernest Barker, *The Political Thought of Plato and Aristotle* (New York: Dover Publications, 1959; orginally published, 1906), pp. 353, 210.

Bishop R. D. Hampden

Benjamin Jowett
(By permission of the Master and Fellows of Balliol College)

Sir Alexander Grant as sketched late in life while
Principal of Edinburgh University

Thomas Hill Green

Walter Pater

John Burnet
(Courtesy of the St. Andrews
University Library)

8

THE VICTORIAN
PLATONIC REVIVAL

"Between Plato and the English nation," declared John Stuart Blackie in 1857, "there is in fact a gulf which cannot be passed."[1] Read in the aftermath of the intense mid–twentieth–century debate over the allegedly totalitarian character of Plato's politics, Blackie's remark would still seem to retain a certain validity. But lack of sympathy for Plato's political philosophy was not the gulf to which the Edinburgh professor alluded; he referred rather to the widespread conviction that Plato's thought was irrelevant for a practical-minded, commercial, industrial nation and to the subsequent neglect of Platonic studies in· Great Britain. The long and extensive controversy over Plato's politics in this century actually became possible only because the gulf that Blackie correctly perceived had been bridged in the interval.

Blackie was by no means alone in his perception of the British neglect of Plato. In 1834 the young John Stuart Mill, in prefatory comments to his partial translations of the *Protagoras, Phaedrus, Gorgias,* and *Apology,* noted there were very few English readers of Plato. In the mid-forties the author of the article on Plato for the *Encyclopaedia Metropolitana* could discover virtually no recent British writers whose opinions on the philosopher he could quote, and he complained of the manner in which "Plato's writings are in the present day indiscriminately treated." About the same time G. H. Lewes, whose philosophical opinions, like Mill's, were at the opposite end of the metaphysical spectrum from Blackie's, asserted that Plato "is often mentioned and even quoted at second-hand; but he is rarely read,

---

1. John Stuart Blackie, "Plato," *Edinburgh Essays by Members of the University* (Edinburgh: Adam and Charles Black, 1857), p. 6.

except by professed scholars and critics." Those persons who had read Plato and who then commented on him hardly encouraged further study. In 1837 Thomas Babington Macaulay, pillorying Plato's wrongheaded method and consequent impracticality in comparison with the productive wisdom of Bacon, informed the readers of the *Edinburgh Review:*

> The aim of the Platonic philosophy was to exalt man into a god. The aim of the Baconian philosophy was to provide man with what he requires while he continues to be man. The aim of the Platonic philosophy was to raise us far above vulgar wants. The aim of the Baconian philosophy was to supply our vulgar wants. . . . Plato drew a good bow; but, like Acestes in Virgil, he aimed at the stars; and therefore, though there was no want of strength or skill, the shot was thrown away. His arrow was, indeed, followed by a track of dazzling radiance, but it struck nothing. . . . The philosophy of Plato began in words and ended in words—noble words, indeed—words such as were to be expected from the finest of human intellects exercising boundless dominion over the finest of human languages. The philosophy of Bacon began in observations and ended in arts.[2]

Clearly, it seemed, Plato was not the philosopher for an age of improvement, progress, and utility.

The state of learned Platonic commentaries and good translations at mid-century confirmed and in part accounted for this situation. In 1850 there were only two modern book-length discussions of Plato in English, and only one of these was by an Englishman. The first was William Dobson's inelegant translation of Schleiermacher's *Introduc-*

2. John Stuart Mill, *Collected Works,* ed. J. M. Robson and F. E. Sparshott (Toronto: University of Toronto Press, 1978), 11:39–41; *Encyclopaedia Metropolitana* (London: 1845), s.v. "Plato"; George Henry Lewes, *The Biographical History of Philosophy from Its Origin in Greece down to the Present Day,* Library Edition, Much Enlarged and Thoroughly Revised (New York: D. Appleton and Co., 1859), p. 187. (Lewes had voiced similar sentiments in a more diffused manner in the first edition of this work; see George Henry Lewes, *A Biographical History of Philosophy* (London: Charles Knight, 1845), 2:30.); Thomas Babington Macaulay, *Miscellaneous Works of Lord Macaulay Edited by His Sister, Lady Trevelyan,* 5 vols. (New York: Harper and Brothers, n.d.), 1:428. For a reply to Macaulay, see George Gilfillan, *A Third Gallery of Portraits* (New York: Sheldon, Lamport, and Blakeman, 1855), pp. 256–65.

tions to the Dialogues of Plato, published in 1836. The other was William Sewell's *Introduction to the Dialogues of Plato* (1841), a collection of brief essays originally printed in *The British Critic,* a high church journal. R. D. Hampden had written a substantial essay for the seventh edition of the *Encyclopaedia Britannica,* and a limited number of much shorter articles had appeared in major journals.[3] As late as the early months of 1865, Benjamin Jowett could complain, "There is nothing good, I fear, in English on this subject."[4] The situation in respect to translations was only somewhat better than that of commentaries. A complete English translation of the dialogues by Floyer Sydenham and Thomas Taylor had been available since 1804. Although these volumes provided Britain with the second complete translation of Plato in a modern language (Italy had the first), Taylor's poor Greek and his own Neoplatonist proclivities vitiated the entire work. Following an attack from the *Edinburgh Review* in 1809, this translation had been relegated to oblivion.[5] Between 1848 and 1854 Henry Cary and Henry Davis produced a new six-volume translation for the Bohn Classical Library, but this effort seems to have aroused little interest; nor did Llewelyn Davies and D. J. Vaughn's frequently reprinted translation of the *Republic* that appeared in 1852. William Whewell's edited and extensively rearranged versions of *The Platonic Dialogues for En-*

3. William Dobson, trans., *Schleiermacher's Introductions to the Dialogues of Plato* (Cambridge: J. and J. J. Deighton, 1836); William Sewell, *An Introduction to the Dialogues of Plato* (London: J. G. F. and J. Rivington, 1841); R. D. Hampden, *The Fathers of Greek Philosophy* (Edinburgh: Adam and Charles Black, 1862), pp. 167–296; Philip Pusey, "Plato, Bacon, and Bentham," *Quarterly Review* 61 (1838): 462–506; John Forster, "The Dialogues of Plato," *Foreign Quarterly Review* 31 (1843): 471–501. Significantly, the article on Plato in William Smith's *Dictionary of Greek and Roman Biography and Mythology* (1846), like the article on Socrates, was written by Christian A. Brandis of the University of Bonn.

4. Benjamin Jowett to John Stuart Blackie, 22 March 1865, John Stuart Blackie Papers, National Library of Scotland. George Grote's *Plato, and the Other Companions of Socrates* had been published a few weeks earlier, but evidently Jowett had not yet seen it.

5. Thomas Taylor and Floyer Sydenham, *The Works of Plato,* 5 vols. (London: R. Wilks, 1804). See also Frank B. Evans III, "Platonic Scholarship in Eighteenth-Century England," *Modern Philology* 41 (1943): 104–08, and Kathleen Raine, "Thomas Taylor in England," Thomas Taylor, *Thomas Taylor the Platonist: Selected Writings,* ed. Kathleen Raine and George Mills Harper (Princeton: Princeton University Press, 1969), pp. 3–48. The devastating critique of Taylor appeared in James Mill (?), "Taylor's Plato," *Edinburgh Review* 14 (1809): 187–211.

glish Readers (1859–61) did not reach a large audience and received almost no commendations from reviewers.[6]

Yet those mid-century translations, however little appreciated, and in the case of Whewell, however unfortunate and unscholarly despite the prestige of the translator, did mark the beginning of a new British appreciation for Plato that by the turn of the century constituted nothing less than a Platonic revival that far outshone that of the Renaissance. More and better translations appeared. Although no single work of Plato's approached the nineteen different translations of Aristotle's *Ethics* rendered over the course of the century, the number of translations of Plato appearing after 1860 was considerable.[7] The most famous of these was Benjamin Jowett's *Dialogues of Plato* in four and later five volumes, which went through three editions (1871, 1875, 1892) and of which several individual dialogues were separately reprinted. In addition to Jowett's work, six complete or partial translations of the *Republic* appeared between 1860 and 1914, and earlier ones continued to be reprinted. There were fourteen renderings of the *Apology* during the period, seven of the *Euthyphro,* and five of the *Meno.* Nor were the Socratic dialogues the only ones so translated. The *Gorgias,* the *Philebus,* and the *Theaetetus* each received three separate translations in addition to those included in versions of the complete dialogues. During the same period of 1860 to 1914—for the sake of comparison—there were fourteen translations of Aristotle's *Ethics,* four of the *Politics,* three of the *Rhetoric,* three of the *History of Animals,* and six of the *Poetics.* The crucial difference between the activity of translation in regard to Aristotle and Plato was that all of the mentioned works by Aristotle had also been translated before 1800 while only after that date were translations of many of the major Platonic

6. Henry Cary and Henry Davis, trans., *The Works of Plato,* 6 vols. (London: George Bell and Sons, 1848–54). This translation seems to have gone through several editions. John Llewelyn Davies and David James Vaughn, trans., *The Republic* (London: Macmillan and Co., 1852), was reprinted at least four times and was still in print after 1900, with a significant new preface added in 1866. William Whewell, trans., *The Platonic Dialogues for English Readers,* 3 vols. (Cambridge: Macmillan and Co., 1859–61).

7. All figures on number of translations are taken from Finley Melville Kendall Foster, *A Bibliographical Survey of English Translations from the Greek* (New York: Columbia University Press, 1918), pp. 26–34, 90–97, and verified by comparison with the catalogues of the British Library and the Sterling Memorial Library, Yale University.

dialogues undertaken, including the *Protagoras,* the *Gorgias,* the *Theaetetus,* the *Sophist,* and the *Laws.* Moreover, alongside this late-century outpouring of new translations there appeared a number of important English commentaries on Plato from writers of such diverse opinions as Grote, Jowett, and Pater.

The story of the teaching of Plato in the universities generally parallels that of the translations and commentaries. In 1831 a character in Peacock's *Crotchet Castle* declared, with only moderate exaggeration, ". . . you must remember that, in our Universities, Plato is held to be little better than a misleader of youth; and they have shown their contempt for him, not only in never reading him (a mode of contempt in which they deal very largely), but even by never printing a complete edition of him."[8] That situation began to change somewhat during the second quarter of the century. F. D. Maurice studied Plato at Cambridge in the twenties under the tutelage of Julius Hare, one of the English translators of Niebuhr. Rowland Williams, the fiery Welshman prosecuted for his contribution to *Essays and Review,* lectured on both Plato and Aristotle at Kings College, Cambridge from 1843 to 1850. W. H. Thompson taught the *Phaedrus* at Trinity College, Cambridge as early as 1844. William Whewell, the master of Trinity and a distinguished philosopher of science, delivered several papers on Plato to the Cambridge Philosophical Society during the 1850s as well as publishing partial translations. Brooke Foss Westcott of Cambridge considered undertaking a complete translation of the dialogues during the fifties but relinquished the task when he heard that Balliol's Jowett had tackled the project. Although Jowett's name will always be linked in Britain with Plato's, it was not he but the Tractarian William Sewell who actively introduced Plato to nineteenth-century Oxford. His discursive lectures on the philosopher, designed to provide an antidote to the dangers of secularism, liberalism, and the general spirit of "improvement," filled Exeter College classes during the thirties.[9] In 1847

8. Thomas Love Peacock, *Crotchet Castle* (London: J. M. Dent, 1891), p. 91.

9. William Archer Butler, *Lectures on the History of Ancient Philosophy,* 2 vols., ed. William Hepworth Thompson (Cambridge: Macmillan and Co., 1856), vol. 2; Frederick Maurice, *The Life of Frederick Denison Maurice, Chiefly from His Own Letters,* 2 vols. (New York: Charles Scribner's Sons, 1884), 1:54; Rowland Williams, *The Life and Letters of Rowland Williams, D.D., with Extracts from His Note Books, Edited by His Wife* (London: Henry S. King & Co., 1874), p. 107; John William Donaldson, *Classical Scholarship and Classical Learning* (Cambridge: Deighton, Bell, and Co.,

Jowett began to teach Plato and told his students, "Aristotle is dead, Plato is alive."[10] After his appointment as professor of Greek in 1853, Jowett regularly lectured on the *Republic* for many years. Across the Irish Sea, William Archer Butler delivered extensive lectures on Plato during the 1840s as part of a general course on ancient philosophy, and James Ferrier and John Stuart Blackie were doing the same in Scotland.

Consequently, after almost two centuries of general neglect the study of Plato reemerged in Britain during the mid-Victorian years. The gulf that Blackie had correctly perceived in 1857 was rapidly bridged. This reawakening of interest in Plato should correctly be regarded as a set of Platonic revivals, because the study of the ancient philosopher was undertaken by at least three distinct groups of writers for three separate though not wholly unrelated purposes. Sewell, Butler, Blackie, Westcott, A. E. Taylor, and other late-century idealists saw Platonic philosophy as a vehicle for upholding vestiges of Christian or transcendental doctrines in the wake of utilitarian morality, positivist epistemology, and scientific naturalism. They appealed to what may be termed the prophetic Plato. Another set of writers including George Grote, John Stuart Mill, and surprisingly enough Walter Pater, associated Plato with the cause of critical, even skeptical epistemology and in some cases with radical social reform. They also criticized major elements of Plato's thought as a means of attacking similar developments in contemporary philosophy and politics. A third school, primarily associated with Oxford and represented by Jowett, Richard Nettleship, Bernard Bosanquet, and Ernest Barker, used Plato's moral and political philosophy to provide a more or less idealist surrogate for Christian social and political values. They hoped

---

1856), p. 253; William Whewell, "On Plato's Survey of the Sciences," "Of the Intellectual Powers according to Plato," and "On the Platonic Theory of Ideas," *Transactions of the Cambridge Philosophical Society* 9 (1856): 582–89, 598–604, and 10 (1864): 94–104; *Dictionary of National Biography*, s.v. "Sewell, William"; John Stuart Blackie, "Plato and Christianity," *North British Review* 35 (1861): 369; David Newsome, *Bishop Westcott and the Platonic Tradition* (Cambridge: Cambridge University Press, 1969), p. 18; Martin Lowther Clarke, *Classical Education in Britain, 1500–1900* (Cambridge: Cambridge University Press, 1959), pp. 111–18. See also *Oxford University Gazette* and *Cambridge Reporter* for the year in question for late-century courses.

10. Evelyn Abbott and Lewis Campbell, *The Life and Letters of Benjamin Jowett*, 2 vols. (New York: E. P. Dutton and Co., 1897), 1:261.

Plato might provide a counterbalance to individualistic liberalism and the egoistic ethics of utilitarianism. Needless to say, these were not hermetically sealed coteries. The work of one group often arose in reaction to that of another, and some commentators, such as Pater, had a foot in more than one camp. Nonetheless, this scheme does indicate the major tendencies and divisions in Victorian and Edwardian Platonic studies. Moreover, the debates among these writers often foreshadowed the twentieth-century controversy occasioned by the publication in 1943 of *The Open Society and Its Enemies* by Karl Popper.

The Prophetic Plato

Like the antimaterialistic spirit that stirred the seventeenth-century Cambridge Platonists (who more nearly resembled Neoplatonists), the original impulse behind Victorian Platonic studies was a determination to defend Christianity, religious sentiments, and idealist epistemology against alleged early nineteenth-century advocates "of sensualism in philosophy, of expediency in morals, of scepticism in reason, and of rationalism in religion."[11] To these defenders of religion, Plato's dialogues and his opposition to the ancient Sophists appeared "peculiarly valuable as exhibiting a contest of Principles eminently characteristic of the present age."[12] Plato was called forth to do battle with the forces of progress and improvement. For example, William Sewell, polemicizing against the Mechanics Institutes and University College London, argued that Plato had intended education to be controlled by a body like the church rather than by secular authorities. He reached this conclusion by interpreting the projected commonwealth in the *Republic* as a prototype of the Christian church and by translating *polis* as *church*. William Archer Butler told his Dublin students that "in Plato, philosophy is only another name for *religion*," and suggested that Plato had defended philosophy and religion against enemies similar to those presently endangering the faith. William Whewell, who strongly urged an idealist philosophy of science, related Plato's epistemology to Coleridge's and concluded that both

11. Sewell, *Introduction to the Dialogues of Plato,* p. 115.
12. Frederick Oakeley, *Remarks upon Aristotelian and Platonic Ethics, as a Branch of the Studies Pursued in the University of Oxford* (Oxford: J. H. Parker, 1837), p. 37.

philosophers supported the existence of intuitive intellectual powers that extended beyond the range of discursive reason.[13]

The Platonic doctrines of the Forms, of Recollection, and of Immortality, which the interpreters of the prophetic Plato usually equated with *the* Platonic philosophy, provided a non-Christian, non-Scriptural underpinning for traditional Christian doctrines and perspectives. Early Victorian writers were familiar with these particular Platonic teachings through Aristotle, who had criticized them, and through the church fathers, who had discerned in them links between Plato and Christianity. As the century passed, Plato stood out as the major non-Christian philosopher to have asserted the necessity for positing the presence of unseen entities or forces without which this world and all that dwells therein would lack meaning or possibly even existence. In 1861 John Stuart Blackie presented Plato as the one sure defense against the reductionist assault on human nature stemming from the physical and social sciences.

> We must either hand ourselves over bodily to J. R. M'Culloch, August Comte, and Charles Darwin, or trim our wings for the old ideal flight under the eagle-captainship of Plato. There is no neutrality possible in such matters. Let us eye the alternative cooly, and make the choice with a wise deliberation: Mind or matter; central plastic force, or circumferential accident; wise choice, or blind law; Plato, or Mr. Buckle.

Plato had taught that through "divinely-implanted ideas" humankind was in touch with the spiritual heart of the universe. Furthermore, according to Blackie, the Good that Plato discussed in the sixth book of the *Republic* was "manifestly not a mere abstract idea, but a living power, an intellectual force, and an energizing intellect,—that is to say, in popular language, a person."[14]

This strain of Platonic interpretation, which passed so easily from Plato to Christianity, although the earliest became the least influential

13. Sewell, *Introduction to the Dialogues of Plato,* pp. 96, 107, 119–20; Butler, *Lectures on the History of Ancient Philosophy,* 2:61–62; Whewell, "Of the Intellectual Powers according to Plato," p. 603, and "On the Platonic Theory of Ideas," pp. 97–104.
14. John Stuart Blackie, "Plato and Christianity," *North British Review* 35 (1861): 369, 377, 373.

element in the Victorian Platonic revival. It could survive the examination of neither a serious Christian nor a serious Platonic scholar. But the possibility of such an interpretation and of a mystical or intuitive philosophy originating from it haunted much Platonic commentary and scholarship. Montagu Burrows warned Oxford students in the sixties that without the balancing sobriety of Aristotle's *Ethics,* "The enthusiastic Platonist may become a mere visionary." Forty years later, just after the turn of the century, David Ritchie still felt required to counter the "popular opinion" that Platonism constituted "a vague, mystical manner of thinking, given to irresponsible raptures and contemptuous of the plodding work of intellect."[15] The use to which certain Anglican theologians put Plato's writings and the late-century union of Platonic studies with British Hegelianism provided sufficient justifications to keep these apprehensions alive. Nevertheless, the later appeals to the prophetic Plato were rather more sophisticated than those of the earlier commentators.

Certain liberal British theologians, of whom F. D. Maurice was the most significant, thought Plato's works provided good reason for believing the revelation of a divine truth to have been more widespread than the Bible recorded and also that the philosophy of Plato could aid their effort to spiritualize biblical doctrines.[16] Behind these views lay the same impulse that informed the liberal Anglican treatment of Socrates. Such opinions were an indirect use of Plato and normally entailed little or no direct commentary on the philosopher. Very few Anglicans were willing to say that Plato had actually anticipated Christian truth or doctrines. Brooke Foss Westcott, a Cambridge don who later became bishop of Durham, was, however, an

15. Montagu Burrows, *Pass and Class: An Oxford Guide-Book through the Courses of Literae Humaniores, Mathematics, Natural Science, and Law and Modern History,* (Oxford and London: John Henry and James Parker, 1860), p. 236; David Ritchie, *Plato* (Edinburgh: T. & T. Clark, 1902), p. 74. A few years earlier St. George Stock had written: "To say that a man is a 'Platonist' does not really give us any definite idea of his philosophical tenets. We infer that he has an enthusiastic belief in the immortality of the soul, grounded on somewhat shaky arguments, and thinks that ignorance lies at the root of evil. There perhaps the matter ends. We should hardly go on to suspect him of being in favour of a community of women among the upper classes of society." St. George Stock, *The "Meno" of Plato with Introduction and Notes* (Oxford: Clarendon Press, 1887), p. 7.

16. Bernard M. G. Reardon, *From Coleridge to Gore: A Century of Religious Thought in Britain* (London: Longman, 1974), pp. 168–215.

exception to this rule. In 1866, reacting against Grote's *Plato, and the Other Companions of Socrates,* Westcott published two articles entitled "The Myths of Plato" in the *Contemporary Review.* He complained that too much recent attention had been directed to the negative side of Plato's work and urged that now the "positive" and "prophetic" side of his philosophy required examination. That aspect of Plato's thought would reveal a recognition of the limits of reason and the necessity for faith. Plato's use of myths in his dialogues had displayed a profound grasp of the unfailing "religious wants of man." The myths testified to his recognition that the issues of creation, immortality, and providence could not be made subject to logical treatment. In that respect, Plato's myths were "an unconscious prophecy, of which the teaching of Christianity is the fulfillment." The life of Christ was "in form no less than in substance, the Divine reality of which the Myths were an instructive foreshadowing."[17] Plato had employed myths when he could not discursively address the problems of life that concerned him. In like manner, Christ himself stood as a concrete example of the ideal life and, as such, taught by example rather than by logical doctrine or discourse. Both Plato and Christ had taught that facts might have moral and religious dimensions unrecognized by science or history.

Although Westcott reprinted his articles in 1891,[18] the matter of Plato's myths created little further interest in Britain until 1904 when J. A. Stewart, the commentator on Aristotle's *Ethics,* published *The Myths of Plato.* The distinctly Christian features of Westcott's comments were gone, but the mysticism remained. Like so many other classical studies of the period, Stewart's book explored the irrational side of human nature as manifested in antiquity. For Stewart the mythical passages in the dialogues presented Plato "the Mythologist, or Prophet, as distinguished from Plato the Dialectician, or Reasoner." The myths were neither allegories nor illustrative stories, but modes of knowledge and discussion qualitatively different from logical or discursively reasoned argument.

> The Myth bursts in upon the Dialogue with a revelation of something new and strange; the narrow, matter-of-fact, workaday

17. Brooke F. Westcott, "The Myths of Plato," *Contemporary Review* 2 (1866): 199, 480, 481.

18. Brooke F. Westcott, *Essays in the History of Religious Thought in the West* (London: Macmillan and Co., 1891), pp. 1–50.

experience, which the argumentative conversation puts in evidence, is suddenly flooded, as it were, and transfused by the inrush of a vast experience, as from another world.

Through these myths Plato appealed to the part of human nature that "is not articulate and logical, but feels, and wills, and acts." The myths provided Plato with "the vehicle of exposition when he deals with *a priori* conditions of conduct and knowledge, whether they be ideals or faculties." Thus Plato induced and satisfied the sense of "Transcendental Feeling" that is one of the features of great poetry, such as Dante's and through the experience of which men and women come near to "Ultimate Reality."[19]

Both Westcott and Stewart sought to assimilate Plato into the tradition of romantic religion rooted in the emotional, nondiscursive side of human nature. For Westcott he was something of an antinomian Christian precursor. For Stewart, in his volume on myths and in his later *Plato's Doctrine of Ideas* (1909), Plato stood at the beginning of the philosophical tradition that in modern times had culminated in the theories of Bergson and others who gave priority to feeling and emotion over discursive reasoning.[20] Stewart's analysis was cut from the same intellectual fabric as the work of Jane Harrison and Francis Cornford who likewise interpreted the classical world through the categories of early twentieth-century French philosophy.

A second version of the prophetic Plato emerged from discussions of his speculative natural theology and owed much to the influence of Hegelian philosophy in the British universities. This interpretation of Plato resulted in some cases from the necessity of commenting on the Idea of the Good and in others from a self-conscious desire to link Plato's speculations to Neohegelian metaphysics. Benjamin Jowett did not initially equate the Idea of the Good with the Christian God as had his contemporary, Blackie. In the early editions of his *Dialogues of Plato* he generally refrained from extensive consideration of the Good, but in 1892 he finally explained that the Good must represent a

unity, in which all time and all existence were gathered up. It was the truth of all things, and also the light in which they shone forth,

19. John Alexander Stewart, *The Myths of Plato,* 2nd ed., ed. G. R. Levy, (Carbondale, Ill.: Southern Illinois University Press, 1960), pp. 1, 25, 44, 74, 69.
20. John Alexander Stewart, *Plato's Doctrine of Ideas* (Oxford: Clarendon Press, 1909).

and became evident to intelligence human and divine. It was the cause of all things, the power by which they were brought into being. It was the universal reason divested of human personality. It was the life as well as the light of the world, all knowledge and all power were comprehended by it. . . . To ask whether God was the maker of it, or made by it, would be like asking whether God could be conceived apart from goodness, or goodness apart from God.

Jowett admitted his paraphrase went somewhat beyond Plato's text but suggested that "we have perhaps arrived at the stage of philosophy which enables us to understand what he is aiming at, better then he did himself."[21] By this remark, which recalled Ferrier's analysis of Socrates and Alexander Grant's explications of Aristotelian concepts, Jowett meant that the Idea of the Good represented a stage wherein philosophy had replaced the categories of mythology, as indicated in the Hegelian pattern of Greek intellectual development. Hegel's philosophy had thus clarified for modern students the larger meaning and significances of Plato's work.

Richard Nettleship, another Oxford commentator on the *Republic*, regarded the Idea of the Good as an "ultimate hypothesis" assuring that "there is reason operating in the world, in man, and in nature." For both Nettleship and Jowett the Good was not exactly God, but rather a concept that helped to alleviate the ontological anxiety arising from the suspicion that the universe lacked purpose. Yet, however much susceptible to this view of the Idea of the Good and however much required by the task of commentary to discuss the concept, neither Jowett nor Nettleship considered it or Plato's other metaphysical speculations to be the heart of his philosophy. Jowett in particular urged that the *Timaeus,* which more than any other single dialogue contained religious and metaphysical elements, be regarded "not as the centre or inmost shrine of the edifice, but as a detached building

21. Benjamin Jowett, *The Dialogues of Plato, Translated into English with Analyses and Introductions,* 3rd ed., rev. and corr., 5 vols. (Oxford: Oxford University Press, 1924), 3:xcvii–xcviii. Unless otherwise noted, all quotations from Jowett's introductions are taken from this edition, which first appeared in 1892. Either the text or the footnotes will indicate when the quoted passage first appeared in Jowett's introductions. If there is no statement to the contrary, the quote may be assumed to have appeared in the first edition of 1871.

in a different style" from the main structure of Plato's philosophy.[22] Although, as will be seen, Jowett in large measure transformed Plato's thought into a surrogate for Christianity, he did not do so on the ground that Platonic metaphysics could in some manner replace the Christian metaphysical foundation that had been undermined by modern science and criticism.

Other late-century writers dissented from this downgrading of the prophetic Plato. R. D. Archer-Hind, in his commentary on the *Timaeus,* and Henry Jackson, in his essays on "Plato's Later Theory of Ideas," which appeared in the *Journal of Philology* during the eighties, saw the *Timaeus* as the "master-key" or "keystone" of the Platonic philosophy.[23] According to Jackson Plato's final view of the world held that "the universe . . . may be conceived as the thoughts of universal mind together with the thoughts of those thoughts."[24] In the hands of a Neohegelian, such as Edward Caird, this interpretation led to the conclusion that the Idea of the Good could not be conceived "except as an absolute self-consciousness, a creative mind, whose only object is a universe which is the manifestation of itself." Caird also believed that by expanding the idea of a realm of morality to the entire universe, Plato had become "the founder of speculative theology." As such, Plato had been the chief architect of Greek theology, which had provided in the course of its evolution the main intellectual and theological categories for the Christian religion and the general religious consciousness of the West. Plato was "the philosopher to whom all *our* theology may be traced back, and to whom it owes most."[25] Yet even Caird did not equate the Idea of the Good with the traditional Christian concept of God.

22. Richard Lewis Nettleship, *Lectures on the "Republic" of Plato,* ed. Godfrey R. Benson (London: Macmillan and Co., 1937), p. 225; Jowett, *Dialogues of Plato,* 3:345.

23. Richard Dancre Archer-Hind, trans. and ed., *The "Timaeus" of Plato* (New York: Arno Press, 1973; first published, 1888), p. 2; Henry Jackson, "Plato and Platonism," James Hastings, ed., *Encyclopedia of Religion and Ethics,* 13 vols. (New York: Charles Scribner's Sons, 1919), 10:59. Jackson's long series of essays, "Plato's Later Theory of Ideas," appeared in the *Journal of Philology* 10 (1881–82): 253–98; 11 (1882): 1–22, 287–331; 13 (1884–85): 1–40, 242–72; 14 (1885): 173–230; 15 (1886): 280–305; 25 (1897): 4–25.

24. Jackson, "Plato and Platonism," 10:59.

25. Edward Caird, *The Evolution of Theology in the Greek Philosophers,* 2 vols. (Glasgow: James MacLehose and Sons, 1904), 1:171, 172, 58. In addition to the

Only well into the twentieth century did a British writer attempt in a serious philosophical manner to draw Plato ˙directly into the mainstream of Christian thought, as had the commentators of the seventeenth century. That philosopher was the idealist A. E. Taylor, whose religious and antipositivist proclivities have already been discussed in regard to his treatment of Socrates. That interpretation of Socrates, which he shared with John Burnet, required a new interpretation of Plato as well because much that had traditionally been ascribed to Plato now became attributed to Socrates. Burnet for his part argued that Plato's own distinctive personal philosophy was that which he had taught in the Academy, that it had remained mostly unwritten, and that it had basically concerned itself with mathematics.[26] Taylor took a different tack. He saw Plato's thought as a direct continuation of Socrates' Pythagorean-oriented teaching. In *Plato: The Man and His Work* (1926) Taylor allowed much of the distinction between Plato and Socrates he had outlined in *Varia Socratica* (1911) to disappear. In the later volume, for all intents and purposes both Socrates and Plato emerged as proto-Christians who had been primarily concerned with the tendance of the soul, which Taylor equated with the modern concept of "the development of 'moral personality'." However, he went further than any other Victorian or Edwardian commentator in his effort to Christianize Plato and urged:

> The *Republic*, which opens with an old man's remarks about approaching death and apprehension of what may come after death, and ends with a myth of judgment, has all through for its central theme a question more intimate than that of the best form of government or the most eugenic system of propagation; its question is, How does a man attain or forfeit eternal salvation?

---

influence of his own Hegelianism and the articles of Henry Jackson, Carid, like other commentators in the latter part of the century, had accepted the chronology for the Platonic dialogues that had emerged from the work of Lewis Campbell and Constantine Ritter. Campbell in 1867 and Ritter in 1888 had established a chronology on the basis of linguistic analysis. This development permitted a more confident systematization of Plato's thought than had been possible for earlier commentators. See John Burnet, *Platonism* (Berkeley: University of California Press, 1928), pp. 8–12.

26. John Burnet, *Greek Philosophy: Thales to Plato* (London: Macmillan and Co., 1943; first published, 1914), pp. 312–13; Burnet, *Platonism*, pp. 15, 96.

In effect this Anglo-Catholic philosopher tranformed the *Republic* into a Hellenic *Pilgrim's Progress*. Nor did he stop at that. He proceeded to argue that as the transcendent source of the reality and intelligibility of all things except itself, "metaphysically the Form of Good is what Christian philosophy has meant by God, and nothing else."[27]

Taylor's assertion marked the high point of the prophetic interpretation of Plato in Britain. It was not accidental that it came in the twentieth rather than in the middle or end of the nineteenth century. Only in the early years of this century had the mainstream of British Christianity among university intellectuals become sufficiently liberal, free of bibliolatry and concern with personal sin, and imbued with a concept of divine immanence to be seriously and philosophically equated with Platonism. Only after Christianity had been "Platonized," or purged of myths repugnant to both rational intelligence and humane morality, could Plato's philosophy itself become Christianized. The nineteenth-century commentators who had espoused a prophetic interpretation of Plato had either retained a belief in the unique character of Christianity or remained so much a part of its theological or institutional framework that they could neither personally nor intellectually regard Plato's philosophy as interchangeable with Christianity. It required a philosopher, like Taylor, whose mature intellectual experience had begun where theirs had ended and who admired the Anglo-Catholicism that idealist philosophy so deeply informed to Christianize Plato. Once again, as so often before, it was a new understanding of the Christian past, tradition, and theology that led to a new interpretation of a part of Greek antiquity. Yet Taylor's work remained rooted in the Victorian conviction that in one manner or another the significance of Greece was to be discerned in making that past age resemble the present as much as possible.

George Grote and Plato the Radical Reformer

The ultimately minor impact of the prophetic interpretation of Plato had not been inevitable. Various Platonic texts were subject to legitimate spiritualistic or mystical reading. In the middle of the nineteenth

27. Alfred Edward Taylor, *Plato: The Man and His Work,* 3rd ed., rev. and enl. (London: Metheun and Co., 1929; 1st ed., 1926), pp. 207n, 265, 289.

century it would have appeared to most observers that such an interpretation of Plato might well carry the day as British university teachers presented Plato along with Socrates as an opponent of the Sophists whose pernicious ideas closely resembled those of advanced modern thinkers. William Archer Butler told his Dublin students in the forties:

> Truth, both intellectual and moral, was beset by enemies in the days of Plato, exactly correspondent to those with whom you are all familiar in the last and current century. . . . and the Theory of Ideas was the first of those mighty appeals to the higher gifts and prerogatives of the human mind by which, under the guidance of the great lights of our race, such assaults have been resisted.[28]

Butler and other British and German commentators, such as Eduard Zeller whose work was becoming well known in Britain, tended to regard Plato's philosophy as a system based primarily on the doctrines of the Forms, Recollection, and Immortality.[29] In all fairness to these scholars who pioneered the modern British study of Plato, it must be pointed out that their familiarity with Aristotle's interpretation of his mentor's philosophy led them to rigidify Plato's epistemology. Even Alexander Grant's learned essay on Plato, published as part of his commentary on Aristotle's *Ethics,* examined primarily the Platonic theories that Aristotle had criticized.[30] This Aristotelian point of departure was important because, as Jowett later never tired of noting, Aristotle had been far more dogmatic about the doctrines of Plato than had been Plato himself.

The direction and philosophical intent of these mid-century Platonic studies are fundamental to an understanding of the significance and novelty of George Grote's *Plato, and the Other Companions of Socrates* (1865). This work in three volumes was longer, more thorough, and more deeply informed by general European scholarship than any other study of Plato in English, and it remained

28. Butler, *Lectures on the History of Ancient Philosophy*, 2:158–59.

29. Eduard Zeller, *Die Philosophie der Griechen in ihrer Geschichtlichen Entwicklung* (Tübingen, 1859), II, pt. 1, pp. 286–698; translated as *Plato and the Older Academy,* Sarah Frances Alleyne and Alfred Godwin, trans. (London: Longmans, Green, and Co., 1876).

30. Alexander Grant, *The "Ethics" of Aristotle Illustrated with Essays and Notes,* 2 vols. (London: John W. Parker, 1857), 1:135–69.

so for over half a century. It could not be ignored even by those who dissented from its analysis. That Grote should become the major British scholar of Plato seemed incongruous to many contemporaries. To John Stuart Blackie it appeared no less inappropriate than Voltaire's composing a commentary on the fourth Gospel.[31] Practically all the reviewers of *Plato, and the Other Companions of Socrates,* with the notable exception of John Stuart Mill, pointed to the apparent paradox of a radical, democratic, utilitarian author publishing a work on the most spiritual and idealistic of ancient Greek philosophers. Not scholarly competence but cast of mind and philosophical proclivity were the issues. Grote was a utilitarian nominalist; Plato was an idealistic realist. Grote held a frequently displayed antipathy towards religion; Plato was the ancient apologist for a religious interpretation of physical and human nature. Grote was the defender of the Sophists; Plato had been their ancient enemy. Grote was the uncompromising champion of the Athenian democracy; Plato had been perhaps its harshest philosophical critic.

Although justifiable on the surface, these observations and apprehensions originated from an incomplete understanding and appreciation of both Grote and Plato. As observed in an earlier chapter, Grote had completed the *History of Greece* with an acutely painful recognition that psychological problems of ignorance, religion, selfishness, family loyalty, and deference had inhibited the proper functioning of Athenian democratic structures in much the same manner that they seemed to interfere with the politics of the British liberal state. Reform of political institutions seemed to require a complementary reform of individual social thought and perception such as Plato himself had advocated. Second, unlike most previous British commentators Grote began to pay attention to Plato's method of

---

31. John Stuart Blackie, *Four Phases of Morals: Socrates, Aristotle, Christianity, Utilitarianism* (Edinburgh: Edmonstons and Douglas, 1871), p. 35. The major reviews of Grote's study of Plato include Alexander Bain, "Grote's Plato: The Negative, or Search Dialogues," and "Grote's Plato: The Affirmative, or Exposition Dialogues," *Macmillans* 12 (1865): 193–208 and 457–72; Edward Caird, "*Plato, and the Other Companions of Socrates,*" *North British Review* 43 (1865): 351–84; Lewis Campbell, "Grote's Plato," *Quarterly Review* 119 (1866): 108–53; George Henry Lewes, "Mr. Grote's Plato," *Fortnightly Review* 2 (1866): 169–83; John Stuart Mill, "Grote's Plato," *Edinburgh Review* 123 (1866): 297–364; William Whewell, "Grote's Plato," *Fraser's* 73 (1865): 411–23.

philosophical inquiry and attempted to separate the method from Plato's substantive metaphysical and political conclusions.

In both respects Grote trod the path of Platonic inquiry first opened in a tentative manner by his friend John Stuart Mill. In an essay of 1834 that introduced his partial translation of the *Phaedrus,* Mill had urged that the major design of Plato's speculations had been "rather to recommend a particular mode of inquiry, than to inculcate particular conclusions."[32] Until the publication of Grote's commentary, no British writer had pursued the implications of that suggestion. In a very real sense *Plato, and the Other Companions of Socrates* occupies the place in Victorian classical studies that Mill's *On Liberty* (1859) and his *Examination of Sir William Hamilton's Philosophy* (1865) hold in mid-Victorian political and epistemological philosophy. Like Mill, Grote was disturbed by the pressures of modern democratic society on the integrity of the individual and by the specter of a resurgence of idealist, transcendental, intuitive social and ethical thought.[33] The commentary on Plato, in addition to fulfilling Grote's earlier promise to complete the story of the intellectual life of Greece, provided an opportunity, such as Mill would seize in discussing Hamilton, to attack with considerable vehemence all forms of intuitive philosophy and the political systems derived therefrom. Grote was familiar with the philosophical activity in the various British universities at mid-century, and he knew that religiously minded scholars were using Plato to combat empiricism and utilitarian ethics. Grote set about to forestall those efforts. He would argue with telling vigor that when Plato was correct, he exemplified critical analytical thought and that when he was wrong, he had embraced intuition. Grote would also contend that on those issues where most British admirers of Plato believed his philosophy valid, it was actually invalid. In addition,

32. Mill, *Collected Works,* 11:62. According to Mill's *Autobiography* (New York: Signet Books New American Library, 1964), pp. 36–38, James Mill had emphasized the reformist elements of Plato while educating his son.

33. Grote praised *On Liberty* as "that admirable Essay; which stands almost alone as an unreserved vindication of the rights of the searching intelligence, against the compression and repression of King Nomos." Grote's concept of King Nomos may have owed something to his reading of Hegel's *Lectures on the History of Philosophy,* as well as to Mill. George Grote, *Plato, and the Other Companions of Socrates,* 3 vols. (London, John Murray, 1865), 1:266n, 254n (hereafter cited as Grote, *Plato*). Manuscript material for these volumes is in the Cambridge University Library, Add. 1932.

Grote would suggest that if clerical commentators employed Plato to support intellectual positions they found congenial, they must also by their method of interpretation accept many ideas and doctrines they would find morally objectionable and embarrassing.

Grote's polemic was not limited to the parochial world of the British universities and Anglican scholarship. He addressed himself to the learned community of Europe and particularly to German scholars who during the first half of the century had taken the lead in Platonic studies. British developments were simply a dim reflection of German scholarship, whose investigators tended to impose a generally idealist system on Plato's philosophy. That Plato's dialogues lacked any single formal system or "any one predicate truly applicable" to all of them constituted Grote's fundamental presupposition and point of critical departure for examining Plato's thought. Grote believed it no more possible to discover the personal Plato than the personal Shakespeare.

> It is in truth scarcely possible to resolve all the diverse manifesta-
> tions of the Platonic Mind into one higher unity; . . . Plato was
> sceptic, dogmatist, religious mystic and inquisitor, mathemati-
> cian, philosopher, poet (erotic as well as satirical), rhetor,
> artist—all in one: or at least, all in succession, throughout the fifty
> years of his philosophical life.[34]

In other words, there was no Platonic "form" of Plato's own thought and philosophy. This position led Grote into an extensive footnote battle with the most learned German scholars of Plato. Schleier-macher, Ast, Socher, Hermann, Stallbaum, Steinhart, Susemihl, and Ueberweg in particular incurred his wrath.

In one way or another each of these German scholars had attempted to impose a system on the dialogues. Generally they had followed either Schleiermacher, who regarded the dialogues as a single precon-ceived whole, or Hermann, who saw them as a system of thought that had developed more or less systematically over the course of Plato's life. The former group of commentators considered certain dialogues spurious because they enunciated doctrines incompatible with the preconceived Platonic system. In Britain Whewell had thus rejected the validity of the *Parmenides* as part of the Platonic canon because

34. Grote, *Plato*, 1:212, 214–15.

that dialogue cast much doubt on the doctrine of the forms.[35] The second group of scholars, although regarding fewer dialogues as spurious, evaluated the doctrines, concepts, and wisdom of a particular dialogue in terms of its place in a purportedly correct order of chronological development. The youthful dialogues, such as the heavily utilitarian *Protagoras,* might consequently be considered as less valuable or philosophically less valid than the more mature, less utilitarian *Gorgias.* The interpreter's own philosophical predisposition had tended to determine the construction of these chronologies. Only in 1867, with the publication of Lewis Campbell's seminal study of Plato's language, was a different approach taken to the chronological arrangement of the dialogues.[36] Campbell's work came too late to influence Grote's study, which was not substantially revised.

Grote dissented from both of the dominant approaches to Plato's philosophy. Rather than considering the dialogues as elements in either a preconceived or an evolving system, Grote treated them as "distinct imaginary conversations, composed by the same author at unknown times and under unknown specialities of circumstances." This rather formalistic approach to the dialogues did not, however, prevent Grote from indulging in a variety of the intentional fallacy. Following Thrasyllus, he divided the dialogues into those of "search" and those of "exposition."[37] The former represented Plato's own development and expansion of the Socratic methodological inheritance; the latter, Plato's own personal philosophy. Grote suggested there had been a general development from search to exposition, but he thought the development had probably been imperfect. On the whole, Grote approved of the dialogues of search, in which Plato addressed himself to problems of epistemology, morals, and politics in a fashion Grote found congenial. He generally criticized the dialogues of exposition, in which Plato expounded ethical and social doctrines that were anathema to Grote.

In the dialogues of search Plato had undertaken what Grote conceived to be genuine philosophical inquiry. Grote directly compared

35. Whewell, "On the Platonic Theory of Ideas," pp. 94–104.
36. Burnet, *Platonism,* pp. 8–12. See Lewis Campbell, ed. *The Sophist and Statesman* (Oxford: Clarendon Press, 1867).
37. Grote, *Plato,* 1:278, 232–33.

the procedure of the searching Platonic Socrates with the method of Bentham. As Grote observed in his preface:

Philosophy is, or aims at becoming, reasoned truth; an aggregate of matters believed or disbelieved after conscious process of examination gone through by the mind, and capable of being explained to others: the beliefs being either primary, knowingly assumed as self-evident—or conclusions resting upon them, after comparison of all relevant reasons favorable and unfavorable.

The dialogues of search, including the *Hippias,* the *Protagoras,* the *Gorgias,* the *Laches,* the early Socratic dialogues, and others, exhibited the negative Socratic dialectic stripping away "affirmative, authoritative exposition, which proceeds upon the assumption that the truth is already known." Grote compared this untrammeled, self-critical search for truth with the procedure of two chemists attempting to solve a difficult problem. One solution or hypothesis would be tried and discarded and then another. The secret of the process was conceiving the truth as genuinely unknown. Grote argued that Plato had no other purpose in the dialogues of search, which usually concluded in skepticism, new questions, or the simple admission of ignorance, than to illustrate the ameliorative, liberating power of the negative dialectic. Plato's message was his very method. The movement of "testing, exercising, refuting, but not finding or providing" constituted the primary weapons for ending the rule of King Nomos, or inherited customs, ideas, and prejudices.[38]

Grote contended that for all their reputation for skepticism the ancient Sophists had not employed a truly negative dialectic. Normally they had known the conclusion they wanted their arguments and reasonings to reach. Grote strongly dissented from Zeller (and by implication from Hegel) who regarded the Sophists as the first Greek thinkers to employ negative dialectic to challenge the common consciousness of the age.

I conceive that the Sophists (Protagoras, Prodicus, Hippias) did *not* do what Zeller affirms, and that Socrates (and Plato after him) *did* do it. The negative analysis was the weapon of Socrates, and

38. Ibid., pp. xn, v, 238, 246.

not of Protagoras, Prodicus, Hippias, etc. It was he who declared
(. . .) that false persuasion of knowledge was at once universal
and ruinous, and who devoted his life to the task of exposing it by
cross-examination.

It was for this reason that Grote contended that what the Germans and
many Anglicans regarded as *Die Sophistik* should more properly be
considered as *Die Sokratik*. The negative analysis so frequently censured by those scholars appeared to Grote to be "both original and
valuable, as one essential condition for bringing social and ethical
topics under the domain of philosophy or 'reasoned truth'."[39] In this
manner, Grote drew Plato as well as Socrates directly into the skeptical
tradition of philosophy and portrayed him as the radical questioner
rather than as the defender of established morality, religion, and politics.

Grote's analysis of the negative dialectic of the dialogues of search
demonstrated that Plato's philosophy need not and should not be
approached as a dogmatic, idealist, realist monolith. In addition to the
Plato of the *Republic,* the *Meno,* and the *Phaedo* who taught the Forms,
Recollection, the Idea of the Good, and Immortality, there was also
the philosopher of the *Theaetetus,* the *Sophist,* and the *Parmenides* who
criticized the doctrine of the Forms, who carefully examined empirical
sense experience, and who made little or no reference to Recollection,
the Good, or Immortality. Grote's own polemical and philosophical
predilections obviously made him sensitive to this variety since it
liberated him from the confines of the prophetic Plato. More important, this mode of interpretation allowed him repeatedly to appeal
from Plato drunk on dogmatism to Plato sobered by the process of
cross-examination.

Grote, of course, acknowledged that in certain dialogues the doctrines of the Forms and of Recollection were present; but he contended
that these doctrines must be regarded as philosophically invalid. Plato's
objectification of every general term or the assumption of a Form
corresponding to such terms "was a logical mistake quite as serious as
any which we know to have been committed by Hippias or any other
Sophist." Plato himself had explored the fallacies of the doctrine of
Forms in the *Parmenides* and the *Sophist,* and Aristotle had, for all

39. Ibid., p. 260n.

intents and purposes, put the capstone on the refutation of the theory. The doctrine of Recollection as representative of an intuitive theory of knowledge was no less fallacious. When expounding it in the *Meno,* Plato had portrayed Socrates interrogating a slave in order to prove that the slave's mind possessed the native capacity to recollect knowledge it could not otherwise have attained. Grote considered this demonstration as neither reasonable nor philosophical, and he explained how modern empirical associationist psychology, such as that of Alexander Bain whose works were mentioned frequently in Grote's footnotes, would account for the incident described in the dialogue.

> If Plato had taken pains to study the early life of the untaught slave, with its stock of facts, judgments, comparisons, and inferences suggested by analogy, etc., he might easily have found enough to explain the competence of the slave to answer the questions appearing in the dialogue. And even if enough could not have been found, to afford a direct and specific explanation—we must remember that only a very small proportion of the long series of mental phenomena realised in the infant, the child, the youth, ever comes to be remembered or recorded. To assume that the large unknown remainder would be insufficient, if known, to afford the explanation sought, is neither philosophical nor reasonable.[40]

This incident in the *Meno* and the epistemological conversations in the *Republic* and the *Phaedo* displayed the dogmatic Plato who had abandoned the negative elenchus of the dialogues of search. In all of these situations there had been no one present to play Socrates to Socrates himself.

Grote regarded the Protagorean doctrine of Homo Mensura, or man the measure of things, as the best antidote to Plato's unacceptable intuitive theories of knowledge and to intellectual dogmatism generally. In both ancient and modern times considerable controversy had

40. Ibid., p. 380; 2:22–23. Grote assisted John Stuart Mill and Alexander Bain in revising James Mill's *Analysis of the Phenomena of the Human Mind* (London: Longmans, Green, Reader, and Dyer, 1869). Grote and Mill also assisted Bain in 1858 in finding a publisher for *The Emotions and the Will.* See Michael St. John Packe, *The Life of John Stuart Mill,* (New York: Capricorn Books, 1954), p. 410.

surrounded and continued to surround this concept.[41] Grote's own analysis roused criticism and opposition even among those who admired his work. Grote interpreted the doctrine of Homo Mensura as reserving the "equal right of private judgment to each man for himself" in determining what was right or wrong, true or false, wise or foolish. He furthermore asserted that this clearly relativistic approach to values and knowledge had been on more than one occasion implicitly embraced by Socrates. In the *Apology,* which Grote regarded as the historic Socrates' own defense, the philosopher had asserted the right to private judgment by promising to continue to pose difficult questions if dissatisfied with the answers proffered by his fellow citizens. In the *Crito* the Platonic Socrates had indicated that although unjust, his condemnation had been legal. He then drew upon the idea of a compact between himself and the city to justify his bondage to the laws of Athens. Although his friends might disagree and urge escape, Socrates regarded himself as bound by the sovereignty of the laws. However, Socrates obeyed those laws for his own personal reasons and not for those of other Athenians or of King Nomos. In regard to this argument Grote contended:

> Here we have the Protagorean dogma, *Homo Mensura* . . . proclaimed by Socrates himself. As things appear to me, so they are to me: as they appear to you, so they are to you. My reason and conscience is the measure for me: yours for you. It is for you to see whether yours agrees with mine.

By espousing the doctrine of the Sophists, Socrates, or Plato through the character of Socrates, had attempted to provide a reconciliation between "constitutional allegiance, and Socratic individuality."[42] Although Homo Mensura might potentially justify radical equality and individualism bordering on anarchy, Grote believed that it had in fact provided the philosophical foundation for the mutual tolerance and forbearance associated with democratic constitutional morality in the past and the present. Homo Mensura alleviated social and political life based on conflict and coercion.

To support this controversial argument, Grote had to refute Plato's

41. See William K. C. Gutherie, *A History of Greek Philosophy* (Cambridge: Cambridge University Press, 1969), 3:170–75, 183–88.

42. Grote, *Plato,* 2:362, 1:305, 304.

own interpretation of the Protagorean doctrine. In a long, ultimately unsuccessful chapter on the *Theaetetus* Grote declared that Plato had misinterpreted the sophistic doctrine by equating it with the theory that all knowledge is sensation.[43] According to Grote's analysis Protagoras had actually intended to say that whether knowledge originated with sensation or in internal faculties, it necessarily involved a relationship between a knowing subject and a known object. A subjective element of judgment was necessarily present in all human knowledge. Furthermore, Plato had mistakenly thought that Protagoras's doctrine implied that every opinion is true or that every person might consider himself infallible. This was a palpably incorrect interpretation because Protagoras had obviously known that he and other persons had entertained different opinions on the same subject at different times in their own lives. Finally, Homo Mensura did not necessarily imply, as Plato seemed to suggest, that human beings holding what must by definition constitute their own opinions would or should refuse to look to other people for advice and new ideas.

What Homo Mensura fundamentally recognized was the essential fact of intellectual reciprocity among human beings that made possible rational discussion and persuasion. Opponents of the right and autonomy of individual judgment could not, in Grote's opinion, support their position. "You cannot," he declared, "escape from the Relative by any twist of reasoning." No matter how a person approached the issue of intellectual authority, the end result was a confrontation with his own personal judgment.

> Whoever denies the Protagorean autonomy of the individual judgment, must propound as his counter-theory some heteronomy, such as he (the denier) approves. If I am not allowed to judge of truth and falsehood for myself, who is to judge for me? ... If you pronounce a man unfit to be the measure of truth for himself, you constitute yourself the measure, in his place: either directly as lawgiver—or by nominating censors according to your own judgment.... You can only exchange one individual judgment for another. You cannot get out of the region of

43. See Mill, *Collected Works*, 11:425–31, and Albert Schwegler, *Handbook of the History of Philosophy*, 3rd ed., ed. James Hutchison Sterling (New York: G. P. Putnam and Sons, n.d.), pp. 380–97.

individual judgments, more or fewer in number: the King, the Pope, the Priest, the Judges or Censors, the author of some book, or the promulgator of such and such doctrine. The infallible measure which you undertake to provide must be found in some person or persons—if it can be found at all: in some person selected by yourself—that is, in the last result, *yourself.*

Subjective judgment and personal decision about truth and falsehood lay ineradicably associated with the human experience and the attainment of knowledge. Furthermore, recognition of that situation did not preclude agreement between people about objective criteria but rather rooted those criteria in "the subjective condition of satisfying the judgment of each hearer."[44]

Grote indirectly attacked the German historians of philosophy and commentators on Plato who, after the manner of Hegel, denounced mere subjectivism in philosophy. They and Anglican writers contended that some kind of universal truth existed that could be recognized by the general reason of humankind of which an individual person's reason was but a part. Grote uncompromisingly replied:

To me this assertion appears so distinctly at variance with notorious facts, that I am surprised when I find it advanced by learned historians of philosophy.... The impersonal Reason is a mere fiction; the universal Reason is an abstraction, belonging alike to all particular reasoners, consentient or dissentient, sound or unsound, etc.... To say that the Universal Reason is the measure of truth is to assign no measure at all. The Universal Reason can only make itself known through an interpreter. The interpreters are dissentient; and which of them is to hold the privilege of infallibility?

This absolute right of individual private judgment could never be popular because it inevitably collided with "the natural intolerance prevalent among mankind."[45] But recognition of the right and reality of private judgment was the foundation for the functioning of both critical philosophy and a free society without which religious, political, and social tyranny could hamper the progress of the human race

44. Grote, *Plato*, 2:359n, 358–59, 363.
45. Ibid., pp. 361n–362n, 362.

and the human mind. In a decade that saw the prosecution of the contributors to *Essays and Reviews* and of Bishop Colenso, the promulgation of the Syllabus of Errors, the spread of German philosophy in Britain, and the publication of Newman's *Apologia Pro Vita Sua,* Stephen's *Liberty, Equality, and Fraternity,* and Arnold's *Culture and Anarchy,* it was not surprising that Grote perceived the need to vigorously defend the open pursuit and expression of truth and the values of tolerance and mutual forbearance.

The logical political outcome of a rejection of Homo Mensura and the government by persuasion and discussion it nurtured was nowhere more evident than in Plato's own projected commonwealths, where private life had ceased to exist.[46] The Guardians of the *Republic* were nothing less than "a military *bureaucracy*" among whom "the whole man is merged in the performance of his offical duties; the entire extinction within of the old individual Adam—of all private feelings and interests." The Guardians treated the lower orders merely "as machines rather than individual men." The situation in the *Laws* had become even more reprehensible. There the city was dominated by "a scientific Professor" or "scientific dictator" who, possessing the certain knowledge that he could not be challenged, laid down the law and cast out those who dissented. The critical, Socratic probing of the dialogues of search was supplanted by "a legislation imbued with the persecuting spirit of self-satisfied infallibility of medieval Catholicism and the Inquisition."[47] Plato's political thought, originating in a faulty epistemology, brought to an end politics as Grote had known and conceived the process and replaced it with authoritarian, bureaucratic administration.

This attack on the suppression of private feeling among the Platonic Guardians seems to contradict Grote's arguments in the *History of*

46. Grote combined an appreciation for the reformist potential in Platonic thought, as previously advocated by J. S. Mill, with a stern condemnation of its repressive elements. The latter were the harshest remarks in English on Plato until the appearance of Karl R. Popper's *The Open Society and Its Enemies,* 2 vols. (London: George Routledge and Sons, 1943). Popper wrote that Grote's study of Plato "greatly encouraged me to develop my rather unorthodox views, and to follow them up to their rather unpleasant conclusions" (1:216). See also Warner Fite, *The Platonic Legend* (New York: Scribner, 1934); Richard H. S. Crossman, *Plato Today* (Oxford: Oxford University Press, 1937); and Ronald B. Levinson, *In Defense of Plato* (Cambridge, Mass.: Harvard University Press, 1953).

47. Grote, *Plato,* 3:211, 215; 2:494; 3:409–10.

Greece and elsewhere in favor of smothering the private person. Without forcing Grote onto a Procrustean bed of consistency, some explanation of this apparent contradiction may be suggested. What he criticized in Plato was the establishment of a ruling elite allegedly devoid of private sensibilities and whose collective expert knowledge and cadre interests were to guide the state and direct the lives of other citizens. The Guardians obviously resembled those sinister political interests of which Grote had always been suspicious. Other, more subtle, factors were also involved in his criticism. During his active political life Grote had sought to devise through institutional arrangements a commonwealth in which political loyalty and patriotism arose from the citizens' spontaneous recognition of their direct impact on the governing process. In his discussions of the ballot and of Athenian politics he had advocated the suppression of private feelings only when citizens voted or otherwise participated in distinctly civic activity. During the rest of their lives private individualism was to flourish and the benefits derived therefrom were to undergird the citizens' interest in the polity. In other words, Grote wanted both a moral commonwealth and one in which private economic self-interest could also operate. Grote seems to have sensed none of the tension implicit in this position. He simply did not understand that a city in which selfishness flourished except on civic occasions would eventually become (or never cease to be) a city in which selfishness dominated civic life as well. His confusion and critical limitation on this issue largely account for his difficulty in explaining the causes of Athenian decline and eventual conquest in the fourth century.

In confronting Plato, Grote had to choose between a society open to competition, critical individualism, and personal selfishness and one closed to such qualities by the imposition of a scientific political elite. That situation also compelled him to come to terms with the twin legacies of the Benthamite intellectual heritage—the criticism of the status quo on the grounds of reason and utility and the solving of social and administrative problems through a central state guided or advised by scientific experts. Grote opted in 1865, without compromise, for the open society and the Benthamite tradition of criticism over that of scientific legislation. The exercise of private judgment and feelings might inhibit the achievement of a moral community, but Grote could not imagine such a community without the use of private judgment by its citizens. As he wrote in regard to Plato's *Laws,* "Now a citizen might be perfectly just, temperate, brave, and prudent—and yet dissent altogether from the Platonic creed. For such a citizen—the counterpart of Socrates at Athens—no existence would be possible in the Platonic community."[48] Grote feared not only the rule of King Nomos but also the dominance of armies, bureaucracies, and unchecked rulers such as the ones he saw in France, Prussia, Austria, and Russia. He had spent too much of his own life in opposition to approve any political arrangement where the life of criticism would cease to be possible.

Although Grote championed the role of the searching, analytical intellect, on more than one occasion he utilized the prejudices of his readers to undermine the religious interpretation of Plato. For example, Grote was quick to expose the feature of Plato's philosophy most certain to embarrass both orthodox and liberal churchmen—the love of young boys.

> The Phaedrus and Symposium have, both of them in common, the theory of Eros as the indispensable, initiatory, stimulus to philosophy. The spectacle of a beautiful youth is considered necessary to set light to various elements in the mind, which would otherwise remain dormant and never burn; it enables the pregnant and capable mind to bring forth what it has within and to put out its hidden strength.

Grote presented the role of *paideros* as merely one element in Plato's thought and made no attempt to render it the sole mode of Platonism. In that manner, he implicitly demonstrated that religious scholars might have more to gain by accepting his indecisive, skeptical Plato than by selecting particular features of Plato's philosophy and then equating them with the whole. Grote also played on the prejudices of clerical interpreters by observing that Plato had conceived marriage as little more than "a special, solemn, consecrated coupling for the occasion, with a view to breed for the public." For Plato, marriage established no permanent bond between the two parties. Furthermore, both Plato and Aristotle—"men who are extolled by the commentators as the champions of religion and sound morality, against what

48. Ibid., 3:460.

are styled the unprincipled cavils of the Sophists"—had insisted on limitation of family size and in certain instances had approved both abortion and infanticide.[49] The fundamental discrepancies between Plato's social views and modern religious moral sentiments demonstrated the very relativity of ethical values against which clerical commentators had directed Plato's philosophy.

More significant than the demonstration of contrasts between Platonic and Christian morality was Grote's contention that Plato had ineffectively championed an unselfish, intuitive ethics of duty. Grote even claimed that Plato often upheld utilitarianism or if not utilitarianism, nonetheless a highly self-regarding moral theory. In the *Protagoras,* Socrates denied the Sophist's view that virtue could be learned from community or religious custom; rather he portrayed virtue as a skill that consisted in rightly calculating pleasure and pain. For the Socrates of this dialogue, "To live pleasurably, is pronounced to be good: to live without pleasure or in pain, is evil. Moreover, nothing but pleasure, or comparative mitigation of pain, is good: nothing but pain is evil." Virtuous activity depended on possession of knowledge that allowed the agent correctly to compare pain and pleasure both immediately and in terms of probable future experience. No person, according to Socrates' position, would carry out some painful act from a sense of duty or of obligation to a higher good unless he eventually expected to reap pleasure from his immediate pain and discomfort. Grote applauded this utilitarianism, but regarded the Platonic version of that ethics as actually more self-regarding than its modern counterpart. The Platonic Socrates had failed to consider "the pleasures and pains (security and rightful expectations) of others besides the agent himself, implicated in the consequences of his acts." Modern utilitarian philosophers, such as John Stuart Mill, had not committed this error. Nor, again, had the ancient Sophists, such as Protagoras, who fully recognized the sense of "social sentiment or reciprocity of regard implanted in every one's bosom" without which "the human race would have perished."[50]

Nowhere had Plato's failure to recognize the necessity of reciprocity in social relationships more completely emerged, in Grote's view,

49. Ibid., 2:223–24; 3:205, 232.
50. Ibid., 2:78, 83, 85. See also 2:83n.

than in the *Gorgias*. In that dialogue, when confronted with the argument that a powerful despot should not constrain his appetites, Socrates had appealed to an abstract ideal of virtue. Grote readily admitted that the Platonic Socrates had here abandoned the utilitarianism of the *Protagoras*. But he contended that Socrates still advocated a highly self-regarding ethics that ignored all other people except the ethical agent himself. There was little or nothing unselfish about the ethical doctrines of the *Gorgias*. Furthermore, even without considering that criticism, the ethical ideal of the *Gorgias* was far removed from everyday life. In drawing the analogy between virtue and the health of the mind, Plato had failed to indicate for what use a mind so maintained should be employed. The reason for maintaining a healthy mind was to enable it to deal with the particular problems of daily living, but Plato had disregarded that fact.

> Immediate satisfaction or relief, and those who confer it, are treated with contempt, and presented as in hostility to the perfection of the mental structure. And it is in this point of view that various Platonic commentators extol in an especial manner the *Gorgias;* as recognising an Idea of Good superhuman and supernatural, radically disparate from pleasures and pains of any human being, and incommensurable with them: an Universal Idea, which though it is supposed to cast a distant light upon its particulars, is separated from them by an incalculable space, and is discernable only by the Platonic telescope.[51]

In the *Gorgias* Socrates sacrificed to an abstract Good not only exorbitant pleasure but also the civilities of normal, healthy social relationships. That separation of the ethical ideal from social reality made Plato's ethics effectively useless.

Grote found the ethics of the *Republic* similarly deficient. In Plato's argument for a mode of justice that human beings should pursue for its own sake Grote again perceived the specter of self-regarding morality.

> The just man is not called upon for any self-denial or self-sacrifice, since by the mere fact of being just, he acquires a large amount of happiness: it is the unjust man who, from ignorance or

51. Ibid., p. 131.

perversion, sacrifices that happiness which just behaviour would have ensured to him.

For the just man to be happy in his justice alone, he must be wholly self-sufficient. But the fundamental argument of the *Republic,* including the basis for initially founding the city, originated in a denial of human self-sufficiency. The concept of the man happy in his own justice alone rested on the "fallacious" analogy between a community that could achieve general self-sufficiency and the individual human being who could not. In both the *Republic* and the *Laws* Plato's ascetic, self-regarding ethics that made justice derive from conformity to an unexamined external standard resulted in "a perpetual, all-pervading drill and discipline."[52] In effect, the ethics of Plato and the politics derived therefrom denied human nature, the social situation, the critical intellect, and the freedom to direct one's own life in the light of personal judgment and of ideas received through liberal discourse with one's fellow creatures. Most assuredly such a philosophy could not provide ethical guidance for men and women in the nineteenth century.

Plato, and the Other Companions of Socrates became almost immediately a primary landmark in Victorian Greek studies and remains still, in W. K. C. Guthrie's words, one of "a few indestructibles" of modern Plato scholarship.[53] Like *A History of Greece,* Grote's volumes on Plato became recommended reading in the universities although, as will be seen, there they soon encountered a major rival in the translations and introductions of Jowett. Although many parts of the work were subjected to revision by later commentators who frequently contested Grote's opinions without mentioning him by name, Grote did thoroughly succeed in preventing Plato from becoming merely the kept philosopher of Anglican idealists and put limits on the manner in which Plato could be made to conform to the desired Anglican configuration. Grote had established Plato as a philosopher of remarkable complexity who could not be reduced to a single intellectual mold. He had set Plato, or at least much of Plato, squarely into the camp of radical philosophical criticism and moral reform and

52. Ibid., 3:133, 142, 443.

53. William K. C. Guthrie, *A History of Greek Philosophy* (Cambridge: Cambridge University Press, 1975), 4:xv.

made him as much a searcher for yet undiscovered truth as a defender of certain knowledge. Grote had also provided the fundamental English critique of Plato's politics from which twentieth-century critics of the philosopher would often find their own point of departure.

During the second half of the nineteenth century, Grote's views on Plato stimulated further analysis and controversy on the part of John Stuart Mill, James Martineau, and Walter Pater. Although in large measure following Grote's lead, each of these writers also carried his own interpretation in a direction that sharply contrasted with Grote's. Their essays illustrate the broad spectrum of late-Victorian opinion on Plato that has been obscured by the general assumption that Jowett and other idealist commentators exercised a monopoly on Platonic studies. The remarks of these other writers also suggest that, despite the apparent logic of the situation, evaluations of Plato's epistemology and metaphysics did not necessarily determine judgments on his politics.

John Stuart Mill reviewed Grote's *Plato* for the *Edinburgh Review* in 1866. As a preparation for the task, he reread the entire works of the philosopher in Greek. In the main, Mill repeated Grote's views. This is not surprising since Grote looked at Plato as a reformer and concentrated on his critical method, as Mill had urged thirty years earlier. Mill praised Grote's estimate of Plato's negative method of criticism and termed that method "incomparably his greatest gift." He also agreed with Grote that the "slippery ground" of Plato's "religious and metaphysical superstructure" remained separate from his dialectics. In this respect Mill accepted the division between the dialogues of search and those of explanation. He saw the latter as the result of Plato's age and his disillusionment. Mill's only major epistemological criticism was his dissent from Grote's interpretation of Homo Mensura.[54]

Mill's view of Plato substantially departed from Grote's in the area of politics, however. Grote remained in the sixties what he had been in the thirties—a radical theoretical democrat and a moderately strong political egalitarian. That outlook had informed his harsh critique of the *Republic* and the *Laws*. By the sixties the elitist vien of Mill's philosophy had again come to the fore. It appeared in his attribution of progress to individual human geniuses in *On Liberty* and in his ballot

54. Mill, *Collected Works*, 11:406. See also 11:425–31.

scheme that weighted the franchise in favor of the educated in *On Representative Government*. The same spirit pervaded his remarks on Plato. For Mill, the real enemy against which Plato had directed his philosophical wrath was not the Sophists or any other particular school of ancient philosophy but rather the "Commonplace," or un-examined acceptance of customary and traditional ideas and opinions. In opposition to the "Commonplace" Plato had set the "exaltation of Knowledge" which consisted of "not Intellect, or mere mental ability, of which there is no idolatry at all in Plato, but scientific knowledge, and scientifically-acquired craftsmanship, as the one thing needful in every concern of life, and pre-eminently in government."[55] What Mill did not explain was that the meaning Plato attached to the idea of scientific training, or the acquisition of certain knowledge on the part of his Guardians was not the same as the meaning nineteenth-century writers and Benthamites attached to it.

Mill in effect advocated a modified form of the scientific dictator-ship and bureaucracy that Grote had so vehemently decried. More-over, he pursued this line of argument with no indication that Grote had discussed the matter in a very different fashion. Among the practi-cal parts of Plato's politics that deserved praise and commendation Mill noted:

> First, the vigorous assertion of a truth, of transcendent impor-tance and universal application—that the work of government is a Skilled Employment; that governing is not a thing which can be done at odd times, or by the way, in conjunction with a hundred other pursuits, nor to which a person can be competent without a large and liberal general education, followed by special and pro-fessional study, laborious and of long duration, directed to ac-quiring, not mere practical dexterity, but a scientific mastery of the subject.

Mill regarded this opinion—a clear defense of modern bureaucratic government—to be "the strong side" of Plato's theory. He acknow-ledged, however, that there was a weaker side that "postulates infalli-bility, or something near it, in rulers thus prepared; or else ascribes such a depth of comparative inbecility to the rest of mankind, as to unfit them for any voice whatever in their own government, or any

55. Ibid., pp. 403, 432.

power of calling their scientific rulers to account." Mill, in sharp contrast to Grote, made absolutely no further criticism of the illiberal face of Plato's politics. He simply regarded Plato's elitism and authoritarianism as "an exaggerated protest against the notion that any man is fit for any duty" to which there was "more or less tendency in all popular governments" whether in Athens or Britain or the United States.[56] Mill shared with Plato a hatred and contempt for the mediocre in public life, as well as an only somewhat modified zeal for the education of an administrative elite. Indeed, as seen in Mill's other works of the period, his fear was that the tendency to mediocrity and equality in democratic society would smother the possibility of the emergence of such gifted individuals.

James Martineau was the most distinguished British Unitarian intellectual of the nineteenth century. He had grown up among those radical Unitarian circles that often bred later utilitarians and extreme political and philosophical radicals such as his sister Harriet and John Stuart Mill's wife Harriet Taylor. James Martineau, though remaining a firm and innovative religious liberal, moved to a more conservative philosophical position, absorbed much German and Coleridgean thought, and eventually set forth an important system of intuitive ethics based on the character of the individual personality and its making of personal moral judgments. In 1866 many people expected Martineau to be named the professor of moral philosophy at University College London because he was clearly the most outstanding candidate. But in one of his most unattractive public actions George Grote, in league with Alexander Bain and others, vehemently and successfully opposed the appointment on the grounds that any philosopher of a religious viewpoint, no matter how liberal, should not teach at that secular institution.[57] Grote's opposition may well have stemmed from distrust of a person who had strayed so far from his radical origins, but he also realized that Martineau advocated the very kind of epistemology against which *Plato, and the Other Companions of Socrates* had been directed.

56. Ibid., p. 436.
57. George Grote to Alexander Bain, 17, 26, and 27 July and 5 August 1866 in Croom Robertson Papers, University College London. See also Martin Lowther Clarke, *George Grote: A Biography* (London: University of London, The Athlone Press, 1962), pp. 154–57.

Martineau discussed Plato in a long essay in *Types of Ethical Theory* (1885).[58] There he presented Plato as a thorough idealist and essentially dogmatic philosopher, and he emphasized most of the elements of Platonic philosophy stressed by the advocates of the prophetic Plato. He argued that the doctrine of the Forms had been fundamental to practically all of Plato's thought and that when the predicates associated with the Idea of the Good were examined, they amounted to a concept of God. Yet Martineau was morally discontent with Plato, within whose pantheistic idealism the individual personality was "but the local emergence of the universal mind." The human personality so conceived could not freely act, choose the better over the worse, or deserve good or ill. Plato's philosophy provided no place for "the *true* moral feeling, based as it is entirely on the distinction between human volition and animal instinct."[59] The implication of this outlook for politics led Martineau to condemn Plato and his implied eradication of the individual with no less severity than Grote, whose metaphysics and epistemology differed so radically from Martineau's.

Along with Hegel, Martineau regarded the whole point of Plato's politics as the suppression of the individual citizen and the subordination of his personality to the state.[60] Martineau contended that this position flowed necessarily from Plato's pantheistic metaphysics that enfeebled the concept of personality and that "regarded particular persons as mere *organs* of a common social life, which, as the higher and more real unity, was entitled to multiply or suppress them, to move and mold them, according to the exigencies of its perfection." In service to the collective state the individual might be required to sacrifice both his personality and his moral character. As Martineau complained:

> To the preconceived perfection of the whole social organism everything is to give way,—not the interests only of the individual,

58. For the best account of Martineau's ethical thought, see Jerome B. Schneewind, *Sidgwick's Ethics and Victorian Moral Philosophy* (Oxford: Clarendon Press, 1977), pp. 237–59.

59. James Martineau, *Types of Ethical Theory,* 2 vols. (Oxford: Clarendon Press, 1885), 1:104.

60. Georg Wilhelm Friedrich Hegel, *Lectures on the History of Philosophy,* 3 vols., trans. E. S. Haldane and Frances H. Simson (London: Kegan Paul, Trench, Trubner and Co., 1892), 2:113.

but his character; and, to be a patriot, he must be content to become, in his own person, the liar, the assassin, nay, the stock-breeder, of his country. And yet the statesman, from whom these sacrifices are demanded, belongs to the class which alone is to realize and represent the consummate form and entire contents of virtue; while from the others on which he exercises his arts of government, are expected only the inferior layers of character,—courage and self-restraint.[61]

No other British commentator so starkly outlined the moral cost of Plato's utopian vision nor the full extent of the moral degeneration of the rulers and the ruled in Plato's commonwealth.

Although Martineau acknowledged that Plato had yielded to none in his opposition to materialism, he had done so by denying all the benefits of personal and moral growth that arose from the family and other private attachments. In somewhat overly florid rhetoric, Martineau denounced the political and social life Plato had advocated.

Strike out from the individual soul the power of love, the light of its romance, the fervour of its ambitions, the tenderness of its cares, the vigor of its purity and faithfulness: take from the mother the office of queen of the nursery, and leave her no function but that of childbearing and wet-nursing to the Republic; and from the father the responsibilities of bread-winner, educator, and king of his own house; and from the child the filial trust and reverence, the fraternal and sisterly heart-affinities which can never be generalised; and the human being is bereft of the most precious springs from which the moral life arises, and can emerge only as a strange medley of the brute, the politican, and the philosopher. A commonwealth of such subjects would hardly, in our estimation, be worth preserving.[62]

Plato's subordination of the individual personality to conformity with absolute reason inhibited the very kind of personal relationships that nurtured moral development and that provided the possibility of moral experience as Martineau and most of his contemporaries understood the term. His criticism would also, of course, have applied to

---

61. Martineau, *Types of Ethical Theory,* 1:75, 106–07.
62. Ibid., pp. 108–09.

Grote's attack on family and other private associations in *A History of Greece.*

Martineau's criticism of Plato is of considerable significance. First, it suggests that those writers who espoused an intuitive philosophy and a moderately idealist metaphysics could be aware of the repressive character of Plato's politics. Martineau found Plato's commonwealth no less dangerous to moral liberty than Grote had found it to political liberty. The Nonconformist experience that Martineau had known, with its absence of many civil rights and its ever-present reminders of Anglican social and intellectual dominance, may well have made him sensitive to the issue of political rights and to the importance of private associations for the emergence of moral personality. Second, Martineau's *Types of Ethical Theory,* published in 1885 by Oxford's Clarendon Press and later reprinted and revised, suggests that it was not from ignorance of the authoritarian implications of Plato's thought that, after Jowett, most Oxford commentators qualified, denied, or simply ignored those illiberal facets of Plato's philosophy. As will be seen, those writers fully intended to use Plato to encourage a collective civic life in which the individualism of the mid-Victorian period would come under the benevolent direction of the state and of a civic elite that resembled Mill's vision of bureaucracy.

Before examining the interpretations of Plato that stemmed from Jowett's teaching and writing, it is necessary to consider Walter Pater's *Plato and Platonism,* published in 1893. Curiously enough, this volume was more indebted to Grote's analysis than to any other single work on Plato, although its political conclusions differed from those of Grote. The close relationship between the thought of the radical utilitarian banker and that of the Oxford aesthete was somewhat less problematical than it might first appear. During the sixties Pater seems to have read deeply in English empiricist philosophy and psychology as well as in Hegelian literature. As noted in an earlier chapter, Pater's concept of myth was deeply indebted to Grote's *History of Greece.* Pater was also thoroughly receptive to the spirit of relativism in philosophy and religion that Grote so admired in the doctrine of Homo Mensura and that he championed in *Plato, and the Other Companions of Socrates.*

Plato and Platonism originated in lectures for Oxford undergraduates who would be examined on the *Republic.* In those lectures and in subsequent essays, Pater combined a somewhat Hegelian analysis of Plato's place in Greek philosophy with the major elements of Grote's analysis of the content of Plato's thought. Pater announced his intention of putting Plato "into his natural place, as a result from antecedent and contemporary movements of Greek speculation, of Greek life generally." Plato's novelty lay neither in the problems he had addressed nor the solutions he had proposed, but rather in the manner in which he had expressed his philosophy. The mode of his philosophizing was new, and for Pater, "... in the creation of philosophical literature, as in other products of art, *form*, in the full signification of that word, is everything, and the mere matter is nothing."[63] Plato's new form was the dialogue, which Pater equated with the essay, the literary mode of expression most particularly suitable for analytic thought. The dialogue or essay emerged after the poem, which had suited intuitive philosophy, and before the treatise, which expressed philosophy that had degenerated into dogmatic systems.

Having sketched this line of development in philosophical expression, Pater momentarily abandoned Plato and moved to the sixteenth century and Montaigne, for whom the essay had provided

> precisely the literary form necessary to a mind for which truth itself is but a possibility, realisable not as general conclusion, but rather as the elusive effect of a particular personal experience; to a mind which, noting faithfully those random lights that meet it by the way, must needs content itself with suspension of judgment, as the end of the intellectual journey, to the very last asking: *Que scais-je?*

Although admittedly Plato's dialogues on occasion reverted to poetry, they were, for Pater, an early version of Montaignian essays. Like Grote, Pater regarded the irony of the Platonic Socrates as perfectly genuine and the skepticism with which many of the dialogues con-

63. Walter Pater, *Plato and Platonism: A Series of Lectures* (New York: Macmillan and Co., 1894), pp. 6, 4. This volume is probably the least discussed of all Pater's works. See U. C. Knoepflmacher, "Pater's Religion of Sanity: 'Plato and Platonism' as a Document of Victorian Unbelief," *Victorian Studies* 6 (1962): 151–68; U. C. Knoepflmacher, *Religious Humanism and the Victorian Novel: George Eliot, Walter Pater, and Samuel Butler* (Princeton: Princeton University Press, 1965), pp. 170–88; David J. DeLaura, *Hebrew and Hellene in Victorian England: Newman, Arnold, and Pater* (Austin: University of Texas Press, 1969), pp. 296–304.

cluded as natural to a mode of expression that primarily tested or analyzed answers. The essay, or the Platonic dialogue, as a literary form was particularly useful in this respect for suppressing error. It also permitted a lifelong pursuit of truth carried on by the individual within himself as well as with others around him. And the chief characteristics of that search conducted by testing and criticizing were "its inequalities; its infelicities; above all, its final insecurity."[64]

To this highly inexact and inherently skeptical way of pursuing knowledge, Pater explained, Plato had linked an absolute standard of truth. From the paradoxical relationship between a skeptical method and an absolute standard there had emerged over the centuries two major traditions of Platonic discipleship. The first was that of Aristotle, the schoolmen, Spinoza, Hegel, and all varieties of Neoplatonists who had been caught up by the theory of ideas and the ideal of absolute knowledge implied therein. But Pater, following Grote's lead, contended, ". . . it is in quite different company we must look for the tradition, the development, of Plato's *actual* method of learning and teaching." The genuine Platonic tradition informed the works of Abelard and Montaigne and those philosophers whose dialectical skepticism had checked the pretensions of both science and modern metaphysics. Those intellects still awaited the achievement of absolute truth that Plato had demanded and that later philosophical systems had failed to provide. As Pater sympathetically observed,

> Such condition of suspended judgment indeed, in its more genial development and under felicitous culture, is but the expectation, the receptivity, of the faithful scholar, determined not to foreclose what is still a question—the "philosophical temper," in short, for which a survival of query will be still the salt of truth, even in the most absolutely ascertained knowledge.[65]

In that suspension of judgment and that cultivation of the philosophic temper lay, in Pater's view, the vital intellectual heritage of Plato and Platonism. Like Grote and Mill, he set Plato directly into the company of those who had pioneered rational, analytic thought and who had preferred to rest in learned ignorance rather than in dogmatism.

64. Pater, *Plato and Platonism*, pp. 157, 166.
65. Ibid., pp. 173 (italics mine), 176.

Anthony Ward has noted that Pater "only feels confident when he can stand a given idea on its head so that it becomes, by an extraordinary gliding process, the opposite of itself before one has quite realised that any change has occurred."[66] Such was certainly his manner of dealing with Plato's doctrine of the Forms. In Pater's analysis that doctrine, traditionally associated with spiritual, idealist, or transcendental philosophy, emerged as a vindication of the flesh and the senses. Here Pater may have been indebted to Hegel's view of the concrete manifestation of spirit. Although Plato sought to impress upon his readers and upon Socrates' interlocutors in the *Republic* the reality of the unseen realm of the Forms, he had, according to Pater, actually been first and foremost a lover of the visible world whose relationship to empirical sense data had been one of love and not hostility.

> The lover, who is become a lover of the invisible, but still a lover, and therefore, literally, a seer, of it, carrying an elaborate cultivation of the bodily senses, of eye and ear, their natural force and acquired fineness ... into the world of intellectual abstractions; seeing and hearing there too, associating for ever all the imagery of things seen with the conditions of what primarily exists only for the mind, filling that "hollow land" with delightful color and form, as if now at last the mind were veritably dealing with living people there, living people who play upon us through affinities, the repulsion and attraction, of *persons* towards one another, all the magnetism, as we call it, of actual human friendship or love:—There, is the *formula* of Plato's genius, the essential condition of the specially Platonic temper, of Platonism.

By taking from the visible world the materials and patterns with which he constructed the inner realm of the human mind, Plato had allowed human beings to explore without fear their inner being and had thus made them "freemen of those solitary places." The realm of the Forms had never been divorced from the already familiar concrete world, and in Plato's philosophy, "all true knowledge will be like the knowledge of a person, of living persons, and truth, for Plato, in spite

66. Anthony Ward, *Walter Pater: The Idea in Nature* (London: Macgibbon and Kee, 1966), p. 26.

of his Socratic asceticism, to the last, something to *look* at."[67] In this manner Plato had transcended the ascetic heritage of the Pythagoreans and of Socrates and had directly contributed to the philosophical redemption of sensation, matter, and the body.

For Pater, the doctrine of the Forms constituted no "prosaic and cold-blooded transcendentalism" but rather was "a way of speaking or feeling about certain elements of the mind." At one point he compared Plato's projection of the Forms with the primitive religious outlook that contemporary anthropologists termed "animism." He also suggested that the Forms resembled "a recrudescence of polytheism in that abstract world; a return of the many gods of Homer, veiled now as abstract notions, Love, Fear, Confidence, and the like."[68] It will be recalled that Pater had previously described the gods of the myths as creations of the human imagination functioning in a finite world, and there is little to lead one to believe he considered the later flowering of polytheism under the guise of Plato's Forms any less imaginary. Behind Pater's lush prose and intellectual eroticism hovered his own profound skepticism and the implicit conviction, shared with Grote, that sense experience rigidly limited and determined human knowledge. For Pater, the philosophy of Plato vindicated and reconciled one to a finite world and did not and could not carry one beyond that realm.

Although Pater agreed with Grote in regard to Plato's method and epistemology, there was substantially less agreement between them on the matter of Plato's politics. Pater portrayed Greek life and culture in Plato's era as torn between great centripetal and centrifugal forces. The latter included the drive to colonize, the pursuit of beauty in sensuous experience, the tendency toward new complexity in human relationships, and the politics of democracy. Each of these factors, which had obvious counterparts in late nineteenth-century Britain, reflected the Ionic experience and the metaphysical outlook of Heraclitus. The centripetal forces in Greek life worked to establish order and stability. They were found in the Doric experience embodied by the Spartan state and the metaphysics of Parmenides. Pater's sympathy lay with the Doric spirit of internalized order, beauty, and courage

67. Pater, *Plato and Platonism*, pp. 125, 128, 130.
68. Ibid., pp. 147, 151.

upon which Plato had seized and which he had incorporated into the *Republic*. That self-imposed political unity served to overcome the flux and uncertainty of the world revealed in Plato's epistemology and fostered by his philosophical method.

> Organic unity with one's self, body and soul, is the well-being, the rightness, or righteousness, or justice of the individual, of the microcosm; but as the ideal also, it supplies the true definition, of the well-being of the macrocosm, of the social organism, the state. ... Remember! the question Plato is asking throughout *The Republic* ... is, not how shall the state, the place we must live in, be gay or rich or populous, but strong—strong enough to remain itself, to resist solvent influences within or from without, such as would deprive it not merely of the accidental notes of prosperity but of its own very being.[69]

Plato's solution, as Pater interpreted it, was to direct Athens back to a simpler, more primitive life in which the individual was part of the community and where justice resided in the maintenance of social relationships within the community. The natural inequality of human beings would constitute the foundation of justice, and the individual citizens would, like the notes of a musical chord, become subservient to the harmony of the whole.

Pater understood that the harmony of the Platonic commonwealth was repressive and demanded an almost complete renunciation of selfhood. He was in agreement with Grote on that point of interpretation, but he dissented from Grote in that he was willing, at least in his mind's eye, to make that sacrifice. Pater rendered it more palatable by portraying the commonwealth as peopled by *voluntary* citizens and as resembling a medieval community. With no justification whatsoever from Plato's text, Pater pictured the citizens of the Platonic commonwealth as declaring to those outside its boundaries:

> We are here to escape from, to resist, a certain vicious centrifugal tendency in life, in Greek and especially in Athenian life, which does but propagate a like vicious tendency in ourselves. We are to become—like little pieces in a machine! you may complain.— No, like performers rather, individually, it may be, of more or

69. Ibid., p. 215.

less importance, but each with a necessary and inalienable part, in a perfect musical exercise which is well worth while, or in some sacred liturgy; or like soldiers in an invincible army, invincible because it moves as one man. We are to find, or be put into, and keep, everyone his natural place; to cultivate those qualities which will secure mastery over ourselves, the subordination of the parts to the whole, musical proportion.[70]

Recognition of the flux in the outer world would lead men and women to renounce their individual freedom and to seek to establish for themselves an enclave of secure order and harmony.

Pater admitted that art would be vanquished from this community, because of a recognition of the seriousness and profound influence that art exerts over the formation of the human character. Still, the city would not remain completely without art or music. Artistic endeavor resembling that of the Middle Ages, with its Cistercian monasteries, its cathedrals, its Gregorian chants, and its sense of Doric order, would permeate all things. For both Pater and Grote (as well as for Martineau), Plato's politics led to the medieval church. Grote saw that institution as an agent of persecution; Pater saw it as an instrument of benevolent order amidst the turmoil of the outer world. The *Republic* had promised "all, or almost all, that in a later age natures great and high have certainly found in the Christian religion." Philosophy in the community of the Platonic commonwealth provided "a satisfaction not for the intelligence only but for the whole nature of man, his imagination and faith, his affections, his capacity for religious devotion, and for some still unimagined development of the capacities of sense."[71] That promise enticed Pater, who in his middle age had moved steadily toward the rituals and spiritual solace of Anglo-Catholicism.

Grote and Pater differed little over the character of Plato's politics; both regarded it as repressing the impulses of the individual. Their disagreement stemmed from their different evaluations of the experience of the free, critical individual human being making his way through the world. For Grote skepticism and criticism were a way of life and a path that eventually led to some kind of truth. His sublime

70. Ibid., p. 246.
71. Ibid., p. 238.

faith in the power of persuasion assumed the possibility of broad areas
of voluntary social and intellectual agreement, and his scientific outlook presupposed a physical world operating according to rational,
discoverable law. At the heart of Grote's skepticism lay a core of
certainty. It was otherwise with Pater, whose skepticism and sense of
relativity were more extreme and radical. Grote had been concerned
with opinions whose falsity might hinder the attainment of truth;
Pater, at least in his early adult life, had, like his contemporary
Nietzsche, been more doubtful of the very possibility of truth as
commonly conceived in the empiricist and scientific traditions. Over
the course of the years, Pater's radical skepticism led him to seek
various possible modes of certainty. That experience quite naturally
permitted him to sympathize with Plato's commonwealth as representing one way in which human beings might deal with the fundamental insecurity and uncertainty of their situation. But it also led him
to suggest, perhaps unwittingly, a near Hobbesian interpretation of
the *Republic*. By portraying the citizens of the *Republic* as voluntarily
renouncing their individuality and entering into an experiment of
living in which they subordinated themselves to the social macro-
cosm, Pater transformed Plato's commonwealth into a Leviathan that
afforded its citizens protection and existential meaning otherwise lacking in the world. Like Matthew Arnold, to whose thought he was
deeply indebted, Pater had grown weary of the "multitudinousness of
things," and he succumbed to the authoritarian temptation.

   The differences in opinion about the role of skepticism and about
Plato's politics that are found in the work of Grote, Mill, Martineau,
and Pater illustrate an important feature of the critical tradition in
Victorian intellectual life. One strain of criticism was of an instrumen-
tal nature, that is, criticism functioned as an instrument to cast into
question various features of the political, social, or religious status
quo. Behind that use of critical reason usually lay the conviction that
some other manner of thought or some other social arrangement was
desirable and should replace the one being criticized. This use of critical reason is particularly associated with the early Victorian generation
of utilitarians, political radicals, and Protestant Nonconformists and
with late-Victorian advocates of scientific naturalism and socialism.
Grote and Mill, with their contempt for King Nomos and their hopes
for political reform, obviously fall into this category. Martineau does

also because his attack on Plato's politics had the object of preserving the right of the citizen to pursue his own life and values and to raise questions not tolerated by the larger society. Pater's brand of criticism and skepticism, especially in his early life, was more nearly existential. He belonged to the generation who came of intellectual age in the late fifties and the sixties. That group inherited the critical tools of the earlier generation, but many of the problems against which those tools had previously been used were solved or no longer seemed pressing. For some members of this second generation criticism became almost an end in itself. There was, as might be expected, a middle ground on which other intellectuals in the last half of the century sought to join criticism with social reconstruction. It was along this path that idealism, particularly at Oxford, moved, and it was along these lines that Jowett and his successors would for almost three intellectual generations interpret Plato. And because the task of social and religious reconstruction seemed so important in the last third of the nineteenth century, it was largely this interpretation of Plato that would carry the day, over the views of Grote that seemed to echo the problems and outlook of a time that was past.

Benjamin Jowett: Plato as the Father of Idealism

Benjamin Jowett was a scholar of two lives. The first was that of an outspoken university reformer and liberal theologian during the fifties and early sixties. The second was his later role as the awe-inspiring master of Balliol College and the major translator and interpreter of Plato for the late-Victorian generation. The two careers were more intimately related than his biographers have usually admitted.[72] In 1870, the year of his election to the mastership and the year before his translation of Plato appeared, Jowett confided to a friend, "I still think there is something to be done in the way of making Christianity, *whether under that or some other name,* a reality. . . . The simple love of truth and of God, and the desire to do good to man have hardly been tried as yet, and people would tell you that they cannot be tried."[73]

72. Abbott and Campbell, *Life and Letters of Benjamin Jowett;* Geoffrey Faber, *Jowett: A Portrait with Background* (Cambridge, Mass.: Harvard University Press, 1957).

73. Benjamin Jowett, *Letters of Benjamin Jowett* ed., Evelyn Abbott and Lewis Campbell (New York: E. P. Dutton and Co., 1899), p. 182.

Jowett knew this simple mode of Christian living faced immense difficulty in the commercially oriented society of the day. He also understood that the historical criticism of the Bible, which he had championed and in the cause of which he had encountered personal persecution and legal prosecution, left many people morally and religiously adrift. Finally, he saw that the reform of the universities would diminish the influence of the Anglican church and that in the future it would be left largely to laymen and secular institutions to set the moral tone of the society. It was into this moral and religious breech that Jowett introduced Plato as a philosopher whose thought could sustain traditional moral values and inculcate a new sense of secular duty among the educated classes of the nation.

The several sides of Jowett's intellectual and university career combined to assure that his translations and introductions rapidly became *the* Plato of late-Victorian Britain. His reputation as a Greek scholar, attained through his New Testament criticism, forestalled significant competitors, and the prestige and influence of his position at Balliol assured that his volumes received attention. Jowett's conscious use of the language and rhetoric of the Authorized Version of the Bible allowed his translations to strike a responsive chord among the religiously minded, as did his vindication of undogmatic Christian ethical values, spiritual truth, and idealist metaphysics. Yet, unlike the advocates of the prophetic Plato, Jowett did not make Plato a Christian; rather, he transformed liberal Christianity into a moral stance that could be justified, at least in his mind, by appeal to the wisdom of Plato. His portrayal of Plato as both a religious thinker and a political reformer opened an intellectual and vocational path that commenced with religious humanism but ended in civic and social service. At the same time the elitism of both Plato and Jowett meshed quite neatly with the growing conservatism of the British intellectual nation during the latter part of the century.

Jowett's *Dialogues of Plato Translated into English with Analyses and Introductions* first appeared in 1871. A revised edition with expanded introductions and corrected translations was published in 1875, and a third edition with still more additions and revisions appeared in 1892.[74] The long title of Jowett's work indicates why it produced such

74. Benjamin Jowett, *The Dialogues of Plato, Translated into English with Analyses and Introductions* 4 vols. (Oxford: Clarendon Press, 1871); Benjamin Jowett, *The Dialogues of Plato, Translated into English with Analyses and Introductions*, 5 vols., 2nd

a broad impact throughout the English-speaking world. He combined translation, analysis, and interpretation in the same volumes, thus establishing a model later followed with similar success by Francis Cornford and Allan Bloom. Jowett's own model was probably commentaries on the English Bible. His translations were small masterpieces of English prose that brought the dialogues into the mainstream of good literature in the same way that Pope's translation had transformed Homer into an English classic. As one of Jowett's biographers declared, "Plato was now an English book."[75] Although the translations received much criticism by scholars, most were not supplanted for half a century, and many still remain the most accessible means for reading Plato in English.[76] A long introduction including paraphrase and analysis prefaced each translation, and not until 1892 was the paraphrase of Plato substantially distinguished from Jowett's analysis and commentary. The commentary often addressed itself to some particular philosophical question in the dialogue or to some other subject that Jowett wished to discuss and for which the introduction provided an occasion. Consequently, a charming essay on friendship was included in the introduction to the *Lysis;* a meditation on immortality prefaced the *Phaedo;* and a long, involved discussion of Hegel's philosophy appeared in the commentary on the *Sophist.*

Just as his intention in regard to Plato was to provide a surrogate for Christianity, Jowett's introductions became a surrogate for his own further original theological or philosophical scholarship. After his prosecution for his contribution to *Essays and Reviews* and his vindication in the vice-chancellor's court, Jowett ceased theological writing except for college sermons. He did not, however, stop thinking about those religious, philosophical, and historical questions upon which he had previously commented. He transferred his forum from theological publications to the introductions to Plato where he could address a wide audience and remain safe from the theological strife that rent the

ed., rev. (Oxford: Clarendon Press, 1875). See note 21 above for information on the third edition and for the manner in which the various editions are cited in the notes.

75. Abbott and Campbell, *Life and Letters of Benjamin Jowett,* 2:7.

76. The most searching contemporary discussion of Jowett's methods of translation was Alexander Grant's in "Professor Jowett's Translation of Plato," *Edinburgh Review* 134 (1871): 303–42. See also David Binning Munro, "Jowett's *Plato,*" *Quarterly Review* 131 (1871): 492–522; anon., "The Study of Plato," *Macmillan's Magazine* 24 (1871): 81–87.

fabric of Anglican intellectual life during the third quarter of the century. His commentaries on Plato, nonetheless, reflected the same kind of intellectual stance that had informed his work as a Broad Church theological liberal. In that earlier role Jowett had often found himself at odds with both the extreme orthodox party within the Anglican church and the extreme rationalists outside it. His position as an interpreter of Plato was quite similar. Jowett opposed both the prophetic view of Plato and Grote's utilitarian, skeptical interpretation. In that respect his Platonic studies stand as one of the last monuments in the latitudinarian tradition of Anglican scholarship.

Jowett approached Plato and his philosophical achievement largely through the categories of German idealist epistemology and Hegel's *History of Philosophy*. Such analysis implicitly repudiated the search for a connection between Plato and Christian revelation and explicitly rejected the evaluation of his thought by the standards of modern utilitarianism. In direct reproach to George Grote, Jowett set out in 1871

> to represent Plato as the father of Idealism, who is not to be measured by the standard of utilitarianism or any other modern philosophical system. He is the poet or maker of ideas, satisfying the wants of his own age, providing the instruments of thought for future generations. He is no dreamer, but a great philosophical genius struggling with the unequal conditions of light and knowledge under which he is living. He may be illustrated by the writings of moderns, but he must be interpreted by his own, and by his place in the history of philosophy. We are not concerned to determine what is the residuum of truth which remains for ourselves. His truth may not be our truth, and nevertheless may have an extraordinary value and interest for us.[77]

These were brave and worthy goals to which, not surprisingly, Jowett was less than faithful. He in fact was concerned about the relevance of Plato's thought, and he did time and again measure it by the standard of utilitarianism in order to suggest the moral barrenness and spiritual inadequacy of the latter philosophy. Furthermore, his historicist analysis permitted him to excuse what he regarded as Plato's

77. Jowett, *Dialogues of Plato,* 1:xi.

shortcomings while appropriating to modern use what he understood to be Plato's wisdom.

Jowett's frequently stated intention of using Plato to combat modern utilitarianism and sensational psychology led him to a much less extreme mode of Hegelian historicism than his student and friend Alexander Grant had employed in his 1857 edition of Aristotle's *Ethics* to attack previous Christian interpretations of the treatise and to suggest its current moral irrelevance. Jowett's historicism was more moderate for two reasons. First, he had initially applied the historical method to the Bible, particularly to the Epistles of St. Paul, to explicate their original meaning for the present day but with no intention of denying their truth or relevance. He approached Plato in the same fashion. Second, although always claiming not to be a "Hegelian," Jowett was firmly attached to the concept of the evolution of the human mind and of particular ideas over time. The development, purification, and amplification of major moral and philosophical concepts represented for him the story of humankind coming to perceive more clearly some mode of eternal truth. Because modern philosophers and thinkers could more fully and correctly comprehend that truth, or those truths, they were able to understand more completely and precisely what Plato had been trying to say and they could remove apparent contradictions or embarrassments from his writings. This concept of intellectual development permitted Jowett to believe that Plato retained current relevance and interest as the implications of his thought were made clear. This view also by its very nature set a premium on the interpretation of Plato.

Certain passages of the introductions and prefaces also hint that combined with this Hegelianism, Jowett also accepted in some unarticulated fashion elements of the Viconian concept of historical cycles which, as in the thought of Matthew Arnold, endowed Athenian philosophy with particular applicability to the contemporary British scene. In 1874 Jowett observed:

> We begin to feel that the ancients had the same thoughts as ourselves, the same difficulties which characterize all periods of transition, almost the same opposition between science and religion. Although we cannot maintain that ancient and modern philosophy are one and continuous (as has been affirmed with more truth

respecting ancient and modern history), for they are separated by an interval of a thousand years, yet they seem to recur in a sort of cycle, and we are surprised to find that the new is ever old, and that the teaching of the past has still a meaning for us.

In the introduction to the *Theaetetus* Jowett appealed to such a cycle of philosophy to dispute Grote's conclusion that the skepticism, or absence of positive result at the close of many Platonic dialogues, indicated that the philosopher believed positive knowledge impossible. Plato's skepticism rather displayed the insufficiently developed state of knowledge and philosophy at the time. Jowett contended, "The writings of Plato belong to an age in which the power of analysis had outrun the means of knowledge."[78] He obviously had in mind the work of the ancient Sophists. This observation was followed in the second and third editions of the introduction by a long discursive essay describing how Kant and Hegel had provided solutions for much of the moral and epistemological skepticism of the eighteenth century. In the context of the essay this latter philosophy was clearly analogous to the skepticism current in Greece during Plato's lifetime.

Having established the historical parallel, Jowett went on to explain, "The importance of the senses in us is that they are the apertures of the mind, doors and windows through which we take in and make our own the materials of knowledge." It was the mind itself, however, that determined the form and character of genuine knowledge and attained "the higher truths of philosophy and religion" that were "very far removed from sense."[79] Jowett's analysis thus indicated that those who still grovelled in sensational psychology and skepticism remained at a stage of intellectual development the inadequacy of which Plato had long ago discerned and from which, more recently, German philosophy had again liberated thoughtful Europeans. Hegelian historicism had allowed Jowett to explain the context of Plato's thought while Viconian analysis permitted him to suggest a modern solution to the recurring intellectual problem.

Through these and other remarks Jowett associated Plato with the moral philosophy and social outlook that in nineteenth-century Britain derived from Coleridge. The idealism of which Plato was the

78. Ibid., pp. xxv–vi; 4:119.
79. Ibid., 4:159, 158.

progenitor in Jowett's eyes was not that of the Forms but rather the more general turn of mind that "places the divine above the human, the spiritual above the material, the one above the many, the mind before the body." Such ethical idealism ennobled human endeavor and could lead to the preservation of what Jowett regarded as the essence of religion—"self-sacrifice, self-denial, a death unto life, having for its rule an absolute morality, a law of God and nature." The great obstacle to this higher life was the selfishness of the world that Coleridge had condemned a half-century earlier and that Plato had deplored in Greek life. As Jowett commented:

> The great enemy of Plato is the world, not exactly in the theological sense, yet in one not wholly different—the world as the hater of truth and lover of appearance, occupied in the pursuit of gain and pleasure rather than of knowledge, banded together against the few good and wise men, and devoid of true education. This creature has many heads: rhetoricians, lawyers, statesmen, poets, sophists. But the Sophist is the Proteus who takes the likeness of all of them; all other deceivers have a piece of him in them. And sometimes he is represented as the corrupter of the world; and sometimes the world as the corrupter of him and of itself.

Plato's bitterness toward the ancient Sophists paralleled and meshed with Jowett's own contempt for those in the Church, business, government, and the larger society whose practices and values made nonsense of honesty in word and sincerity in deed. Jowett was voicing his own and Coleridge's discomfort when he wrote that Plato believed "the whole world appears to be sunk in error, based on self-interest." In a private letter of 1875, Jowett admitted to having made Plato's views congruent with his own and to having "attacked a good many of my private enemies under the disguise of the Sophists."[80]

Jowett employed his commentary on Plato not only to condemn the immorality of commercialism and self-interest but also to preach the necessity of an ethic of self-sacrifice and duty to a higher collective social good. He once told Balliol students, "There never will be a millennium on earth until we make one." But before his fellow citi-

80. Ibid., 2:19; Abbott and Campbell, *Life and Letters of Benjamin Jowett*, 2:311; Jowett, *The Dialogues of Plato*, 4:287 (passage reflects small change made after the first edition); 2:99; Abbott and Campbell, *Letters of Benjamin Jowett*, p. 194.

zens could undertake the task of moral and social reconstruction, they would have to renounce the ethical philosophy of utilitarianism and the psychology of associationism and sensationalism which by their very nature could never raise human beings beyond a commonplace image of themselves. In 1875, reacting to the ever-increasing influence of scientific naturalism, Jowett declared:

> As knowledge is reduced to sensation, so virtue is reduced to feeling, happiness or good to pleasure. The different virtues—the various characters which exist in the world—are the disguises of self-interest. Human nature is dried up; there is no place left for imagination, or in any higher sense for religion. Ideals of a whole, or of a state, or of a law of duty, or of a divine perfection, are out of place in an Epicurean philosophy. The very terms in which they are expressed are suspected of having no meaning. Man is to bring himself back as far as he is able to the condition of a rational beast. He is to limit himself to the pursuit of pleasure, but of this he is to make a far-sighted calculation;—he is to be rationalized, secularized, animalized: or he is to be an amiable sceptic, better than his own philosophy, and not falling below the opinions of the world.[81]

Those philosophies that glorified the cult of self-interest and extreme individualism left humankind to wallow in its own lowest common ethical denominator and in effect vanquished the moral ideals that had in the past called forth yet undiscovered potential for human nobility and achievement. Although Jowett did not say so, he might also have noted that Aristotle's *Ethics,* though hardly of a reductionist character, could not effectively lead human beings beyond current social cus-

---

81. Benjamin Jowett, *Select Passages from the Theological Writings of Benjamin Jowett,* ed. Lewis Campbell (New York: Henry Frowde, 1902), p. 183; Jowett, *Dialogues of Plato,* 4:173. From the mid-seventies on, Jowett became increasingly disturbed by the growing influence of reductionist scientific naturalism. In January 1875, he wrote to Edward Caird, "I sometimes think that we Platonists and Idealists are not half so industrious as those repulsive people who only 'believe what they can hold in their hands,' Bain, H. Spencer, etc., who are the very Tuppers of philosophy and yet have gained for themselves fame and name." Abbott and Campbell, *Letters of Benjamin Jowett,* p. 190. For a discussion of the scientific outlook that Jowett scorned, see Frank Miller Turner, *Between Science and Religion: The Reaction to Scientific Naturalism in Late Victorian England* (New Haven: Yale University Press, 1974), pp. 8–37.

toms. It had been the absence of zeal for reform and righteousness in
Aristotle that convinced Jowett that Plato must become the new
philosophical text of Oxford education.

To make good his presentation of Plato as the defender of an ethic of
duty, Jowett had to confront Grote's vigorously argued position that
Plato's philosophy itself had frequently been utilitarian in direction. In
answer to Grote, Jowett maintained that Plato had sometimes displayed certain utilitarian paradoxes, such as in the speech of Socrates in
the *Protagoras,* to illustrate "moments or aspects of the truth by the
help of which we pass from old conventional morality to a higher
conception of virtue and knowledge."[82] Once utilitarian analysis had
dissolved the rule of traditional morality, the way lay open for the
construction of a new intuitive ethics based on duty. That Plato had
himself entertained such a concept of ethical evolution suggested itself, according to Jowett, in the philosopher's strong repudiation of
utilitarianism in other dialogues. Jowett in effect imposed on Plato's
analysis of Greek thought the three eras of intellectual development
that Hegel had ascribed to the general emergence of Greek philosophy. Jowett also implicitly argued in a Viconian fashion that
nineteenth-century utilitarian morals similarly fulfilled little more
than a temporary critical transitional function. The wish was, of
course, father to the thought. Jowett hoped that his descriptive
analysis of ethical development might become prescriptive for his
own day. And to the extent that idealism rather than utilitarianism
replaced Christian ethics and political philosophy at Oxford and elsewhere for over two generations, he succeeded.

Jowett encountered difficulty, however, in providing a satisfactory
philosophical justification for an ethics of duty based on the text of
Plato. For example, Jowett defended the nobility of the asceticism
championed by Socrates in the *Gorgias* and without naming him
criticized Grote's interpretation of the dialogue. Jowett understood
the value of the dialogue and of its examples of self-sacrifice as residing
in the moral ideal they set before readers. Of Socrates' speeches on the
happiness of those who suffer willingly, Jowett commented:

> He is speaking not of the consciousness of happiness, but of the
> idea of happiness. When a martyr dies in a good cause, when a

82. Jowett, *Dialogues of Plato,* 1:126 (added to the second edition).

soldier falls in battle, we do not suppose that death or wounds are without pain, or that their physical suffering is always compensated by a mental satisfaction. Still we regard them as happy, and we would a thousand times rather have their death than a shameful life. Nor is this only because we believe that they will obtain an immortality of fame, or that they will have crowns of glory in another world, when their enemies and persecutors will be proportionally tormented. Men are found in a few instances to do what is right, without reference to public opinion or to consequences. And we regard them as happy on this ground only.... We are not concerned to justify this idealism by the standard of utility or public opinion, but merely to point out the existence of such a sentiment in the better part of human nature.

Jowett insisted that Plato had intended to argue that "in some sense or other truth and right are alone to be sought, and that all other goods are only desirable as means towards these." No matter how reprehensible, self-regarding, or deluded the idea of voluntary suffering might appear to writers of Grote's persuasion, there could be no doubt that Plato's ascetic ideal remained "one of the conceptions which have exercised the greatest influence on mankind."[83] Jowett essentially declared that the pursuit of duty entailing self-sacrifice did occur among human beings and that it defied rational explanation.

Jowett's words rang with eloquence and sincere conviction, but he failed to comprehend that a sense of duty in and of itself defines neither the quality nor the righteousness of the object or action toward which duty is directed. He failed to recognize that in part, at least, the purpose of ethics is to help human beings to decide rationally what to do at a particular time and place. Jowett praised the life of duty and pointed to examples of it, but neither from his own reasoning nor from Plato's text could he provide a rigorous philosophical defense of the life of sacrifice. In that respect, Grote had once described Jowett as well as Plato when he warned readers of the *Republic* to look "upon Plato as a preacher—inculcating a belief which he thinks useful to be diffused; rather than as a philosopher, announcing general truth of human nature, and laying down a consistent, scientific theory of Ethics."[84] For

83. Ibid., 2:295 (small change after the first edition); 2:296.
84. Grote, *Plato,* 3:156.

Jowett, a life of duty that included the values of both Christian charity and aristocratic paternalism was vindicated by the self-evident nobility it displayed and the personal responsibility for the higher life of the society it called forth among an elite group of citizens. The essence of Christian morality remained true no matter what the fate of the documents of revelation. To criticize Jowett for his philosophical shortcomings is to miss the point of his life and endeavor. He was not in truth a philosopher; he remained always a clergyman, a teacher, and a moralist.

Although Jowett employed Plato's philosophy as a surrogate for traditional Christian ethics, the Greek vessel contained what by Victorian standards were elements of moral sediment profoundly repugnant to Christian and middle-class moral sensibilities. The most significant of these were Plato's comments on love between males in the *Phaedrus* and the *Symposium*. Ancient pederasty posed to the appreciation of some Greek literature and philosophy a moral difficulty analogous to that presented by slavery to the defenders of the Athenian constitution. Although Shelley had written a tolerant essay on the subject, his views did not set the tone for educated mid-Victorians.[85] Grote had used the homosexuality in Plato's philosophy to embarrass clerical interpreters who were frequently perplexed by the morally troubling passages. W. H. Thompson, a respected Cambridge classical scholar and master of Trinity College, stated his incredulity in regard to certain of Socrates' remarks in the *Phaedrus*.

> It seems impossible that Plato can seriously have entertained the paradox that the παιδῶν ἔρως was a necessary step towards moral perfection. All that can fairly be gathered from his words is, that those who struggle victoriously with appetite, will come out of the conflict the stronger and happier than they were before it commenced—that the trials of the soul are the occasions of its triumphs.[86]

Thompson in his anxiety had simply fled from the text.

Jowett shared Thompson's discomfort. In his commentary on the

85. James A. Notopoulos, *The Platonism of Shelley: A Study of Platonism and the Poetic Mind* (Durham: Duke University Press, 1949), pp. 404–13.

86. William Hepworth Thompson, *The "Phaedrus" of Plato with English Notes and Dissertations* (London: Whittaker & Co., 1868), p. 163n.

Epistles of St. Paul, Jowett had alluded to the practice of homosexuality in the ancient world and described it as "a great gulf fixed between us and them, which no willingness to make allowance for the difference of ages or countries would enable us to pass."[87] In the first edition of *The Dialogues of Plato* (1871) Jowett ignored the issue of male love in the *Phaedrus* and treated the subject as presented in the *Symposium* more or less as he had in his Pauline commentary. He observed that Alcibiades had combined in his speech "the most degrading passion with the desire of virtue and improvement." He also noted that the Platonic Socrates, unlike perhaps the historic Socrates, had regarded "the greatest evil of Greek life" not "as a matter of abhorrence, but as a subject for irony."[88] Jowett made a substantial departure from this viewpoint for the second edition of his translations (1875). There (and in the third edition), in the introduction to the *Phaedrus,* he contended that modern readers must make certain adjustments in their reading of the text if they were genuinely to grasp the meaning that Plato ascribed to erotic relationships between males.

> To understand him, we must make abstraction of morality and of the Greek manner of regarding the relation of the sexes. In this, as in his other discussions about love, what Plato says of the loves of men must be transferred to the loves of women before we can attach any serious meaning to his words. *Had he lived in our times, he would have made the transposition himself.* But seeing in his own age the impossibility of women being the intellectual helpmate or friend of man (except in the rare instances of a Diotima or an Aspasia), seeing that, even as to personal beauty, her place was taken by young mankind instead of womankind, he tries to work out the problem of love without regard to the distinctions of nature.

In regard to Socrates' speech on love in the *Phaedrus,* Jowett assured readers of the third edition of the dialogues (1892) that there was no "need to call up revolting associations, which as a matter of good taste

87. Benjamin Jowett, *The Epistles of St. Paul to the Thessalonians, Galatians, Romans, with Critical Notes and Dissertations,* 2nd ed., 2 vols. (London: John Murray, 1859), 2:77.
88. Jowett, *Dialogues of Plato,* 1st ed., 1:486. (Jowett retained these statements in the second edition but removed them from the third.)

should be banished, and which were far enough away from the mind of Plato." Later generations of the ancients, Jowett contended, had condemned love between males, and Plato himself had criticized all depraved forms of it. What Plato had condoned, Jowett explained in the introduction to the second edition of the *Symposium,* was a relationship in which the male participants "deemed the friendship of man with man to be higher than the love of woman, because altogether separated from the bodily appetites."[89]

In effect, Jowett's remarks on male love acknowledged that Plato had said what he said about love between men without admitting that Plato had meant what he said in the way that he had said it.[90] Jowett's idea, shared with other Hegelian commentators, that a later age was able to comprehend more fully the thought of past epochs provided one ground for his reading of these troubling passages. But of more immediate relevance was his previously developed method of interpreting the Scriptures which also owed much to Hegel. Both the Bible and Plato contained texts that were in sharp variance with modern morality and modern knowledge. The advance of physical science and moral sensibilities required the Bible to be read in a sense other than the literal one. Jowett once explained that the interpreter of the Bible had to attempt to enter the mind of the prophet, evangelist, or apostle and "to distinguish the words of Scripture from the truths of Scripture."[91] As he wrote in regard to the reading of the Psalms:

> There must be a silent correction of the familiar words of the Psalmist when we use them, if they are to express the truth for us.

89. Jowett, *Dialogues of Plato,* 3rd ed., 1:406 (italics mine), 1:415, 535.

90. Over the years Jowett seems to have become increasing concerned about the possible moral impact of the sexual passages upon students. This situation may have arisen because of the apparently more open character of erotic relationships among male university students toward the close of the century. At one point he intended to write an essay on Greek love for inclusion in the third edition of *The Dialogues of Plato* that would have argued that Plato used the idea of love between males metaphorically. He was dissuaded from this course, it would seem, by a letter from John Addington Symonds. See John Addington Symonds, *The Letters of John Addington Symonds,* ed. Herbert M. Schueller and Robert L. Peters (Detroit, Mich.: Wayne State University Press, 1969), 3:345–47, 365. See also Kenneth James Dover, *Greek Homosexuality* (Cambridge, Mass.: Harvard University Press, 1978).

91. Benjamin Jowett, "On the Interpretation of Scripture," *Essays and Reviews,* 12th ed. (London: Longman, Green, Longman, Roberts, & Green, 1865), p. 497. Much of this essay bears on understanding Jowett's reading of Plato. Furthermore, throughout the introductions to Plato Jowett frequently notes that certain passages must be interpreted as one would interpret a difficult or unclear passage of the Bible.

For we know that God is not sitting, as He is represented in some pictures, on the circle of the heavens, but that His temple is the heart of man; we know that He is not the God of one nation only, but of all mankind; we know that God helps those who help themselves.[92]

After a long, courageous career attempting to persuade fellow Christians of the need to read the Bible in this manner, it is not surprising that Jowett applied the same method to the interpretation of Plato. In both cases the task of the interpreter was to glean the unchanging moral truth of the insights of the ancient writers that lay encased in the language and moral conventions of an earlier time and place.

One of the first questions that an articulate Victorian reader asked about any serious book or text was its moral intent. Once that purpose had been established, the text was read in that light. Even the work of poets of questionable moral propriety, such as Goethe and Heine, could and did in this fashion become moral guides. By this process Victorian critics and scholars largely concealed from themselves the character of their own activity as much as they did the literal content of the work being read. In the case of the Bible they masked the fundamental theological transformation they were actually effecting; in the case of Plato they hid from themselves the immense moral distance lying between Greece and their own day. Both modes of unconscious self-deception were essential and intrinsic to the moral and intellectual enterprise being undertaken.

This method of reading an ancient text in the light of its purported moral intent and through a rationalizing historicism carried over into Jowett's interpretation of Plato's political philosophy and produced far-reaching results for the study of Plato throughout the English-speaking world. Jowett's political thought, like his theology, partook of the Coleridgean spirit. Both Coleridge and Jowett sought to forge a spiritual and ideological ideal of the state as a countervailing force against the social and moral dissolvents of commercialism and modern natural right philosophy.[93] As Christians—an affiliation too often forgotten because of their battles with more orthodox believers—they

92. Jowett, *Select Passages from the Theological Writings of Benjamin Jowett*, p. 42.
93. On Coleridge's political thought, consult David P. Calleo, *Coleridge and the Idea of the Modern State* (New Haven: Yale University Press, 1966), and John T. Miller, *The Social and Political Thought of Samuel Taylor Coleridge* (Ph.D. diss., Yale University, 1977).

saw the social and political world blighted by sin or human corruption that was to be, so far as possible, circumscribed by political institutions. This outlook on the human situation led Jowett and more nearly secular idealists after him to value the moral rigor of Plato's political thought. They found obvious resonances of their own elitism and collectivist ideal of the state in Plato, and they then imposed on Plato their own moral intentions and political goals. As a result, they came to discount or to rationalize the distinctly illiberal elements of the *Republic* and the *Laws* that had so disturbed Grote and Martineau.

Jowett found himself particularly attracted to the *Laws,* which epitomized Plato at his repressive worst. Jowett's admiration for the treatise stemmed directly from his own pessimistic philosophical anthropology; as he commented, "There is none of Plato's works which shows so deep an insight into the sources of human evil as the Laws."[94] Jowett tempered and sometimes simply excused the repressive institutions in the *Laws* on the ground that Plato's intention had been clearly moral and religious. The philosopher's plan for inquisition into the lives of private citizens represented what Jowett first termed "the weakest point"[95] but later called simply a "weak point" of a philosophy that displayed the incapacity to discern "the boundary line which parts the domain of law from that of morality or social life."[96] In his usual historicist manner, Jowett excused this excess as a result of the conceptual incapacity of Greek thought itself in the fourth century B.C. to distinguish properly between ethics, which dealt with private behavior, and politics, which was concerned with the public person.[97] Jowett admitted that in Plato's eagerness to restrain the disintegration in Greek society, he had failed to understand "that without progress there cannot be order, and that mere order can only be preserved by an unnatural and despotic repression."[98] Yet with all these qualifications Jowett still discerned a positive side to the persecution of irreligion advocated in the *Laws* because "the spirit of persecution in Plato, unlike that of modern religious bodies, arises out of the

94. Jowett, *Dialogues of Plato,* 1st ed., 4:17. In the third edition, Jowett significantly revised this statement to read, "No other writing of Plato shows so profound an insight into the world and into human nature" (5:xxvii).
95. Ibid., 1st ed., 4:165*.
96. Ibid., 3rd ed., 5:ccii.
97. Ibid., p. lxxviii.
98. Ibid., p. cxxxvi (first appeared in second edition).

desire to enforce a true and simple form of religion, and is directed against the superstitions which tend to degrade mankind."[99] Plato's intent had been worthy even if his methods were perhaps too extreme.

Jowett's relative lack of indignation about Plato's authoritarianism is not altogether surprising. The personal experience of religious persecution that Jowett had suffered disposed him to favor state action in such matters because it had been the decisions of secular courts during the fifties and sixties that eventually brought an end to the heresy-hunting of the various Anglican religious parties. And it was the Public Worship Act of 1874 that set limits on the activities of the Anglican ritualists whom Jowett and other religious liberals regarded as harbingers of revived superstition. Moreover, although like other university liberals of the sixties he had favored a careful expansion of the franchise and the opening of the government and civil service to newly educated classes, Jowett was not a democrat. He remained all his life a thoroughgoing elitist and paternalist. Jowett desired enlightened change and progress, but he did not want reform at the cost of order.

For Jowett, Plato's political thought upheld the idea of the state against democracy and rampant commercial competition. In Plato's political dialogues he found a concept of government that confirmed the views he had imbibed from Coleridge and Hegel and which in large measure he shared with Matthew Arnold. For Plato, ". . . justice is the order of the State, and the State is the visible embodiment of justice, under the conditions of human society," Jowett had written in 1871. This point of departure indicated that Plato thoroughly rejected, and in the *Republic* specifically refuted, the concept of the state as having originated in human conflict. The philosophy of modern natural right that formed the philosophical basis of secular liberalism and classical economics had long been anathema to Jowett. Commenting on its ancient counterpart, found in the position taken by Thrasymachus in the *Republic,* Jowett protested:

Such a philosophy is both foolish and false, like that opinion of the clever rogue who assumes all other men to be like himself. And theories of this sort do not represent the real nature of the State, which is based on a vague sense of right gradually corrected and enlarged by custom and law (although capable also of perver-

99. Ibid., p. cciv.

sion), any more than they describe the origin of society, which is to be sought in the family and in the social and religious feelings of man.[100]

Plato's epistemology, ethics, and politics brilliantly contrasted with the political philosophy of a nightwatchman state and the mechanistic concept of human life and personality that flowed from the thought of Hobbes and Locke into mid-nineteenth-century liberalism, economics, and utilitarianism.

Jowett stood as the chief heir and acted as the primary link between the early nineteenth-century protest of paternalistic romantics against the disorder of industrial society and the late-Victorian university generation. Like others in the Broad Church party, he combined a Coleridgean concern for restraining commercialism with a Hegelian and Carlylean concept of statesmen-heroes larger than ordinary bourgeois life. Jowett drew Plato directly into this modern tradition of paternalism and a strong, elite, meritocratic state. He thoroughly admired the Plato of the *Laws,* who seemed "like some politicians of our own time, to be half socialist, half conservative" and whose thought encouraged "a struggle against evil, and an enthusiasm for human improvement." In the introduction of 1875 to the *Gorgias* Jowett sketched the character of the statesman who would carry forward policies of social and political reconstruction.

A true statesman is he who brings order out of disorder; who first organizes and then administers the government of his own country; and having made a nation, seeks to reconcile the national interests with those of Europe and of mankind. He is not a mere theorist, nor yet a dealer in expedients; the whole and the parts grow together in his mind; while the head is conceiving, the hand is executing. Although obliged to descend to the world, he is not of the world. His thoughts are fixed not on power or riches or extension of territory, but on an ideal state, in which all the citizens have an equal chance of health and life, and the highest education is within the reach of all, and the moral and intellectual qualities of every individual are freely developed, and "the idea of good" is the animating principle of the whole. Not the attainment

---

100. Ibid., 3:vi, xxix (first sentence introduced in third edition).

of freedom alone, or of order alone, but how to unite freedom with order is the problem which he has to solve.[101]

This passage would seem to call for the emergence of a moral Bismarck. It also recalls William Mitford's praise for the early tyrants of Greece and for Philip of Macedon, who Mitford believed had restored civil order to the turmoil of the Greek democratic cities. The echoes from Mitford are not wholly accidental because Jowett, like Mitford and Coleridge after him, hearkened, perhaps unknowingly, to the old complaints of the Country party ideology about the selfish commercialism of English society and government.[102]

Jowett's image of the true statesman meshed with his vision of the new national leaders he hoped would emerge from the reformed universities. Through their education they would be liberated from the philosophy of selfish individualism and would become imbued with the spirit of self-sacrificing paternalism. This concept of the new responsible, meritocratic leader was another reason that Jowett distrusted the Platonic dominance of the state less than did Grote or Martineau. Jowett was reasonably sure that the modern cadre of British guardians would be his friends and former students and that they would thus share his ideals and sound intentions. The farseeing bureaucracy that Mill had praised in his essay on Plato actually did come to be trained at Jowett's Oxford, but ironically it was educated according to an idealist philosophy that Mill abhorred. And over the years a disproportionate number of young men educated in the *Literae Humaniores* school, with its late-century emphasis on Plato, entered the civil service. Jowett and his successors carefully used their political influence to see that the examinations favored persons so educated.

Through his introductions, Jowett set a tone that long dominated the British analysis of Plato's political dialogues. He taught a generation or more of teachers and students to find lessons for contemporary life in Plato, to regard him as an idealist bulwark against selfishness and utilitarianism, to rationalize the elements of political repression,

101. Ibid., 5:cxxxiv, cxxxvi; 2:308–09.
102. For the important relationship of Coleridge's thought to the Country party ideology, see Miller, *Social and Political Thought of Samuel Taylor Coleridge*. There is no reason to believe that Jowett was familiar with those eighteenth-century writers, but, to the extent that he was dependent on Coleridge, his thinking reflected much of their moral protest.

and through Plato to view themselves as the servants of a higher social ideal. His commentaries are little read today, but in conjunction with Green's political writings they exercised a profound influence over the later Platonic criticism of Richard Nettleship, Bernard Bosanquet, and Ernest Barker. The works of Nettleship and Barker remain standard works on Plato's philosophy and are widely consulted by readers who have little or no recognition of the Victorian and Edwardian intellectual and political preoccupations they reflect and embody.

Richard Nettleship was a student and then a tutor at Balliol. He is now familiar only through his posthumously published *Lectures on the "Republic" of Plato.* The memoirs of the period speak of him as a teacher with a remarkably gentle disposition and an engaging talent for inducing his students to think. [103] During his lifetime he published only a single essay, a discussion of education in the *Republic,* and the biography of T. H. Green that prefaced Green's collected works. In August 1892, Nettleship perished from exposure while attempting to scale Mont Blanc. Several years later Godfrey Benson, a former student, culled the notes that he and others had taken during Nettleship's lectures in the mid-eighties and in 1897 published the volume on the *Republic,* which went through several subsequent editions.

Nettleship and his students belonged to that generation of late Victorians drawn from the middle and upper-middle classes who retained only the barest remnants of a traditional Christian faith but who also carried within themselves what Beatrice Webb described as a sense of sin about the economic hardships and social conditions of the working classes. The teaching and writing of T. H. Green had convinced them that questions of politics and economics could not be separated from moral issues. Green along with Jowett had also led many of them to believe that the educated classes bore a special responsibility for the moral reform and improvement of society. This message stood in direct opposition to most mid-century political economy and the philosophy of individualism. Nettleship was familiar with all of Green's writing, and Green's thought strongly informed his lectures on the *Republic.*

Nettleship characterized Plato as a philosopher who had thought long and deeply about human life and who had then become "in-

103. *Dictionary of National Biography,* s.v. "Nettleship, Richard Lewis"; "R. L. Nettleship," *The Oxford Magazine* 11 (1892–93): 8.

tensely anxious to reform and revolutionize it." In portraying Plato as a revolutionary reformer, Nettleship in a sense followed the steps of Grote, but he moved in a very different direction from Grote when it came to defining the character of the revolution that Plato had sought to effect. Nettleship's treatment of Plato in this regard illustrates how by the end of the century the Oxford idealists had stolen the reformist card from the earlier generation of utilitarians and political economists. Nettleship countered Grote's view of negative criticism as the chief vehicle for reform by asserting that in addition to believing that everyone must find the truth, the true philosopher must also believe that "the truth is to be found." According to Nettleship, the irony of Socrates, which Grote had equated with a confession of genuine ignorance, arose instead "from a genuine sense of the inexhaustibility of knowledge." And the dialectical method of Plato resulted not only in critical distinctions but, more important, in "a state of mind to which all things presented themselves as a perfectly connected order—an order in which every part down to the smallest detail . . . was seen by the mind to be eventually connected with every other part and with the principle which makes them all one."[104] These epistemological principles derived from Green's critique of the empiricist reduction of knowledge to disconnected sense experience. For Green's philosophy and for Nettleship's interpretation of Plato this epistemology provided the foundation for a social philosophy that stressed the interdependence of human relationships.

Nettleship contended that although the *Republic* appeared to be "a book of political philosophy," it was actually "a book of moral philosophy" that inevitably led to politics. The primary question of the *Republic* was quite simply "How to live best?" Because no human being can dwell in complete isolation, that question resulted in specifically political considerations. The epistemology that Nettleship had attributed to Plato suggested that the mental life of the individual human being necessarily involved constructive activity as well as passive sense experience. Consequently the analogy drawn by Socrates in Book II of the *Republic* between the justice of the individual and the justice of the polis indicated a concept of social life wherein "all institutions of society, class organization, law, religion, art, and so on, are

104. Nettleship, *Lectures on the "Republic" of Plato*, pp. 6, 15, 44, 288.

ultimately products of the human soul, an inner principle of life which works itself out in these outward shapes." Society was thus an emanation of the human mind rather than the result of a search for physical security. Although Plato, like the political economists, regarded society as originating from the principle of division of labor, he had conceived that division as "a moral principle" leading to social cohesion rather than to separation and selfish individualism. Nettleship argued that for Plato:

> Society depends upon a double fact: the fact that no man is sufficient for himself, and the complementary fact that other men want him. While every man is insufficient for himself, every man has it in him to give to others what they have not got. This is what we may call the principle of social reciprocity; the limitation of the individual goes along with the fact that he supplements the limitations of others.[105]

Nettleship had simply interpreted the division of labor in terms of giving rather than of receiving, and he had then carefully refrained from substantial inquiry into the motives for the giving.

Throughout his commentary on the *Republic,* Nettleship quietly suggested other redefinitions of the traditional vocabulary of utilitarianism and political economy. In doing so, he incorporated those terms into a political theory and ethics that supported unselfish sacrifice of personal comfort and a collectivist concept of society. He argued that for Plato the individual achieved justice through "concentration on duty" which meant that "everybody would do what was best for himself and what was best for others." Nettleship skirted the obvious problem, then haunting much of academic ethical philosophy, of the frequent incompatibility between personal happiness and collective social good. Nettleship denied the existence of any meaningful contrast between the good of the individual citizen and of the community at large in Plato's commonwealth. He also denied that Plato had actually called for his citizens or guardians to sacrifice their individuality to the community.

> There is no such thing as an individual in the abstract, a human being literally independent of all others. Nor, conversely, is there such a thing as a community which is not a community of indi-

105. Ibid., pp. 5, 4, 68, 71.

viduals, or a common life or interest which is not lived or shared by men and women. Nor is individuality, in the true sense of the word, diminished by participation in this common life or interest.... When a man so completely throws himself into the common interest that he can be said to live for others, he does not lose his individuality; rather his individuality becomes a greater one. In this sense it may be said that what Plato had in view was not the abolition of individuality, but the raising of it to the highest possible pitch through *esprit de corps*.

Plato's ideal had been that of citizens dwelling together with a sense of unity and common purpose such as modern British citizens experienced "under great excitement at great national crises."[106]

Needless to say, Nettleship had imposed his personal concepts on both Plato and his own students. Plato's guardians do not consciously or unconsciously live for others, but the young men who came to late-Victorian Oxford were susceptible to that imposed unselfish ethic, especially when it was tied to the idea of national service. By joining individualism "in the true sense of the word" to military metaphors and a rhetoric reminiscent of Christ's remark about losing one's life to save it, Nettleship transferred the concept of individualism from its usual association with peaceful economic competition to the requirements of an age of imperialism and social reform. Nettleship ignored Plato's requirement of long philosophical training for his guardians and emphasized instead the military and gymnastic education he had advised. For Nettleship, Plato's "test of a man's goodness and of his greatness is the extent to which he can lead a common life (...), or can identify himself with, and throw himself into, something not himself." Plato had provided for such a life by his plan for a community of goods among the guardians. Nettleship explained that Plato's proposal bore no meaningful relationship to contemporary communistic schemes but rather resembled the medieval monastic ideal "that a man can only serve God by avoiding certain temptations which tend to prevent him from serving God, and that therefore, as it has sometimes been put, a man should live outside the world." The life of the guardians resembled "a kind of military monasticism" in which the community and its good had been substituted for God.[107]

106. Ibid., pp. 151, 164, 177, 178.
107. Ibid., pp. 299–300, 170, 136.

The monastic example, or model, as a metaphor for explicating Plato provides an important key to the late-Victorian interpretation of the philosopher. It appeared in the work of Jowett, Pater, Martineau, Bosanquet, and Barker, as well as in Nettleship's.[108] To illustrate the character of the commonwealth envisioned by Plato through comparing it to the medieval monasteries was clearly anachronistic. Although the monastery provided a nonrevolutionary example of the sharing of goods, a more important reason lay behind this explication of the *Republic*. From the time of the earliest conservative romantic protest against the industrial order, medieval society had, in the work of Southey, Pugin, Oastler, Disraeli, and Carlyle, provided a major contrasting model to the emerging world of capital and competition. Consequently, when collectivist commentators on Plato sought to employ his thought to oppose individualism and competition, it was natural for them to interpret his commonwealth through the medieval social categories previously used in polemics against modern commercial society.

The example of medieval society suggested to the historically minded of these commentators that a competitive society did not embody eternal social laws but the conditions of a particular time and place. As Jowett commented, "We boast of an individualism which is not freedom, but rather an artificial result of the industrial state of modern Europe."[109] The idealized life of the Middle Ages, which had penetrated so much Victorian social thought, gave greater credibility to the possibility of a noncompetitive social life that these writers hoped to extrapolate from Plato. On more than one occasion Nettleship and Barker compared the general thrust of Plato's reform with that advocated by Carlyle in *Past and Present*. There Carlyle had contrasted the life of a medieval monastery guided by the remarkable monk, Abbot Samson, with the contemporary industrial order that lacked direction, leadership, and humanity. Carlyle had called for people of action who, like Abbot Samson, possessed a knowledge of

108. Jowett, *Dialogues of Plato,* 3:cxciv, clxxii; Pater, *Plato and Platonism,* pp. 230, 252–54; Bernard Bosanquet, *A Companion to Plato's "Republic" for English Readers,* 2nd ed. (London: Rivington, Percival & Co., 1895), pp. 176–77, 183; Ernest Barker, *The Political Thought of Plato and Aristotle* (New York: Dover Publications, 1959; first published, 1906), pp. 137–38.

109. Jowett, *Dialogues of Plato,* 3:clxxviii.

the reality of the universe beneath the world of appearance and who could thus govern wisely and bring order out of the current spectacle of human misery and social chaos. The later reformist writers moved easily from Carlyle's idealized monastery to Plato's idealized commonwealth because both the ancient and the modern social critic embraced an idealist metaphysics and epistemology, a contempt for democracy, and a belief in elitist political leadership. Moreover, by the latter part of the century Carlyle had come to enjoy a reputation, like that also ascribed to Plato, for having combined a spiritual perception of the universe with a strong desire for fundamental social reform.

Although the link with Carlyle's politics exists, Nettleship and most of the other late-century Platonic commentators were political collectivists rather than statists. Nettleship for his part retained an almost Christian view of the value and ethical integrity of the human personality, but he had come to believe that the personalities of individual men and women could most fully realize themselves through a collective social experience. Nettleship attempted not to confuse the personal well being of citizens with the good of the society, and he believed that Plato himself had not made that error. Throughout his lectures he insisted that by the virtue of the state Plato had intended to indicate the "qualities of individual men" and not those of "some non-human entity." Although Nettleship saw the positive benefits of a healthy collective social life, he refused to countenance any outright sacrifice of the individual to the collectivity. For example, he criticized Plato's plan for the family not only on the obvious grounds of middle-class social convention but also from the conviction "that human nature is limited in the degree to which it can really lead a common life." In the same context, he added, "What is more, if human nature is over strained in this way, it does indeed live a common life in a sense, but it does so at the cost of its own higher individuality."[110] The latter mode of individualism, somewhat similar to Martineau's, was what Nettleship truly prized, and although a healthy social experience could nurture such moral development, it should not be confused with it.

In large measure, it was Nettleship's paternalistic concept of society that also permitted him to accept or at least to tolerate the censorship

110. Nettleship, *Lectures on the "Republic" of Plato*, pp. 146, 178–79.

Plato had advocated in the *Republic*. Benjamin Jowett had thoroughly rationalized the exclusion of poets that Plato championed in Book X of that dialogue. Refusing again to acknowledge that Plato had really meant what he said, Jowett suggested:

> Plato does not seriously intend to expel poets from life and society. But he feels strongly the unreality of their writings; he is protesting against the degeneracy of poetry in his own day as we might protest against the want of serious purpose in modern fiction, against the unseemliness or extravagance of some of our poets or novelists, against the time-serving of preachers or public writers, against the regardlessness of truth which to the eye of the philosopher seems to characterize the greater part of the world.

Nettleship was more forthright and admitted that Plato had urged censorship and had approved known falsehoods in a manner repellent to the modern mind. Nettleship justified these practices by associating Plato's educational project with the concept of "nurture." Nettleship thought there were occasions when, for the good of students or citizens, political leaders or educated persons might approve and propagate stories and information that were not wholly true. Such was the case particularly with considerations of the Bible. In a sentence that might have come from the pen of Mrs. Ward's fictitious Robert Elsmere, Nettleship wrote, "To us, as to Plato, the problem of early religious education is, How to express the highest truth in the most appropriate and least inadequate forms."[111] Historically false biblical stories could be taught as illustrations of moral truth. The child's mind could be trusted to assimilate what was valuable, and later education could rectify the historical error.

Nettleship further argued that although the nakedness of Plato's censorship was regrettable, his proposals did not wholly lack wisdom or insight into human nature. Plato had properly recognized that it is "often justifiable to allow people to retain beliefs which contain substantial truth, although the form in which it is put is not the truest." In good Hegelian fashion Nettleship contended that truth could and did

111. Jowett, *Dialogues of Plato,* 3:clxiv; Richard Lewis Nettleship, "The Theory of Education in Plato's *Republic,*" Evelyn Abbott, ed., *Hellenica: A Collection of Essays on Greek Poetry, Philosophy, History, and Religion* (Oxford and Cambridge: Rivingtons, 1880), pp. 71, 105.

exist in different forms, and he concluded "We have at the same time to try and make the form as adequate as possible, to make the truest truth true to everybody."[112] Yet Nettleship remained largely dissatisfied with this position. The appropriateness of what truth for which people was a vexing and highly debatable issue. Lying itself was not an admirable practice, and at best it was a compromise with human weakness. Despite his paternalism and Hegelian recognition of different kinds of truth and stages of consciousness, Nettleship could not quite abandon the belief in a single truth; nor in good conscience could he teach civic virtue based on falsehood.

The comments of Jowett and Nettleship on censorship and falsehood in Plato's politics must be viewed against the intellectual background of nineteenth-century Oxford as well as in relationship to concern with honorable and dishonorable or liberal and authoritarian political behavior. From the years of the Tractarian movement on, the questions of the nature of truth and the meaning of verbal expressions in matters of theology, ecclesiastical oaths, and biblical criticism had haunted and often poisoned the intellectual atmosphere of the university.[113] Some of the Tractarians had believed in the doctrine of reserve in theology. Newman's Tract XC had made thoroughly problematical what a clergyman meant when he voiced acceptance of the Thirty-nine Articles. As already suggested, the injection of the methods and conclusions of the higher criticism further confused the meanings that people attached to the words of Scripture. And even those whose fabric of religious faith had become threadbare or completely worn away were often unsure whether such a state of unbelief should permeate the entire social order. It was from these religious considerations and practical ecclesiastical problems that Jowett and Nettleship approached Plato. This situation is one reason why their views of Platonic censorship seemed so compromised and compromising to later critics and readers who approached Plato solely from the standpoint of political experience and political philosophy.

In the decade after Nettleship delivered his lectures, the role of the just, or ethical, personality within the larger community, as it had

112. Nettleship, *Lectures on the "Republic" of Plato*, pp. 135–36, 136. See also p. 106.

113. James Livingston, *The Ethics of Belief: An Essay on the Victorian Conscience* (Tallahassee, Fla.: American Academy of Religion, 1974).

been emphasized by both him and Jowett, played an increasingly smaller role in discussions of the *Republic*. For example, in 1895 Bernard Bosanquet suggested in his *Companion to Plato's "Republic"* that government commissions now carried on the activity of Plato's just statesman. The state itself rather than ethical citizens as such had become the administrator of the good. Moreover, the sense of a hierarchical society implicit in Nettleship's paternalism and Jowett's elitism became much more explicit and rigidified in Bosanquet's thought. In the *Philosophical Theory of the State* (1899), he contended Plato's fundamental political conviction had been that

> every class of persons in the community . . . has a certain distinctive type of mind which fits its members for their functions, and that the community essentially consists in the working of these types of mind in their connection with one another, which connection constitutes their subordination to the common good.

Bosanquet, whose references suggest some influence from the eugenics movement, went on to declare, "There is no sound political philosophy which is not an embodiment of Plato's conception." In his monumental edition of the Greek text of the *Republic,* James Adam carried this idea further by suggesting, "Where each individual has the work to do for which he is best qualified, one fruitful cause of discontent and sedition is removed."[114] Both Bosanquet and Adam in effect approved and prescribed Platonic regimentation without, like Walter Pater, actually admitting that it was regimentation. Neither commentator was willing to confess that the ambition to do that for which one may not be qualified has stirred the human heart more often than the desire to fit into one's proper station. Bosanquet's views on Plato clearly reflect the hardening of social attitudes and class lines that, as political and social historians have noted, was occurring around the turn of the century.

Ernest Barker's *Political Thought of Plato and Aristotle* (1906) drew together most of the late-Victorian and Edwardian strands of Platonic political commentary and illustrated the fusing of views on Plato and

---

114. Bosanquet, *Companion to Plato's "Republic,"* p. 203; Bernard Bosanquet, *The Philosophical Theory of the State,* (London: Macmillan and Co., 1899), p. 7; James Adam, *The "Republic" of Plato Edited with Critical Notes, Commentary, and Appendices,* 2 vols. (Cambridge: Cambridge University Press, 1902), 1:198n.

on contemporary politics. This book and his later *Greek Political Theory: Plato and His Predecessors* (1918) were almost wholly derivative works, both of which have continued to be consulted by teachers and students of Plato to the present day. Barker, like Jowett, Nettleship, and Bosanquet, was a Balliol scholar. He was also a Nonconformist.[115] Although he later converted to Anglicanism, Barker had been an active Congregationalist throughout his college years and early professional life. Consequently, he drew upon both the idealist tradition of political philosophy and the Nonconformist tradition of the chapel as a moral community when he formulated his views of positive freedom and social solidarity.

In all of his work Barker examined the issues of Greek political thought with the intention of illuminating their relationship to modern politics. He wrote:

> We do not . . . come to the study of the philosophy of the [Greek] city-state, as to a subject of historical interest: we come to the study of something, in which we still move and live. The city-state was different from the nation-state of today; but it was only different in the sense that it was a more vital and intense form of the same thing. . . . In studying it we are studying the ideal of our modern States.[116]

The Greeks had regarded the polis as an ethical entity that united the individual citizen and the state into a single moral purpose. That ideal proved attractive to Barker, as it had to Richard Livingstone, Ernest Gardner, Lewis Farnell, Alfred Zimmern and others of the Edwardian generation.

According to Barker's analysis, Plato had cleared the way for the emergence of an ethical concept of the state by defeating the Sophists whom, in 1906, Barker portrayed as the ancient analogue of the eighteenth-century philosophes and the nineteenth-century utilitarians. Through their contractual view of politics and conventional concept of morality, the Sophists and Socrates had first articulated the tension between the individual and the civil order that constituted "the precedent condition of all political thought." But carried to an ex-

---

115. Ernest Barker, *Age and Youth* (London: Oxford University Press, 1953).
116. Barker, *Political Thought of Plato and Aristotle*, pp. 15–16.

treme in either their ancient or modern forms, these theories could lead to the disintegration of the state. Into the midst of this intellectual and political skepticism had entered Plato, rather resembling the British idealists who confronted the thought of the mid-Victorian utilitarians, radicals, and liberals. Plato directly opposed the contractarianism of the Sophists and the disruptive individualism of Socrates. Plato had urged the Athenians to recognize "the inevitable nexus which binds man to man in a State, and—as a corollary—the absolute claim of the State upon its members." Toward this end, Plato had proceeded in the *Republic* to treat "man as a member of the State, and ... the State as a moral community."[117] Barker quite simply transferred to Plato the political theory of T. H. Green and Bernard Bosanquet. The religious, ethical humanism that Jowett had hoped to preserve through a vague sense of service to God and humankind here became replaced by service to the state. Morality was something that extended beyond the ken of the individual citizen but not beyond the community.

In addition to linking Plato directly to the protest against a democratic, commercial, pluralistic society, Barker also imposed on his thought many of the contemporary political catchwords of the new Edwardian liberalism. For example, Plato was said to have argued, "No longer should individualism infect the State: a spirit of 'collectivism' (...) should permeate the individual." Plato's plan for an elite cadre of guardians and a society wherein each citizen performed the function best suiting his abilities was intended as a device "to create efficiency—to restore integrity, and, with it, harmony." Not only had Plato more than two thousand years earlier campaigned for an efficiency state, but he had also been perplexed about the possible incompatibility of efficiency and democracy that troubled liberal Edwardian intellectuals.

Where there are representative institutions, one can unite the democratic principle of rule by the people with the Socratic and Platonic principle of rule by the Wisest and Best. Accordingly, it may be said that Plato was not criticizing democracy in its essence, but in a particular (and perverted) manifestation.[118]

117. Ibid., pp. 2, 70, 84.
118. Ibid., pp. 86, 87, 89n.

Like Jowett and Nettleship before him, Barker compelled Plato to fit the collectivist, idealist mold by imposing special definitions on words from ordinary political discourse. In this case he was defining *democracy* ("in its essence") to meet the presuppositions of those Edwardian writers who sought to forge a political structure combining a democractic electorate with an elite mode of leadership and administration.

The Edwardian liberalism that permeated Barker's commentary also largely accounted for his criticisms of Plato. Liberal ideology as a creed for social reform halted well before advocating genuine socialism or absolute state dominance. But Plato had not accepted such limits. Therefore, Barker regarded the commonwealth of the *Republic* as "a benevolent depotism" in which Plato had pushed the idea of justice as duty to an unacceptable extreme. Plato had forgotten that for the individual citizen to realize his potential in and through the state, the citizen must retain some sense of identity besides his relationship with the state. Plato had correctly spotted certain evils that his projected community of property and family structure among the guardians might eradicate but his solutions were a cure worse than the disease. Property, according to Barker, was necessary for a knowledge of self.

> It is exactly this power of knowing ourselves as separate individuals which Plato really destroys, when he abolishes property; for property is a necessary basis for any conscious sense of an individual self. This then is one flaw of Plato's communism, that by abolishing the basis of *any* sense of self, it takes away the possibility of the *true* sense of self which he inculcates.

Consumed by "the zeal of the State," Plato had annihilated for his guardians the very modes of secondary associations that allow human beings to fulfill their higher instincts through social life.[119]

In his second study of Plato, which was a much revised edition of the earlier volume, Barker abandoned his condemnation of the Sophists. He also suggested that in the *Laws* Plato had projected what amounted to a police state. Moreover, the commonwealth of the *Laws* carried out state religious persecution which Barker, like Grote, compared to that of the medieval church. The policy of Platonic persecu-

119. Ibid., pp. 103, 156, 159.

tion presupposed a perfect congruity between citizenship and ideological or religious opinion. Barker, whose opinions on Plato's repression resembled those of his earlier fellow Nonconformist Martineau, did not believe such a precise unity was possible. Echoing Grote and Mill, as well as Martineau, Barker asked:

> Can a creed based on human reason, as Plato's creed was, ever claim the infallibility, and the right to be vindicated by persecution, which the medieval Church held herself justified in claiming because she believed her creed, and her interpretation of that creed, to be divinely inspired?[120]

It may have been the experience of the Great War, the suppression of pacifist dissent, or the retrenchment of the civil liberties under the Defense of the Realm Act that stirred Barker's conscience. More than likely it was a matter of liberal common sense. Whichever it may have been, Barker spent much of the rest of his professional life defending and explicating the pluralistic character of the modern nation state.

To return to the thought that opened this chapter, it may be said that Barker's two studies, largely because of their derivative character, displayed the obstacles that remained on the various bridges built between Plato and the English nation during the Victorian age. Although theologians and idealist philosophers appropriated the theological side of Plato, in one degree or another British intellectuals continued to be discontented with Plato's politics. It did not require the later polemics of Crossman and Popper to alert twentieth-century English readers to the authoritarian potential of Plato. In 1906 Barker had written:

> To Plato Political Science starts from absolute principles, and arrives at equally absolute conclusions. His principles have their truth: they have also their qualifications. Life ought to be directed by them: it can only be directed by them partially, even if we postulate with Plato an ideal ground for their operation. There is something French in Plato's mind, something of that pushing a principle to its logical extremes. . . . When we turn to Aristotle, it hardly seems fanciful to detect more of an English spirit of com-

120. Ernest Barker, *Greek Political Theory: Plato and His Predecessors* (London: Methuen and Co., 1951), pp. 342, 368.

promise. He has his principles—true "for the most part"; he seeks exactitude—"as far as the nature of the subject admits." Where Plato turned Radical under the compulsion of the Idea, Aristotle has much sound Conservatism: he respects property; he sees good in the family. He recognizes the general "laxity" of actual life, the impossibility of concluding man wholly within the pales of any scheme. He recognizes, above all, that a Government can only go so far as a people follows. . . . This is a principle which Plato had not realized: he had forgotten (rather than despised) the people; but he had left them out of his scheme none the less. His State has some of the features of a despotism; nor would it have been any the less galling in practice, because it was the despotism of an idea.[121]

Such hostile criticism was admittedly interwoven with often lavish praise for Plato, but it was nonetheless present and not in this passage alone. The ambiguity toward Plato's view of authority, the state, a governing elite, and individualism that appears throughout Barker's analysis reflected and embodied the same ambiguity toward those political questions that informed contemporary Edwardian liberalism.

Edwardian liberals whose political philosophy stemmed in large measure from the Platonism and neohegelianism of Balliol scholars sought to reappraise the Victorian ideological inheritance of individualism, utilitarianism, and self-help. They believed the state must assume a more extensive role in the life of its citizens. They also wanted to preserve basic English liberty. In the politics of Plato and of Aristotle they discerned an appreciation of the state as a moral entity that could foster the good life for larger numbers of citizens. They also saw in the Greek philosophers the ideal of a responsible, largely meritocratic governing elite. The Edwardians believed they could pursue this vision of the good life and postulate such a responsible political elite without simultaneously postulating authoritarian government, and in that effort they were largely successful. They generally embraced the spirit of pragmatic political moderation that Barker

121. Barker, *Political Thought of Plato and Aristotle*, pp. 162–63. The French thinkers with whom Barker associated the uncompromisingly first-principle approach of Plato were John Calvin and Rousseau.

in 1906 ascribed to Aristotle in contrast to Plato. They read Plato with considerable disbelief and with a certain lack of seriousness. For all of his virtues and wisdom they still regarded him as a "utopian" who had set forth visionary societies. They did not believe that the kind of vast social and intellectual revolutions required to create such societies could or probably even should take place. They regarded the state as an essentially benevolent instrument that might help to restore a sense of community and social cohesion that had diminished through the industrial and urban developments of the past century. In that respect the late nineteenth and early twentieth century commentaries on Plato helped these politically minded intellectuals to sort out for themselves the proper and improper areas for state action. Thinking about Plato helped them to think about themselves. Plato aided them in coming to see a new role for the state in modern industrial society and also in setting certain limits on that enlarged state. In that respect, although differing profoundly from their Edwardian predecessors, Richard Crossman's *Plato Today* (1937) and Karl Popper's *Open Society and Its Enemies* represented a continuation of the same kind of clarification of modern political issues through discussions and criticism of Plato.

EPILOGUE

The Victorian study of the Greek heritage occurred in an arena of thoroughly engaged scholarship and writing. Disinterested or dispassionate criticism was simply not the order of the day. Historians and commentators openly and avowedly used discussions of Greek art, religion, literature, philosophy, and history as vehicles to address contemporary issues far removed from the classics. The educational system, which emphasized the Greek language and the literature and history of ancient Greece, prepared an audience within the political and social elites of Britain who could appreciate and respond to these studies, histories, and commentaries. And in this period before scholarship had become thoroughly professionalized, readers normally expected the consideration of the past to carry implications for the present.

This rootedness of Greek studies in modern questions was the obvious source of polemical distortion of knowledge about Greece. But more important, it was also the less obvious reason for much sound scholarship and correction of distortion. Victorian scholars of Greek antiquity were not the self-deluded victims of their own historical situation. Because Greek civilization seemed or was alleged to have so much relevance for the contemporary Victorian world, there existed a strong impetus for achieving more and more precise knowledge about Greece. During the century there consequently developed a creative and critical dialectic between polemic and genuine understanding. Controversy and distortion arising from ideological or religious orientation became a self-generating engine that drove scholars of differing opinions back to the original sources in pursuit of new evidence or new interpretations. Mitford harshly indicted Athenian democracy from a particular eighteenth-century English political outlook. Grote responded not simply with new ideology but with a more critical reading of the relevant ancient documents. His political stance led him to recognize the Athenian Assembly as something other than a

447

mob and to see religion as an operative factor in Greek civic life. But evidence for those views certainly existed in the text of Thucydides as well as in Grote's radical political philosophy. Later writers with still different political views would further cull the ancient sources in hopes of correcting Grote. In the long run this amassing of evidence and its critical evaluation, achieved by engaged scholars convinced of the modern relevance of their work, raised up stout, if not necessarily impregnable, barriers against new, flagrantly ideological and polemical interpretations of the Greeks.

The impulses behind most of these engaged discussions of Greek civilization were conservative in character. Victorian and Edwardian writers attempted to combat cultural and political pluralism through the commendation of the purported social and spiritual solidarity of the Greek polis. This analysis of the political and moral unity of the polis was intended to overcome modern tendencies toward subjective morality and romantic art on the one hand and utilitarianism and radical politics on the other. Arnold's Hellenism, the art criticism of Westmacott, Waldstein, and the Gardner brothers, the interpretive tradition for Aristotle's *Ethics,* and the idealist reading of Plato similarly invoked prescriptive images of Greek civilization that supported the social and moral values of the traditional British elites as models for the new middle class leaders of the nation or that aided the traditional elites in reaching an accommodation with the new political realities of the day.

The general approach to Greek political life similarly sustained this conservative bent of analysis. Until the publication of Grote's *History of Greece,* British treatments of Athens were almost uniformly hostile. Although Grote sharply challenged that interpretation, he and his emulators ignored or rationalized the problem of slavery and its implications for the modern British social question. Although Grote himself had genuinely radical purposes in his analysis of Athenian democracy, his work was immediately interpreted as a vindication of the mid-Victorian political system as he portrayed Athenian politicians in a modern, stable parliamentary guise. By the close of the century, the analogy between Athenian and British politics led to a new conservative use of the ancient polis to criticize the modern liberal state from the standpoint of social imperialism. Even Alfred Zimmern's *Greek Commonwealth,* though supporting an activist state and policies of social welfare, was conservative in its appeal to the bonds of feeling, religion, and family.

To the extent that it served as a surrogate for Christianity the Greek heritage fulfilled another conservative function. For writers of such diverse opinions as Hampden, Arnold, Gladstone, Green, and Murray, the experience of ancient Greece provided a source of information on the natural, or secular, history of humankind that supplemented, confirmed, or replaced elements of sacred Judeo-Christian history. This interpretation of Greece permitted the perpetuation of traditional Christian values apart from the documents of revelation through the discernment of those same values in the natural developments of the Greeks. This prescriptive appeal to the emergence of civilized humanity in Greece represented a secular version of Christian providential history. It permitted a writer to accept a secular or non-Christian view of human development without abandoning the hope or expectation of finding purpose or prescriptive patterns in human history. This outlook also provided a kind of alternative anthropology that blunted the impact of scientific anthropology which carried human origins to a remote primitive or animal past.

Most of those aspects of Greek culture or of modern Greek scholarship that might have challenged dominant Victorian intellectual or moral values were ignored, suppressed, or in some way domesticated. Both clergymen and lay scholars recognized the skeptical implications for the Bible of Wolfian approaches to Homer. They consciously used that apprehension over the Scriptures to inhibit extensive consideration of Wolf's theory and later of Grote's analysis of the Homeric epics. Grote domesticated Athenian politics into a parliamentary framework, and Gladstone attempted to tame the heroic ferocity of the Homeric heroes into Christian gentility. Mythographers excised the unsavory portions of the myths and later transposed them into solar tales. Frazer and Harrison confronted the terror and orgiastic character of chthonic and Dionysian rites, but they removed much of the fearfulness by relating the rituals to the food supply or by finding positive psychological value in the religious ecstasy of the ancient worshipers. The homosexuality implicit in certain Platonic dialogues was regretted or denied, while the authoritarian politics advocated in other of the dialogues and criticized by Grote was transformed into a beneficent paternalism by Jowett and his successors. A significant dualism characterized all these approaches to embarrassing features of Greek civilization. Commentators publicized all the political flaws reported by Herodotus, Thucydides, Xenophon, and Plato, but they hid the moral flaws revealed in the myths, literature, and philosophy. In both situations the principle of conservative selectivity was upheld.

Despite the generally conservative social and political implications of Greek studies, strongly progressive or modern intellectual impulses informed this activity. Commentaries on Greek history and civilization were major vehicles for leading British thought into the mainstream of modern European intellectual life. Matthew Arnold, drawing largely on the thought of his father, set a little-recognized Viconian stamp on the cultural consideration of fifth-century Athens and created a secular ideal that gradually supplanted the religious ideals associated with Judea. Grote injected a strongly Comtean analysis of Greek religion and intellectual life into his interpretation of the myths that produced broad results throughout both Greek studies and Victorian literature and criticism. Jowett's introductions to Plato's dialogues also introduced Hegel's thought to hundreds of readers who would never have attempted to read the German philosopher. Frazer's *Golden Bough* led scores of humanist scholars to an appreciation of the role of anthropology in understanding literature. In their discussions of Greek religion and philosophy Jane Harrison and Francis Cornford brought English readers into contact with Nietzsche, Bergson, and Jung. Studying Greek antiquity might be a traditional and conservative activity, but the method of that study and the social or historical philosophy informing it could and did act as solvents on inherited modes of thought and analysis. This role of Greek studies as a conduit for the transmission of modern thought into British universities and other British intellectual circles should not be underestimated.

Throughout the century both the conservative and the progressive tendencies within the Victorian exploration of the Greek heritage were closely related to events and developments in the world outside classical scholarship. The rediscovery of the Greek heritage by British intellectuals in the late eighteenth and early nineteenth centuries coincided, and not accidentally so, with the vast transformations being wrought by those myriad forces designated by the terms liberal democracy, industrialism, and enlightenment. The art, history, literature, religion, and philosophy of Greece furnished British intellectuals with new points of departure and cultural reference for thinking about themselves and the new situations they confronted. The projection of their own concerns and problems onto the Greek experience, whether from a Christian, Viconian, Comtean, or Hegelian standpoint, was one means of bringing order into their own lives and thought. As W. H. Auden observed just over thirty years ago, "The historical discontinuity between Greek culture and our own, the disappearance for so many centuries of any direct influence, made it all the easier, when it was rediscovered, for each nation to fashion a classical Greece in its own image."[1] In this manner the exploration of Greek civilization provided an avenue for the evaluation of the modern British experience, and as that experience changed the understanding of Greek antiquity was often modified accordingly. In turn, Greek studies came to bear profound marks of Victorian religious, philosophical, and political preoccupations, the not always faint outlines of which may still be discerned in the scholarly examination of the Greek heritage in our own day.

1. W. H. Auden, "Introduction," ed. W. H. Auden, *The Portable Greek Reader* (New York: The Viking Press, 1955; first published, 1948), p. 2.

INDEX